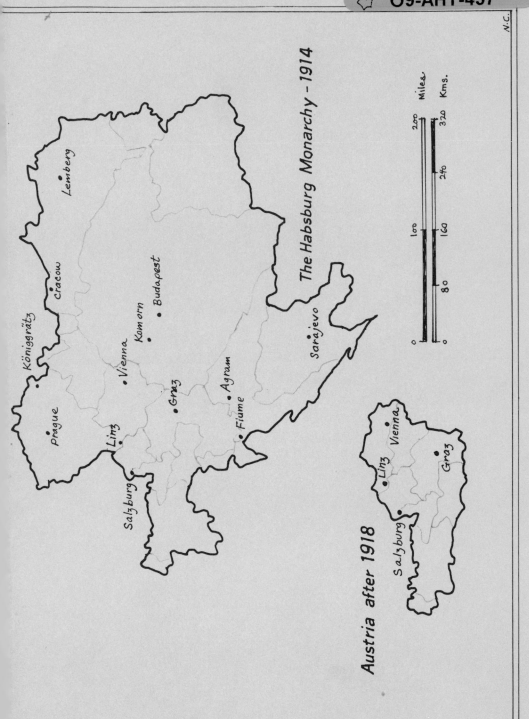

The Habsburg Monarchy – 1914

Austria after 1918

Miles
Kms.

THE EAGLES DIE

Franz Joseph and Elisabeth in the first years of their marriage and
Elisabeth in mourning (probably after the death of Rudolf)

THE
EAGLES DIE

*Franz Joseph, Elisabeth,
and Their Austria*

GEORGE R. MAREK

1817

HARPER & ROW, PUBLISHERS

NEW YORK, EVANSTON, SAN FRANCISCO

LONDON

Designed by Sidney Feinberg

To Emily and her Vienna

Contents

Illustrations

MAP

Foreword

To the librarian: Please catalogue it under "B" and not "H";
the book is biography, not history. It is a portrait of a man and a
woman, a consequential man and a beguiling woman, who were
fortune's fools. It is the tale of two people who lived at the sunset
of an epoch. One of them, a sovereign of little malice and intermittent kindliness, was forced by his tradition and the bent of his
mind to act in so retrograde a manner that one can say that he
hastened the sinking of the sun. During his reign an empire slid
into the dusk, and he could not understand the reason for its
fading. Nor did he understand what caused the deep division between himself and his queen. More than a historical tragedy, more
than the political chronicle of a man who ruled what the novelist
Robert Musil called "the second-weakest great power in Europe,"
the story of Franz Joseph and Elisabeth is a personal tragedy, a
tale of mismanaged love and marriage.

Another kind of division occurred during those years. While
statesmen quarreled and groups hacked themselves into bickering
factions, artists and scientists united, locked their doors, and
emerged with extraordinary achievements. Weakness was compensated by strength; building increased side by side with crumbling;
mindless adherence to the old was opposed by a daring reach for
the new. Compensation—it is a characteristic of civilization which
has appeared often enough in history to make one suspect that it

appears not by chance alone. The Franz Joseph years provide a remarkable example of compensation, the parallel of which to our own time is too obvious to need underscoring.

The cold and the warm currents clashed and rocked the bark. It was not a calm period—but was there ever a calm period?

As to its main events, though I stress the personal and biographical note, I do include a presentation of the political twists of a reign which began with a revolution (1848) and ended with a war (World War I) from which we have never really emerged. Franz Joseph's politics of long ago have a bearing on today's struggles. At any rate, in writing about a ruler one must write of ruling. I have limited myself to the chief affairs which shaped or shook the enormously complex conglomerate of races and nationalities that was the Austro-Hungarian monarchy. In doing so, I had to omit many men and women then important, ministers and generals, revolutionaries and philosophers, writers and industrialists. A cast of characters of thousands would have crowded and confused the spectacle. Leon Edel, who wrote the five-volume biography of Henry James, said: "The art of biography, at least as I practice it, is an art of leaving out."[1]

So much has been written about the history of Austria that one slinks past the shelves of unread and unreadable books with a guilty conscience. Extensively though I have read, I cannot claim that I know *half* of the available publications. Less has been written about Franz Joseph. The standard works are two: a three-volume biography by Egon Cesar Conte Corti, which—though it contains a wealth of facts—reads as though Corti had written it kneeling, so worshipful is it; and a more temperate work by Joseph Redlich, who wrote his biography after it was all over and he was teaching at Harvard University. Elisabeth has been considerately treated by Corti and more searchingly by Joan Haslip, whose biography I have greatly enjoyed. (Other works which I have consulted are listed in the bibliography.) As any biographer does, I have tried to go back to original sources, making several trips to Vienna, Ischl, Budapest, and other places, and I have translated freshly all the material used. I was lucky enough to find eighty-five unpublished letters from Franz Joseph to Katherina Schratt; they helped me to establish what I believe to be the truth about a relationship with which the historians have played a sentimental game of hide-and-seek.

In Vienna I came across a spectrum of reactions, typical of Austria. One old Austrian count responded to my questions, which were of a personal nature, "I don't know, and if I did I wouldn't tell you. Such things don't belong in a biography." But usually I found great willingness to speak frankly, and some people put themselves to much trouble to satisfy my inquiries.

To thank them is a pleasant duty. In Vienna I was helped by Dr. Hanns Leo Mikoletzky, then the director of the Austrian State Archive; by Mr. and Mrs. Kurt Stümpfl, the curators of the Ischl villa; by Dr. Rudolf Neock of the State Archive; by Dr. Waldstein-Wartenberg of the same institution; by Dr. Gottfried Heindl of the State Theaters; by Professor G. Stourzh and by Professor Adam Wandruszka of the Vienna University's Historic Institute; by Father Lorenz Gyömörey of the Austrian Center for Culture; by my friend Armin Robinson; by Hans W. Polak of the Paul Zsolnay Verlag; by Mrs. M. Janos of the Vienna Bildarchiv; in England by Mr. Robert Mackworth-Young, the librarian of Windsor Castle, who made it possible for me to quote from Queen Victoria's Journal.

On the other side of the Atlantic I received valuable guidance from Professor Robert A. Kann of Rutgers University and from Dr. Heinrich A. Gleissner, Consul General of Austria in New York. Dr. Ada Truppin aided me with medical knowledge. Kenneth P. Sneider drew the maps of diminishing Austria, and Walter Hitesman encouraged me while warning against too scholarly a stance. Frances Lindley of Harper & Row proved how a good editor can be both critical and encouraging; I used most of her suggestions, as I did those of Phyllis Jackson and Mrs. Peter Costigan. My wife and Mrs. Costigan patiently typed the several versions of the manuscript; the only thing I have in common with Tolstoy is that I too have needed to rewrite eight times.

Finally I want to thank the people on the third floor of the New York Public Library at Forty-second Street. No European library in which I have worked can compare in service and helpfulness with this institution. If this be chauvinism, let it be.

I have been inconsistent in the use of names, using the original versions when the person seems well known to the English reader, but translating less familiar appellations. I speak of "Kaiser Wilhelm," but use "Frederick William IV" in mentioning the ineffective Prussian king; I vary as well in giving the titles of books, plays, or paintings, speaking of Kafka's *The Trial* but of Schnitzler's *Liebelei*.

The Calendar at the end of the book may help the reader to place events chronologically, since I have tried not to encumber the text with too many dates.

"Biography is the only true history," wrote Carlyle. I hope he was right.

GEORGE R. MAREK

New York, 1973

Kings are for nations in their swaddling clothes.
    —VICTOR HUGO: Speech in the French Assembly

The world is growing weary of that most costly of
all luxuries, hereditary kings.
    —GEORGE BANCROFT, American historian

Both quotations from 1848, the year Franz Joseph ascended the throne.

THE HABSBURG MONARCHY FROM 1848 TO TODAY

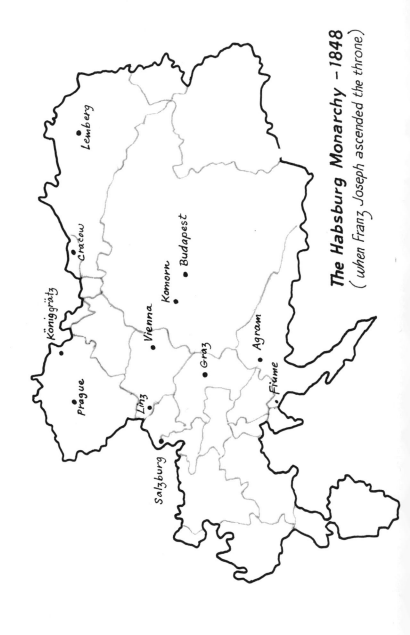

The Habsburg Monarchy – 1848
(when Franz Joseph ascended the throne.)

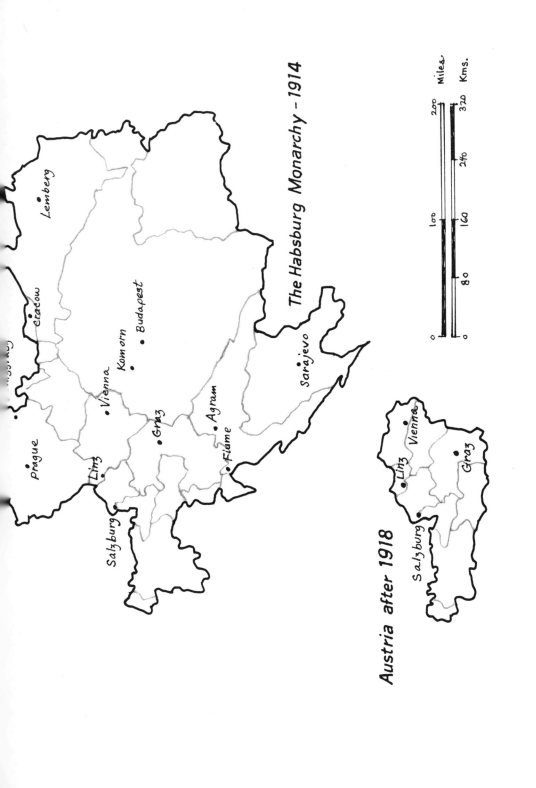

The Habsburg Monarchy – 1914

Lemberg
Cracow
Budapest
Komorn
Vienna
Prague
Linz
Graz
Agram
Fiume
Sarajevo
Salzburg

Miles
Kms.

0   80   160   240   320
0   100   200

Austria after 1918

Linz
Vienna
Graz
Salzburg

THE EAGLES DIE

Gustav Klimt: *Portrait of a Lady* (oil painting) . A superb representation
of a well-to-do young Viennese woman around the turn of the century.

CHAPTER I

Franz Joseph's Viennese

ONCE UPON A TIME, in a country which then seemed far away and during a span of years so heavily freighted with the bale of events that between its beginning and its end the distance seemed as great as the distance between antiquity and the Middle Ages—in a place and time, then, which have assumed for us aspects of the legendary, there lived a King. In his youth he was lithe and sat straight to horse; in his old age he sat in his office, bald, bent, and trembling, and wrote on paper of inferior quality memoranda to which nobody paid much attention. As a member of a dynasty, one of his first concerns was that of succession. The scepter had hardly been handed to him before he began to search for the mate who would bear him children. She had to spring from a royal house, her ancestry stainless, and she had to profess the same religion as he. The choice was restricted. In a neighboring country he met a young girl with whom he fell in love at first sight and whom he brought home as his bride, though his mother objected that the girl was too young, too flighty, and too inexperienced for so great an honor. The Queen was acknowledged as the most beautiful woman in Europe and people came from near and far to gape at her magnificence. But the Queen was less than a queen. Hers was a tortured mind in a glorious body, Helen's looks with Cassandra's soul, half self-adoring, half self-despising, an errant being who punished herself physically and mentally, who mastered superbly any subject or skill she wished to master and learned nothing which could be useful to her. Through restless and purposeless travel, through reckless and unsteady expeditions, she fled from the duties imposed upon her by her position. She fled as well from her husband. In short, the two lived unhappily ever after.

The King was more than a king. He was an Emperor, ruling the largest and in many ways the richest country in Europe, a vast territory ranging from the heat-oppressed lagoons of Venice to the top of Bohemia's cold forests, and embracing in its boundaries an artificially trussed-together conglomeration of polyglot national-ities—Germans, Hungarians, Czechs, Ukrainians, Croatians, Serbs, Poles, Slovenes, Bosnians, Rumanians, Italians—most of them be-ing little content as members of the Empire and none of them loving his neighbor as himself.

The Emperor was Franz Joseph, a Habsburg. The Habsburgs had reigned since the thirteenth century, and their dynasty com-prised rulers who were little more than warlords, as well as rulers who were reforming philosophers. Franz Joseph, neither a warlord nor a philosopher, ruled longer than any other Habsburg and indeed longer than any other head of state except Louis XIV. He ascended the throne in 1848, when he was eighteen years old, and he died in 1916 at the age of eighty-six, in the middle of the war which was to efface his monarchy. We, non-Austrians living no-where in its vicinity, are today both suffering and benefiting by events, decisions, discoveries, and thoughts arrived at during Franz Joseph's regime. It would be too much to say that he reshaped the world—the world was reshaped by too many men and buffeted by too many forces for responsibility to be assigned to any single figure—yet it is demonstrable that Franz Joseph's endeavors as well as his botches still have a bearing on our lives. In a cemetery of the little village of Vienna, New Jersey, a man lies buried who died because of him. In Prague and Budapest and Belgrade families now live in fear because of conditions which he triggered when he issued those commands which in the end commanded him. Europe is still paying for his mistakes, and that means that the world is paying. On the other hand, there arose in Austria during his reign men and women who, working sometimes in overt opposition to their sovereign's aims, made greater contributions to civilization than Austria has made in all the years since his death. We live longer, our health is firmer, we know more about the human mind, our concert halls are enriched by more than a score of compositions, the world's literature has taken a new direction, because of these men who lived so near his palace that they could have ambled over, but of whose existence the Emperor was largely unaware.

Franz Joseph believed that all men were created unequal. Though he got much of his wheat from Hungary, his coal from Bohemia, his finest fruit from the Po valley, he thought that the Czechs were bothersome louts, the Hungarians gaudy trouble-makers, the Italians tricky intriguers. As to the Serbs or Croatians —they were unwashed barbarians, and when their delegations came for an audience, he received them but he opened the windows after they left—or rather he commanded that they be opened. Truly civilized people spoke German. No, even that was overstating it: truly civilized people spoke Viennese, the comfort-able, melodious, careless dialect which had given house room to other languages—to French Napoleonic expressions and to Italian descriptive words and in which even an antique Roman noun found use: people greeted each other with *"Servus"*—"Your Slave." In Viennese the German language was sweetened and rendered cozy, and diminutives stuck in the speech like raisins in a pudding. Nobody called potatoes by the harsh German *Kartoffel:* they called them *Erdäpfel,* apples of the earth. The speech was picturesque and so was the city.

Franz Joseph himself was picturesque, studiously so. In essence he was the King of Vienna. He labored continuously to make the city more picturesque. He concentrated on the Viennese whatever affection he was capable of, though apart from formal occasions he seldom spoke to any inhabitant below the rank of Imperial Royal Major. He sat in the Burg, the ancient palace of the Habsburgs, and when he had a free moment, he looked down upon the comings and goings of the people below. His summer residences were near enough to his capital for him not to step beyond the Viennese ambience. He traveled rarely to the rest of his realm, and when he did, there had to be a specific reason: a speech before the Hungarian Parliament, an army maneuver in Galicia, a hunting party in Croatia. He never made much of an effort to understand the non-German-speaking regions of his empire, which made up two-thirds of it.

To the outside world as well, Austria meant Vienna. When Queen Victoria thought of the country and demanded reports from her ambassador, the imperial city was in her mind. When a United States senator went east on his European itinerary, he would be pleased to go and see the Stephanskirche or the Spanish Riding School; perhaps he traveled on to Budapest. But who would visit Cracow or Mährisch-Ostrau or Bozen?

The world had (and still has) a curious idea of what a Viennese was like.* The picture is as wrong as the belief that all Frenchmen engage in an enviable *ménage à trois,* that all Englishmen are taciturn and stiff, and all Germans are methodical and just love to work. A Viennese is supposed to be gay, lighthearted, easygoing—*gemütlich* is the overused word—living his life without thinking of tomorrow, a smiling hedonist. When he is young, he has an affair with a "sweet young thing," whom under no circumstances does he ever marry. Later he does get married, whereupon he sits for hours in the *Kaffeehaus.* On Sunday the whole family goes walking in the Vienna woods and listens to the bird song. When they can afford it, father and mother go to the *Heurigen* in Grinzing, where they sing the old songs and drink the new wine, become sentimental, shed tears, eat themselves red in the face on fried chicken, and return home by the last streetcar, the one that has a blue light in the rear. Every Viennese is an expert on music, can hum both Mozart and melodies about May a-borning, loves the opera, and is a graceful dancer, although the only dance he cares about is the waltz.

This is the operetta view of Vienna, as promulgated by Johann Strauss, Father and Son, by Suppé, Millöcker, and later by Lehár. The view antedates even those three-quarter-time melodists: Schiller wrote of Vienna as the land of the Phaeacians, the pleasant island which Ulysses visited, where "Sunday is perpetual and the roast is forever turning on the hearth." It is a one-seventh view, not being applicable to the other six days. True, at one time the

---

* In this discussion of Vienna and the Viennese I have chosen the period of the late nineteenth century, though many characteristics remain unchanged even today.

Viennese did love gaiety, they practiced leisure with skill, they danced, and they were devoted to music as long as the music made not too heavy a cerebral demand. But by the time Franz Joseph came along, some of the geniality and much of the insouciance had disappeared in a city which had twice been invaded by Napoleon, its money devalued, its poor become very poor. Rhythms harsher than those of the waltz pulsated through the life of its citizens. *Die Fledermaus* (1874), "typically Viennese," plays in a never-never land. There never was a Vienna that fizzed as blithely.

It is much nearer the mark to define the Viennese temperament as inclined toward melancholy. It is forlorn rather than gay. The wit which the Viennese uses liberally to help him cover his melancholy is bitter, fearful, supercilious, spoken with a shrug of the shoulders and expressing a "what's the use?" resignation. He luxuriates in resignation. He runs himself down. He belittles his achievement. He deprecates his worth. Yet if another agrees with his self-deprecation, he takes umbrage. There are historical reasons for this: Vienna had been menaced from the West—by Frederick the Great in the eighteenth century and by Napoleon in the early nineteenth—and before that from the East by the Ottoman Empire. Fortified by bastion and moat, it nevertheless lay insecurely between inimical pressures and its life was hardly ever carefree. This outpost of a city was—and to a certain extent still is—a mixture of Occidental and Oriental influences. The inner city belongs firmly to the West; yet a few kilometers to the east the aspect changes. Metternich said that the Orient began just left of the Rennweg (one of Vienna's principal streets). The mixture produced people unsure of themselves.

This lack of security leads to continuous questioning, to an excessive looking into oneself, to a pensive mockery. Vienna's greatest writer of comedies, Ferdinand Raimund, is marked "by the deep-seated melancholy beneath his wit."[1] Johann Nestroy's plays, "thoroughly irreverent," indulge "in much burlesque of the tragic efforts of the time."[2] These are no accidents. Dusk, parting, death, impotence, the transitoriness of friendship, the evanescence of love, the volatility of happiness, the impermanence of peace— these are the themes which pervade Viennese poetry. The light is veiled, passion passes. Franz Grillparzer, Austria's national poet and dramatist, wrote of renunciation: "What is earthly fortune?—A shadow! What is earthly fame?—A dream!"[3] Rainer Maria Rilke wrote: "Who speaks of victory? To survive is everything."[4]

As for the man who is not writing poetry, the middle-class citizen, he complains. "Er raunzt," to use the Viennese expression: he "bitches." The Viennese is always complaining. Nothing and nobody is ever right—no, never!—whether it be the director of the Opera or the new traffic commission or the tailor who has cut the Sunday suit. Hermann Bahr, an author of the Franz Joseph era, wrote: "A Viennese is one who is dissatisfied with himself, one who hates the other Viennese, but can't live without them."

The road of life is full of holes, and there is no point in repairing it. Far better to make a detour. The simple, straightforward way rarely appeals to the Viennese temperament. If he wants a job, he does not ask for it. He tries to find somebody who knows somebody who is a distant cousin of the boss. He runs around looking for recommendations. He is impressed by connections and titles. Indeed, titles in Vienna were the coin used in social traffic. Everybody had a title. (It is still substantially true.) A man pursuing an official career slowly climbed up a ladder where his title became ever more polysyllabic. If you took care of a small railroad station—which meant more or less that you came out with a red cap on your head and saluted the engineer of the express as the train roared by—you would not only become station master but in due time *upper* station master. Hardly any physician was a plain doctor; you were a *Dozent,* a professor, a privy councillor. In the restaurant you never called for "the waiter"; you addresssed the lowest of the waiters as "Herr Ober." If the man talking to you knew what you were, he promoted you automatically to one rank above the one to which you belonged. If you were vice president, you were called president. A bookkeeper was a "Herr Direktor." When you hired a *fiacre,* the driver looked you over, and depending on how you were dressed, he called you "Herr Doktor" if you were poorly dressed, "Herr Baron" if you were decently dressed, or "Herr Graf" if your sartorial opulence impressed him. The topmost rung of the title ladder was the titleless title: the mere mention of your name preceded by the definite article, the implication being that you were so well known that identification became superfluous: *the* Billroth, *the* Slezak, *the* Freud.

Bits of excessive and meaningless politeness sat like stones in the rivulets of Viennese conversation. Richard Strauss said: "People are false everywhere, but in Vienna they are so pleasantly false." The standard greeting to any woman higher on the social scale than a charwoman was: "I kiss your hand, gracious lady." This was followed by a peck on the hand, later to become a phrase without accompanying action. Pious people kissed the hand of the priest, children the hands of parents and grandparents, a young woman the hand of an older woman. When two people met on the street, a sluicegate of polite expressions was opened, each asking the other the state of "your precious health" and that of "your highly honored gracious lady." The flood of phrases gave you time to think who for God's sake it was you were talking to.

Social distinctions were punctiliously observed: you belonged where you belonged. A plain bourgeois, even if he could afford it, did not eat at Frau Sacher's Restaurant nor take his *Jause,* his five-o'clock tea (which in point of fact was coffee with whipped cream and two or three pieces of pastry) at Demel's. These places were reserved for the aristocracy, the upper members of the army, and a few millionaires. The man from the middle class ate at Meissl und Schadn, or Hartmann's, or at the Linde, and had his *Jause* at Gerstner's. If he went to the theater, he did not sit in the first two rows of the Burgtheater or the Opera; these rows were reserved for people whose family names began with a *von* or for visiting diplomats. The boxes at the opera were owned by the aristocratic families—Pallavicini, Liechtenstein, Fürstenberg, Montenuovo—and were not for sale.

The Viennese family man—let us call him "Otto," because Otto is a popular Viennese name—was often a tyrant, and the two subjects about which Otto felt tyrannical were food and quiet. Food was of dramatic importance, and any man who was not finicky about it would be despised by his wife and his servants. In his youth Franz Joseph was admired because he could eat as much as a longshoreman. Viennese cooking is an art which, if it does not rival the subtlety of the French or the variety of the Chinese table, includes astonishing marvels. There are no fewer than thirty-two varieties of boiled beef, and the headwaiter at any good restaurant knew which variety of *Tafelspitz* a steady customer preferred and served it with his choice of chive sauce or applesauce laced with horseradish. Meals usually ended with a warm, rich, and fattening dessert. Here variety was almost endless, including such creations as *Palatschinken* (crepes), *Kaiserschmarrn* (broken-up crepes), *Marillenknödel* (dumplings filled with apricots), *Milchrahmstrudel* (cheese strudel with a cream sauce). One of the most popular cakes consumed at the *Jause* was (and is) the *Gugelhupf*, a yeast cake which gave its name to a hospital for the insane, a round building constructed by Joseph II in the eighteenth century. To this day the heraldic emblem of Vienna seems to be the Sacher torte, a cake of chocolate and jam.

The main meal, at midday, had to be served on the dot, beginning with the soup. (That and the start of the opera were the only two events which took place punctually.) If the food was not to Otto's liking, he was capable of pulling the tablecloth from the table and throwing the dishes onto the floor. The household quaked. With every meal rolls rather than bread were eaten. Tradition has it that the rolls shaped like a crescent moon, the *Kipfel,* were invented by a baker after the Turks were driven back. The rolls or bread had to be absolutely fresh. They were baked twice a day, and after 2 P.M. nobody would dream of buying the rolls baked in the morning. Most Viennese ate five times a day: a breakfast of coffee and rolls, a "fork breakfast" at about ten o'clock, the main midday meal, the *Jause* at five, and a relatively simple supper around eight or after the theater.

After the midday meal, a short siesta was obligatory. It was high time for a rest, since Vienna rose early. The milkman came at 6 A.M. Factories opened at seven. School started at eight. During Otto's siesta the children had to be as quiet as grass growing. The Viennese did not cater to their children, nor were they good educators, being too impatient and nervous to consider that children might have problems. Children were lovable as long as they were cute and clean, but they were not to be forward (*vorlaut*). When they came of school age, they went to schools which were often harsh and dull and in which they were inoculated with a great many disconnected and incomprehensible facts, including the facts of Austria's history so distorted as to give most Viennese children the impression that Austria had won all her wars.

Stefan Zweig, who was a boy during the last period of Franz Joseph's reign, remembered his own school:

> . . . For us school was compulsion, barrenness, boredom, a place in which one had to swallow exactly measured portions of knowledge. . . .
>
> Not that Austrian schools were all that bad. On the contrary, the study plan was carefully designed after a century of experience, and had it been attractively presented, it could have formed the basis of a fruitful and reasonably broad education. Yet it was just the precision of the plan, the inflexibility of the blueprint, which made our school hours so dreadfully barren and unliving. The cold teaching apparatus was never regulated for the individual; like an automaton it was measured only by numbers, by marks of "good, satisfactory, unsatisfactory." We learned our curriculum and took our exams to show what we had learned. In eight years no teacher ever once asked us what we would like to learn. The lifting inspiration for which every young person secretly longs was absent. Jejune prosiness was expressed in our school building, a typical functional edifice plastered together fifty years before as cheaply and as thoughtlessly as possible. With its cold, badly painted walls, the low ceilings of its classrooms, not relieved by a picture or any decoration which might have pleased the eye, the all-pervading smell of the toilets, this barrack of learning resembled a piece of furniture in an old hotel which many had used and many were still to use without giving it a glance or a thought. Even today I cannot forget the stale, glum smell which was so characteristic of this building as well as of all Austrian official buildings . . . a smell of overheated, overfilled rooms, the windows of which were never properly opened. The smell remained first in one's clothes and then in one's soul.[5]

Perhaps Zweig's description is too somber. Even in the building he describes one or two dedicated and inspiring teachers were to be found.

Otto was not a joiner. The associations, clubs, and mass gatherings beloved by the Germans held little attraction for people who enjoyed company in twos and threes but rarely in large groups. What Otto liked to do was to saunter in the city's streets before his midday meal or after his work, hands clasped behind his back in a gesture he may have copied from Beethoven, who may have copied it from Napoleon. He followed a fixed route which invariably included the Kärntnerstrasse, the principal street, which led from the Stephanskirche to the Ring. His hat was doffed to left and right as he greeted acquaintances. There was no end of hat lifting in Vienna. Otto liked to be well dressed—clothes meant a lot to him; he often wore his cylinder during the day as well as the evening, and he carried an important-looking black briefcase which may have contained nothing more important than a sandwich or the schedule of future opera performances. Eventually he halted at his favorite *Kaffeehaus,* where he read the newspapers furnished by the establishment. Vienna had many newspapers, reflecting its many political parties, and for the price of a demitasse one could read them all, stretched as they were on handy reading racks. A friend would come, and together the two men would discuss politics in an undertone. Each *Kaffeehaus* had its specific clientele: artists met in one, bankers in another, lieutenants in a third. Bricklayers, policemen, jewelers—they all had a favorite *Kaffeehaus.* The *Kaffeehaus* served as a club, as a conference room, and as a place for lovers' meetings; it was warm, smoke-filled, and shabbily comfortable. Often Otto would invite a business acquaintance to meet him at the *Kaffeehaus;* "invite" meant that each paid his own bill.

In the evening Otto liked to play cards—tarok was the favorite game—but he retired early. Vienna retired early. At ten o'clock the doors of the houses were locked. If you came home after ten, you had to wake the porter, who shuffled out sleepy and grumbling in slippers and a robe that smelled of cabbage, unlocked the door for you, and, after having been tipped, gave you a bit of a candle to light your way upstairs. The porter obviously disapproved of night owls.

The big topic in Otto's house was: Where do we go for summer vacation? The Viennese of Kaiser Franz Joseph liked to travel—within a prescribed and modest circle. The children needed fresh air, because the air of the city was "dangerous," at least in Otto's opinion. It was true that Vienna did not enjoy a good health record. The city was paved with cobblestones; the traffic chipped minute particles off the stones and these found their way into the atmosphere. The high incidence of tuberculosis—Vienna's endemic disease—was ascribed to this pollution. Otto took his family to the mountains, the nearby Semmering or the lake district of Carinthia or the beautiful but rain-soaked Salzburg region or the verdant Tyrol. Or, as a change, they would go to the seashore, to Ragusa (now Dubrovnik). The more adventurous would visit Venice, the still more adventurous would have a try at Paris. A Viennese would not dream of going to Budapest unless he had to go on business. The caviling he indulged in at home changed abroad to the opposite, scorn for whatever was not Viennese. Right outside Vienna's city limits began the "province." A Viennese put a world of contempt into the word "provincial." A man with a Bohemian accent was as standard a figure of comedy on the Viennese stage as the doctor from Bologna on the Italian stage. To hear them tell it, nobody in Prague ever read a book.

Though Vienna was a melting pot of diverse nationalities—"At the Danube the Moor becomes a Viennese" was a popular saying— the Viennese did not feel comfortable with foreigners. Whatever went wrong in Vienna, the fault was traceable to foreign influences. Jews, even if they had been born in Vienna, were "foreigners." Anti-Semitism was but ill suppressed and was secretly encouraged by the army and at some periods by the Church. In due course we shall meet Vienna's brilliant but anti-Semitic Mayor Karl Lueger; let it be said that Franz Joseph could not stomach him. Of course Franz Joseph was not alone; there was no dearth of voices which protested, sometimes gently, sometimes loudly, often ironically, against the hoary prejudice. Yet although the bacillus lay in the blood stream of a people of insecure constitution, only intermittently did it produce a high fever. Most of the time anti-Semitism served but as another excuse to be piled on excuses. Otto was not only suspicious of the Jews but envious of them. He could not understand their positive view of life, their nervous energy, their derision of military glory. "Jew"—or rather his worst incarnation, a "Galician"—was the reason why business was bad, or a new tax was levied, or a property went down in value. On the other hand, when somebody in the family became

ill, Otto tried to find a Jewish doctor to come to the house. By and
by he came to concede the enrichment the Jews brought: Altenberg, Beer-Hofmann, Schnitzler, Zweig, Karl Kraus in literature
and journalism; Goldmark, Mahler, Schönberg in music; Reinhardt in the theater. These men could and did work in and for
Vienna, though Otto preserved his distance. Vienna had room for
diversity.

Otto went to church partly because he believed it was good for
him and partly because he did not dare not to go. The Catholic
Church could influence a man's career through power which
reached into the corners of commerce. There were few major
commercial enterprises in which the Church had no investment.
Its wealth was shrewdly used. Joseph II, the reformer Emperor,
had attempted to appropriate some of its Austrian possessions and
to put limits on its simony. By the time Franz Joseph came to the
throne, the Church had worked its way back to wealth. It got
money, a good deal of it, from the Austrian Imperial Royal
Treasury, and from the collections which were exacted from the
faithful more punctiliously than their prayers.

In the Vienna of the late nineteenth century one could still
find many an old priest, white-haired and rosy-cheeked, whom
everybody in the district knew and who knew everybody's problems. Children ran out and curtsied to him when he took his walk,
his head covered by an old-fashioned cylinder, his black cassock
strewn with tobacco crumbs because he was still taking snuff. The
janitor standing before the door took the pipe out of his mouth
and asked after the health of "Your dignified highness." He gave
the children cheap little colored pictures of the saints and offered
lozenges to the women. His day began at five o'clock in the
morning and ended at eight o'clock at night with a multitude of
tasks in and outside his church; he worried about the district
school, the orphan asylum, the musical committee, the funeral
facilities

He was carefully supervised by a bishop, who in turn reported
to a delegate directly responsible to Rome. These delegates were
diplomats of such determination and sophistication as to make
Austria at periods virtually a possession of the Vatican. They could
not have operated had they not been supported by the Emperor;

that support was given partly because he was a believer and partly because he had learned his history lesson and knew what troubles Rome could engender in a disobedient country. The bishops, elegantly robed and purse-proud, were always watching. Any infringement of the tacit bondage was communicated up the ladder. Atheism, while it existed, was hidden and did not show its head until very late in Franz Joseph's reign. He despised an apostate.

The Church delivered value for value received. In addition to the comfort, the sense of belonging, and the solace it offered the Viennese poor, it gave them the joy of spectacles. The splendor of sound of the Masses by Haydn, Mozart, Beethoven, the jeweled reliquaries, the magnificent processions, the sonorous sermons, the organ music dipped in incense, these were the antidotes to the six-day grayness. Practically the whole Viennese population turned out for the Corpus Christi procession in June. At five o'clock in the morning the air was filled with the pealing of bells and the girls got up to put on their summer clothes and straw hats decorated with real flowers. In every window there were flowers, lighted candles, pictures of the saints, and a picture of the Emperor. The band began to play loudly, and a long row of carriages and pedestrians, ordered strictly according to rank, started to move. The officers and soldiers were in parade uniform and the mayor, wearing the gold chain of the city of Vienna, was seated in the state coach, pulled by six horses. The splendor of his coach was exceeded only by that of the coach of Franz Joseph, which was all gold and was drawn by eight white horses trained to move with the precision of ballet dancers. The princes, the archdukes, the dukes, and the lesser aristocracy followed. As the procession started in the inner city, Franz Joseph alighted from the carriage and walked all the way. Through narrow old streets, across wide squares, past the Lobkowitz Palace, the train made its way, at its center the silk baldachin under which the monstrance was carried, surrounded by flags and guarded by halberdiers who seemed to have been recruited from some medieval play. Three times they halted, at the altars of three churches. Franz Joseph knelt at each stop, a candle in his right hand, his left resting on the pommel of his saber. The cardinal blessed the people. It was Catholicism's show of shows, and it was what the Viennese call a *Hetz*, a spree. On Maundy

Thursday the populace was treated to the ceremony of the Emperor bending down to sprinkle water over the feet of several carefully selected indigent old men. To be sure, the washing was purely symbolic, a ritual to indicate the humility which Franz Joseph did not in the least feel.

As powerful as the Church was the military. The professional army was coddled and protected, and was allowed to obey a law of its own. Its rights ranked above civilian rights. When an officer and a civilian met on a narrow sidewalk, the civilian had to step out of the way. If he did not and was a man of substance—"capable of giving satisfaction" was the technical term—he was likely to be challenged to a duel. The duel at dawn was the outlet for the bellicose instincts of the lieutenant who had been trained for war but found his country at peace.

Austria had the worst army but the best-dressed one. The lancers (*Ulanen*) sported a waterfall of gold braid tumbling from the back of their tunics; in the winter the cavalry officers wore fur coats held together by a silver rope and in the summer put on light mantles of blue crisscrossed by gay shoulder straps; the Royal Hunters appeared in gray ensembles with green facing; the artillery was furnished with a uniform which won the prize at the Paris Exposition of 1900; the infantry marched in tight-fitting red trousers; for gala occasions guard officers donned snow-white jackets and covered their heads with toques from which gushed a fountain of green or white feathers. The horses were as finely caparisoned as the men and seemed as vain. Parades strutted almost daily, their obvious purpose being to demonstrate Austria's might, not so much to the enemy without as to the malcontent within the frontiers. To Franz Joseph a carelessly dressed soldier was a traitor; he himself was always the perfectly turned-out officer and hardly ever appeared in civilian dress. A row of closets contained his uniforms, hundreds of them, and a special valet was charged with their care.

Military service was compulsory; most of Vienna's young men loved to serve. It was their chance at an existence within a fixed span of time where everything was measured for them and they did not have to make decisions for themselves; an outdoor life enjoyed, with all its boring drill, before the walls of the office or the factory enclosed them. The timetable of life was clearly printed and thought seemed superfluous. It was as well their chance at uncensored sexual experience. The barracks were located in small villages, far away from the metropolis, and there one could find peasant girls who would not resist a uniform or say no to the "defender of the fatherland." Otto had served his "one-year voluntary" in Hungary; in his later years the word "Hungarian" conjured up for him an odor of woman's breasts, the sweat of horses, the dust of hot country roads, and black boot polish.

The professional officers, the lieutenants and first lieutenants, despised the likes of Otto; civilians were invented to serve the military, not the other way round. With civilians one could be, indeed one ought to be, condescending. But civilians with money were useful. The lieutenant was forever in need of money. He was badly paid and sometimes lost a month's wages in a night's gambling session. Otto's wife could count on the lieutenant to be the extra man at her dinner party; the lieutenant needed the meal and the dozen roses he sent the next day were cheaper than the menu of a decent restaurant. He sat next to a young girl from a good family, the one who was a bit faded.

As the officer advanced to major, lieutenant colonel, colonel, and up the scale, as his hair grew grayer and, in spite of a corset, his paunch became noticeable, he moved closer and closer to the fulcrum of the military, to the Hofburg. The easiest road by which to reach the Emperor was the military road. Franz Joseph spoke of "My army." To him it was part family, part toy, part Christmas-tree decoration, part castellan of Habsburg tradition. For considerable periods of his reign, Austria was a peaceful state, playing like a child with the fire of war. When war came, the child got burned, the army failed. Nonetheless, as soon as the peace treaty was signed, the army became important once again.

The other cog on which the wheel of Vienna's life turned was officialdom. The officials wore a uniform of their own—black suit, bowler hat, gray tie with a pearl stickpin, real or false depending on the rank—and they were more numerous than soldiers. Their lives consisted of a ritual of petitions, requisitions, appeals, solicitations, interpellations, and applications, each carefully penned, couched in a lumbering jargon of its own, with the proper stamp affixed, signed and countersigned. Matters which could have been decided on the instant and which involved a trifling expenditure of a few gulden became occasions for lengthy memoranda; these papers drifted through government bureaus and into crammed wooden files, but never into waste-paper baskets. In the lexicon of the functionaries the favorite word was "Impossible." Every Viennese knew that this was only the first answer, the expected move of a delaying tactic. The petitioner kept on and usually got what he needed, got it by logic or influence or charm or sheer persistence. The officials were often pedantic and self-important, but rarely nefarious. If you could find out what the official's hobby was—philately, lepidoptery, numismatics—and could discuss it with him, you could twist him around. Bribery wouldn't do it. Vienna's functionaries were remarkably honest. Very few cases of corruption occurred in the whole complicated system of Austrian bureaucracy; they valued their respectability and their titles too much for that. When their wives entertained, titles flew around the room, though the food and wine served were modest enough. A bowl of fruit was placed on the table, but the guests did not touch it. Everybody knew that it was there for decoration and that it was to be sent back to the grocer the next morning. There was always a next morning. Parliaments came and went, ministers were exalted and dismissed, ambassadors schemed and resigned, but below the heights the bureaucrats shuffled the documents, remained steady, did their work, slept well, and were the real regents of the empire. Only foreigners tried to butt their heads against the paper wall; the Viennese lived within it.

Hermann Bahr in his book *Austriaca* (at first suppressed by the censor) wrote that some important functionaries—the court councillor (*Hofrat*) and the section chief (*Sektionschef*)—felt that their real duty was to sabotage "responsible government established by the Emperor and the people," just to make sure that they themselves would not lose power:

> Our Emperor doesn't say much and one never knows what he is thinking. The Germans envy us for that. But there are disadvantages. A few [officials] use this condition to arrogate a mysterious power to themselves and to give themselves an importance to which they are not entitled. They pretend that somehow or other they

know the Emperor's wishes. What *they* want they demand by as-
suring us that it is the will of the *Emperor.* . . .

One of the chief functions of our bureaucracy is to render ridiculous or impossible decisions by parliament or by the ministers. It is
quite a system: they want to prove that it is of no use to have right
on your side, if you don't have the bureaucrats with you.

The "operetta view" of Vienna postulates that its women are
beautiful, lively, and blond. The men liked them *"mollert"* (a
word derived from the Italian), soft-fleshed, soft-skinned, and
a trifle hefty. A realistic view must be less gallant. As many homely
and hard-skinned women were to be found in Vienna as in any
city, though it is probably correct to say that the Viennese were—
and are—a better-looking race than the Berliners or the Frankfur-
ters. Cosmetics were confined to a discreet application of rice
powder and a little eau de cologne. The natural look was fashionable; they did not wrap themselves in a sexual penumbra, eyelids
half closed; they presented themselves with frank charm, eyes wide
open. Nor did they possess the instinctive chic which was inborn
in Parisian girls. Women of bourgeois income, and even most of
the wealthy ones, had their clothes made at home. The "house
seamstress" came, usually an elderly lady from Bohemia. Several
serious conferences ensued. Then, with the aid of some picture
clipped from a Paris journal, the seamstress, her mouth full of
pins, tried to create the creation. When she got through, it had the
"made-at-home" look.

It was different with hats. They were imported from Paris and
constituted the most important article of a woman's wardrobe.
They were multicolored, multitiered islands covered with flora
and fauna and seemed ready to float off had they not been
anchored by long rhinestone-studded hatpins. They were creations
of woodland fancy, silk and taffeta setting a woman's face in a
frame of frond and dell.[6] Outdoors, women wore a veil, a last
reminder of Oriental purdah, but they took it off indoors, while
they rarely took off the hat as long as somebody was around to
admire it. When the wearer of the dreamy hat got old, she sometimes replaced it with a plain felt cloche, as shapeless as it was
unbecoming. That meant either that her husband had arrived and
become a *Hofrat*—or that she had given up competing.

The Viennese girl from a middle-income family was neither as uneducated nor as innocent as she is depicted in the sentimental romances of the time, though her intellectual curiosity, like her piano playing, had a way of fading after marriage. Her occupation with her husband bordered on the fanatic. In nine marriages out of ten she was subservient to the male and in due time became a rather corpulent cricket-on-the-hearth. She was always talking about *mein Mann;* she would lay a pound of pride as well as an ounce of fear into those two words.

Viennese women were frugal. They locked up the butter and the wine, carrying their keys in a great bunch. The key ring constantly got mislaid and there was a frantic search through the house. The maid usually found it. All but the poorest families had one servant, the more affluent ones at least two, a stout cook (Polish or Czech) and a chambermaid who came from the country to the big city. There she fell in love, was left in the lurch by the infantry sergeant, wept profusely, and told her mistress all about it. The mistress listened willingly to the tale of the perfidy of men. Most women were on an easy footing with their servants, though the lady of the house gave her servants cheaper food to eat than the food she served her family.

On her shopping expeditions a Viennese woman usually took a friend or a servant along. To stand alone in front of a store window was not considered quite respectable. Department stores did not exist. Each store featured a specialty, and most women were personally acquainted with the owners. When they went in, they preceded their shopping with an expansive chat about the owner's family and his plans for the summer. Most stores displayed a sign: FIXED PRICES. This merely served as a challenge to the shopper to begin her bargaining. If she did not haggle, she felt she had not done herself justice. Only the members of the aristocracy did not bargain, but neither did they pay cash, and kept the store-keepers waiting for their money. Ordinary people paid at once and in cash; charge accounts were unknown.

The thinnest and most diaphanous layer of Viennese society was the top layer, the fabulous families which were called *die Adeligen,* "the noble ones," whose male representatives appeared either turned out by the best English tailor and with a monocle clamped in their faces—or in torn hunting costumes and mud-stained boots, while their women would either spend a fortune at the couturier or roam around the palace in a dress a servant girl might disdain. By no means everybody who possessed a patent of nobility, by no means all those whose names began with a *von,* were considered *"adelig."* You could earn the prefix by merit, deeds beneficial to the state, or money spent for the common weal, but you would not thereby ascend to that pinnacle where stood a scion whose grandfather had been a prince in Maria Theresa's time. It made little difference whether this scion was a pigeon-livered wastrel, his brain comatose, his legs spindly; if he was a Kinsky or a Palffy, he was an object of admiration to all who did not know him. There were no more than two hundred families in Austria who could pass the test of true aristocracy. Their ancestors had built Vienna's baroque palaces; their sons preferred to spend their time at the Jockey Club, Vienna's one exclusive club, which ·tood in back of Sacher's and which no casual or common visitor had ever entered. They were there when they were in Vienna; but in fact they spent little time in Vienna. In the autumn they had to be present for the hunting in Bohemia or Moravia, the winter had to be spent in Paris and on the Riviera, the early summer in London; only Franz Joseph's two court balls at carnival time, the Derby in May, and an occasional charity affair required that they show themselves. These appearances sufficed to streak the Viennese sky like fireworks. The Viennese, coal heavers or councillors, were bedazzled by their luster.

The industrial millionaires who appeared in the latter half of the nineteenth century pretended to derogate the "harebrained hoard" of the nobles, but in truth they were overjoyed if they could manage to be on friendly terms with a prince or an arch-duke. It did not happen often: the high castes did not shake hands with the lower castes. Franz Joseph was willing to "sell" the millionaires titles and orders, but neither he nor a member of the highest aristocracy would sit down with them at lunch. In turn, the millionaires formed a closed circle of their own and, perfecting their own brand of snobbishness, invented their own legend. When they got together, the word "money" was hardly ever spoken: they saw themselves as patrons of the arts, as breeders of race horses, as collectors of old crucifixes, as anything except businessmen.

Symptomatic of the stratification of Vienna's society were the vehicles which transported the citizens on their errands and pleasures. The finest were the "court equipages," sumptuously painted coaches, either "four-seaters" or "two-seaters," drawn by four or two horses and displaying on their sides the Austrian double eagle. These were used by the court itself and its top functionaries. The liveried coachman wore a special two-cornered hat, and he held his whip as if it were a scepter; a lackey sat beside him. The court equipages brought visiting foreign diplomats to the Emperor's audiences and the teachers to the Habsburg children. Actors and singers as well, if they had earned the title of "Imperial Royal," were entitled to a court equipage; it was so specified in their contracts. The carriages for the "All-Highest Person," the Emperor, his wife and children, were painted black on top, green below, and had green and gold wheels. The other court carriages were painted green and brown, and the wheels were gold- or red-striped. The sentries at the gates were thus able to see at a glance whether the guard had to be called to present arms. Wealthy citizens kept carriages of their own, but the coachman wore a cylinder, to distinguish him from those with the two-cornered hat. If you did not own a carriage, you could hire one called an "unnumbered"; it pretended to be a private carriage. For ordinary use you could jump into either a *"Fiaker"* with two horses, or a cheaper *"Einspänner"* with one horse. Fares were a matter of bargaining. By and by a few horse-drawn omnibuses began to operate—but most men went to work on foot.

If you used the omnibus, you tipped the bus conductor. In Vienna you tipped everybody: the servants if you were invited for dinner, the mailman, the chimneysweep, the messenger—usually an old man with a white mustache and a red cap—who stood at the corner ready to perform any kind of errand; the usher in the theater, the janitor, the woman who guarded the public comfort station (you could relieve yourself in either first class or second class, with or without toilet paper). Vienna was a city of small change. When you wanted to pay your bill in the restaurant, you called for the "pay waiter," you told him what you had eaten, including the number of rolls or slices of bread; he totaled it all up on a tiny sheet of paper with a tiny stub of a pencil, and then you gave him some change. Tipping united all the Viennese.

Two men were welcomed by all classes of society; as the years went by, each became one of the prominent sights of Vienna, as familiar as the "Pest Column" in the Graben, as popular as the Prater promenade. One of these was Ludwig Lobmeyr, whose father had begun selling glassware in a little store and who around 1865 had become a glass manufacturer; his chandeliers hung in the best salons and illuminated Vienna's theaters. Lobmeyr, a bachelor, devoted his life to the perfection of Viennese craftsmanship; he commissioned young artists to design table services, ashtrays, drinking glasses, and vases, and took a leading part in developing "Vienna porcelain." He was the guiding spirit behind and chief contributor to the Austrian Museum (now the Vienna Historical Museum), which was founded on the principle of the Victoria and Albert. Being a bachelor, he ate at the Hotel Imperial: exactly at noon he would leave his office on the Kärntnerstrasse, and when the policeman saw him coming he stopped the traffic so that Lobmeyr could cross the street unhindered.

The other was Ludwig Bösendorfer, son of Ignaz, the piano manufacturer. The Bösendorfer piano rivaled in quality the Steinway or the Érard, and Ludwig, with his beautiful white beard, impeccably dressed in black, was a man everybody knew and everybody asked for favors. In 1872 he built in the Palais Liechtenstein a concert hall with superb acoustics, seating 588. Bülow gave the opening recital; after him appeared Liszt, Rubinstein, Mottl, Weingartner, Scaria, and others.[7]

It is significant that both these personalities, Lobmeyr and Bösendorfer, were businessmen who had something to do with art.

It has been said that Vienna was a city where legend was stronger than reality. The Viennese was forever turning his back on reality. Facts were his enemy, illusion his friend. He looked for the amaranthine flower among the dry grass of his existence—or, if he had no hope of finding the fabled blossom, he at least looked for the four-leaf clover. He was not by nature a doer or a fighter;

the army, which absorbed so much of Franz Joseph's care, was at times a fictive instrument, its trappings more real than its power. When personal or national failure came to a Viennese, he wrapped himself in a cloak of plaint and submission. He vacillated between a soft irony and a determined frivolity. Since frivolity sounds louder than irony, the city earned a reputation for being gay. Superficially it was. Yet its gaiety was as much a flight from actuality, as much an escape from daylight into twilight, as its pessimism. A Viennese loved to make believe. His make-believe helped to render the make-do bearable. The beautiful blue Danube was not blue, and by the time the river reached the outskirts of the city it was not particularly beautiful. It was all a fancy, and Vienna was a city where fancy was bred. It was a city of dreaming. Here the interpretation of dreams was to be developed into a new science.

Because the typical Viennese sought to hold reality at a distance, he welcomed unreality as expressed in certain arts, the more illusory the more beloved. Music, the opera, the theater played substantial roles in the life of Vienna, though here again one must be careful not to prettify description or exaggerate Vienna's artistic probity. Vienna was rightly called "the City of Music"—it had earned that title late in the eighteenth century—not because it gave birth to great musicians but because great musicians worked there. Many of the "Viennese composers," from Mozart on, were not born in Vienna: they came from Bonn or Hamburg or Kalischt in Bohemia. That is unimportant; what is important is that they went to the Imperial City because they found an audience there. Yet it is easy to overestimate the size of that audience. It is not true that "everybody in Vienna loved music." The public for symphonic or chamber music might have been relatively larger than that of Moscow; nevertheless it was a limited public. Lanner or Johann Strauss, the sentimental Schrammel Quartet or the slushy gypsy bands, found more partisans than did the Vienna Philharmonic Society, which early in the 1840s was formed from the "Imperial Court Opera Orchestra."[8] Mozart knew that Vienna's taste was more superficial than Prague's. Beethoven complained (somewhat unjustly) that the Viennese cared only for

Rossini and more Rossini, Brahms's *Requiem* was hissed (in 1868), Mahler had to seek approbation outside Vienna. The demand for entertainment may by-pass art which needs understanding before it can become "entertaining." In Vienna, as everywhere, the demand for entertainment and the willingness to enter into the meaning of a work of art were both present. Who would question, however, that the first public was larger than the second?

The Opera was popular not so much, or not entirely, as a dispenser of music as a dispenser of magic. It was the local palanquin under the cover of which fairy tales were enacted. A thousand Viennese who had never been inside the opera house knew about its machinations, the power play of its directors, its scandals, the fortunes and misfortunes of its singers. And each of the thousand had a comment to make. The Opera was a rallying place, a symbol, a sports arena, a tourist sight, a conversation piece, a mill for gossip. Who was sleeping with whom—the outsiders had the inside story. The waiter conversing with a visitor spoke of "our Opera" in somewhat the same tone as Franz Joseph spoke of "My army." One "went to the opera," not always to hear a particular opera; the petty official was in the gallery, Otto and his wife sat in one of the back rows of the lower floor called the parterre, the wealthy in the front rows except the first two—and the students squeezed into a narrow enclave, the standing room. Officers went for half-price, and those who knew the right people went for nothing. The children were taken to *Hänsel und Gretel* or Nicolai's *The Merry Wives of Windsor,* later to be exalted by that "music beyond music," *Tristan.* Italian opera had always been, and continued to be, popular, and young and old shed a tear at the last act of *Traviata,* performed in German. Mozart's *Don Giovanni* and *Figaro* were performed in German translations as well—wretched translations—and often aroused more respect than love. The military ogled the ballet *Die Puppenfee* appreciatively.

Yet most plain Viennese became musically fervid when they heard or sang Viennese songs, some old, some newly manufactured, some home-felt and poignant, some mawkish and mushy. "Vienna, Vienna—only you will always remain the city of my dreams"—it was another expression of flight from reality. As English writers, Dickens or Lamb or Gissing, wrote eloquently of food, English food in reality being nothing much to write about, so did the Viennese glorify in song a city of their imagination.

The theater—for that Vienna mustered unqualified enthusiasm. If you called somebody a *Theaternarr,* a "fool for the theater," it was a compliment much relished. The theatrical tradition was rooted in Vienna's history; it included dirty slapstick farces which were given in suburban theaters, comedies with magic and music, "song-plays" in which dialogue alternated with sung numbers and which eventually came close to opera, naïve prose plays with a moral, sour satires stuffed with allusions incomprehensible to a non-Viennese, high tragedies in blank verse. When Franz Joseph ascended the throne, the Burgtheater had some seventy years behind it,[9] but it was still to rise to its best work. The finest and most mellifluous German was spoken there, and to be a member of its company put the stamp of approval on an actor. The Burgtheater's subvention was generous, even in hard times, and it was able to stage not only the German classics but Shakespeare, Molière, Calderón, Sophocles, and when the time came the new problem dramas of Ibsen and Shaw. Its repertoire was truly international and it helped to develop such great actors as Adolf Sonnenthal (Lear and Nathan der Weise), Charlotte Wolter (Lady Macbeth), later Josef Kainz (Hamlet and Faust). All the same, the Viennese criticized the theater, though lovingly. Alfred Berger, a director during Franz Joseph's time, said that there existed three insoluble problems: the squaring of the circle, a *perpetuum mobile,* and a satisfactory Burgtheater director. Somebody else said that the population of Vienna consisted of 1.7 million potential Burgtheater directors, each and every one ready to assume the office, each and every one convinced he could do better than the incumbent.

A generic description of a human complex never can be wholly true. It must allow for as many exceptions as a German grammar. The exceptions multiply when one deals with societies within a society: such is the picture of the Vienna of Franz Joseph, a city of which the bourgeoisie formed the core around which moved, and against which rubbed, the aristocracy, the workmen, the military, the thickening layer of the newly wealthy, the bureaucrats, the entertainers of high and low stature, and so on, no one society being integrated in or absorbed by the other. Can we say that these societies possessed a common characteristic, can we define a "Viennese character"? Otto Friedländer has attempted to do so:

> A Viennese lives for his leisure occupation. That is the true goal of his life. Vienna is a city of people who have chosen the wrong profession.
>
> The relationship in which men stand to their work is one of lukewarm convenience—not one of passion. Only seldom is their love expended on their official or legitimate activity, the reason being that the Viennese possess little self-assurance and little confidence in their own abilities. They believe in tradition, in the well-trod ways, in connections, not in accomplishments. So they become lawyers, merchants, physicians, teachers, etc., if these professions seem to offer them favorable opportunities; then they hate the profession which gives them their daily bread. They suffer and so does their work. Perhaps it is less a question of guilt than of natural inclination; the predilection of most Viennese pushes them towards art—usually towards music or the theater. The whole world could not use as many musicians and actors as Vienna could or would like to produce. The Viennese artistic longing must remain unfulfilled, a frustration.[10]

If it is true that a people get the government they deserve—a truism not to be taken unquestioningly—it is also true that to understand the man who governs we must understand the governed. In Franz Joseph's upbringing, in his tradition, in his mind, in his character, lay seeds of decay. These seeds could not have taken root had he been unable to plant them in receptive ground. But the ground was receptive, the destructive sap rose in the trunk, and the defoliation of the Austrian Empire proceeded until the trunk itself toppled. The process took more than a half-century and was slowed by some seemingly glorious summers. They were false summers, producing far-off storms which were mistaken for summer lightning.

Yet, while political rot set in, there flourished an astonishing intellectual life. How did that happen? What nourished it? Was it because the Viennese possessed what may be called a predisposition for creativity? Did the government's indifference help or hinder the nonpolitical creative men, the physicians, painters, poets, university professors, musicians? They led a separated existence and formed still another society within the Viennese concourse. Did the separation from communal concerns help them move strongly upward, while Austria moved weakly downward? Was the division between reality, being the exercise of statesmanship and concern with economic development, and unreality, being the exercise of a special and often isolated imaginative faculty, healthful? Were the atony of the state and the vigor of Viennese creativity connected?

These questions belong to a biography of Franz Joseph, a man who loved uniforms and cared little for the white coat of the scientist or the thinker's cap.

Franz Joseph when he ascended the throne (after a drawing
by Leopold Kupelwieser)

CHAPTER II

Fever in Europe

ANYBODY WHO COULD or would peep beyond the wall of his own little garden was able to tell that all was not well with the European world of the 1830s and the 1840s.

What was it that was wrong? Life for many—indeed for most except the underpaid laborers—seemed tranquil enough: Napoleon was safely dead, the Congress of Vienna had established some sort of order, industry was flourishing, no war devastated the fields. What was the cause of so general a discontent? Was it a new self-assertiveness, an increasing consciousness that the role of kings could no longer be accepted unquestioningly? While most men were still willing to be governed by a sovereign, many wished to have a hand in the business of governing. The old concept that "Rex est lex"—"The King is the law"—was being questioned. Yet it was being questioned only vaguely and indecisively. A more immediate concern, a more active cause for worry, was the machine. Would the machine rob people of their bread? It looked as if the shoemaker was going to have to shut his little shop because a factory in Bohemia was turning out acceptable shoes more cheaply. It looked as if fewer bricklayers were going to be employed as soon as the builders learned how to use the new concrete mixtures. At any rate, what did the future hold for the little man?

Pustulating spots appeared on the body politic, the cure for which none of the governments dared prescribe, the cure seeming

31

more painful than the disease. Many of the disorders, occurring here and there without apparent plan, were plain protests against "progress," provoked by fear of the cogwheeled monsters which man had invented and which now, it seemed, would make many men superfluous: a nail factory in Thuringia was destroyed by workers who feared mechanization, the weavers of Silesia held a mass demonstration against the introduction of weaving machinery, ironworkers on the Rhine wrecked one of the large foundries, sailors on the Danube stopped river traffic for a time as the larger steamship companies threatened to deprive them of their livelihood.

Perhaps the malady was temporary, perhaps it would all pass over, perhaps threats and severity, the police and the militia, would manage to restore quiet. As yet, more windows were broken than heads. As yet, more words were hurled than stones. The fever, though measurable, stood just a few strokes above normal, resembling a mild influenza. It might have been assuaged by sensible measures. But sensible measures were what nobody undertook, his excellency, the Minister, loathing the reformer, and the reformers themselves jockeying for power and self-glorification.

Protests spawned by unemployment and inadequate wages widened into deliberate movements. "Insurrection of thought always precedes insurrection of arms" wrote Wendell Phillips. Down south in the Kingdom of the Two Sicilies the people forced Ferdinand II to give them a written constitution and parliamentary rule. Up north Frederick VII was coerced into similar concessions by the Danes.

It was France, that eager host of revolution, which inflamed the sporadic disturbances into an epidemic. "When France has a cold," said Metternich, "all of Europe sneezes." It was from Paris that the contagion spread, carried by contact among the nations of the Continent, because no nation could any longer be put into an isolation ward.[1] By the time the heads of government realized what was happening, it was too late: the fever had mounted, the Revolution of 1848 was in full frenzy.

The year before, a group of Parisians had organized a series of "reform banquets." They met at dinner, made long speeches criticizing the French Chamber and the King himself, and asked for universal, unrestricted suffrage. That was really the sum and substance of what they proposed: they believed that if everybody had the right to vote, peaceful reforms could be enacted. The antigovernment forces were better at talk than at action, and they were not strong because they were divided into factions: the moderate liberals of the old school, the republicans, the socialists, and a few radicals who had read their Marx and Engels and who belonged to the newly organized Union of Communists, with headquarters in Brussels. It was the government itself which strengthened and united them by refusing to listen. On February 22 further "reform banquets" were forbidden. That was the rallying signal the opposition needed. Laborers, artisans, students, bakers, and candlestick makers massed, built barricades in the streets of Paris, and with one voice no longer requested but now *demanded* reforms. King Louis Philippe, deaf up to then, took fright and called for a new ministry to investigate what could be done. It was too late for investigation; the people no longer trusted the King. Thousands of French, young and old, idealists and opportunists, grouped in the suburb of St. Antoine, the historic quarter of revoluton, marched on the city, and flooded the boulevards. A shot was fired—nobody knew by whom—it was answered by other shots, horses shied, street fighting began, hysteria became general, the National Guard could not or would not keep order, and before the day was over, enough men were killed for the infuriated people to take up the corpses and march with them through the streets, holding them high as symbols of martyrdom. Nothing now could stem the insurrection, and Cinna the poet was torn for his bad verses. Two days later Louis Philippe abdicated and fled to England, stripped of title, realm, and, what was worse, of money. The Republic was proclaimed

Events in Berlin mirrored those of Paris with curious similarity. There Frederick William IV was King, an uncertain king, lost in medieval and moist reveries, mistrusting his advisers, a monarch who had been offered the opportunity to unite the small German states and muffed that opportunity, because he could not bring himself to be either a strong conservative or a strong liberal but instead took one step to the right and one to the left on slippery ground. He watched the demonstrations organized in Baden, Württemberg, Darmstadt, Mannheim, and other German cities. He saw that Bavaria was in an uproar. The Bavarians, usually easygoing, now openly resented their King Ludwig I, who had insisted that his mistress, Lola Montez (born in Limerick, Ireland, as Marie Dolores Eliza Rosanna Gilbert), be given a patent of nobility. That was not so bad, and it wasn't that the people didn't condone the sixty-two-year-old king's passion for his thirty-year-old *fille de joie*—why should he not have a little *joie?*— but Lola had managed to divert considerable funds from the Bavarian treasury to the Montez bank account. Ludwig fought for Lola, answering the students' protests by peremptorily closing the university; that move was hardly calculated to pacify Munich's citizens, and soon enough (March 20, 1848) Ludwig had to abdicate. Lola fled over the border.

These manifestations were duly reported to Potsdam, but still Frederick William hesitated. When he finally agreed to a reorganization of the regime, to be mapped out by a National Diet, when he finally promised the end of censorship, when he announced that he would consider proposals for a new written constitution, his words came too tardily. Resentment ran away with reason. As in Paris, so in Berlin the pavements were torn up to form barricades: across them citizens faced the army. There was silence on both sides until, through fright, fatigue, through the very fact that guns were loaded and cocked, through none knew what miscalculation, a few soldiers opened fire. Fierce fighting began. "I saw the barricades of 1830 and those of 1848 [in Paris], but no spectacle as terrible as that of this day has been revealed to me," wrote Adolphe de Circourt, French chargé d'affaires in Berlin. One hundred and eighty-seven men were killed, many more wounded, prisoners treated cruelly. Frederick William, who loathed bloodshed, issued a tearful appeal to his "dear Berliners." The dear Berliners wouldn't be fobbed off. More violence was imminent, until Frederick William, much to the dismay of his army officers, ordered the troops to withdraw. Now further humiliation was in store for him. The people carried the bodies of the dead civilians, their wounds exposed, into the courtyard of the palace. The King and the Queen were made to salute them. "Only the guillotine is missing now," said the Queen. Two days later Frederick William rode through the streets of Berlin wearing a black, red, and gold sash (the revolutionary German colors), visibly uncomfortable, though enthusiastically followed by friends and the foes of three days previous. Everybody realized that it was a defeat for an absolute monarch, a victory for constitutional rule. Would the victory last? "Revolutions begin with infatuation and end with incredulity," wrote the French statesman François Guizot.[2]

The 1848 revolutions in Prussia, France, the German states, in Sicily, Naples, Piedmont, were organic movements "as natural a growth as an oak." Their aims were at first supranational and included better security for labor, limitation on dynastic power through elected representatives, and freedom of speech. These ingredients were present as well in the cauldron which boiled up in Austria, but there additional components embittered the mixture. In the first place the Austrian Empire was old and encrusted with tradition, a crust not easily melted away. Second, it was large—in territory larger even than France—and any of its problems became a large problem. Third, it was a conglomerate of nationalities, most of them inimical to one another and all of them, that is all those not "Austrian" in the German-speaking sense, inimical to Vienna. The longing to form national entities, based on race and language, was as keen as all the other desires put together. Fourth, where was one to direct protest, where suggest reforms? Austria was governed by an embrangled bureaucracy which the historian Bertier de Sauvigny described as a "helter-skelter of ministries, council-offices, chambers, chanceries, departments—the jurisdiction of one contradicting that of the other." Fifth, Austrian policy had for years been designed by a high priest of conservatism, that severe, smooth, and most secure of statesmen, formerly Napoleon's adversary, now grown old but still a keeper of the absolute tradition, still a believer in the divinity of kings or, better, in the necessity of having the populace believe in the divinity of kings. That was Clemens Metternich.

It was Metternich, not the Habsburgs, who had led Austria

from defeat and shame to a position of power and eminence. His plan, by no means illusory, was to confer leadership of all Central Europe on a Habsburg and to have Austria assume European hegemony. Only a king, vested with authoritarian power, could keep Europe at peace. Only a king could weld a people into a prosperous unit. Democracy was absurd because nations are "children, nervous women, or silly creatures." "Monarchy is the only form which appeals to my mentality." Sovereignty of the people? That represented to him "the worst enemy of social order." Revolutions? He knew three kinds: those against persons, those against particular institutions, and those, the so-called social revolutions, which undermined the structure of human society. All three were abominable, steps into the past and not the future: he called revolution a "volcano," "cancer," "the Flood." Revolutions were caused by governmental weakness, and one needed to treat them with forbearance but excise them by force: "One may pardon, but not grant amnesty." No, it was not through revolutionary ideas springing from a few hotheads that progress could be achieved, but only by the work of an enlightened monarch "who would really govern." To circumscribe a monarch by a parliament or permit representation by "self-seeking commoners" was tantamount to an infraction of the responsibility of the anointed ruler. It would result in a disservice to the ruled; it would abandon the common man to a fate which would be as changeable as the direction of the wind.

Metternich despised mystics, ideologists, doctrinaires who were "most adept at ruining everything and least adept at saving anything." "The world today is plagued by a particular disease: it is called mysticism. Like all epidemics it will pass." He would rather do battle with radicals than with liberals. "Liberals only deserve contempt." He was sure he was right: "The science of government can be reduced to principles as fixed as the laws of chemistry." He knew the formula; England (under Lord Palmerston) was wrong, and America's institutions might be healthful in America but would not do in Europe. As to Austria:

> Every political body needs a strongly founded government for its health and for life itself. When such a body consists of parts which are separated by nationality, customs and habits of its people, when

it is further divided by local laws and administration, then it cannot do without the force of a [central] government which is forever active and watchful.[3]

To save Austria from the influx of revolutionary ideas, he made use of an extraordinarily efficient police and spy system. That system, as well as under-the-table donations to domestic and foreign newspapers, helped him stay in power. No university professor entered Austria's frontier without the police having obtained his dossier. No political agitator could slip past the guard. Anybody who had been active in socialist circles in France or Germany was promptly spotted and either arrested or thrown out. The police opened private letters at will and reported subversive contents. (The police were so punctilious that they opened Metternich's love letters to his long-time mistress, the Countess of Lieven—*without*, however, telling Metternich about it. Metternich's amorous correspondence, like his love life, was ample and international: he had three Austrian wives, three French and three Russian mistresses. He wrote French, English, and German with equal fluency.)

Censorship was ubiquitously exercised. Austria's leading writers signed a manifesto protesting against stage censorship (1845). In Austrian plays "no illegitimate children may appear, no fathers may quarrel with their sons, no sons with their fathers. All kings have to be portrayed as benevolent. Was it not impossible to create anything truthful under such strictures?" Grillparzer was the first to sign. The protest was filed and forgotten.

This sedulous salesman of the status quo, this dexterous diplomat and single-purpose philosopher, wielded such influence that the encyclopedias define the period of 1815 to 1848 as "the age of Metternich." Yet, useful though he had been in the struggle against Napoleon, adroit though his leadership had been at the Congress of Vienna, effectively though he then had worked in the cause of European peace, Metternich, too, grew old, his logic stiff with age, his system no longer serviceable in a new kind of struggle. He could not keep Austria aseptic. Grillparzer wrote an epitaph for him which, needless to say, was never used:

> *Hier liegt, für seinen Ruhm zu spät,*
> *der Don Quixote der Legitimität,*

der falsch und wahr nach seinem Sinne log,
zuerst die andern, dann sich selbst betrog,
vom Schelm zum Toren ward bei grauem Haupte,
weil er zuletzt die eignen Lügen glaubte.

(Here rests, too late to mend his fame, the Don Quixote of Legitimacy. He lied, both falsely and truly, according to his conviction, betraying first others and then himself. He grew from a rascal to a fool with gray hair, because in the end he believed his own lies.)

2

Looking back from the revolutionary year of 1848 toward the redrawing of the map which had been accomplished at the Congress of Vienna in 1815, one can perceive Austria-Hungary as a vast heterogeneous empire. The sovereigns who had conquered Napoleon—finally, after years of bloodshed—wrangled over who was to get what territory, and Metternich proved a superb, suavely stubborn negotiator in Austria's cause. He was helped by the fact that Field Marshal Karl Schwarzenberg had taken command of the allied troops battling Napoleon at Leipzig in 1813 ("The Battle of the Nations") and had vanquished the unvanquishable Bonaparte. Glory to Austria and its Emperor, Franz I, who had twice fled from Napoleon, but now was transmuted into the hero of the hour, riding a white horse!

What *was* Austria-Hungary in 1815, when the negotiators went home?

It consisted of Upper and Lower Austria, Styria, Carinthia, Tyrol, and Salzburg, the German-speaking motherland. Bohemia, Moravia, Silesia, and Hungary (which included Croatia) had become part of the realm long before, in 1526. Though at one time, before Napoleon, most of Poland had belonged to Austria, it now got back a not inconsiderable portion of it, Polish Galicia. (The little republic of Cracow was left free by the Congress; it was later swallowed up by Austria, with the approval of Russia and Prussia.)

In southern Europe Austria scored its greatest territorial gains: Dalmatia, western Istria, several islands in the Adriatic Sea which had formerly belonged to Venetia, Venetia itself—the important city of Venice at its hub—the province of Lombardy—which meant Milan—all became Habsburg property. Since members of the Habsburg family sat on the thrones of Tuscany, Parma, and Modena, and since Austria exercised influence in the Papal State as well as in the Kingdom of the Two Sicilies, it meant that Italy was virtually an Austrian province. Austria did have to relinquish its sovereignty over portions of the Netherlands and a few small holdings on the Rhine. Altogether, however, the country emerged from the Congress much enriched. In addition, the statesmen meeting in Vienna dreamed up the idea of a "German Confederation," a grouping of the smaller German states. Austria was to assume the presidency of the diet of this Confederation; in other words, the Habsburgs were to play a leading part in German affairs.[4]

Franz I died in 1835. Metternich at that time was sixty-two years old, as shrewd and as powerful as ever. Franz was succeeded by his elder son, Ferdinand. But Ferdinand was emperor in name only: he hardly functioned. The Viennese in their kindlier mood called him "Ferdinand the Good-natured." His nature made little difference, since he was an epileptic and close to an idiot. His thick tongue could not squeeze out two connected sentences, and his favorite amusements were to wedge his bulk into a big waste-paper basket and roll around in it, or to catch flies with his hands. The poor creature with his hydrocephalic head could not manage to lift a glass with one hand or open a door or descend the stairs. "Great God!" wrote the Czarina Alexandra in her diary, "I had heard so much about him, about his small ugly shrunken figure and his huge head void of any expression except that of stupidity— but the reality beggared all description." And this was the Emperor of Austria. He reigned for thirteen years. It was Metternich who really reigned: he himself called Ferdinand "a lump of putty."[5]

To everybody's astonishment, Ferdinand's physicians had permitted him to marry, though it was doubtful that he could perform the sexual act. He married a twenty-eight-year-old princess, Maria Anna of Sardinia, and the court was speculating whether there would ever be any children. (There were none.)

During his wedding night he suffered five epileptic attacks. They were now becoming ever more frequent, and everybody around him lived in dread of when the next paroxysm would strike.

Ferdinand's brother, Archduke Franz Karl, was married to Sophie, daughter of Maximilian I, a Wittelsbach, who was King of Bavaria; he died in 1825. The year before her father's death, Sophie's wedding to Franz Karl had been celebrated—she was nineteen—and she moved to Vienna to spend the rest of her life in the Habsburg Hofburg. For eleven years she hoped that her brother-in-law Ferdinand would be declared unfit to reign, in which case her husband would ascend the throne and she would acquire what she most dearly desired, an imperial crown.

Sophie never forgave Metternich his assent to Ferdinand's becoming Emperor. She felt that he could have prevented it; more, that he could have used his influence in favor of her husband, who, if no marvel of wisdom, charm, or ability, was at least a normal man. Metternich said that he had carried out the wish of his dying friend and monarch Franz I; more probably he felt that with so feeble a ruler in the Hofburg he would continue to be indispensable. Whatever the truth, Sophie detested him—as a man. But she looked up to him as a statesman. Indeed, he formed her political ideas, and she proved an adept pupil: like him she distrusted any form of democracy, like him she despised "anything which is called a Constitution," like him she had little use for the Hungarians, who early sought parliamentary reforms. Though she disliked Metternich's highhanded behavior and his loose treatment of women, Sophie took good care never to criticize him openly; she soon became too skilled a politician to voice her opinion incautiously. Not even in her letters to her mother did she speak of Metternich; she knew that even those letters could be opened by his spies.

Sophie had not always been a political creature. Her portrait as a young girl gives the impression of a sunny and zestful girl, her face, not exactly pretty, enclosed by a merry-go-round of curls which framed her dark, intelligent eyes. Court gossip had it that she was in love with the Duke of Reichstadt, Napoleon's son. He, L'Aiglon of Rostand's play, lived virtually as a prisoner in the Hofburg, a wan, pallid, and poetic youth—he was six years younger than Sophie—marked for an early death. He died of tuberculosis a few weeks after Sophie's second son, Ferdinand Maximilian, was born. Some of the court gossips found—or pretended to find—that this son resembled L'Aiglon to a remarkable degree. They were probably wrong. Sophie and the young duke may not have been lovers. It may have been merely an unfulfilled love, the romantic longing of a girl which centered on the fragile frame of a moribund boy who bore the name of Napoleon.

An unromantic marriage with a mediocre man, a man who read nothing, learned little, did little, was interested only in hunting, as well as the dispiriting atmosphere of the Habsburg home and the irritation of being hectored by a Metternich, turned Sophie from a woman into a strategist. She perceived that her husband would never become Emperor. Neither Metternich nor any of the other peers of the realm would stand for replacing a feeble-minded sovereign with a man who wanted to be left in peace, who had no wish to assume the burden of a ruler. Very well—if her husband was ambitionless, she was not. She wanted power. He could give her children, and one of those children—presumably her first-born if he was male—would eventually mount the steps of the great throne. Thus she dreamed, this was what she worked for, for such a cause she turned herself into a resolute and obdurate planner, a Bible in her hand and a plot in her head. She formed alliances with the high clerics, becoming censorious in her religion, and a prude. She was "sorry" for the charming Sophie Müller, an actress of the Burgtheater, because as Juliet she had to recite "verses of doubtful propriety." All the same, Sophie kept appearing at the theater, with or without her husband in tow, partly because she loved the theater and partly because she knew that the Viennese admired theater devotees. Unlike the Viennese, she became ever more stiff-necked and determined. They called her "the only man at the Habsburg court."

On August 18, 1830, her first child was born, a boy. At once the harrowing question posed itself: was he normal? Or was he cursed with the disease so greatly feared by the Habsburgs, epilepsy? Epilepsy had entered the family by way of Maria Louisa, a princess of Bourbon Spain and mother of Emperor Franz I. Both Archduke Karl, the hero of the Battle of Aspern, and Archduke

Rainer, Beethoven's friend, suffered from it. It was then believed—
erroneously, medical science now maintains—that epilepsy was
inheritable. What of Sophie's first-born? Was he to be condemned
like his uncle? No, it appeared that he was normal and sturdy.
Solemnly, with bejeweled bishops and red prelates assisting,
Sophie named him Franz—the Joseph was added later—and began
to treat him as a future king. (Five years after Franz Joseph's birth
she had a daughter who *was* epileptic. The child died, hardly five
years old.)

As soon as Franz Joseph was old enough to understand, he
began to be indoctrinated in the art of ruling. His teacher,
summoned by Sophie, was old Metternich.

3

Let us return, now, to the revolutionary year 1848. Those revolutions which are fathered by ideas—revolutions which are pro-
founder than riots—are bound to leap over frontiers, selecting and
binding together men who think alike and suffer similarly though
they speak different languages, wear different clothes, live under
differing conditions, and may in nonrevolutionary times be indifferent to one another. Multicellular groups formed themselves
in geographically remote parts of the Austrian Empire. They all
wanted more or less the same thing: separation from Vienna,
meaning separation from absolutism, or more specifically separation from Metternich.

Nationalism rose in Hungary, Bohemia, Italy—all parts of the
Austro-Hungarian realm. Nationalism was the emotional mantle
covering the practical demands for steadier employment and
better wages. Nationalism meant huddling together to keep one
another warm. Nationalism was an ideal easily understood, an
ideal of self-assertion, psychologically serviceable, though few
thought its consequences to conclusion. Too often all that happened was that one flag was lowered, another hoisted; but to many
thousands it represented liberty—that vague and seductive term—
and the demand for it was never to die down.

Hungary's spokesman was Ludwig Kossuth. An eloquent

spokesman he was, his oratory now rubbing salt into wounds, now promising the healing ointment, his words a mixture of politics and poetry. He looked the part of the revolutionary hero: a larger-than-life face framed by an intensely black beard, dark eyes which managed a whole repertoire of accusing glances, a voice which rode the singsong of the Hungarian language like a circus rider. He had been trained as a lawyer and had served as a member of the Hungarian Parliament (an old institution of which the Hungarians were proud but which represented more glitter than accomplishment). He had there uttered enough inflammatory remarks for Metternich to throw him into jail. After three years in prison, public pressure won him freedom and he set to work to formulate Hungarian policy. He proposed: first, an abrogation of the privileges enjoyed by the landed aristocracy, those magnates with their vast estates on which peasants worked in virtual serfdom; second, the end of censorship; third, a constitution which, though still subject to the final authority of the Emperor, would assure Hungary an indigenous government. Hungary for the Hungarians—but what was first a wish for home rule soon became a cry for complete independence. The house was to be repaired by being sawed in two. From the Habsburg point of view, such a proposal was unanswerable or was answerable by the only means they understood: the army marched off to fight. In turn Kossuth assembled his own troops. The war was on.

Prague was the scene of the first Pan-Slavic Congress. There, too, proposals and negotiations proved insufficient to calm a people too long considered inferior; there, too, armed conflict began, though the imperial troops made short work of their dilettantish enemies.

In the Italian states the longing for liberation pulsed with greater vitality, gaining tension by being forced to exist subcutaneously. Now men of remarkable ability came along to release the tension. Camillo Cavour, a superb organizer and subtle brain—his cousin described him as "a bar of iron painted like a reed"—pleaded through his newspaper *Il Risorgimento* (*The Reawakening*), from which the movement took its name. Lombardy rose. In its principal city, Milan, the people demonstrated against Austria by refusing to smoke, tobacco being a monopoly of the Austrian state. Then they attempted to tear the cigars from the lips of soldiers marching defiantly in the streets. In March, the childish boycott grew into organized resistance, a Piedmontese army came to protect the city, the cries of *"Libertà!"* were shouted in the hoarse voices of the Milanese, and old Marshal Radetzky was forced to withdraw to the fortified sector bordered by Verona and Mantua. There he and his Austrian troops sat for the time being, waiting for reinforcements or a miracle. "The character of the Italians has changed as if by magic," he reported home. "Fanaticism is everywhere." When he needed meat for his soldiers, he sent a detachment to confiscate it: "Just in time I discovered that the meat had been poisoned." In Venice almost fifty thousand volunteers joined against Austria. "The Republic of Venice" was proclaimed under Daniele Manin as President. Giuseppe Mazzini, at first a visionary, had learned the possibility for power which lay in people once organized; he had formed the clandestine "Young Italy" groups, which now shed their masks. In Venice, Padua, Rome, Naples, they hacked in two the double eagle affixed to Austrian embassies and burned it.

How could the arms and legs of the empire be infected and its heart remain undisturbed? The fever reached Vienna.

4

After the victory over Napoleon, Vienna had enjoyed some twenty years of vigor. New schools sprang into being (including the Polytechnic Institute, which was to become famous) ; the first steamers plied between Vienna and Budapest; Beethoven's Ninth had its premiere; Grillparzer, Raimund, and Nestroy produced lively and significant plays; the Austrian Mint was built; the first railroad began to operate; the city was brightly illuminated with new gas lamps; and the waltz became acceptable as a social dance.

But prosperity was not deep-seated: a few bad harvests, increasingly tough competition from Prussia, where coats and beds were being manufactured more efficiently, reconstruction made more difficult by the mounting price of British steel—and the curve turned downward. The purchasing power of the gulden, a jittery coin, declined; more and more workers faced unemployment—suddenly this greengrocer and that cloth merchant had to close his door—and before the Minister of Finance or the mayor fully realized what was happening, depression had oozed from the poorer quarters to the center of the city. It was no time for carnivals, the theaters were half empty, and gloom was widespread. Beggars stood at the corner of the Kärntnerstrasse and prostitutes slunk in the shadow of the Stephanskirche. In the outlying districts, some of the unemployed started to loot butchers' and bakers' shops. In 1847 a few soup kitchens were set up, but they offered only a petty alleviation. Discontent mounted and was given voice by the students of the university. On March 13, 1848, the Diet of Lower Austria was scheduled to hold its session in a building in the Herrengasse. The day before, two student deputies had handed a petition to the Emperor Ferdinand, demanding among other changes the dismissal of Metternich and his Minister of Police, the notorious Joseph Sedlnitzky. (The day before, Sedlnitzky had declared: "Nothing is going to happen in Vienna.") Ferdinand with a thick tongue had answered: "I shall consider." That was that.

Early in the morning of the thirteenth, the students marched to the Herrengasse. The news of the march leaped through Vienna, and people began to stream out of their houses, not a few simply because they wanted to be part of the show, part of the *Hetz*. The revolt had begun, but it was as yet only a "Viennese revolt"; with all its sincerity there was something operatic about it, something picturesque, with the students in the uniforms of their various affiliations, the workers in their traditional blue caps and blouses, and a group of staid burghers in cylinders and morning coats.

There they all stood, waiting. What satisfaction would they obtain from the men meeting inside? While they waited, some of their leaders climbed on boxes and addressed the crowd, which by this time had swollen to about ten thousand. Somebody read Kossuth's last speech in translation. Somebody else shouted, "Down with Metternich!" The shout was taken up, and anger begot anger. There was nothing else to do but to be angry.

Suddenly, one heard the march step of the military. The

Grenadiers were coming, commanded by Archduke Albrecht, with instructions to clear the streets. When the people saw the soldiers, they grabbed whatever they could—stones, pieces of wood, broken lanterns, clumps of filth—and pelted the regiment, screaming their hatred. Albrecht was wounded by a wooden log. A salvo of shots was fired. In an instant the Herrengasse was empty, but four men lay dead on the pavement and another was gravely wounded.

The scattered crowd now swarmed all over Vienna, their fury directed against Metternich. The students broke into the Arsenal and took guns, swords, or any other weapon they could find. Factories were set on fire, machinery was smashed. The people then veered toward the imperial residence, and finding a strong garrison there barring access, they stood and howled.

In the Hofburg a family council had gone on all day. The assembled Habsburgs feared that Vienna would see a repetition of the Paris revolt, the monarchy turned into a republic, the Habsburgs stripped and banished. What was to be done? Ferdinand, poor lump of a man, was being besieged with proposals from right and left. Archduke Ludwig, his uncle, was all for using force: Marshal Alfred Windisch-Graetz, the hardest and grisliest leader of the Austrian command, should be charged with suppressing the rebellion at all costs. No concession must be tolerated. Johann, Ludwig's brother, was all for conciliation: Give the people a hearing, dismiss Metternich. Franz Karl, Sophie's husband, had no opinion. Cousin Albrecht, wounded, stammered that Metternich's resignation was the only solution. Sophie, who kept calm and confident—"the only man at the Habsburg court"—agreed with Albrecht, in opposition to other delegates and the army representatives, including Windisch-Graetz, who declared that his soldiers could easily mow down the "hoodlums." Reports brought in during the day sounded more and more grave. By late afternoon even Ludwig felt that Metternich must be got rid of. They sent for him.

He appeared at six o'clock, dressed in court costume with a green redingote and leaning on a cane with a gold handle. He advised: full opposition, no sign of weakness. He spoke for more than an hour. Nobody listened. Then, without raising his voice, without betraying one sign of emotion, he agreed to his dismissal.

Archdukes and courtiers thanked him profusely. He waved thanks away: "I protest against calling my action a generous one. I act according to what I feel is right." Let no one say in the future that he had carried monarchy away with him: "Nor I nor any man has shoulders strong enough to carry monarchy away. If monarchies disappear, it is because they themselves give themselves up." With that, he bowed and walked slowly away, leaning on his cane and enclosing everybody in his condescending smile. When he arrived home, his wife said to him, "Well, are we all dead?" "Yes," he replied, "we are all dead." He sent a messenger to Salomon Rothschild and borrowed a thousand ducats to finance his escape. During the night of the fifteenth, he left Vienna in a hired fiacre and fled to England.[6]

An officer, preceded by a flag-bearer, walked all night through the streets of the inner city, crying out the news of Metternich's dismissal. In the morning the people shouted with joy. All day long a real Viennese celebration went on.

5

It was not enough. Throwing one man out of the window did not relieve the crowding of the discontented. They kept pressing in on Ferdinand. Though he now promised "all the reforms wanted," the more he promised, the more was demanded. The Habsburgs shilly-shallied; they could not accommodate themselves to the concept of a world in which they were no longer to rule unchallenged as "All-Highest—by the Grace of God." After centuries of wearing the cloak of absolutism they froze at the idea of shedding it. The court did not mean what it promised: it tried insincere compromises, it tried delaying tactics, and the people saw through the deceit. New cabinets were formed and dismissed with short shrift. Neither cabinet nor King dared to act courageously while the anti-Habsburg movement rolled on.

News from Budapest,[7] from Venice, from the fortress in which Radetzky was waiting, from Prague, where during a day of fighting a stray bullet killed Windisch-Graetz's wife—all of it was bad. "Every day a terrible message," wrote Sophie in her diary. "God have pity on us!" By early May the climate of Vienna had become so unsalubrious that the royal family thought it prudent to pack up and leave. Ferdinand then could not easily be reached by renewed exactions, which now included the proposal that Austria join a "German-national" union. Under cover of darkness on May 17, the court stole away and moved to Innsbruck: there, among the conservative Tyrolean peasants in their lederhosen, they would feel safer. As to young Franz Joseph—he was to be sent to the Italian front. That was his mother's idea, a subtle idea, since it would dissociate him physically from the Habsburgs' now tainted reputation. At the right time she would present her son in pristine freshness. Under Radetzky's tutelage he would acquire some knowledge of warfare, Radetzky was sure not to expose him to too much danger, and in the event that the Italian revolt would in the end be suppressed by Radetzky's army—and Sophie was sure that it would—her son could return a hero. How the old general felt who, beset with problems, now had a precious Habsburg fledgling at his side is not recorded.

At the end of May, a new wave of revolt swept through the city. The barricades seemed to spring overnight from the pavements, like mushrooms after the rain. Workers and students banded together; now there was no longer anything picturesque about these marching groups. All was in dead earnest. Something *had* to be done. Somehow the Viennese had to be pacified. Perhaps another compromise? Still another cabinet was hurriedly formed: after swallowing hard they set down the principles of a constitution which included the right to vote and the abolition of censorship. A Reichstag, a parliament, was to be called in July to deal with the details and turn them into law.

The fight seemed to be won.

But it was not.

The Reichstag, which duly met on July 22, could not cope with the work. No decisions, more delays, more frustration. In August the royal family returned to Vienna, though Ferdinand was kept virtually under house arrest in Schönbrunn. In the same month there were further workers' demonstrations, with further bloodshed.

The climax came in October. It was triggered by the sympathy

the Viennese felt for the Hungarian cause, an instance of selfless-
ness rare in Viennese history. An imperial army had been assembled to fight Kossuth's army in Hungary. The leader of the
imperial army was Governor ("Banus") Josef Jellačić, a Croatian
who hated the Hungarians as much as the Hungarians hated the
Croatians, a bald, stout, beady-eyed fanatic. To support his efforts,
troops were to be sent from Vienna: the first battalion consisted of
Italians who left, docilely enough. The next was a group of
Viennese Grenadiers whose barracks were located in a suburb.
When it came time to march to the railroad station, a crowd of
jeering civilians accompanied them. A second crowd occupied the
station, tore up the rails, and made it impossible for them to leave.
An alternate road across the Danube was rendered impassable by a
blockade of the bridge. The Grenadiers now acted in an unexpected and "shocking" manner: they refused to obey orders and
fraternized with the people. A hurriedly summoned military detachment attempted to enforce the Grenadiers' departure. The
soldiers shot aimlessly into the crowd, the wounded moaned, the
Grenadiers embraced the workmen, the people shouted, the sabers
glistened, the smoke made eyes tear, men thrashed about brandish-
ing lengths of iron rail, spades, and axes, the bells of St. Stephen's
pealed menacingly, and crowds and soldiers reeling with the
ebullience of violence, faces swollen with fury, stormed back over
the city. They halted at the War Ministry building and chanted
"Latour, Latour." Theodor Latour-Baillet was Minister of War:
he had given the command to send the troops to Hungary and to
support Jellačić. The mob dragged him from the building and
hung him on a streetlamp. One man hit him across the face with a
saber, another plunged a bayonet into Latour's chest, others tore
the clothes from his body, women dipped their handkerchiefs in
his blood, and finally several men tore the genitals from his
corpse.[8] Where now were the ideas of constitution and representative law? They were hysterically debased, transformed into
stabs of hatred against one man, sixty-eight years old, who was no
more than a functionary of the system.

Once more the court moved and in great haste, this time to the
fortified town of Olmütz in Moravia. It was the early morning of
October 7. A strong army detail convoyed them, no fewer than

seven thousand soldiers. Franz Joseph, back from Italy, rode with the soldiers. Fear, too, rode with Ferdinand, Franz Karl, and Sophie. It was in effect a flight, not different from other flights of defeated royalty. They arrived in Olmütz after a nerve-racking journey of almost seven days.

Were they beaten? Was it the end of the Habsburgs? Was the dented crown to be stowed away in a museum? No. Habsburg determination stiffened in face of what seemed a desperate situation. In Vienna the revolutionary forces had the upper hand, but from other parts of the fevered realm came contrary news: encouraging indications that a great difference still existed between rash insurrections and the tenacious, methodical work of slaughter and suppression by the imperial army, led by tenacious, methodical men. A group of Grenadiers might mutiny, but the army was still loyal and obedient. Windisch-Graetz had stamped out the Prague revolt on June 17, and at Custozza old Radetzky, after being twice beaten, had won a decisive battle and retaken Milan. How could it have happened otherwise when six thousand Italians were pitted against nineteen thousand Austrian army regulars?

Stronger reasons than a victory or a defeat in this or that post underlay Habsburg confidence. They were aware how deep lay the sinew which bound the Austrians to the family which had governed them for six centuries. That "inert force of History," tradition, dwelt in the body of a Habsburg subject. One could hate a Metternich, one was capable of violating a Latour, could trip up a cabinet, one could even raise a clenched first toward the Hofburg itself, but one was not ready—not yet—to do without the majesty of a king, to smash the golden statue, to live life void of the father image which the sovereign represented. From the Habsburg point of view, how right they were to keep their confidence while ducking temporarily into shelter! By and by the less ardent, the more conservative—the small merchants, the middle-class burghers—tired of fighting and wearied of marching. Their ears smarted from the oratory. They longed for "order" under kingly command, they wished to end the anarchic state of Vienna, with its torn-up streets, and turn the beloved city once again into the Kaiserstadt, where the coffee was first-class.

Essentially the attack had not been directed against monarchy itself. Golo Mann, reviewing the Revolution of March, 1848, writes:

> The "March achievements" were the result of a momentary loss of nerve on the part of the rulers, not their decisive defeat. Furthermore, the victors themselves did not want a real victory; they did not want a revolution in the French sense. The words "everything is granted," heard so often with joy in Germany at the time, show that people wanted freedom to be granted by the traditional authority. Reform, compromise, "agreement" were the German liberals' favorite terms; only a few radical democrats raised the question of what should happen if the two partners, "crown" and "people," failed to agree.[9]

As in Germany, so in Austria. In both countries the revolution itself began to weaken. Great revolutions begin as a drive by a small group of men, themselves driven by a clear purpose. As the adherents multiply, the original group is joined by men not so clear, not so pure of purpose, and fractionalized by conflicting opinions. Enter the impractical men, the half blind, enter the radicals through another door, and of course enter those with an ax to grind. In Frankfurt, where a "German National Assembly" had been sitting for many a weary month, attempting to solve some of Germany's as well as Austria's problems, deliberations ground to a slow halt. In Vienna the revolution lost clarity of purpose and strength of ideals. A sad story, an oft-told tale. "The overwhelming pressure of mediocrity . . . will mitigate the most violent and depress the most exalted revolution," wrote T. S. Eliot.

Nor were the revolutionary leaders as able as the practiced statesmen. Oscar Jászi, in his analysis *The Dissolution of the Habsburg Monarchy,* states:

> The absolutism of many centuries so completely choked all movements of the popular forces and eliminated so entirely all political criticism and civic education that those peasant, citizen, and intellectual elements which now appeared for the first time on the scene of public life were lacking in all political preparedness and in all systematic effort toward the realization of those great aims which they suddenly faced.

The shrewd, conservative men of aristocracy and wealth gathered around the Habsburg throne. They didn't give two gulden for the far future; they wanted to protect their own immediate future. Probably some of them were so far gone in the Metternich malady that they might have sincerely believed in the rightness of their intransigence. They might have despised Ferdinand, but they knew that they could remain potent only by standing near a throne on which *somebody* was sitting. A leader among these realistic politicians was Prince Felix Schwarzenberg, nephew of Karl, canny, audacious, elegant, sophisticated, lean, and handsome, with veiled eyes, whose love affair with Lady Jane Ellenborough—her husband was England's Keeper of the Seals—had added to his titillating reputation. "A cold soul," his secretary called Schwarzenberg.[10]

Yet Vienna was not ready to give in. The citizens fought on, hoping for a union with Kossuth's men, who were supposed to be on the way. They were on the way—but they never reached Vienna. Instead, Windisch-Graetz descended from the north, Jellačić from the east. This is how Schwarzenberg saw the situation at the most critical moment (from his report to Olmütz) :

> The fate of the monarchy hangs by a thread. If Jellačić will not arrive in time, if he is not successful in preventing the Hungarians from locking arms with the Viennese insurgents, if Windisch-Graetz is unable to hasten his march to the capital, if it is impossible to conclude a quick peace with Sardinia—which I think most improbable—so as to liberate our Italian army, then I really do not know how we shall find the means to deal with the revolution. The several examples of mutiny by troops in Lombardy, in Hungary and Vienna, trouble me more than I can say. Yet we must not lose courage, and we must be very careful not to show our apprehension to others. We are like a man who gambles *va tout* though his purse is *en déveine*. . . .

Windisch-Graetz did arrive in time. He surrounded and shelled the city. A writer of the period, Berthold Auerbach, has left us a diary of events in Vienna in those last days of the year of revolution.[11] It is a pathetic document of confusion and frustration. He describes the fear which paralyzed the people, how one could not know who was a partisan and who a policeman in plainclothes, how the imperial soldiers, themselves Viennese, entered the homes of former neighbors, pillaged, and bayonetted old women, how the insurgents lost confidence in their leaders, how he, Auerbach, climbed again and again up the steeple of the Stephanskirche and, looking through a telescope, searched frantically for the Hungarian troops. They did approach on the fourth day of the siege. They were annihilated in sight of the Stephanskirche.

On the thirty-first of October the city capitulated to the imperial troops. Vienna's revolution was over. It was all over. The Habsburgs won their *va tout* gamble, or almost all of it, for Hungary remained rebellious. The cannon was mightier than the cry. Discipline was deadlier than earnestness. But it was the fever that had been brought under control, not the disease. The disease would break out in future years.

The gains subtracted from the losses showed a balance in red. What gains there were consisted of a lightening of the load of the enant farmer: the rights of the landowner were circumscribed. In other respects—the right to walk to a polling place, the right to be represented by elected delegates, freedom from the gag of the police censor—nothing was accomplished. Had revolution succeeded, in one form or another, the history of Europe might have pursued a happier course.

An idle thought! Yet, as one thinks of the men and women uselessly killed in the streets of Vienna, Prague, Paris, Berlin, Milan, and though history has served up many a crueler horror tale since then, one cannot help remembering how tragic a year was 1848—a tragic year for Austria especially, though the denouement was still generations away.

6

Schwarzenberg arrived in Olmütz to announce the victory. He had conferred with Windisch-Graetz (his brother-in-law) , and he came with a plan, one which dovetailed with Sophie's ambition. First, all concessions made by Ferdinand were to be canceled because they had been wrung from him under duress. Second, they felt it advisable, indeed necessary, to get rid of Ferdinand. He was too ill, too weak, and was now too hated to continue to reign. A new emperor was needed whose scepter had not been dipped in the mud of revolution. By right of succession the crown should have passed to Sophie's husband. But Franz Karl, though only forty-six, was not the man. He was, to put it plainly, too stupid even for an emperor. Schwarzenberg did not say so, but the implication was clear. The right choice was Sophie's first-born, eighteen-year-old Franz. He could appease the people by his youth, he could serve as a symbol of a new era, though in point of fact it was going to be the old, old era, and he would be muscular enough to resist further unrest. To the people he would seem uncommitted. He had made no public statement, promised no promises. It was Sophie's triumph. She and Schwarzenberg went to Ferdinand and demanded point-blank that he abdicate. Ferdinand gulped, lay down on a couch, folded his arms, closed his eyes, and stuttered yes.[12] Franz Karl proved less tractable, but after repeated remonstrances Sophie "persuaded" her husband. Schwarzenberg suggested that the future Emperor add "Joseph" to his name, partly to distinguish him from Franz I and partly to remind his subjects of Joseph II, the reformer, long dead, whom it was now the fashion to revere.

On December 2, at eight o'clock in the morning, the family, as well as Schwarzenberg, Windish-Graetz, Jellačić, and the ministers were bidden to appear before Ferdinand. They had been told to "dress in gala"; they probably guessed what was in the wind. When they had all assembled, the Habsburgs seated, the door opened and Ferdinand appeared, supported by two adjutants. He was slowly pushed up to the throne, amid total silence. A sheet of paper was handed to him. With a thick voice, halting several times between words and mispronouncing syllables, he read: "Important reasons have led Us to the irrevocable decision to lay down Our crown in favor of Our beloved nephew, Archduke Franz Joseph, whose High person We now declare of age, etc., etc. . . ." Franz Joseph knelt before Ferdinand, who whispered to him, "God bless you, remain steadfast, God will protect you." Franz Joseph straightened up and arose as Emperor, and Ferdinand half-tumbled from the throne. The documents were then signed.

Schwarzenberg went out onto the balcony and addressed the regiment assembled in the courtyard. It was a cold morning and the soldiers were glad of the opportunity to wave their arms and cheer. The band played the Austrian national anthem, which Haydn had composed for Emperor Franz, *"Gott erhalte Franz den Kaiser."* The words no longer fitted Franz Joseph.

At eighteen years and three months, he had become Emperor through circumstances in which revolution and a mother's ambition played their roles. As his motto he chose *"Viribus unitis"*— "With united strength." Of strength, his court could still claim a good deal; of "united," little.

Sophie, Franz Joseph's mother, as a girl

CHAPTER III

The Education of an Emperor

A MOTHER HAS four sons. All four are tended with equal care, brought up in the same house under the same economic conditions, subjected to similar schooling, exposed to the same cultural milieu; yet each of the four develops characteristics, and evolves into a personality, sharply diverse from the other. Who does not know that pattern, and who has explained it satisfactorily? The answer usually given, one which does not explain, is that there can be no equality, that circumstances cannot be similar, that unrecorded, unidentified, and unidentifiable influences impinge on growth and bent.

Sophie's first son was Franz Joseph, born after she had been married six years and had undergone two miscarriages. She was then twenty-five. Ferdinand Maximilian followed Franz Joseph after two years; he turned out to be sensitive, studious, intellectual. Karl Ludwig was the next son, born in 1833, only a year after Maximilian; he grew up to be a half-mad religious mystic, which didn't prevent him from having three wives. Ludwig Viktor was the last born; twelve years younger than Franz Joseph, he became a debauched homosexual who never did a stroke of work and finally immured himself in a castle near Salzburg. Franz Joseph hardly ever spoke to him.

Of four sons, then, two would be deemed "normal," though differing in personality from each other, while two would show the crippling characteristics of a heritage of inbreeding, from both the Habsburg and the Wittelsbach side.

The influence of his father on Franz Joseph was negligible; it was his mother who guided and formed him. She gave him the care and concentration which in her nature served as substitutes for sexual love, since she did not love her dull husband, nor did she care for casual bedfellows, the chief passion of her mature life being that "polish'd perturbation . . . so troublesome a bed-fellow," the crown. To reach it through her son, she set her course as determinedly as a lover does walking to his mistress. She was never distracted by being able to see another point of view. Wilhelm von Weckbecker, later adjutant to Franz Joseph, said she had "by all odds the finest political head among the members of the royal family." Finest, that is, for the achievement of her object, the continuation of the dynasty. She did not know what it was to be soft or compliant. "I could have borne the loss of one of my own children more easily than I could the shame of submitting to a bunch of students," she said after the last revolt of 1848. She may even have meant it! She feared nobody, except perhaps an arch-bishop. She may have been, she probably was, a believer, but she used her faith for a practical purpose. Crown and crucifix were allies; both were the instruments of sovereignty, talismans to keep the unruly at bay. Hers was a militant Christianity. In Sophie's mind the kingdom of heaven was reached by way of an anteroom, the kingdom on earth.

During his reign, Franz Joseph was to call frequently on "the Almighty" to come to the assistance of the "All-Highest."

The household of a prince who is to be formed into a king is no simple matter. The child was given into the care of an official governess, a baroness who conferred constantly with Sophie and to whom a retinue of eight reported: a nurse, an assistant nurse, two lackeys, a special cook, a chamberwoman, a maid to serve the chamberwoman, and a scullery maid. Two physicians called weekly to examine the prince, and every childish upset must have fright-ened Sophie. He was a sturdy child and a handsome one. Indeed, Franz Joseph inherited little of the Habsburg physical character-istics: he had neither the protruding lip nor the prominent nose.

He never went to school, never had casual playmates, never

knew what it was to trundle a hoop through the streets of Vienna or to trade postage stamps in the park. He played mostly with his brother Maximilian, who was impetuous and highstrung and tended to lord it over his older brother. When Franz Joseph was six years old, Sophie decided to replace his female staff with a male contingent: Count Heinrich Bombelles (of whom Metternich said that he was one of the few men who knew instinctively Metternich's wishes, a dubious compliment) was appointed "official instructor," along with an assistant instructor; plus a "personal valet," a groom, two lackeys, an "apartment overseer," his helper, and a chambermaid. Bombelles was a stern keeper of the tradition.

In addition to the three R's, Franz Joseph was taught German, religion, French, and geography. These thirteen hours of weekly instruction were increased in his ninth year to thirty-seven and soon after to fifty. Study periods began at 6 A.M. He learned Hungarian, Czech, drawing, chemistry, and political history—a lot of political history—as well as Italian. Attempts to teach him music met with total indifference. Literature bored him. On the occasion of the centenary of Goethe's birth, in 1849, he wrote to his mother that "we could have done without this useless festival; we have better things and people to celebrate." His brothers and Georg of Saxony were proposing to see Goethe's play *Torquato Tasso;* they were looking forward to it, but it would *"ennuyer"* him to death. Like most boys he learned enthusiastically how to fence and swim; his bodily coordination was extraordinary. At first he was timid about mounting a horse, but he overcame his fear and learned to ride superbly.

He played with toy soldiers. For his fourth birthday Sophie gave him a fine hand-painted set. He didn't break or lose one of them. By and by the collection was added to, until every Austrian regiment was represented. The boy knew every button on every uniform. He was taught early how to play war. Later, in his teens, he began to receive serious military training, to understand maneuvers, signals, strategies, weapons, the functions of the four principal military branches. When he was thirteen, he was appointed colonel of a regiment of dragoons; they remained "his dragoons." Henceforth he could play with live instead of tin soldiers. By that time instruction had changed to indoctrination,

Lesson time for Franz Joseph in the presence of his mother and three teachers

the imparting of knowledge to the imparting of monarchic principles, the presentation of a panorama of the world to a peephole view in which the double eagle formed the center. An engraving of one of Franz Joseph's "school hours" exists; in spite of the artist's obvious desire to make the picture pleasing, it is fairly sour. The young boy sits there, stiff and deadly serious, Sophie to his left, her glance calculating beneath the ringlets, and three teachers surround him like three police judges; one of them, black-gowned Canon Joseph Columbus, seems to have been sent by the Inquisition. The scene takes place in the gayest of Empire rooms, with round porcelain stove, elaborate chandelier, and voluptuous frescoes.

Franz Joseph was soon taken to make official appearances, at which he behaved with dignity and self-reliance. Yet he was still a child; he could still clown and be humorous, a quality he lost all too quickly. A little note from his fourteenth year is preserved, written to his brothers when he was confined to bed:

To those who dwell below Us.
Impertinent Creatures!
How could you dare not to inquire how my Highness is feeling? I deign to inform you impertinent fellows that I am quite blue-red, that I feel well enough, and that I am still kindly inclined toward you. With exemplary graciousness I deliver my respects to Prince Hetzius [Maximilian] and send him a kiss. He who is dissatisfied with your impertinences,

ARCHDUKE FRANZ

Given with condescension from Our bed, the 15th of the Easter month, Anno 1844.

When he grew into a young man, he was supposed to be a whirlwind dancer, though one does not know how factual are the testimonies left in the memoirs of various court ladies. The beautiful Countess Elisabeth Ugarte, ten years older than he, wrote: "I danced each time with our delicious Emperor. It created quite a sensation. . . . He is agreeable in conversation and improves each time one talks to him." Another early description of him was given by one who could hardly have been overawed, King Leopold I of Belgium. He wrote to Queen Victoria:

In his warm blue eyes one can read much temperament and courage. On occasion he is able to demonstrate a certain pleasant merriment. He is svelte and graceful, and even in the whirl of dancers and archdukes, all of them in uniform, he stands out.

His social manner is . . . free of pompousness and awkwardness. He gives himself simply, and when he is in a good mood, as he was with me, quite sincerely and naturally. He commands an audience without consciously giving himself the aura of authority. Just the same, something surrounds him which lends him authority, and which is often missing in those who have authority. I think he could be severe if he needed to be. He has daring.[1]

When he was eighteen, he looked older than his age and he had become as virile-looking as a young Roman from the Augustan period. Or, to borrow from *Henry IV,* he looked like an eagle having lately bathed. His hair was soft and dark blond, his forehead high, his eyes wide awake, his nose straight, his whole face as orderly as a lawbook: in short, he had the good looks of the non-intellectual who has been well scrubbed since infancy. His ears were too large, however. He was proud of his military figure, and later in life he dieted. He never became fat.

Sophie, frequently though she folded her hands in prayer, was not puritanical. She understood a young man's needs. Undoubtedly she arranged for him to obtain sexual companions, since he could hardly go out and find them for himself. The girls of the opera ballet were willing objects of aristocratic admiration, and they were discreet. They used to go to the Stephanskirche for the noon service, which in popular parlance became known as the "ballet Mass." There appointments were fixed, and from time to time a court equipage brought one of them to the Hofburg.

Franz Joseph's sexual education may have been unconnected with the ballet: an oft-repeated story tells that his "official instructor" selected for him a Bohemian peasant girl, healthy, good-natured, and pleasant. An agreement was reached with the parents of the girl: she was to be married to a minor court official of her choice and receive a substantial dowry if she would first go to bed with the young Habsburg. The matter was carefully staged to give Franz Joseph the impression that he himself had met the girl by chance. During a maneuver in Bohemia he did meet the girl, he started to speak to her in Czech, he liked her, she liked him—and it happened quite naturally. Many years later he saw her again with her husband at some court function or other, recognized her at once, but could not speak to her.

Though the little idyll is probably true, it is doubtful that Franz Joseph experienced a profound love affair in those early years. Summoned to the throne when he was little more than a boy, he is supposed to have said: "Must I do without my youth?"

2

For the task before him, he—or rather Sophie—gathered counselors who had both feet firmly planted on the road to retrogression. They were statesmen dressed in Metternich's leftover garments. The old man in far-off England must have rubbed his hands in satisfaction as he addressed a flood of admonitory letters[2] to Franz Joseph's court. As was to be expected, Felix Schwarzenberg became Prime Minister. Count Franz Stadion, a protégé of Windisch-Graetz's and no favorite of Schwarzenberg's, was jammed into the position of Minister of the Interior, thereby creating internecine friction from the start. The fox among the seven top ministers was Alexander Bach, Minister of Justice. He was one of those adroit men who have the answers but not the conviction. He could design the house of government with the door on the left as easily as on the right. In point of fact, he had previously designed a liberal plan which he now filed away without one reminiscing glance, to come forth with a new blueprint in which all rooms led directly to the throne room. Though this plan was as old-fashioned as the periwig, it shocked the president of the Court Chamber, Karl Friedrich von Kübeck Kubau, who became one of Franz Joseph's advisers as well.

Kübeck did not agree with Bach,[3] Bach did not agree with Schwarzenberg, and Windisch-Graetz, who was still commanding the army, did not agree with any of them. He, who was "pig-headed and tough" and "brought up in the tradition of a Bohemian nobleman," believed he was entitled to a privileged position and he was damned well not going to submit his decisions to any rank lower than His Imperial Majesty himself. He thought he knew more about the business of government than the others, while the others thought they could be more successful in leading an army than he. When Franz Joseph opposed him in the name of "the duty We have toward the monarchy," Windisch-Graetz replied, "Would Your Majesty deign to remember that you would have *no* duty if I had not been on the scene?"—an impudent reply he would have hardly have dared to make in later years. Each of the men saw himself as the star tenor and wanted to sing the main arias. They would combine their voices in only one chorus, the hymn to Habsburg.

How should that hymn be sung? On that they could agree: it had to be a monophonic apostrophe to the person of the Emperor. These men were neither fools nor knaves: they were convinced of the rightness of their policies. The argument of autocracy lay then—and lies today—in the magic word "order." Order, internal peace, respect for the law had to be reestablished if Austria was to survive. The country could not live on if the students continued to pelt the militia or the workers continued to jam machinery. Communism was as yet but a feeble force, but the *Communist Manifesto,* published by Marx and Engels in the revolutionary year of 1848, was not unknown to the Austrian statesmen. More serious than the threat of communism, if the Czechs, the Hungarians, the Italians were hell-bent on governing themselves, there would soon be no Austria left—or only the root without the tree—and what would become of the empire which served as the bulwark east against the Turk and north against the Czar, that greedy potentate who was quite prepared to push his power into all of Slavic Europe? If nationalism were to prevail, would not all minorities living in national units be suppressed, the Serbs in Hungary, the Germans in Bohemia? So liberal a poet as Grillparzer sensed the danger:

> *Der Weg der neuern Bildung geht*
> *Von Humanität*
> *Durch Nationalität*
> *Zur Bestialität.*

(The road of modern culture leads from humanity through nationalism to bestiality.)

Schwarzenberg, the most brilliant of Franz Joseph's advisers, saw the task as more than that of forcing the empire together again and gluing the seams. He envisioned "a trialistic edifice of Middle Europe, consisting of Austria, Prussia, and a combination of four smaller realms"—the very opposite of nationalistic units. Whatever the ultimate aim, no results could be achieved without a supreme commander. It was not self-interest alone—or it was only partly self-interest, the desire to live in a world in which they could remain standing on top of the structure—which bound the Schwarzenbergs, the Bachs, *et al.* to the young Franz Joseph.

However, let us be prudent. Let us see if an Assembly could formulate principles which, while making or rather pretending to make some concessions, would not be at variance with authoritarian rule. That might mollify some of the discontented. Thus Schwarzenberg—and Franz Joseph agreed. After the riots in Vienna the Reichstag had been transferred to Kremsier, near Olmütz. The Kremsier Reichstag worked out a proposition which granted national groups the right of being represented by their own delegates, acknowledged that all languages spoken within the empire were equal, and gave permission to every "land of the crown" to hold its own conclave. This, though it did not mean much, was tantamount to an admission that the empire was divisible into national groups. Unsatisfactory! Unsatisfactory to Schwarzenberg and Franz Joseph. The Reichstag finished its work on March 4, 1849, and three days later—only three days later—its proposal was declared void. The monarchy was defined as a "free, independent, indivisible, indissoluble, constitutional, Austrian, hereditary monarchy." An absurd contradition in adjectives—like ordering a cup of black coffee with cream in it, unsweetened but with sugar.

Franz Joseph not only knew about these moves and countermoves, but he took an active part in the moving. From the first he governed. Enough dissension swirled around him to force him to make decisions. He was decisive by instinct. He was the central star in deed as well as name, type-cast from the first, looking, acting, thinking the strong king. His courtesy was deliberate and unvarying, but he hid under it a quantity of condescension. This mirror image of Vienna possessed little Viennese mildness. He was even then the man in uniform. In his initial "Emperor's Manifesto" he said that he wished to work "for the rejuvenation of Austria" and that he wanted to "share rights with representatives of the people" It was his first lie, a tragic lie that carried the seed of destruction. Franz Joseph had no intention of ceding any of what he believed to be a monarch's rights to "representatives of the people." In saying that he would—wrote Joseph Redlich—he showed *mala fides*, "bad faith." One cannot excuse him because he was young: "He was ripe and prudent beyond his years." Perhaps the lie was not wholly his: "It was Schwarzenberg's, who stood at his side as Prime Minister." Yet it "lay deeply in Franz Joseph's nature to embrace the lie" and "make it his own without feeling or voicing opposition to it."

The Viennese believed him—what else could they do?—and he turned his attention to stamping out the revolution. Prague was conquered, Vienna was conquered, Italy was to be cleaned up next. Charles Albert, King of Piedmont and Sardinia, challenged Radetzky to a showdown. He broke the armistice and went to war. Radetzky had foreseen this possibility, had gathered fresh troops and strengthened his old ones, and now broke out of the quadrangle and pounced on Charles Albert. He defeated him at Novara. Charles Albert abdicated. Radetzky returned to Milan. The peace contract was signed on August 6, 1849. Only Venice under Manin was still resisting, but it, too, was subjugated later that year after an intense siege.

The Hungarians held out. They had not only their Kossuth but a talented young general, Arthur Görgey. From the *pusztas* and remote villages he mustered his fighters, hot-blooded and defiant, and they threw back the Austrian troops so effectively that by the beginning of April Görgey stood before Budapest, menacing the capital city where Windisch-Graetz was ensconced. It looked as if soon not one Austrian soldier would remain on Hungarian soil. On April 14 the Hungarian Parliament proclaimed Hungary a republic, under Kossuth, and declared Franz Joseph dispossessed.

The shock waves of the news spread through the Empire. What was to be done? How could those proud Hungarians be tamed? To lose Hungary? It was unthinkable, a major disaster which at all cost had to be prevented. One owed Windisch-Graetz a great deal, but it became clear that he was no match for the insurgents and had to be relieved of his command. Could that be done by "kicking him upstairs," making him Prime Minister, of course with Schwarzenberg's consent, who would then be appointed to an even higher post? Such was the suggestion of Count Karl Grünne, chief adjutant of the Emperor. Here Franz Joseph stepped in with a decisiveness remarkable for a nineteen-year-old. Perhaps he had studied Caesar's *Commentaries*. The order he issued has a Caesarian tone:

> Windisch-Graetz cannot become Prime Minister. All parties at present are against him, and we must not forget that we are still standing on top of a volcano. It is likewise impossible that he remain chief army commander. The old stick-in-the-mud routine can not continue. The conduct of the war must change. If not, I myself will go down and clean up the mess. In case the Field Marshal [Windisch-Graetz] is vanquished, not only he but all the other defective elements must instantly be dismissed. Ordnance General Welden must be dispatched hurriedly with reinforcements, without a moment's delay. Then I myself will go down and do my best to refresh the spirit of the troops. Then we will win.[4]

That was the end of Windisch-Graetz, who of course blamed everybody—especially his brother-in-law, Schwarzenberg—but himself. Sullenly he withdrew into oblivion. Replacing Windisch-Graetz with Ludwig Welden did not suffice. Welden had to report, "With a broken heart I must communicate to Your Majesty the fact that I have not been able to change conditions." Five days later: "We have been bested by the enemy in every respect; he has displayed enormous military force. No other course remains but to retreat the army *à cheval* to Pressburg. We must depart." Vienna itself, Welden thought, was exposed to "the Hungarian hordes."

At this dire moment Franz Joseph had to look for help. He looked for it where he hated to look for it: he appealed to the Czar. Nicholas I had closely watched Austria's worsening difficulties; the worse things became in Hungary, the more he smiled. Clearly here was Russia's chance to jump into the breach, and to fill it with its own minions. The rest of Poland, the top of Hungary—the Czar already saw them in his mind's eye as Russian possessions. And more! Russia could extend its influence to all the Slavic people, dig deep into Serbia and Croatia, and by pursuing this right angle threaten the Turks who threatened it. The opportunity was there for Russia to break out of Asia, so to speak, and climb into Europe, using Austria as the ladder. Franz Joseph was not oblivious of the Czar's intention. Nonetheless he needed him just then, and he addressed him on April 16:

> Sire: I pray that you believe me when I say that in the midst of the painful tribulation which Providence has heaped on me, I have derived comfort and hope from the certainty that I can count on the unwavering friendship of Your Imperial Majesty. It is a precious legacy left to me by my predecessor.[5]

In short, help us!

Two weeks later the Russian troops marched into Galicia. The Czar himself took command and arrived in Warsaw on May 2. Franz Joseph left Olmütz, went to the front—though Welden thought that gesture imprudent and unnecessary—and then met the Czar in Warsaw. There they discussed strategy: the Russians, as a separate unit, were to fall on the Hungarian army from the north, Jellačić from the south, and General Julius Haynau (whom Franz Joseph had appointed as Welden's successor) was to attack from the west. The two Emperors were generous with grandiloquent phrases; having surfeited each other in mutual loving protestations, they, or rather their staffs, haggled over who was to pay what costs. Nicholas made sure that his troops were not to move before full supplies had arrived. He also extracted a promise from Franz Joseph that Austria was to help Russia should the Turks in future years prove obstreperous.

The Czar commanded 190,000 soldiers; the avalanche was reinforced not only by 150,000 Austrian troops but by non-Magyar groups living within Hungary whom Kossuth, who had made himself virtual dictator, had treated much the same as Austria treated its minorities.

The combined forces rolled over the country. What price bravery, against that much metal and powder? By July the rocks of resistance were ground into gravel. Franz Joseph personally took part in the fighting, as he had said he would, but how much actual danger he was exposed to is questionable. After a final battle at Világos, where 30,000 Hungarian soldiers capitulated to the Russian army, the war ended. Kossuth abdicated, and after having secretly buried the sacred crown of Hungary,[6] he fled to Turkey, then to England, and finally to the United States, where he was hailed as a "hero of liberty." In later years he twice attempted to stir up his compatriots, but his voice had lost its power. In exile, the revolutionary firebrand had become a bore.

For the moment, then, Hungary was subdued. Nor did Russia obtain all the Czar had desired; the Western powers put a damper on his ambition, and once the war was over, Austria's thanks were not as freely proffered as Nicholas had expected.

Schwarzenberg, who had foreseen and helped shape Austria's diplomatic course toward Russia, remarked cynically: "Our ingratitude will know no bounds."

3

While Franz Joseph was occupied in Hungary, the Frankfurt Diet, an assembly of German and Austrian delegates which was begun with high hopes, and dragged on and on, kept trying to find a solution to the problem of the split-up German states. A proposal was put forward for a union of all German-speaking peoples, with Prussia's Frederick William IV as "Supreme Head" (*Reichsoberhaupt*) : it represented an old mystic hope, which Hegel and other philosophers had voiced. Frederick William would not respond with a straight answer; pressed again and again, he finally refused, though, like Caesar refusing the crown, "he would fain have had it," offering the countersuggestion that a "greater Germany" be formed under Franz Joseph's aegis. Schwarzenberg saw the ruse: Frederick William wanted Austria to bolster a weakened Prussia. Schwarzenberg recognized the possibilities inherent in a union of the Germanic peoples; he was too shrewd a statesman, however, not to acknowledge that the scheme was futile as long as Prussia was regarded with suspicion and distrust by other German states. Austria had troubles enough of its own. Then, too, the plan would have brought Franz Joseph into direct conflict with Louis Napoleon; France could hardly tolerate so formidable an Anschluss. Frederick William tried blandishments: "The plan would put Your Majesty at the head of a totality of seventy million people." Franz Joseph evaded: he was as yet too new, too inexperienced, to shoulder the task. Besides, wasn't the German land itself disunited? Could all those German principalities, plus the multilingual Austro-Hungarian Empire, ever be merged—and live together in peace? It was the imperial pot calling the royal kettle black.

In the end, after all the speeches, the debates, the chimerical proposals for unity, and one fine plan after another was drafted, modified, and torn up, nothing was settled. Germans had to wait for a later day and a later man to form a nation. The Frankfurt Diet, said a Spanish diplomat, began life as a goddess. It ended as a poor prostitute in a side street.

4

The revenge which followed the revolts "did paint the fearful difference of incensed kings." In the six months following the armistice, Lombardy had to pay Austria 27 million gulden (an enormous sum, perhaps equivalent to $60 million in today's purchasing power). Italian women who sang patriotic songs were whipped and beaten with wooden sticks, after which a bill was presented to the local magistrate for the cost of "broken staffs and bandages." Men were jailed in the *carcere duro*. In Venice and Milan the rebel leaders were executed. Austria policed press and stage with new severity: the strings of censorship were drawn tight. Protest had to masquerade. In 1850 Verdi proposed producing an opera to be called *La Maledizione* to a libretto based on Victor Hugo's play *Le Roi s'amuse*. The Venetian censor forbade its production, alleging "republican tendencies." Verdi and his librettist, Piave, then softened the plot and called the work *Rigoletto, Buffone di Corte*. (François I thus became "the Duke of Mantua.") It was an even greater success in Venice on March 11, 1851, than *La battaglia di Legnano*, on a patriotic subject, had been in Rome two years before.

Unhappy Hungary, having cost more men and money to subdue, was more severely chastised. A reign of terror began; people said that the Czar had saved Hungary for Franz Joseph but in doing so had turned it into Siberia. The brutality represented official policy, not excessive zeal on the part of this Austrian general or that Austrian judge. An example was to be made to terrify future dissidents—such was the official command. When Schwarzenberg was advised that clemency might be the wiser course, he was supposed to have answered: "I agree, but first let's hang a few." They hanged quite a few: on the anniversary of the murder of Latour, thirteen Hungarian generals were executed and a great number of officers jailed. The tribunals handed down 114 death sentences and 765 prison sentences.[7] Premier Ludwig Batthyány, a moderate statesman, proved a problem to the tribunal: they couldn't find enough incriminating evidence against him. But then he tried to commit suicide, wounding himself in the neck with a dagger; so they thought they might as well shoot him. The documents in the case were spirited away to Vienna and locked up in a secret file. His wife appealed to Sophie, begging for clemency. Sophie never answered the letter. The Czar, though he approved of Batthyány's execution, could not go along with the wholesale condemnations. It was too much even for him; he wrote on the margin of a report: "The death sentences for those who gave themselves up to our army represent an infamy and are an insult to us. I feel deeply hurt." General Görgey, however, was merely banished, since he had ordered a Hungarian regiment to lay down its arms and thus contributed to shortening the war.

The most cruel of the avengers was General Haynau, a sadist who was nicknamed "General Hyena." He came into conflict with Schwarzenberg as well as the Russian leaders, but nothing would deter his psychopathic thirst for blood, abusing women, shooting officers. He shocked Europe. When later he went to England and visited a brewery there, the draymen attacked him and covered him with dirt, shouting, "Down with the Austrian butcher!" Lord Palmerston was "not sorry for what has happened."

In later years Franz Joseph's biographers have tried to excuse the Draconian measures by saying that he personally did not know about them, that they were all concocted by the camarilla around him. The evidence suggests that this could not have been the case. He was too much the man in charge, he read every directive and memorandum issued by his advisers too carefully, he himself signed too many of the punitive commands, to be ignorant of what was going on. It is true that in the beginning a memorandum was issued stating that it was the will of His Imperial Majesty that "only the most dangerous and damaging individuals were to be [automatically] condemned to death," but this sentence was quickly changed and Franz Joseph signed the order. Perhaps in the beginning his desire for revenge was temperate; but revenge "feeds on its own dreadful self. Its delight is murder," as Schiller wrote in *Wilhelm Tell*.

Franz Joseph's initiation was lamentable. In the first year of his reign, his realm was plunged into civil strife. The task of ending the strife by bandaging the wounds and not by cutting deeper proved too much for him, as the revolution itself proved beyond the understanding of the Metternichs or the Schwarzenbergs. Metternich had thought on the very day of his dismissal that all they needed to do was to "clean up the nuisance" in the streets; the Viennese were much too good-natured and too frivolous to be serious about a revolt.

A few Viennese started the fire. But even when thousands marched toward it and threw their existence and their very lives into the conflagration, they—that is, the rulers—did not look for its cause. Did Franz Joseph know that Austrian laborers had virtually no recourse to the law and that nine-year-old children could be required to work ten hours a day? Did he know that when he mounted the throne the price of potatoes and peas had risen almost to the prices of the Napoleonic famine?

When the revolution was suppressed, it was understandable that a Windisch-Graetz, whose wife had been watching the fighting from a window, half hidden by a curtain, when a bullet killed her—none knew whether by accident or design—would be filled with thoughts of revenge. But what of Franz Joseph, who had not suffered personally? Two thousand Viennese had been slain by imperial troops, most cruelly by Jellačić's Slavic soldiers; 2,400 had been arrested later. In Hungary women of high society who had been imprudent enough to speak up against Austria were publicly whipped; among them was the wife of the Magyar aristocrat Maderspach, who had sheltered Hungarian soldiers. Maderspach killed himself. Alexander Petöfi, Hungary's great poet, was killed and his corpse was never found. Did all this not call for clemency? Not to Franz Joseph. Yet, strangely, his temperament was not deeply cruel; he was not an Attila, as his later life proves. The evidence suggests that it was fear which motivated him, a young man's fear—and fear is so much stronger in the young than in the old—the fear of losing what he had been taught to regard as his possession by God's decree, the fear of defeat which seems irremediable when one is nineteen

So he hacked about him. And it was only after the fear had been quieted that Franz Joseph turned around and became a "kindly ruler." As such he wanted to be known, as such he saw himself, as such in many later years he was. Only seldom did cruelty emerge as he tried to re-form and cement together the vessel of his realm. He learned to do it, though the vessel remained frangible, and though more than one shard broke away.

Caricature from *Revue Comique*, Paris 1849: "The three props of Austro-Croat civilization," showing Jellačić, Radetzky, and Windisch-Graetz

CHAPTER IV

Years of Mixed Blessings

No ONE CAN ESCAPE the calendar, not even those who long for the year 1. Franz Joseph continued to believe what he had been taught to believe and what he loved to believe. Yet the events which pressed upon him, the new demands spread before him, changed the character of his kingship, without his being fully conscious of it. He did not "give in," he did not retreat from absolutism. But once the realm was again more or less of a piece, once the '48 insurrections and the '49 executions were done with, the style of his governing changed. It could not have happened otherwise, even though 1848 had proved a failure from the progressive point of view, and an age of reaction set in. Tolstoy wrote: "The higher a man stands on the social ladder, the more people he is connected with and the more power he has over others, the more evident is the predestination and inevitability of his every action."[1] One needs to understand this statement in its large and time-stretched sense; then it becomes true that no man can remain untouched by the course of broad cultural or economic developments, be he ten times an emperor. Necessity is the mother of history. Franz Joseph adapted himself to necessity and became an emperor of peace, though the peace was often no better than the sleep of a sick man who awakes in the hours of the night and longs for daylight.

European society transformed itself drastically in the 1850s, the machine being the transformer. The population explosion combined with the growing prosperity of the middle class to create new demands for gloves and winter coats, bricks and iron girders, salt and coffee. The craftsman in his cottage was replaced by the laborer in an impersonal factory. The old sources of power—water, wind, and human muscle—were replaced by steam and gas and soon by electricity. In ten years the output of coal in Austria trebled. The Siemens brothers laid the foundation of the German electrical industry. In 1849 a new reinforced concrete was perfected; in 1850 R. W. von Bunsen invented a new burner; in the same year E. C. Carré developed a vacuum freezing machine and the first submarine cable was laid between Dover and Calais; in 1851 in the U.S. Isaac Singer patented a sewing machine; three years later A. Gesner introduced a new industrial substance which he called kerosene. The building of railways, ships, roads, and bridges made communication easier. In 1849 a Hungarian entrepreneur, I. Széchenyi, built a modern suspension bridge between Buda and Pest; a grand regatta was held to celebrate the opening and Franz Joseph attended, though somewhat reluctantly. Four years later he inaugurated the new railroad from Vienna to Triest constructed not only for commercial reasons but as a means of quick troop transport to Italy—just in case. It was Austria's important link to the sea; it led over the high mountains of the Semmering and represented a triumph of engineering. In Triest, Baron Karl Ludwig von Bruck had built an excellent harbor. Franz Joseph was beginning to toy with the idea of reshaping his imperial city. He had the example of Paris before him: in 1853, at Napoleon III's instigation, some of the old Paris was being pulled down and new broad boulevards were being constructed by Georges Haussmann, who also designed the Bois de Boulogne. Beautification was not Napoleon's only motive: he thought that broad streets would be more difficult to barricade in the event of another revolution.

Pride in technical wonders was comprehensively displayed at the Crystal Palace, erected in London to house the "Great Exhibition" of 1851. Science, said Prince Albert in his opening speech, would weld mankind together into a community of nations. How could people misunderstand one another now that it was so easy to communicate by telegraph?

Franz Joseph encouraged industry. He labored conscientiously to promote what he understood as the welfare of his people, concentrating on the economically more advanced German regions. He protected the new factories by favorable laws. He made it possible for Austrian industrialists to become wealthy and for those who worked to become well-to-do. He himself worked hard, indeed much too hard. Even in his twenties he sat long hours at his desk, steeped in the details of administration, often unable to perceive the larger design by devoting too fussy an attention to crossing the *t*'s and dotting the *i*'s. His seriousness was unrelieved by lightness or by humor. He hardly ever went to the theater or the opera; when he appeared at carnival time, he danced only representationally, putting a damper on the festivity; he was formal in his dealings with people, and he seemed to relax only when he was on horseback, riding with speed and elegance. He had no friends with whom he was at ease, except perhaps Albert, Prince of Saxony, who was "intelligent, antiliberal, and a soldier, body and soul," as Franz Joseph told his mother. "If Franz Joseph were not an emperor," said the Prussian delegate, "he would be much too earnest." At any rate, he made the Viennese go to work earnestly; from being lackadaisical they swung to the opposite extreme, so that he soon issued a law making Sunday a compulsory rest day. His wish to have everybody appear in church had something to do with that.

Though, to quote Tolstoy again, "a king is history's slave," that does not mean that he cannot govern decisively, nor that he is unable to nudge history to follow a certain path. Franz Joseph was now in complete authority; he seemed predestined for rule. Only his mother could say him nay. Even Schwarzenberg was being careful. Metternich was recalled from exile and received in triumph in Vienna, and Franz Joseph closeted himself with his erstwhile adviser—the young man listening to the soft voice of the old statesman, now grown very feeble—but then made up his own mind. Franz Joseph was the most powerful figure in continental Europe, possibly in the world. Only the Czar was as purple-laden. Frederick William was a small-dimensioned king compared to Franz Joseph; Napoleon III, an upstart, was just beginning to turn France from a republic back to a monarchy, while England's constitution inhibited Queen Victoria in her more willful moments. In 1851 Franz Joseph did create a sort of "advisory parliament," but nobody was left in any doubt as to what its functions were to be. The task of government, it announced fulsomely, was to "fortify in every respect the moral principle of imperial authority and to widen the limits of a power which had proved itself useful for centuries." It went on to preach, "Concessions do not change the minds of the inimical; they weaken the efficiency of government, and encourage revolutionary elements to pursue their nefarious game." Harsh words! As to a constitution, so often proposed and frequently put on paper, it had never meant much and meant nothing now. A constitution can be significant only if it expresses the condition and wish of a society—and this one was penned as an exercise in apologetic essay-writing. After scratching out this word and that, Franz Joseph abolished the attempt altogether. "All perspicacious men," he announced in August 1851, "realize that the constitutional principle of England or France cannot be applied to the Austrian state." Nine days later he wrote to his mother: "A great step forward has been taken. We have thrown the constitution overboard. Austria now has only *one* master. Now we will have to work even more intensely."[2] Sophie wrote in the margin, "God be praised." Later she called the move an *"heureuse culbute"* (a happy somersault).

Franz Joseph assumed, as well, the supreme command of the army. When Schwarzenberg died the year after—only fifty-two years old—Franz Joseph did not replace him; he became in effect his own Prime Minister.

Up to the last, Schwarzenberg had been the ablest of the executants of that creed of absolutism which Metternich had advocated. At the beginning of 1852 Schwarzenberg feared he was going blind: this was a fate the proud prince could not endure. His physician assured him: "You are not going blind—but I'm afraid you may suffer a stroke one of these days." "That," said Schwarzenberg, "is a death to which I agree." On the fifth of March his sister-in-law, Eleonore Schwarzenberg, asked him whether he would come to her soiree that night. "Certainly I will come, if I am alive." He attended a meeting of the ministers, then went to a florist to select with particular care a bouquet he was sending to a beautiful Polish lady, then went home to change his clothes—and died of a stroke. Franz Joseph hurried to his house but arrived too late. The next day Franz Joseph wrote to Sophie in Graz bemoaning the loss and praising his dead friend. Yet the end of the letter is unexpected and significant: "Now I'll have to do more things myself, since I cannot rely on anybody as I used to rely on Schwarzenberg. But perhaps that is all to the good." He relied on himself, then, both in foreign and in domestic policy. It was not a wise reliance, not altogether.

In matters of interior administration he established a ubiquitous civil service. He felt comfortable with the bureaucrats, and they with him. He felt at home, too, in the council chamber of the Church. Gradually the Vatican moved closer to the Hofburg. Pius IX, at first a liberal pope, became estranged from and outright inimical to "liberalism, progress and modern civilization"; he favored Austria as "safe." Franz Joseph gave the Church concessions which it had not enjoyed since the seventeenth century. It was enough, said a Viennese agnostic, not only to make the great Joseph II turn in his grave, but to make him rise as a ghost to haunt the Stephanskirche. The Church controlled the Austrian school system almost completely, it influenced censorship, it established a legal system of its own, and it determined Austria's matrimonial laws.

Yet, with all constraints, with all the caution required, with all the do's and don't's issued by the functionaries, life in Austria was not unpleasant. The years from the end of 1849 through 1858 were untroubled by major wars, though not spared by storms of some severity. Once he had established his supremacy, Franz Joseph proved not to be a tyrant. Rather, he was a paper tyrant, not an iron one. If you kept your mouth shut and obeyed regulation 132B, you had nothing to fear.

He was not beloved. But he was accepted. He was accepted particularly by the bourgeois element, soothed by prosperity. If you ran a store on the Kohlmarkt or were employed as a *Concipient,* recording the minutes of ministerial meetings, you could bring up your family decently, take a Sunday walk in the woods, and go to the opera once in a while. It was different with the workers in Vienna's suburbs, and very different in the now silent Hungarian villages, or the noisy alleys of Venice's slums.

Franz Joseph and Nicholas, Windisch-Graetz and Radetzky, Jellačić and Schwarzenberg, had for the time being conquered the revolutionary and pinned him to the ground. They were in the habit of calling a revolutionary, in Metternich's phrase, "a snake in the grass of the state." They had scotch'd the snake, not kill'd it.

2

On February 18, 1853, a bright day, Franz Joseph took a noonday walk accompanied only by one of his adjutants, Maximilian O'Donell. He walked up to one of the high plateaus adjacent to the wall which surrounded the inner city; it was a favorite spot of the Viennese, a sunny and pleasant promenade from which one could get a view of the city. There was nothing unusual in the Kaiser's taking a walk: it was traditional. Joseph II had roamed the city in disguise, like an Occidental Harun al-Rashid, and Franz I had mingled with the people. Franz Joseph stepped to the wall to observe a regiment going through its exercises on the other side. He did not notice an insignificant young man sitting on a bench nearby. The man had come there every day for fourteen days. Suddenly the man jumped up, drew a knife from his coat, and threw himself on Franz Joseph. A woman standing a few paces away screamed, and Franz Joseph instinctively turned toward the noise. The gesture saved his life; the assassin's knife slipped and wounded the Emperor in the neck, the collar of his uniform reducing the force of the blow. Immediately the man prepared to strike again, but in the intervening second O'Donell had drawn his saber and flung himself on the unknown, throwing him to the ground. Another citizen came running and helped O'Donell hold the man fast till the police arrived. Franz Joseph was dazed but had not lost consciousness, and, seeing his assailant belabored by both men, he stammered, "No, don't hit him." Then the blood began to soil his uniform, Franz Joseph felt faint, and O'Donell led him away to the nearby palace of Archduke Albrecht. The doctors arrived in a few minutes.

Vienna was in a turmoil. A wide conspiracy was suspected, and the portals of the city were closed, the railroad stations surrounded, the outgoing trains brought to a standstill. Two regiments occupied the inner city. People rushed to the Stephanskirche; that evening at six o'clock a Te Deum was sung. Sophie appeared and wept.

The identity of the assailant was soon established. He was a Hungarian, a tailor's apprentice by the name of Johann Libényi, and he had acted all by himself, without a conspiracy. As he was led away he shouted, "Éljen Kossuth!" ("Long live Kossuth!"). He was executed within the fortnight.

In the meantime Franz Joseph's condition had worsened. The wound bled profusely and he partially lost his eyesight. His fever mounted. After a week, however, his strong constitution began to assert itself, though it was a month or more before he regained full health.

Nothing like it had ever happened before. No reigning Habsburg had ever been assailed, though perhaps in the Middle Ages a poisoning or two might have occurred. The deed, solitary as it appeared, was a visible symptom of the fact that a deep disturbance was continuing underground. When Franz Joseph recovered, there was no general rejoicing, even in Vienna, though the court staged a spectacular loyalty demonstration. In the suburbs they sang a ditty to the effect: "Tailor, why did your needle stick so badly?"

The assassination attempt was, of course, discussed by the European sovereigns. Queen Victoria noted in her journal:

March 6th, 1853 . . . Talked [to Lord Aberdeen] of the Empr. of Austria and the fear expressed by surgeons and physicians here, that from the nature of the injury, though he may to all appearances seem well, he might die suddenly at any moment. . . .

March 17th, 1853 . . . The absurdities believed abroad, but principally at Vienna, are such, that one can hardly credit them. Amongst others is the following: on the knife with which the Empr. was stabbed, and on those used in Milan, which were of Birmingham manufacture, it was found that they were stamped "Palmer and Son," upon which people declared it was "Palmerston," and that Ld. Palmerston had had them made on purpose!!

Hungary was in a "catastrophic mood." A memorandum had been handed to Franz Joseph, signed by twenty-four Hungarian nobles, stating that the country could not exist in its present condition. Bitterness concentrated itself against General Haynau. In the summer of 1850 he wanted to have twenty-three Hungarian deputies tried for high treason because they, along with others, had voted for the abdication of the Habsburgs. Schwarzenberg said no, enough blood had flowed. Haynau considered Schwarzenberg's order interference with his own jurisdiction. He announced—he must have been half-mad with the lust for vengeance and swollen with self-importance—that he would appoint his own tribunal. All the men were condemned to death—and then he personally and promptly granted amnesty to all of them. This curt farce proved too much for Franz Joseph. Haynau was dismissed, though Franz Joseph allotted him 400,000 gulden for his services. (A like sum was given to Windisch-Graetz and Jellačić; Radetzky got 500,000.) Yet Haynau's dismissal did not quiet those troubled people living east of Vienna.

Franz Joseph's physical wound healed, but the attempted assassination left a psychological wound which cut deeper than the knife and which he did not get over for many years, if he ever did get over it. Like a healthy man who remembers a former illness with egocentric fondness, he began to remember grievances with the pleasure that is part of pain. He was surer than ever that he was right and he now peered with mounting mistrust at those who dared to disagree. He carried himself like a ramrod and he walked in isolation. He could not unbend. A layer of cold air enveloped him; only seldom did it blow away. At this time he took up hunting as a hobby. He was a hunter, not a slaughterer of animals, though he was pleased with his marksmanship when he hit the stag cleanly. What he really loved was the walk in the woods. It gave him the sense of being alone, or the semblance of it, since retrievers, lackeys, and adjutants had to stand nearby. To be *menschenscheu*, "shy of humanity," is a difficult defect in a man who must grant audiences to fifty people a day.

3

Franz Joseph's foreign policy in those years was what foreign policy often is, a compound of cunning and evasion, showing the mobility of a weather vane, with today's promises withdrawn tomorrow, the object being to attain a state of equilibrium during which Austria's economy could develop. What was expedient was moral. That the European situation was as unstable as a child's toy house built of blocks, and that therefore he had to seek expedients, even Franz Joseph's severest critics could not deny.

Even when the wish for a "Greater Germany," a coherence of German-speaking people, had been most alive in Franz Joseph's and Schwarzenberg's minds,[3] they saw the difficulties, difficulties so great as to counsel extreme caution. In the first place Austria was not going to give up any of its non-German population. Second, they feared that Prussia would simply use such a union to lord it over the other German states. (How right they were in this was shortly to appear.) Metternich warned repeatedly: "The ambitions of the Prussians are nothing but selfish aims, hiding under the pretense of liberalism. . . . The words spoken in the Berlin Parliament are significant: 'Prussia cannot be second in a union.' Not being second leads to only two possibilities, either their resigning from the union or their capturing first place by force."[4]

Third, Franz Joseph knew that he would meet opposition not only from the Czar but from France and England; none of these countries could look with favor on such a strong combination, upsetting the balance of power. Fourth, Franz Joseph and Schwarzenberg distrusted Frederick William personally. Schwarzenberg called him "sentimental, untruthful and simpering." "From the highest minister to the lowest subject," he reported from Berlin, "nobody believes in the character or the words of this monarch." Nevertheless, Franz Joseph and Frederick William met in September, 1849, assured each other of their mutual esteem, called each other "dearest relative" (Frederick William was married to Sophie's sister and was therefore Franz Joseph's uncle) , and then parted without having arrived at much more of an agreement than a customs union which would facilitate the transshipping of goods. Neither the Prussian nor the Austrian sovereign would cede an iota of sovereignty. Neither one nor the other could descend from the doctrine that to dominate another country spells well-being for the one that dominates. The standard of living might have been raised for millions of people had unification become reality. Fewer people might have died in fewer wars. But true consonance was a concept that could not be understood, not by an Austrian emperor, nor by the most provincial of provincial electors, nor—most importantly—by the very men and women who had most to benefit by it. Even had the two monarchs been able to agree, their peoples would have repudiated an ultra-national amalgamation; students would have marched, orators would have orated, "patriots" would have mounted the barricades. In that sense, again, "a king is history's slave."

Trouble between Prussia and Austria quivered through the year of 1850, the meetings of His Imperial Majesty and His Royal Majesty and the unctuous documents floating in diplomatic pouches between Vienna and Berlin notwithstanding. Loyalties changed as rapidly as partners in a square dance. In February Austria proposed a German unification program to Bavaria, Saxony, and Württemberg. Prussia was left out. In March Frederick William summoned a meeting in Erfurt to form a confederation in opposition to Austria's. In May Austria answered by attempting to revive the Frankfurt Diet under Schwarzenberg. In September the game of "trump that" was beginning to be played with more than words, the overt occasion being an incident which took place in the electorate of Hesse-Cassel. There the people had long chafed under the rule of as degenerate a prince as was to be found in the German states, a man who had once sold his subjects as soldiers to Britain. Now the people had risen to throw him out and the local Chamber had refused him safe-conduct. Austria took the position that this was an offense against the sovereignty of princes, while Prussia assumed the "liberal" pose. Probably neither Franz Joseph nor Frederick William lost an hour's sleep over the ideologies involved; it was obvious that Prussia was using the occasion as a test case to prove its authority over a minor German state. Franz Joseph acted promptly; he met with the kings of Bavaria and of Württemberg and concluded an alliance with them against Prussia (October 11). Prussia moved troops into Hesse-Cassel from the north, Bavaria from the south. Both sides readied for war. Franz Joseph and Schwarzenberg had received a secret promise from Nicholas that Russia would support Austria, but just to make doubly sure, the Emperor of Austria once again went traveling, journeying far to meet Nicholas personally. The meeting took place, significantly, on Russian territory, in Warsaw on October 30. A smiling Nicholas entered, dressed in a Hungarian uniform. It was the Czar's not so subtle reminder of the debt Austria owed Russia for suppressing the Hungarian revolt. On the same day the order for a general mobilization of the Austrian army was issued. Now the intimidated Frederick William backed down; concerted Russian-Austrian opposition, he feared, would prove too powerful. Presently he took up his pen, and dipping it in ink and maudlinism he wrote Franz Joseph one of his typical letters:

November 26, 1850

My dear wonderful Kaiser!
Could it really be true what they imagine in all Germany, namely that you are surrounded by a small party of men who are inimical to Prussia and want a war?

Two days later, the so-called Punctation of Olmütz was signed by Prussia and Austria; it did not substantially advance the solution of the problem of German unification, while representing a defeat for Prussian prestige. Order was restored in Hesse-Cassel; the Czar went home and presumably changed his uniform to one of Russian cut; Frederick William called off the troops, remained in Berlin, nursed his grievance, and encouraged his military experts to improve the Prussian army. A new invention, the "needle gun," seemed a promising weapon. Franz Joseph heard about it and asked his experts to report on it: the report was negative. The gun, they said, was impractical, its deterioration too rapid, the needle breaking too easily.

4

How discouraged the historian becomes when he has to relate discord after discord, rift after rift! As he turns the pages of the chronicles it seems to him that a nation staggers from the preparation for a war to the fighting of it to the recovery from it. The years seem to consist of three winters to one spring, so seldom is the weather clement.

Franz Joseph was a soldier to whom a saber seemed a thing of

Honoré Daumier: *The Inventor of the Needle Gun Foresees the Future*
(lithograph), drawn in 1866
Metropolitan Museum of Art, Rogers Fund, 1922

beauty; but he was not a soldier-king in the sense that he deliberately sought conquest. As we have said, the period was one of comparative peace for Austria; yet even then an especially vicious war was being fought, lasting three years, that did not leave Austria untouched. In that same span of time Brahms began the composition of his Piano Concerto No. 1, Walt Whitman wrote *Leaves of Grass,* Theodor Mommsen published his *History of Rome,* Herbert Spencer applied Darwin's doctrine to *Principles of Psychology,* Hermann Helmholtz taught in Bonn his principle of the conservation of energy and measured the velocity of nerve impulses, Henry Bessemer invented a new process for making steel, Gustave Flaubert published *Madame Bovary,* Richard Wagner composed *Die Walküre,* Courbet, Delacroix, Daumier, and Ingres were enriching French painting, David Livingstone discovered Victoria Falls, Richard Burton set out to find the source of the Nile, and Johann Strauss, Jr., was gaining fame as the Waltz King. Plentiful as were these achievements, would the sum not have been more fruitful had not most of Europe been worried about a peninsula called Crimea, so remote that few Europeans had ever seen it? Did another Brahms or another Flaubert perish in the cannonade of Sebastopol?

Few wars were based on flimsier excuses or were started on more hollow pretexts than the Crimean War, and few had less determinate issues. What was determinate was its toll: suffering, starvation, cholera, useless bravery, and death, death for almost half a million young men. These have joined the supernumeraries on the stage where the brute spasms are enacted, and we have since learned to give the spectacle with a larger cast. Three memories remain: a poem "The Charge of the Light Brigade," by Tennyson; the work of a nurse they called "The Lady of the Lamp," whose name was Florence Nightingale; and the *Sebastopol Sketches,* which established the young Tolstoy's early fame. Nobody won the Crimean War; the country which, politically, lost most through it was the one least engaged in it: Austria.

For many years a division had existed between monks of the Greek Orthodox faith and Roman Catholic priests. Occasionally the differences became so severe that Turkish soldiers had to part the clerics to prevent fisticuffs. Traditionally the Greek Orthodox churchmen stood under the protection of Russia, while the Roman divines looked to France for support, the Vatican and the Tuileries being allied. Nobody worried much about the Greco-Roman dispute or its theological issues. Nobody, that is, until the Czar announced that the followers of the Greek Orthodox faith in the Ottoman Empire—some 11 million of them—were being suppressed and "exposed to terrible sufferings." He, Nicholas I, Czar of all the Russias and Defender of the Faith, "could not tolerate this" and would demand "proper satisfaction from the Turkish government."[5] The challenge was consistent with Nicholas's character, both as a fulminating autocrat and a mystic theocrat, combining the worst features of both. Most of the European rulers, including Franz Joseph, were not fooled; they could discern the Czar's real purpose. Russia wanted expansion and felt itself strong enough to get it by force. What it wanted especially were those important Dardanelles, which would guarantee Russia free passage from the Black Sea to the Mediterranean. Such a move could lead to Russia's becoming one of the major powers of the West, a rival of Austria, and a competitor of England's sea power.

Nicholas demanded to know from Franz Joseph whether Austria would go along with the proposed move against the Sultan, whom he called "the sick man on the Bosporus." He did not fail to remind Franz Joseph of the gratitude Austria owed Russia. Franz Joseph now stood before a "devilish question," as he wrote to his mother. He answered Nicholas evasively: one ought to proceed cautiously, great danger lay in offending both England and France, and so on. Before the letter arrived, Nicholas had acted.

On the nineteenth of April, 1853, his emissary to Turkey, Prince Alexander Menshikov, handed a note to Turkey claiming a Russian protectorate over Christians living in the Ottoman Empire. There was but one answer to that ultimatum: Turkey rejected it. On the last day of May, Nicholas's soldiers occupied the lower Danubian principalities, preparatory to proceeding against Turkey. In the meantime he had held out a further bait to Franz Joseph to try to draw him into active alliance: would it not be a good idea, he said, for Austria to "occupy" (meaning annex) Herzegovina and Serbia, so that both of "our great countries" would gain sovereignty over all the Slavs?

England was incensed. Her ambassador to Turkey, Stratford de Redcliffe, Viscount Canning, one of Queen Victoria's finest diplomats, had long felt profound antipathy toward Nicholas and now passionately defended the integrity of Turkey. The British public supported their Queen, who was heart and soul against Russia's move and who rightly called the war "incredibly popular" with her subjects. They were aware of Nicholas's despotism, they knew about the snows of Siberia, they had read of the dread "Third Division" of the secret police. At Oxford and Cambridge the students had learned of the punishment which the Czar had imposed on Dostoevsky because he was found guilty of joining a secret society with socialist tendencies. He had been condemned to death, a sentence which was lightened at the last moment to four years of imprisonment at hard labor in Siberia (from which Dostoevsky was not allowed to return for ten years). Idealistic considerations aside, England could of course not allow Russia to get the upper hand in the Mediterranean. When the Czar told Queen Victoria that he wished only to aid the "sick man," Sir John Russell, then head of the Foreign Office, replied that the sick man would undoubtedly expire through the kind ministrations of his well-wishers. With the full approval of Parliament, the fleet was ordered to stand by at the Dardanelles. After some futile attempts at negotiations, Turkey declared war on Russia. The Russians first annihilated the Turkish fleet, but the British ships, now joined by those of France and one or two from Sardinia, penetrated into the Black Sea. Napoleon III joined England because he welcomed the opportunity to get on friendly terms with the country where France's business interests were at stake. An alliance with England would bestow political respectability on him. A nod from Victoria, who up to now had disliked him, was much to be desired. What was more, he felt a personal grudge against Nicholas, who had never managed to address him as "brother," as was traditional among crowned heads; Nicholas called Napoleon, whom he considered an upstart, merely "good friend." Such considerations influence momentous decisions.

Frederick William acted as expected. He had one Russian day followed by one Turkish day. He managed to vary between pro and con and in the end to be neither and to stay out of the conflict.

At the same time, he quickly entered into an alliance with his enemy of yesterday, Franz Joseph, who could, if need be, protect the Prussian flank against Russia. In this treaty he was greatly aided by a new diplomat who had won his confidence, Otto von Bismarck. Bismarck, however, realized that the treaty did not mean much and that Franz Joseph could not be pinned down to a definite promise. Bismarck trusted neither the Emperor of Austria nor his diplomats. It was then that he first decided that "in the long run it was impossible to get along with Austria."

Franz Joseph found himself between the devil and the deep black sea. He could not deny his moral obligation toward Nicholas. But neither could he tolerate Russian encroachment on the Danube base. Nor could he stand by while Russian troops advanced into Galicia, from which they could conveniently travel south. On the other hand, Austria could not well afford to concentrate its military strength in Galicia to oppose Russia, because such deployment of fighting power could weaken the monarchy's position versus Prussia or, worse, make necessary the withdrawal of units from restive Italy. It was dangerous as well to offend France, because France was active in Italy and could make trouble in Austria's Italian possessions. Franz Joseph felt, then, that he could neither join England and France and Prussia openly nor support Russia's aims. He did neither—and drew discredit from both sides. When Lord Palmerston announced, "Austria will go with us, up to a point," a snicker went through the House of Commons, and Palmerston continued sarcastically, "She will go with us . . . *in spirit.*"

The Czar continued to try to win Franz Joseph. Would you enjoy it, he wanted to know, if France and England were to govern in Constantinople? Was it possible that Russia, in the holy cause which it wished to defend, should have no allies? He wrote to Franz Joseph: "Do you seriously intend to make common cause with the Turks? Apostolic Emperor, does your conscience permit this? . . . If you think that I could ever be convinced to tolerate the subjugation of the liberated Christian under the yoke of the Musselman, go ahead! Become one of my enemies. . . ."[6]

No definite answer to this letter was forthcoming, so Nicholas sent to Vienna a confidential messenger who was to hand Franz

Joseph a document personally written by the Czar: it contained an assurance to the Czar that Austria would preserve neutrality even if and when the operations of the war made it necessary for Russian troops to step over the Danube. Franz Joseph was to sign this. The document further held out the promise that all "regions of Turkey which would eventually be declared independent would be placed under a joint protectorate of Russia and Austria" —in plain language, that if Russia were victorious and Austria permissive, they would bag part of Turkey.

Franz Joseph called a conference of his ministers. There was much talk and much head-shaking. After deliberating far into the night, they recommended that Russia's proposal be denied. In this recommendation they merely agreed to what Franz Joseph had already made up his mind to do. When the Czar received the answer, he berated Franz Joseph, accusing him of the secret intention to attack Russia, the same Russia which "a few years ago offered you spontaneously the tribute of its blood in order to bring back your misguided subjects."

On the eighth of May, 1854, Franz Joseph ordered troops sent to Galicia to prevent the possibility of a Russian invasion. In the meantime, Russia had occupied the Danube principalities; Franz Joseph demanded that Nicholas withdraw from them. The Austrian ambassador to St. Petersburg, Count Esterhazy, now had the opportunity of observing Nicholas in a paroxysm of fury. "The Kaiser evidently has forgotten," screamed Nicholas, white with anger and sawing the air with spread fingers, "what services I rendered him. I have no more faith in him. Our mutual confidence is over." He spoke of "unparalleled perfidy" and of future revenge.

On December 2, 1854, Franz Joseph signed a four-point agreement with Britain and France which demanded: (1) Russia's abandonment of any claim over the Sultan's Christian subjects; (2) revision of the rights over the Dardanelles in favor of the Allies; (3) free passage at the mouths of the Danube; and (4) integrity of the Danubian principalities and of Serbia. If these demands were not met before the end of the year, Austria was to "take the necessary steps" to enforce them. In return, Austria's Italian possessions were to be guaranteed for the duration of the war. The Czar ignored the ultimatum. But Franz Joseph did *not* "take the necessary steps"—he did not go to war. Empty threats redound on the threatener: Franz Joseph became known in the palaces and parliaments of Europe as the man who breaks his word. That was the price he paid for keeping Austria "neutral," his army uninvolved in the Crimea.

He confessed to his mother that in turning against Nicholas he felt some twinges of conscience. They were as slight as were the reasons he advanced for his action (or lack of it), the real reason being that he did not dare to face the enmity of England and France: "It is difficult to act against erstwhile friends. However, everything is possible in politics. Russia has been at all times our natural enemy in the Orient. . . . First of all I have to be an Austrian, and leaving aside my personal feeling for Nicholas, I am happy that Russia is now showing weakness."[7] A craven attitude—spawning retribution.

The Crimean War was in full swing. Its varying fortunes do not concern us here. It was a foregone conclusion that Russia could not succeed in its rapacious expedition, though the Czar blamed Franz Joseph because he had pinned down Russian troops in Galicia. The real conqueror was cholera, the victims all five of the powers involved.

At that, it took almost a year of a frantic siege before the Russian fortress of Sebastopol fell into ruins. Before it capitulated, Nicholas suddenly died; several historians believe that he committed suicide, despondent over the Crimean failure.

The peace treaty was signed in Paris on March 30, 1856. The war had not changed anything very much. Turkey's independence was upheld, Russia had to cede Bessarabia, the Black Sea was declared neutral, and free shipping on the Danube was permitted. What did happen, as one writer has put it, was that Prussia, acting much the same as Austria, managed to remain friendly with everybody, while Austria managed to antagonize everybody.

If there was a winner, it was the little Kingdom of Piedmont. Victor Emmanuel was by this time its king, Cavour its Prime Minister. They had lost only twenty-four men in the war—as against France's loss of a hundred thousand. Yet Napoleon III, to spite Austria, saw to it that Cavour was allowed to sit at the Paris conference, though at the lower end of the table. The peace treaty was signed with a feather plucked from an imperial eagle (*aquila heliaca*) captive in the Paris Zoological Garden. Symbolically, the feather could have been plucked from the Austrian double eagle.

5

One needs to speculate what effect Europe's general scorn had on Franz Joseph the man, now twenty-six years old. Sir Hamilton Seymour, envoy to St. Petersburg, wrote that "there was no doubt that Franz Joseph felt his isolation deeply." However much he protested as Emperor that "everything is possible in politics," as a man he knew that he had betrayed a friend. Franz Joseph had wept when Nicholas honored him with a high Russian decoration. He had called him "brother" with more than formal conviction. Though made of softer substance than the zealot Czar, he had agreed with many of Nicholas's ideas. Now Nicholas was dead, and neither the fat and fatuous Napoleon III nor the erratic Frederick William, who was slowly veering toward madness, could serve as equivalents, even had they been less inimical to Austria. First the attempt on his life, now the disdain of France and England and of Russia—at the Paris meeting the Russian delegate had openly called Austria "a mongrel dog"—the deprecation of a Seymour or a Bismarck, created in Franz Joseph a feeling of inferiority which, in the classic pattern of that complex, expressed itself in the wish always to be in the right. That wish made him fluctuate between doing nothing and coming to decisions peremptorily. Since he was not stupid, he was as often in the right as he was in the wrong. But almost always he was lonely. Since he was not trusted, he could not trust. Since he could not give, even those close to him could not give to him. Impeccably dressed, he granted glossy audiences at which he spoke at people, not with them. Two halberdiers stood motionless before the audience chamber, lances erect, helmets shining; they guarded His Apostolic Majesty. The man guarded himself.

Yet there was now one person in his life whom he truly loved: Elisabeth. Even she was not destined to share his thoughts.

Elisabeth as a young girl (after a contemporary lithograph)

CHAPTER V

The Young Elisabeth

HER NAME WAS ELISABETH, but they called her Sisi. The nickname fitted her, with two clear *i*'s mingled with two slender *s*'s. Her body, very tall, was as finely proportioned as a statue of a wood nymph, except that being always in motion, darting and running rather than walking and striding, there was little that was statuesque about her. Her father had admonished her that she should "float like an angel"; her temperament was too lively for her to be able to obey the precept. She was small-bosomed in an age when women were proud of their full breasts, and naturally tiny-waisted in an age when women corseted themselves mercilessly. Her eyes were blue and so bright that they seemed to give out light even in a gloomy room. When she was troubled, the blue eyes changed to an uncertain gray, dropping a curtain on her feelings. Her hair was as long as the Lorelei's, but it was not golden, varying between a dark blond and a light brown. Her complexion was as delicate as white lilac. She blushed easily, and when she did it was "as if her veins ran lightning," to use Byron's phrase, a poet she read as a girl. She laughed easily, too, when she was a girl, and this puzzled her elder sister Helene, nicknamed Nené, who was serious and a little self-important. The young Elisabeth could by no means be called self-important, being as shy as she was merry.

It is not true that

She in beauty, education, blood
Holds hand with any princess of the world.

In beauty, yes; in blood, perhaps; in education, no. She was the
daughter of Duke Max of Bavaria, who married his cousin Ludovika of Bavaria. Ludovika was Sophie's sister; therefore Franz
Joseph was Elisabeth's cousin. Elisabeth was also related to Ludwig II, King of Bavaria: they were second cousins. Sophie, Ludovika, Max, Franz Joseph, Elisabeth, Ludwig II—they all could
point to one ancestor, Maximilian I, the important Wittelsbach
King of Bavaria, who died twelve years before Elisabeth was born,
on December 24, 1837. (She was therefore seven years younger
than Franz Joseph.) They were all related and all of royal blood,
and that blood was commingled.

Elisabeth was the fourth child to be born to Ludovika and
Max, and five more were to follow, three more girls and two boys,
nine children in all. One may wonder where Max got the time and
inclination to father the nine: Ludovika did not love him, nor did
Max pine for Ludovika. She was angry that her husband showed
no sign of dynastic ambition. Her sisters had made brilliant
marriages: the eldest, Elisabeth, married King Frederick William
IV of Prussia; her twin, Amalie, was the wife of King John of
Saxony; Sophie was the mother of the young man who had become
Emperor of Austria; and Sophie's twin, Marie, was married to
Frederick August II, who had been King of Saxony before the
reign of King John. Royalty stood all around her, while Ludovika
herself had to settle for the meager title "Duchess in Bavaria."
Rumor related that Ludovika had expressed her disappointment
on her wedding night by locking her bridegroom in a closet. But
evidently he had emerged to father that brood of children. Max
cared nothing for the royal purple; he preferred torn garments.
Disguised as a strolling minstrel, he would visit fairs and peasant
weddings, strum a guitar, and sing simple songs, while the child
Elisabeth danced and played a tambourine, deftly catching the
coins thrown to her. Many years later Elisabeth once showed a
lady at court a few coins that she had saved from those childhood
days, saying that "it was the only money she had ever earned
honestly." She cherished and admired her father, and she was over-

joyed when she could be with him. That happened rarely, because Max was away from home more often than he was at home. He went traveling, one willing lady after another accompanying the debonair duke to Greece, Turkey, Egypt, Nubia. He chased after exotic experiences, Bavaria holding little attraction for him other than a few agreeable peasant girls by whom he sired quite a few illegitimate children. In Cairo he bought four little Negro slave boys, brought them home to Munich, and had them baptized. He was fond of playing the zither, and his favorite virtuoso on that instrument occasionally got taken along on a voyage; once the two of them played duets on top of Cheops pyramid. Max was an expert rider, and when he was at home he performed circus stunts with his horse. He would dearly have loved to earn fame as a poet: he wrote a quantity of poems and verse plays; they were all bad, even for a duke.

Home was an ugly, square castle called Possenhofen, some seventeen miles from Munich, at the border of the blue Starn-berger Lake, its ugliness compensated for by an expanse of forest and field, framed by the Bavarian Alps. There, amid the yellows and the blues of flowers and the white of snow, she grew up, running through the woods, escaping to the outdoors from the schoolroom, to the delight of her father, who thought bookish education unnecessary for pretty girls, and laughed at Ludovika's remonstrances. Elisabeth loved the tame animals around her: they gave her a whole series of dogs, a pony, a hind, a lamb, and a pet rabbit as playmates. She could sketch a little and began to draw impudent caricatures of her governess and more respectful ones of the animals. It was difficult to teach her French, more difficult to teach her English, and hopeless to teach her the piano. But she did like to write poetry, imitating her father. With all her shyness she was intensely occupied with herself, even as a young girl, looking often and questioningly in her mirror. Hardly fifteen, she fell in love with a young man "with dark brown eyes" who gave her his picture. Ludovika found out about it; the young man was sent away and died soon after, though not of a broken heart. He was followed by a "Count F.R." with blue eyes; more poems were the result. She was not yet sixteen when she met Franz Joseph. She was undoubtedly a virgin, in mind and disposition carefree and trusting, in behavior open and natural, characteristics which ill equipped her to be an empress.

2

Franz Joseph, or rather his mother, was in search of an empress. The dynasty had to be preserved, children had to be produced. The choice had to fall on a princess from a royal house, and since no candidates could be found in Russia or France, only two seemed possible: either a princess of Prussia or one of Bavaria. Accordingly, Franz Joseph went to Berlin when he was twenty-two to look at Anna, Princess of Prussia, a niece of Frederick William IV. He liked her well enough, but she didn't like him much, and besides she was already engaged to a prince of Hesse-Cassel. So they used the excuse that she was a Protestant and wouldn't become a Catholic, and forgot the matter.

Sophie then wrote to her sister and proposed the idea of a marriage between her son and Nené. As always with Sophie, political considerations entered into the plan: to bind neighboring Bavaria to the Austrian monarchy was a promising move, particularly now that Austria was having its troubles with the Czar and could use another friend. A meeting was arranged in Ischl,[1] the spa which lay conveniently near Munich. Franz Joseph, his mother, adjutants, and a detachment of guards journeyed to Ischl with all due pomp. Ludovika appeared with her two eldest daughters and the appropriate retinue. Max was away. The girls' luggage had not arrived yet, but Sophie insisted that no time be lost. She sent her personal hairdresser to arrange Nené's coiffure—Sisi arranged her own hair—and they all appeared in traveling clothes for presentation to the young Emperor. He, svelte, rested, handsome, accoutered in a general's uniform, correct from top button to spurs, bowed to the girls. The conversation was desultory; embarrassment hovered in the room, since everybody was well aware of the purpose of the meeting. Sisi alone seemed unconcerned; after all, she was only a spectator. Franz Joseph looked at her—and from then on had eyes for nobody else. Lunch was announced. Franz Joseph sat next to Nené, but his glance strayed toward the lower end of the table, where, it seemed as if miles away, Sisi was sitting with her governess. Of course everybody noticed. Sisi blushed and could not eat. Nené, inwardly furious but outwardly composed, probably asked what was going on in Constantinople.

Such is the record of their first meeting. There exists another description, more romantic, which because it is improbable may be true.[2] According to this one, Franz Joseph was walking in the woods around Ischl before he thought the Bavarian contingent had arrived, when suddenly there appeared out of the forest a young girl clad in white, her long hair streaming down her shoulders; she saw him, smiled with pleasure, and threw her arms around him. From that moment on, Franz Joseph was in love with her.

Well, perhaps that version is too improbable. However it happened, he did fall in love with her. and early the next morning he announced to his mother that he was going to marry not Nené but Sisi. Sophie raised all kinds of objections: she was too young, a child really, too giddy, unable to fulfill the role of representation. This was the nonsense of the moment, a first, all too heady impression. He should think it over. There was nothing to think over. For once the son did not obey the mother. Sisi, or nobody.

That evening a court ball was to be held, to which both retinues, along with newly arrived guests—Queen Elisabeth of Prussia, Prince Karl of Bavaria, and others—were invited. Franz Joseph's aide-de-camp, Wilhelm von Weckbecker, described the scene in his memoirs:

> His Majesty did not dance the first dance. Neither did the two princesses, Helene who was intelligent but not pretty and Elisabeth, who was as pretty as a picture with her sixteen years, but still almost a child. Before the second dance, a polka, I got a message from Duchess Sophie that I ought to dance with Elisabeth. Up to now she had danced only with a dancing master, and for her debut she would need somebody who could lead her firmly. [Sophie] introduced me to the Princess, who was adorable but ill at ease. She whispered to me shyly that she didn't know whether she could manage it without her dancing master. I reassured her, but I myself

was a little uncertain, knowing from experience that Bavarian princesses didn't dance very well. . . . Fortunately, Elisabeth seemed
to possess a sense of rhythm. What was my astonishment when I
observed that the Emperor did not dance the polka either, but
stood and devoured the fascinating Elisabeth with his eyes, as like a
sylph she glided past him. After the dance I whispered to O'Donell:
"I think I just danced with our future Empress." O'Donell agreed.
Later the Emperor danced with both princesses. But the cotillion
he danced with Elisabeth. That made it definite.

That did make it definite, the cotillion being a sign of special
favor. He gave Elisabeth not only the "cotillion bouquet," as was
the custom, but all the other flowers which by the rules of etiquette he should have distributed among the ladies. The engagement became official two days later, Franz Joseph's birthday.

After mass on the 18th, the official congratulatory reception took
place. The entire Suite was presented to the future Empress. Grünne
spoke eloquently. The Princess was so moved and embarrassed she
could hardly get out a word. After the banquet Duchess Ludovika
said to me that she feared the heavy task her daughter would have
to face: she was ascending the throne virtually from the nursery. She
was worried, too, over the merciless judgment of the women of the
Viennese aristocracy.[3]

There is no question that Franz Joseph loved Elisabeth. It was
a love which endured in him through misunderstandings, miseries,
estrangements, and infidelities. Yet it was a poor love. He was
incapable of giving better, being too much the Emperor, too little
the man. The desk became more compelling than the bed. He
could not form, after the first brief enthusiasm, a part of a partnership, and after a while she didn't help either, becoming herself a
disturbed creature, constricted as a woman. She was too immature
physically when she married, while he was too disabled psychologically. However certain and determined he appeared when he
wooed Sisi, he was too inexperienced for marriage, at least for a
true marriage of minds, and clumsy as a lover at the side of a girl
who was little more than a child, half-awake and half-aware. No
true mental communion existed between the two, and probably
their sexual communion left something to be desired. (Rumor has

it that Franz Joseph made violent love to her during the wedding night and that Elisabeth, shocked and perplexed, did not respond. There is of course no way of proving the truth of this.)

There *is* some question that Elisabeth was in love with him. She was overwhelmed by the honor, bewitched by the position, dazzled by the gold, allured by the crown, and she must have been attracted to the elegant cavalier Franz Joseph then was. But was she in love? "I do love him," she said to her father; "if only he weren't an emperor." She offered him a love which she tended carefully, as if it were an indoor plant, but she could not give him spontaneity or abandon. In her, too, a reticence resided which might have been unlocked by the right man and the right skill. She was afraid of being touched: she was not erotically awakened. She had been brought up in great freedom—perhaps because nobody cared much—and now she was taken out of the woods and brought into an indoors where ceremony hung in the stale air and where every gesture and every step dripped viscous precedent. She was not unaware of what awaited her. "I shall be the most ignorant queen in Europe," she said. She was not the most ignorant, but perhaps the most easily wounded. Between her engagement and her marriage she went home and confided to the pages of her secret diary a poem, addressed to the swallow:

> O swallow, lend me your wings,
> Take me along to far-off fields;
> How gladly would I loose my chains,
> How joyfully the binding band [etc., etc.].

It is a girlishly naïve poem, and it is not the poem of a girl in love.

Whatever her doubts, she accepted her role. Her time was too occupied now, some eight months before the wedding, for much introspection. She had to sit for three different artists to have her portrait painted before Franz Joseph was satisfied that he had one good enough to be shown publicly. A crop of royal relatives paid visits, and Franz Joseph himself came to Possenhofen as often as he could free himself from the worsening situation in the Crimea. One after the other the splendid gifts arrived, brought by splendidly uniformed couriers; a diamond brooch in the shape of a bouquet of rosebuds, his miniature set in a diamond frame, an ermine coat, a parrot from the Schönbrunn menagerie, and so on. He himself brought her the famous diadem, necklace, and earrings of opal and diamonds which his mother had worn at her wedding. Sophie, however, sent a rosary and objected when Sisi thanked her with the familiar *"Du."* Even Franz Joseph used the *"Sie"* form to his mother. The trousseau had to be planned, tried on, and finished; it included 163 chemises, 72 petticoats, 168 pairs of stockings, 240 pairs of gloves, 16 hats, 31 evening dresses, and 4 ball dresses. Twenty-five trunks were sent to Vienna.

She was assigned a tutor in Austrian history. He came three times a week. He happened to be a Hungarian, and Sisi learned that there was more to Austria than Vienna. He awoke in her an enthusiasm for Hungary; she enjoyed her lessons.

Inventories were drawn up, contracts written, and the dowry stipulated; it was a considerable one: 50,000 gulden (about $100,-000). Franz Joseph on his part deeded her an outright gift of 100,000 gulden plus a *Morgengabe* ("morning gift") of 12,000 gold ducats ($240,000). The "morning gift" followed an ancient custom, a gift by the husband to the wife to compensate her for the loss of her virginity.[4] Since a budget had to be established, Franz Joseph told the Treasury to assign 100,000 gulden yearly to the Queen. This sum was officially called "pin money" and was earmarked for costumes, hats, and other "small purchases." In case he died Elisabeth was to receive 100,000 gulden annually as a pension.

As the day drew near when Sisi was to be brought to Vienna for the wedding, she once again expressed her feelings in verse:

> Farewell, you quiet rooms,
> Farewell, you ancient castle.
> Those first dreams of love—
> They rest beneath the waters of the lake.

A ship, decorated with flowers from bow to stern, brought Elisabeth down the Danube to Vienna. People stood along the shores of the river to watch the bridal ship float by. Before the vessel had quite landed, Franz Joseph jumped onto it and embraced and kissed Elisabeth. As he escorted her to the equipage, the dignitaries of the court saluted her, their tired hearts beating a little faster under their gray beards, while the people who had gathered by the thousands and were standing in the valley near the Leopoldsberg, the hill which is Vienna's outpost to the west, broke into such cheers as to outroar the cannons. Eight white Lippizaner horses drew the carriage through the streets. where other thousands had assembled to pelt the couple with flowers. The church bells rang. Elisabeth, very pale, sat, smiled, and nodded. She wore a pink lace gown and a broad hat decorated with roses, but the rose color could not hide the pallor of her face. The Viennese called her "the rose fairy princess." That evening, when any young man called on his Marie and said, "I love you," it was understood that he meant "I love you, as long as I cannot have Elisabeth." On that day Franz Joseph was completely in love with her. So was the city.

Elisabeth was taken to Schönbrunn. There she found that her entire staff had been selected for her, obviously by Sophie, and one by one they were introduced to her. Her chief lady-in-waiting (*Obersthofmeisterin*) was the Countess Sophie Esterhazy-Liechtenstein, a fifty-six-year-old sour-faced woman of doubly aristocratic origin, who later turned out to be one of Sophie's spies. Sisi was handed a voluminous document entitled "Ceremonial Procedure for the Official Progress of Her Royal Highness, the Most Gracious Princess Elisabeth." She was to study it that evening.

Early the next morning the entire court was up, the men dressed in gala uniforms, the women in the crinoline gowns which that arbiter of fashion, the Empress Eugénie, had recently reintroduced in Paris society. The slow and glittering spectacle seemed as if it were a replaying of a scene of the eighteenth century, a pageant Rigaud could have painted in luminous colors. Franz Joseph and Elisabeth were driven to the old castle, the Theresanium, which traditionally served as the building from which a Habsburg bride was to emerge for her ride through Vienna. There Elisabeth and her mother mounted the special carriage, made of glass and decorated by Rubens, which was used for nuptial occasions. As Elisabeth emerged from the building and saw the crowd, she was overcome by a wave of pain and she started to weep, but she got hold of herself, and the procession made its way through a Vienna whose pavements were covered with flowers. Flags waved from every house, the soldiers formed a continuous aisle; behind them the people, shoving and shouting, forgot the threat of mobilization and war. The next day was set aside to prepare Sisi for the wedding ceremony. Two more documents were handed to her, one of them giving her "Most Humble Reminders" for the wedding procedure, the other, nineteen pages long, detailing the various ranks of the guests and how and with what precise greeting they were to be received.

The wedding took place on the twenty-fourth of April, 1854, in St. Augustin's Church. Elisabeth, in her white bridal dress embroidered with gold and silver and decorated with myrrh flowers and white roses, looked beautiful enough to elicit a general gasp of admiration from an audience used to beautiful women. The famous diadem was in her hair. Nearly a thousand people squeezed themselves into the church. More than a thousand candles lit the scene. The heat was intense. Cardinal Rauscher officiated and spoke so long and so fulsomely that the Viennese promptly nicknamed him Cardinal Plauscher (Cardinal Loquacious) . He was assisted by seventy archbishops and bishops.

They returned to the "Hall of Ceremony" in the Hofburg. Franz Joseph led his bride to the "Queen's Throne" beside his own, and the long ritual of the *Baisemain* followed: Austrian and foreign dignitaries, advancing in the order of that nineteen-page memorandum, placed a discreet kiss on the right hand of the Queen; her hand rested on an embroidered cushion. The banquet which followed was as endless as royal wedding banquets usually are, a babel of languages, a series of platitudinous toasts, an atmosphere as frozen as the ices that were served. Sophie was at Elisabeth's side, whispering instructions.

It was very late when Ludovika conducted her daughter to the bedchamber; twelve pages holding golden candelabra stood along the way. Ludovika, assisted by Countess Esterhazy and four maids, undressed the bride. A half-hour later Sophie led her son into the room. By that time Elisabeth could no longer bear the exchange of polite inanities with her mother-in-law. She pretended to be asleep. Sophie felt insulted.

As a final instruction, Elisabeth had been told that she was expected to appear at the family breakfast the next morning. That was a shock to her; she didn't want to show herself after the wedding night. She protested feebly. In vain—it was a tradition and there was nothing to be done about it. At that breakfast Sophie is supposed to have asked her how well her son had performed the sexual act. Elisabeth broke into a fit of weeping.

The wedding formalities were by no means finished. Two days later, the great Coronation Ball was held in the Hofburg. An augmented orchestra was conducted by Johann Strauss, Jr. At twenty-nine the younger Strauss had become sufficiently famous to be asked to present his waltzes at so important an occasion, though it was not forgotten that he had sympathized with the revolutionaries of 1848. Later, when he applied for the title of "Imperial Royal Court Ball Music Director," a title his father had held before him, he was refused.

After the Coronation Ball the round of ceremonies continued; Elisabeth had to receive the delegations from various parts of the realm, and for each occasion she had to be dressed in the appropriate national costume. It seemed to her that life was an unending sequence of dressing and undressing. Since she often had to stand, she needed comfortable shoes. Having found a good pair, she had to discard them quickly. A queen was supposed to wear a pair of shoes only once, and at most not more than six times.

3

A long struggle between her and her mother-in-law now began. Their mutual antipathy was deep-seated and irreconcilable, Elisabeth calling Sophie "Madame Mère" to the court and "that bad woman" to the one or two friends she trusted. Sophie called her "that Bavarian provincial." As the years went by, the chasm between the two deepened; it was never to be bridged.

There was no honeymoon. After the wedding the couple went to the Habsburg country seat, the beautiful palace of Laxenburg (which Bellotto had painted in the eighteenth century for Maria Theresa), but Sophie went along. She watched, she admonished,

she instructed, believing that she was "doing her duty" and helping to form a girl into a queen. Sisi was allowed no free or
unpremeditated gesture; at all times she had to appear representative, bedecked and bejeweled. "It is not fitting for an empress" was
Sophie's favorite stricture. "It is not the custom" was the usual
reply by members of the staff, all of whom owed their appointments to the steely mother.

> I had to sit next to the Empress at meal times. Those were the
> Emperor's orders. She was still exceedingly shy, and she was to be
> trained in small talk. The choice of her chief lady-in-waiting, de-
> cided by Sophie, seemed to me unfortunate. On the one hand this
> woman treated the young Empress in the manner of a governess; on
> the other hand she felt it incumbent on her to initiate Elisabeth into
> all kinds of family gossip of the high aristocracy, matters in which
> the Bavarian princess understandably took little interest.[5]

There was little privacy in the Hofburg. Elisabeth was appalled
by the toilet arrangement for the ladies-in-waiting, who had to use
a toilet hidden behind a screen in a passage guarded by male
sentries. When she asked that this be changed, Sophie answered,
"Your Majesty evidently thinks you are still in the Bavarian
mountains."[6]

Franz Joseph left early every day to go to Vienna and attend to
business. Sisi was left alone. "World affairs do not stand still
during a honeymoon," he said to her. She cared nothing about the
Crimea or world affairs. She wanted to go with him and leave
Laxenburg, that "sad spot." Sophie: "It is unseemly for an Empress to run after her man, to gallop hither and yon like a cavalry
sergeant."[7] At a gala dinner Elisabeth took off her gloves before
beginning to eat. That seemed a major transgression, which was
"humbly" pointed out to her. In this case she won: the rule was
amended and the Empress of Austria was permitted to dine glove-
less. After a while a meal with her could hardly have been a
scintillating occasion:

> I pity the poor Empress. . . . Morally she is . . . terribly dis-
> pirited, almost melancholy. . . . Frequently she secludes herself the
> whole day and weeps. . . . She eats astonishingly little, so that we
> suffer thereby, for the meals, with four main dishes and four des-

serts, coffee, etc., never last more than twenty minutes. She does not go out when melancholy besets her, but sits at an open window all day, excepting a canter on her horse for one hour, at most.[8]

Elisabeth's melancholy and her perplexity were more pronounced in the first stages of her marriage, when she was still trying to find a way to make the union work, still attempting to be a wife, and still earnestly learning to be a queen, than later, when she had found a solution which removed her, body and soul, from the struggle. Occasionally she felt rewarded by pride in her exalted position and by the beauty and wealth of the trappings in which she was swaddled. Perhaps, at one moment or another, she felt a physical outgoing to the personable young man beside her, who was so spruce on the throne and so tedious at *Jause* time. But these moments were fleeting. Once more she confided her sadness to awkward poems:

> What are the delights of spring to me
> Here in this far and foreign land?
> I long for the sun of my home,
> I long for the banks of the Isar.

Or, worse:

> O had I never left the path
> Which might have led me to my freedom.
> O had I never vainly strayed
> On the broad road of vanity!
>
> I am awake and am in prison
> I see the chains that bind my hands.

The second poem was written fourteen days after her marriage.

When in the autumn following their marriage Elisabeth began to show visible signs of carrying a child, Sophie wanted her to appear publicly on all possible occasions in dresses which emphasized her condition. Elisabeth felt the reticence usual with young women of her age and wished to dress so as to conceal her secret as long as possible. Sophie wanted to proclaim the fact to all the world; to her the successor to the throne was all-important. What difference did the prudery of a young girl make? Another Habsburg was to be born. Glory be to God! The God of Imperialism.

The friends of the dynasty—and more important its enemies—had better know it at once.

Sophie's motives in creating the conflict, some of them conscious and some of them instinctual, went beyond the jealousy of the possessive mother. She did hold on to her first-born by an exceptionally tough umbilical cord. She found in him the compensation for a joyless marriage and in his good looks a relief from her husband's plainness. Unprepossessing now—she had become stout and her hair had turned gray—she envied the girl's startling beauty. Starched in the tradition and etiquette of centuries, she found Sisi's naturalness and impulsiveness offensive. While neither woman could conceivably be called "democratic," Sophie could not lean down from her high perch to shake hands with a coachman, while Sisi was able to banter with her riding master. As Sophie grew older, she became haughtier. She became as well increasingly influenced by the man who wore the chasuble. Sisi's rather casual Catholicism would not do.

Sophie was more than what the Italians call *un madro,* a male mother. Her affection for her other sons was less domineering, her treatment less exacting, because it was Franz Joseph who was the Emperor; she had made him so, and on him she concentrated the rays of her will. In her subconscious it was she who was the Empress, not Elisabeth. Woman, wife, mother, she was potentate by proxy. Her family was Austria-Hungary, not to be loved but to be held together with chains whose strength had been demonstrated by history. She could not accept that her son's wife might be less firm of purpose.

While Sophie possessed the sweep of the imperator, she was not above fighting with a needle, a woman's weapon which can be as wounding as the sword. In a hundred little incidents she pricked Sisi's life. Among Sisi's beloved animals—horses, birds, and the dogs she wanted to bring with her to the table—were a couple of pet parrots she had brought from Bavaria. Sophie wrote to Franz Joseph in late June, 1854:

> I believe that Sisi ought not to concern herself so much with her parrots. If a woman is always looking at animals, particularly in the first months [of pregnancy], the children are apt to resemble them. It would be better if she looked at herself in the mirror, or at you. *That* kind of looking would please me.

Why did the husband not put a stop to it? Franz Joseph was no conventional meek Michael, deeply though his mother influenced him. He shared Sophie's absorption in government. The crown was Sisi's rival. Perhaps there is an even simpler explanation: he was too busy to bother. He was at best a nighttime husband, his daytime thoughts being political. Such a man in such a position needs to learn the value of the intimate; Franz Joseph did not learn it until it was too late. In judging Franz Joseph's heart it is interesting to cite an entry in Queen Victoria's journal, written about that time:

> . . . General Radowitz (whom Albert saw for some time) to dinner. . . . I asked the General what he had heard of the young Empr. of Austria, whom he had known as a child. "He has a cold heart," he replied, but he believed the Emperor to be serious, clever, distinguished, very well educated, & with a great knowledge of languages & military affairs. He was very determined, possessed of an iron will, so that he would risk anything, to carry through what he once considered to be right. This, I think is rather a misfortune.

Sisi's first child was born on March 5, 1855. It was a girl. She was baptized with all pomp and circumstance and was given the name of Sophie (Sisi was not consulted). A representative of every major European government appeared at the baptismal feast, Russia being pointedly absent. Sophie had chosen the retinue of the nursery, including the wet nurse, the cook, and the attending physician, Privy Councillor Dr. Johann Seeburger, who was a special confidant of Sophie's. Sisi had nothing to say, nothing to do. The nursery was set up next to Sophie's quarters and far away from Elisabeth's. If Elisabeth wanted to see her baby, she had to climb a long staircase; when she got there, Sophie was usually present. In short, the child was taken from the mother.

Three months after the birth, Sisi went home to see her mother and Nené. Whether she confided in them we do not know; we only know that she returned dutifully to Vienna to take up the struggle again.

The struggle became sharper when the second child was born, July 15, 1856. Again it was a girl, christened Gisela. Two daughters, no son—the whole realm was disappointed. Elisabeth now insisted that the children be moved to rooms directly connected with hers, her anxiety increasing when the baby Sophie showed frequent signs of being sickly, without Dr. Seeburger's being able to diagnose the cause. Franz Joseph wrote his mother, who happened to be in Laxenburg, that he had decided to move the nursery to the "Radetzky rooms," because they were "more commodious and more practical" and Elisabeth didn't have to climb stairs.[9] He then took Elisabeth on a little voyage to Styria and Carinthia, the beautiful Alpine regions. While there he received two furious letters from Sophie: she was insulted that her grandchildren were being taken from her and she threatened to move away from the Hofburg. Had her son lost confidence in his mother? Elisabeth cared more about her horses than her children, Sophie wrote. Franz Joseph proved adamant, though he begged his mother, "Be tolerant with Sisi." Elisabeth won her point—but obviously her relations with her mother-in-law did not improve. Nor did Sophie really let go of the children, wherever they were located.

Surrounded by animosity, always having to watch her every word and gesture, living in a thicket of tattlers, linked to a man who could not give her the tenderness she craved, Elisabeth became more and more self-absorbed. She found nobody in those first years of her marriage with whom she could communicate on terms of easy friendship. Etiquette determined whom she could receive: of the aristocratic families of the realm, only 23 men and 229 women had what was called "free access," meaning that they could appear at a "circle" and address the Empress. But these circles were formal occasions, and Elisabeth could not or would not establish a one-to-one relationship, being herself ungiving. She remained a stranger. She made no intelligent effort to enter into Vienna's life or to understand her husband's problems. She loathed being surrounded by a protective guard; if she wanted to go shopping for a shawl on the Graben, policemen were stationed all around, and if she felt like visiting a museum, she had to announce her intention the day before and the museum director would clear the rooms of all visitors, while he accompanied her bowing and mumbling. She loved to go riding. It was unseemly for her to ride alone or in the company of just one man, Sophie declared.

After a while Elisabeth gave up any attempt to proffer her

hand to Sophie. Her loneliness was partially of her own making, and it expressed itself in an intensive pursuit of her own person. She did not take lovers, the expected action of the lonely woman. Perhaps her sexual instincts were not strong enough; more probably they turned inward. She began to make a cult of her beauty, gazing like Narcissus at her own image. Slowly, over the years, her preoccupation with herself embraced almost all her sexual content. The care of her face, hair, and figure became a ritual. Ketterl, a *valet de chambre,* remembered: "For the dressing of her fabulously beautiful and wonderful hair an entire apparatus was readied. Indeed, washing the hair was an affair of state. Each time we used a quantity of raw egg yolks and twenty bottles of the best brandy." Similarly, from her niece, Luisa of Tuscany:

> The dressing room would be covered for the occasion with a white cloth spread over the carpet. The Empress seated herself on a low chair in the center. The hairdresser, clad completely in white, would begin to brush and comb. After the hair was arranged, the hairdresser would carefully gather up all the stray hairs from the floor, the clothes, the brush and the comb. Then they would be counted and the Empress would be told how many hairs had fallen out. If in her opinion there were too many, she would become perturbed.[10]

She was like a woman who cannot forget that her hair is being disarranged even while a man is making love to her. Having been transplanted from green mansions into a carpeted bedroom, she could not make the adjustment. Nor could she find the exit. Not at first. Those of us most accustomed to freedom are often least able to realign ourselves in circumstances where regulation rules. The most free become the most bound. So this girl, by nature guileless, closed herself off and constructed a private chamber for herself, the walls of which were full-length mirrors. The admiration of her own beauty, which came close to autoeroticism, consoled her for an unsatisfactory marriage and served as a defense against Sophie.

Partly by accident, partly by design, partly by unconscious instinct, she drifted toward a course of action which, she knew, would be particularly unwelcome to Sophie: she would espouse the cause of the Hungarians. Sophie could not stomach the Hungarians. If Franz Joseph was, in effect, the protector of Vienna, she, Elisabeth, would become, in effect, the patron of Budapest. She would try to gain the admiration of these strange and beautiful people living in a strange and beautiful country. This plan, vague at first, came to her during her first state visit. Such visits are sales tours undertaken by royalty to convince the branch offices that the home office has not forgotten them.

The tour to Hungary was preceded by a trial run, to the Italian provinces.

4

Italy needed the attention. The reports were not cheerful: even the most efficient censorship could not silence the imprecations against Austria or stop the jokes the Italians were retailing, the butt of which was invariably the asininity of one Habsburg or the other. The university teachers told and retold the history of ancient Rome's fight for liberty; the audience at La Scala applauded with obvious relish the bloodier passages of Verdi's *I Vespri Siciliani,* the opera which had its Italian production in 1856 (after the censor emasculated some parts of it) ; and the young people sitting in the cafés fell silent as soon as an Austrian official entered. Whatever unarmed hostility could accomplish by black looks and bitter mien was accomplished. Perhaps the authority of kings, a reassuring word spoken by Franz Joseph, would lessen the tension. Perhaps a personal appearance by Elisabeth, in all her beauty, might charm Italy's young men. Elisabeth agreed readily, since such a voyage would free her for a time from Sophie's domination. She took along her little Sophie, now two years old, but she left the baby in Vienna.

The first city to be visited was Triest, which they reached on November 20, 1856. The Adriatic Sea was at its bluest, the sun shone, the harbor was turned into a field of Austrian flags, and all preparations augured happily. Yet even during the preliminary ceremonies in City Hall, a mysterious fire broke out. It was nothing very much, just a small accident really, the fireworks to be used that night having ignited. But was it an accident or was it sabotage? The police thought the latter. The official program proceeded: the royal pair were to show themselves to the populace, seated on the deck of the traditional festive float, the *Galeggiante,* which was to sail down the harbor. The vessel was surmounted by a huge crown made of crystal. Suddenly the crown broke into a thousand pieces. Was this, too, an accident?

In Venice the Austrian officials had worked for months to get everything ready for the grand reception. The dining hall of the royal palace was swathed in white and red cloth, the Austrian colors. Too late somebody noticed that the floor of the hall had been covered with a *green* cloth, giving the effect of white, red, and green, the Italian colors. When the Emperor and the Empress landed on the Piazzetta to make their way to St. Mark's Church, the huge square was completely filled. There was silence from the Italians, a silence made all the more obvious by a few "Hochs!" and "Hurrahs!" dutifully pushed out by Austrian soldiers. The British consul reported to London: "The only thing the people felt was curiosity to see the Empress. Everybody here had heard how wonderfully beautiful she was."

The leading Venetian families had suddenly found that they had pressing engagements away from Venice; at the reception given by Franz Joseph and Elisabeth, only 30 of the 130 patrician families appeared. As their wives and daughters alighted from the gondolas in their full court attire, the Venetian rowdies standing around pelted them with insults.

Yet, showing courage and sense, Franz Joseph and Elisabeth remained in Venice, went through the scheduled program, Elisabeth particularly doing her best to appear gracious. At her suggestion, Franz Joseph issued, five days after his arrival, an amnesty for a number of political prisoners. It had its effect. The day after, when Franz Joseph and Elisabeth showed themselves, they were greeted with applause. The British consul noted the improvement in the mood of the people and ascribed it solely to "Elisabeth's youth and charm." Though she did not feel well, the wet climate getting on her nerves, she seemed to derive satisfaction from meeting the challenge flung out by the Venetians. She was warned of the danger of a gross insult or, worse, an attempt at assassination. She ignored the warnings and appeared in the streets, speaking to all who would speak to her.

She was less successful in Milan. There, in northern Italy's most important city, elaborate preparations had been made to spin the illusion that all was harmony and peace. The Austrian police had distributed one lira per person to several thousand Milanese. The bribe proved insufficient. The population turned out en masse but it kept silent en masse. Not a single "Evviva!" Not a sign of welcome. The men kept their hats on. In the evening a performance had been scheduled at La Scala. Outside the opera house the people stood and hummed *"O mia patria,"* the chorus from Verdi's *I Lombardi.* The boxes at La Scala were owned by Milan's aristocratic families. The Austrian officials, wanting to make sure that they would not remain empty, had notified all box holders that they were either to appear or to put the box at the disposal of Austrian functionaries. Virtually all the families had answered yes, they would use their box. In the evening, the boxes were filled—with the families' servants, wearing black or red gloves: it was the custom to wear such gloves on occasions of mourning. Milanese society women received anonymous letters, warning them that should they appear at the imperial functions, the newspapers would publish details of their past and current love affairs. At the imperial reception, only a fifth of the bidden guests appeared. Here, as in Venice, Franz Joseph decreed an amnesty and a trifling reduction in taxes. Here, as in Venice, Elisabeth did her best. But Milan remained hostile, and it was particularly painful for Elisabeth to be told that people were saying she had taken her little daughter along only as insurance against a possible attempt on her life.

From the report of the British consul: "Though officially the visit of the Emperor was described as highly successful, the fact remains that by far the greater part of the well-to-do and intelligent Lombardians showed their dislike plainly. This state of affairs is to be regarded seriously." Nevertheless, Elisabeth had proved her usefulness. If anybody could placate the dissidents, she could. It was decided to make her the pivotal figure in the progress to Hungary. Franz Joseph and she set out for Budapest early in May. She made one condition: she would take both her children, both little Sophie and baby Gisela. Madame Mère objected strenuously: children should not travel. Elisabeth, now stubborn, thought this but another move on Sophie's part to bind the children to her. She insisted on having her way. Dr. Seeburger came along.

5

The Hungarians responded to her and she to the Hungarians. Something in their temperament appealed to Elisabeth. They seemed to be visitors in their own city, their natural habitat the steppes from which they brought indoors a reminder of feral freedom. They seemed to have just dismounted from their perspiring, lean horses, and their black eyes seemed still to be glancing at wide horizons. The men were the handsomest Elisabeth had seen, with their short leopard cloaks slung over one shoulder, their uniforms encrusted with gold and jewels, a single white heron plume rising like an exclamation point from their shakos. As yet Elisabeth spoke their language imperfectly, yet she fell in love with Hungary. The Hungarians knew how to pay her homage, partly for policy, but partly because they genuinely admired her. They were aware of the family quarrel and remembered the animosity which Sophie had shown them during the 1848 revolution. It did not take them long to decide that if ever they were to win an effective ally, it was to be the Empress, not the Emperor. They set out deliberately to win her friendship. They offered her prize dogs, fine horses, jewels, and, a little later, the use of a magnificent castle and hunting preserve, the castle of Gödöllö.

From Budapest the royal pair traveled to the town of Debreczin, one of the chief centers of Hungarian agriculture. On the road the people stood and shouted loud tributes to Elisabeth—it was a curious contrast to the reception accorded her in Italy—and the young men rode their horses at top speed alongside the procession, now overtaking her coach, now dashing toward her at a furious pace, as if they were attacking, only to halt smartly at the last moment and wave their hats. For the first time in many months, she was happy.

When she arrived at her destination, a telegram was waiting

for her. It was from Dr. Seeburger. The children had been left in
Budapest, and Sophie had shown signs of illness, which the bun-
gling doctor first attributed to nothing more serious than teething,
but soon the child began to spew blood, and Dr. Seeburger now
had to notify the mother that the child's health gave him cause for
anxiety. Franz Joseph and Elisabeth immediately turned around
and hurried as fast as they could back to Budapest. They found the
child weak, her eyes glazed, her condition obviously critical. Elisabeth did not leave the child's bedside, and for eleven terrible
hours she watched her die, probably of typhoid. Elisabeth
screamed in despair, accused herself first for having brought the
child along and then for having left her. The voyage to Hungary
was terminated. She and Franz Joseph returned at once to Vienna.
Franz Joseph, too, was in misery, as much over his wife's suffering
as over the death of his child. The worst moment came when
Elisabeth met her mother-in-law again and saw in her eyes, or
thought she saw in her eyes, the silent accusation. At least Sophie
was tactful enough not to say anything. Elisabeth's mother and
three sisters came from Bavaria to try to comfort her, but she
would have no comfort and she allowed no one to come near her.
Alone and wretched, she would go riding in the woods, digging
her spurs into her horse, then return to the palace and lock herself
in her room. Thoughts of suicide obsessed her. She refused to eat.
Dr. Seeburger justified himself by announcing that Elisabeth had
ignored his advice. Sophie, it must be said, did not believe him.

Under the circumstances, it was senseless to resume the interrupted journey to Hungary. Franz Joseph, with a heavy heart, set
out by himself. Perhaps the tragedy brought about a more conciliatory attitude on his part toward the Hungarians, and in turn
the Hungarians felt sympathy for the two sovereigns, especially for
that nineteen-year-old girl to whom too great a measure of hatred
and death had already been apportioned. In his softer mood Franz
Joseph relaxed some of the punitive regulations against the Hungarian rebels; quite a few of the men who had taken part in the
revolution were permitted to return to their country. Chief among
these was Count Gyula Andrassy. Wealthy, dashing, elegant,
Andrassy was one of the most magnetic representatives of the
Magyar aristocrats. He was also highly intelligent and a progres-

sive statesman. He had fled from Hungary, been condemned by an Austrian court and hung in effigy, spent the intervening years in Paris enjoying life, and now (June, 1857) was not only permitted to return but was restored to his rank and estates.

During the following winter Elisabeth announced that she was once again pregnant. Franz Joseph, overjoyed, now treated her with tenderness and consideration, assigning to her the apartments she wanted. News of the Empress's condition was spread abroad, and from all parts of the monarchy letters came to advise her what she ought to do during her pregnancy so that the baby would be formed into a boy. Ancient formulas arrived from distant farms and obscure villages—when the moon was full she was to melt some lead, drop it in water, and if a piece took the shape of a penis she was to carry it herself to the altar of the Madonna. Elisabeth took some of them seriously, not being entirely free of superstition.

While the births of the first two children had been relatively easy, the birth of the third child was difficult. Her labor lasted more than twenty-four hours, and the pains were so severe that her cries could be heard throughout the palace. When finally, with tear-drenched face and exhausted limbs, she asked after the baby, her husband could bend down and tell her that it was a boy. The heir to the Habsburg throne had been born. He was christened Rudolf. The year was 1858. Elisabeth and Franz Joseph had been married four years.

The famous portrait of Elisabeth by Franz Winterhalter. First painted in 1865, when she was twenty-eight, it was later copied in several versions.

CHAPTER VI

The Realm Diminishes;
Elisabeth Grows Up

IF FRANZ JOSEPH'S FULL TITLES were to be declaimed, as they were on some state occasions, the recital would seem endless. It would begin: "Emperor of Austria, Apostolic King of Hungary, King of Bohemia, of Dalmatia, of Croatia, of Slavonia, of Galicia, of Lombardy and Illyria, King of Jerusalem, Archduke of Austria, Grand Duke of Tuscany and Cracovia, Duke of Lorraine, of Salzburg, of Styria, of Carinthia, Carniola and Bukovina, Grand Prince of Transylvania, Margrave of Moravia, Duke of Upper Silesia, of Lower Silesia, of Modena, Parma . . ." and continue on and on. Some of the titles had already become fictitious—what was Franz Joseph to Jerusalem or to Lorraine?—but now others were to fall away and become phrases spinning in a void.

The unification of Italy was one of those rare developments in which history consorted with logic. It made sense. Yet the doing of it was difficult enough to have required a political magician. To pull together states which in the Renaissance had fought one another with loud clashes of lances, to unify groups which were in the habit of forming alliances and enmities as unstable as March weather, to drill through the high walls of envy which Italian cities had built around themselves, to recapture provinces which had been thrown into the kettle of foreign foragers—in short, to form a nation of bristly bits and gaudy pieces—was an achievement which, like most historic achievements, had to be brought about partly by unselfish action and partly by egotistical propulsion. The desire to become a nation, united by language and geography, had been growing in many Italian minds. Garibaldi, a soldier, gave it the sharp taste of pride. Manin wrote the words of exhortation. But it was Count Camillo Cavour who translated desire into practical action. A worthy disciple of Machiavelli, inspired by Alfieri and Foscolo, Cavour saw what needed to be done, and he did what he did because he loved his peninsula—and because he wanted power and glory for himself. The dual motivation helped to make him effective. His eyes were not beclouded by unrealizable dreams, his voice did not become hoarse uselessly shouting *libertà*, he moved calmly and diplomatically, his goal being both the general good and personal advancement. Cavour had been trained in mathematics, and he applied rationality to what he called the "moral sciences."

During the Crimean War he threw in his lot with the Allies, at small cost to his kingdom; thereby he earned a relationship with Napoleon III, who, to be sure, was no great thinker—"The Little Napoleon," Victor Hugo dubbed him—but clever enough to recognize a bargain when he saw one; Cavour gained as well the respect of Lord Clarendon. Once he had become Prime Minister of Piedmont, he worked toward the modernization of his state, modeling himself on the pattern of the English nineteenth-century liberal. Here was a man who recognized that change was not only desirable but within reach. That change, he said, must be moderate; he had no patience with fire-snorting reformers. And time and again he pointed out to French and British statesmen that the revolutionary ground swells in Italy endangered not only Italy itself but the peace of all Europe. It was a good argument, a practical one. At the Congress of Paris, which followed the Crimean War, Cavour managed to have his own ideas vigorously expressed by Lord Clarendon, while he himself spoke modestly and with restraint. He went home from Paris with the good will of France and England tucked in his portfolio and managed to remain on reasonably good terms even with Russia. Only Austria remained hostile. That was precisely what Cavour wanted.

He persuaded Napoleon III that Austria—that nest of absolutism—could never be made to see reason, that Italians would never be content to live under Austrian rule, and that the only solution lay in chasing the Habsburgs out of Italy. In 1858 Cavour and Napoleon reached a secret agreement that France would come to the aid of Piedmont if Austria were to attack. The agreement was, to put it plainly, a conspiracy which, though initiated by Napoleon, was mostly Cavour's invention. They concluded their understanding at a clandestine meeting in Plombières, a spa where Napoleon III was taking a cure. Cavour arrived there in the best conspiratorial style, complete with false beard and faked passport. The *sine qua non* the French Emperor laid down was that neither France nor Piedmont should appear as the aggressor: he wished to appear innocent in the eyes of England, whose Queen was working for European peace.

In return for France's aid, Napoleon III would be conceded influence in certain Italian territories, while the estates of the Vatican would be reduced and, what was more significant, Nice and Savoy—more French than Italian—would be given to France. For this plan to work, Austria had to be goaded into a war. Cavour understood this perfectly. Through the press and through local leaders he saw to it that new logs would be thrown on the fires of discontent. Discontent, hatred of "those Austrian despots," burned in Venice and Milan, in Modena and Parma, in Padua and Vicenza.

Luck played in Cavour's favor. As often as not luck lies in the mistakes of your enemy. (See Tolstoy, again.) Franz Joseph at this time was much influenced by a war party, headed by Count Karl Grünne, who could do no wrong in Sophie's eyes, and seconded by Count Ferdinand Buol-Schauenstein, the Foreign Minister, a red-faced and pugnacious bully. They pressed Franz Joseph, trotting out the old philosophy that to forbear is to forgo and that the only salutary measure was a passage at arms if Austria was to retain its sovereignty in the Italian lands. The army was to be strengthened in the South and a new general, Franz Gyulai, was to be entrusted with the supreme command. When Gyulai said that he did not feel himself up to accepting such responsibility, Grünne wrote him: "What are you thinking of? You'll certainly be able to accomplish what that old ass of a Radetzky was capable of at eighty."

These warlike preparations gave Cavour the excuse to arm and offered Napoleon III the opportunity to assist Cavour. The cannons were drawn up by both sides, but as yet there was no war.

In vain did prudent minds counsel moderation. Franz Joseph had appointed his brother Ferdinand Maximilian as governor general of Lombardy and Venetia, but what Maximilian advised, though he was on the spot, was held at little value:

> After a year of careful and in every respect wakeful examination, I must express to you that this land has just cause for complaint. Much here is not as it ought to be. . . . I know that imposing might is the best bulwark against all who have violated their allegiance. . . . Nevertheless I must confess that a just, sage, and wherever possible mild treatment is to be recommended.[1]

Or, more frankly, to his mother:

> The other day when I went to Milan I experienced a sense of deep shame. I was all the more humiliated because we both [he and his newly wedded wife Carlotta] were treated with much good will— as respectable private persons. . . . One thing they did accomplish in Vienna, if that indeed was their purpose: there is no longer a party of opposition. *Everybody* now belongs to the opposition, the military, the officials, the clerics, etc. There is but one voice in the land, the voice of disapproval, and I am powerless against it. I do not feel fear because a Habsburg does not feel fear, but I am ashamed and I keep silent. . . . We live here in utter chaos. Only the complete calm which, with all of my twenty-six years, I pretend to possess keeps things hobbling along. Around me everybody has lost his head . . . and sometimes I ask myself if in all good conscience I ought blindly to obey the directives from Vienna. . . .[2]

Later, and more urgently:

> I beg your Gracious Majesty to see to it that somebody preaches calm and moderation to Gyulai. . . . No ostentatious show of troops! True power does not need to provoke. If we don't provoke and show determination without fear, we will perhaps be able to solve the present catastrophic crisis.[3]

Never to know, he wrote, how the day would end, surrounded by inimical hosts, uncertain whether he would hear catcalls if he went to the theater, or indeed if he would return alive from a promenade, such was his existence. But his brother would not listen.

Franz Joseph and his staff could not believe that little Piedmont would dare to take up arms against Austria or that that "arch-crook" (Franz Joseph's appellation), the little Napoleon, would deliver what he had promised in the secret agreement, the salient points of which the Austrian diplomats had discovered. Presently Russia proposed that the differences be arbitrated by a congress to which all continental powers would be invited. Franz Joseph declared that before he would participate in such a meeting, Piedmont would have to disarm. Buol urged that Piedmont be confronted by an ultimatum. When Franz Joseph discussed the question with Metternich, the old negotiator said: "For God's sake, Your Majesty, no ultimatum."[4] Franz Joseph replied, "It was sent yesterday."

It was sent on April 23, 1859, and it demanded that Piedmont disarm within three days. It was the signal for war.

Austrian troops crossed the Ticino and marched into Piedmont. Napoleon III, fulfilling his obligation, landed at Genoa on May 12 with an army of 120,000 which joined the 60,000 soldiers Cavour had managed to raise. The first attack by the Franco-Piedmontese forces, near the village of Montebello, was carried out with such ferocity that Gyulai withdrew to the Quadrangle. On June 4 the French attacked at Magenta. They fought house by house for four days. Forty-eight thousand soldiers opposed the superior Austrian force of 61,000—superior not only in men but in cavalry and artillery—and pushed them back. On June 8 Napoleon III and Piedmont's King Victor Emmanuel, now become a symbol for a united Italy, made their entry into Milan. The people went wild with enthusiasm.

Now it was all Gyulai's fault, naturally. He was relieved of his command "for reasons of failing health." In order to instill new courage in his troops, Franz Joseph himself decided to take command. He hurried to the front, but while he could encourage men he could not correct deficiencies of material or confusion in logistics. "When we marched to battle the day before yesterday," wrote an adjutant to his wife, "the troops had had nothing to eat for twenty-four hours." The decisive battle was fought at Solferino. It was the most terrible of carnages, taking its place in history with such stygian horrors as Borodino and Waterloo. All day long it swung to and fro, and as it swung it killed, until the Austrian army was forced to retreat, while a violent thunderstorm broke over man and horse. Twenty-five thousand men were killed, 15,000 wounded. It seemed the end of Austria in Italy.

Not quite. Napoleon III's true nature now asserted itself, and, by-passing Victor Emmanuel as well as Cavour, he arranged to meet Franz Joseph at Villafranca on July 11 to "talk things over." The two monarchs agreed that Lombardy was to be ceded to Napoleon, who would turn it over to Piedmont; the other Italian states (such as Modena, Parma, Tuscany, and Bologna) would form a federation in which a plebiscite would be held; Austria was to retain Venetia. One can only speculate on Napoleon's motives in seeking such a compromise. Perhaps he was reluctant to see Italy become too independent. He was conscious, too, of the growing disapproval of the conservative Catholics and the clergy within France itself, most of whom sympathized with Austria. Furthermore, Prussia hinted that it might proceed against France should Napoleon become too involved. Finally, Napoleon might have been prompted by sheerly humane considerations: another battle of Solferino, another day of staining green grass red, was unthinkable.

When the results of the armistice were announced, the Italians were deeply disillusioned. From being a knight in armor Napoleon became overnight a despised double-dealer. Cavour tried to continue fighting, but Victor Emmanuel accepted the conditions, whereupon Cavour berated the king and resigned.

The peace treaty was signed in Zürich on November 10, 1859. It took only a little more than two months after that for Victor Emmanuel to swallow his personal dislike of Cavour and recall him to his post. With Cavour's help Garibaldi marched on the South— the famous "Expedition of the Thousand" which drove out the rotten Bourbons, the last representative of whom was impotent Francis II, married to Elisabeth's sister Maria—and the integration of Italy went on apace. In March, 1861, the first all-Italian Parliament met in Turin. The Kingdom of Italy was there proclaimed, with Victor Emmanuel as King.

That Franz Joseph conducted the war ineptly is evident. The Austrian ineptitude may be traced to overconfidence inspired by size, Fafner's "I lie and possess." But even if Franz Joseph had won the war, he could not have won in the end. Whatever may be conquered, the *Zeitgeist* cannot be conquered. The pull which brought forth Italy was as certain as the pull of gravity. It operated independently of this man's ability or that man's lack of it. Cavour used the aspirations of the times; that was his genius. Franz Joseph fought the aspirations; that was his tragedy.

The defeat of Solferino not only cost the monarchy some of its richest and culturally most advanced territories but it menaced Austria in other ways: Hungary took it as a signal to stir uneasily once again; Prussia declared that it was no longer feasible to assign a leading role to Austria in any attempt to unite the German states; the Czar let it be known that he felt nothing but *Schadenfreude*—and the Viennese felt ashamed and resentful. When Franz Joseph showed himself at a parade in Vienna, his reception was icy; quite a few Viennese kept their hats on, while others shouted "Abdicate!" and still others, after glancing over their shoulders to see that no policeman stood nearby, exclaimed "Maximilian! Maximilian!" having heard that Franz Joseph's handsome brother had shown great courage in Milan. When Franz Joseph appeared at the Opera, the public pretended he wasn't there. Sophie sobbed: "My poor, poor son."

Franz Joseph's advisers were demoted or dismissed. Grünne, Sophie's protégé and Elisabeth's enemy, was replaced by Count Franz Folliot de Crenneville. A new Chief of Staff, General Ludwig Benedek, was appointed. He was a gruff, plain soldier, and the army liked him. Investigations were conducted to find out why supplies had not reached the army in time and why certain weapons had not functioned properly. Instances of graft and malfeasance were discovered, and a number of men were thrown into jail.

Scandal covered the Ballhaus, the seat of ministerial government, the War Ministry, and seeped even into the Hofburg. The inquiries were long, complicated, and of little use, the stables being scoured after the horses had gone. The general gloom continued. The Swiss ambassador in Vienna summed it up in a report to Bern:

This peace with its dishonorable conditions has made a terrible impression here. I believe that the dynasty has never suffered a severer blow. If the Emperor returns with the idea to continue this present system of government . . . the monarchy faces a sad future. The system is morbid through and through and must break. I spoke with many patriots today; they no longer feel the nimbus which emanates from the person of the Emperor. In bitter words they express themselves about the ignominy to which Austria has been subjected.[5]

Could Franz Joseph recover from this ignominy?

2

Small comfort awaited him when he came home. During the war Elisabeth, lost and lonesome, had pleaded with her husband to let her join him at the front. That was hardly possible: "I cannot set my army a bad example"; nor could he be sure of her safety while the exigencies of the campaign made him move from one post to the other. All Vienna now knew about her quarrel with Sophie, and Sisi, knowing that they knew, became mentally depressed, wasted herself in useless coming and going, spent as much time in the imperial stables caressing her horses as she spent on her own person, arrived late at every appointment, and in fact did nothing. Franz Joseph pleaded with her:

My dear, dear angel—I beg you, for the sake of the love which you have dedicated to me, take hold of yourself. Show yourself occasionally in the city. Visit public institutions. You have no idea how you can help me thereby. It will encourage the Viennese and firm their spirit, of which I have need. . . .[6]

She did nothing of the kind but instead went riding, sometimes alone, sometimes with a handsome English riding master, Henry Holmes, "dear Mister Holmes." Sophie must have complained, because Franz Joseph wrote, "Apropos of your riding, I thought about it. I can't permit you to ride with Holmes alone. It is unseemly."

At the depth of her sadness she said, "All I ask of humanity is that it should not interfere with me." Yet while she turned further away from Franz Joseph as husband and lover, while she dug herself deeper into the gray mood, she still felt for him the affection born of intimacy, and a sympathy which vibrated strongly, now that he was meeting peril and defeat. She feared for his safety, dreaming of a hundred dangers, not those from the enemy alone, but disease, infection, overwork, a train accident. He had constantly to reassure her. And to admonish her:

> My dearest angel!—Sisi! I can't begin to tell you how much I long for you and how much I fear for you. Your awful way of life . . . worries me to distraction, because it will ruin your health. I beg you, relinquish it and rest at night, which is nature's time for sleeping, and not for reading or writing, And don't ride so much and so fast. . . .[7]

He longed for her now that he was away, but once back and once more encapsulated within Habsburgian walls, it was *aria da capo* and he was unable to do the one thing which would have helped her: break his mother's hold. Elisabeth came to him and declared that she was seriously ill. What was wrong with her? She feared her lungs were affected and that she might be tubercular. This was a common Viennese fear. The physicians who examined her could not find the slightest evidence of infection, aside from a red throat. True, she was pale and painfully thin—but why would she not eat? She couldn't and she wouldn't face those court dinners:

> . . . To live completely within her regimen she hardly ever appeared at the court table. The Emperor was forced to dine only with the male members of his staff. By and by he too avoided those occasions and wolfed down one dish or the other on the day's menu while seated at his desk. On the exceptional occasions when the Empress did appear at the table (e.g., in Schönbrunn or Ischl), she ate nothing. She had her own cook and her own meal hours, similar to those of a jockey.[8]

With her starvation diet, it was unavoidable that she was subject to colds and anemia. She told Franz Joseph that she could not bear to spend the next winter in Vienna. She needed to get away, to a southern, warm climate. What she meant of course—and he might even have understood it—was that she needed to get away from the existence forced upon her. Franz Joseph proposed several of the resorts of southern Austria; she would have none of them. Nothing Austrian, nothing familiar, would satisfy. She proposed a voyage to the farthest point which seemed to her possible, the remote island of Madeira. She knew that for an Empress to leave her country at a sad time and for a prolonged period would create a bad impression among the people, and if she did not know it, Franz Joseph must have pointed it out to her. But she was deaf to his pleas; she would go, whatever the consequences. It was the first of the odysseys she was to undertake, which would remove her from the Hofburg for longer and longer periods.

Her escape to Madeira may not have been a capricious flight. We must look for a deeper reason than "caprice" to understand Elisabeth's decision to leave her husband at a critical juncture, to relinquish her attempts at making the marriage work, to abandon her role as a queen—only later was she to resume it—and to deliver her children once and for all to her mother-in-law.

While Franz Joseph was in Italy, the letters which passed between them testify to an acceptably normal marital relationship, though more ardent on his part than on hers. Here were husband and wife, separated, but still husband and wife. When Franz Joseph returned, Elisabeth was ready to welcome and comfort him. Returning vanquished and shamed, he needed consolation.

This was a peculiar characteristic of their relationship: when he wrote to her he did so with a tenderness and softness which vanished when they were face to face. His letters, at least those of the early years, almost contradict his behavior. Absence, which often makes the heart grow less fond, increased his love; presence choked it, or drove it underground. Elisabeth might have learned to understand the paradox had it not been that something happened which changed their relation. Between July, 1859, and the autumn of the following year, the bond tore. Why?

It is probable that Elisabeth discovered that Franz Joseph had been untrue to her. Court gossip had it that the woman was a Polish girl whom he had known before his marriage. This cannot be proved; it is merely oft-repeated and traditional hearsay. No letters or reliable documents exist.[9] Marie Wallersee-Larisch, Elisabeth's niece, wrote in her memoirs that Elisabeth "discovered her husband's liaison with a Polish countess, and her love for

Franz Joseph received a shock from which it never recovered." But Marie was not an altogether trustworthy witness.

If it be true, how terribly Elisabeth must have suffered! Estranged from her children, spied on by Sophie, feeling herself useless or made useless by force of circumstances, she had still possessed one ineluctable excellence: her wonderful beauty. And now she had to learn that this beauty was not enough and that her husband, grown weary of her sickliness and nervousness, had sought satisfaction in the caresses of another woman, perhaps more skilled in making love than she, or more willing to make love. In this case, it would have been inconsistent with Elisabeth's character to blame herself, even partly. Bewildered, injured, up to that moment used to adulation and the wide-open glances of admiring men, but now deeply wounded in that very quality of which she was most proud, she first hit out at Sophie and Count Grünne, whom she suspected of promoting the affair, and then broke down in body and soul. Her one thought was—away. Away from him, away from the miserable court, away from Austria.

She did not then understand her own sexual shortcomings, any more than he understood that she was no longer a little girl but a woman whose vivid and active mind desperately sought useful occupation. He would not let her share any of his governmental problems. Typical was his pronouncement: "The only reason that Sisi is interested in the Hungarians is that they are picturesque."

Was he really untrue to her? If one believes in the adage, "Where there is smoke . . .," one would answer in the affirmative. Alma Mahler relates this story (it belongs, however, to a later period) :

> The Emperor also demanded the re-engagement of the singer E.B.-F., with whom he had had a passing affair, but whose voice was no longer extant. "Good," Mahler said, "but I will not let her come on." To which Prince Montenuovo replied that it was the Emperor's express wish that she should, and a long-standing promise also, and in any case her salary would come out of his Majesty's private purse. "Then I suppose she'll have to," Mahler replied. "But I shall have it printed on the programme 'by command of his Majesty the Emperor.'" He heard no more of it. And it must be set down to the credit of the old régime that his audacity did him more good than harm.[10]

Elisabeth's escape may have been propelled by a reason even grimmer than casual adultery. For weeks she had observed that her wrists and knees showed an ugly swelling. Neither Dr. Seeburger nor the court physician Dr. Skoda was able to ameliorate the condition. Suspecting something, she is supposed to have decided to consult a physician unconnected with the court. She went to him heavily veiled and under a false name. He told her that she was venereally infected. If this be a fact, the infection must have been a light one, for both she and Franz Joseph were perfectly healthy in after years. But her fright, her disgust, the nauseated mortification she must have felt, could explain her almost hysterical departure. It could as well explain the future relation between Franz Joseph and Elisabeth. Though eventually she forgave him, though she came to pity him, though to an extent they were reconciled, she never again could love him. And he? He treated her with great consideration throughout the rest of her life, with a generosity that met without demurring all of her fantastically extravagant demands, and with a tolerance at variance with his nature. Was this expiation?

Here again we have no documents, only whispered tradition. The Austrian historians whom I have consulted believe that the facts are as I have stated them. At any rate, the sequence of events is clear: Elisabeth visited her family in Possenhofen in July, 1860, and for a brief spell Franz Joseph kept her company. During that summer Garibaldi and his thousand occupied Sicily and from there menaced Naples, where Elisabeth's sister Maria (now called Maria Josepha) was queen. Elisabeth begged her husband to send troops to Naples to help her sister and her sister's husband, but after Austria's recent defeat, Franz Joseph could not and would not embroil himself again in Italian affairs. The Neapolitan couple were abandoned and had to flee. On September 7 Garibaldi entered Naples. Elisabeth, shedding many tears, had returned to Vienna, while Franz Joseph went to Warsaw to confer with the Czar. Before that conference Elisabeth seems not to have formed any plan of flight. Though bemoaning her sister's fate and probably blaming Sophie for Franz Joseph's decision not to interfere, she gave no inkling of her wish for a separation. Did something change her mind while Franz Joseph was in Warsaw? Did

Franz Joseph see the Polish countess again and did Elisabeth hear of it? When he returned he found a frenzied and haggard Elisabeth who insisted on leaving.

3

No Austrian vessel was available for the journey, so she applied to Queen Victoria to lend her a ship. Victoria generously and at once offered her the use of her own private yacht. "Dearest Child," Victoria wrote from Windsor on November 17 to her eldest daughter, the Princess Royal:

> . . . You will have heard how ill the poor, young Empress of Austria is so that she is obliged to go to Madeira. We have given her the *Victoria and Albert* to take her there, as being the only really fast and comfortable vessel and she goes over tomorrow to Antwerp to carry the beautiful, fragile young Empress alone without husband and children to a distant land! May it not be too late. . . .

The voyage to Madeira proved exceedingly stormy but Elisabeth, alone of all her retinue, was impervious to seasickness. She seemed to thrive on and take satisfaction from the fury of the sea. Perhaps the turbulence of nature opposed and calmed the storm in her soul. When the yacht finally came within sight of the dark cliffs of Cape Garajao, her health had already improved.

Count Carvahal, who owned half Madeira, offered her a princely villa. She refused it and rented a small, isolated house standing on top of a cliff. From its veranda she could see the closed horizon of a vast sea and, directly below, a tropical garden from which palms and laurel and mimosa tried to climb toward the rocky summit. It was peace. "The sea is my father confessor," she wrote; "it restores my youth, for it removes from me all that is not myself."

Everything possible was done to please her. Three ladies-in-waiting and three counts, all of whom adored her, ministered to her wishes. (One of them was Count Imre Hunyády, a handsome Hungarian who instructed her in that language. She liked him and spent much of her time with him. When this became known he was recalled. Elisabeth did not mind particularly and forgot him.) Eight ponies were put at her disposal. She admired a huge English sheepdog, whereupon a dog of the same breed was promptly ordered to be shipped to her from England. She watched the island's birds and made a few of them captive in cages around the house. She was trying to surround herself with her childhood. It was as happy a period for her as she could manage. Her throat was fine, she was well, and the cough which had plagued her when she arrived at Madeira disappeared. Yet every so often melancholy, combined with longing for her children, crept over her, and then she would give orders to depart, only to countermand them the next moment.

She remained at Madeira until the end of April, that is, more than four months. All that time, in letter after letter, Franz Joseph begged her to return. He sent for a detailed map of Madeira, just to understand where she was and to follow her on her excursions. He missed her very much. When she finally ended her stay, she wanted to return incognito, by way of Spain, taking the ordinary slow train to Seville, but she was recognized and a large official delegation waited for her at the Seville railroad station, much to her annoyance. She wanted no ceremonies, refused to stay in the royal palace, refused an invitation from the King of Spain, and presently continued her journey through Gibraltar, Majorca, and Corfu. Here was another island that gave her delight. With its orange trees and cypresses, the bluest of blue waves, the profusion of juicy yellow buttercups, she found Corfu even more beautiful than Madeira. She very much wanted to stay; she could not. Franz Joseph—on the imperial yacht, with an escort of five battleships!— was hurrying toward the island to take her home. When he saw her, eyewitnesses reported, he wept.

Bronzed by the southern sun, the twenty-three-old Empress radiated health. Not for long. Almost from the moment she was ensconced once more in Vienna's palace—even when she moved out and declared she would live an "unofficial existence" in Laxenburg—she declined and fell into her "fastness." Her cough returned. She could not eat, she felt weak, she developed a low fever, she believed she was going to die. One cannot know the cause of her relapse: was it unwillingness to resume marital relations, was it her hatred of Sophie which by now had intensified to mania? The wildest rumors flew through Vienna: the Empress was mortally ill, the doctors were supposed to have said she had only six more weeks to live. The Wittelsbach family physician was called from Munich; he forbade her to talk so as not to irritate her throat. Shortly it was announced that her doctors had recommended that she go to Corfu. They recommended no such thing: Ambassador Lord Bloomfield said it was obvious nonsense and that no physician in his right mind would recommend Corfu in the summer, when malaria was prevalent.

Whatever dangers Corfu might hold, she had been enchanted by the island, and there she went, having spent just a few weeks in Vienna. This time the farewells were tearful. Were they ever going to see her again? She seemed so very ill. Even Sophie wept. Elisabeth was accompanied by Dr. Skoda, whom she promptly dismissed. Once again the cough disappeared, she was free of fever, she took endless walks, she swam in the sea, and at night she sat on the beach while her dogs draped themselves contentedly at her feet and she gazed at the moon. She read a great deal, Shakespeare and Heine.[11]

In Corfu she had a visit from her sister Nené, who had recently been married. Perhaps Nené thought how fortunate she had been that Franz Joseph's choice had not fallen on her; she surely guessed, or if she did not guess Elisabeth told her, the fragmentation in her sister's soul. How often in Elisabeth's letters to the children did the phrases recur: "Don't forget your Mamma . . . think once in a while of your Mamma!" Perhaps Nené pumped courage into her, though it took a long time before Elisabeth was to summon it effectively.

She spent the whole summer of 1861 in Corfu, and Vienna was gossiping about a definite break between Emperor and Empress. Partly to contradict such harmful rumors, partly because he loved and missed her, Franz Joseph sent Count Grünne to Corfu to try to persuade her to come back, if not to the Hofburg, at least to Austria. He could not have chosen a messenger more maladroit. She loathed Grünne and at first refused to see him. When she did receive him and he told her of the Viennese rumors, she replied that it was he and Sophie who were responsible for the rumors. It was he and Sophie who had made her life impossible; they had robbed her of her children and humiliated her with Countess Esterhazy, a vulgar tattletale. Grünne withdrew and tried again on another day. Elisabeth no longer could master her nerves and spat at him that he was a panderer, that he had introduced women to her husband whom ordinarily he was not likely to meet, that he had done his best to destroy her marriage. Presently she realized she had gone too far and apologized. Count Grünne left, his mission unaccomplished.

Some two months later Franz Joseph did what he should have done in the first place: swallowing an emperor's and a man's pride, he went to Corfu to beg Elisabeth to return. They arrived at a compromise. She would not return to Vienna but they would both go to Venice, the children would be sent there, and they would spend as long a period in Venice as Elisabeth desired. They would be together as man and wife.

While they were in Venice, Elisabeth managed to persuade Franz Joseph to dismiss the Countess Esterhazy, and to appoint a new governess for the children. It was a small victory, but it was a victory. Not until almost four years later, after many another skirmish with Sophie, and after Elisabeth had become politically indispensable to Franz Joseph, was she able to win decisively. It was then, in the summer of 1865, that she handed her husband an amazing memorandum, which she asked him to sign:

> I demand that I be given complete autonomy in everything which concerns my children: the choice of their surroundings, the place where they are to live, the complete guidance of their education . . . up to their majority. Furthermore I desire that all matters which affect me personally will be determined solely by me, such as the choice of my surroundings, the place where I am to live, any changes in the house, etc.

He signed.

While she was in Venice, she began her collection of photographs and drawings of Europe's most beautiful women. Presently every one of Austria's foreign embassies was notified to gather pictures for her. The ambassador in Constantinople was told that the Empress wanted not only the portraits of famous Oriental beauties but those of the women of the Sultan's harem. It was strictly forbidden to acquire these, but nevertheless he managed to get a few and smuggle them out. (The albums containing Elisabeth's collection are still extant and are now in an archive in Budapest.) Was this curious hobby prompted by her narcissistic leanings? Did she want to know: "Who is the fairest in all the land?" or rather, "in all the lands?" Perhaps—and if one puts that curiosity alongside her expressed wish to meet beautiful women wherever she traveled and her later desire to surround herself with attractive women—it could also have been an expression of unconscious lesbianism.

The men to whom she felt herself drawn in those years shed a psychologically significant light on her personality: in one way or another they were maimed creatures. In Bad Kissingen, a fashionable resort which Elisabeth frequented because it gave her still another excuse to stay away from Vienna, she made the acquaintance of the blind Duke of Mecklenburg. She took him for walks, and they, the young woman and the old man, discussed the meanness of life and the unimportance of death. Among the poems she wrote was one which she framed and hung in her bedroom:

> *Ob gross, ob klein erscheint, was wir gethan*
> *Wenn wir beschlossen unsere Erdenbahn*
> *Wie schnell ist ausgefüllt die leere Stelle!*
> *Wie viel machts Unterschied im Ocean?*
> *Ein Tropfen weniger oder eine Welle.*

(Whether what we have accomplished at the close of our earthly existence appears great or little—how quickly is the empty spot refilled! What difference does it make to the ocean? A drop less, or a wave.)

In Kissingen, too, an Englishman, John Collett, who was almost completely paralyzed, fell in love with her. At first he did not know who she was and took her for an English girl. He sent her flowers, wrote poems to her, and begged for a lock of her hair. She was touched by his love, and he introduced her to the books he treasured and the English poets he admired. She took it all in with responsive sweetness; it was a relationship unencumbered by danger to her. But she would not give him a lock of her hair. She had made a vow, she wrote, never to give such a memento to anybody. Anyway, "I can only tell you that you esteem me much too highly. I do not hold myself at half the worth you do, when you think of me and write to me. . . ."[12]

A special tenderness lay in Elisabeth's heart for her second cousin Ludwig, son of Maximilian II of Bavaria, eight years her junior. She had admired him since he was a boy. She was drawn to his mind, which wanted to live in a forest primeval, steeping itself in saga and knightly legends, feeding on beauty as it exists only in a poet's imagination, and which, world-weary and diseased, was finally to come to grief and extinction. Like her, he was irresponsible; like her, a fugitive from reality; like her, extravagant; like her, mistrustful where he might have trusted and wholly trusting where he could better have used caution. And like her, he was a being of exceptional magnetism.

Ludwig felt for Elisabeth the adoration and devotion which a homosexual can feel for a beautiful woman. She in turn basked in his admiration and was led by him toward music and poetry. He opened wide to her the world of the arts. She entered that world eagerly, and much of the fulfillment which she later derived from it she owed to Ludwig's instruction. There were occasions when his enthusiasm proved oppressive to her: unannounced visits late at night when he sat and did not want to go home and had to be coerced to leave by a ruse; his appearance at the railroad station, waiting sometimes for hours, just to greet her; the enormous bouquets of jasmine, his and Elisabeth's favorite flower; as well as the books, the wine, the trinkets which he sent. Sometimes Elisabeth criticized him. When Ludwig left Bavaria at a moment when the country was in critical danger of war, when he turned his back on everything just to call on Wagner in Triebschen and beg his "God-like friend" to return to Munich, Elisabeth wrote: "I hear the King has gone away again. If he would only concern himself a little with government, in these terrible times!"[13] She could even make fun of him: "He kissed my hand so often," she wrote to Rudolf, "that Aunt Sophie [Elisabeth's sister], who was spying through the door, asked me afterwards if I still had my hand. He was again dressed in an Austrian uniform [obviously as a compliment to Elisabeth] and heavily perfumed with Chypre."[14] Yet her censure was a loving censure. She knew his sorrow. Did she know that he was a homosexual? I am convinced she did, though she never discussed it openly, and I believe that she believed he might be brought around to normalcy. Henry Channon, in *The Ludwigs of Bavaria,* wrote that Elisabeth "remained the only person whom he ever trusted. . . . Their friendship brought happiness to two unhappy people, but they encouraged each other's neurotic tendencies, and in a sense it was a liaison of complicity since they shared and condoned strange secrets."

Ludwig was called to the throne in 1864, when he was eighteen, exactly the same age as Franz Joseph at his accession—but unlike Franz Joseph he had had no political training, no instruction in government, no preparation in statesmanship. He was an immature boy living in a dream world, declaiming the tragedies of Schiller while riding his horse. And suddenly, from being allowed a few talers of pocket money a week, he found himself able to dispose of vast sums. He dreamed of fantastic architectural projects. That almost his first act was to rescue Wagner was an achievement which in retrospect outranks the achievements of most of his contemporary sovereigns, however mawkish his impulse might have been. Elisabeth shared some of his love for Wagner's work: when Wagner gave a series of three concerts in Vienna in December, 1862, and January, 1863, Elisabeth appeared as patroness and sent him a gift of a thousand gulden.

As Ludwig continued to reign, as the conflict with his ministers and his people sharpened, as he emptied the coffers of the Bavarian treasury, Elisabeth kept hearing tales of his eccentricities. The Austrian ambassador to Bavaria, Count Blome, described Ludwig's bedroom in his castle of Hohenschwangau: he had a lamp made in the shape of the moon which he could regulate so as to simulate the moon's phases from new to full. The lamp shed its light on a miniature fountain which bubbled night and day. The table on which his supper was served rose magically through the floor, quite as the old fairy tales would have it.

Ludwig was a creature of night. He would arise at 2 A.M., would wander over to the Royal Riding Academy, which at his orders was kept fully lighted, saddle his horse, and ride round and round till the break of dawn. Blome reported a performance of Schiller's *Kabale und Liebe* (*Love and Intrigue*) at which King Ludwig sobbed uncontrollably. "He shows more imagination than brains. . . . An exaggerated self-importance, stubbornness and inconsiderateness toward others make themselves felt more and more. . . . Music and literature are the predilections of His Majesty; as to the former, he cares more about the texts than the tones, since he is not really musically gifted."[15] This was of course a reference to Wagner, whose "impudent demands for money" and "improper pronouncements" Blome resented as much as did the Bavarian ministers. On the day of the declaration of the war of 1866, Ludwig retired to his "Rose Island" in Starnberg Lake and for three days refused to receive the ministers. On one of those nights he lighted fireworks for his solitary amusement. "One begins," declared Blome, "to think the King mad." But Elisabeth defended him and thought Blome's judgment unnecessarily severe.

He came nearer madness when he proposed marriage to Sophie, Elisabeth's sister. Perhaps he thought at first that he could change himself and prove his manhood, that he would be able to have sexual relations with Elisabeth's sister because she *was* Elisabeth's sister. It is certain that he chose Sophie because she reminded him of Sisi: she, too, was beautiful. But what could Ludovika and Max, her parents, have been thinking of when they gave their consent? Were they that ignorant? Or that ambitious? Did the prospect of another queen in the family rob them of all sense so that they were willing to sacrifice a daughter?

So Ludwig let himself drift toward the altar. He was all enthusiasm when it came to selecting the new furnishings or planning the wedding ceremonies, though he called on his bride only seldom and as often as not unexpectedly at night. When it was rumored that he might be coming, Ludovika had Possenhofen lighted and the entire staff had to stay awake. As the time drew near, Ludwig became more and more frightened, postponed the day of the wedding week after week, then determined that if he could not end the wretched business he would kill himself with cyanide, and finally wrote Sophie: "Dear Elsa [using Wagnerian nomenclature]: Your parents wish to end our engagement. I accept their proposal. . . . Your Heinrich." Then Ludwig threw Sophie's bust out the window and wrote in his diary on October 7, 1867, "Sophie terminated. The gray fog lifts. Liberty I longed for. Liberty I thirst for, after recovery from a painful incubus." Poor Sophie, by nature gay and happy—undoubtedly she loved Ludwig —was shamed before the world. Yet the next year she married the Duke of Alençon. On the eve of this wedding, Ludwig suddenly appeared to congratulate his former fiancée, and after a few minutes just as suddenly disappeared again. Elisabeth was understandably incensed over Ludwig's treatment of her sister. "I have no words to characterize such behavior," she wrote. Yet she forgave him.

The bond between them remained unbroken. Much later, in 1875, Ludwig wrote to Crown Prince Rudolf:

> You Fortunate and Enviable one, you to whom it is given to dwell near the adored Empress—oh, please, place my tribute at her feet and beg her in my name to remember her faithful slave, who has always and will forever worship her. . . .[16]

Finally, in 1886, Ludwig was forced to abdicate. Soon after, a group of soldiers, two physicians, and several male nurses equipped with a strait jacket came to fetch him, but he eluded them and walked into Starnberg Lake. When he and his personal physician were found drowned—was it suicide or an attempted flight?—when the whole tragic fate of the companion of her youth was told to Elisabeth, she said, "He was not mad. He was a lonely man enclosed in a world of ideas. He should have been treated with kindlier feeling; perhaps the gruesome end could have been avoided." The following year she went to Bayreuth. She was especially moved by *Parsifal,* and she talked to Wagner's widow Cosima, exchanging memories of Wagner and Ludwig.

Ernest Newman wrote:

> It is a curious reflection today that Wagner and Ludwig were each of them really and truly understood only by the other and by one woman in addition. In the King's case the woman was his cousin, the beautiful and intelligent Empress Elisabeth of Austria, whose life was as tragic as his own; in Wagner's case it was Cosima. The strain of melancholy and the sense of frustration in Elisabeth gave her, and her alone in his immediate circle, the key to Ludwig's unhappiness.[17]

These men—Ludwig, Collett, and others—did no more than awaken in her capacities which had lain dormant. She had room in her mind for both vanity and poetry. Her drive for learning was a steady force, her intellectual curiosity one of the mainsprings of her being. And all she did or learned sprang from a genuine impulse; she did not pose, she did not pretend. In a later year Karl Hasenauer, one of Vienna's foremost architects, said of her: "One needs a thorough knowledge of history, art, and science to be able to converse with her; her learning is astonishing."

As Elisabeth matured intellectually and her horizon widened, she outgrew her earlier indifference to affairs of state. Though, as she said, ordinary politics still disgusted her, she wanted to contribute something to the basic thrust of government, the problem of nation getting along with nation. A queen cannot forget that she is a queen. She wanted a cause. She found it, a cause shot through with romantic color.

She admired the Hungarians because they persevered in their struggle for independence. She loved them because in looks, flourish, valor, they seemed to her an exotically lucent people—they reminded her of what she imagined the Argonauts had been when they set sail for the Golden Fleece. She used to quote the Hungarians' favorite proverb: "Outside Hungary there is no life; if there is any, it is not the same."* She decided that here was her task, here she could help. With new seriousness she plunged into learning Hungarian. She studied while her hair was being done, she studied while she was being dressed, she studied during her daily hour of exercise, which she now performed in a little gymnasium especially constructed for her. With that same determination with which she dieted, she mastered the language. In the same little black book in which she entered her daily weight—she never kept a diary because she "feared the curiosity of posterity"—she wrote Hungarian verbs to be learned by heart. As she grew proficient, Dr. Max Falk, one of her Hungarian teachers, made her translate from French the correspondence between Joseph II and Catherine the Great, no easy homework. One day she said to him, "Yesterday I was busy all day with receptions and in the evening I

* It existed originally in Latin: "Extra Hungariam non est vita, si est vita, non est ita."

had to go to a state concert. After that I was so tired that I went to bed. Then I suddenly remembered that I had not done my Hungarian homework. So while I was lying in bed I tore a leaf out of an album lying on the night table and wrote. Please excuse it if my composition is written in pencil."

Elisabeth's love for Hungary did not remain a secret to that country's leaders; they nourished it by showing her a warmth which grew into worship. On the other hand, Franz Joseph was astute enough to use Elisabeth's popularity in his attempts to close the rift between Vienna and Budapest.

In Hungary, as everywhere in the heterogeneous empire, political opinion ranged from the desire for compromise to the radical demand for separation from Austria and the founding of an independent Hungary. The head of the conservative party was a lawyer, Franz Deak, an honest and a modest man, whom his people trusted. He believed that complete separation would spell "Hungary's death, a death without resurrection." His friend, Count Gyula Andrassy, agreed with him. As already noted, Andrassy had fled to Paris after 1848 and had been hanged in effigy. (In Paris he came to be known as *le beau pendu*.) When he met Elisabeth, he was in his early forties, and he who had been used to the cream of beautiful women in Paris and London thought her "the prize of all womanhood." She in turn fell under his spell, as well she might. He seemed to her the very symbol of romantic insouciance, glowing with the light of his own past and his country's history. In court assemblies his tall figure towered above all others, and he bowed with the ease of the man of wealth to the manner born. He was delightfully fluent in conversation, but able to bore into a difficult problem with the utmost seriousness, his dark eyes assuming a scholar's intensity. For a time Franz Joseph was suspicious of him, a suspicion in which his inherited dislike of everything Hungarian may have been sharpened by a twinge of jealousy.

Further to steep herself in the understanding of Hungary, Elisabeth now desired a Hungarian girl as a companion, as a "court lady." A long list of members of the high Hungarian aristocracy was submitted to her, but she chose a relatively simple girl, a member of the gentry, seemingly for no better reason than that

she liked her mellifluous name. Her name was Ida Ferenczy.
Elisabeth asked for Ida's picture, liked it, and asked her to come to
Vienna. She was to be the one. A difficulty arose because the girl
was not of sufficiently noble birth to be given the rank of "court
lady." They got around that by giving her the title "Reader to
Her Majesty." Ida stayed with Elisabeth for many years and
proved utterly devoted to her.

Elisabeth told Andrassy, "When things are not going well in
Italy, I feel sorry. But if misfortune were to strike in Hungary, it
would kill me." On her name day in 1865 she went to the Bene-
dictine Abbey in Martinsberg, where the cloak of St. Stephen,
Hungary's first king, was kept as a holy relic. She repaired the
cloak with her own hands.

Elisabeth played a difficult political role, more difficult than
she at first imagined. She felt that only a liberal attitude toward
Hungary could avoid an open break; Franz Joseph felt that only
stern centralization could preserve the monarchy. He did not
then, and at bottom never did, understand any system but the one
in which he had been brought up and which, so to speak, had
exercised a prenatal influence on him. He could envisage only two
conditions: either order vested in the sanctity of the ruler—or
chaos. Pressed as he was, he did make a few concessions. In 1861 he
established a Diet of two chambers, one Austrian and the other
Hungarian, which would report to a national and central Parliament. It was a cumbersome structure, and nobody was happy with
it. The struggle continued, but less acrimoniously because Deak
and Andrassy and the others knew that they had a friend at court
who could speak up in the bedroom.

It now became fashionable to learn Hungarian: members of
the Vienna court rushed to obtain teachers and sprinkled their
Viennese dialect with Hungarian expressions. Delegates went back
and forth between Budapest and Vienna. On January 8, 1866, a
"grand deputation" led by Hungary's chief cardinal appeared at
the Hofburg. Elisabeth had once again returned to Vienna. Surrounded by eight newly appointed Hungarian court ladies, she
received the deputation—Andrassy, of course, among them—
dressed in the Hungarian national costume: a dress of white silk
with a lace apron, set off by a gaily embroidered velvet bodice; on

her head the Hungarian cap, on top of which rested a crown of diamonds. The men were stunned. Sophie was shocked.

The visit was returned by Franz Joseph and Elisabeth. Elisabeth made a speech to the assembly, speaking Hungarian with only the slightest of foreign accents. The British consul in Budapest reported: "It would be difficult to describe the effect of the Empress' speech in the restrained words suitable for an official report."[18] Franz Joseph added to the enthusiasm by pardoning most of the revolutionaries of 1848, including Kossuth. The pardon came eighteen years late, and it pardoned many a dead man. And, between gesture and reform, the gap remained. He would not concede a self-contained government to the Hungarians. A few days after the Budapest reception he wrote to his mother:

> I hear that once again the Viennese are indulging in their usual pastime: to be scared. Now they fear I am going to make concessions here, establish a ministry, etc. Obviously I haven't the faintest intention of doing so. . . .
>
> Sisi is of great help to me here, through her courtesy, her exquisite tact, and her excellent Hungarian, by which the people are able to hear many an admonition from a pair of pretty lips.[19]

During the Prussian war of 1866 Elisabeth returned to Budapest with the children. Franz Joseph wanted them there for safety's sake. From there Elisabeth bombarded her husband with pleas, ever more insistent in tone, that he do what he did not have "the faintest intention of doing," seek a compromise. She could not bear to watch "incompetent men," prompted by "senseless hatred," run the imperial wagon deeper into the mud. Would he not at least see Deak and Andrassy and listen to their ideas? Andrassy ought to be appointed Minister of the Exterior: the people trusted him and he would be able to keep internal peace. She knew instinctively the temper of the people; she was sure that her judgment was correct.

> Just now I returned from Königsegg, where I had a discussion with Andrassy, naturally quite alone. He expressed his views clearly and decisively. I understood them, and I am convinced that if you would trust him—*wholly* trust him—it would still be possible to save ourselves and the entire monarchy, not Hungary alone. In any case,

you *must* talk to him. And that at once. Each day conditions can so change that he might no longer accept responsibility; to do so at this moment does require a certain sacrifice on his part. Do speak with him immediately. You can do so without reservations; you are not confronting a man—that I guarantee—who wants to play a role at all costs, or one who chases glory. On the contrary, he is risking his present very favorable position. . . . For the last time I ask you for the sake of Rudolf, do not neglect this last opportunity. . . .

I have asked Andrassy to tell you the unvarnished truth [about the sharpening of dissatisfaction in Hungary] and to put you completely in the picture, even if it is unpleasant. I beg you, telegraph me immediately after receipt of this letter to tell me if Andrassy should take the train to Vienna tonight. . . . If you say "no," if at this hour you refuse an unselfish counsel, then you will act dishonorably toward us all; . . . then, whatever will happen, I have no other redress but to comfort myself with the knowledge that one day I can say to Rudolf honestly: "I did everything within my power. Your misfortune is not upon my conscience."[20]

"Your misfortune is not upon my conscience"—the woman writing this was a different Elisabeth from the girl in the Bavarian woods or the fugitive in Madeira. Her new seriousness and courage were the symptoms of a new capacity to understand the world. That capacity was nourished as much by the attraction she felt for Andrassy—it would not be exaggerating to call the attraction love, though they never had sexual relations—as by intelligence. At last she had made a place for herself, beyond being wife and removed mother. At last she knew that she could be useful. Her "unselfish counsel" was a mixture of the reasoned and the felt. She understood. All understanding is a mixture, produced in a silent alembic.

Had there been no Elisabeth, had she not felt herself drawn to the Hungarian nobleman with the beautiful eyes, had she not, once determined, insisted on solving the issues her way, had her hold on Franz Joseph not been sufficient to have him give in to her, then the monarchy would have broken in two and Austria-Hungary would have ceased to exist. Of that there is no question, just as there is little question that Franz Joseph did not understand the real causes involved: the pressure of nationalism, the desire of a people for government of the home by the home.

The evening on which he received Elisabeth's letter, Franz Joseph telegraphed to her (in code) : "Have secretly summoned Deak. Therefore don't commit yourself too far with Andrassy."

But he did receive Andrassy:

Beloved Angel: Pray fervently that God may inspire me to do what is right and what is my duty. Yes, today I am expecting G. A. I shall listen to him attentively and let him speak out. Then I'll sift him closely to determine whether I can really trust him. The old man [Deak] is no longer in Pest and has to be fetched from the country, so that he cannot arrive here before tomorrow or the day after. Anyway, I prefer to see A. first alone. The old man is very clever, but he never had much courage. . . .[21]

The interview with Andrassy was not a success. Franz Joseph felt that "his ideas were too imprecise," and though he was undoubtedly sincere, he lacked the power to convince non-Hungarians of the soundness of his intentions. Besides, he regarded the problems unilaterally, from the Hungarian point of view. What about the other nations?

It is difficult to judge how much, if at all, Franz Joseph was influenced in his negative judgment by jealousy, how much by his innate reluctance toward change, and how much by logic. Here again the mixture of reason and emotion may have been at work. At any rate, in the letter he immediately wrote Elisabeth (at half-past five in the morning), he postponed decision and suddenly swerved to her personal life:

I am grateful for your description of the Villa Kochmeister [which Elisabeth had rented], which seems to be very pretty. But I am concerned about the glass door of your room. Surely one could look in when you perform your ablutions. That frightens me. Have a curtain made to cover the whole door. I beg you, take care of your health and spare yourself, or you will really become ill and that would be terrible. . . . Your faithful little fellow.[22]

Elisabeth would not be put off. Andrassy advised her to speak tête-à-tête with Franz Joseph and never mind writing letters back and forth. She packed, left Budapest, and appeared in Vienna. Andrassy was to follow the next day. He noted in his diary: "If our cause meets with any success at all, Hungary will owe greater thanks than it can surmise to our 'Beautiful Protectress' who watches over us."

It came to an outright quarrel between Elisabeth and Franz Joseph. She had to tell Andrassy, "I harbor no further hope of seeing my effort crowned by success." The Emperor, nervous and almost frantic because the Prussian war was lost, could not see it her way. The best she obtained was a promise that he would grant Andrassy another hearing. She left almost at once, to go back to Budapest. He pleaded with her to return. She would not. The letter with which he answered her refusal is the only letter in which the man who loved her—in spite of everything—sounded a bitter note:

> Many thanks for your letter of the 5th [August], the only purpose of which is to prove to me, with a mass of reasons, that you wish to, and that you will, remain in Ofen with the children. . . .
>
> Well, I shall have to comfort myself and to bear with patience my being alone. I am used to it. I have learned to bear much and one gets used to everything. On this point I won't say another word; otherwise our correspondence will become too boring, as you rightly remark. I shall await with composure your eventual decision.[23]

Elisabeth's response was to mount her horse and to ride wildly for hours in the Hungarian landscape. She felt ill; she too was lonely; she couldn't sleep. Two weeks later he regretted his intransigence and wrote her: "You, my treasure—and what a treasure!—I miss you so much. Don't leave me alone for so long, my Sisi. Don't let me pine so long. Come to me soon."

In September he had to appoint a Minister of the Exterior. It was not Andrassy on whom his choice fell. He feared the reaction in Vienna should he name a Hungarian. On the other hand, he did not want to offend the Hungarians further by choosing an Austrian. He therefore summoned to Vienna Baron Ferdinand Beust, who as Prime Minister of Saxony had shown extraordinary ability in smoothing over the complicated relations of the South German states with Prussia and Austria. Saxony was allied to Austria, and Franz Joseph knew Beust well. What attracted him particularly was Beust's hatred for Bismarck, a sentiment which was returned in full by Bismarck, who said that if Beust's vanity were to be amputated, nothing at all would remain of him. To be sure, Beust did not exactly underestimate himself—after his appointment he said that he had been summoned as the laundress to wash clean the dirty linen which had accumulated for centuries and was befouling Austria's air—but he *was* a remarkable man, moderate in his views, far-seeing, and an adroit diplomat whom even the suspicious Napoleon III respected. Franz Joseph needed him badly and chose him though he was a Protestant. It turned out to be a wise decision.

Almost the first move Beust recommended was rapprochement with Hungary. And he convinced Franz Joseph. He completed what Elisabeth, Deak, and Andrassy had begun. Rather, it was the weight of evidence and counsel, as well as the force of external circumstances, which tipped the scale. No one counselor did it, no one friend or enemy, though Beust in his memoirs gave himself most of the credit. The signal-fire for the beginning of a dual monarchy was lit. Austria was changed into hyphenated Austria-Hungary.

Work to hammer out a new constitution began at once. It established virtual autonomy for Hungary in domestic affairs while holding on to the concept of unity in international matters. It gave Hungary its own cabinet, with the Prime Minister—Andrassy was appointed to the post[24]—responsible directly to the "King of Hungary," Franz Joseph. The monarchy was divided into Transleithania (Hungary) and Cisleithania (Austria),[25] both parts equal in rights, sharing the army, the navy, and a finance ministry. Taxes and duties on goods were to be unified, their amounts to be decided by delegates of *both* countries. The army and navy were to look to the Emperor as their supreme commander, but the cost of their upkeep was dependent on budgets established by joint committees. While German remained the official language of army and government offices, Hungarian was now to be considered equivalent and "military orders could be given in both languages." (Hitherto Austrian officials generally had refused to learn Hungarian, and quite often communication between educated men was carried on in Latin.)

On February 17, 1867, in the central hall of the National Museum in Budapest, the Hungarian delegates, sixty-seven of them, listened in deep silence as the royal document detailing these proposals was read. At the end they rose and applauded

Gyula Andrassy in the costume of a Hungarian magnate. Photographed in 1867, the year of the "Hungarian Compromise."

frenetically. Only Kossuth from his exile let it be known that he disapproved. He accused Deak—the noblest Hungarian of them all—of having sold out to Austria. This merely helped to turn Austrian opinion toward the settlement.

The famous "Hungarian Compromise" (*Ausgleich*) was ratified on May 29. It marked the end of wholly centralized government. But it preserved the empire. The head of that empire and his Queen were now to be formally crowned as King and Queen of Hungary.

For representational purposes Elisabeth and Franz Joseph came together again. To the world they seemed united, though Elisabeth could not help indulging herself in one "I-told-you-so" dig: "More and more I come to understand," she wrote to him on the day of ratification, "that I am exceptionally clever, though you do not sufficiently value my brains." It was written only half in jest. A week later he joined her in Budapest and the rehearsal for the ceremony could proceed.

June 8, the day of the coronation, dawned at 4 A.M. At that hour twenty-one cannon shots rang out over Budapest to proclaim a spectacle such as the city had never seen. Every house was decorated with the Hungarian flag, the display of which had up to now been forbidden. The sun was shining, and before the procession started, reported Janka Wohl, an eyewitness,

> the tall figure of a priest, in a long black cassock studded with decorations, was seen to descend the broad white road leading to the Danube, which had been kept clear for the royal procession. As he walked bareheaded, his snow-white hair floated on the breeze, and his features seemed cast in brass. At his appearance a murmur arose, which swelled and deepened as he advanced and was recognized by the people. The name of Liszt flew down the serried ranks from mouth to mouth, swift as a flash of lightning. Soon a hundred thousand men and women were frantically applauding him, wild with the excitement of this whirlwind of voices. The crowd on the other side of the river naturally thought it must be the king, who was being hailed with the spontaneous acclamations of a reconciled people. It was not *the* king, but it was *a* king. . . .

In three weeks Liszt had composed a Coronation Mass for the occasion. It was an inconsequential work.

At 7 A.M. the procession emerged from the royal palace. Elisabeth wore a gown of white and silver brocade, on the bosom of which jewels rayed out like a sunflower; it had been created for her by Worth of Paris. Franz Joseph, in a white uniform, was weighted down by St. Stephen's cloak. Six hundred horsemen representing fifty-two regions, each in the costume of his region, rode before him. Two hundred magnates in medieval apparel followed. The prelates of the Church walked under red baldachins. Arrived at Buda's parish church, Franz Joseph dismounted. Andrassy held St. Stephen's crown first over Elisabeth's head and then placed it on Franz Joseph's head. While a Te Deum sounded, Franz Joseph stepped outside onto a platform, and holding a crucifix in his left hand, he raised three fingers of his right hand and swore to uphold Hungarian law. He then remounted his white horse, charged up Coronation Hill, sprinkled with clumps of earth from the various parts of Hungary, pulled St. Stephen's sword from its scabbard, and pointed it toward the four cardinal points to symbolize his resolve to protect the country from danger from whatever direction. *Hic et ubique.*

No ceremony in nineteenth-century Europe had been as glittering as this: even the cool London *Times* waxed lyrical:

> We almost see the pale and careworn look of the Imperial and Royal candidate, as, faint with his "thirty hours' fast," he kneels at Mass in the old parish church of Buda: we almost feel the three to four pounds' weight of the holy and precious diadem which must press his brow during the whole of a ten hours' solemnity; we interpret the deep colour mounting the lovely countenance of the Empress as her neck and shoulders are bared to allow of her being anointed, not on the forehead, like the King, but according to inexorable prescription "under the right armpit"; and we hear the roar of the ordnance, the peal of the bells, the clatter of the splendid cavalcade, in which one of the magnates is to appear in a complete suit of solid silver plate armour; another is to wear jewelry on his coat to the amount of £6,500, while the mere caparisons on the charger of a third are valued at £8,000.

Once having accepted the plan of the dual monarchy, Franz Joseph did his best to make it work. According to Edward Crankshaw in *The Habsburgs,* "He kept his side of the bargain more loyally than the Hungarians kept theirs." The Hungarians were no more generous than other nations in treating their minorities, the Serbs, Slovenes, Poles, and the Germans living within their frontiers. The Hungarian Compromise did not produce Hungarian tolerance.

4

"One must treat Bismarck with the greatest caution. It is hard to imagine how stubborn this statesman is, how completely he is led by his hatred for Austria." This from a report by Count Johann Rechberg, Austrian Foreign Minister.

The 1866 war between Prussia and Austria was linked with the Hungarian *Ausgleich*. It resulted in a further diminution of the realm, less consequential for Austria in territory than in reputation. It was a war in which Bismarck acted both as Merlin and as exorcist.

Bismarck's fractious mind, churning behind his pale eyes, burned with a double desire: the desire to make Prussia great and to make himself great. The second ambition he could achieve through the first. To achieve it he had to expunge Austrian influence from the German lands, an influence which had formed an integral part of Habsburg history, which had been affirmed as a mandate at the Congress of Vienna, and the renewal of which was still in the forefront of Franz Joseph's thought. Austria's motto, engraved in stone on the Hofburg, was A.E.I.O.U.—"*Austria est imperare orbi universo*" ("To Austria is the whole world subject"). The boast had never been wholly true. But it had been true that Franz Joseph's forefathers held sway over the vast Holy Roman Empire, which included all Catholic Germans, that Austria did *imperare* German territories, and that the dream of a reverse Anschluss—Germany to Austria, not Austria to Germany—had never died. It was time, Bismarck thought, to awaken from the old dream and to face a modern world, a world in which the Germans were to be united and led by strong, progressive Prussia, while Austria was to be pushed to the East. Beat Austria! It could be done. Prussia was strong, or would be made so by him; Austria was soft. Bismarck, who was not moved with concord of sweet sounds, hated the music of the soft Austrian dialect.

Even before he became Chancellor in September, 1862, he had expressed himself openly—and openness was not usually a characteristic of his—to Disraeli. He said that as soon as the Prussian army had been brought to a respectable condition, he would seize *any* pretext to declare war on Austria, to dissolve the German Diets, to subdue the smaller German states, and to weld the German-speaking people into a unit, with Prussia as the master smith. He had to wait four years before he could begin, and when he did begin he not only fought Austria but opposed his own king. Wilhelm I felt a kind of loyalty toward Franz Joseph; Bismarck had little use for loyalty and less for sentimental attachments. The year after Bismarck became Chancellor of Prussia, Franz Joseph made an attempt to unite the German states: the old ambition was to be subjected to one more trial. The time seemed right, the necessity pressing: Poland was in revolt against Russia, Napoleon III protested as he was bound to do under the terms of an agreement with the Czar, Russia threatened to move westward into Prussia, the German principalities were bickering—in short, the sovereigns once more were playing a dangerous game of ninepins with the lives of their subjects. Once more, then, a Frankfurt meeting was proposed, Austria presiding. Once more it would be suggested that German lands merge into a single economic and military might. Wilhelm I was taking the waters in Baden-Baden when the King of Saxony arrived to invite him to the meeting. "What!" said Wilhelm. "Thirty German princes and a king as a messenger! Of course I cannot refuse." "You *must* refuse," Bismarck opposed in a series of violent arguments. Participation in Frankfurt would be tantamount to conceding German leadership to Austria. It was unthinkable; it would be fatal for Prussia. On the other hand Austria's defeat would unfold Prussia's glory.

Bismarck won his argument. He bludgeoned Wilhelm into agreeing. As he left the King's chamber, Bismarck broke off the door handle, smashed a pitcher against a wall, and then burst into a fit of uncontrolled sobbing. But Wilhelm stayed away from Frankfurt, and without Prussia nothing could be accomplished.

The mental picture one has of Bismarck is that of "blood and iron," an iron man, obdurate, undeflectable, strong, as if his Sunday suit had been a coat of mail. Yet this ursine man could be as nervous as a whippet. In public pronouncements he left no room for doubt; he gave the impression of being utterly sure of himself. In private he often broke down, showed the classic symptoms of neurosis, doubted, and was sorry for himself. Both genius and disease were in him. Contradictions abounded in his personality. He was a halting orator but a superb writer. He was a fanatic Germanophile and hated the French, but he wrote a French as rhythmic as that of an eighteenth-century Parisian essayist. He sat and read the Bible, but this did not prevent him from lying and from practicing unscrupulous cynicism. Private honesty was one thing, public behavior another. He loved animals and trees, and he despised human beings. He selected his co-workers adroitly, but then could not bear to have men who were too capable around him, and he dismissed them. He had to be first, and none was to share the credit. In his own mind people were always taking advantage of him; he was always being insulted. When opposed he escaped into illness. As Golo Mann describes him: "He suffered from ailments such as phlebitis, insomnia and nervous pain in the face during most of the time that he was politically active, and made a great deal of fuss about it. When he encountered opposition he suffered from cholecystitis [gall-bladder trouble], jaundice and convulsions."[26]

This does not jibe with the portrait of the man of iron, yet he was that, too, and iron-bound was the structure he planned. He had tripped Austria's ascendancy, but he had not yet assumed European leadership. Indeed, no one had: Europe after Crimea was in a chaotic condition. Luck came to aid Bismarck; rather, he knew how to use luck. A relatively unimportant problem, the problem of Schleswig-Holstein, gave him the chance. It was an old dispute. To whom should these duchies on the Elbe belong? They had been appendages of Denmark for centuries, and though in the general revolution of 1848 they had risen against Denmark, nothing had come of the revolt, and by the treaty of London in 1852 the Danish union had been confirmed. Now conditions had changed: Frederick VII, the Danish King, had died in November, 1863, and his successor, Christian IX, wished to incorporate

Schleswig into a "Greater Denmark." This was a breach of the London agreement. Bismarck seized on it as an opportunity to show Europe that Prussia would not tolerate any infraction of international treaties (particularly if such an infraction went against his interests—but obviously he kept quiet about *that*), and he proposed proceeding against Denmark. He told Franz Joseph: "Come with us. Help us and we'll help you with your troubles in Italy." It was a cynical proposition. Bismarck wrote confidentially to Robert von der Goltz, Prussian ambassador in Paris: "You do not trust Austria. Nor do I. But I think it is right to have Austria with us now; we will see later whether the moment of parting comes and from whom."

The Austrian-Prussian war against Denmark began in February, 1864, and no one came to Denmark's aid; Bismarck had gambled on England's and France's indifference. He was right. The war, interrupted by fruitless conferences, ended in October. It took almost a year before any kind of agreement could be reached, but finally in August, in Gastein—why is it that bellicose agreements were usually concluded in spas and resorts?—some kind of uneasy decision was reached: Austria was to administer Holstein; Prussia, Schleswig. A plebiscite was to be held to determine the eventual status of both provinces. But no plebiscite was held, and soon it became clear to the most obtuse of statesmen that Bismarck wanted to tuck both duchies under a Prussian hat. An infuriated Franz Joseph said that he "forbade any interference whatever in the administration of Holstein." The quarrel between Austria and Prussia, yesterday's allies, broke into the open. Even when Napoleon III appeared in his favorite role, that of mediator—Bismarck called him *une incapacité méconnue*—he not only failed at a peaceable resolution but saw that the differences between Prussia and Austria were becoming more acerbic. Bismarck accused Austria of insisting on an unfair settlement of the Schleswig-Holstein question, of interfering in German affairs in ways detrimental to Prussia, and of arming against Prussia in secret. None of these accusations was substantially true, and all contained some truth. Franz Joseph hated to go to war, but he realized that the bear of Berlin was ready to bite and he wasn't going to be bitten. Both sides armed.

Italy seized the disturbance as an opportunity to get rid of what remained of Austrian power. Victor Emmanuel considered Austria's presence in Venetia as irritating as a speck in his eye. An Austrian army had to be put on a war basis in Italy, and Franz Joseph appointed Archduke Albrecht to keep order. He negotiated with Napoleon III and won from him a promise of strict neutrality in the coming Prussian altercation, though at a great price: after the war, Austria would cede Venetia to Napoleon III, whether or not Franz Joseph were to win against Prussia. It is probable that he foresaw that in any case Austria could not hold on to her Italian possessions for long; the unification movement was engulfing. The insane part of it all was that Italy offered to buy Venetia for 400 million gulden, while Bismarck said he would purchase Holstein. Franz Joseph refused both offers.

While Bismarck was preparing the army for war, he secretly fomented strife in Hungary, sending spies and agitators to Budapest.[27]

So it went, war preparations on both sides, accompanied by insincere "last-chance" offers; protestations by both sides of the necessity that "we must negotiate" and no intention on either side to do so; wooing of the smaller German states by both Austria and Prussia with the result that they were helpful to neither; appeals to France and even to Queen Victoria—all fruitless. The Austrian army gathered in Bohemia to meet the Prussians. Franz Joseph had given the command in the north to Ludwig Benedek, who did not want any part of it. He implored the Emperor to send him to Italy, where in his youth he had fought successfully and where he knew every tree and bridge. Bohemia was strange territory to him. On the eve of the battle Benedek wrote to his wife, "It would be best if a bullet hit me." Franz Joseph insisted that Benedek, not Albrecht, take the command. He had a reason: he feared that the Hungarian soldiers particularly would not go through thick and thin for Albrecht, who was besmirched by the recollection of the part he had played in suppressing the Hungarians in 1848. That memory was still green in many minds.

Bismarck's army was commanded by Helmuth von Moltke, who, though four years older than Benedek (he was sixty-six), was young enough in spirit to understand the new methods by which wars were being fought. Moltke was and looked like a scholar, and his conversation sounded as if he had never stepped outside the study. He knew many languages and their literature. He knew the antique world, history, geography, sculpture, architecture. He was to live on to the age of ninety-one and become one of the great masters of German prose. Yet this man could walk away from his books, mount the commander's hill, and become a brilliant strategist. He took advantage of a new weapon: mobility. He split up his army, kept it flexible, and transported the units where they would be least expected. He was enabled to do so by the development of the Prussian railroad system, which was better than the Austrian.

When the two armies finally faced each other at Sadowa (Königgrätz), each side represented an aggregate of nearly a quarter of a million soldiers. Yes, nearly a half-million men were involved, over a matter of two little duchies! Of course neither Bismarck nor Franz Joseph worried about the welfare of Schleswig or Holstein. What was at stake at Sadowa was European leadership. Both sides fought with senseless bravery. One Prussian regiment, which had gone into battle with 30 officers and 9,000 men, emerged with 2 officers and 400 men. At the end of the battle, an Austrian corps advanced to the tune of a regimental march, and in just twenty minutes it lost 279 officers and 10,000 men. The new Prussian needle gun, which the Austrians had turned down, proved a devastating weapon which could be fired from three to five times faster than the Austrian guns. Bismarck was on the battlefield. So was Wilhelm, quite intoxicated with the roar of war. He got in everybody's way, until Bismarck gave the King's horse a sharp surreptitious kick in the flank. The horse galloped off with Wilhelm. When the battle was over, Moltke wrote to his wife that most of the "entire field was covered with corpses of humans and horses. . . . The wounds were horrible to behold. An officer implored me to kill him. . . ."

This was the battle which has been described as the first blitzkrieg and which, like Solferino, changed the course of European history. It was one of the shortest wars on record. The main fighting lasted no more than eight days, from June 26 to July 3, 1866. Because it got Austria out of Germany, because it allowed Bismarck to demonstrate to all German states that for their future they had better count on Prussia rather than Austria, the formation of Greater Germany, which had been talked about off and on for fifty years, was now to progress in fifty weeks. When the sun set on July 3, 1866, Benedek had to telegraph two words to Franz Joseph, "General rout." When Franz Joseph read it, an eyewitness related, he became "as white as his uniform." Benedek's career was finished. He stipulated in his will that he wanted to be buried in civilian clothes. Moltke wrote his widow a heartfelt letter paying tribute to Benedek's courage.

All this over Schleswig-Holstein, of which Lord Palmerston said later that the true causes had been so complicated that only three men in the world understood them: now one was dead, one was mad—"and I have forgotten what the causes were."

The Prussians now threatened to advance into Austrian territory and to menace Vienna itself. The Viennese fled in droves, even as they had years before when Napoleon I was on the move. The despair was general, relieved only by the news that Archduke Albrecht had won a victory over the Italians at Custozza; and later that the admiral of the Austrian fleet, Wilhelm Tegetthoff (the Viennese are proud of him to this day, and a huge monument to him stands at the entrance to the Prater), had destroyed a good part of the Italian fleet at Lissa. It really did not matter much. The real question which faced the country was: How deeply would Bismarck demote his enemy? Was Austria to become Prussia's vassal? Queen Victoria noted in her journal for December 7, 1866, that Lord Bloomfield told her: "The Emperor had grown ten years older, and was terribly cast down."

It was at this moment that Bismarck showed his genius. He did not want to destroy Austria. His sweeping view made him realize not only that Austria was a necessity of European existence but that if he proceeded on a conqueror's course, the other nations, including England, would react strongly against Prussia. Napoleon III was already making threatening noises. No one could live in peace with a Germany to which Austria was subjugated. And Bismarck had no wish to repeat the fate of Napoleon I.

Where force had been effective before, mildness would now be more effective. Wilhelm I was all for marching on to Vienna and for carving off a sizable chunk of Austria, including the German part of Bohemia. Bismarck fought his king, standing before him like a giant, his face red and swollen, arguing till deep in the night, and at the height of the argument furiously seizing and breaking plates of fine porcelain. It is inexplicable that Bismarck, whom at the bottom of his heart Wilhelm disliked, was not carried off to jail. On the contrary, he won his point.

The terms of the peace treaty, which was signed in Prague, were amazingly lenient. Franz Joseph lived up to his promise and ceded Venetia, which was combined with Victor Emmanuel's Italy. Schleswig-Holstein was to become Prussian, except for North Schleswig, where a plebiscite was to settle the matter. Austria had to pay war damages of 40 million talers ($50 million) and to abjure its influence with its South German allies. Prussia incorporated the principalities of Hanover, Hesse-Cassel, Nassau, and the city of Frankfurt into its domain, all of which represented a modest demand by a victor, as such demands go.

The day after the peace was signed, Bismarck thought of turning yesterday's foe into tomorrow's friend. Austria, he planned, would become an ally in the shaping of a new Germany and a new Europe. He was going to live with the neighbor. He knew when to cock a gun and when to lay it aside. And how well he knew his Germans! "If we do not make excessive demands," he wrote to his wife, "if we do not believe that we must conquer the world, we will achieve a worthwhile peace. But we become intoxicated as quickly as we become despairing. And I have the thankless task of diluting the fizzing wine with water; I have to make them understand that we don't exist by ourselves in Europe, but with three nations who hate and envy us."

5

Political fate dealt Franz Joseph a further blow. Troubles came not single spies, though the death of Ferdinand Maximilian in Mexico represented to him more of an offense against the structure of sovereignty than a sorrow over the loss of a brother.[28]

What business had a gentle, soft-spoken, dreamy Austrian aristocrat to accept an emperor's task in a country torn by strife, a country thousands of miles distant and totally unknown to him, whose language he did not speak, and the mentality of whose people he did not fathom? The transplantation was as absurd as growing a lilac bush and a cactus in the same pot of earth. His going there was an egregious example of the daily occurrence that the human mind can make itself believe anything it wants to believe. An hour's realistic reflection could have told him that Mexico's throne was made of mud and would crumble at the first storm.

France's financial investment in Mexico was large: its commercial interests demanded protection. Napoleon III feared not so much the republic which was then Mexico's legitimate government, unsteady and divided though it was, as he feared the possibility of action by the United States—the Monroe Doctrine stipulating "no interference of European powers on the American continent"—or worse, the reconquest of the country by Spain through troops stationed in Cuba. A monarchy was the answer, provided the Mexican people assented; it would satisfy Mexican capitalists, ally the country to France's industry, but keep Washington quiet. French soldiers were swarming over Mexico—a country five times as large as France—and their stay had to be safeguarded. Conservative Mexican statesmen, such as Hidalgo and Gutiérrez, supported the monarchic plan. Juárez, they thought, was now rendered impotent, fled to the hills with a few guerrillas. A group of wealthy émigrés called on Maximilian and Carlotta in their sea-girt palace, Miramar, and offered them the crown. Carlotta's ambition, her longing to wear a diadem similar to that of her sister-in-law Elisabeth, is usually blamed for their willingness to set sail from Miramar to the unknown. It is probable that Maximilian was as eager as she: he needed and wanted a purpose in life. That purpose was presented to him as idealistic and noble, a ruler ministering to a confused people. He believed the story, being himself an idealist.

Some of Maximilian's early letters from Mexico reveal a curious fantasy, as he tried to compare Mexico to his accustomed surroundings. It was a dream of home, dreamed by a European:

> The country is really very beautiful; the surroundings of the capital city have the aspect of unforgettable Lombardy [nothing could be

less like!], marvelous meadows, beautiful trees and plenty of water. We live alternately in the enormous Palais Nacional in the city and in Chapultepec, the Schönbrunn of Mexico. It is a charming summer palace built on basalt rock and surrounded by the giant trees of Montezuma. It affords a view which could only be compared to Sorrento. . . .[29]

Or again:

Carlotta gives a ball every Monday; a flora of the most beautiful women enhances it and one diplomat after another comes to call. Our kitchen is one of the best in the world [his cook was Viennese], as is the court cellar. The diplomats gorge themselves and drink so much that after dinner they manage to emit only inarticulate sounds.[30]

He honestly tried to understand Mexico, traveling up and down the primitive roads and speaking Spanish with a German accent. But how grossly he missaw it!

I live here in a free country in which principles predominate which at home you wouldn't even dare to dream at night. . . . Even if Mexico in some respects is backward, in social questions we are far ahead of Europe and of Austria especially. A spirit of democracy prevails here with such force and conviction as you [in Austria] may perhaps obtain after fifty years of concentrated struggle.[31]

Only gradually did he realize how he had been duped, how the plebiscite which had indicated Mexico's desire for a ruling prince had been falsified, how bare was the cupboard of the Mexican treasury, how it was all a delusion.

Before Maximilian left for Mexico, Franz Joseph had warned him. He told Maximilian that "under no circumstances could Austria embroil herself in Mexican affairs." Such a statement was politically justified, Austria hardly being able to spare a soldier, in view of the situation in Prussia. Yet the "hands-off" policy may have been motivated as much by the man as by the ruler. Franz Joseph had not forgotten the cries of "Maximilian" when he returned from Italy. He was aware that Sophie loved her younger son with undemanding and smiling love, that she would refuse nothing to her "absurd Max," who was more of a Wittelsbach than a Habsburg. Elisabeth, too, understood him and sympathized with his artistic bent. Maximilian and Elisabeth got on too well for Franz Joseph's liking. Jealous, then, of his lighter-hearted and more intellectual brother, Franz Joseph was not exactly displeased to have Maximilian out of the way, though of course he could not foresee the tragic outcome and though the jealousy never rose to the surface. He had forced Maximilian to renounce his right of succession should Franz Joseph die prior to his son's majority (no Emperor of Mexico could ascend the throne of Austria as second-best), having journeyed personally to Triest for this purpose. It led to an open quarrel between the brothers, who as children had been such good friends. After Maximilian signed, he wrote a secret letter which stated that he had agreed to the renunciation under duress; he deposited the letter with the *Mexican* Embassy in Vienna, of all strange places, perhaps because he trusted no Austrian bureau. Maximilian's lot was now definitely linked to Mexico. When he left, he carried with him another letter: Napoleon III had written it in his own hand. It assured Maximilian that he could "count on my friendship and full support."

In fewer than three years the Mexican Fata Morgana dissolved. Napoleon III needed his troops at home—and left Maximilian without support. Maximilian tried his unselfish best, but unselfishness was the wrong diet. He offended the clerics by being a liberal, and he offended the republicans by being a Habsburg. Juárez was gathering new forces. Carlotta hurried to Europe; she implored Napoleon to fulfill his promise. At first he would not even see her. When he did see her, the tears streaming down her face, he shrugged his shoulders. Carlotta, half-frantic, sped on to Rome. Would the Pope help? He could not, he replied. "Holy Father," she said, "I will not budge from your doorstep until you grant me help." "Then you must stay," rejoined the Pope, and ordered two beds to be put in the Vatican library, one for her and one for her lady-in-waiting. Morning came. Attendants called on her—and discovered that she had gone mad. She thrashed about, was put into a strait jacket, and led away. She lived out her life—sixty more years of it (she died in 1927 at the age of eighty-seven) —interned and insane.[32] She imagined herself Empress still and demanded a fresh pair of gloves every day.

Maximilian was executed "for treason" on June 19, 1867. He asked to be shot through the heart, so that no one might see a Habsburg writhe in pain. The guards shot badly—into his face.

Franz Joseph got the news on the thirtieth, not quite two weeks after he had been crowned King of Hungary.[33] His grief was decorous, but not much more, even after he had read Maximilian's farewell letter to him; it was the letter of an unclear and unfortunate romantic who thanked him for his "brotherly love and friendship."

Franz Joseph sent a ship to Mexico under Tegetthoff's command to bring back his brother's corpse, and Maximilian was buried with all military splendor six months after his death. That they knew how to do in Austria, put on a splendid funeral, with laudatory speeches. Franz Werfel, writing *Juárez and Maximilian* in 1924, gave him a juster speech:

> Guilt is not to be great enough for one's deeds. Failure is guilt. My idea of a radical monarchy was unreal. Therefore the error, the lie must be in myself: guilt. The age of royalty is over. In the ship-wreck of the privileged classes poor little kings who are not kings must perish. The hour of the dictators has come. Juárez.

The years of Franz Joseph's young manhood—from his thirtieth to his thirty-seventh year—must be charted in a descending graph. He lost Italy, he lost his influence in Germany, he was forced to divide his realm into a dual monarchy, his brother was killed—and the woman he loved unclasped love's coherence. Yet his will to govern remained unabated. There was recompense in misfortune. He began to understand his country better, or at least a part of it, and to push it toward new health. According to his creed, he, as the head of Habsburg, was the only man who could command the task. He pursued that task with all energy. He was still "as strong as any man in Illyria."

The Vienna Art Museum, begun in 1872

CHAPTER VII

Linden Trees in Vienna

REHABILITATION BEGAN TIMIDLY. The administration tightened its belt. It practiced picayune economies, the kind of ridiculous little savings which are hastily ordered by big business in a year of small profits. Government bureaus had to issue decrees on *single* sheets to save paper, envelopes had to be turned and used twice, army coats were to be single- instead of double-breasted to save buttons, and so on. Franz Joseph said that "the imperial household must set an example," and reduced the food budget of the Hofburg, whereupon Elisabeth's private cook (female) declared that if she didn't get the wherewithal she needed with which to prepare decent meals, she would leave at once. Elisabeth took the cook's part, and the command was rescinded. (No cook has ever been afraid of a king.) Before the Hungarians presented the hunting preserve of Gödöllö to Franz Joseph and Elisabeth, he wrote to her:

> If you wish, go to Gödöllö and pay a visit to the wounded. But don't inspect it as if you were considering purchasing it. I have no money at present and in these hard times we have to be very saving. Even our family estates are terribly devastated by the Prussians and it will take years before they can recover. For next year I have reduced the court budget to five million, which necessitates a cut of two million. Almost half the stable must be sold. We must live modestly.
>
> Your sad little fellow[1]

Elisabeth did not pay much attention to such strictures, knowing full well how wealthy her husband was. She spent two-thirds of the year following the *Ausgleich* in her beloved Hungary, much of it in Gödöllö. There Franz Joseph visited her whenever his duties, become more complicated through defeat, would allow him. His losses, his sadness, his disappointments, had brought the milder and more conciliatory side of his nature to the surface. The character of so positive a man could not change fundamentally. The phases of his traits, though, moved tidally. When outward circumstances flowed at neap tide, his better self stood at spring tide. The autocratic part of him submerged, letting the more tractable, the patient part, come to the fore. He was fortunate at this time to be surrounded by able and patient men: Beust was patient, Andrassy was sensible, and Déak was generous. When Franz Joseph asked Deak what conditions Hungary demanded to smoke the pipe of peace, Deak replied, "Nothing more *after* Sadowa than before."

Elisabeth, too, softened and gave the marriage a second chance. They lived together again, and on April 22, 1868, a fourth child was born, a daughter, a "fat little thing with such thick dark hair one could comb it" (as Franz Joseph told Rudolf), and was christened Marie Valerie. This child, Elisabeth determined, was going to belong to her and to her alone. She had "lost" Gisela, who loved her grandmother. Rudolf had been entrusted to the care of a military tutor whose idea of hardening a child and "turning him into a hero" was to pretend that there was a wild boar lurking behind the wall ready to attack him. Now Rudolf was nine years old and was a nervous, high-strung boy. He suffered nightmares and often wet his bed. Elisabeth managed to have the tutor changed, his new one being Joseph Latour, a man of liberal leanings. Perhaps the change came too late.

Valerie was not going to be taken away by Sophie or anybody else. Elisabeth fussed over her like a Jewish mother. She became hysterical when the slightest upset bothered the baby. She quarreled with the wet nurse because the child had a stomachache for two days. "I was terribly frightened, I shuddered . . . I don't have one peaceful moment," she wrote to Ida Ferenczy (Elisabeth was home in Possenhofen), and she telegraphed for a new nurse. The old one told the Empress of Austria what she thought of her.

"Not even God could have got along with her," was Elisabeth's response.

She was helpful to her husband in a new effort to form an alliance with Napoleon III. Franz Joseph must have swallowed hard before he came to this decision. He disliked the "fat intriguer" as much as ever, but he knew that Austria stood at present isolated from Berlin and was viewed with supercilious suspicion by St. Petersburg. So he stretched out his hand to the man who had opposed him in Italy and was at least partly responsible for his brother's death. Politics make strange hand-shakers. Elisabeth represented Franz Joseph at the first meeting, which took place in Salzburg. There Eugénie and Elisabeth, Europe's two most beautiful women, came face to face, one fair and tall, the other shorter and dark but equally eye-filling, with "the eyes of a *pietà* and the mouth of a coquette"; they looked each other over, were tactful with each other, exchanged careful comments about people they knew, each telling the other "secrets" which the other knew to be no secrets, and then went their ways, neither breaking out of her golden cocoon. Later, in October, 1867, Franz Joseph journeyed alone to Paris and conferred with Napoleon. He derived more satisfaction from the Paris Exhibition, then at its height, than from the conferences. He found the Exhibition "overwhelmingly beautiful," and was dazzled by the lights of Paris which flared from thousands of gas jets strung along the iron railings of balconies. Why could he not create similar splendor in his Vienna? He inspected a machine called a dynamo, shown by the new German firm of Siemens and Halske, and he was much impressed—as was everybody—with a fifty-ton steel cannon which Krupp had manufactured for the King of Prussia. He peered through a powerful new microscope which had aided a French chemist, Louis Pasteur, to prove that fermentation depended on the action of living organisms and to solve the mystery of the silkworm disease, thereby substantially helping southern France's economy.

There is no evidence that Franz Joseph was especially impressed by Austria's most important export commodity, produced by a man more persuasive than any diplomat. Johann Strauss, Jr., was the hero of the Paris Exhibition. He had been introduced by Pauline Metternich, Metternich's daughter-in-law, friend of

Eugénie, and the most extravagant, snobbish, and capricious of Parisian hostesses. Pauline presented Strauss to the Parisian *haut monde* at a soiree arranged by her at the Austrian Embassy. For this occasion she had browbeat the Austrian treasury into giving her 165,000 francs—in spite of all exhortations to economize—and she had talked the mayor of Paris into getting a special pipe laid which was to carry water into the embassy. Thousands of roses were banked on top of the staircase, and through that bank flowed an artificial cascade. At the right moment Napoleon and Eugénie made their entrance to the tune of a Strauss march. Pauline had even persuaded Baron Rothschild to lend her his personal cook, a man who had never before practiced his magic outside Rothschild's palace.

At the Exhibition auditorium Strauss conducted his waltzes for dancing dandies and crinolined ladies. Asked for something new, something special, Strauss brought forward a waltz which he had performed a few months before in Vienna. Then it had been sung by a male chorus to stupefying words, a crass political poem which promised better times to come; and the Viennese audience, weary and ashamed of its country's fate, had received it with indifference. Now, in Paris, Strauss played "On the Beautiful Blue Danube" without any words. It became the theme song of the Exhibition and, in a sense, Austria's national anthem. Everybody was enraptured by the "Fleuve d'azur." Edward, Prince of Wales, was so impressed that he hummed the tune to his mother, and Strauss was asked to come to London. Queen Victoria found him "very agreeable." Franz Joseph paid no attention to him. Was the reason indeed Strauss Jr.'s political persuasion? Did Franz Joseph remember that during the 1848 outbreak the younger Strauss sided with the revolutionaries—opposing his conservative father, who had composed the "Radetzky March" and a march to honor Jellačić—while the son had been guilty of performing something called the "Revolution March"? There is extant a record of the police interrogation of the younger Strauss on December 6, 1848; why, the police wanted to know, did he play the "Marseillaise"? Strauss Jr. evidently had courage; he replied that he played the piece because it was good music and good music was what concerned him. Franz Joseph may have recalled the incident. Or he may have been indifferent to *any* music, even the "Blue Danube Waltz."

2

He turned his attention to the home front. He gave fresh thought to the problems existing within the borders: it was a task of drawing lines which would lead from remote cities to the focal point of Vienna.

The reforms included: (1) assigning to Parliament a more active role in the shaping of laws; (2) trial by jury for alleged violations against censorship; (3) abolition of corporal punishment, for both the military and civil population: no more whipping or beating; (4) ending certain restrictions leveled on the Jews; (5) providing compulsory elementary education free to all children of all nationalities; and (6) modernizing the army. This last measure was particularly dear to Franz Joseph. Officers were required to study tactics anew, equipment was improved, discipline was sharpened. Universal military service was introduced in 1868.

Perhaps the most significant reform lay in Austria's wriggling itself loose from the embrace of the Vatican. The monarchy was and remained a Catholic country—religious instruction remained compulsory—but the clasp became less tight; the Concordat was unhinged and later, in 1870, altogether canceled. The privileges of the clergy were shaved away. Old Cardinal Rauscher, Franz Joseph's teacher, fought the reforms tooth and nail and was supported by many of the entrenched aristocrats. Opposing him, Count Anton Auersperg spoke eloquently to Parliament of "ecclesiastical slavery" and conjured up memories of Joseph II and his reforms. In September, 1867, the teachers of the Viennese schools met and passed a resolution asking that the schools be released from bondage to the Church. The Viennese demonstrated as they were wont to do, marching to the Hofburg and demanding "freedom from Rome." A new marriage law was proposed by which civil marriage was legalized and marital trials could be brought before a secular court. (Divorce, however, was not legalized except in special cases.) In a dramatic meeting the upper house passed the marriage law—and the Catholic prelates promptly marched out of the meeting. On the day the law was passed all Vienna was illuminated. Beust had supported the law. An enthusiastic Viennese accosted him on the street, knelt, clasped his knees, and cried, "You have liberated us from the fetters of the Concordat." "Thank you," Beust replied, "and will you now in turn liberate my legs."

How Sophie must have grieved at seeing Austria put this distance between itself and the Vatican! Franz Joseph used the declaration of the Vatican Consilium that "the Pope was infallible speaking *ex cathedra*" as the reason for his decision. Pope Pius IX called the reforms "destructive, abominable, and damnable." It did not comfort his mother when Franz Joseph told her that he hoped in the future to make another alliance with the Church, but "with the present Pope that is impossible." She did not understand, or did not want to understand, that the liberal elements within the monarchy were pressing for separation of church and state, and that he was sensible enough to perceive justice in their demand.

Not all the reforms worked as well in practice as they looked on paper. Distrust of Vienna and intimidation by priests did not stop: the black-robed men still threatened the fires of hell effectively, and they were listened to not by peasants alone. The rising consciousness of nationalism threw obstacles on the road of the empire's recovery: the Czechs wanted rights equivalent to the Hungarians', the Poles in Galicia were not sure where their loyalties lay, the Italian deputies from Triest and southern Tyrol refused to attend meetings of the Parliament—and so on in disputations which Franz Joseph had to arbitrate, now by threats, now by compromises.

Nevertheless the realm made remarkable progress in seven fat years following the Prussian defeat, Hungary particularly developing its agrarian economy. In June, 1869, John Jay, American minister in Vienna, wrote to Hamilton Fish: "From the defeat of Sadowa Austria has arisen to the astonishment of Europe and of itself, with modern ideas, free principles, and a new life."

In these years Franz Joseph's plan for the enlargement and beautification of Vienna began to be translated from edict to actuality, from pen to spade. He had thought of the plan for a long time. He knew that in the minds of his people, as vividly as in his own mind, Vienna was more than a capital city: it was a one-word symbol for a way of life, a concept which one either loved or hated—and often both loved and hated. The city had once served as a bulwark against the Eastern foe, then as an arbor in which a Haydn, a Mozart, a Beethoven, a Grillparzer, walked and thought, and was now a local habitation into which flowed the questions of multilingual nationalities and from which emanated the answers. Whatever it was, Vienna was not, not as yet, a true metropolis. It could show the visitor isolated marvels, the eighteenth-century Belvedere or the magisterial Stephanskirche, which like a dowager traced its lineage back to the thirteenth century, or the superb Court Library which Fischer von Erlach had designed—but to get to these masterpieces the visitor had to walk through ugly streets, some of them as narrow and dirty as a Croatian village and smelling a lot worse. The inner city was still surrounded by a wall which had outlived its usefulness as fortification and restricted the breathing of the city. Parliament met in a ramshackle wooden building, and the old university erected in Maria Theresa's reign had not functioned as a building since the revolution of 1848. Outside the wall the suburbs felt isolated, like guests not seated at the main table. Franz Joseph had seen Paris. Was there any comparison between Vienna and Paris?

On Christmas Day, 1857—Franz Joseph had been Emperor for only nine years—there appeared on page one of the *Wiener Zeitung* a detailed edict. It began:

> It is My Will that the enlargement of the inner city of Vienna be undertaken as soon as possible, with the object of connecting it with the suburbs and of regulating and beautifying My Residential City, the capital of the realm. To that end I grant the destruction of the circumvallation and fortifications of the inner city, as well as of the adjacent moats. . . .

The idea of modernizing *Alt Wien* did not, of course, meet with universal approval. No new project lacks its chorus of head-shakers. The *Besserwisser* (in the expressive German phrase), "people who know better," were sure that Vienna's intimate attractiveness would evaporate in open spaces. Grillparzer, morose and always at odds with the authorities, wrote a quatrain asking what use it was to pull down the wall when the whole country was hemmed in by a Chinese wall. The debate lasted for years, but in the meantime the work progressed. The razing of the bastions began at the end of 1858, and the clearing was completed, or almost so, in six years. Architects were asked to submit ideas in an open competition—eighty-five such plans were considered—to suggest how the areas freed by the destruction of the wall and the filling in of the ditches were to be used. The central feature of the plan adopted was a majestic curved avenue, the Ringstrasse, which was not a ring but a street in the form of a horseshoe, its open end facing the Danube Canal, its apex facing the Imperial Burg. The Ringstrasse is as daringly conceived and as successfully executed a boulevard as the pride of building has produced, surpassed not even by the Champs Élysées.[2] Because it is curved it offers the pleasure of the unexpected: traveling along its expanse is like being in a theater, with yourself moving and the scenery stationary, new vistas constantly disclosed. What gives the Ringstrasse more than pride and pomp, what gives it charm, what allows you to love it, is its lavish green. The linden trees, copious with leaf and flower, have invaded the street itself. They are an integral part of it, as if they were out for a city stroll, a timeless stroll of which they never weary. To the left and the right of them stand the important edifices; these are set in green plantations of their own or are neighbored by parks, the largest of them being the City Park (Stadtpark) , which was begun in 1861 and where today stand the monuments to both Schubert and Johann Strauss, Jr. The public buildings were created in an orgy of building which lasted more than twenty years. (At that, the whole plan was never executed.) The money to construct them was raised by selling desirable sites along the Ringstrasse to the new industrialists. The contracts stipulated that their palaces had to be completed within four years and had to dovetail with the general design. In return, certain taxes were forgiven them for as long as thirty years. Building did not stop even when business turned bad and the stock market crash of May 9, 1873, the so-called Black Friday, caused a general panic. Franz Joseph continued to raise building funds as a public works program.

The Emperor himself approved the architects and, in his office in the Hofburg, pored over blueprints. He wasn't at all sure of what he was going to get, but he was all enthusiasm as long as the buildings reflected the "greatness of the Empire." As a special contribution to Vienna's growth he caused a model aqueduct to be built which brought clear, ice-cold water from the high Alps to the city. As a result, Vienna has—or had until recently—the best water of the major European cities.

These were the buildings completed to reflect the greatness of the Imperial City:

BUILDING	CONSTRUC-TION BEGUN	COMPLETED	ARCHITECT
Opera	1861	1869	Siccard von Siccardsburg and Eduard van der Null
Two "Court Museums"			
Art Museum			Gottfried Semper and
Museum of Natural History	1872	1881	Karl Hasenauer
City Hall	1872	1882	Friedrich Schmidt
University	1873	1883	Heinrich Ferstel
Parliament	1873	1883	Theophil Hansen
Stock Exchange	1874	1877	Semper and Hasenauer
Burgtheater	1874	1888	Semper and Hasenauer

(In addition, the Votivkirche should be mentioned, though it is some distance removed from the Ringstrasse and was begun in 1856 [completed 1879], before the general plan was developed. The architect was Heinrich Ferstel. The Votivkirche was built as a memorial, celebrating Franz Joseph's escape from the assassination attempt of Libényi.)

The Opera was opened on May 25, 1869, with a performance of *Don Giovanni*. As usual on gala occasions, ceremony received more attention than music. To be there those who paid anything at all paid 25 gulden (about $50) for a seat. Charlotte Wolter, one of the celebrated actresses of the Burgtheater, stepped on the stage dressed as "Vindobona," the spirit of Vienna, and declaimed a Prologue which at the last moment had been badly mangled by the censor to snip from it all political references. It was followed by a procession down a grand staircase in which members of the Court Opera represented the various races and peoples of the monarchy. They formed a circle of unity—very symbolic and very untrue. Franz Joseph, accompanied by members of his family and with the King of Hanover as his guest, bowed from the great Imperial loge. But Elisabeth was absent, still in Gödöllö, though the opening had been postponed a week in the expectation that she would appear; she could not face the tumult.[3] As soon as he could after the lights went down, Franz Joseph snuck out: a whole evening of Mozart was more than he could take.

Even before the premiere it appeared as if the Opera, the first of the monumental buildings, would prove a disastrous mistake. It stood below the level of the Ringstrasse, squat and heavy, and was immediately dubbed "the sunken trunk" and "an architectural Königgrätz." Two winged horses surmounted the building. A typical Viennese *Besserwisser* came forth with the observation that mythology knew only one Pegasus and two Pegasuses were nonsense. To which somebody in some coffeehouse rejoined that in Vienna any respectable person took a fiacre (with two horses), and why should art travel like a poor man? Yet the two horses proved too plump and small. They were removed, sold to America,[4] and replaced by taller and slimmer models. Still, the façade of the house, with its indeterminate Franco-Venetian-Gothic style, came in for plenty of abuse. Worst of all, it was discovered that many seats in the third gallery and some in the fourth afforded but a quarter-view of the stage.

The criticism overwhelmed the chief architect of the building, van der Nüll. In despair he hanged himself. His co-worker, Siccardsburg, was suffering from heart trouble; grief over the death of his friend aggravated his condition—two months later he too was dead. Neither had heard a performance in the building they created, but both must frequently have heard the lampoon which was going the rounds (in Viennese dialect) :

> *Der Siccardsburg und van der Nüll*
> *Die haben beide keinen Styl!*
> *Griechisch, Gotisch, Renaissance,*
> *Das ist denen alles ans!*

> (Siccardsburg and van der Nüll,
> Both of them have no style!
> Greek, Gothic, Renaissance,
> It's all the same to them!)

But as the years went by, the sunken trunk proved to be a superb container for music. Its defects became less, its festive virtues more, apparent. The alchemy of time was at work. Past performances coated the auditorium with a soft patina; the marble was warmed by sound. The Vienna Opera was like a dumpy girl who, as she becomes older, grows glamorous, thanks to charm and experience.[5]

The most successful of the buildings are the two Court Museums, each standing like a Renaissance cassone within reach of the statue of Austria's great queen, Maria Theresa, as if each contained her trousseau. These museums, as well as the theater for spoken plays, the Burgtheater (which was completed later), are the work of two architects, Semper and Hasenauer, who did know the difference between "Greek, Gothic, Renaissance." In the Burgtheater they gave the audience a chance to stroll during the intervals and to nibble a bite (all-important in Vienna): the theater's finest feature is its promenade, with its polished parquet floor, its walls hung with paintings of famous actors, and its wide view of the Ringstrasse. The ornate marble staircase which the audience ascends helps to stimulate the expectant mood, the acoustics are good, and altogether the theater can compare itself with such prize creations as the Fenice in Venice or La Scala in Milan. Yet the new Burgtheater came in for its share of criticism. Because iron was largely used, and wood as little as possible, the actors said that their voices sounded too loud and that tender passages lost their effect. They complained that the new, elaborate ventilation system created drafts. According to Helene Bettelheim Gabillon, an actress, the actor Ernst Hartmann ostentatiously walked through the auditorium, and raising a wet finger to determine the direction and strength of the current of air blowing through the house, commented: "Perfect breeze for sailing."

Hugo Thimig (father of the Thimig dynasty of actors which included Helene, Hans, and Hermann) collected the signatures of his colleagues in a petition to Franz Joseph, asking that the theater be "rebuilt." Franz Joseph summoned him to an audience at half-past seven in the morning:

> He gave me a big cigar wrapped in silver paper. When I said that it would be too heavy a smoke for me he replied, "If it doesn't

kill *me* you can risk it." He continued: "Well—you have something
to say to me?" I began, "First, Your Majesty, my deepest thanks to
permit me to be the simple spokesman for the lamentations of your
actors. Permit me to tell Your Majesty that, though I speak without
an official mandate, I voice the opinion of all members of the Burgtheater, many of whom would not dare to speak up frankly. The
new theater is beautiful and magnificent—" "Yes, yes," interrupted
the Emperor, "beautiful and magnificent—that's only the param-
pulium (he meant praeambulum), get to the point." "It cannot be
used for the presentation of the tradition of the old Burgtheater, it
is too large, too high. . . ."

Franz Joseph then listened patiently to Thimig's detailed
specifications of the defects. Thimig departed satisfied—and nothing was done about the theater. The actors got used to it.[6]

The "new" City Hall seems a Gothic imitation of or importa-
tion from the Brussels Square, and the university is a bland block
in the Renaissance style, without even an irritating feature. Worse
is the Parliament, which takes itself very seriously and is a confec-
tioner's attempt to re-create in nineteenth-century Vienna a building which might have stood in ancient Athens. It was hardly
improved when a vulgar statue of Pallas Athena was later placed
in front of it. The Viennese explained that the goddess of wisdom
had to be placed outside the house since no wisdom could be
found inside it.

Take any one of the buildings of the Ringstrasse and not one is
an original piece of work. It is all neo—neo-antique, neo-Renais-
sance, neo-Gothic, rubbed with the salve of nineteenth-century
romanticism. Yet take all the buildings together, take the Ringstrasse as a whole, add to it such memorial details as the remains of
the last bastion opposite the university, where, high up, stands the
Pasqualati House, in which Beethoven lived, and you receive the
impression of harmony, stateliness, and largess. You draw a deep
breath. The parts are faulty, the sum of the parts adds up to one of
the world's most beautiful cities. I have suggested that one reason
is the adroit use of green, the four rows of linden trees, the grassy
plots, and the continuous alternation between stone and gardens.
Perhaps there is more to it. Whether they knew it or not, the town
planners employed space in daring articulation. The Ringstrasse is

a triumph of variegated space, plentiful enough to set off each
building and not so overwhelming as to fatigue the eye. Space
itself, interrupted and modulated, creates pleasure. Perhaps it was
all a lucky accident, but there it is, the Viennese paradox: they
mixed up styles imported from Athens, Brussels, Florence, France
—and it all came out whole and right.

It all came out right for Franz Joseph. During the "building
years" he began to regain much of the hold which the loss of Italy
and the Prussian defeat had cut away. The nimbus of imperial
majesty, badly smoked over, began to gleam again. The Prussian
military attaché, Lothar von Schweinitz, a careful and unprejudiced observer, wrote in his memoirs:

> I was able to observe how the Emperor, who had been unpopular
> in the highest degree when I first came to Vienna, began to gain
> the good will and later the love of the people of the capital city.
> Dynastic feeling, inborn in the Viennese, was revived and has now
> [in the 1870s] spread markedly.

Franz Joseph built for representational reasons. He even built
a new wing onto the old Burg to underscore Habsburg perma-
nency. He did not foresee the true result: several of the buildings,
specifically the Opera, the Burgtheater, the Art Museum, the
university, and one called the House of Artists (Künstlerhaus),
became havens for new minds. They offered a place and a back-
ground for an intellectual development and artistic unfolding
with which the Emperor had no connection and of which he had
no understanding. It happened almost in spite of him. He had
wanted to clothe Vienna in parade uniform. The uniform was
used as working garb.

3

The building project offered an anodyne to the wounds which the
Prussian needle guns had inflicted. Revenge? There was now
hardly time for such a word. The interior reforms occupied Franz
Joseph's attention as well as that of his topmost councillors, Beust,
Andrassy, and a new minister—though an old comrade in ideas to

Franz Joseph—Count Eduard Taaffe. Prompted by wisdom and by weakness—and it was part of his wisdom to acknowledge weakness—Franz Joseph stayed within his frontiers and aspired to no major role in the conflicts being fought outside. His theater now was his own land, a dual monarchy, a scene large enough. He remained neutral. Yet nothing had been forgotten—nothing ever is—and as Franz Joseph, proud and cool, took his seat at the head of the conference table, he knew that as he was nobody's friend and could not afford to be, so he could find no friend among the other sovereigns.

While neutrality was dictated by prudence, his personal feelings could not be so dictated. Whom did he dislike most? Choleric and self-important Victor Emmanuel, whose troops occupied Rome on September 20, 1870, added the Holy City to united Italy, and thus ended the secular power of the Pope? Sophie still begged Franz Joseph to help the Pope. Franz Joseph silenced his mother by declaring he could do nothing "in Europe's present condition," while Pius IX fulminated that Austria was now in the power of a Protestant, Beust. Or was it Czar Alexander II whom Franz Joseph viewed with greatest distrust, since Franz Joseph himself was guilty of having broken his word to the Czar's predecessor? Napoleon III? After his visit to Paris, Franz Joseph had not learned to like Napoleon better or to palliate his dislike of Bismarck, in spite of Bismarck's propitiating gestures. Where were his sympathies to nestle in the grim clash which was now dividing Napoleon and Bismarck?

Bismarck needed the Franco-Prussian War to allow him to continue and to crown the work he had begun, that is, the unification of Germany. Only a war, he reasoned, could truly make the Germans stick together, and specifically only a war could draw Bavaria into the orbit. In a sense the Franco-Prussian War was a continuation of the Prusso-Austrian war. (Or are all wars of aggression continuous, even when they change enemies?) Its purpose—or at least a part of its purpose, another part being to show who was the stronger—was to wipe out internal scruples by dangling before the doubters a goal of common cause, however illusory the goal might be and however unpardonable. Bismarck took arms against Napoleon on the slightest of provocations (though it was Napoleon who issued the formal declaration). Would Bismarck have done so could he have foreseen that this war would kindle a hatred which was to burn for almost a century and remnants of which are still glimmering? Probably. Franz Joseph's sympathies were not with his kinsfolk, the Germans, not with the people whose language he spoke, not with the country from which his wife had come, but with France, whose government, he knew, had become cankered and debilitated. It didn't matter that he loved Napoleon less, because he loathed Bismarck more. Over and over again in his private letters he expressed his sympathy with France. How dearly he would have liked to help dig a hole into which Bismarck would tumble! Elisabeth tried to comfort him: "Well, perhaps we shall have to vegetate a few years more until it is our turn—what do you think?"[7] He dared not interfere, all the more so as he had been given plainly to understand by the Russians that "if Austria violates its neutrality, we shall do the same." After the first defeats of the French, an envoy of Napoleon, de Vaugelas, came to beg Franz Joseph for help:

> Franz Joseph paced up and down his workroom, his mien dark and troubled. I tried to explain to him in a few words the urgency for help, which we had expected he would grant us. He interrupted me and exclaimed, "Why has everything been decided overhastily? You knew very well that I would need six weeks to mobilize. . . . It is impossible for me to strike, what with the Italian menace in the south, the certain danger in the north, and a protracted mobilization effort which could leave me defenseless." The Emperor was terribly emotional. And suddenly I saw heavy tears coursing down his cheeks.[8]

As blow followed blow, as the French army capitulated at Sedan and Napoleon was taken prisoner and forced to hand over his sword, as Eugénie fled to England, and Paris was bombarded, and as, finally, on September 5, 1870, the French Republic was proclaimed, Franz Joseph grieved. Richard Metternich in Paris echoed Austrian feelings when he wrote, "Quel cauchemar! et quel avenir avec cette omnipotence de Bismarck!"

Early in 1871, in the Hall of Mirrors in Versailles, Wilhelm was proclaimed the first Emperor of Germany. Franz Joseph wrote of his "haughtiness, his vanity, and his sanctimoniousness,"[9]

though he confided this opinion only to his mother. It took Bismarck but a little over two months to give the new Germany its
Constitution. Now Austria had no choice but to live in concord
with Germany. Emperor Wilhelm I, hiding his true feelings, went
to pay a state visit to Franz Joseph in Ischl. Franz Joseph, hiding
his true feelings, congratulated him on his victory and suggested
that the three emperors in whose hands the fate of Europe lay—
Germany, Russia, and Austria—should meet to form an entente.
The meeting of the three emperors duly took place in September,
1872, in Berlin. (At this meeting Franz Joseph appeared in a
Prussian uniform—"It seems to me as if I were going to the battlefield against myself," he said—and the Czar donned a Hungarian
uniform: the usual symbolic masquerade.) After war came the
conference, after cannons conversation. All three protested fealty
to one another, meaning for the moment what they asserted,
without wiping from their memories the hurt of past defeats or
obliterating from their minds the dreams of future conquest.

One victim of Franz Joseph's new Germanophile policy was
Beust. He was demoted and assigned to a sinecure in London. The
Viennese grumbled, but it did them no good. Similarly, Richard
Metternich, known foe of Bismarck and friend of France, was recalled from his post at the Paris Embassy. Andrassy became Beust's
successor, to Bismarck's satisfaction. Andrassy admired Bismarck.
The Viennese mumbled that now Austria was going to be Magyar-
ized, but again it didn't do them any good. In short, after all the
bitterness, the hatred, and the dead of Sadowa, Austria's future
now lay not in conflict with Germany but in collaboration.

The conclusion was as immoral as the war itself had been. In
the Franco-Prussian War, a civilized nation had sunk to a new low
in an era which was supposed to be animated by humanity and
reason. Future carnage was presaged by the efficiency of Bismarck's
war machine. He had even perfected a new spy system by which
Prussian officers, disguised as harmless tourists with palette and
easel, made exact note of battle sites while pretending to sketch
the French landscape. This was no longer a conflict of soldier
against soldier. The civil population of Paris was systematically
starved, French villages were burned, partisans were shot. While
such bestiality was rampant, the first ships were taking advantage

of one of modern man's great engineering feats, the Suez Canal, Schliemann was beginning to excavate Troy, and Charles Darwin was reading the proofs of *The Descent of Man.*

As frequently happens in countries which have been spared from serving as battlefields, a boom developed in Austro-Hungary. After peace between Prussia and France had been signed, the neutral country benefited. Exports rose, grain from Hungary nourished the Parisians, coal was shipped to Berlin. New industries sprang up, manufacturers proliferated, shares on the Vienna Bourse rose day by day, almost all the Viennese—except those of the lowest laboring class—felt good and prosperous.

To demonstrate the progress that Austria had made in the last years, Franz Joseph determined to open a World Exposition in Vienna. It was to be a show of brave proportions, for which a huge round building, the Rotunde, had been constructed in the Prater. It was opened on May 1, 1873, by Franz Joseph and Elisabeth. Hotels, cafés, restaurants, and places of amusement had been built far in excess of the requirements of normal times. New railroad cars had been bought. Seven million tourists descended on Vienna. No fewer than seven hundred American firms and civic organizations exhibited. Among the American novelties shown were an Indian wigwam and a bar which served American drinks. As Arthur Jay May wrote, "Not since the historic Peace Congress of 1815 had the Hapsburg capital acted as host to so many crowned heads and other celebrities." Among the crowned heads whom Franz Joseph and Elisabeth entertained were the Czar and the Czarina. Elisabeth, forced for a time to do the honors in Vienna, did them with good grace, though she couldn't quite hide her boredom; at least she could wear a succession of glorious gowns. After the Russians, Victor Emmanuel appeared, surrounded by so large a guard of plumed adjutants that he looked like the trainer of an aviary of tame birds. Elisabeth, though by this time used to the fog of political hypocrisy, could not face the erstwhile enemy of her sister and her sister's husband. She refused to show herself, pretending that she had an upset stomach. Perhaps she did. Victor Emmanuel did not believe it.

The Vienna World Exhibition was pursued by ill luck. An epidemic of cholera broke out. News of it was suppressed, but people learned about it all the same and, not being told the truth, exaggerated the danger and packed up in a panic. The fiacre drivers of Vienna went on strike. Nine days after the opening of the fair, the stock market crash came. There had been rumblings of insolvency, false expansion, and dishonest manipulations before, but little attention was paid to them in an aura of moneyed euphoria and a boom which few recognized as transient. Now disclosure followed disclosure; it appeared that even high military officials, even one or two ministers, even one of Franz Joseph's adjutants, had participated in the dubious dealings. Dozens of companies went bankrupt, shares of inflated enterprises—such as railroad shares—tumbled to midget values, business credits stopped. The little people, the investors from the coffeehouses, the maids and the grocers, the clerks and the widows, lost their savings. They stood around the Bourse or tried to force their way into it, some weeping, some shouting with rage. In dark houses men killed themselves.[10] Whose fault was all this? It was the fault of the Jews. Of course it was the fault of those "foreigners" who had come from Poland and Galicia to trade. The slump reawakened Vienna's latent anti-Semitism, sharpened by envy of the Rothschilds' sagacity: they had not only warned against reckless speculation but had refrained from it and therefore emerged from Black Friday relatively unscathed. Newspapers, supported by the more radical members of the Catholic clergy, went in for Jew baiting. It was from this root that the poisonous weed of the Christian Socialist party grew.

Black Friday was an early manifestation of the economic interdependence of one country on another. The depression spread worldwide, leaping from Vienna to other European centers and causing the withdrawal of foreign investments from the United States. In turn, this led to a financial panic in the United States, which had essentially the same causes as the Vienna panic: speculation and overproduction.

The Vienna Exhibition did not recover. When it was closed, it showed a deficit of 15 million gulden ($30 million). But Austria and the world did recover, and in a remarkably short time. The mines kept on producing, the locomotives kept on puffing, the inventions kept being translated from laboratory to marketplace, the building urge continued unabated, the birth rate increased and the children needed food and shoes and schools and toys, and the farmers drove their old wagons, heaped with wheat and pulled by dray horses, to the docks of modern steamships.

Steam was still the chief driving power. Now, around the latter half of the century, a new wonder worker entered the industrial scene, and while frightened old men said that it was presumptuous for man to steal lightning from the gods, a throng of young scientists examined the uses of electricity. Samuel Morse had invented the telegraph in 1833; it was followed by the wave theories of Heinrich Hertz, Thomas Edison's microphone and phonograph, Alexander Bell's telephone, a multiplicity of electric motors, and the first electric tramway. The world promised to become cleaner, its work easier, though a few thinkers predicted that it was going to be a more impersonal world in which many a man would become a digit in a statistical table.

In short, industrial expansion moved forward with too powerful a thrust to be stopped by the morass of a Black Friday. What aided the expansion, paradoxically enough—or perhaps not, so paradoxically—was a new demand by labor for more decent wages, working conditions less demeaning, and hours shorter than the eleven-hour day, six days a week, which was the norm. This demand had been voiced loudly by Karl Marx and moderately by Ferdinand Lassalle, both writing and proselytizing in Germany.

Their teachings took hold even in Austria, a country whose commerce was still predominantly carried on by small merchants in small shops or by artisans with one or two apprentices. Large factories and mills were still rare. But large or small, the men and women who worked in shops and factories, those "gay and carefree" Viennese, lived anything but *gemütlich* lives. There was nothing gay or carefree about their dwellings, rickety suburban rooms—often a whole family had to make do with one room, the kitchen in the corner—rooms with a rancid smell and a crucifix on the wall. A communal outhouse served as a toilet, and water still had to be fetched from a public pump.

Gradually the people in the poorer districts moved, so to speak, a little closer to the Ringstrasse. Gradually Austria showed progress, not through the sham show of a World's Fair, but through

social thought applied horizontally.[11] Gradually the economic
weather became more stable.

On December 2, 1873, Franz Joseph celebrated the twenty-fifth
anniversary of his ascension. He told the Viennese magistrate:
"Tell all the inhabitants and citizens of Vienna that the love of my
people represents my life's happiness." They were the usual banal
words a sovereign speaks on such occasions. Yet they turned out to
be not altogether empty words, though it still took some years
before one could speak of love between the Emperor and his small
subjects. With improved conditions came improved love.

In the next decade more smiles were to be seen under Vienna's
linden trees.

4

But in those same years Franz Joseph committed a deed which
introduced into the body politic a terminal cancer unseen, unfelt,
undiagnosed for many years: that deed was the occupation of
Bosnia and Herzegovina.

Permission for the occupation seemed merely a box of candy
given Franz Joseph for being a good boy and not interfering in the
fight between two bad boys, Russia and Turkey. In reality the
matter was far more subtle, and the negotiations, tricks, power
plays, and double-dealings which led to it were as complicated as
the ploys in a game of "Go." It would be wearisome to retrace the
details, but in brief this is what happened:

In 1876 the Sultan of Turkey, Abdul-Asis, was murdered, the
Turks having discovered that their country was totally bankrupt.
He was succeeded by Abdul-Hamid II, who promised reforms but
turned out to be no less of a despot than his predecessor. Russia—
that is, Czar Alexander II—had never got over her defeat in the
Crimean War, nor had she ever abandoned her ambition to obtain
power in the Balkans, drive the Turks eastward, and thereby
expand toward the Mediterranean. Russia now used the pretense
of furthering the "Pan-Slav movement" (the unification of all
Slavs into one state) to declare war against Turkey. Alexander II
announced that it was his "human duty"—conquest is always

"human duty" or "holy duty"—to clean up Turkey's chaotic conditions, an act "the world would judge fundamentally proper, human and necessary."[12]

Russia's superior might conquered the Turks in less than one year. In 1878, the Peace of San Stefano formed Rumania, Serbia, Montenegro, and Bulgaria into independent states, while Bessarabia and other territories were ceded outright to Russia and reforms were planned in Bosnia and Herzegovina. What it amounted to was the weakening of Turkish influence in Europe and the rise of Russian hegemony over the Slavs. Such increase in Russia's power was greeted with heavy frowns by the major European nations, by Great Britain especially, who hated Russia's move to the south and wanted no part of the Russian navy in southern waters. What would happen to the Suez Canal, the major portion of the shares of which Disraeli had bought? A very black crisis developed, Britain's fleet was ready to move, it looked like a general European war. Queen Victoria told Disraeli that she would rather "lay down the thorny crown" than see Britain "kiss the feet of the great barbarian" (Alexander). She could well say so, knowing that the people were with her. At this dangerous impasse the genius of Bismarck asserted itself once again. For the first time in ages, certainly for the first time since the Napoleonic threat, all the governments agreed to sit together at a conference table. Bismarck acted as mediator. War had to be avoided. Great Britain, Germany, Austria-Hungary, France, Italy, Russia, and Turkey sent their representatives to Berlin,[13] Andrassy represented Franz Joseph; he puzzled the British diplomats. In his scarlet and gold Hungarian costume he reminded them of the leader of a gypsy band; they soon learned that he was anything but a mountebank. He was of great help to Disraeli—who at first had described him as a "picturesque looking person"—and Disraeli acknowledged his support. The conference was difficult, but in a month of wrangling (June 13 to July 13, 1878), the Peace of Berlin was concluded. It was peace, though far from a perfect peace: Russia smoldered under its conditions, but for the time being could do nothing but store up her resentment against Germany, against England, and especially against Austria, which had so large a Slavic population. Russia had to give up her claims over the Balkans, but she did get Bessarabia. Serbia, Rumania, and Bulgaria, though greatly reduced, were confirmed in their independence; England was to assume the management of Cyprus, while Austria was permitted to occupy Bosnia and Herzegovina. In a word, the Balkans were carved up—for safety's sake.

Before the Russo-Turkish conflict began, the Czar had proposed to Franz Joseph that Austria "annex" Bosnia and Herzegovina. The annexation, tantamount to an outright rape, had been discussed in a secret meeting between the two Emperors in July, 1876. The annexation was Austria's reward for assuming "benevolent neutrality," whatever that phrase might mean. Franz Joseph had accepted the proposition gladly; here, it seemed to him, was some compensation for the loss of Italy. For such a prize he would manage to stay "benevolently" neutral. Andrassy disagreed: he was all for going to war with Russia and to stop once and for all the Czar's sneaking into rooms with western exposure. In a conference of ministers Andrassy, usually elegant and circumspect in his speech, lost his temper and said, "The Russians are up shit creek (*Scheissgasse*), and one ought to take care that they don't escape." (The remark was duly noted in the minutes of the meeting.) The Emperor refused Andrassy's counsel and Andrassy handed in his resignation, which was not accepted. In the end, Franz Joseph agreed that it might be wiser to suppress the word "annexation" and to announce to the world an "occupation." The word was used in the Pickwickian sense; the difference was purely formal, an occupied country being in effect an annexed country. Everybody knew that Austria was never going to *dis*occupy the territory.

In July, 1878, immediately after the Berlin meeting, an Austrian army detail entered Bosnia and Herzegovina. The takeover was going to be easy. It was not: the Austrians found sabotage and guerrilla warfare at every bend of the road, descending from every mountaintop, and hiding behind every tree. The people resisted— and if they had no guns they threw knives, and if they had no knives they threw stones. Franz Joseph had to send fresh troops— more than a hundred thousand soldiers!—to intimidate and to wipe out the hidden nests. But by September the soldiers had done their work and the two provinces belonged to them.

Not really. These dark-veined and fiery people never forgave, though Austria later governed them sensibly and well. They had always been somebody's property—first Hungary's, then Turkey's, now Austria's, and no questions asked. Who were they, after all? Illiterate mountain shepherds. Peasants in hempen shoes. Ignorant miners. They knew enough to enclose themselves in rancor. Within that enclave the rancor hardened as the years passed by, to break out in a malignant tumor thirty-six years after and spread by metastasis to all of Europe.

Katherina Schratt as a young girl, probably in the title role
of Kleist's *Das Kätchen von Heilbronn*

CHAPTER VIII

Elisabeth and
the Placid Triangle

Sophie died. Her death came too late. It came too late to allow husband and wife to mend the fissured union. By the time Sophie closed her censorious eyes, Elisabeth had separated herself mentally and physically from Vienna, from her representational duties, from concern with the future of her country, and, most of all, from any feeling for Franz Joseph that could truly be termed love. Even with Sophie no longer present at the breakfast table, there remained an inert distance between them. He was trussed by his own bonds, his reserve. She could not step out of the cold cave into which she had fled. He still loved her, and understood her no better than before. They knew each other well and didn't know each other at all. They remained intimate strangers.

Sophie had been politically active and physically vigorous until the very last. She went to a performance at the Burgtheater and afterward sat on the balcony of her apartment to cool herself in the May air. There she fell asleep. When she woke in the morning she felt ill. She was put to bed, and after a long struggle, to which Elisabeth, who had been called back from Merano, was witness, she died at a quarter past two on the night of May 28, 1872, at the age of sixty-seven. In Vienna people said, "We have lost our real empress." Elisabeth duly wept a few tears. The true situation was summarized by Marie Festetics, one of Elisabeth's new ladies-in-waiting, who noted in her diary a few days after Sophie's death:

Her ambition drove a wedge between husband and wife and forced him forever to take sides either with mother or with wife. Only by the grace of God was an out-and-out break avoided. She wanted to nullify the influence of the Empress on the Emperor. It was dangerous doing, for he loves his wife.

Countess Marie Festetics had entered Elisabeth's retinue the year before and soon became as trusted a friend as Ida Ferenczy. Andrassy had recommended her, which to Elisabeth was recommendation enough. At their first meeting Elisabeth had received Marie dressed in blue, a huge mastiff standing at her side. Marie was not only a handsome woman—Elisabeth could not have liked her had she not been physically attractive—but a cultivated companion, almost matching Elisabeth's mentality. Her instinct for judging the people who were turning about the Empress was exceptionally good. Now and then she was able to pull Elisabeth from her despondent moods. Now and then she managed to disagree with Elisabeth; Marie was no sycophant. Her diary is one of the valuable sources of Elisabeth's history.

Though Elisabeth's relationship with Marie became close, distance, not closeness, now marked her attitude toward most of humanity. As Freud was to define many years later, one of the symptoms of a psychic wound is the unwillingness to give oneself in intimacy even to those whose good will one cannot doubt. Even Andrassy and Ludwig II did not escape a cold look now and then. Her instability showed itself in her moods, catch-as-catch-can jumps between depression and exhilaration, extreme seriousness and exaggerated gaiety, severity and a flirtatiousness which was not really consistent with her character. Only in one way did she act consistently: she had to be on the move. On the occasions when necessity forced her to go to Vienna, she did so unwillingly. She wrote to Ida: "Except for you and my horses, I will find only unpleasantness there."

She was still a woman, and some of her charming traits remained with her—her sense of the ludicrous, her impulsive generosity, her laughter over the pompousness of the ministers, her love of the poetic. She could still be jealous of her husband, in spite of her indifference to him. In 1869, Franz Joseph and Elisabeth were supposed to officiate at the opening of the Suez Canal, as were Napoleon and Eugénie. At the last moment Elisabeth decided not to go but to remain in Gödöllö. Then she regretted her decision, the more so as Franz Joseph wrote to her of the thousand-and-one-night luxury with which Sultan Abdul-Asis received him in Constantinople, with "the greatest possible charm one can imagine in a host," and described to her the fabulous Arabian horses, the white steeds of the Sultan. She was worried about Franz Joseph's being with Eugénie: "Now you are with your beloved Eugénie. I am extremely jealous when I think how you are now acting the charmer while I sit here alone and cannot even revenge myself."[1] Franz Joseph answered that Eugénie was no longer quite so beautiful, having become too stout. Andrassy was with the Emperor, and Elisabeth got word of one of his amorous adventures with an Arabian woman, when he had been surprised by the unexpected return of her husband and had to flee precipitously minus his trousers. Elisabeth wrote him a joshing poem, which Andrassy answered with another piece of doggerel, of course telling her that there was not a word of truth in the story.

When she was not in Gödöllö, she wandered all over Europe. Where was she not in those years? The mere itinerary is dizzying: the Riviera, Baden-Baden, Heidelberg, London, Athens, Smyrna, Corfu, Wiesbaden, Amsterdam, four times in England, in Ireland, Munich, the palace of Miramar (Triest), Budapest, Rome, Normandy, up and down the Adriatic and the Mediterranean. Maurice Barrès wrote: "Her voyages did not resemble the peaceful and deliberate regularity of migrating birds; they were rather the planless darting to and fro of an unanchored spirit which beats its wings, allowing itself neither rest nor design."[2] She used the Habsburg yacht, the *Miramar,* to cross the seas. She had a round glass pavilion built on deck; there she sat and looked out over the ocean. During a storm at sea she had herself tied to the mast like Ulysses.

The purposes of her voyages to England and Ireland were riding and hunting. She loved English country life as lived by the aristocratic fox-hunting set—the only set with which she came in contact—red coats, early morning hunt breakfasts, hallooing, panting dogs, and all. She was not only an intrepid rider, she was a frantic one, despising dangers and obstacles which frightened the men. The more difficult the chase the more she enjoyed it. "Lots of stretchers," she reported gleefully, while she remained unharmed and the cynosure of the lords and ladies. (In Normandy she did have a bad accident; she was thrown from her horse and suffered a concussion. Franz Joseph was beside himself with worry, as he could not get away from Vienna to be with her. "What am I to do in this world without you, the good angel of my life?" he wrote, thoroughly frightened. She recovered in a few days.) The only nuisance in England was the necessity of spending time with Queen Victoria. Elisabeth found Victoria "unsympathetic." The feeling was probably reciprocated. Did Victoria, now dumpy and trying in vain to hide a double chin, envy her beauty? Did Elisabeth have but a scant comprehension of Victoria's dedication to her task? At any rate, the two women had little to say to each other. Victoria twice invited Elisabeth to dinner: twice she refused, a slight to which Victoria responded at a later date by sending word that she was too busy to receive Elisabeth. "If *I* had such bad manners . . .," Elisabeth petulantly wrote Franz Joseph, forgetting her own bad manners.

In Ireland she found the terrain even more to her liking, and she would have gone there more often had she not been told that as the representative of a Catholic realm she would have to be careful not to appear to take sides in the English-Irish disputes—Home Rule was being much debated—and not to arouse Victoria's suspicion. Back to England she went.

The expense of one of her English voyages—traveling as she did with her own retinue and her own horses—is documented as 106,516 gulden (more than $200,000), and that of her one Irish sojourn as 158,337 gulden (more than $300,000), a fortune indeed! She came under attack in the foreign press and from the new German Socialist party. A businessman wrote her saying that what she spent in *one* day on a hunt would finance his entire business: would she not give him the money? She pretended to be impervious to such criticism. She was not.

She rented one of England's finest hunting preserves, Easton Neston in Northamptonshire. One of her hosts, Lord Spencer, suggested that a young officer of the Twelfth Lancers, a Captain George Middleton, act as her hunting guide. Nicknamed "Bay," he was known as one of England's finest riders to hounds. He was one of those independent Englishmen who make a show of being independent: neither rank nor wealth impressed him. Before he met Elisabeth he told Lord Spencer, "What do I care about an empress? I'd rather go my own way, though of course I'll accept the assignment." Short of stature, strong, elegantly dressed, swinging his riding crop, a bowler hat placed at a rakish angle on his head, large blue eyes and small mustache—he was a figure who could have stepped from the pages of *Punch,* the welcome extra man at any dinner party, in spite of the fact that he had become slightly deaf through an early riding accident. His determination not to be impressed received a jolt when he met Elisabeth. He was enraptured by her, as she outpaced him in recklessness, provoking difficulties, tireless in the saddle, expert as any huntsman. And she? At first she was amused by his indifference to the honor accorded him. She set out to meet his challenge and to charm him. Then she became infatuated. They spent day after day together. The thirty-year-old Bay seemed to rejuvenate her: she was nine years older than he, a grandmother, Gisela's first child having been born two years previously, but she acted like a twenty-year-old. The gossip flew from London to Budapest, but her husband gave not the slightest inkling that he knew or cared. Nor did he interfere, though the name of Captain Middleton constantly cropped up in her letters. So they rode together, he lost in admiration of this woman beside him, dressed in a tight blue habit which accentuated an improbably narrow waist, a diamond star on her bosom, her hair piled high beneath a tall cylinder, wearing three pairs of gloves to protect her hands.[3]

Elisabeth was so absorbed that when Rudolf came to England she paid scant attention to her son. In turn Rudolf deliberately turned his back on Bay Middleton when he met him at a party at which the Prince of Wales was present. Elisabeth said nothing. The Middleton-Elisabeth relationship lasted almost six years, though by and by it cooled. Were they lovers? We do not know. The probabilities are that they were not, that it was an infatuation, not an affair. But one cannot be certain.[4]

Bay Middleton married and died, six years before Elisabeth did, a death that was to be foreseen: he broke his neck in a riding accident. They probably kept the news from Elisabeth.

Obviously, her passion for riding was an expression of her need for being in motion; but it was also an expression of her desire to excel. What she undertook she had to master. Proficient though she was, she began to take lessons from a circus rider (a girl by the name of Elise Renz who, Elisabeth assured Franz Joseph, was a perfectly "respectable girl"), and presently she could perform complicated stunts on horseback. She bought four trained circus ponies. She carried with her a little red notebook in which she criticized her performance. One of her dogs served as an interested spectator. A succession of dogs is mentioned in her letters—one and all big animals—"Shadow," "Mohammed," "Plato."

When she went sightseeing in foreign cities, she did so hurriedly but with complete absorption. She went about incognito and unguarded, accompanied only by Marie or Ida, without a thought for her safety. In Paris she climbed on a bus, and having no idea of how much the fare was or what the coins denoted, emptied her purse into the conductor's hand, saying, "Take what is necessary." In London she was fascinated and a little repelled by Madame Tussaud's Cabinet: Franz Joseph was one of the figures.

While she loved ocean swimming, she found it difficult to achieve it in the resorts she visited. People used to watch her through binoculars; to confuse them, a lady-in-waiting put on the same bathing suit she wore. But she soon gave it up, so great was her dislike of being stared at.

She now followed the most extreme of diets, sometimes nourishing herself for an entire day with six glasses of milk. Nothing else. This milk had to be obtained from special cows, and in the account book of the Austrian Finance Ministry one finds an item of "traveling expenses for cows." In Aix-les-Bains she bought two cows and the bill (1473.53 francs) went to the Ministry for Foreign Affairs. The gift of an unknown admirer, a Count Manna, was of little use to her: he stipulated in his will that Elisabeth was to be regularly supplied with *pannetone,* the famous Milanese yeast cake, until her death. It was really carrying owls to Athens, since Vienna is the home of the *Gugelhupf*, the finest yeast cake of them all. Elisabeth loved sweets but barely touched them, except once in a while a water ice flavored with violets.

She would undertake walking tours which left such companions as Ida and Marie exhausted. She would march for six, seven, eight hours, once fully ten hours. Except in the midst of winter, she did not wear petticoats. In summer she took her walks wearing only a dress over her naked body and no stockings. She began to feel sorry for Ida and Marie and allowed them to be carried in sedan chairs, and her private physician would occasionally come along riding a donkey. When her feet became swollen from those long marches and pained her a great deal, she consulted a Dr. Metzger in Amsterdam who forbade her to walk, ride, or fence for six weeks. She didn't obey his regimen, but at least he got her to eat a little more sensibly. Later she reverted to her starvation diet. Again, this was a pattern with her: she would consult one physician, then the next, then the next—and then ignore all medical advice.

Increasingly, preservation of her beauty became her obsession. Occasionally, Marie Larisch related, she would wear a mask at night which was stuffed with raw meat.[5] During strawberry season a paste of strawberries was prepared with which she massaged her neck and face. She took baths in warm olive oil. She sometimes slept with her hips wrapped in wet rags to preserve her slimness. She slept on a hard bed without pillows. She disliked perfume, and none of her retinue was allowed to wear it. She wore no rings on her fingers, not even her wedding ring, but strung them on a chain around her neck.

Her extravagance grew with her restlessness. She did not have much taste, and when the shopping fever was upon her she bought works of art and antiquities with little discrimination. She who was sensitive toward poetry and responded to music derived scant inspiration from pictorial art and only on the rarest of occasions visited the Breughels or the Dürers which were to be seen in the Vienna Museum. What she really liked was pictures of horses. There were many such in her apartments in Schönbrunn, and she said to Ida, "These are my true friends." In Paris the Venus de Milo did thrill her, though she regretted that the Greek ideal ran to full hips and breasts. But she began to look at other Greek sculpture, and her interest grew into enthusiasm when she saw the Acropolis. The "Hermes Villa" near Vienna and her palace in Corfu, built later, were expressions of her love for Hellenic antiquity.

Whether for riding or building her tastes were expensive. She frequently asked for more money than her yearly allotment, and Franz Joseph always granted her demands. Yet, according to what Baron Albert Rothschild told Count Erich Kielmansegg, after her death it turned out that she had a fortune of several million gulden, of which neither the Emperor nor the Finance Minister had any knowledge. While she had been demanding additional money, she had apparently used part of her allowance to invest with the Rothschilds.

The most fashionable and the most popular painter in the Austria of the 1870s was Hans Makart. He was as famous in Vienna as John Singer Sargent was to become in Boston, without possessing a quarter of Sargent's talent. He specialized in painting nudity with clothes on. He painted portraits of beautiful Viennese women in seductive poses. He painted historic scenes in which women threw flowers or their lovely selves at the feet of a conqueror. He painted mythological scenes peopled by Ariadnes and Minervas (for whose faces and bodies socially prominent ladies lent their own faces and bodies). No matter what he painted the result was the same: female flesh, a ripe lot of it, shimmering through rich garments, breasts half hidden, half revealed, thick colors, and peacock feathers, shells, flowers, ferns, thistles, jewels everywhere. His reputation as a rake added to his progress, so that soon the Makart style pervaded Viennese homes, rich and poor, and the period was spoken of as the Makart Age. He was painting *Venice Pays Homage to Caterina Cornaro,* which was to be exhibited at the Vienna World Exhibition, when Elisabeth appeared unannounced in his studio—an abode popularly known as the "Palace of Seduction," overdraped, overcouched, overperfumed— and asked to see the picture. She said nothing more. Makart said nothing. She stood for a minute silently contemplating the painting, then turned to him and said, "I am told that you own a pair of Scottish greyhounds. May I see them?" The animals were brought, the Empress thanked Makart, and left the studio without saying a word about either the picture or the dogs.

Her love for animals did not confine itself to her horses or dogs. Virtually nothing which cantered or crawled or flew was abhorrent to her, not even the mouse, traditionally feared by women. Elisabeth was greatly amused when a mouse frightened Valerie's nurse out of her wits. She reported to Franz Joseph:

> Last night there was a great hunting expedition in my old room. Children, women, lackeys, and a lady-in-waiting chased a mouse with brooms, sticks, and rags; it was a real steeplechase, during which the poor little thing fell into Horseguard's [a dog] trough.[6]

Madness held a peculiar fascination for her. She, a member of the house of Wittelsbach, in which the disease had shown itself more than once, must have feared its threat in her dark moments. She thought of her cousin Ludwig II, who with the years became more of a recluse, a stout, sallow-complexioned dreamer, pining after the dead Wagner, incurring debt after debt through building the castles of Neuschwanstein and Herrenchiemsee,[7] and toying with the plan of building in Bavaria a reconstruction of the "forbidden city" of Peking. She heard that he now often dined alone, pretending that Marie Antoinette was his dinner guest. She was frightened as well by Ludwig's brother, Otto of Bavaria, who was mad, mad medically, and in 1873 was confined in an insane asylum. Elisabeth frequently visited institutes for the insane, in Vienna, in Munich, and Bedlam in London. Were these visits another escape from life, as were her visits to the hospitals for the wounded and the victims of cholera, visits undertaken modestly and carried through stoically? Were these contacts with disease and death self-punishment or an expression of a death wish? Once, in a self-mocking mood, when Franz Joseph asked her what gift she would like for her name day—she received gifts that day because her birthday fell on the day before Christmas—she answered him, "Since you ask what I would like, I will tell you: either a tiger cub—the Berlin Zoological Garden possesses three such—or a medallion. But what I would really like best would be a completely equipped insane asylum."[8]

What were the gossiping duchesses, the fawning adjutants,

what was Franz Joseph to make of this combination of vanity and naturalness, naïveté and mistrust, childish delight and adult intro-spection? She adored going to the circus and took great delight in the antics of trained monkeys; watching them, she could laugh more than her children. At the same time, she read Plato, and when Nietzsche's *The Birth of Tragedy* first appeared, she read that. The new Burgtheater began to perform Ibsen almost as soon as the theater opened its portals. His social dramas, *The Pillars of Society* and *An Enemy of the People,* aroused intense distaste among that part of the Viennese audience which could not recon-cile Ibsen with the rolling verses of Grillparzer. Elisabeth, how-ever, was intrigued. Her favorite Shakespeare play was *A Mid-summer Night's Dream,* and she had the scene of Titania stroking Bottom's head painted above the entrance of several of the castles and palaces she inhabited. "We are forever caressing the ass's head of our illusions," she said.

Illusion wove through her attitude toward her children. Gisela she did not love, and Rudolf she loved only from afar. Even after Sophie's death she was unable to establish a meaningful relation with them. Nevertheless, I believe that Marie Larisch put it too harshly: "The Empress says that she became Rudolf's mother only through an accident. Everything which has been written about her great love for him is sheer fiction. Mother-love was an emotion unknown to my aunt. Valerie, however, was the exception. Elisa-beth believed that her children aged her."

Gisela turned sixteen in 1872, and at that age, just a few months older than her mother had been when she met Franz Joseph, she became engaged to Leopold, Prince of Bavaria. The wedding took place the following year, the year of the Vienna Exhibition. Elisabeth, everybody agreed, far outshone the bride. In that year the Shah of Persia came to Vienna, less, he said, to see the Exhibition than to see Elisabeth. She appeared in a long white robe embroidered in silver and set off by a startling belt of purple velvet, her hair loosely held by a band of diamonds and amethysts. When the Shah entered, he first remained rooted to the spot, then slowly put on a pair of gold-rimmed spectacles, inspected her methodically from head to foot without paying attention to either Franz Joseph or the surrounding courtiers, and then circled around Elisabeth five or six times, murmuring, "Mon dieu, qu'elle est belle!" Forgetting etiquette, he then took Elisabeth's arm and pulled her into the banquet hall. With so exciting a mother, it is understandable that Gisela wished to get away to lead her own life.

Little Valerie inherited her mother's love for flowers and her mother's taste for poetry. Elisabeth saw to it that in whatever palace they lived Valerie had her own garden, which she tended with all the conscientiousness of a parson's wife. When mother and daughter were separated, they exchanged flowers. Valerie wrote poetry, though her poems were no better than her mother's. "She is more than a daughter to me," her mother said; "she is an intimate friend." Valerie early learned Hungarian, and Elisabeth was accused of bringing up the Habsburg daughter as a Hungarian girl. The two often spoke Hungarian together; it was another bond between them.

Rudolf was going on fifteen when Gisela got married. He was a precocious fifteen, not an especially good-looking boy, but bright and quick-tempered, looking at the world with sharp eyes. He reminded a contemporary of a small wolf, a green fire glimmering in his eyes. When he was twelve years old, he had begun shooting rabbits, grouse, and whatever else he could espy. Undoubtedly he imitated his father and to a certain extent his mother, but unlike his father, hunting to him was more than a sport. He took pleasure in killing for the sake of killing: in the many drawings in which the boy pictured himself as a hunter, he included a great blob of red. He knew early what role he was to play; the part lay naturally for him, and political science, political history, the uses and abuses of government, and the privileges and duties of the ruler were schoolroom subjects which he eagerly swallowed, even as a teenager. He took in stride the severe pedagogical pressure brought to bear on him. By the time he was fifteen, he had been taught by no fewer than fifty tutors. One of them, who taught him Hungarian, was Bishop Hyazinth Ronay, who had been on the side of the revolutionaries in 1848 and who, like Andrassy, had been banished. Perhaps it was from Ronay as well as from the liberal Latour that Rudolf absorbed ideas at variance with his father's conservatism. Perhaps it was merely the usual oedipal protest.

Whatever the reason, Rudolf handed Latour several essays at Christmas time, 1872, in which he voiced opinions which must have astonished even Latour: the aristocrats and the clergy are forever plotting under cover, their sole object being to force the common people to remain stupid so that they can continue to lord it over them. Aristocratic society—what was it? Nothing but a pus-filled abscess on the body of the state. Nine years later, when he joined the army and was stationed in Prague, he wrote:

> In Vienna one finds crookedness, thievery, brutality, arbitrariness, corruption, weakness of the state. The most important positions are held by riffraff. I contemplate all this with equanimity. I am merely amused to find out how long before such an old and solid building as Austria will collapse.

Two years before that, he had written to Latour, whom he trusted:

> Our Emperor has no friend. . . . He knows little about the views and opinions of his people. He believes we are now in one of Austria's happiest epochs. They tell him so officially, he reads it in the clippings from the newspapers which are marked in red for him. . . . There was a time when the Empress discussed serious matters with the Emperor. . . . Now the exalted Lady cares for nothing but sport. Three or four years ago the Emperor was more or less reconciled to the nineteenth century. Now he is again harsh and suspicious, as he used to be in the time of poor Grandma. Who knows what is going to happen?[9]

"The Empress," "the Emperor," "the exalted Lady"—it is a young man writing about his parents. He was twenty-three then. He had grown a mustache similar to the one his father sported, and he was constantly stroking his mustache exactly as Franz Joseph did.

2

A wife's absence turns a husband into an awkward bachelor, be he ever so solid a king. The charm which Elisabeth's femininity had brought to the halls of the Hofburg evaporated to leave behind immovable air. The spoonful of relaxation and the pinch of humor which, despite all formality, Elisabeth had introduced at court functions no longer seasoned the occasions, and dinners were as stiff as the faces of the lackeys behind the chairs.

Baroness Maria Redwitz, daughter of a then popular author, described them:

> Dinner was at six o'clock. One had to appear fifteen to twenty minutes before, since the Emperor always came early and the entire retinue had to be assembled. . . . As he entered everybody stood for a moment, then with a gesture of his hand he invited the princesses into the dining room. . . . Because the Emperor was served first and ate rapidly, the guests swallowed the food at a frantic pace.[10] Of course nobody addressed him. If he posed a question one answered as succinctly as possible; in that sense there was never any "conversation." How well I understood that the witty, intellectually vital Empress could not bear such a banal atmosphere.

Again:

> After dinner one repaired to an adjoining room where a fire was burning in a large tile oven. The Emperor sat down close to the fire, and the others formed a semicircle around him. He smoked and asked a few questions of the silent company which were answered mostly by "Yes, Your Majesty" or "No, Your Majesty." I had previously heard how barren this "sit-by-the-fire" was and felt sorry for the monarch who . . . submitted himself to such boredom. Later I came to understand that he didn't want anything else.[11]

He buttoned up tighter in his uniform. He ruled with impersonal sobriety. As pressure by his people forced him gradually to move his realm a little nearer the concept of a constitutional monarchy, he observed the letter of the law as punctiliously as a bank teller counting change. His punctuality, a psychologically significant trait, grew into an obsessive ritual. At public functions he appeared not only at the prescribed minute but at the very second, like the Count of Monte Cristo. Before he went to such a function, the official equipage made a trial run to fix exactly the time needed for him to arrive at his appointment.[12] Court ceremony continued to be strictly observed at the audiences Franz Joseph held twice a week. A master of ceremonies instructed the person to be received while he waited his turn. He was to bow three times: first, when the double doors were opened; second, midway between the door and the Emperor; third, ten paces in front of the Emperor, where he was to halt. After the audience he was to make his exit without ever turning his back to the Emperor, repeating the triple obeisance.

Such solemnity, inherited from the Spanish court, was nothing if not vestigial. There was safety in memoranda, comfort in clockwork routine. All was precise in the Hofburg. He drove emotion inward or expunged it altogether and remained a ruler who kept his distance from a people who were essentially imprecise, warm, and very, very sentimental. Elisabeth's defection opened not only a physical vacancy but a psychological one. It was not so much a vacancy in the bedroom—that could be replenished by baronesses eager and willing—as a stretch of emotional wasteland that she left behind. One cannot help speculating that the fate of Austria might have taken a different turn had Elisabeth remained and decided to be more than a queen in name only.

Of course they pretended that nothing was amiss, and for a time he did so even to himself. At first his letters remained loving, and he urged her to come back. She did come back from time to time, stayed a few days, and was off again. She returned for their silver wedding celebration on April 24, 1879, which took the form of a spectacular festive procession, designed by Makart. As in medieval times, the various guilds, the bakers, the innkeepers, the tailors, the builders, the printers, paraded before Franz Joseph and Elisabeth. They were dressed in ancient costumes, and the head of the printing guild, dressed as Gutenberg, held aloft a tablet on which the words "Fifteen Days on the Danube" were engraved. This was the title of a just-published book by Rudolf.

The guilds were followed by a procession representing the arts. Makart, impersonating Rubens—no lesser painter would suffice— rode at the head. Since he did not know how to ride, they had to put him on an old white nag, but at that the horse shied, Makart lost his hat, and nearly got pricked by his own sword. A triumphal chariot fashioned after a design by Dürer followed; on it posed Vienna's most beautiful women and Vienna's best-known actresses, including an attractive young actress named Katherina Schratt.

In diplomatic circles it was said that the imperial pair celebrated not "vingt-cinq ans de ménage; mais vingt-cinq ans de manège" ("not twenty-five years of a household but twenty-five years of horsemanship"). Hardly was the festival concluded when Franz Joseph left for Hungary and Elisabeth went riding.

He threw himself into work. He would arise at four in the morning and be at his desk at five. Sometimes he had his meals there, paying scant attention to when and what he ate. There was no need for him to read all those petitions, proposals, complaints, budgets, and ambassadorial letters, no need to plow through that crop of paper. His staff could have done it perfectly well. But he did it because from the details he distilled an opiate. "A government of statesmen or of clerks? Of Humbug or of Humdrum?" Disraeli wrote. Austria had both. To be sure, the problems did not diminish. Andrassy, grown old, had to be replaced. Taaffe, Franz Joseph's choice, did not suit the "German Liberals," a strong party who disapproved of the Bosnian occupation. The Czechs demanded new concessions, some of them entirely justified. Russia remained inimical and France uncertain. Bismarck continued his overtures, and in the September of the silver wedding year he came to Vienna to confer. Again former enemies became friends, or pretended to. From that meeting grew the German-Austrian alliance, signed on October 7, 1879. It obliged either country to come to the other's aid, employing all its military power, should either be attacked. (That meant Russia.) It also guaranteed peace between the German and the Austro-Hungarian Empire. It was Bismarck's triumph, obtained by him with great difficulty, since Wilhelm I bitterly fought any measure inimical to his nephew the Czar. Bismarck worked for weeks to convince Wilhelm of the advisability of this Austrian alliance, but he never was entirely convinced, and the agreement was kept a secret document. The term was specified as five years. In effect it lasted to the end of World War I.

Marie Festetics sensitively summarized the Franz Joseph of those years:

> The Emperor possesses intelligence and quick understanding. Yet he gives his imagination no time to develop. Thus he sometimes acts abruptly, overworked as he is and incredibly devoted to his duties. For him only primitive concepts exist. Beautiful, ugly,

dead, living, healthy, young, old, clever, stupid—these are all separate notions to him and he is unable to form a bridge leading from
one to the other. . . . His ideas know no nuances.[13]

He called Elisabeth's ideas "cloud-climbing" (*Wolkenkrax-
lerei*) , using the word in a pejorative sense.

3

One understands Elisabeth's cloud-climbing—her longing for the
open, a longing for flight traceable to her childhood—when one
peers into those moments of family life after the diplomats departed and, in Goldsmith's words, "our own felicity we make or
find." Little felicity could be made or found in the Burg. Ceremony ended, the facilities for living were restricted indeed.
Stephanie, Rudolf's wife, described them in her memoirs:

> There were neither bathrooms nor water closets in the Hofburg,
> not even running water. For my ablutions I used a bathtub made of
> rubber. On two wooden stools stood two pails filled with water
> which was poured on me. The dirty water and the chamber pots
> were carried away through passages where passers-by could encoun-
> ter them. . . . Our kitchen was on the same floor as our living
> quarters, separated only by one room which always smelt of cook-
> ing. The food was crude and did not agree with me. Yet there was
> quite a revolution when I hired a French cook. After three years of
> quarreling, I finally succeeded in changing the medieval con-
> veniences, and at my own expense I had two completely equipped
> bathrooms built. For that I was severely criticized. . . . Horrible
> petroleum lamps which burned out after a few hours gave forth an
> evil smell. A rain of soot drifted into all the rooms, or the cylinders
> broke and we sat in the dark and waited for them to be replaced.[14]

Perhaps we must discount this description, because Stephanie
was a chronic complainer—the poor woman had enough about
which to complain. All the same, inside that fortresslike imperial
residence life did not reflect the story-book picture the Viennese
painted of it, all silk and lights and luxury, with Franz Joseph
smiling at bare-shouldered beautiful women who never walked
but moved in dance step!

In the city itself, however, a new gaiety bloomed. The depression of 1873 had had the usual effect of convincing people that life beckoned to be enjoyed that very day, since who knew when another Black Friday would arrive? One waltz after another came from Johann Strauss's pen, and Viennese life imitated Viennese music, the second act of *Die Fledermaus* serving as the theme song for clinking glasses, even if in real life the glasses were not filled with champagne. In Franz Joseph's palace the routine may have been severe enough; yet even there, and at least twice at carnival time, the Hofburg demonstrated of what splendor it was capable.

The Court Ball was the great event to which hundreds were invited. It took place in the large and small *Redoutensaal*, exquisite rooms in the Hofburg which at other times were used for concert and theatrical performances and where Mozart, Haydn, and Beethoven had appeared. The guests were chosen by the "imperial steward" and the list submitted to Franz Joseph: it consisted of members of the aristocracy, the diplomatic corps, privy councillors, generals, heads of civil departments, members of Parliament, men who had been awarded an order of distinction, and so on. Officers at all times had access to such a function. In addition, debutantes from high society would be presented. The ball started at six and ended officially at ten, though the young people stayed after the Emperor and his retinue had taken their leave and dancing—waltzes, *polkas françaises,* quadrilles, lanciers —really got going. The guests were divided among several rooms according to a strict ceremonial. When Franz Joseph and Elisabeth entered—frequently an archduchess substituted for Elisabeth—they marched through the main *Saal* amid breathless silence, and then went to each of the rooms in turn, where the guests were introduced to them. The presentation was topped off by the "diplomat cercle," a round of ambassadors and envoys as well as of *étrangers de distinction* (as the ceremonial had it), which formed around the Emperor. This done, Franz Joseph and his retinue appeared on a balcony and he gave the sign for the first waltz to begin. The Empress placed herself on a sofa and summoned those ladies she wished to honor. Franz Joseph, instead, made his way among the dancing couples, saying something polite to one or the other, bowing to this countess or that. For four hours he never once sat down. He and all members of the military were dressed in white gala uniforms. It was all intensely glamorous and intensely boring.

More intimate and more exclusive was the "Ball at Court," to which only aristocrats of the highest rank were invited, the so-called Sixteen Quarterings, meaning those who could trace their ancestry to eight male and eight female noble forebears; then the most important ambassadors of foreign countries and, to make dancing bearable, a sprinkling of young Viennese lieutenants from the best families. Dukes danced with duchesses, barons with baronesses; everybody knew everybody, and they addressed one another in the familiar form, and only in French, a stilted, eighteenth-century French. Each lady was given a bouquet of flowers with the ribbon tied in a traditional way; it was called the Maria Theresa bouquet. At supper a soup was served supposedly prepared after a secret recipe of Maria Theresa herself.

The swirl and the sway, the real fun, were to be found in the balls where the not-so-elite got together. These balls, called with typical Viennese promotion Elite Balls, were organized by diverse groups, the railroad employees, the painters, the fiacre drivers, the coal merchants, the Poles, the Czechs, the Hungarians, the local regiments. They were the occasion for masks, for unbuttoned behavior, when the unknown young man approached the unrecognized girl, addressed her by *du,* danced with her all night, and took her home in a fiacre as the pale February sun came up. These late echoes of Dionysian revels were as often as not played in decorous rhythm, the outcome nothing more than a passing flirtation. There were exceptions, of course. One whispered of balls in secret places held by secret societies in which men and women danced nude. Schnitzler described such a revel in the harrowing short story "Nocturne." Yet the prevailing theme was merely a flutter, a little flight from the workday.

Elisabeth once took such a flight.[15] The escapade, innocent enough, again reminds one of the second act of *Die Fledermaus,* which, by coincidence, was to have its premiere the year after. At carnival time in 1874 (Elisabeth was then thirty-seven), she took it into her head to visit an Elite Ball in secret. She hid her plan from her husband—indeed the facts came to light only after both of them were dead—taking only Ida into her confidence. Late one night, after everybody was safely asleep, Elisabeth got up, dressed in a domino costume of heavy yellow brocade, too opulent for the occasion, and hid her own hair under a red wig. She put on a mask from which black lace hung, so that nothing of her face could be seen. She called herself Gabriele. Ida and she entered the ballroom, went up to the balcony, and observed the dancers. Nobody paid attention to them, and presently Elisabeth began to get bored. Ida suggested that "Gabriele" point out to her any man in the hall whose looks pleased her. Elisabeth pointed to a young, good-looking fellow who was dancing below. Ida slipped downstairs, entered into a conversation with him, and soon convinced herself through the answers he gave that he did not belong to court society. He seemed safe enough. Ida said, "Do you want to do me a favor?" "Yes, certainly." "I have a friend here who is sitting quite alone in the gallery and is bored to death. Do you want to entertain her for a few minutes?" "Of course," responded the young man. He went up and introduced himself to Elisabeth as Fritz Pacher, a clerk in one of the ministries. Pacher was no fool and felt from the first moment, judging from the richness of her dress, from her whole bearing, from her way of speaking, that the woman to whom he had been brought was somebody exceptional. They chatted in constrained tones for a while and Elisabeth asked him curious questions: What did the people think of the government? What was the general opinion of the Emperor? Had he ever seen the Empress? How was she judged? The idea went through his head that he was addressing the Empress, but it was only a fleeting idea and he dismissed it as being too fantastic. He told her that he had seen the Empress riding her horse in the Prater, that she was an incredibly beautiful woman, that she was being generally criticized because she appeared so seldom in public, and that her passion for horses and dogs seemed to him exaggerated, though he understood that she had inherited the predilection from her father, who was supposed to have said, "If I weren't a prince I would become a circus rider." Elisabeth interrupted him to ask, "How old do you think I am?" "You? . . . You are thirty-six years old." Somewhat taken aback, she answered, "You are not very polite," and presently she added, "You can go now." But he would not go. It wasn't fair to have him called away from dancing, to have her ask a dozen questions, and then to dismiss him peremptorily. Elisabeth agreed, and, loosening up, the conversation became more animated. They spent the next two hours dancing and promenading. Pacher did not press her, sensing that the woman with him was a mysterious being, unused to crowds, as every time somebody brushed against her, he felt her tremble. He happened to mention Heine: it appeared that Heine was the young man's favorite poet. Quite charmed by him now, she asked him many questions, about his family, his life, his hopes, and finally who he thought she was. He replied: "You are a great lady, probably a princess. I can see that by your behavior." Had he guessed correctly? Elisabeth laughed. "One day I will tell you who I am, but not tonight. We shall see each other again. Could you come to Munich or Stuttgart for a rendezvous? You see, I have no home and I am forever traveling." "I shall come wherever and whenever you wish." He wrote down his address for Elisabeth, and she said, "Promise that after you have seen me to my carriage you won't return to the ballroom any more. Not tonight." He promised, and as they descended the staircase he exclaimed: "I must know who you are!" and tried to lift the lace of her mask. At this moment Ida threw herself between the two and spirited Elisabeth away. To cover their traces they had the carriage go to the suburbs. Far out, in a tiny street, the carriage halted, Ida descended and looked around, and having made certain that they were not being followed, they returned to the Hofburg.

A week later Pacher received a letter from Munich. (The date on the letter is written in Elisabeth's handwriting, but the rest of the letter is in a disguised hand.) The letter said that she had promised to let him have a sign of life and here it was; she was sure he had been waiting for it and that he was thinking of her. He answered as he was bidden to a box number at the post office. The correspondence was kept up on Elisabeth's side in a disguised handwriting and always posted in places where Elisabeth was not.

A month after her first letter Elisabeth wrote to him again, pretending that she was in England:

Dear Friend: How sorry I am for you! Because you haven't had any word from me in such a long time, your life must have been empty and time must have hung heavy on your hands. Yet I was not able to write to you. I felt deadly tired. My thoughts could not lift themselves, and day after day I sat at the window and for hours stared into the hopeless fog. Then suddenly I became as giddy as a debutante and rushed from one party to the next. Did I think of you? That's my secret. I have no obligation to still your curiosity, you conceited youth. . . .

My watch says it's after midnight. At this moment are you dreaming of me, or are you humming songs of longing into the still night? In the interest of your neighbors, I hope the former.

She asked him to reply to the General Post Office in London. Something—was it the bantering tone of her letters, was it that he recognized that the handwriting was disguised?—must have aroused Fritz's suspicion. This is apparent from Elisabeth's next letter:

Why don't you think that my name is Gabriele? Do you have an aversion to the name of that beautiful archangel? . . . You seem to have taken it into your head that I am not in London. If only I were again in Vienna, I assure you I would have a better time there.

In this letter she asked him to send her his photograph, and to assuage his doubts she gave a description of her life in England, not a word of which was true. She hoped that he would enjoy his vacation at the Italian lakes, where he planned to go with his mother and sister.

I know that even there you will think of me, in spite of your mother and sister. I have woven myself into your life quite unconsciously and naturally. Tell me, would you now like to unravel the thread? Now you can still do it. Later, who knows?

As to his insistent demand to know her "biography"—all she would say was that were she to relate it, it would not bore him. Yet she was not going to disclose her secret until they knew each other better. Today she would only tell him that the most thrilling experience of her life was her stay in the Orient. Thus she played with him, spinning fantasies, partly like a child, partly like a cocotte. Elisabeth had not yet been to the Orient. She tried further to muddy the clues by telling him that she hated dogs. Yet Fritz felt that something in her letters did not ring true. He did not wish to confront her directly with his idea of her identity, nor was he positive, but in his next letter he made some vague reference to an Empress called Elisabeth. At this, Elisabeth took fright and broke off the correspondence.

Eleven years passed. Elisabeth was now forty-eight, several times a grandmother. Once again she had taken up the writing of poetry, expressing in varied meter and sad stanzas her one longing, the longing to be free, "as free as the seagull." (Only a minute quantity of these poems is extant, Elisabeth having destroyed most of them in a self-critical moment.) In her poetic mood she remembered Fritz and the carnival night. She composed a poem, "Long, Long Ago," and she called it "The Song of the Yellow Domino." Without sending the poem, she wrote to Fritz Pacher's old address, asking him to send her his present address and his latest photograph. Fritz's astonishment is easy to imagine:

> Dear Yellow Domino,
>   Nothing could have surprised me more than a sign of life from you. To say "I fell from the clouds" is to express it much too weakly. What hasn't happened in all these eleven years?! Surely you are still as beautiful and as proud as ever. I instead have become a married man, bald, respectable, but happy. My wife resembles you in height and figure. I have an adorable little daughter.
>   If you think it right after these eleven long years, you really could take off your domino without fear, and bring clarity into the mysterious adventure which, of all the events of my life, has most fascinated me. . . .

He did not send his picture and she did not answer for four months. Even then she did not tell him who she was, but simply repeated her request for a photograph of "the fatherly baldhead." Fritz apparently resented her lack of openness and wrote back that he was sorry that after eleven years she still found it necessary to play hide-and-seek with him: "after such a time, anonymous correspondence loses its savor."

Elisabeth did not reply to this letter. Yet two years later (June 3, 1887) Fritz received an envelope franked with Brazilian postage stamps. In it he found a single printed page, the poem Elisabeth had destined for him. That was all.

Now Fritz was sure. Who could have written to him from Brazil, and who could have penned such a poem and had it set in type? He replied with another poem entitled "To the Unknown One," in which he wrote that, clever though she was, she was not clever enough, because "figure and walk and word and thought carried the mark of Highness." He had penetrated the disguise of the yellow domino; he knew who she was.

It is a telling episode in its very triviality and inconsequence. Her need to be admired led her to the edge of chance, not beyond. She wanted the fiction of love rather than its physical embroilment.

4

Katherina Schratt was a real Viennese girl, round and soft, fed by an inner spring of gaiety, light-hearted, vivacious, the kind of girl who when she walked arm in arm with a man molded herself along his frame and looked up into his eyes. She was neither exceptionally handsome nor exceptionally clever; yet without being out-and-out coquettish she made the most of her femininity through her conviction that a man must be catered to. She was the sort of woman who would always have flowers on the breakfast table and never appear there except in carefully arranged disarray.

She was an actress who did not at all fit the picture of the loose-living, free-giving *bohémienne* to be found in the novels of her day. She was methodical, a good housekeeper, an excellent cook, prim, and quite capable of pronouncing prissy homilies. She was a devout Catholic. One of her favorite pastimes was doing jigsaw puzzles, the more complicated the better; she used to lay the pieces out on a large table.[16]

Katherina was not a great actress, but her charm made up for her lack of depth, and she had a successful career in a variety of comedy roles. After an apprentice year, she owed her rise to the opportunity given her by Heinrich Laube, a brilliant man of the theater, first the intendant of the Burgtheater and later the head of the rival Stadttheater. There, in March, 1873, she made her Vienna debut in Kleist's verse comedy, *Das Kätchen von Heil-*

bronn. The *Neues Wiener Tagblatt* found her looks "poetic" and her acting distinguished by "inborn, unstudied grace." At her debut one of those unfortunate accidents occurred which turn out fortunately: she fell and twisted her ankle. The attending physician counseled against continuing the performance, but Laube decided to the contrary and furnished her with a cane, inserting two verses into Kleist's text:

> GOTTSCHALK: What ails you, lady?
> KÄTCHEN: My foot does play me tricks.

The public understood and liked her all the better for her pluck. In December of the same year Katherina played another Kate, in *The Taming of the Shrew.*[17] Franz Joseph and Elisabeth saw her for the first time at this performance, a gala held for the Emperor's twenty-fifth jubilee. She probably was a tame Kate.

Twelve years were to elapse before Franz Joseph made her acquaintance; in the meantime she married and had a son; and, the marriage proving unhappy, she and her husband agreed to separate. At the Ball of the Industrials, at which Franz Joseph often made an appearance, he conversed with her for quite a few minutes. Tongues began to wag. That conversation took place in December, 1885; she was then thirty-two years old, he fifty-five. He was attracted to her, and he suggested to her that she have her portrait painted at his expense; it would be his tribute to a fine, typically Viennese actress. The fashionable painter Heinrich Angeli was given the commission and on May 20, 1886, Franz Joseph sent him a note setting his and Elisabeth's visit to his atelier for the next day at one o'clock; they wished to see what progress he had made. Schratt was sitting for the portrait when Their Majesties were announced. She got stage fright and wanted to hide, but it was too late: Franz Joseph and Elisabeth had entered.

Two days later he wrote to her. It was the first of the hundreds of letters which passed between them:

> May 23, 1886
> My dear Lady: I ask you to accept the enclosed souvenir as an expression of my warmest appreciation of the fact that you have given yourself the trouble to sit for the Angeli portrait. I must emphasize

again that I did not dare to demand such a sacrifice from you and therefore my pleasure over your gracious consent is all the greater. Your devoted admirer—

He enclosed an emerald ring.

The Angeli portrait shows her in décolleté, with composed and regular features, an uninteresting face redeemed by large eyes and just the suggestion of a smile, long dark hair cascading over her neck. In a word—pleasing.

With this letter began a relationship which, with some considerable interruptions, lasted to Franz Joseph's death. She was his best friend and often his only friend. Some of Franz Joseph's official biographers have tried to make it appear that it was a platonic friendship, while others simply have avoided discussing the question.[18] There is little doubt in my mind that Katherina Schratt took the place of a wife, that they shared sexual as well as companionable experiences, that he not only loved her but was in love with her, at least for some years. I cannot prove this statement, since proof does not exist—no witnesses peered into her room—and since the evidence of contemporaries is contradictory. I derive my belief from his behavior toward her and from the tone of his letters, which sound—though in muted accents and in the minor mode—a harmony such as two people can produce only when their relationship is more than that of friends. His letters to her—her letters to him have been destroyed—are not love letters, yet they are letters of love. He was too introverted a man to pour out his feelings in passionate streams, and he was too circumspect and sometimes too embarrassed to pen eloquent endearments. He must have known the probability that these letters would be perused by posterity. All the same, as one reads the letters one is struck by sentiments which denote the normal man-woman relationship, and later by an aura of domesticity, of keeping house together. Jealousy, worry over losing her, fear of having offended her, longing for her, protestations of being too old for her, sharing of secret thoughts, dependence of one on the other—they are all in the letters and they have the flavor of love. They outweigh their moralistic assertions that they were "not doing anything wrong" and that they were "just good friends." Whom was he fooling—himself?

. . . Your half-portrait with hat, in morning dress, with the famous angel around your neck [a jewel he had given her] I had framed especially to keep it here and to look at it constantly. This portrait, so like you, reminds me of unforgettable hours. . . . [1887.]

Today fourteen days have elapsed since I talked to you and Sunday it will be as long since I saw you if only from afar. This period seems to me an eternity. . . . [January 11, 1888.]

An equivocal letter, typical of the correspondence:

To my greatest joy I received this morning your long, sweet, dear letter of the 12th, for which I thank you with all my heart. . . . If I didn't know that you are always truthful with me, I could doubt its contents, especially when I look into my mirror and see my old, wrinkled face. . . .

That I adore you, you must know. At least you must feel it. My feeling grows all the time, ever since I experienced the great happiness of knowing you. . . .

Our relationship must, in the future, remain as it is now if it is to endure. I hope it will endure, because it makes me so very happy. You say that you must hold yourself in check. I will do the same, even if it isn't easy for me. I do not want to do any wrong. I love my wife and do not want to abuse her trust in you or her friendship for you. I am too old to be a brotherly friend, so you will permit me to be a fatherly friend. . . . Your letter I will treasure as a precious jewel and as a proof of your love. Preserve for me the place I occupy in your great heart. My thanks for advancing me to the rank of "angel first-class." I shall try to merit this new distinction. [February 14, 1888.]

Four days later:

Again you suffer twinges of conscience and are terribly afraid that I look on you as a seductress and could become angry with you. The latter is impossible, and as far as the former is concerned, it is true that you are so beautiful and lovely and good that you could become dangerous to me, but I remain strong. Since I received your letter and know your feelings, I am both happy and tranquil. Clarity is always the best thing; even when it is not quite correct it is good. And now I am saved from my stupid jealousy which plagues me so often. . . .

I cannot tell you how often I read and reread your *dangerous* letter. Please lock up this letter along with the others *extra* carefully. [February 18, 1888.]

That you have another cold, that is certainly bad luck. Surely you've been careless: no umbrella, thin shoes or some other of your usual lack of precaution. . . . I find it comforting that this time I didn't give you the cold. . . . [September 14, 1889.]

Often I torture myself with the thought that you no longer love me, not even a little, and that your goodness and your friendship for me have changed. [December 16, 1889.]

My first courier won't arrive until about eight o'clock, and so I take advantage of the early morning hours to address a few lines to you, and to tell you that I think of you constantly and that I long for you incessantly. [November 8, 1890.]

Franz Joseph learned that she was attracted by the handsome Count Philip Eulenburg, German ambassador to Vienna:

You know I have long been afraid of this, because the ambassador is very *aimable*—much more intelligent and amusing than I am. He may soon push me out of your heart. That is why black thoughts pursue me constantly. It is high time that you quiet me down and that I once again see your dear, clear eyes. [March 5, 1896.]

Once in a while their emotions did overflow their prudence and they wrote each other what they called "letters of thought" (*Gedankenbriefe*), which were letters not of thought but of feeling and which they urged each other to destroy.

He knew the times of her menstrual period, which he called "your quiet week" (*stille Woche*). "Your quiet week ought to postpone our meeting," he wrote to her from Cap Martin (March 14, 1894); and another time, "Your quiet week arrived a day too early, according to my calculation." Such intimacy suggests a more physical relationship than just being friends.

At other times the letters are filled with the minutiae of life, descriptions of his hunting successes, impressions of nature, reports on the weather. "Silly prattle," he calls them. He fusses constantly about her health; when she has a cold he wants her physician to notify him daily. "Your cute little nose must be a bit pink," he writes in Viennese dialect. He hardly ever mentions his imperial task; politics is a subject strictly avoided, though several times he cancels an appointment with her, regretfully because of "my duties."

However these letters are to be scanned, one fact is certain: Elisabeth not only knew about the relationship, she encouraged it. As Rebecca West wrote: "She introduced . . . Katherina Schratt into his life very much as a woman might put flowers into a room she felt to be dreary." That is the remarkable feature of the triangle: the three participants drew it in agreement. It helped Elisabeth as well as Franz Joseph. Her conscience troubled her for leaving him alone, and Schratt's presence helped to salve her conscience. At the beginning she fairly pushed him into it by inviting Katherina to be with them, and at all times she was gracious to her. Franz Joseph wrote Schratt: "Repeatedly the Empress has spoken approvingly and charmingly about you, and I can assure you that she likes you very much. If you would know this marvelous woman better, you would reciprocate her feelings." One time Katherina's son, Toni, then twelve years old, received a scurrilous anonymous letter about his mother. Though the police immediately investigated, they could not discover its author. When Elisabeth learned of the incident, she invited Toni and Katherina to the imperial villa in Ischl. She then took a walk with Toni, while Katherina and Franz Joseph followed behind, and spoke to the boy intimately and sweetly, praising his mother and telling him that only depraved minds could write such letters. Later she saw to it that Toni received presents of tarts and cakes from the *Hofkonditorei* (court baker) .

Only rarely did resentment against her rival come to the fore. How easy it is to understand the jealousy of a woman even when she no longer wants a man! How easy it is to understand that Franz Joseph did not understand! He quoted to Katherina a letter he had received from Elisabeth:

> Yesterday I received a letter from the Empress, dated Sept. 28, from Algeria where she arrived that very day. She writes about you: "Last night I dreamed about the friend [female]. I had invited her for tea and forgot to order the tea."

In short, this was no love affair hiding in secret corners. Franz Joseph, in finding Katherina the female friend he needed, did not forget Elisabeth. He wrote Schratt:

> Your simple new hairdo in the third act was particularly becoming. It reminded me that the Empress wore her hair in a similar fashion in her young days.

He did not try to conceal his early morning visits to her. In Ischl he had a special door built in his villa from which he could walk directly to the garden gate of her villa, the key to which he carried in his pocket. He came at seven or eight in the morning, and she had to be ready and dressed, the coffee brewing on the stove. Sometimes she went to early Mass just so they could greet each other with a look. Once on a February morning she fainted from the cold, and he could not come to her aid in the public church. She went to see him in the Hofburg two or three times a week, had afternoon coffee with him, chatted or merely sat while he continued working. When Elisabeth was in Vienna, Katherina was occasionally invited to dinner. Valerie noted in her diary that sometimes they were four at dinner: her parents, Katherina, herself. Valerie was ill at ease; Elisabeth thought it pleasant.

Once, when Elisabeth felt it her duty to stay with him and he and Valerie thought that she ought to go and see Dr. Metzger in Wiesbaden to consult him about her rheumatic pains, he asked Katherina to help him with a trifling ruse. She was to telegraph that she was coming to see him—Katherina happened to be in Mentone—and thus convince Elisabeth that her departure would not leave Franz Joseph "alone and cheerless."

The two women even dieted together. Franz Joseph thought those scales which they both used punctiliously were an invention of the devil. Katherina complained that she was suffering with "galloping fat-ulence" (*galoppierende Fettsucht*). Elisabeth adopted the expression and warned Katherina not to take "turtle extract" (thyroid pills) ; it was bad for the heart.

Katherina worried about him with wifely solicitude. She cooked for him. She supplied him with expensive Havana cigars which he liked to smoke but which he refused to buy for himself. She was always thinking of gifts to give him, and one Christmas she sent him a mechanical nightingale, no doubt a reference to "The Emperor and the Nightingale." She made his workroom gay with the first violets of spring, and arranged with Max Schling (who in his young days was the court florist and later went to New York) to deliver a pot of four-leaf clovers when he needed luck politically. She gave him a small mirror, which he kept on his desk and on which she had had engraved in her handwriting: "Portrait de la personne que j'aime." He told her one day that the previous night he had returned late from a Court Ball and had been unable to sleep, being plagued by thirst. He did not want to wake his valet. She saw to it that from then on a bottle of iced champagne and a box of biscuits were placed in his bedroom.

However intimate they might have been in private, in public she behaved circumspectly, addressing him in no other way than "Your Majesty." When he visited she kept away her own friends, chiefly people of the theater. (Thimig was an exception.) But she regaled him with all kinds of gossip, not only of the theater but of her whole little world—what the porter said about the new taxes and how the hairdresser judged the new Ringstrasse buildings— and he used to listen with half an ear and smile. Though people tried to get at her by hook or crook, she was clever enough never to interfere in the running of the state, never to recommend anybody for a government post. "I do not believe she ever exercised the slightest political influence on the old monarch," wrote Count Lützow, even though "one frequently met in her salon young gentlemen dressed in cutaway and cylinder and a subservient mien." Once she asked Franz Joseph if he would award the Order of Merit to the famous comedian Alexander Girardi—the one who was the most successful interpreter of the leading role in Raimund's *The Spendthrift* and who popularized the flat straw hat called in Vienna "a Girardi." Franz Joseph replied, "Gladly, as soon as the proper minister under whose jurisdiction the matter falls has recommended such a distinction." He did nothing about it, and it took another year before the document came across his desk. At the beginning of their relationship, he did break his rule once and asked the director of the Burgtheater to renew her contract, after Katherina told him that she was having difficulty in the negotiations. Many years later—she was then forty-seven and perhaps a little too old to play youthful comic parts—she asked him again. He refused, and this caused a rupture between them. He would not give in—bureaucrat himself, he could not make himself interfere with the decision of another bureaucrat—and Katherina was duly pensioned off. Before she retired, she was given what she had so much wanted, the chance to play a tragic role. She wanted to play Ibsen; instead she appeared in the leading part of a serious drama by a new playwright: *The Heritage* by Arthur Schnitzler.

Financially he treated her well. And tactfully. Early—in 1887—he wrote her:

> The carnival is nearing its end; it demands fine outfits; such out-fits are expensive; you ought not to get into debt; and therefore I would be most thankful if you were to accept the enclosed little sum to help you defray the cost of your wardrobe. . . .

Two years later:

> I have arranged it so that after my death you will be free of [finan-cial] worries. Details I will tell you in person. . . .

She was given a yearly allowance which Kielmansegg estimated at 30,000 gulden (about $60,000). Would such an amount, along with the jewels and other gifts, not be a further indication that their relationship was more than friendship?

He disapproved of only two of her pastimes. She loved moun-tain climbing; he was afraid that some accident on some glacier was going to befall her. He begged her not to take risks. The other was a more serious matter: she was a passionate gambler, and when the mood seized her nothing could hold her back. He knew how many of his officers, bored to death in some Croatian village, were ruined by gambling debts; he knew the fever. He pleaded with her not to be a fool.

Nothing less imperial than the Franz Joseph–Schratt affair can be imagined. Here was no royal lover storming at the gates and commanding subjection. Here was no Lola Montez, no Madame de Pompadour taking into her hands the reins of a kingdom. From the letters emerges a picture of suburban smallness, a middle-aged man seated at a little table with a young *Hausfrau*, contentedly consuming a *Schnitzel* she had prepared. It was no *grande passion* but the sort of liaison the Viennese fiacre drivers could understand. Franz Joseph gained popularity by it; the Viennese called him Herr Schratt.

He never presumed on his privileged position. He never acted the King with her; on the contrary, toward her he showed a modesty unique in his relationships; neither Elisabeth nor his children experienced it. "Your letters are far superior to mine in style, spirit, and handwriting," he wrote her. Perhaps they were. He did not pretend to her; he wrote quite frankly to the actress about his lack of interest in what was the passion of her life, the theater. Even Duse's acting did not carry him away. He heard Verdi's *Falstaff* and lasted to the end: "Kindly marvel over this extraordinary accomplishment," he wrote Katherina. He took Valerie to *Die Walküre;* he stayed two hours "and took a nap from time to time." "I go to the opera as a sacrifice for my country. After all, I function only as an advertisement to sell tickets." An exhibition of paintings he saw at Cap Martin (probably of Impressionists) he described to her as "real junk."

The royal lover—if that is what he was—told his beloved that he was suffering from corns on his feet. He didn't want to have them cut, as he was afraid of blood poisoning, and wasn't she lucky not to have corns on *her* feet?

Elisabeth's mother herself once said that her daughter was "too uncomfortable a wife for Franz Joseph." When he changed companions he changed for one all too comfortable. His personality divided: one part of it, the bourgeois part, the one which so to speak wore slippers, became happier. The regal part, the one which wore boots and spurs and medals, stayed the same. Katherina did not try to change it. For that he was grateful, and the relationship endured. "My very much loved angel," he called her in a letter written when he was seventy years old.

5

Elisabeth, of whom it could almost be said that she "clung to the whistling mane of every wind," did come to rest for a time. She found that rest in the far away and the long ago, often the goals of fleeing spirits. She had read the *Iliad* so fervently that she knew almost all of it by heart. Now she eagerly followed every bit of news which came from Schliemann's camp: every turn of the spade seemed to unearth an astonishing marvel, large or small, gold or stone. She wanted to tread this "haunted holy ground," to see it all for herself. In a voice filled with emotion she quoted Byron's

> Fair Greece, sad relic of departed worth!
> Immortal, though no more; though fallen, great!

"My body is still here," she wrote in 1885, "but my soul has flown to Troy. If only I could go there!" She kept after Franz Joseph to put the *Miramar* at her disposal and, as usual, he acquiesced, though not without misgivings, since conditions in that part of the world and especially in Turkey and its Aegean islands had worsened. "The Empress intends to make a sea voyage to the Orient," wrote Rudolf to Latour, "at a moment which is most ineptly chosen." All the same, she departed, her first stop being a return visit to Corfu. She was once again enchanted with the island, and she conceived the idea of building a retreat for herself there. The Austrian consul to Corfu, Alexander von Warsberg, was a Greek scholar who had written a highly regarded book, *Ulyssean Landscapes;* with him Elisabeth explored the corners of Corfu and the neighboring islands. Here was the harbor in which, legend said, the angry Poseidon had turned a ship to stone, and there was Santa Maura where Sappho died. The yacht sailed on, and Elisabeth visited Mykonos, Delos, and Santorini.

Just before the *Miramar* was to steam up the Dardanelles and to Smyrna, Elisabeth received a telegram from Franz Joseph telling her that because of political differences the Austrian ship could not penetrate into Turkish waters or land at Smyrna. But she could still visit Schliemann's excavation. She saw what she had longed to see: the frightening gold masks, the miraculous wine cups, the stern stone reliefs which had emerged from the earth. She gazed at the palpable mementos of the *Iliad* and stood weeping before a mound of earth which was supposed to be the grave of Achilles. She apostrophized the spot in a poem. What was it to her that Russia was once again fomenting trouble in the Balkans, that the Czar was behaving as if Bulgaria were a state owing him tribute, that he had sent a Russian general there to arrest Bulgaria's Prince Alexander and put himself in charge, that Moscow still had fixed its sights on Constantinople and that Franz Joseph had to confer with Bismarck and with a sharp needle sew the international fabric which seemed forever to be coming apart?

The captain of the *Miramar* decided that notwithstanding the orders from Vienna he had to drop anchor at Smyrna to take on coal. The rumor of Elisabeth's being on board spread through the city, the Austrian consul threw himself into his gala suit, the people assembled at the harbor, the municipal band started to play, one and all wanted to catch a glimpse of the Empress. She arranged to have her hairdresser, a Frau Freifalik, don a festive costume and, seated in the official landing boat of the yacht, travel up and down the harbor to receive the plaudits and the cheers of the public—while Elisabeth herself, with a companion, dressed in simple clothes, took a little bark, landed in the city, and recognized by no one went sightseeing and shopping to her heart's content. From Smyrna she went to Rhodes, to Cyprus, and to Port Said. Then she returned to Gödöllö. There she was again plagued by rheumatic pains which threw her into such despondency that she contemplated suicide.

Valerie was growing up. She was in love. The young man of her choice was the reasonably attractive but not particularly distinguished Archduke Franz Salvator of the Tuscan branch of the Habsburgs. It made Elisabeth feel old to see her youngest ready to marry. She was going to lose her—it was the end of intimacy between the two, since separation was inevitable—but however Valerie's marriage was to turn out, Elisabeth determined never, under any circumstances, to become a mother-in-law, to be a Sophie, and she said so to Valerie. Yet she could not quite suppress her possessive instinct toward the one child she loved. A sad scene must have been played between the two, which Valerie remembered in her diary: "I really love only you," Elisabeth said to her. "When you leave me, my life will be finished. . . . One loves in this way only once in a lifetime. . . . You had to be my own, my one and only child, my treasure on whom nobody had any claim but myself. All the capacity to love which my closed heart possessed I concentrated on you."[19] Once more she sought release from her unhappiness in poetry. Her poems were given to printers sworn to secrecy and were set in type; a few copies were printed, and these were locked up by Elisabeth in an iron casket. Virtually nobody knew of their existence; Valerie did.

Hither and yon she was driven, or rather she drove herself, to a remote spot in Hungary, again to London, to Gastein, back to Corfu, to English watering places. Sir Compton Mackenzie remembered that as a child in Bournemouth he saw a tall slender woman dressed in brown alpaca sitting on a beach alone, "with a small lace parasol, staring out to sea, then writing, writing, staring out to sea again." (He told this to Edward Crankshaw.) In 1887, she journeyed to Ithaca, the island of Ulysses, every stone of which she explored. "My fatigue was greater than any I had ever experienced in my travels to the Orient, which were hardly easy ones," Warsberg, whom she had bidden to accompany her, noted in his diary.

On December 24 of that year, Elisabeth reached her fiftieth birthday. It was the year that Franz Joseph's relationship with Katherina Schratt first became firm. Elisabeth was still incredibly young-looking, her face unwrinkled, her figure as lithe as ever. She could no longer indulge her passion for riding; she now threw herself into a passion for learning. She studied Shakespeare in English and began to learn modern as well as ancient Greek. Her first teacher was one recommended by Warsberg. This Professor Romanos was followed by other teachers, chief among them Konstatin Christomanos, a small, hunchbacked, sensitive, and poetic young man, whose dark disposition was in tune with his pupil's, and who trotted after her wherever she went. He was a homosexual. He wrote no fewer than three books of reminiscences of his life with the Empress, to whom he was utterly devoted. Elisabeth had a way of drawing such devotion to her. For hours the two of them walked up and down in the garden, Elisabeth declaiming Greek sentences and Christomanos correcting her. Eventually he became too officious for her taste, quarreled with members of her retinue, and was dismissed. Yet he managed to teach her so well— or she managed to learn so well—that her knowledge of Greek was profound enough for her to be able to translate Heine into classic Greek and *Hamlet, King Lear,* and *The Tempest* into modern Greek, surely an astonishing feat.

From her passion for Greece sprang her plan to build her palace on Corfu. She worked on the project for several years. She selected as the site Homer's "wide-viewed prospect" on a hill which was Corfu's highest point. She commissioned a sculpture of "the dying Achilles" to stand in the marble entrance hall. On the ceiling Franz Matsch[20] painted a huge fresco, *Achilles Triumphant*. She called the place the Achilleion. She filled it with furniture in antique style, marble putti, stucco reliefs, modern bathrooms, electric lights which used bulbs in the shape of fruits, surrounded it with terraces which afforded an unobstructed view of the ocean, and guarded her privacy by a large garden. The Homeric dolphin became the insignia of the palace: towels, napkins, glasses, dishes were marked with the Austrian imperial crown above which a dolphin rode. There is but one word to describe the Achilleion: *Kitsch*. It is as falsely Greek as the Vienna Parliament, and worse in its pretentiousness. It cost millions, and Franz Joseph directed that the cost be covered by his private fortune and not by public funds. When it was finished, Elisabeth took but brief joy in it. Presently she wearied of it and asked Franz Joseph to have it sold. So capricious a decision, he wrote her, would create a scandal: "Valerie and her no doubt numerous children won't starve, even without the money" such a sale would bring. The matter was dropped. Elisabeth resumed her life of wandering.

Caricature of Franz Joseph which appeared in *Vanity Fair* in 1877

CHAPTER IX

"Muddling Through"

TELL ME WHO your ministers are and I'll tell you what kind of a ruler you are—that surely can apply to Franz Joseph, during whose reign so long a line of politicians served that one is tempted to exclaim, "What! Will the line stretch out to the crack of doom?" The line did stretch out to the crack of Austria's doom.

These men, these prime servitors of the state, can tell us something of the mind of the man who appointed them. Their number may suggest the complexity of the problem, but their quality indicates that Franz Joseph did not feel comfortable sitting in conference with too powerful or too positive a personality. Felix Schwarzenberg had been such a personality, but that was in the early days.

Since the time of Schwarzenberg, and though the prime ministers ran a wider gamut than from A to B—wider than Andrassy to Bach—not one of them dominated the Emperor and not one of the men guiding Austrian policy could have been termed a genius of statesmanship. Wilhelm I had a tough will of his own and hardly looked on Bismarck as a bosom friend; yet with all the differences between the two, Wilhelm enabled Bismarck to function. There was no Bismarck in Austria, no Disraeli, no Gladstone, a man whom Victoria liked no better than Wilhelm liked Bismarck but whose contribution she valued; and as to Clemenceau—anybody as fierce as "The Tiger" would not have lasted a month in the Hofburg. Franz Joseph was like a star actor who mistakenly surrounds himself with a cast of less than stellar caliber. What prompted him was not conceit but conviction: no man must be so tall as to be able to throw a shadow on the crown.

It was understood that his officials were to preserve a certain amount of anonymity, though inevitably the ablest among them became known to the people. "It was understood"—that impersonal grammatical construction was widely used by the Austrian officials, their communications reading "It is declared . . . ," "It is forbidden . . . ," "It is decreed. . . ." The "I" and the "We" belonged to Franz Joseph.

It is undoubtedly an exaggeration to say with Redlich that "Franz Joseph literally never saw or listened to a free and independent man." Yet ministers and ambassadors, generals and judges, were watched—and they knew it. Once a week Franz Joseph granted a private audience to Baron Johann Kempen, Chief of Police (in the 1850s). Franz Joseph, though he did not spy or pry in the common practice of the dictator, though he did not precisely encourage surveillance, did nothing to stop it.

One could not describe him as dictatorial—he was, in his middle years, too kindly for such an appellation—nor would the word "dogmatic" fit him exactly; yet he ruled by dogma as dogma ruled him. He tolerated dissent up to a point, allowing Socialists or Germanophiles to rake the ground, as long as he sat fast, his principles indivisible, inviolate. Censorship and secret scrutiny existed, yet the newspapers were allowed considerable latitude and they could scold and chide and turn thumbs down so long as those thumbs, smeared with printer's ink, did not touch the throne. If "Denmark's a prison," then was Austria one, a goodly one in which the confines, wards, and dungeons were often fitted with silk and eiderdown.

He was now so self-enclosed that he preferred writing directives to speaking them. He wrote briefly, in a precise script, on sheets of plain paper which he would sometimes tear in half, frugally to save the other half. At the end of the day the wastepaper basket would be collected and its contents burned; it is a testimony to the loyalty of Franz Joseph's valets that no memorandum he wanted to dispose of has ever appeared. As impersonal as this procedure was, so was his behavior at table. His adjutant Albert Margutti relates that loud laughter was censored by a reproving look and that he found no pleasure in "funny anecdotes" which some inexperienced soul mistakenly thought he ought to relate to enliven the dinner. Franz Joseph felt that this was "a disregard of the nimbus of the ruler."

And yet—we have seen that with Schratt he was easygoing, amenable, even humble, showing a modesty which went beyond the *"politesse des rois."* Nor was this modesty wholly prompted by a fear of losing his friend. Was it not rather the desire to unbend felt by a man who found it difficult to unbend? He carried his pride in a large coffer; yet there were moments, though they were rare, when he would dearly have wished to travel with lighter luggage. In some corner of his soul was hid a longing for an iridescent lightness, the frivolous touch, the irresponsible. Why else did he feel drawn to such jaunty and debonair men as Moritz Esterhazy or Beust or Milan of Serbia or (later) Berchtold?[1]

Born to the Viennese tradition and steeped in it, Franz Joseph, who became a symbol of *Alt Wien*, nevertheless shared little of the light side of the city. It could not be said of him, as it was said of the Viennese, that they considered "the situation desperate but not serious." Not by his position alone, but by his disposition, his psychological constitution, he leaned toward problems and consequently problems moved toward him. While his citizens sang songs at new-wine outings, Franz Joseph read dry documents. When a Viennese sat down to his breakfast and perused his morning paper, while he drank his coffee and ate his *Kipfel,* he was aware that the Emperor had been long awake, taking care of "everything." He represented both a shining deity moving in a remote empyrean and a man who was a neighbor. It was a comfortable Viennese paradox, and that is how Franz Joseph wanted it. Once in a while, however, and then only dimly, he envied the ability of some of his subjects to float on top of the day. And his governing sometimes veered, now assuming a laissez-faire stance, now one of stubborn harshness.

His personal courage was beyond question. Assassination was an ever present specter; he had the recent example of Alexander II before him, as well as an attempt on the life of Wilhelm I, and surely he remembered Lincoln's assassination in 1865. No guard could be tight enough to protect the life of a sovereign. In 1882 the five-hundred-year celebration of Triest's belonging to Austria was being celebrated; Franz Joseph and Elisabeth journeyed there, and just in time the police discovered that a certain Gugliemo Oberdank was planning to kill them. Later, Czech fanatics planted a bomb under a railway bridge on the road from Prague to Reichenberg over which Franz Joseph was to travel. Yet Franz Joseph went about practically unguarded. He stood on the open balcony, quite exposed. He simply did not think of death, not death by force, and rode and spoke and opened ceremonials for any Hungarian or Pole or madman to fix him, gorgeously caparisoned, within his gunsight. He made the necessary speeches in Prague or Klagenfurt, and he had enough self-critical judgment to know that he was a terrible orator. "For once I spoke pretty well," he confided to Katherina Schratt, "without a prompter and without getting stuck." The Viennese told the story (apocryphal) of his reading a speech at a birthday celebration for Wilhelm II. Nearing the end of the speech, he read, "And now, ladies and gentlemen, I ask you to join me in a triple salute: Kaiser Wilhelm, hurrah! hurrah!"—long pause while he turned the sheet of paper—"hurrah!"

He became bored by all those functions he had to attend. He wrote to Elisabeth and Katherina a phrase which became standard with him: "Aussi möcht i." It is low Viennese dialect, translatable as "Lemme outa here." All the same, he attended. And he never got over his love of ceremony. When his daughter Gisela, a princess of Bavaria since her marriage, dined with him, Franz Joseph appeared wearing the star of the Bavarian order of St. Hubert and the entire retinue had to wear their Bavarian medals. One night he fell ill and his personal physician had to be called in the middle of the night. The doctor threw on a dressing gown and rushed to Franz Joseph's bedside. Franz Joseph could hardly talk because of the pain, but he managed to stammer "Full-dress suit" (*Frack*) to the doctor.

Though he was distant and seemed unconcerned with ordinary human troubles, he could summon pity and compassion. A dreadful calamity befell Vienna on December 8, 1881. That night, in the large Ringtheater, the second performance of Offenbach's new opera, *The Tales of Hoffmann,* was to be given. A fire broke out on the stage, and the stage manager in a panic shut off all the gaslights, thinking vaguely that would help the situation. The whole house was suddenly plunged into darkness. What followed has long been regarded as one of the worst holocausts in the history of such disasters:

It was a quarter to seven when the first spectators precipitated themselves through the main portal on to the street, emitting cries of terror. "Fire!" Already clouds of smoke were billowing from the front windows of the fourth story. The gas jets in the interior of the theater had been extinguished, and the audience, most of which had assembled, particularly in the galleries, found themselves suddenly plunged into darkness, while everybody, pale and aghast, rushed to the exits. The panic became uncontrollable. People appeared at the windows of the first and second stories imploring help. On the street a crowd assembled, calling the names of relatives who they knew had gone to the theater. A wild tumult ensued above and below. "Wait! Wait! The fire brigade is coming! Wait!" In the meantime, the fire broke through the roof and leaped into the sky with brilliant shoots which bathed the infernal scene in a yellow light. Finally, after ten minutes which seemed an eternity, the signals of the fire brigade could be heard. Pump after pump, water wagon after water wagon, and other rescue apparatus were drawn up. Dire seconds elapsed until the tarpaulin was unfolded. Eighty-four persons who were standing on the balcony jumped down, one after the other, women and children quivering with fear, hesitating at first and finally forced by necessity to jump. At half past eleven the whole interior of the theater was burned out and the caved-in remains formed a huge mass of embers.

. . . In the galleries only those persons could save themselves who were fleet of foot and were familiar with the stairs. Among those who remained, a desperate battle for salvation sprang up.

. . . Incessantly corpses were carried out of the house until half past one. They were clumps, carried by hospital servants to the Hotel Austria, three or four persons heaped on one litter. At the moment of going to press, 104 corpses had been counted. They were

The 1881 fire in the Ringtheater (after a drawing by Theodor Breitwieser)

transported to the Allgemeine Krankenhaus. The last corpses which were removed from the burning theater were glued one to the other; indubitably the unfortunate ones fought with one another to reach a way out.[2]

At the end the dead numbered not 104, but 384. From a nearby window Anton Bruckner watched the conflagration; it made so deep an impression on him that for the rest of his life he had a morbid fear of fire; even the lighting of a match disturbed him. Franz Joseph hurried back from Gödöllö to initiate the investigation into the fire's origin and to determine what solace could be offered the families of the dead. The Viennese loudly blamed Taaffe as the guilty one, for not having ascertained that safety regulations were properly observed. The press editorialized in vehement words—"irresponsible," "incompetent," "venal"— and Rudolf accused Taaffe. After punctilious examination, Franz Joseph exonerated him. It appeared, however, that the director of the theater, Franz Jauner, was guilty of carelessness—he had not seen to it that the pails intended to contain water had been filled (not that it would have made much difference)—and he was condemned to prison. He had recently been ennobled; he was stripped of his title and the directorship of the theater. King Albert of Saxony pleaded for Jauner. Franz Joseph answered that "the extent and horror of the catastrophe as well as Jauner's carelessness demanded a punishment which, according to general and to my feeling, could not be adequately encompassed by any fine."[3] Two weeks after the Ringtheater disaster, Franz Joseph announced that he had ordered the building of a large edifice, to be known as the House of Atonement (*Sühnehaus*). It was to be an apartment house with a chapel at its core. It was to be paid for entirely from Franz Joseph's private fortune, and the rental income donated to charity. The house was built, dedicated by Franz Joseph in 1886, and stood as a memorial, until on April 11, 1945, it was hit by a bomb and—a grim example of lightning striking twice—burned completely. Nothing is left of it.

Two further actions resulted from the Ringtheater fire: the major theaters of the world immediately improved their fire regulations—the "safety curtain" came into use—and a new and highly efficient "volunteer fire brigade" was organized in Vienna. *The*

Tales of Hoffmann became a bad-luck opera in Viennese superstition, and it was years before it was given again.

2

However posterity may admire Franz Joseph's milder qualities, as a ruler he must be charged with a tragic fault. Therein lay the seed of Austria's disintegration, there the kernel of destruction. Disintegration was not inevitable, the empire might have continued to exist; but he would have had to change, he would have had to learn that the world had changed, he would have had to embrace the concept of self-determination. The least of us find it difficult to change ourselves; how much more difficult it is for a ruler. Could he have done so? It is an idle question, as it is ironic to know that whatever the sufferings the Czechs, the Poles, and the Hungarians had to endure under his rule, they were plunged into worse once a cynical and unscrupulous communist tyranny took over. What would Elisabeth think were she to see how gray, wrinkled, and pallid her beloved Budapest has become?

The biographer must not speculate; he must tell the story. The fact is that Franz Joseph continued to believe that if he would only be sufficiently Habsburgian, the lion would lie down with the lamb, the man in Linz with the man in Lemberg. Continuity, continuity—he cultivated that ancient plant even as he saw the seeds of discontinuity sprout in his "sea-walled garden, the whole land." Like Richard II's gardener, Franz Joseph's gardener could have said (had he been a Shakespearean spokesman) :

> "O, what pity is it
> That he had not so trimm'd and dress'd his land
> As we this garden!"

He would not "dress" his land. Nor would he deracinate sick roots and plant new ones. The wish for self-government seemed to him a futile wish. There was no home away from home, Vienna being every Austrian's home. Weakening centralization meant weakening everybody's lot. Why did the Czechs and the Slovenes want it? To improve living conditions? He understood the necessity for ameliorating the conditions of the poor, but that could be accomplished only by the father figure, the one and only sovereign. Of what use were all those debates in Parliament? A lot of impolite noise. Indeed, Parliament never played a significant role in Austrian life, and that was due to Franz Joseph's purposeful weakening of it. As a youth he had disliked the Hungarians: he did so no more. He was not interested in the Hungarians as Hungarians—or in the Poles or the Czechs—but as subjects of the crown. They were all subjects, and though he himself was thoroughly Viennese, he harbored no racial prejudices. Nor was he in the least anti-Semitic. There was nothing wrong with the Jews, as long as they paid their taxes and as long as the Rothschilds and the Mendelssohns invested in Austrian industry. (He had hardly met a Jew, except members of the Rothschild family.) The only thing which made the Jews less desirable was their inclination to become intellectuals. Intellectuals made poor soldiers. Franz Joseph was not so stupid as to sympathize with an anti-Semite of the period who pronounced that "science is what one Jewish writer copies from another," but he was almost as indifferent to science, or rather abstract exploration, as he was indifferent to music or painting. When Richard Krafft-Ebing, professor in Graz, published his *Psychopathia sexualis* in 1886, the importance of which was at once recognized, and the book was called to Franz Joseph's attention, he thought that it was about time that somebody wrote a new Latin grammar.

He never opened any of the new books written by his contemporaries, not even those which made pleasanter reading than Krafft-Ebing. Whatever little leisure he allowed himself he devoted to hunting, exchanging his uniform for a pair of lederhosen—rumor had it that his valet wore them first to "age" them—and a green comfortable jacket. The villa that was built for him in Ischl was in effect a hunting lodge. It is one of the most tasteless residences ever built for a king. He loved it. The walls are covered with the antlers of the stags he shot, hundreds of them, all neatly tagged with the date; the furniture is brown and lifeless; the paintings of cows and horses and landscapes would be knocked down for a pittance at some side-street auction if they were ever put on sale; and the most prominent work of art in the central room which faces the garden is a bronze group depicting a fox hunt, with a very dead fox, indeed. This monstrosity was a gift from Queen Victoria. The gardens are as beautiful as the Kaiservilla is ugly; exotic trees from distant parts of the world were planted there. Later Franz Joseph had a large swimming pool built for his grandchildren; he enjoyed seeing them splash about.

He had no idea what the swimming pool cost, or anything else. Katherina Schratt once showed him an emerald ring she had bought. "Your Majesty, guess what this cost." "Five gulden?" "Five gulden!" "Well, then, ten." "Ten? It cost two thousand gulden." "Two *thousand?* A very good bargain!"[4]

The death of his uncle, the old Emperor Ferdinand, in 1875 made Franz Joseph the sole heir of Ferdinand's fortune. This, according to Franz Joseph himself, amounted to a capital of 14 million gulden ($28 million), which produced a yearly income of a million gulden. These were figures to him, unreal, though useful in paying Elisabeth's expenses.

On the other hand, he did know what the army cost. Whatever the amount he considered it a bargain. His affection for it was no longer motivated by much hope that it could conquer a strip of Russia or reacquire an Italian plain. It was there to help him hold the realm together. He loved the men in uniform because they were in his mind a symbol of order, degree, rank, command easily distinguishable.

> Take but degree away, untune that string,
> And, hark! what discord follows.

Franz Joseph would have understood Ulysses' discourse in *Troilus and Cressida.* He gave everybody his correct title and felt as at home in an army bivouac as in Katherina's salon.

3

To return now to the procession of ministers: After Beust was dismissed in 1871, a cabinet under Count Karl Hohenwart was formed. He was a mild, cautious, and idealistic cleric who earnestly attempted to guide the monarchy toward federalization on the United States model. He was supported by A. Schäffle, a forward-looking and knowledgeable economist and sociologist who spoke up bravely and said that the liberals were not always right, the Germans not invariably superior, and that the "so-called inferior races [the Slavic races], whom it was the fashion to ridicule, could create a higher culture and produce more talented and interesting personalities than I had thought possible." That tore it. The Austro-German liberals screamed that they were being sacrificed, the Vienna newspapers ranted that western Austria was being subjected to the Slavs. All the same, Franz Joseph made an honest effort to reconcile the Czechs to a union and to give them equal status by declaring that he was willing to take the coronation oath, as he had done in Hungary, thereby turning the Dual Monarchy into a tripartite state, the third part being "the Kingdom of Bohemia." That declaration gave the Hungarians a pain in the solar plexus, specifically Andrassy, who argued that ceding to Czech demands would cause Hungarian revolts, weaken the army, debilitate finance, and make confusion more confounded. A "Slavicized Austria" was an impossibility. As Franz Joseph was pondering these warring opinions, the Slavs in southern Austria revolted and the military had to be called on to put down the insurrection. Franz Joseph, astonished and angry, changed his mind. Hohenwart was dismissed—his ministry lasted but five months—to be succeeded briefly by Prince Adolph Auersperg, who moved with rash revenge against the Czechs, arresting Prague journalists and confiscating copies of Franz Joseph's own edict, circulated only a short time previously, in which he had acknowledged "the rights of the Bohemian kingdom." In turn the Czechs boycotted the next parliamentary elections—and on went the tugging, using the force which was needed for the nation's weal to inflame nationalistic woes.

When Andrassy took over, Franz Joseph did have a minister more confident, clever, and flexible than his predecessors. Yet this rider from the open fields was not unprejudiced; Hungary was his home and the Hungarians could do no wrong. He did not want to hear a word about *his* countrymen suppressing Slovenes or Croations living in Hungary. Nevertheless, Andrassy's mentality was broad enough for his work to prove beneficial: peace, friendship with Germany—that above all—better relations with England, avoidance of open conflict with Russia, were his aims in exterior policy, conciliation of nationalistic squabbles the goal of his interior program. There was one difficulty: Franz Joseph did not like him. Andrassy's high charm wove a sufficient spell to skirt severe quarrels, but Franz Joseph could not accept him fully, having accepted him in the first place through Elisabeth's advocacy.

The Prime Minister he came as near to liking and trusting as any was Count Eduard Taaffe. He had all the qualifications which would make him appeal to Franz Joseph's character: he came from a family of aristocrats which could trace their lineage back to the dawn; his career had been a step-by-step climb on the official ladder—he had been successively governor of Salzburg and Upper Austria, then Minister of Defense and of the Interior—he was a stickler for etiquette, even his handwriting being neat and exact; he was in no sense a "political philosopher" and avoided using theoretical phrases; he worked for the day and let the morrow be sufficient unto itself; he combined Viennese mockery with German earnestness, confronting each problem with the saying, "It can be done," while he pretended that he took nothing seriously; he could muster a smile for virtually everybody and be everybody's friend, so that the churchmen found him sympathetic to their cause while he helped to detach Austria from the Vatican, and the German nationalists thought that he understood them while the Hungarians and the Poles regarded him as their spokesman at court; he listened with equal attentiveness to the War Minister who wanted his budget increased and the Finance Minister who predicted bankruptcy; and even the anti-Semites supported him, though one of his chief advisers was a Jew named Blumenstock. In short, he was a moderator, a conciliator, a bargainer, an expert at soothing and smoothing, whose favorite proverb was, "It is never eaten as hot as it is cooked."

Taaffe's ministry lasted for fourteen years, a long time. He was able to enclose the heterogeneous interests in a ring which came to be known as "Taaffe's Iron Ring," within whose circumference factions fought and scratched and threatened—without, however, breaking through the ring. Taaffe's fourteen years—1879 to 1893—

were years of diplomacy. The opposing elements were held in check. That is all: they were held in check, they were, so to speak, bargained underground. Taaffe called his policy *"fortwursteln."* It is Viennese slang, denoting the ability to make compromises, to "muddle through." Franz Joseph was satisfied. Elisabeth, who did not like Taaffe, was not. She who rarely ever criticized her husband's policy thought that Franz Joseph had become "a tool in the hands of an acrobat, used by him [Taaffe] as a balancing rod." She still longed for her Andrassy, who had retired at the beginning of Taaffe's tenure (1879), prideful as ever. He said that he would rather leave the stage of the world still a star than to play secondary roles in a provincial theater. He returned to his estates in Hungary and from there watched Taaffe grapple with the problems. Sometimes he wrote Elisabeth a warm letter and sometimes she answered. As a wealthy magnate he kept open house and entertained visitors in glittering style. Occasionally he mounted his horse and fled into solitude. He wrote a fair and judicious history of the Hungarian Compromise, and died in 1890, honored by all of Hungary. Elisabeth mourned him for the rest of her life.

4

On March 13, 1881, Czar Alexander II was riding in the court sled when a bomb was thrown at it. Several of his retinue were severely wounded; the Czar wanted to go to their aid, rushed out, and became an easy target for a second bomb, hurled by a woman. He was killed on the spot. Franz Joseph grieved over the death of a monarch, even though he had not been his friend, but then he said, "Perhaps it will be easier to negotiate with his successor." It made little difference to him that this successor, Alexander III, was a simian, ignorant, drunken tyrant who encouraged pogroms, stifled the universities, burned books, slept on a heap of furs from which he made his own bed, and would soon die of alcoholism. Franz Joseph began to negotiate an alliance with Russia and Germany. The negotiations were successful, and the "Secret Three-Emperor League" (Wilhelm I, Alexander III, and Franz Joseph)

was signed in 1881 and renewed in 1884. To bolster this agreement, the historic "Triple Alliance" between Austria, Germany,
and Italy was forged the following year, thanks to Bismarck's
expert hand. When in 1887 peace was once more in danger,
Austria quarreling with Russia over its interference in Bulgaria,
and Franz Joseph was beginning to mobilize his army, it was
Bismarck once more who saved the situation through the famous
"Reinsurance Treaty" with Russia. Bismarck wanted no trouble
over the Balkans. Had war broken out there, Germany, by the
terms of the Triple Alliance, would have been obliged to come to
Austria's aid against Russia. Bismarck had said years before that
the whole Balkans were not worth the bones of a single Pomer-
anian grenadier. He was willing to cede Russia a certain amount
of influence in the Balkans if he could avoid an armed clash.
Hence the Reinsurance Treaty with all its elaborate quid pro quo.
How complicated it all was! Oversimplified it meant that Russia
promised neutrality toward Germany unless Germany attacked
France. In return, Germany promised neutrality toward Russia
unless Russia attacked Austria.

Finally it seemed as if the peasant could till his field without
fear. The various pieces of paper on which the various treaties
were penned seemed to form themselves into one word: peace. Yet
the paper contained the devil's flaw: when one piece fell away the
whole tore. Bismarck was dismissed by Wilhelm II. The Kaiser of
the crippled arm, grandson of William I, "dropped the pilot" (all
Europe stared at the famous cartoon) ; and one of the first acts of
Wilhelm II's new Chancellor, Leo Caprivi, was to repudiate the
Reinsurance Treaty. That drove Russia toward France and England and left Austria and Germany between what Edward Crankshaw has described as "the jaws of a monstrous trap," Russia
forming one jaw, France and England the other. The trap

> was to crush the body of Europe just thirty-five years later, destroy-
> ing the grandson of the Germany signatory, the nephew of the Aus-
> trian signatory, the grandson of the Russian Tsar. Designed by two
> men, one a man of genius, the other a statesman of very considerable
> parts, for the sole purpose of maintaining the peace and the integ-
> rity of Europe, signed by two monarchs, also desiring peace, but
> above all honour, it contributed more than any other single act to

the greatest holocaust in history and, at a later stage, to the super-session of Europe as the centre of the universe by the two young giants, America and Russia, who, even before they could relish their remarkable translation, themselves discovered to their untold cha-grin that each, separately, was unable to command a world which also contained Africa and Asia.[5]

Even before Franz Joseph tried to improve Austria's exterior position, he continued to work with his Prime Minister to amelio-rate domestic conditions. He turned his attention once more to Bohemia.

Taaffe's renewed attempt to create something like the Hun-garian Compromise with the Czechs ran into many difficulties, because not only did the Austro-Germans rail against it, but the Czechs themselves were divided into young and old factions. Franz Joseph insisted that the Czechs be placated and used the "Old Czechs," who included the landed aristocrats loyal to him, to hold the "Young Czechs," the hotspurs, in line. Czech deputies were persuaded to attend the Parliament sitting in the autumn of 1879; they had been absent for sixteen years. With their help, Taaffe pushed through the "Language Ordinance," which made Czech equivalent to German in its use in official communications be-tween Vienna and Prague. This was a considerable step forward. It helped young Czechs obtain jobs in government bureaus, and, in turn, this aided the task of administering Bohemia. Up to then government officials, or most of them, spoke only German. As Gustav Strakosch-Grassmann, an Austrian historian, wrote:

> The lack of acquaintance with country and people of those officials who are sent into the provinces to administer them is a mat-ter of much consequence. Without any or with only the scantiest knowledge of country and people, without a knowledge of the lan-guage, but with much self-assertion (one must make the acquain-tance of these elegant gentlemen in the political administration who with so much poise always play the fine cavalier and emphasize their superiority), the young and older representatives of the politi-cal authorities walked into the provinces. Behind their glittering and supple appearance there was nothing but bottomless ignorance.[6]

Now Bohemia had at least a few administrators who under-stood the conditions of the province. Other benefits followed:

because Czech became a "respectable" language, the University of Prague increased the chairs from which Czech was spoken and new local institutions of learning were opened.

Yet by that law of perversity which postulates that every enlightening reform creates a shadow side, the Language Reform was used by the militant Czechs to suppress the Germans who were living in Bohemia. Belligerent both, they could not come to terms. The Germans called the Czechs "snakes," the Czechs called the Germans "lice," the Germans thought the Czechs ignoramuses, the Czechs thought the Germans philosophic rogues. The Germans flirted with Bismarck, who would have none of them, and the Czechs ranted about secession. "Bohemia is being sucked dry by Austria, which resembles a vampire," shouted one of the extremists, Edward Grégr. The United States Consulate in Vienna reported to Washington in 1886:

> The irrepressible parliamentary conflict between the slavery and the antislavery parties [in the U.S.] was not waged with more acrimony and determination than the political strife now in full progress between the German and the Bohemian subjects of the Austrian empire. There is not a political move on the European chessboard which to the participants in this internal warfare seems of any importance whatever in comparison with the great and overwhelming question whether the German-Austrians or the Czech-Austrians shall obtain predominance in the Empire.

Franz Joseph did not lose patience with either faction. Though he called the young Czechs "queer customers" and the Bohemian Germans "presumptuous," he continued unshaken in his belief that only by holding on to Vienna could either side manage to exist. Would the Czechs prefer staying put to being swallowed by either Germany or Russia? Taaffe persevered and proposed to accommodate Bohemia into two judicial zones. Whereupon the young Czech deputies, insisting on controlling the whole judiciary, seized the manuscripts of speeches prepared by the German deputies and tore them up; books, inkstands, rulers were hurled through the hall, fistfights broke out, a noose was placed on a statue of Franz Joseph, and the students marched in Prague singing the "Marseillaise" and the Russian national anthem.

Yet in spite of all the difficulties, some kind of truce was achieved. What helped was the growing business prosperity in Bohemia. The textile industry, shoe manufacturing, the production of good and cheap china and glass, sugar refineries, breweries at Pilsen and Budweis, mining of coal and graphite, machine shops, the largest of them at Pilsen being headed by Emil Skoda, combined to turn Bohemia into one of the most vital areas of the Empire. Workers were still poorly paid and many emigrated to the New World, while young women sought employment as cooks or nursemaids in Vienna. Still, even the industrial laborer's lot gradually improved and the middle class became stouter and wealthier.

Prague University showed new vigor and produced a number of fine scholars, among them Thomas Masaryk. He had studied in Vienna, published a number of sociological tracts, and at the age of thirty-two was appointed professor of philosophy at Prague University. He opened to his students the essentials of Western thought, being catholic in his appreciation of diverse philosophical systems and sensitive to the contributions made not only by German minds, Kant or Leibnitz, but by Locke, Hume, Montaigne, Pascal. He was an enthusiastic democrat, though his enthusiasm was clear-eyed and realistic. He married an American girl and discoursed often on the ideals of Jefferson. He had courage, intellectual honesty, and practical sense, despising hyperbole and florid talk. He examined the old Königinhof Manuscripts on the basis of which Czech scholars had proved that Czech literary culture antedated German culture and proved that the manuscripts were a forgery. The Czech "patriots" fulminated that he had been bribed by German interests to derogate his country's heritage. He held his ground—"Our pride must not be based on a lie"—and he was eventually shown to be right.

He demonstrated even greater courage when he defended a Jew, Leopold Hilsner, who was accused of murdering a Czech girl to obtain blood for ritual services. These accusations of ritual murders were lies hoary with the hatred of ages. In the eighteenth century in Poland, for example, between 1710 and 1760, nine trials for this crime are recorded and the accused were tortured,

flayed alive, or impaled on a stick. The Jews had appealed to Pope
Benedict XIV, who had ordered an investigation. The papal
nuncio in Warsaw had reported that in no case was there any
evidence of guilt. Yet once again, at the end of the "enlightened"
nineteenth century, the ritual murder canard reared its head and
many people, and not ony illiterate peasants, believed it. Masaryk
examined the evidence and proved the charge against Hilsner
false. The best he could accomplish, however, was to commute
Hilsner's death sentence to life imprisonment,[7] and Masaryk was
persecuted by his own countrymen. For a time he could not give
his lectures at the university, the police had to barricade the streets
leading to his house, and his boy had to go to school flanked by
two constables. Masaryk battled on, a moderate and modest patriot,
became a member of the Austrian Parliament, and with straightforward eloquence promoted the Bohemian cause. He never
ceased to plead that the Germans living in Bohemia needed to
unite with the Czechs, that their enmity was no more reasonable
than a child's tantrum. At the age of sixty-eight he was elected the
first president of the Czechoslovak Republic. He died in 1937,
eighty-seven years old.

Franz Joseph's treatment of the Poles in Galicia followed a
course similar to his policy in Bohemia; he approved plans for new
railroads, building factories, and improvement in the production
of petroleum. He particularly pleased the Poles by elevating the
Archbishop of Cracow, a popular and kindly priest, to the rank of
a Prince. In the south of the Monarchy (Carniola and Carinthia)
Taaffe made shrewd concessions to the Slovenes, which included
declaring *their* language too an official language.

5

Every community leads a double life, the life to satisfy the day and
the life to plan the morrow. In the Vienna of the 1880s the separation between the two was marked. The tourist arriving at the
Grand Hotel experienced the proverbial Vienna: he could hear

Johann Strauss, now turning sixty, his hair and imposing mustache dyed black, married to his third wife, forever jotting down musical ideas on loose sheets of paper, on menus, laundry lists, and bedsheets, working all night and sleeping much of the morning—he could hear this worshiped musician, who with all the worship was prone to fits of depression, conduct in the Prater. He could, if he managed to obtain a ticket, see a performance of *The Gypsy Baron,* on which Strauss had worked for two years, while he had composed *Die Fledermaus* in forty-three nights; this operetta, written for Girardi, satirized the yokel from Hungary (Zsupan), and Girardi was superb in it. He could attend one of Pauline Metternich's exuberant "Prater festivals," a riot of flowers, decorated equipages, and dancing couples; in the Prater he could enjoy Viennese cooking at several new restaurants, including one managed by a Herr and Frau Sacher. These Prater festivals were given for charitable purposes, and the first of them proved so popular that 268,000 tickets were bought, by about a quarter of Vienna's population. The visitor would certainly have gone to hear, in one *Kaffeehaus* or the other, the new Schrammel Quartet (two violins, an oboe, and a guitar). Two brothers, Hans and Joseph Schrammel, had perfected a new style of playing old Viennese ditties. Crown Prince Rudolf was a great admirer of theirs and could listen to them until three o'clock in the morning, as he got more and more inebriated. Balls in the Schwarzenberg Palais, parades on the Schmelz field, gambling at the Casino in Baden—there was no end to diversion. If the visitor searched for entertainment more nourishing, he was able to hear the Vienna Philharmonic play Brahms's Third Symphony or hear Leschetizky or Liszt play the piano.

At the new Burgtheater Adolf Sonnenthal acted King Lear and Nathan der Weise. Sonnenthal, according to Egon Friedell, represented "the complete and round expression of the bourgeois ideal: sonorous, solid, and sentimental. The world was then play-acting humanity and liberalism. Sonnenthal embodied these sentiments on the stage. Knighted by the Emperor, he was a knightly apparition." The Viennese nicknamed him "Jupiter."[8]

Franz Joseph went to the Burgtheater not so much to see a

performance as to see the splendid new curtain: Katherina Schratt and her little son had served as models for two of the allegorical figures. He wrote to Katherina:

> I saw the beautiful, well executed curtain by Fux. Your portrait is a bad likeness, Toni's is much better. "Jupiter" was present as well, and more mannered than ever. I really ought not to say this because that is against discipline and the respect which you owe to your chief. [Sonnenthal was temporarily in charge of the Burgtheater.] Let my uncalled-for remark remain between us.

Side by side with waltz rhythms, side by side with entertainment superficial or profound, new movements stirred under the linden trees. The *Zeitgeist* took up residence in the Ringstrasse, and no more than any other metropolis could Vienna escape the forces which were pushing the world. Not only in the outer sections of the Iron Ring but in its center new social ideas boiled and bubbled. Two leaders arose to head two opposing movements. One demanded Anschluss, the other a form of socialism.

The head of the pan-German movement was a fierce-tempered, pathologically vicious fanatic, Georg von Schönerer. His father had been knighted and left the son considerable wealth which he had earned as a railroad builder. Schönerer worshiped Bismarck and all that was German. In Parliament, where he represented the very district from which Hitler was to spring, he began a series of hypnotizing speeches, the contents of which never varied: the Germans, whether born in Austria or in Germany, were racially superior, the Slavs were by nature inferior, and it was totally useless for Taaffe or anybody else to seek a way of getting along with inferiority. "One hears talk of equality between Germans and Slavs. It is as if one compared a lion to a louse because both are animals." Expectedly, a virulent anti-Semitism was one of the chapters of Schönerer's primer. In 1882 he proposed a bill which would have prohibited Russian Jews from entering Austria. Six years later, when the newspaper *Neues Wiener Tagblatt* announced the death of Wilhelm I prematurely, a small band of hoodlums organized by Schönerer raided the plant of the "Jew sheet" and assaulted the staff for spreading false news about "our" sovereign. The newspaper sued, and Schönerer was convicted, stripped of his title of nobility and of his seat in Parliament, and imprisoned. All that accomplished was to convert him into a martyr.[9]

In the same year that he proposed the anti-Jewish bill, Schönerer worked out the so-called Linz Program. In that document anti-Semitism was still carefully concealed, so that it is understandable (or *almost* understandable) how two Jews, both of them educated and distinguished men, were among the signers. One was Heinrich Friedjung, later one of the best of the Austrian historians; the other was Dr. Viktor Adler, who was shortly to become the leader of the opposing movement. Like many radical programs, the Linz Program made some sense in the beginning: it advocated state ownership of the railroads, a graduated income tax, taxes on luxuries, regulated working hours for male laborers as well as for women and children, separation of the schools from the Church, and so on. It contained less incontestable proposals as well, such as separate statehood for Galicia, springing from Schönerer's *"Deutschland über Alles"* creed. That creed even included abolishing the Christian calendar. Years were not to be counted from the birth of Christ but from the Battle of Teutoburg Forest in A.D. 9, which the Germans, under Arminius, won over the Roman legions under Varus. Like most programs conceived in a bed of hate, the Linz Program soon grew into an ogre.[10]

Bismarck despised Schönerer's "German National party." Not only was he too wise a statesman to swallow such indigestible lumps of malice, not only was he still convinced that Austria-Hungary was "a necessity of life," not only did he perceive that an Anschluss program would be unworkable, but he also feared that if the Slavs were to be separated, they would gravitate toward Russia and Russia would become an even more powerful threat than it already was. Franz Joseph agreed. He too loathed the movement. And yet he did not stamp it out but tried to maneuver and tack around it. As long as Schönerer did not commit lèse-majesté he was allowed to operate.[11]

While Schönerer became irrational, his opposite, Viktor Adler, became reasonable. Not that he was free of tortuous psychological twists: he never got over the self-hatred of the Jew, a form of self-punishment particularly prevalent among Viennese intellectuals;

and though he adopted Protestantism, he could not find there the solace he so earnestly sought. He first became a physician and early debated against Sigmund Freud. Then, influenced by Karl Marx and Engels (whom he visited in London), he determined to devote himself to messianic endeavor, and between 1887 and 1889 spent much time in jail for his efforts to organize a workers' party. Adler's program was, essentially, the establishment of an eight-hour day and extension of the vote to everybody. Only a part of Austria's population could vote. Casting a vote cost a fee; it was altogether a circumscribed process reserved for the privileged. Adler wanted unlimited suffrage. He was eventually elected to Parliament, and though always forceful and undeterred, he never became a spitting radical, and kept his voice low. He understood the value of moderation through personal observation. In 1882 two workmen murdered the hated shoe manufacturer Joseph Merstallinger; this murder caused a wave of panicky persecution, and in this climate twenty-nine Socialists were convicted of treason by the Vienna courts. "Acts of terror are worthless," said Adler; "they merely retard progress. To better the economic, social, and political fate of the proletariat we need a broadly organized legal effort."

It can be counted to Franz Joseph's credit that, though he then thought universal suffrage an absurdity by which numbers wiped out experience (he was to change his mind later), he felt a certain liking for Adler. And, curiously, Adler admired Franz Joseph.

On the first of May, 1890, Adler organized a huge demonstration of his "Social Democratic party." It was to take place in the Prater, on the very day when traditionally the "Flower Corso" was to be held. The police expected violence, the military was called out, shops were closed, women and children were warned to stay off the streets, and just to make doubly sure, Adler was summarily interned in Cell 32 of the Vienna jail. From there he wrote to his friend Friedrich Engels:

> The idiots think that I will go promenading in the Prater on the first of May carrying bombs in my pocket. At any cost they wanted to put me out of the way. It was a long afternoon, and only late in the evening did I hear the signal which told me that the military had returned to the Alser Barracks. Toward ten o'clock in the eve-

ning my warden came and remarked, "Everything went off peacefully and they say it was magnificent." I knew that a decisive battle had been won. Austria's proletariat had awakened.

Time was still to elapse, the nineteenth century was to turn into the twentieth, before that awakening led to daylight action.

In addition, then, to dealing with the problems peculiar to Austria, Franz Joseph faced a world movement which he could as little deflect as the waves rolling against his sea-walled garden. It was to come, the change by which the aristocracy lost its power, the middle classes strengthened theirs, eventually to have it wrested from them by the laborers who, through unification and education, "assembled lonely plaint into coherent thrust."

Yet with all the change some form of continuity was possible. Hope, according to the proverb, makes a good breakfast but a poor supper. All the same, in those times hope was in plentiful enough supply to nourish people with continuous sustenance. Franz Joseph was as hopeful as any man. He never let go. He continued to improve the Imperial City—the regulation of the Danube bed, protecting the city against floods, and the construction of the Danube Canal were among his accomplishments—and he helped develop Austria-Hungary from a backward agrarian country to an industrial producer, so that Austria's goods could compete on the European market—though Austria never reached Germany's efficiency—and Austria's economy was no longer largely dependent on the amount of rain in the current year. Hungary was remarkably successful in working itself out of the financial doldrums. For fifteen years, from 1875 to 1890, its economic and political affairs were supervised by Coloman Tisza, a gnomelike, carelessly dressed dynamo of a man with long, untidy hair, who looked at the world through large blue eyeglasses and who was so effective an organizer that he virtually ran the country. Though in the beginning Tisza had been an enemy of the *Ausgleich,* and though Franz Joseph first regarded him with suspicion, he soon reached an understanding with the Emperor. Together they expanded Hungary's railroad system and improved its agricultural methods.

Counteracting the dispersing tendencies, Franz Joseph might have succeeded in "muddling through." His prestige was still enormous. Upon the King! People still wanted to lay on the king their lives and souls. Often Franz Joseph's mere appearance sufficed to calm an altercation and make deputies come to agreement. The idea he personified was still powerful, and white-haired men of substance, summoned before this seemingly impersonal figure, stammered with stage fright or, more precisely, with throne fright. The king still governed, however much the Schönerers stormed in Parliament. The concept of monarchy was still valid, not only in Austria but in Germany, Russia, Italy, England. Franz Joseph, now nearing sixty, was at the height of his vigor, erect on his horse, erect at his desk, erect before his people. He was strong enough to prevent fragmentation among the congeries of nationalities. He might have left his son an intact Austria, had not an event intervened which, foreseen by no one and understood by no one, shook him to the core of his being.

Crown Prince Rudolf, at the age of twenty

CHAPTER X

Rudolf's Tragedy

ALMOST AS MUCH has been written about the deed done on a cold and wet January night in 1889 at the hunting lodge of Mayerling as about the whole long reign of Franz Joseph. The mystery, at first covered with lies, then purposely obfuscated and never fully clarified, has captured the world's imagination and spawned romances, novels, plays, films, poems, memoirs, no end of newspaper stories, along with attempts at factual reconstruction.[1] Two questions have confronted—and still confront—the historian. The first: *What* happened at Mayerling? The second: *Why* did it happen?

Among the theories advanced are the following:

1. Rudolf killed his passionate blond mistress, Mary Vetsera, and then himself because they could not be united. He was married and unable to obtain a divorce. Even had he been able to do so, she was not of sufficiently high nobility to serve as a consort for the Crown Prince. Hopeless love, therefore, was the reason for the death pact.

2. Rudolf killed himself in a fit of depression prompted by the fear that he was going mad. He had been deeply troubled by the death of Ludwig II, by Otto's insanity, and by the increasingly strange behavior of his mother. He believed that he was destined to share the fate of the Wittelsbachs. That fate he could not face.

3. He had contracted syphilis and wanted to end his life before he would suffer the final consequences of the disease.

4. He had just quarreled violently with his father, accusing Franz Joseph of purposely keeping him from taking part in governmental decisions, of keeping him idle and useless. This quarrel had taken place the night before Rudolf went to Mayerling and had been so fierce that courtiers standing outside the chamber had overheard their voices shouting at each other, although Franz Joseph rarely shouted.

5. Rudolf was involved in a plot conceived by his Hungarian friends to overthrow Franz Joseph. Hungary was to be separated from Austria, Rudolf was to be crowned King of Hungary, and Archduke Johann Salvator of the Tuscany branch of the Habsburgs, who was supposed to be in league with Rudolf, was to succeed Franz Joseph as King of Austria. The plot had been discovered and there was no way out for Rudolf but to do away with himself.

6. He did not commit suicide at all but was murdered, and Mary was an incidental victim of this murder. The instigator of the assassination was his own father, who wished to get rid of his son because the son plotted against the father.

7. It was all a put-up job. Rudolf did commit suicide for political reasons, but it was made to look like a love tragedy. In point of fact, Mary Vetsera did not die and the corpse of another girl was substituted—with the cooperation of the court and the police. Because Mary knew too much about Rudolf's political activities, she was spirited away in an Austrian warship and was taken to America, landed in Texas, married a farmer there, and raised a family.

8. Rudolf's suicide was an affair of honor, what was then called "an American duel." Mary wanted to die with Rudolf, but she was not the reason Rudolf had to die. The real cause was his seduction of a Countess Aglaia Auersperg, wife of a Prince of the realm. Aglaia's brother challenged Rudolf to a duel in which the one who drew the "black bullet" obligated himself to commit suicide within six months.

9. Murder—a jealous revenge by a half-mad forester, who first castrated and then killed Rudolf.[2]

10. Accidental double murder. Baron Henry Baltazzi, an uncle of Mary, forced his way into the room and confronted Rudolf. Rudolf grabbed a gun and wildly discharged several shots, one of which killed Mary. Baron Henry then killed Rudolf by hitting him over the head with a champagne bottle.

11. Mary was the illegitimate daughter of Franz Joseph. She didn't know it and Rudolf didn't know it. But when their love affair became known, Franz Joseph told the facts to his son, and Mary's mother to her daughter. Mary and Rudolf, having unwittingly committed incest, decided to blot out their shame.

12. Mary was pregnant. Rudolf agreed with her that death would be preferable to living on and bringing a child into their divided world.

Obviously, much of this is rank sensationalism, and invented. What are the facts?

The latest of the books which have attempted to seek sober elucidation is a work by Fritz Judtmann (now deceased), who spent five years sifting anew all evidence available in the Vienna archives, the police reports, the letters left by Rudolf and Mary, testimonies of cab drivers, valets, physicians, guards, relatives of Mary Vetsera, the memoirs of Rudolf's wife Stephanie, and of Mary's mother, Helene Vetsera, the immediate and later statements by Countess Marie Larisch, who was deeply implicated in the Mary-Rudolf relationship, the findings of the court commission sent to Mayerling, statements by Count Taaffe,[3] confidential memoranda sent by the embassies to their sovereigns (including a report by the Prince of Wales to Victoria), correspondence with the Vatican, and so on. The book is entitled *Mayerling: The Facts Behind the Legend* (London, 1971).[4]

Though Judtmann's research clears up some details of what happened, it does not materially help us to understand *why* it happened. Perhaps if we were to attempt to examine Rudolf's personality, if we were to regard his psychological constitution, we could come a step nearer to understanding the motives.

Rudolf's biographer, Oskar Mitis, wrote that for once fate might have put a philosopher on a Habsburg throne. Possibly that put it too hopefully, but certainly Rudolf bent toward that study "which takes all knowledge for its province." He read Descartes and Voltaire, studied botany and ornithology, geography, physics, sociology, history. He prepared himself for his eventual task by learning several of the languages spoken in the Empire, Hungarian, Polish, Czech, in addition to French and English. He was almost as fluent in Hungarian as his mother, and the two corresponded in Hungarian. He traveled extensively and related his experiences in a book, *Travels in the East,* which was translated into several languages. One of his travel companions was Carl Menger, the prominent Austrian economist. While they were in England in 1878 they published anonymously an essay, "The Austrian Aristocracy and Its Constitutional Mission," in which they compared the irresponsibility of the Austrian nobility to the civic conscience of the British. Under Rudolf's direction, a huge work on the ethnography and history of the Habsburg Empire was prepared: it ran to twenty-four volumes and, though overly patriotic, is still regarded as a valuable reference work.

His amassing of knowledge may have served Rudolf as compensation for an early life in which the ordinal of Habsburg existence hindered normal access to his father, while absence estranged him from his mother. How sad it is to read in the schedule which was kept for the boy the entry: "10 to 11 A.M.—See Their Majesties"! As a baby he was spoiled by his grandmother's adoration, to fall as a boy into an emotional tundra. As a youth he may have loved his father—he probably did—but Franz Joseph was not a father but an apparition, seldom seen. His mother walked in beauty, surrounded by court ladies; she possessed little understanding of the male child, her love concentrated in Valerie. "I could not answer you before," wrote the twenty-year-old Rudolf to his cousin Ludwig II, "because I never managed to talk to Mama alone. During the journey she did not feel well, confined herself to her compartment, and appeared only at meals, which however were partaken of in company of her suite. In London I never saw Mama alone." Rudolf admired her and shared her dislike of their starched Habsburg relatives and their waspish wives. "Interested in all intellectual pursuits" (as the London *Times* described him), he understood Elisabeth's love for poetry and went to considerable trouble to obtain for her the original manuscripts of some of Heine's poems. Though intellectual empathy existed between the two, he could not reach her in intimacy; no queen's closet scene occurred between them. Altogether, Rudolf sought his intimates outside the home.

As a result, he never trusted anyone completely, though he had friends with whom he shared his philosophic and political ideas. It was difficult for him to separate the Horatios from the Rosencrantzes and Guildensterns: he was, after all, the heir, the man who could become the next Emperor at any moment. Everything was done to cater to him, though as a boy he was given little freedom. Even his introduction to sex was planned: there exists a document, signed by several tutors, which describes in dry officialese Rudolf's being told the facts of life (December 27, 1871, when he was thirteen) . One of his early loves, the Princess Maria Anna of Tuscany, whom he adored when he was nineteen, died of tuberculosis.[5] The sadness of it may have driven him to flickering experiments, to an overdriven eroticism. His profligacy, a need for conquest as compelling as Don Juan's, could have been an expression of his desire for intimate contact. Even in the first years of his marriage he had a number of affairs. That, conversely, he was a jealous husband is consistent with his psyche. Stephanie wrote:

> The Crown Prince was extraordinarily suspicious. When he was at home, I could not leave him for a moment. I had to remain in his room, even when he received army people or visitors I didn't like. . . . I was not allowed to write letters; even those addressed to my parents were read before their dispatch. The Crown Prince gave orders that during his absence no one except my ladies were to be admitted.[6]

Though he was not conventionally handsome, he was irresistible to women. His moist eyes, the black mustache Hungarian-style, the straight back, the trace of melancholy in his expression, now and then wiped away by great laughter, his dashing style of dressing with his cap at a provocative angle, his vitality, as well as the fact that he *was* the Crown Prince, made Stephanie's sister, Princess Louise of Coburg, who in her memoirs implied that their relationship was more than that of relatives, describe him as "more than handsome, he was seductive . . . he was disturbing." According to the account of Berta Szeps, he did love again and seriously, a beautiful Jewish girl living in Prague. She, too, died.

Mary Vetsera reminded him of her. His marriage to Princess Stephanie of Belgium represented a purely political alliance; she was the daughter of King Leopold II of the Coburg dynasty, who did not love his daughters but was forever seeking to augment the power and the wealth of the family through important marriages. Elisabeth detested the Coburgs, and Bismarck called them "the stud farm of Europe." (When Rudolf went to Brussels to ask for her hand, he was supposed to have taken a Viennese actress-friend along.) Lack of love is not entirely certain—there exists one letter to Latour in which he says that he loves Stephanie—but surely he could not have found great satisfaction in a match with a girl who was mentally and physically almost a child. She was plump, had red arms, small eyes, a sullen and haughty expression. At her marriage she walked down the aisle with "all the daintiness of a dragoon." The marriage had had to be postponed when it was discovered that Stephanie, fifteen years old, had not yet menstruated. When the ceremony did take place, on May 10, 1881, Rudolf seems to have been unwilling to enter the bridal chamber; he was supposed to have said that his bride bored him. Boring she was, a dumpy, uninspiring girl, who, like Rudolf, had been brought up in a loveless atmosphere and was quick to see herself as the insulted and the injured. She described her wedding night:

> Our rooms (in Laxenburg), into which we were immediately conducted, were situated in the Blue Court, opposite the Palace Church. I was expecting beautiful and pleasant quarters, since I read in the newspapers that there were fourteen rooms which for weeks had been renovated and newly furnished. As we entered, a musty, clammy, icy air took our breaths away. Nothing seemed in readiness. . . . There were no rugs, no dressing table, no bathroom, just a washstand on a three-legged stool. . . . What a night! What pain, what disgust! I knew nothing. . . . I froze, I trembled with the cold, then feverish waves coursed through me. . . .

Stephanie could share neither his high thoughts nor his low tastes. Rudolf sometimes took her along dressed as a peasant girl when he frequented suburban dives, but she could not endure "the smell of tobacco and garlic" nor find pleasure in the "sentimental, ordinary *Schlager*" the men were singing.

According to Count Monts of the German Embassy at Vienna

(quoted by Judtmann) , Rudolf overstrained his body with sexual adventure and resorted to alcohol and the hypodermic needle. Krafft-Ebing treated him for a "nervous complaint." When he was twenty-eight years old, he fell ill. This illness, it is now generally agreed, was of venereal origin, "a gonorrheal infection which he passed on to his wife." Stephanie noted:

> I myself did not suspect the cause of my complaint. Everything was hushed up upon orders from above, and the doctors were sworn to secrecy. Only later did I discover that the Crown Prince was responsible for my complaint. He too had been gripped by the terrible disease which never yet stopped at anyone. . . .[7]

Rudolf probably was not entirely cured of the disease. In bitter moments he seems to have contemplated suicide—before Mayerling—while in the next moment he veered toward the love of life and a consciousness that he was to become a man of destiny.

Because he was known to be a student, a liberal, a freethinking spirit, because in a word he was everything his father was not, he was subjected to the distrust of the court camarilla. They believed that his "madness" must not unwatched go. Rudolf knew it: "From day to day I observe more clearly with how narrow a circle of spies, of denunciation and watchfulness, I am surrounded." Yet in one respect Rudolf, who wanted only to work for peace and against nationalism, agreed with his father: that was his interest in the army: "The army is the one binding substance which, in these chaotic times, still represents the idea of the state. It is Greater Austria. One ought to protect it, develop it, favor it. That should be the endeavor of all liberals."[8]

Nevertheless he saw salvation only in a world which would have no need for an army: "There will be wars until the people and the nations have completed their development, until they at last unite themselves, and mankind has become one great family."

Rudolf's political mind, a mind embracing wide horizons yet too naïvely idealistic, can be gleaned from his writings and from his correspondence with the editor of the liberal *Neues Wiener Tagblatt*, Moritz Szeps; he was the man whom Rudolf came as near to trusting as anybody and he gave Rudolf the chance to express himself by opening the pages of the newspaper to him. Rudolf wrote, anonymously of course, of his admiration for the wealth France had contributed to the human spirit, with its Voltaires and its Diderots. As strongly as he felt toward France, so strongly did he dislike Germany's bellicose arrogance, and when he was sent to Berlin, it was difficult for him to behave with ordinary politeness toward Wilhelm II. He had great sympathy for the aspirations of the Slavs in the empire and, like Elisabeth, was especially drawn to romantic Hungary, however much he censured the Hungarians' treatment of minorities. From Austria's connection with the Vatican only grief and obscurantism could come, he believed. He mocked the prelates and the bishops. The Church must be stripped of its holdings, just as the aristocrats must be more equitably taxed and their estates parceled out among the peasantry. Above all, he wanted to realize "Victor Hugo's dream of a United States of Europe."

> The principle of nationalism is based on common animal instinct. It is essentially the victory of fleshly sympathies and instincts over spiritual and cultural ideas. . . .
>
> I consider all enmity based on nationality or race a great retrogression. . . . [July 26, 1882, when he was twenty-four years old.]

> Dark and ugly times await us. One can almost believe that old Europe is outdated and is beginning to disintegrate. A great and thorough reaction has to set in, a social upheaval from which, after a long illness, a wholly new Europe may blossom. [November 24, 1882.]

Yet he was a patriot:

> However gray the times threaten to become, I believe steadily in the future of our country. . . . Austria must exist; no other state can take its place, and the space upon which we stand cannot be made to disappear. [January 1, 1885.]

Rudolf loathed Austria's growing anti-Semitism. He reported to Szeps (a Jew) that a bunch of aristocratic rowdies who went around Prague, probably when drunk, smashing the windows of Jewish shops were arrested, spent the night in jail, but got off with no worse a punishment than an "admonitory sermon." That was scandalously unjust; he was going to write an article exposing the matter. He did write one concerning similar incidents in Hungary, when in 1883 the peasants rioted against the Jews.

Once the Jews are robbed, the castles of the lords will fall as spoils of the peasant war. Fire is indiscriminate: it consumes houses of magnates with the same appetite that it does Jewish homes. The mask of civilization will melt like wax, if we do not have the courage and the will to proceed against excesses such as we have now tolerated in Hungary, shaming our century.

On the other hand Rudolf himself was capable of scabrous pranks, to some of which he was led by Archduke Otto, son of Franz Joseph's brother Karl Ludwig. Otto was the *enfant terrible* of the Habsburgs, a handsome ne'er-do-well. (The Viennese, who were rather fond of Otto, laughingly told how on one occasion he had emerged from a *chambre séparée* at the Hotel Sacher, wearing a cap, gloves, and his saber—but otherwise completely naked.) Otto, Rudolf, and possibly Franz Ferdinand were riding in the Prater when they came across a funeral procession. They bade it halt and amused themselves by jumping their horses over the coffin. The incident was aired in Parliament by deputy Engelbert Pernersdorfer, though he did not mention names. A few days later two officers went to Pernersdorfer's house and gave him a thrashing. The police were called in. Rudolf wrote to Stephanie:

> The police gave me a few uncomfortable hours. They discovered some clues, including what regiment was responsible for the thrashing. They couldn't find the men, since we spirited them away, one to south Hungary, the other to Herzegovina. It needed all my nerve and foxiness to extricate myself. . . . Now we are again quite safe. . . .

Prince Heinrich Reuss, German ambassador to Austria, wrote, "The personality of the Crown Prince is very impressionable. Views which he feels intensely and voices openly he suddenly dismisses as rapidly as he assumed them. Therefore the ministers do not fear his disapproval, of which he makes no secret." Bismarck, a better judge, knew better: "His political understanding is uncommon; it astonished me. It proves that in spite of his youth he thinks independently and seriously. We did not always agree, but he knew very well how to make his points and I noticed particularly how circumspectly he did it."

Beautiful principles but no realistic plan; yearning for betterment, but plunging into lower depths; a sense of responsibility drowned in drunken nights; a fine brain but one not strong enough to fuse the visionary with the possible—such was Rudolf. This prince of peace was always shooting, toying with revolvers he kept in his room; on his table lay a human skull. He played with death, haunted by Ludwig's suicide. He was not afraid to die; yet he, an atheist and Voltairean, wondered about a life hereafter. The elements remained unmixed in him, and his great gifts were hampered by great weakness.

He suffered because he was an idle son. Other princes experienced a like fate and bore it with equanimity or sloth or through the pursuit of pleasure. Rudolf, too active a thinker, could not be content in being unthinkingly dissolute. Victoria's son was saved because Disraeli, after much difficulty, persuaded the Queen to give him some part in governmental affairs, and when he was thirty-four he was sent on a tour of India. (Yet he was sixty before he became Edward VII.) Rudolf was not given much even of a pretended task, only the slightest of representational duties. He wrote an analysis of Austrian political conditions, sent it to Latour, and asked: "Will the Emperor take this, my small work, seriously, or will he leaf through it before falling asleep and file it among the other documents, considering it a piece of eccentricity to be expected from and cut in the pattern of a visionary?" Franz Joseph filed it. He would not let Rudolf sit in council, nor ask his advice, nor confide in him. He waved him off with a wave of his imperial white hand. A few months before his death, Rudolf wrote to Szeps: "Every year I become older, that is, less vital and less able. . . . This eternal period of preparing yourself, this continuous waiting for the time when construction can begin, sap my creative energy!" How did he feel when he saw Wilhelm, "that Hohenzollern upstart," become Emperor of Germany that very year, at the age of twenty-nine?

Through frustration, vainly seeking satisfaction by slipping between the satin sheets of various beds, by hunting and traveling, by essays the authorship of which he could not acknowledge, by alcohol and possibly by drugs, there proliferated in Rudolf's mind, crawling like caterpillars over his thoughts, a swarm of dark and bitter feelings directed against the man who made him lead that useless life. Rudolf hated his father and feared him. Rudolf also

Rudolf in Hungarian uniform

loved his father and admired him. The conflux of feelings can be sensed in much of what he wrote and said and did. Likewise, he loathed Taaffe, whom Franz Joseph had chosen. Surely the loathing had a more personal origin than political divergence.

He could, in fact, be carelessly imprudent in showing his hatred of Taaffe. On January 28, 1883, Taaffe banned the sale of Szeps's newspaper, the *Neues Wiener Tagblatt,* in the government-owned tobacco shops, a move which spelled financial ruin for the paper. Two days later, a court ball took place and Rudolf came from Prague to attend it. Secretly he summoned Szeps for an interview. In the dead of night, through unlit corridors and down a hidden staircase, Rudolf's valet guided Szeps to Rudolf's apartment. Still wearing his gala court uniform, Rudolf received the editor, the valet served supper, Rudolf commiserated with Szeps. The Crown Prince ate little but drank a lot of champagne and gradually poured out his own unhappiness, his bitter disappointment in Austrian affairs, his violent opposition to Taaffe's policies, his fears for Austria's future. All this happened a few yards away from where the ball which Taaffe was attending was still going on. The interview ended at dawn. Surely Taaffe knew about it. Surely the Crown Prince had been spied upon. Rudolf returned to Prague, and Szeps found a way to save his newspaper.

The year before Mayerling, Rudolf went hunting with his father. Always ready to shoot at anything within sight, he carelessly discharged his gun and only just missed shooting Franz Joseph, wounding the Emperor's loader, who was standing behind him. Franz Joseph was furious with him, not so much because Rudolf showed himself to be a bad shot but because he knew that the incident would furnish stuff for gossip all over Vienna. Later that year Rudolf had a bad fall from his horse. He begged his doctor not to tell his father about it. The fall seems to have worsened the headaches from which he was suffering and for the relief of which morphine was prescribed. It was a dangerous prescription.

In this love-hate, an oedipal complex springing from a subconscious web more complicatedly branched than sexual impulse, is to be found the operating motive for the Mayerling tragedy. The subconscious desire for revenge destroyed Rudolf. Revenge, specifically the wish to wreak vengeance on a parent by destroying oneself, is one of the strongest drives leading to suicide. In an analysis of "The Psycho-dynamics of Suicide," by Sidney S. Furst and Mortimer Ostrow, one reads:

> *Revenge.* Finally, and perhaps best known, are the fantasies in which suicide represents the ultimate act of revenge aimed at a disappointing object, or a real or imagined persecutor. Here, in effect, suicide is homicide which has been turned against the self. The interplay between murderous impulses and suicidal drives and, in particular, the mechanisms whereby one is interchanged with the other, were not understood until Freud formulated his theory of sadism in *Mourning and Melancholia* in 1917, by which time the vicissitudes of aggression were more clearly recognized. Freud postulated that in pathologic depression the subject identifies with a hated and loved object. The identification, or psychic incorporation, expresses the love. When, as a result of loss, disappointment, or rejection, the love turns to hate, the tendency to suicide may become overwhelming. By destroying himself, the subject also destroys the object, who is inside him and yet remains united with him. If, in addition, there is guilt toward the object, suicide becomes even more appropriate and compelling. For then in a single act, not only is the object destroyed, but the guilty self is justly punished for hatred and murder.[9]

The analysis offers a hint as well of the motive which led Rudolf to seek companionship in death and to kill an innocent victim: it speaks of "the interplay between murderous impulses and suicidal drives." A loved object can substitute for the hated object: in killing Mary, Rudolf may subconsciously have killed Franz Joseph. Then, too, Mary was there to buttress Rudolf's nerve, to give him the courage which comes with company. Had it not been Mary, it might have been Mitzi. The need for revenge ravaged Rudolf so greatly that he had to turn not only against himself but against another being, one with whom he was linked by sexual contact.

It can be proved that hopeless love (Theory 1) was far from the motivating cause. It is extremely doubtful that Mary was pregnant—the affair was too recent for her to be sure, having begun on January 13 and ending on January 30—though there was considerable contemporary gossip to that effect (Theory 12). Even had she been or thought herself to be, there was no need for suicide: as Wandruszka observed, "A crown prince had every opportunity to dispose of the embarrassment of an illegitimate child. The history of all European dynasties, including that of the house of Habsburg-Lothringen, furnishes plenty of examples of such disposal, but not one of suicide for such a reason." However, Wandruszka does not entirely rule out the possibility that had Mary been pregnant, she might have set her course toward tragedy:

> From all we know of Mary it is improbable that she would have consented to any "arrangement" [to get rid of the child]. Nor would she have agreed to relinquish her lover. A human being inclined to the fantastical is governed more by emotion than by reason. Evidently she possessed not only a strongly erotic radiance but considerable force of will, a force which far exceeded that of the Crown Prince who, though greatly her intellectual superior, was yet weak in soul and health, shattered by his unfortunate relationship to his family, to his father as to his wife.[10]

All the same, it is unlikely that she had become pregnant. While Rudolf undoubtedly was in a depressed state, he was not insane. His depression was not sufficiently deep to make the madness theory (Theory 2) tenable. It is fairly certain that he did not have syphilis (Theory 3). The gonorrheal infection, passed on to Stephanie, must have been curable, since she married again. No good evidence exists for the quarrel with his father (Theory 4); Judtmann considers it one of the many legends which have sprouted around the tragedy. One of Stephanie's ladies-in-waiting did report that she heard from a valet that some days previous to Rudolf's departure for Mayerling he quarreled with his father and that Franz Joseph said to him, "You are not worthy to be my successor," but this is a hand-me-down tale, mere gossip, unconfirmed. Rudolf was supposed to have written to the Pope asking for an annulment of his marriage and the Pope was supposed to have forwarded the letter to Franz Joseph. On receiving the letter, Franz Joseph was said to have had a violent altercation with his son. No such letter has been found in the Vatican or the Vienna archives. As to the Hungarian plot (Theory 5), here again not a shred of evidence has been found in spite of almost a century of research. It is true that at one time there was some talk of Rudolf's being offered the crown of Hungary, but the matter was dropped long before Mayerling. What of the murder hypothesis, specifically a murder directly or indirectly instigated by Franz Joseph (Theory 6)? A weird plot has been suggested, the mastermind of which was supposed to have been Archduke Albrecht, intimate of Franz Joseph. Rudolf, who had been accused of outright disloyalty to the Emperor, was summoned to appear at a family dinner at which the dirty linen was to be washed and it was hoped that father and son would come to an understanding. When Rudolf failed to show, Albrecht sent two officers to Mayerling. Late at night when Rudolf was sitting alone and drinking cognac, the two men broke a window, entered, placed a revolver on the table, and said that Rudolf would know what to do with it. This was the command, traditional in the army, for "voluntary" self-destruction. Instead, Rudolf seized the revolver, fired several shots, and wounded one of the officers while the other took the bottle of cognac (the champagne bottle mentioned in Theory 10 would not have been heavy enough), and hit Rudolf over the head with such force as to kill him. Hearing the shots, Mary rushed in from the bedroom; a stray bullet killed her. This involuted story has been brought forward as recently as 1971, with many detailed "proofs," by Alexander Lernet-Holenia. It does not ring true, the stray bullet business being altogether unbelievable. Nor would it be consistent with Franz Joseph's character to have instigated the murder of his son. Franz Joseph was no Cesare Borgia. All the murder theories (Theories 6, 9, and 10) seem false because the medical and circumstantial evidence decisively points to suicide.[11] Theory 7, advanced by a woman who claimed to be a descendant of Mary Vetsera and wrote from Texas to Vienna, is certainly fiction, as in all probability are Theories 8 and 11. It *was* suicide.

In seeking the main motive for the suicide, one returns to the psychological explanation of revenge, revenge on the father. In diagnosing "revenge" one may add that the subconscious force was accompanied by other, conscious impulses. Suicide is not simple. Weariness of life, satiety, anger at Austria's political tendencies, the frustration of his inactivity, guilt feelings toward Stephanie, bad health—they all may have played a part. How can the reasons for such an act be logically listed? Though Rudolf was not insane in the medical sense, can a man be called sane who destroys not only himself but an innocent and loving companion?

In the last year, Rudolf's physical condition had markedly worsened. His hair was thinning and he suffered from a bad sty. His handwriting, as Edward Crankshaw has observed, rapidly deteriorated. He drank more than ever and he looked older than his twenty-nine years. Body and mind moved toward darkness.

2

I will try to give as clear an idea as I can of the Mayerling events by passing in review the more important persons involved. Here, then, are some of the dramatis personae:

Mitzi Caspar:

The year before his death, Rudolf had an affair with Mitzi Caspar, one of Vienna's known and expensive prostitutes. She was an agreeable, laughing young woman who enjoyed life and in whose company, as well as in whose embraces, Rudolf found pleasure. At one time or other he spoke to her of suicide. She did not take such talk too seriously. Suicidal impulses were not uncommon in Vienna; they were an echo of that romantic negation which started with *The Sorrows of Young Werther*. Not only disappointed lovers or men in financial trouble, but students who failed in their *Matura,* the final school exam which one had to pass in order to enter the university, threatened to do away with themselves. After a while, when Rudolf persisted in bringing the subject up with Mitzi, she got worried and went to the police president, a Baron Franz Krauss, and told him about it.

Franz Krauss:

Krauss refused to become involved—it was no concern of the police—and instead of thanking Mitzi he warned her that she would be subject to considerable unpleasantness should she breathe a word of the matter to anybody. He then protected himself and did his duty by keeping careful records of subsequent conversations with various people acquainted with Rudolf. These records are extant.

Baroness Helene Vetsera: A wealthy widow, mother of Mary. She was obsessed by social ambition; she dreamed high, she dreamed of entering that closed circle at the center of which stood Franz Joseph. Elisabeth thought her ludicrous and was suspicious as well of her two brothers, the Baltazzi brothers, both of Levantine origin, both wealthy. Franz Joseph himself, usually indifferent to the social maneuvering around him, was not unaware of Helene Vetsera's ambition. Marie Festetics noted in her diary that the Emperor said to her, "The way that woman goes on about Rudolf is incredible. She chases him everywhere. Today she even gave him a gift."[12] That had occurred when Mary was only eight; Helene was apparently trying to use Rudolf to introduce her to the Hofburg. She was so obvious a schemer and her reputation was so dubious that the wife of the Austrian ambassador in London refused to receive her. There was no danger of Rudolf's falling for Helene Vetsera's charm; she was too old for him. But little Mary was, again to quote the Festetics diary, "coming up—slowly, to be sure, but one builds from the ground up."

Mary Vetsera: Her daughter.

When Rudolf met Mary, she was seventeen, a soft round girl promising Oriental sensuousness, a girl with a porcelain complexion, "soulful eyes with such long lashes," and the look which is called *schmachtend* in German. She fell head over heels in love with Rudolf; it was an immature, romantically overcolored passion compounded of remnants of French novels and fairy tales. A few letters she wrote during a journey to Paris and London, before she knew Rudolf, show that she was a nervous, high-strung creature. The noise of Paris was "driving her crazy." She wrote good French and acceptable English; she was not uneducated. Was she an innocent, wide-eyed virgin, as infatuated as Emma Bovary and ready to share Emma's fate? Or was she, as her mother's daughter, a girl who had learned early to capitalize on her sex appeal, a calculating coquette? Historians have uncovered a previous infatuation of Mary's with a young English officer whom she met in Cairo, and there was talk in Vienna that Mary's mother tried to marry her to the elegant Duke Miguel of Braganza, a widower living in Vienna. None of this can be put forward with certainty; the one fact which need not be doubted is the genuineness of

Mary Vetsera, seventeen years old

Mary's love for Rudolf. It all happened quickly: they met in November, 1888, and we know that they first slept together on the night of January 13. Mary gave Rudolf a gold cigarette case with the engraved words: "In gratitude to a kindly fate! January 13, 1889."

To her, as to Mitzi, Rudolf spoke of suicide. The two planned to go to the hunting lodge of Mayerling near Baden, south of Vienna, there to be united by death. Many years later (after World War I), an ashtray was found, on the bowl of which were written the words, "Better a revolver than poison. A revolver is more certain." The words are apparently in Mary's handwriting. Mary's willingness to enter into the pact remains a riddle. One can only guess that she was so greatly enamored, her mood one of so feverish an exaltation, Rudolf's influence on her so hypnotic, that she would have done anything he asked her. That is not a satisfactory explanation: one must simply say, as the historian often has to say, that human beings can act in ways which make no sense at all.

Count Josef Hoyos: A friend of Rudolf who was present at Mayerling, as was

Prince Philipp of Coburg: His brother-in-law, husband of Stephanie's sister Louise. To him Rudolf described how Mary once came to him in the Hofburg clad in nothing but a nightgown, with a fur coat thrown over it. He told this story to his wife's brother-in-law!

Joseph Bratfisch:

The coachman of an "unnumbered" fiacre Rudolf frequently used. (The name could have been invented by a German Dickens: it means baked fish.) Rudolf trusted Bratfisch and was fond of him; he could whistle Viennese songs like a streak.

Johann Loschek: Rudolf's valet at Mayerling.

Countess Marie Larisch:

She was one of Elisabeth's nieces and frequently in Elisabeth's company. An unscrupulous, predatory woman, she no doubt acted as go-between in the affair. She was a friend not only of Rudolf but of Helene Vetsera, and the confidante of Mary. Elisabeth was fond of her niece, and it is difficult to understand what could have been Marie's motives in promoting a liaison of which Rudolf's mother would certainly have disapproved. One hypothesis has it that Marie Larisch herself was in love with Rudolf, that at one time they had been lovers, and that she was still willing to serve him—but that is a hypothesis only, and too reminiscent of *Dangerous Acquaintances.* Probably a more reasonable explanation is a plain financial one: Helene Vetsera as well as Rudolf helped the Countess with money. It is known that the Countess was often in debt and that she attempted to hide those debts from her husband.

These were the chief protagonists involved. Let us observe their movements:

Night of January 27–28: Rudolf spent the night with Mitzi Caspar. One of Baron Krauss's minions, detailed to spy on Rudolf, reported this.[13] That fact alone would tend to eliminate the romantic notion that Rudolf died for love of Mary. Among the farewell letters Rudolf wrote, one supposedly brimming with tenderness (the letter itself has been destroyed) was addressed to Mitzi. Among his last instructions he wrote: "Whatever money is found give to Mitzi Caspar."

Morning of January 28: Rudolf spent the morning in his rooms at the Hofburg. He was waiting, he told his servant, for a telegram and a letter. They arrived one after the other; he crumpled up the telegram and was overheard by the servant to say, "It has to be." Those who believe in Theory 3 interpret the remark as Rudolf's reaction to the discovery of the Hungarian plot. It may be quite as applicable to a confirmation he received that all the details of the flight to Mayerling had been settled and that he was now committed. That flight had been meticulously sketched out in advance by Rudolf and Mary, with Countess Larisch's help. It wasn't easy to get the girl away from her mother and transport her in secret to the trysting place.

The plan and sequence of moves were as follows: About ten o'clock in the morning, Countess Larisch called at the Vetsera home. She was going to go shopping with Mary, she said. They did go shopping, visiting a linen shop, but then drove to the Hofburg, where Mary and Rudolf talked briefly. After the interview, the two women drove to the shop of the fashionable jeweler Rodeck on the Kohlmarkt. Countess Larisch went into the shop alone.

Mary stayed outside in the cab, left the cab, and took another cab to a suburban inn, where Rudolf met her. From the inn Bratfisch drove them both to Mayerling, where they arrived in the early afternoon. Nobody had seen her. Only Loschek and Bratfisch knew of her presence.

From Rodeck's shop Countess Larisch drove back to the Vetsera home, with her story ready. She told the mother that Mary had disappeared from the cab and had left a cryptic suicide note in the cab. She confirmed this later to the police. But it is not certain that such a note was ever written. The Countess's story was a fabrication, prearranged, and it is impossible to separate what happened from what the Countess said had happened. She told the mother that there was no cause for worry: Mary was in good spirits, laughing and gay, and any talk of suicide was nonsense.

Here the plan went awry. Helene Vetsera took the matter seriously. Indeed, the Countess found the mother quite hysterical, Mary's sister Hanna having discovered a note in Mary's room: "Dear Mother: By the time you read this I shall be in the Danube." Mary seems to have had a positive passion for announcing her intentions, which surely indicates that her state of mind was far from "normal." Was she motivated by a subconscious desire to prevent her death? Was it a form of boasting of her love? Was it defiance?

The mother claimed then and later that she had had no inkling of Mary's affair with the Crown Prince. This seems unlikely: Viennese gossip swarmed too busily not to have reached the ears of a Helene Vetsera, herself a gossip. But we may give her the benefit of the doubt in believing that she knew nothing of Mary's flight.

Countess Larisch told her that the police ought to be notified and then persuaded the mother to let her call alone on Baron Krauss, who was a friend of hers, and enlist his help in finding Mary. How stupid Helene Vetsera must have been! She allowed herself to be persuaded. Countess Larisch immediately drove to police headquarters. We know what happened there, since Baron Krauss wrote a detailed memorandum of the interview. The Countess told Krauss that the idea of suicide was not to be taken seriously and that she had reason to assume that the girl had cooked up the whole plan, including the suicide note found in the cab, in order to go away with her lover; that lover she "believed" to be the Crown Prince. The moment the Crown Prince's name was dropped, Krauss again became uncomfortable. These were matters too hot for him to handle. When Larisch asked him to have a search made for Mary Vetsera, he replied that he did not possess sufficient information to warrant official action.

If official action were required, then the mother would have to make a formal report of her daughter's disappearance. A search could then be instigated, but there would be no way of keeping the news from the Vienna newspapers, and obviously the consequences for Mary's reputation would be serious. The minutes of the meeting which Baron Krauss kept implied two things: first, that he did not believe that Countess Larisch was telling the truth; and second, that at any cost he wanted to stay away from becoming involved with a royal sex scandal. Later there was a second interview, and Countess Larisch, before leaving Vienna to rejoin her husband, wrote Krauss two confused letters, the only reason for which could have been her extreme fear. She must suddenly have realized that the flight to Mayerling represented something more sinister than the usual lovers' escapade. She must have wished to God that she had not been as deeply involved as she was. Hence her rush to the police, her two almost incoherent letters, her altogether strange behavior. Enmeshed in her lies, Marie Larisch left Vienna as soon as she could, and then Helene called on Krauss and officially notified the police that the girl had disappeared.

January 28, about 1 p.m.: Before taking any action, Krauss thought he had better obtain official sanction. Consequently he called on Taaffe, who listened impatiently, as he was just about ready to go to lunch. The Prime Minister believed that the Vetsera mother was herself involved in the business, "since the mother's and also the daughter's pasts were not free of reckless escapades." No further steps were taken for the moment.

It may be conjectured that Krauss felt some foreboding that a tragedy was in the making. Nevertheless, leaning on the word of his superior, he did nothing, since he knew how embarrassing it could be to interfere with the person of the Crown Prince. (This inactivity stands as an ironic parallel to the inactivity of the police on the fateful day in Sarajevo, on June 28, 1914.)

Rudolf and Mary spent the afternoon, evening, and night together at Mayerling.

January 29, in Mayerling: This was the day for which Rudolf had scheduled a hunt. He had invited Hoyos and Philipp to go hunting with him. The two guests traveled by the Südbahn to Baden, leaving Vienna at 6 A.M. Alighting at Baden, they took a carriage to Mayerling, where they arrived at eight o'clock. The Crown Prince greeted them after a few minutes, and the three had breakfast together. He said that he had such a cold that it would be better for him not to go hunting lest he become seriously ill. It was the truth; he did have a cold. The Crown Prince dismissed them graciously, bidding them good hunting. On the evening of that day Rudolf, as well as Philipp, was scheduled to appear at a family dinner in the Hofburg which was to celebrate the engagement of Valerie to Archduke Franz Salvator of Tuscany. The only outsider invited was Prince Reuss. Rudolf was supposed to sit at the right of Franz Joseph. During the day, Rudolf sent a telegram to Stephanie, asking her please to make his excuses, that he had such a heavy cold that he wanted to stay put. The fact that the dinner was scheduled to begin at six o'clock and that the telegram was dispatched as late as 5:05 P.M., arriving in Vienna at 5:10, indicates Rudolf's disregard for the amenities to be observed toward his father, a disregard which, though perhaps not calculated, must have been more than mere carelessness. Franz Joseph gave orders not to change the seating arrangement but to leave Rudolf's place empty. Perhaps he would show, after all.

During the day Rudolf received several telegrams from Hungary keeping him abreast of the parliamentary debates being held in Budapest. They concerned a new army bill. Rudolf discussed the matter with his two friends when they came back from the hunt. Mary remained hidden.

The Prince of Coburg returned to Vienna in time for the family dinner, after taking tea with Rudolf, who apparently was in excellent spirits. Count Hoyos stayed at Mayerling and dined alone with Rudolf.

January 29, Vienna: More than a day had elapsed. There was no news of Mary, no word to her mother, no help from the police. Helene Vetsera was becoming desperate. What was she to do, where was she to turn? She went over Krauss's head and asked for and obtained an interview with Taaffe. The Baroness wanted to know whether she should try to speak to Franz Joseph himself. That was most inadvisable, Taaffe replied coolly. Imagine how you would feel if your report turned out to be untrue. You possess no proof that Mary is with the Crown Prince. He is supposed to be present at a family dinner tonight. Let us first wait and see if he shows up.

Taaffe did instruct Krauss to make some inquiries, and accordingly several plain-clothes police agents were sent to Mayerling to find out—discreetly—whether the Crown Prince was there and whether he had a female companion. They were so discreet that they didn't find out anything; perhaps they didn't try very hard.

Night of January 29 to early morning of January 30, Mayerling: Rudolf retired early that night. He instructed Loschek not to admit anybody to the bedroom, "even if it were the Emperor himself." Loschek naturally interpreted this as Rudolf's wish to enjoy an undisturbed night with Mary. Loschek arose early the next morning. To his intense surprise, Rudolf appeared at 6:30 A.M., dressed in a robe. He told Loschek that he was going back to bed but that Loschek was to wake him punctually at 7:30. He then returned to his room, whistling to himself, and, contrary to his custom, he locked the door behind him.

When shortly after 7:30 Loschek tried to wake him, there was no response. Repeated knocking proving fruitless, Loschek asked Count Hoyos what he should do. The Count felt that they ought to let Rudolf sleep. In the meantime, Prince Philipp arrived back from Vienna. It got to be eight o'clock, and past, and the three men were gripped by a vague sense of fear. The silence seemed to throw a spider web over the morning. Something was wrong. Why was there no answer from the bedroom? Should they force the lock? Perhaps Rudolf was ill. Loschek then told them that Rudolf was not alone, that Mary Vetsera was in the room. Even so—. The men decided to break down the door, but since the friends did not wish to appear to spy on Rudolf, Loschek alone was to look into the room. Loschek tried to remove the lock but finally had to smash one of the door panels. Through the aperture he glanced into the bedroom, withdrew in horror, and told them that the two were lying dead in bed, Rudolf in a pool of blood.

Should they call a doctor? They realized at once the danger of the scandal: under the circumstances they felt that Loschek ought to enter the room and ascertain whether there was a trace of life remaining in those two human beings. Loschek, reaching the lock through the smashed panel, succeeded in opening the door and went in. He rushed out at once and stammered, "They are both dead. They have been poisoned with strychnine." It was the first supposition and it was a believable one, since strychnine poisoning can cause hemorrhages.

Philipp, who loved Rudolf, went to pieces. So great was his grief that he was unable to act, and it remained for Count Hoyos to deal with the situation as best he could. He summoned Bratfisch and told him to drive to Baden as fast as his horses could gallop. Hoyos arrived at the Baden railroad station a few minutes after nine. The express train from Triest was coming through at 9:18. It stopped at Baden to discharge passengers, but it could not take on passengers. Hoyos spoke to the stationmaster, who wanted to know by what authority he was to go against regulations. In his perturbed state the Count let himself be trapped into dropping a hint that the Crown Prince was dead. He swung himself onto the train. The stationmaster immediately telegraphed the news to the Vienna head of the banking firm of Rothschild, Baron Nathaniel Rothschild. The Rothschilds were the largest stockholders in the Südbahn, and it is a curious fact that they knew about the tragedy before either Franz Joseph or Elisabeth did. It is another curious fact that the stationmaster telegraphed that Rudolf "had shot himself." That was nothing but a guess, and it happened to be correct.

January 30, morning, Vienna: The train arrived at Vienna at 9:50 and Hoyos took a cab to the Burg. He immediately went to the Lord Chamberlain of the Crown Prince, Count Bombelles, and made his report. Together the two men went to see the Empress's

Lord Chamberlain, Baron Franz Nopcsa, and then the three of them went to the Emperor's aide-de-camp, Count Eduard Paar. Obviously the purpose of this coming together was not only to seek company in misery but to share the responsibility of breaking the tragic news to Franz Joseph. In the end the four men decided to inform the Empress first. I find it telling that they went first to the mother, who as a woman presumably ought to have been spared as much as possible, rather than communicating the message to the father and head of state. They delegated Baron Nopcsa to call on Elisabeth, he being closest to her.

Ida Ferenczy was the only one allowed to enter Elisabeth's apartment without previous notice. She knocked at the door of the room and in a tear-choked voice begged Elisabeth to receive Baron Nopcsa, who had to see her right away on a matter of urgency. "He can wait," replied Elisabeth. She was busy listening to her teacher, who was reading aloud some verses of Homer which she was learning by heart. Ida broke into sobs and insisted that Elisabeth see the Baron: he had bad news to report of the Crown Prince. The Baron entered and told Elisabeth that Rudolf was dead, poisoned by his mistress. That is what they all believed, that he had been poisoned. The kindly old man burst into tears, and when he left Elisabeth, he nearly fell at the door.

Elisabeth, now at the moment of crisis, showed the finest side of her nature. Horrified, unbelieving, writhing in pain, she buried her head on the couch, crying, "No, no, no"—but at once she got hold of herself as Franz Joseph was announced. "Do not let him in," she said to Ida. "Give me a moment." She dried her tears, and then opened the door to Franz Joseph. They were alone. Nobody knows what words passed between them. Elisabeth then personally conducted her husband to Katherina Schratt, who happened to be in the palace. She thought Schratt might comfort him. She then asked that her daughter be brought to her. Valerie came and Elisabeth told her that her brother was no more. Valerie at once said, "Did he kill himself?" The sister knew him better than the mother. The last of the immediate family to be called was Rudolf's wife. Both Franz Joseph and Elisabeth received her. Stephanie sat there between the two, miserable, confused, ashamed. She was besieged with questions by the parents, "some of which I could not and others would not answer." When she told them what she knew of Rudolf's condition, they did not believe her. In vain did Stephanie recall to them that she had previously tried to speak to Franz Joseph about her unhappy marriage. In vain did she appeal to Elisabeth: "The Empress closed her mind to all I was saying. . . . I felt that she was turning away from me, that in her eyes I bore part of the guilt of the tragedy."

Elisabeth's ordeal was not over. By a coincidence, Helene Vetsera was in the palace at that very moment. Had a playwright so arranged the scene, he would have been accused of stretching the arm of coincidence beyond endurance. She was waiting in Ida Ferenczy's apartment to beg her to use her influence to arrange an interview with Elisabeth. The last person in the world Ida wanted to see was Helene Vetsera. But the woman simply would not be sent away. She sat motionless, weeping and saying over and over again, "Only Her Majesty can help me find my child." Now Elisabeth stood before her, contained, outwardly calm. In a soft, sad voice she spoke: "Baroness, you will need all your courage. Your daughter is dead." Helene cried out wildly and sank down at Elisabeth's feet. Elisabeth looked at her, a harsh light passed over her face, and in a voice that seemed to have emerged from a star she said, "My Rudolf is dead too." Helene, too, was sure that Mary, in a transport of love, had poisoned the Crown Prince. At the end of the interview, Elisabeth put her hand on Helene's arm and whispered, "Remember from now on and forever, Rudolf died of a heart attack."

January 30, midday, Vienna: That was the story given out to the newspapers. Taaffe himself wrote the official bulletin. Not a word was said about Mary; merely that "His Imperial and Royal Highness, the most Serene Crown Prince, the Archduke Rudolf, died suddenly of heart failure," etc., etc. The Austrian papers appeared with their front pages framed by a black border.

Franz Joseph and Elisabeth never questioned that the poison story was accurate, that it was Mary Vetsera who had killed their son. Hoyos, before he hurried back to Vienna, had only thrown a hasty glance into the bedroom, where the blinds were drawn. Even had he examined the scene more closely, he would not have been competent to establish the exact cause of the deaths.

Now, however, the post-mortem examination had to begin and an official report had to be made. A medical commission of five physicians was sent forthwith to Mayerling, headed by Dr. Hermann Widerhofer, Franz Joseph's personal physician.

January 30, afternoon, Mayerling: Widerhofer entered the room with Loschek at his side. The candles were still guttering from the previous night. Widerhofer threw open the shutters. The sight that greeted him made him, a medical man used to the sight of death, ill with horror. He found Rudolf in a half-recumbent position, the top of his skull blown off and parts of his brain spattered all over the room. Lying on the floor was the army revolver he had used. A glass standing next to Rudolf still contained some drops of brandy. A hand mirror was lying on the bedside table: it was deduced that Rudolf had held the mirror up to his head in order to be sure that he would aim correctly. Mary Vetsera was lying stretched out on the bed, her hair arranged loosely over her shoulders. There was a bullet wound near one of her temples; the bullet had been fired from a short distance. Aside from this wound, her head did not appear to be disfigured. She was half-naked, and Rudolf had placed a rose between her folded hands. Widerhofer's investigation established the fact that Mary had died from six to eight hours before Rudolf.

The sequence of events could now be reconstructed. Rudolf had shot Mary early during the night and then spent the rest of the night trying to get up enough courage to kill himself, all the while drinking brandy. When he appeared at six o'clock in the morning with a cheerful countenance—when Loschek saw him—he knew that a dead girl was lying behind the door, and his purpose in telling Loschek to wake him at 7:30 was to set the final moment beyond which he could not allow himself to live. Had he not done so, he might at the last not have had the strength to commit suicide. This is supposition, but a reasonable one. The notes Mary left behind exude a feeling of exultation and willingness to die, while Rudolf's letters, especially those written at Mayerling, give forth an aura of reluctance and regret.

(Many years later, when Loschek was eighty-three years old, he dictated a statement detailing his recollection of that night. He stated that he heard *two* shots at about 6:10 A.M. It is quite possible that the old man's memory failed him; but it does seem strange that he would be mistaken about the time of the shot or shots. So dreadful a shock remains engraved on the mind. The point has never been cleared up. The fact that Hoyos did not hear the shots can be explained by his being lodged in a house some distance away from the main house. There are other inconsistencies between Hoyos's and Loschek's memoranda, as to timing, examination of the bodies, etc. In the main, however, the events seemed to have happened as related here.)

January 31, morning, Vienna: Widerhofer now faced the gruesome task of informing Franz Joseph. At six o'clock in the morning, he made his report. Widerhofer began to speak of the bullet. "What bullet?" asked Franz Joseph. "The bullet with which Rudolf killed himself." "Don't talk nonsense!" said the Emperor. "My son died of poison. There was no bullet." He became furious, the veins stood out on his forehead, and, losing control, he actually threatened Widerhofer. But to the physician truth was more important than a king's wrath. He told Franz Joseph the whole truth, using only one little lie—if it was a lie—that the condition of Rudolf's brain might eventually indicate a temporary derangement. Franz Joseph had to hear not only that his son and heir had killed himself, but that His Serene Highness the Crown Prince, a Habsburg, a direct descendant of all those Apostolic Holinesses who had reigned over the Holy Roman Empire, was a murderer. Franz Joseph collapsed and wept. After a while, bitterness overcame him and he is supposed to have sobbed, "He died like a tailor!" (In German the word *Schneider* is often used as a synonym for coward.)

A final humiliation was in store for Franz Joseph. Rudolf had left a number of farewell notes, including a letter to his wife and one to Elisabeth. He left no letter, no note, no greeting, not a single word, for his father.

January 31 and the days following, Vienna: From here on, Franz Joseph, Taaffe, Krauss, the police, the censors, the men who issued the official bulletins, in short the entire machinery of the court, plunged into lies. These lies grew frantic in the endeavor to stamp the scandal underground. Documents were secreted, letters destroyed, witnesses intimidated, leaving room for rumor to run wide and high. In the end the lies only succeeded in making everything worse.

A new story was released to the newspapers that Rudolf had met with a hunting accident; this superseded the heart attack version. Every mention of Mary Vetsera was suppressed. A cordon was placed around Mayerling to prevent the journalists from entering.

January 31, Vienna: Count Paar had called on Helene Vetsera and hinted to her that she would be well advised to leave Vienna at once. However he put the matter, she obeyed and left immediately for Venice. She was so exhausted that she got no farther than halfway and then turned back. The next day another messenger appeared to suggest that she would be doing Their Majesties "a favor" if she stayed away during the time of Rudolf's funeral. She said she would do so if requested by an official emissary from the Emperor. That evening, Count Taaffe himself called on her—so important was it to Franz Joseph that she be unavailable for questioning—and she allowed that the Prime Minister was of sufficiently high rank to do what was asked of her. Off she went; she never saw her dead child.

Night of January 30–31, Vienna: Rudolf's body was transported in a closed, black-draped freight car to the Hofburg. The autopsy was performed, the death mask taken. The head was artificially repaired with wax and cosmetics. The process began at 8 P.M. and lasted until midnight. The writing of the report probably took until the early morning hours. Then an official bulletin, announcing "suicide by revolver in a state of temporary derangement," was issued. Still nothing was said of Mary. Franz Joseph saw his son at 7 A.M., and for a quarter of an hour stood in silence by Rudolf's body, nervously pulling his mustache.

January 31, Mayerling: The authorities now went into action to deal with the most difficult part of the problem, which was how to hide the fact that Rudolf had killed Mary. It seems preposterous, but they all, Court Commission, police, Taaffe, Franz Joseph, the doctors, still believed that the knowledge of Mary's presence at

Mayerling could be suppressed, that the secret could be kept. To succeed, Mary's body had to be spirited away. That was the first step, to remove her from Mayerling, where sooner or later the journalists would have found the grave and connected her with Rudolf's death. It was decided to bury her, hurriedly and clandestinely, in a cemetery at the nearby Shrine of Heiligenkreuz. The legal subterfuge which was used was that the Mayerling building was "extraterritorial," a property of the imperial household where neither political nor police authorities had jurisdiction. It was a transparently thin excuse, but anything would do to help them obliterate the traces and to prevent an official police investigation. Such an investigation would have been unavoidable had murder been admitted. Thus, the body was made unavailable to honest examination and a falsified post-mortem was prepared: it read that Mary Vetsera had committed suicide. This created another problem, because, as a suicide, it was difficult to get permission to have her buried in a Catholic cemetery. The problem was handled as the lesser of two evils: the Commission managed to "persuade" the abbot of Heiligenkreuz to permit the burial.

It is almost unbelievable that Franz Joseph would lend himself to such miching mallecho. But he did: he not only lent himself to it, he was active in the machinations. Anything, any lie, any offense to custom and usage, any disregard of common humanity was preferable to facing the truth and the scandal.

In fact, the court called a halt to any further investigation of the Mayerling events.

Mayerling, night of January 31, and Heiligenkreuz, February 1: Mary's mother had insisted that somebody from the family be present at the burial. Accordingly, Mary's Uncle Alexander Baltazzi and Count Georg Stockau, a brother-in-law, went to Mayerling. Mary's body had been cleaned, and now the two men carried the corpse, dressed in a fur coat and hat, into a closed carriage. They put Mary upright between them, the carriage started off, and they drove, holding the body bobbing from one side to the other, as best they could. The ghastly ride covered the four miles which marked the distance between Mayerling and Heiligenkreuz. It was night—but if anybody had glanced into the carriage, it would have looked as if two older men were traveling in company with a young girl.

A terrific rainstorm beat down on the fields during the night, soaking the ground and preventing the grave from being dug in time. In the morning, the gale was still blowing, and the men who were at the cemetery lent the gravediggers a hand. Finally, at around nine-thirty in the morning, the grave was ready and the coffin could be lowered. No death certificate had been issued, and the body was not inspected upon its arrival at its destination. A provisional coffin and a provisional grave had to suffice, changed later to a newly built vault. While the burial was in progress, a detective kept informing headquarters of every step by frequent telegrams in code, showing how nervous the Austrian officials were that something might go wrong at the last minute. The final telegram was sent at 10:00 A.M.: "All finished."

Vienna, February 1 and thereafter: The Austrian press did not swallow the official story. They suspected, if not the truth, that something was fictitious. The "unofficial" newspapers, meaning those that were antagonistic to the government, published wild rumors: Rudolf was shot by a poacher, he was killed during a drinking bout, and so on. On February 1 the *Neue Freie Presse* came out with the jealous-forester story. All copies of the newspaper were confiscated. On the same day, Szeps's paper, the *Neues Wiener Tagblatt,* published an article entitled "The Last Bullet"—and the entire issue of that paper was likewise confiscated.

The authorities fought in vain. They could not regulate out of existence an event of such worldwide importance that the best journalistic talent was put to work to ferret out the truth. The *Münchener Vorabendblatt* published a long analysis of the case on February 8. They came close to reporting correctly the circumstances of the double death. It can be surmised that they got their facts from somebody in the Court Commission or Rudolf's retinue. The paper was imported into Austria, and the article had the effect of a thunderclap. The police dearly wished to prohibit the newspaper from using the Austrian mails, but they realized that such an action would be futile, since it would have to be applied to virtually all foreign publications.

Later, when Helene Vetsera wrote her memorandum and had it privately printed, it was reported to Krauss that the London *Times* intended to publish the memorandum. The Foreign Office in Vienna sent a ciphered telegram to the Austrian ambassador in London, asking him to do his best to persuade the *Times* not to publish. Curiously enough, the *Times* acceded to the request.

One press report had it that Elisabeth, now insane, kept hugging a pillow to herself, saying to everybody, "Isn't the new Crown Prince beautiful?" A flood of fiction began to appear, novels and short stories with such titles as "The Huntsman of Mayerling" or "Darling of Austria and the Women," each publication trying to outdo the other in lurid details.

Fully nine years later, the Countess Larisch (now remarried to an opera singer and living in Munich[14]) wanted to publish her version of the story. Franz Joseph tried to prevent publication by offering Larisch a sum of money, and sent an agent to negotiate with her. The agent was unsuccessful: her memoirs appeared, entitled *My Life*. They were as false as they were self-justifying.

Vienna, February 1: As soon as Andrassy heard the news, he left his estate in Hungary and, weak and in pain though he was, journeyed to Vienna. He did not call on Franz Joseph, but walked into Ida's apartment. There Elisabeth saw him. He tried to speak words of comfort to her. They discussed the consequences of Rudolf's death to their beloved Hungary, but came to no conclusion. Then Andrassy left as quietly as he had appeared. Franz Joseph was not told of the visit.

Elisabeth said to Valerie: "All the people who have had nothing but evil to say of me, ever since I came here, now have the satisfaction of knowing that I shall pass out of existence without leaving a trace of myself in Austria."[15]

Vienna, February 5: On February 3 Rudolf's coffin was moved to the Hofburg Chapel, and on February 4 and 5 the chapel was opened to the public. Rudolf lay in state. A vast crowd collected. People fought to catch a glimpse of the coffin, they pushed and shoved, some fainted, and the police had to restore order.

At 4:00 P.M. on February 5, six gray Lippizaner horses

pulled the hearse to the Capuchin Church, the burial church of the Habsburgs. Neither Elisabeth nor Stephanie nor Valerie was present at the services.

The story has persisted to this day that the Pope would not consent to a church burial for the Crown Prince. Franz Joseph was supposed to have fought bitterly with the Holy See, and was reported to have sent a two-thousand-word telegram to the Vatican, after which the Pope relented. This has been proved almost certainly to be fiction. No such telegram was sent, and the decision to allow the church burial was arrived at in Vienna between Franz Joseph and the Hofburg chaplain, with the approval of the papal nuncio. Later some of the high clergy did stay away from a memorial Mass, and in the conservative Catholic provinces, such as the Tyrol, the clergy did show its disapproval. But Leo XIII himself sent a telegram of condolence to Franz Joseph. Galimberti, the papal nuncio, told Reuss, who told the British ambassador, who told Lord Salisbury, that his conscience was clear: he needed only to believe the official story. Still, it was the first time that a papal nuncio in full regalia had lent his presence to "the funeral of a murderer and a suicide."

When the coffin had been placed in the Habsburg crypt, Franz Joseph knelt down and kissed it. He clenched his hands; that was the only sign of emotion he betrayed. He then straightened himself and walked stiffly away.

Vienna, February 9, night: Late at night, Elisabeth got up, dressed—everybody else had retired—left the palace unobserved, hailed a passing cab, and asked to be driven to the Capuchin Church. She was heavily veiled. She pulled the bell. It took some time before she aroused a monk, who opened the church door and did not immediately recognize her. "I am the Empress," she said. "I wish to see my son." The monk took her to the guardian priest, who ordered torches to be lit, and by their light conducted Elisabeth to the crypt. She asked to go into the crypt alone. The priest tried in vain to dissuade her. She descended the steps. The two men waiting above heard her cry out, "Rudolf." Then all was silence. After a while she emerged, her face drawn and set, and without saying a word, she disappeared into the night. That, at least, is the story which has been told. It may be legend.

February, Vienna: The letters Rudolf left behind and his testament were now examined. Judtmann gives a list of eight farewell letters (and four from Mary), but if these contained an explanation of his conduct—which is doubtful—the information is lost, most of the letters having been destroyed. Rudolf's letter to his mother, for example: Elisabeth kept it, but according to her explicit wish it was burned after her death. His letter to his wife is a pathetic but superficial note.

DEAR STEPHANIE:

You are rid of my presence and burden; live happily in your own way. Be good to the poor little girl [their daughter Elizabeth] who is the only thing that remains of me. Give my last greetings to all my acquaintances, especially Bombelles, Spindler, Latour, Wowo [pet name for Baroness Welden, who had been his nurse], Gisela, Leopold, etc., etc. I am going calmly to my death which alone can save my good name.

Embracing you most cordially, your loving

RUDOLF

"Death which alone can save my good name" and in another letter, "I must die—it is the only way of leaving this world like a gentleman," these phrases are equivocal and could be used to serve any theory. Let us note again that in the letter to Stephanie, Franz Joseph is not mentioned. And could a man who had just committed murder leave the world "like a gentleman"?

Rudolf also left instructions that all letters to him from Marie Larisch "and the little Vetsera" were to be destroyed. However, a letter from Marie Larisch to Rudolf was found in the pocket of one of his uniforms; it proved her complicity. From then on she was never again received by Elisabeth or Franz Joseph, and her letters to Elisabeth were returned unopened. Elisabeth was deeply perturbed by the betrayal of the niece whom she had befriended and trusted. How could she, she asked Valerie, "retain any belief in life or love or friendship?"

3

Now that Rudolf was dead, Franz Joseph threw over him a cloak of fictive recollection—as a widow does who recalls as a paragon the husband with whom she had not been happy. In his letters to Schratt he called him "the best son" and "the most faithful subject." These are the untruths from which we press drops of solace. The son was lost and, equally horrendous, or possibly more horrendous, the heir was lost. The dynastic thread had been cut; it would have to be knotted by somebody else's son. There was no hope that Elisabeth at the age of fifty-two could bear another child, even had their marital relations resumed a normal course. Franz Joseph reviewed the tragedy over and over again in his mind. In March he wrote to Katherina Schratt:

> In the afternoon he [Dr. Widerhofer] spent more than an hour with me. Once again we discussed thoroughly all the sad events, tried to establish a connection, searched for the reasons. No use at all. There is no point to it. But I can't think of anything else, and talking about it affords one a little relief.
>
> Well, here I am again, at the same sad chapter. Forgive me. I know you understand me. . . .[16]

Franz Joseph must have asked himself many times, "How could he do this to me?" "How could he so disgrace the Habsburg line?" Elisabeth, who drew close to him during those weeks, could find an answer no better than he. Together they mourned and were ashamed, she, Valerie, and Franz Joseph. He wrote to Schratt, "The Empress especially finds it hard to soften her grief. Yesterday she again had a very melancholy day. At our little dinner for three she cried a lot, and of course Valerie then started to weep."

From now on Elisabeth almost always wore black. She developed a nervous tic and hid her face behind a fan. That is how the Viennese encountered her when they did encounter her: a black figure, pale, beautiful, distant.

The shots discharged at Mayerling echoed through the

realm. Rudolf dead made more of an impression on the Austrians than Rudolf alive. His action, people felt, "bode some strange eruption to our state." His spirit usurped the conversation in coffeehouses and parliament and workshops. A blanket of dust—promising a storm but not delivering it—lay over the country. Franz Joseph did not know how to clear away the cloud. "The Emperor begins to understand less and less about more and more," said the German ambassador. He never recovered from the shame, not entirely. After Mayerling he was never quite the same.

Egon Schiele: *Self-Portrait*. This gifted artist might have become one of the important painters of the twentieth century had he not died at the age of twenty-eight in the influenza epidemic which swept Vienna in 1918.

CHAPTER XI

Compensation

IF A MAN'S RIGHT HAND is weakened by illness or injury, his left hand does more work, grows stronger. The principle of compensation applies as well to man in society, to the behavior of a group. Failure in one endeavor will often lead to, or will at least be assuaged by, success in another. Man seeks some accomplishment to which he can point with pride. Whether as an individual or as a member of a people, he needs the satisfaction which excellence can give. The coveting of success, a desire for elevation above the ordinary, is an ingredient of his constitution. When a man or a group fails to satisfy this desire in one enterprise or direction, he or the group must turn in another direction. Man or society cannot exist flatly. One cannot live with the concept of "the average." Hence, compensation: in a period where the artistic talent of a nation is feeble, scientific talent may flourish. When a country finds itself in economic straits, it may create its best literature. Defeat in war may bring about reform in social legislation. If no painters or poets are born to a nation, it may produce fine watches and good chocolate. Compensation is a law of nature in its physical aspect and a law of civilization in its cultural aspect.

Periods of strength and periods of weakness do not follow an orderly schedule. They may coexist. There are times—such as in

Elizabethan England—when the sun shines warmly, the skills work hand in hand, and the poets are as vigorous as the statesmen. There are times—such as in prerevolutionary France—when dissatisfaction and unhappiness divide men, the weather is blustery, the fields of thought lie fallow—and then suddenly, from fallow fields and in inclement seasons, men arise who find new answers to old problems.

While attempts have been made to explain compensatory movements—by changes in the direction of the Gulf Stream or changes in eating habits—they are impossible to account for. How did it happen that the light suddenly shone in the Venice of the eighteenth century, after it had been dimmed for a century? No neat pattern exists; history is not written in a bookkeeper's script.

All the same, the historical panorama shows that where and when there is weakness, there is strength as well, and if satisfaction is not to be found on one road it will be sought on another. The depression of the 1930s in America produced a remarkable new literature, and the economic weakness of the country was compensated by a new resolution in governmental thinking. Arnold Toynbee, in *A Study of History,* observed: "One of the devices by which Life achieves the *tour de force* of keeping itself alive is by compensating for a deficit or surplus in one department by accumulating a surplus or incurring a deficit in another."

Austria, whose political heart was beating with lessened vigor, whose political body was enfeebled as the nineteenth century drew to a close, developed an extraordinary wealth of nonpolitical achievement. As the state decayed, men of talent turned from it toward other pursuits. It is almost miraculous how much was achieved in Vienna in music, drama, poetry, architecture, medicine, and a new science dealing with the psyche. When Franz Joseph began to rule, Austria was continental Europe's mighty state. When he died, Austria was in process of being wiped out of existence. The decline was long; the line moved slowly downward, and as the political graph descended, the intellectual graph climbed. The rise was notable particularly in the years after Rudolf's death, when the politicians clawed at one another, while the "nonpoliticians" helped one another. In the twenty years from 1890 to 1910 Austria piled up more creative treasures and contributed more benefits to world civilization than in the sixty years before or after. They were halcyon years for inventive minds. What they produced is still indispensable.

So saporous was this harvest, so sharply did it contrast with the meager results produced by court and Parliament, that one is tempted to ask whether governmental weakness does not benefit artistic strength, whether by compensation intellectual life is not stimulated when the power and the glory are dimmed. No generally applicable hypothesis can be deduced, but it is suggestive that most of the artists of that period in Austria were ignored by most of the government officials, from Franz Joseph down, that they in turn ignored the officials, and that many of them worked in overt opposition to the "establishment." The life of the country seemed to fall into two camps. The Hofburg and the Parliament seemed acres removed from the university and the *Musikvereinsaal,* however near one another they actually stood.

Franz Joseph, who never read one of Rilke's poems nor listened to a Brahms symphony, suspected the "intellectuals," that strange and ridiculous breed. This suspicion, or at the least this indifference, which frequently hardened into opposition, stimulated Austria's life of the mind by its very opposition. The creative men seemed to huddle together to form a resistance movement. The coldness outside their circle stimulated warmth inside it. Toynbee calls it "the stimulus of penalizations": "Penalized classes or races generally respond to this challenge of being excluded from certain opportunities and privileges by putting forth exceptional energy and showing exceptional capacity in such directions as are left open to them—much as the blind develop exceptional sensitiveness of hearing."

One condition favoring a creative climate did exist: a public was there to enjoy, appreciate, or disagree. The composers and writers did not play to empty houses. Audiences came, readers bought books. Audiences and readers included numerous segments of Viennese society; they were not confined to a special clique, though of course they did not comprise a majority of the citizens.

2

After the death of Beethoven in 1827 and Schubert's death the following year, the habitat of music seemed to shift from Vienna. For fully a generation no great composer resided near the Stephanskirche. Would a new tenant appear, could the tradition be carried on?

In 1862 Brahms, twenty-nine years old, stocky and sturdy and already carrying such samples of his genius as the First Piano Concerto, arrived in the city. He soon became the man you could trust. His music, cast in a conservative mold, linked to Beethoven and Schubert, gracious yet sad, appealed to Viennese taste, which always has favored the traditional and does today. The critic Eduard Hanslick, himself a traditionalist, became Brahms's champion. Brahms hardly needed a champion: soon after his arrival his Sextet was performed with great success, and when he appeared as a pianist, such confident vitality flowed from his stubby fingers that no one in the hall could remain quiescent. Still, it did not hurt to have the Petronius of Vienna's musical taste on your side.

Hanslick's essays, so brilliantly written that they were read throughout the musical world and were reprinted in America in *Dwight's Journal of Music,* have not outlived his mistakes. He is remembered, unjustly, not because he loved Brahms but because he hated Wagner. His antipathy to Wagner cut deeper than purely artistic dissent: he must have feared the sexual force which suffused Wagner's music. He disliked any art born of nighttime thoughts; even Verdi's *La Traviata* was rejected by him, because phthisis "belonged in the hospital, not in the opera house."

What that little man with his hook nose and his bushy white eyebrows did was to stimulate dissent and thereby heighten the lustiness of Vienna's musical life. What happened at the opera and the concert hall was important to both the Guelphs and the

Ghibellines. The discussions at the Café Mozart flowed on for hours, and even the "piccolo" (as the busboy was called) held firm to his opinion. Thus encouraged, the Vienna Philharmonic, under Hans Richter, acquired new virtuosity, and Wilhelm Jahn inaugurated "the dawn of a most brilliant and prosperous era in the Opera's history."[1] When *Parsifal* was first given in Bayreuth in 1882, Wagner recruited his cast from singers of the Vienna Opera: Materna, Winckelmann, Reichmann, and Scaria.

As Brahms walked down the Kärntnerstrasse, hands behind his back, derby hat pushed back, his coat patched and wrinkled as if it had passed the night in a dustbin, his trousers too short and unceremoniously snipped off at the ankles, as he puffed on rather than walked, children would follow him, knowing that his pockets were stuffed with candy which he was going to give them sooner or later. Most of the promenaders knew him, and so did the prostitutes who were standing near the Stephansplatz. Many of them knew him well; he could not enjoy intimacy with a respectable woman. He became wealthy, but he preserved an exaggerated simplicity, living in two mean rooms; he would generously aid relatives and friends in need—"Remember," he wrote to his stepmother, "that I have more money than I need"—but would be stingy enough to put insufficient postage on his letters, to waste time figuring out how he could smuggle in his cigars without paying duty, to be content with a supper of a tin of sardines, the oil of which he drank right out of the tin. When late in his life the Ministry decided that his merits ought to be acknowledged officially, and he was awarded the Order of Leopold, he refused to pay the ceremonial visit of thanks at court and was only persuaded with the utmost difficulty by Prince Reuss that such a visit was obligatory. He wouldn't wear gloves, because surely Franz Joseph would not inspect his hands, but, pressed once more by his friends, he finally fished out an old pair, no longer immaculately white, and put on the left one. Early in the morning he dressed in evening clothes for the occasion, and then sat all day, grumbling. He wanted to walk to the Hofburg, but when he was told that he really shouldn't appear before the Emperor in muddy shoes, he reluctantly hired the cheapest—"one-horse"—cab. He was forever belittling his own work. "Once more I have merely chucked together a set of waltzes and polkas," he said to his friend and biographer, Max Kalbeck. The set of waltzes and polkas turned out to be the Fourth Symphony, and he pretended to discourage his publisher from issuing the score: "The work will be printed when its immortality is already finished." But this was playacting, and if he could be as coy as a kitten, he could be as jealous as a cat. In truth, he was proud and touchy and often envious, and he was capable of quarreling with so faithful a friend as Bülow because he thought him insufficiently submissive. "He is an unregenerate egotist, without realizing it," Joachim said of him.

Brahms never lost his gruff North German manner, nor his Hamburg accent. Yet he became the leader of the renaissance of Viennese music and a prophet in his adopted country.

On the other hand, Anton Bruckner, the most magisterial symphonist after Beethoven, had to go outside Vienna to gain recognition. The Viennese public would not take seriously this little schoolteacher from Linz, and it was not till late in his life, after his Seventh Symphony had impressed Leipzig and Munich, that the local concertgoers began to perceive the stature of their compatriot, though they knew him to be a uniquely superb organist and though a few of the young musicians—Hugo Wolf, Gustav Mahler, the conductor Franz Schalk—understood and loved him. It was easy to make fun of Bruckner: he was an ungainly man, speaking a peasant's dialect, with a head which seemed to belong on a Roman coin, a nose which began to trace an emperor's profile and then lacked the courage to go on, and blue eyes which were forever expressing timid astonishment. That head was placed on a body which was too small to carry it. Everything about his appearance was ill-fitting. He dressed in a black suit of a cut fifty years out of date, and from the back pocket of his baggy trousers he would draw a seemingly endless red handkerchief stained with remnants of snuff. Unlike Brahms or Mahler, who were educated men, Bruckner's mind was concentrated on the staves of music paper; he was uninterested in poetry or science or painting or philosophic conversation of the kind beloved by the Viennese. He seemed a simpleton, and he was a genius.

He was excessively devout, constantly making the sign of the cross and kneeling when the Angelus sounded. Thus he composed, as it were, under the eye of God, who helped him, timid of life, to be bold in music. There is something incantatory about his work, as if a high priest who did not have to worry about holding the attention of his audience had penned these notes. Bruckner thought high thoughts while drinking a glass of beer. Perhaps his occasional fulsomeness served him as compensation for his meager external life. Perhaps he recognized his prolixity: he had a curious habit of numbering each bar of his compositions, as if he were in search of arithmetical order. Indeed, he was always adding: the number of steps of a staircase, the number of cups of coffee standing on the tables of a *Kaffeehaus,* the number of fiacres passing the corner. He longed for written proof of his ability. He was ecstatic when, as a young man, after an examination in organ playing, one of his examiners exclaimed in admiration, "He should have examined *us.*" After that he insisted on submitting to at least eight additional examinations, in each case asking for a written *Zeugnis,* a testimonial document, and celebrating each occasion as a triumph. No doubt his maladjustment, which twice or three times brought him close to a nervous collapse, had a sexual origin. He was very much attracted to women, but the objects of his desire were almost always young girls under twenty, and they would have none of him. When he was nearly seventy, he underwent an experience as ridiculous as that of Mr. Pickwick with Mrs. Bardell. A chambermaid in a Berlin hotel claimed he had promised to marry her, and it was true that he actually became engaged to her for the length of a whole afternoon. He had to be extricated by a friend who generously undertook the task of buying the girl off. Bruckner remained unmarried.

In his diaries are records of how many carnival balls he attended, how many waltzes and polkas he danced; and these notations are intermixed with the numbers of *A*'s (*Ave Marias*) and *V*'s (*Vater unsers—Pater Nosters*) he said.

He admired Wagner so much that he was virtually subservient to him, and he probably suffered more from the loud propaganda of Vienna's noisy *Wagnerverein* than he did from

Hanslick's vituperation. His Third Symphony was dedicated to Wagner, and accepted for performance by the Vienna Philharmonic, only to be discarded after one rehearsal. When he was fifty-three, he himself conducted this symphony: most of the Viennese audience walked out. When it was over, only about a dozen people were left in the hall; one of them was Mahler.

Bruckner was sixty-two when his Seventh Symphony was successfully performed in Vienna by Hans Richter. And it was in that year that Franz Joseph, who had heard him play the organ in Ischl, finally awarded him an order and a small stipend. When Franz Joseph asked what further favor he wanted—the conventional and meaningless question asked at such audiences—Bruckner is supposed to have replied, "Please, Your Majesty, tell Hanslick not to write all those terrible things about me." The story may be as apocryphal as the one concerning a rehearsal of his Eighth Symphony, when the conductor turned to him and said, "Is this note supposed to be a C or a C sharp?" and he replied, "Whatever you like, Herr Kapellmeister."

By the time success came to him, when the Seventh Symphony and the *Te Deum* were acclaimed in Berlin, when an honorary degree was conferred on him by Vienna University, when the Society of Friends of Music in Vienna elected him to membership, and he was given the freedom of the city of Linz, in short, when the honors came, they came too late. He was by that time ill and marked for death. During his illness, he composed the marvelous "Adagio" of the Ninth Symphony, which stretches to a remote but penetrable horizon.

Valerie, who liked him, offered him free lodging in the Belvedere. He moved there in July of 1895. His mind became clouded and he was increasingly subject to religious mania. In October of the following year he died, without having completed the Ninth Symphony. He was laid to rest in the church of St. Florian, beneath the organ which he had played so often.

This seemingly ingenuous man, who after the performance of his Fourth Symphony rushed up joyfully to the conductor, Hans Richter, and offered him a gulden as a tip—Richter wore the coin on his watch chain ever after—left a heritage of music worth countless gulden. However plump the symphonies may appear here or there, they are works of a tall and an ecstatic master.

3

Like Bruckner, with whom he is often wrongly bracketed, Gustav Mahler was born in the provinces, in a little village situated, as it were by mistake, between Moravia and Bohemia and representing a German dot on a Slavic map. That region of Austria, forever beset by local dissent, also produced Sigmund Freud, the great musicologist Guido Adler, and Franz Kafka. The evil fairy standing at Mahler's cradle burdened him, in addition to the expected difficulties, with the uneasy feeling of homelessness, of not belonging. "I am thrice homeless," he once confessed to his wife, "as a native of Bohemia in Austria, as an Austrian among the Germans, and as a Jew throughout the world. Everywhere I am an intruder, never welcome."

But he *was* welcome, he *was* successful, and his plaint hints at a self-pity which lay like a cloud over the sky he tried to touch. His inner conflicts consumed him, and twisted his inspiration just as it reached its highest plane. As one listens to his music, one often gets the impression of a question asked but not answered, of a promise given but not kept. "The eternal beginner," he called himself. Immense apostrophes to nature, sublime confidence in man, promenades in "the kingdom of beauty" (Bruno Walter's phrase), alternate with "country matters," naïve *Ländler* which are not really naïve—Mahler could not be truly naïve—and lose themselves in thickets. It is as if Redon were to paint like Rousseau. Yet once we accept his occasional lack of clarity or his banal moments, we can love Mahler because, questioning himself as deeply as he did, he voiced our own deep questions. He sought to express in music primal beginnings as well as ultimate destiny, but he was well aware that the riddle remained a riddle and that he was bound to be frustrated. He has been elected the musical representative of our age, a spokesman for frustration, a modern mystic.[2]

His mysticism and his preoccupation with death—which

found its most poignant expression in *Das Lied von der Erde*—derived from his Jewish heritage, his contemplation of nature being kin to that of Spinoza, and it clotted in the atmosphere of Vienna, in the aura of a country destined for death. Mahler was as much the Viennese as the Jew. He was Don Quixote of the Ringstrasse who fought not windmills, but the mills of the gods. That is not to say that he could not be gay or laugh, but that he, like many of the Viennese minds, the poets, the psychologists, the novelists, the satirists, the painters, gazed at his soul in a magnifying mirror. Some of them gazed too long.

Though he doubted himself, he led a life of extraordinary accomplishment and experienced the satisfaction of success—contrary to what some biographers would have us believe. He was born to poor parents who had twelve children. Of these five died of diphtheria at an early age, one sister (Leopoldine) died of a brain tumor at the age of twenty-six, one brother (Ernst) died at the age of thirteen of the heart trouble which seemed endemic in the family; and one brother (Otto), who gave great promise of becoming a fine musician, committed suicide at the age of twenty-six. Mahler was well acquainted with death. But if he harbored within himself a death wish, this was balanced—as Freud said of the death wish—by Eros, the positive drive of the love that seeks to preserve life. That drive enabled him to complete his nine symphonies and his songs, to become a powerful, if erratic, conductor, and to be appointed at the age of thirty-seven the director of the Vienna Opera, where he was to remain for ten years.

When Mahler took over at the Opera House, once again the old miracle of the living theater renewed itself. It was a miracle created by luminous idealism. Everything he touched, every work he staged or conducted, sounded fresh and looked newly bathed. "What most theater people call tradition is nothing but slovenliness," he said—as Toscanini was to say years later: "Tradition is the last bad performance." He sought for a new unification of the musical and dramatic content of an opera by gathering around him a group of new talents—not singers alone, but directors, musicians, designers, all of whom he inspired to deliver beyond what they thought themselves capable of. Schönberg said of him that "the productive force within him enables him to form an exact picture of what he wants in the performance. He will compromise as little as he does with his own creative work. His way of re-creation differs but a little from his way of creation, though the path may be different." Marie Gutheil-Schoder, Selma Kurz, Lucie Weidt, Erik Schmedes, Hans Breuer, Leo Slezak, Richard Mayr, Georg Maikl, these were some of the young singers with whom he worked. As principal stage designer he engaged Alfred Roller, who threw out the netted trees and papier-mâché castles. Franz Schalk and Bruno Walter joined him as conductors. Bruno Walter wrote: "Mahler freed Mozart from the lie of preciousness as from the boredom of academic dryness. He gave him the dramatic seriousness and truth which belong to him. . . . He changed the public's lifeless respect for Mozart's operas to an enthusiasm which shook the house with its demonstrations." He extracted new cooperation from the audience: in a Vienna where practically everybody except Franz Joseph always came late, you had to come on time; if not, you had to wait until the entracte before being admitted. Mahler was even successful, for a time at least, in doing away with the claque.

He was happy working at his three tasks of composing, conducting, and directing. He had no illusions and he had every illusion. "I know I am beating my head against a stone wall," he said, "but I shall nevertheless make a hole in the wall." The repertoire he produced comprised about a hundred operas; his taste was conservative, oriented toward the classics. (A few of the novelties he produced were Smetana's *Dalibor,* Tchaikovsky's *Eugen Onegin,* Leoncavallo's *Bohème,* Strauss's *Feuersnot.*)

He had been director of the Opera for five years when he met and fell in love with Alma Schindler. She was twenty and he was already forty-two, and he adored her with the passion of his all-or-nothing temperament. Alma was as artistically adventurous as Isabella d'Este, but, more important, she was as beautiful and as sexually active as Raphael's *La Fornerina,* with her dark hair, her dark eyes, and her smile punctuated by two dark points at the sides of her mouth. She was an excellent pianist, a minor but pleasant composer, and a perceptive critic of her husband's scores. She championed the new painters who were arising in Vienna, her stepfather, Carl Moll, being a member of the group of painters who formed themselves into the "Vienna Secession," which produced such artists as Gustav Klimt, Otto Wagner, Josef Hoffmann, Egon Schiele, and later Oskar Kokoschka. Alma profoundly influenced Mahler.[3] In turn Mahler's work influenced Viennese literature and the visual arts. No art is an island. "I believe in the drawing together of all the arts," Mahler wrote.

The crisis was as profound as his achievement was exultant. It came in 1907. In that year his daughter Maria Anna, five years old, died of diphtheria.[4] Grief nearly destroyed Mahler. At the same time his position at the Opera was undermined by the growing hostility of the press. He had become too uncomfortable a man to have around, forever warring against easy routine performances. And of course he had made mistakes. On the fifteenth of October he conducted his last performance at the Opera, *Fidelio*. It was badly attended. He wrote a farewell to all members of the opera house:

> . . . In the heat of battle, the excitement of the moment, it was inevitable that all of us should have suffered wounds and committed errors. But once a piece of work was accomplished, a problem solved, we forgot our pain and we felt ourselves richly rewarded, and that even without the external signs of success. All of us have progressed, and with us the institute to which our endeavors were wholly devoted.

The day after this notice was pinned on the bulletin board it was torn to shreds. Mahler left to accept an engagement at the Metropolitan Opera. Though at the Metropolitan he was able to work with such artists as Caruso, Chaliapin, Scotti, Destinn, Sembrich, Farrar, he was not happy with the catch-as-catch-can staging or the comings and going of the socialites in the loges. After two seasons he resigned. He was appointed conductor of the New York Philharmonic. There he triumphed.

But his health deteriorated. Emotional disturbances marred his life with Alma. In 1910 he decided to seek help from Freud. He broke the appointment three times, both desiring and dreading the interview. Finally the two men met at Leyden in Holland. (Freud's notes about the meeting are extant.) Freud noted that

Mahler's mother had been a suffering, morose woman, and that Mahler was subconsciously seeking that same quality of sadness in his wife. As to his fear that he was too old for Alma—Freud said that it was Mahler's very maturity which attracted her. The recollection of a childhood incident suddenly sprang up in Mahler: he told Freud that his father had often ill-treated his mother and on one occasion when the child had witnessed a particularly ugly quarrel he had rushed out of the house and in the street had run into an organ grinder, grinding out the old ditty *"Ach, du lieber Augustin."* All his life that cheap tune came back and sounded in his brain in moments of tension. It was this which prevented him from being certain that he had achieved his goal as a composer.

Freud's counsel, or Mahler's own recuperative powers, or both, strengthened him so that he was able to restore his marital equilibrium—indeed, his love for Alma flooded anew—and he was able to complete the Eighth and the Ninth symphonies, as well as revise the Fourth and Fifth. The Tenth remained a fragment.

In April of 1911 Mahler returned to Europe from America, and on the advice of his doctors the mortally ill man was brought back to Vienna. They felt that he would die more peacefully in the city which he could never call home but which was his home in spirit. He died on May 18 and was buried in Grinzing, next to the grave of his daughter.

Mahler's ill treatment in Vienna is often ascribed to Austrian anti-Semitism. (Mahler conveniently became a Catholic when he assumed the directorship of the Vienna Opera.) The accusation in my opinion is not tenable. That he was a Jew didn't help him—but Mahler's rise and fall repeated a Viennese pattern, regardless of religious prejudice. "One has to be dead to be allowed to live," Mahler once said. The Viennese have regularly first extolled, then denigrated, their great men—read Mozart's or Grillparzer's story—and named streets after them posthumously.

4

Brahms, Bruckner, Mahler, and Johann Strauss by no means complete the catalogue of musicians working in the Austria of the second half of the nineteenth century. Hugo Wolf carried on the gentle tradition of the German *Lied,* suffering because he could be no more than a lyric composer, but soothed by the balm of believing in his immortality. And yet that he wrote so beautiful a song as *"Anakreons Grab"* did not satisfy him; he grieved over the failure of his opera *Der Corregidor,* tried again, and never completed his second operatic attempt. He contracted syphilis when he was seventeen and eventually became insane. One day he was discovered in front of the Opera House proclaiming that he had been appointed the new director and was waiting for an audience with Franz Joseph. Some friends led him to an asylum, where he died, only forty-three years old.

Bedřich Smetana was the pioneer spirit in establishing a Bohemian school of music. He was an Austrian patriot—in his youth he even composed a *Triumphsymphonie* celebrating Franz Joseph's marriage—but he loved Bohemia more than he did Vienna. He founded a dramatic academy for Czech theater in Prague, established a music school there, conducted at the Prague Opera House, and when he composed *Ma Vlast (My Fatherland)* , a cycle of six symphonic poems, it was Bohemia which represented his "fatherland." His two chamber works, the quartet *Aus Meinem Leben* and the poignant Trio in G Minor, are his finest music, but he is best known for his opera *The Bartered Bride,* which Mahler brought to New York in 1909. (His other operas, such as *Dalibor, Libusa, The Kiss,* long neglected, are now coming to the fore in Europe.) He and Dvořák gave their music a sylvan tinge, deriving the sounds from woods and fields. Like Hugo Wolf, he died insane, like Beethoven deaf—a sad and senseless end.

Antonin Dvořák, a cultured and a lovable man, composed in a style more international than Smetana's. Still, as Philip Hale wrote of him, "His music was best when it smacked of the soil, when he remembered his early days. . . ." He lived wholly in music, the teaching and composing of it, and he could compose everywhere and at all times, except during a thunderstorm. He was so frightened of a storm that he turned pale, sat stiffly at the piano, and attempted to drown the noise of thunder by hammering out loud chords.

He was befriended by Brahms and recommended by him to

the publisher Simrock, who commissioned Dvořák to write an orchestral work based on Bohemian folk themes. The *Slavonic Dances* (1878) established his fame. He was honored in England, feted in America, invited here and there, but he remained rooted in his beloved Prague. When he was sixty the taciturn and modest man finally received official Austrian recognition: he was appointed to the upper house of Parliament, a purely honorific appointment. He traveled to Vienna with a friend to attend the one and only session he did attend. On the way there he said virtually nothing, as usual. When the train passed the Wittingau marshes, his friend commented on the swarms of midges which obscured the landscape. Dvořák made no reply until, days later in Vienna and walking on the Ringstrasse, he suddenly said, "Probably because there's so much water." In the Parliament the delegates came to congratulate him. He growled something indistinct —and went home, carrying off some sharpened pencils. He told his wife that the pencils would help him compose. In a serene life he composed several operas, nine symphonies (of which he suppressed four), a famous cello concerto, an almost equally famous violin concerto, choral music including the *Stabat Mater,* and some thirty chamber works which musicians regard with especial fondness. If he was not an exciting composer, he was one who dispensed much pure pleasure. He does so still.

A mere chronological tabulation, even if not complete, will give an idea of the musical wealth of the period. Beginning, arbitrarily, with the Hungarian *Ausgleich* and ending with the first decade of the twentieth century, the inventory reads:

(Unless noted otherwise, the year indicates date of composition.)
1867 Johann Strauss, Jr.: "The Blue Danube Waltz"
1868 Bruckner: First Symphony—premiere
      Brahms: *A German Requiem*
1869 Bruckner: Mass in E Minor—premiere
1871 Bruckner: Second Symphony
1873 Bruckner: Third Symphony
1874 J. Strauss: *Die Fledermaus*
1875 Smetana: *Ma Vlast*—premiere
1876 Brahms: First Symphony
      Bruckner: Fifth Symphony

1877   Brahms: Second Symphony
1881   Brahms: *Academic Festival Overture*
       Bruckner: Sixth Symphony
1883   Brahms: Third Symphony
       Dvořák: *Stabat Mater*
1884   Mahler: *Songs of a Wayfarer*
1885   Brahms: Fourth Symphony
       Bruckner: *Te Deum*—premiere
1891   Mahler: First Symphony—premiere
1893   Dvořák: *Symphony from the New World*
1900   Mahler: Fourth Symphony
       Dvořák: *Rusalka*
1902   Mahler: Fifth Symphony
1903   Schönberg: *Gurrelieder*
1904   Janáček: *Jenufa*
1905   Lehár: *The Merry Widow*
1906   Bartók: *Hungarian Folk Songs*
1907   Oscar Straus: *A Waltz Dream*
1908   Bartók: First String Quartet
       Mahler: *Das Lied von der Erde*
1909   Mahler: Ninth Symphony
1910   Alban Berg: Third Quartet
       Mahler: Eighth Symphony—premiere

5

Austria's contribution to medicine in those years was as significant as its enrichment of music. The doctors were more generously rewarded with titles and honors than the artists—provided they were conservative. Even in medicine, however, the segregation between science and the court was clearly marked. Vienna had two "schools" of medicine: the official one which served the Habsburgs, the military, and the chief functionaries; and a new school of scientific doubters whom Archduke Karl Ludwig once called "the godless witch doctors."

However fortuitous the connection between music and medicine may be, such a connection was personified by one man, as high-minded a healer as medicine has produced, who yet found time enough away from the hospital to become a proficient pianist, to earn respect as a sensitive critic of Vienna's young writers and adviser to them, and to respond to music with the strength of his soul. This was Theodor Billroth (1829–1894), a surgeon who developed new methods of anesthesia, invented the resectioning of the ulcerous stomach, made revolutionary progress in operations on the larynx and the esophagus, produced a new antiseptic bandage, and initiated a school for nurses which helped to make nursing a respectable profession. Under his leadership the Vienna Clinic became an international center for surgery; his assistants were eagerly sought by Europe's universities. Billroth had to a high degree what stellar physicians too often lack, compassion. He himself was no stranger to illness and sorrow, his first-born being a deaf-mute who ailed for years until he finally died. Billroth, whom all Vienna looked up to, never ceased to deplore "the ignorance of knowledge"; in his study, where the light often burned till two in the morning, he worried over each failure more than he rejoiced at his brilliant successes. Brahms was his great friend. Billroth understood that spinate character and was proud of the relationship. Their correspondence extended over thirty years, and though Brahms was not eloquent in words, the letters are inspiring to read. Brahms used to have his new chamber music first performed in Billroth's home. Hanslick called this the *jus primae noctis*.

Billroth represented the exceptional best of the Viennese character: a passion for achievement in his work combined with great love for the arts. Let one of his letters to Brahms serve as a description of a typical day of his life:

Vienna, March 5, 1890
11:30 P.M.

Today was a stormy day and a prevailingly harsh one, as usual every minute occupied. I awoke early with a cut on my finger. The bell didn't stop ringing and I could hardly eat breakfast in peace with my wife and the children. Messengers arrived from various hotels asking for consultations [from visitors expressly come to Vienna to consult him]. Then calls on private patients operated on yesterday. Then the Clinic. Assistants, surgeons, staff members—everybody wants something. Jesus—it is twenty minutes past ten! Let's go! To the Auditorium. Two hours of being the schoolmaster and of operating. Hardly had I left the operating room when I was besieged from all sides. Finally home, 20 minutes to eat. Then a very difficult operation which lasted more than two hours! Cautious courage—finally victory—it was successful. Quick—two glasses of cognac. Then home: six patients, some with trifling complaints—some incurable. Lies, lies as comfort. 15 minutes with the family for 5 o'clock tea, a half-hour rest, what a pleasure! I finished Widmann's book [a book describing a journey to Italy which the poet J. V. Widmann had made with Brahms]. Then to the Renaissance Concert [where old a cappella music was being performed]. For an hour and a half I derived great satisfaction from this quiet music. . . . Home, a little peace, good humor, a comfortable family supper. Now six business letters, absolutely necessary. At last! *Enfin seul!* That is how I had to fight for every moment in which I might read Widmann's charming book, that is how I have to fight for the moment to thank you that you sent it to me. . . .

How happy are people who are able to define for themselves the limits of their achievement and manage to move within these limits. Perhaps happiness lies in subconscious resignation. I cannot be so content. I am an old man but any limit is unbearable to me. I long for something—I myself don't know what—and this longing prevents any tranquil enjoyment. It is very stupid—but I can't change.

Recently the finale of your C Minor Symphony [No. 1] moved me anew and profoundly. . . .

Well, enough of these lamentations! Believe me, I am always the same—

Your faithful
TH. BILLROTH

Billroth was only one of a score of physicians who were to transform Vienna into a mecca for all medical students; until World War I it was the place to which one had to go to burnish one's knowledge.

Carl Rokitanzky, born at Königgrätz, the village where the Austrian army suffered its defeat at the hands of the Prussians, came to Vienna, became a professor at the age of forty, and performed during his career some eighty or ninety thousand autopsies, on the basis of which he drew brilliant parallels between postmortem findings and clinical manifestations of disease. He was one of medicine's pioneers, virtually the founder of pathologic anatomy. Unlike Billroth, he was indifferent to therapy; all his striving was concentrated on finding truth empirically. Though he himself was deeply religious and believed that men must follow Christ in learning to endure pain, he took a leading part in the effort to stop compulsory religious instruction in Austrian schools. His friend and disciple, Josef Skoda, a year younger than Rokitanzky and likewise a Bohemian, developed the diagnosis of chest diseases through percussion and auscultation which is still employed after a century and a half. In his clinic, too, the watchword was still *"Primum non nocere,"* the first thing is not to do harm, that is, refrain from interfering with natural healing processes. Hermann Nothnagel, who perfected the measurement of blood pressure in diagnosis, was a different sort of doctor: he believed in helping nature, and he made many useful contributions to pharmacology. He was personally one of the kindest of men, setting out in sleet and rain at all hours of the night to comfort his patients. A tragic physician was the Hungarian obstetrician, Ignaz Semmelweis. In those days mortality in childbed ran incredibly high: he discovered the cause of childbed fever. But few would listen to him, he fought acrimoniously with his colleagues, and he died, insane and friendless, at the age of forty-seven, before his creed had gained acceptance. In the year he died Lister introduced carbolic acid, and soon afterward the antisepsis Semmelweis had pleaded for was generally adopted. Ferdinand Hebra developed dermatology and created in Vienna so renowned a school for skin diseases that patients came from all over the world.

Ernst Brücke (1819–1892) was a man of prodigious breadth of culture. He raised physiology from a practically nonexistent branch of medicine to an essential part of the science and trained thousands of students during his long career. Like Billroth, he combined a passion for the arts with medicine. He became an expert on Renaissance art and wrote several papers on Michelangelo, who was one of Freud's favorites as well. He invented one of the early phonetic alphabets and published studies of German poetry and the structure of the Hindi language. Like Rokitanzky he served in the Upper Parliament, but declined a member's privileges, and fought the fight against the clergy. He was a Protestant, yet in spite of this handicap he became rector of the University of Vienna, the first non-Catholic to be elected to the post.

Freud was his pupil, and he not only trained Freud in detailed observation and the avoidance of false interpretations of microscopic findings, but he stimulated in the younger man his interest in art and literature. Freud revered Brücke, who was indeed one of the most astonishing polymaths of his century. One had to go back to the philosophes of the Enlightenment to find his like.

Theodor Meynert was one of the early psychiatrists, examining the brain's anatomy in a primitive little laboratory of his own, not the least disturbed by the noise of his children playing. He sought a physical solution in his treatment of madness, refusing the psychological approach as useless, since it transcended "the bounds of precise scientific investigation." Nevertheless, according to Jones's biography, Freud respected him as the most brilliant genius he had ever encountered. It was his successor, Richard Krafft-Ebing, who first probed scientifically the psychology of sex life.

Krafft-Ebing coined the word "masochism," basing it on the confessions of Leopold Sacher-Masoch, a writer who specialized in stories of struggle in which women subjugated men. What he wrote was largely autobiographical: only when tormented by his partner could he derive sexual satisfaction. He signed a contract with a woman of Viennese society, a Baroness Fanny Pistor, obliging himself to be her unconditional slave for six months. He then described this relationship in a novella, *Venus in Furs*.

Though Krafft-Ebing's work anticipated Freud's in some respects, Freud's most important predecessor and his most influential supporter was Josef Breuer (1842–1925), an internist who numbered Brücke and Billroth among his patients, and who made such important contributions as the definition of the function of the vagus nerve in breathing and the role of the canals of the inner ear in controlling equilibrium. He was an overly modest man, personally unambitious, even-tempered, generous—in the early years he frequently helped Freud with money—a pure man of science. Toward the end of 1880 Breuer began to treat for hysteria a twenty-one-year-old girl, Bertha Pappenheim, whom later, in writing the history of the case, Breuer called "Anna O." Bertha suffered from insomnia and paralysis of the legs and believed herself to be pregnant. Lying helplessly in her bed, she began to talk to him—she was a highly intelligent girl—recalling her childhood and her nursing of her beloved father, now dead. With infinite patience he listened, guiding her but slightly or not at all, and occasionally employing hypnosis. She called these sessions her "talking cure" and "chimney sweeping." After months of this, her symptoms disappeared, and after a year and a half she was completely restored. Breuer divined that hysteria could be caused by what he called "retention," the unconscious storing of "unassociated ideas," ideas of guilt, and that if one could make these suppressed ideas emerge into the conscious, a "cathartic" process would take place. A dozen years later—as long as that—Freud persuaded Breuer to collaborate on the *Studies in Hysteria,* published in 1895. But Breuer never again ventured on a "talking cure," being too shaken by his first experience.[5] It has been suggested that Breuer's refusal and his unwillingness to subscribe to a theory of the sexual origin of neurosis were due to a childhood trauma in his own life, his mother having died in childbirth when he was three years old. At any rate, Freud carried on, though for some time he was unsure, trying one method or the other, cocaine injections, electric massages, and so on. Years later Freud said in an address at Clark University, "If it can be counted as a credit to have brought psychoanalysis into being, the credit does not belong to me. . . ." He maintained that he was considered the inventor only because the opponents aimed their fire at him, not at Breuer. Even after he split with Breuer he acknowledged the older man's prompting.

The flow of extraordinary medical talent continued for a long time. We have mentioned only a few of the outstanding men; they were followed a little later by, among others, Adolf Lorenz, the orthopedist who devised "bloodless surgery" which led to the correction of club feet; Lorenz Böhler, Jr., the founder of modern accident surgery; the psychiatrist Julius Wagner-Jauregg, who used malaria to treat paralysis; the radiologist Guido Holzknecht; the ophthalmologist Ernest Fuchs; the anatomists Emil Zuckerkandl and Julius Tandler; Béla Schick, whose diphtheria skin test profoundly influenced the practice of immunization and helped to stamp out that dread child's disease; the otologist Heinrich

Neumann, and Josef Halban, the gynecologist (husband of the famous coloratura soprano Selma Kurz) . A remarkable percentage of these physicians were Jews, who yet made their way in an anti-Semitic climate. At one time Julius Tandler's memory was expunged from the annals of Viennese medicine (though he had been Vienna's health commissioner) along with that of other Jewish doctors. Today the Althanplatz in Vienna, named after an Austrian nobleman, has been renamed the Tandlerplatz.

Franz Joseph favored the doctors who behaved themselves decorously. He seldom employed one of the luminaries, preferring for his own needs a member of the profession whose family tree was traceable, who had done his military service, and who was a good Catholic.[6]

He left the scientists alone, but the ministers and bureaucrats manipulated them. One needed *Protektion* to succeed to a leading post. One needed "pull" to have oneself hoisted into a chair at the clinic, to become a *"Dozent,"* then an "associated professor," and then a full-fledged "professor." Plain "Doctor" would not do—and even the most idealistic of the scientists knew that with Vienna's love for titles a title represented a necessary covering for your head. The title hunt was on, and the minister who could confer it, the university being under governmental jurisdiction, had to be catered to. Many a mediocrity who knew how to use the system was given the opportunity to pontificate at the university, because he treated the *Hofrat* and his entire brood without sending a bill, or because he gave discreet advice about the *Hofrat's* abnormality. On the other hand, the strong idealists learned how to get along with the system and how to draw supportive talent to Vienna. These doctors knew what they wanted. Rokitanzky insisted on Billroth's appointment against violent opposition. Breuer insisted on supporting Freud.

6

At this late date what can be said of Freud, the literature about whom has grown to a ton of paper,[7] who gave his stamp and impress to our age, who survived derision to rise to Jupiter's pedestal in the Pantheon of healers, to doubt whose word was at one time a traitorous act, who is as often quoted and misquoted by people who have never read him as is *Hamlet,* and whose genius was encompassing enough to allow disagreement now?

Like Leonardo or Newton or Einstein he perceived a region which had been there all the time but which nobody had noticed, and he ventured into it. No—that is not quite true. Men had noticed it, or felt its presence, but had shied away from it. Plato had examined dreams in *The Republic* and had observed how "the wild beast in our nature, gorged with meat and drink, starts up and walks about naked, and surfeits at his will; and there is no conceivable folly or crime, however shameless or unnatural—not excepting incest or parricide—of which such a nature may not be guilty. In all of us, even in good men, there is such a latent wild beast nature, which peers out in sleep." But Plato had not attempted to explore further. Freud explored. Half-humorously he once compared himself to Columbus: "I am not really a man of science, not an observer, not an experimenter, not a cogitator. By temperament I am nothing but a conquistador, an 'adventurer' if you want the word translated, with the curiosity, the audacity, and the tenacity of such a nature."[8]

Is it hindsight to say that Freud would have been inconceivable in any place except the city of Vienna and at any time except the time of Franz Joseph? As I have tried to show, the Viennese were always prone to self-probing, even in the days of Austria's strength; more so in the days of Austria's weakness. Their gaiety sat on top of brooding melancholy, and they constantly sought to come to terms with the two conflicting characteristics. This occupation with oneself led, as Freud wrote, to "determinism, skepticism, what the people call pessimism." That pessimism was expressed in a Viennese saying: "Life is like a baby's shirt, short and dirty." To alleviate the short and dirty life they turned sometimes to Catholicism and its promise of paradise; just as often they were skeptics who, as is the way of skeptics, fell for miracle cures. It is characteristic that they were long fascinated by hypnosis, as Dr. Franz Mesmer, whose theory of magnetism Mozart spoofed in *Così fan Tutte,* found to his advantage. Mesmerism mesmerized the Viennese of the eighteenth century, when the doctor's treatment of the hysterically blind singer Maria Paradis set the whole city agog.

Dreams and dreaming were subjects frequently treated in Austrian literature. Pamphlets of dream interpretations could be bought at the stationer's, and Frau Müller rushed to the fortune-teller to consult her about last night's dream. Schnitzler dealt with the interaction of dream and reality, and in his *The Veil of Beatrice* he probed as a poet what Freud was to probe as a scientist. One of Schnitzler's early one-act plays of the *Anatol* series is entitled "Questioning Fate" and deals with hypnosis. To the publication of the *Anatol* plays Hofmannsthal contributed a dedicatory poem which adumbrates the mood of intellectual Vienna:

> Thus we play theater,
> Playact our own feelings,
> Ripe before their time,
> Tender and *triste,*
> The comedy of our soul. . . .
> A few listen but not all,
> A few dream, a few smile,
> And a few sip a sherbet. . . .
>
> (*Also spielen wir Theater,*
> *Spielen uns're eignen Stücke,*
> *Frühgereift und zart und traurig,*
> *Die Komödie uns'rer Seele. . . .*
> *Manche hören zu, nicht alle,*
> *Manche träumen, manche lachen,*
> *Manche essen Eis. . . .*)

They enacted "the comedy of our soul" until a genius showed them that this comedy was a serious business, until he showed them what were the results of the suppression of "the wild beast in our nature."

The root of Freud's concept was planted in the soil of an Austria which, while producing gay flowers, was becoming sodden. There it grew, nourished by malaise and doubt. A premonition of the end of an era, a foreboding of that decline which Mayerling represented, a mood ill-at-ease, drove the poets to twilight musings, the social philosophers to attempts at correction, the doctors to efforts to relieve pain, and the psychologists to the endeavor to clarify the dark diseases of the mind. Compensation was at work.

Freud came along at the right time. A genius creates the *Zeitgeist*, but the *Zeitgeist* helps to create the genius as well. Yet in the beginning he ran up against much opposition in Vienna, and this opposition has been ascribed both to his being a Jew and to the shock of the sexual theory he advanced. Infantile sexuality, incest, fetishism—these were horrendous ideas with which to tangle. Once a stranger accosted him, asking, "Are you Dr. Freud?" Freud admitted the identity. "Then let me tell you what a dirty-minded, filthy old man you are." That was supposed to be the general opinion.

Both statements are only partly true. One need not deny the prevalence of anti-Semitism by observing that in spite of it a Breuer or a Schick was respected, successful, even beloved. As to Freud's sexual etiology, it was Jean-Martin Charcot in Paris (with whom Freud studied) who first said of neurotic conditions, "Mais dans des cas pareils, c'est toujours la chose genitale, toujours, toujours, toujours"—and few were scandalized. It is improbable that in a city where prostitution was openly regulated by the police,[9] where a man could take a girl to any of a dozen hotels and obtain a room for an hour or two (they were called *Stundenhotels*), where a Sacher-Masoch lived, a discussion of sex and its abnormalities could be all that shocking. What was shocking was Freud's tracing sexual drives to early infancy, to involve the child's relationship to his parent, parent to child. What—an innocent little child feel sexual desire? Terrible! Yet not even his uncovering of the early causes of the formation of character and behavior could fully account for the hostility with which he was at first met.

It was rather Freud's own nature which aroused the opposition. He would not compromise, he would not chase after titles, he would not play the Vienna academic game, he would not promise cures as of a certain date. He would not promise cures at all. Once he formulated his theories he was intransigent: you believed them and were his disciple—or you disagreed and were banished. This

happened even when he himself changed a theory, as he not infre-
quently did. The breaking off of friendships runs as a pattern
through his life. He behaved like the endowed creator he was,
showing the amalgam of stubbornness and self-questioning which
allows little questioning by others. Seeing patients often for as
many as twelve hours a day, and then writing his notes for an
additional three hours, he was obsessed: he could not live "without a dominating passion—in fact, without a tyrant, to use Schiller's expression." That passion—he wrote even before the
publication of *Studies in Hysteria*—"is psychology, which has been
the goal beckoning me from afar" and in the service of which "I
know no moderation." Often he was discouraged: "If establishing
so few points as are needed to solve the problem of neurosis neces-
sitates so much work, energy and mistakes, how dare I hope to get
a glimpse, as I once fondly expected, into the totality of mental
function?" He understood neurosis, being himself something of a
neurotic. He did his best work when he could suffer along with his
patient. His furor, the fixation of the man who gives birth to a
great idea, drove him on. In the early days he inspired his few
followers, intrepid doctors one and all. They met on Wednesday
evenings: "A spark seemed to jump from one mind to the other,
and every evening was like a revelation."[10] Yet as time went on,
disagreement penetrated the circle. Freud would not tolerate it;
he had an inner need to be regarded as the paterfamilias of
psychoanalysis, and despite his reluctance to assume official posts,
he was pained when his name was omitted from a scientific paper.

He was capable of self-serving judgments. He disliked
America; the strange continent intimidated him, and he was
unable to read the books about America which his friend Ferenczi
had brought him. The day before he sailed for America he fainted.
"Perhaps his inadequacy with the language gave him a feeling of
inferiority, and Freud did not like to feel inferior."[11] Perhaps
with all his love of traveling he did not want to leave familiar
surroundings in which he felt secure. He was as afraid of trains as
some people today are afraid of planes. For the great work he did
he needed every possible reassurance, sometimes hardening into
arrogance.

It is understandable that such a man could not knuckle under the university politicians, that he offended those who would not at once accept his discoveries—their very newness set up a certain amount of resistance—and that for well over a decade he felt himself to be a pariah of medicine. He both hated and loved Vienna. "I hate Vienna almost personally, and in contrast to the giant Antaeus I gather fresh strength as soon as I remove my foot from the soil of my *urbs patriae*," he wrote in 1900. But it wasn't so: much later, after World War I, when Freud was famous and could have gone wherever he pleased, he told the writer Ernst Lothar: "Like you I love Austria and Vienna, although, unlike you, I know its abysses." He continued: "Austria-Hungary is no more, but I would not wish to go elsewhere; emigration is not for me. Instead I shall go on living with the truncated body, clinging to the illusion that it is still complete." When the Nazis burned his books, when Hitler invaded Austria, and when, in 1938, Roosevelt and Mussolini intervened in his behalf, he had to be practically forced to leave Vienna. In London, he survived only a little more than a year.

He was then, essentially, a product of fey Vienna and the Franz Joseph period.

He was Viennese enough—at least once—to know that he needed the title of "Professor" for pecuniary reasons, if for no other. The story of how Freud became Professor Freud is told by Ernest Jones. It is a real Viennese story:

> In January 1897, after he had been a *Privatdozent* for the unusually long period of twelve years, he wrote that rumor of his once more being passed over in favor of younger colleagues left him quite cold, but it might hasten his final break with the University. In the next month, however, he reported an interview with Nothnagel, who told him that he (together with Krafft-Ebing and Frankl-Hochwart) was proposing him for the position of Associate Professor, and if the Council of the Faculty did not agree, they were determined to forward the recommendations themselves to the Ministry. He added, however: "You know the further difficulties; perhaps we should achieve nothing more than 'putting you on the carpet.'" What gratified Freud was that he was able to retain his opinion of them as "decent men." He then had to prepare for the purpose a dossier of his published work, one which has since been published.
> Nothing came of it. The anti-Semitic attitude in official quarters

would have been decisive in itself, but Freud's reputation in sexual matters did not further his chances. Against these considerations the splendid work he had done in neurology and his European standing as a neurologist counted as nothing. In the annual ratification in September, he and his group were ignored in 1897, 1898, and 1899. In 1900 all the names proposed were ratified with the sole exception of Freud's. But he was pleased that his friend Königstein had at last been accepted.

Four years passed during which Freud took no steps. Then came the great visit to Rome, after which he says his pleasure in life had increased and his pleasure in martyrdom diminished. Dignified aloofness, no doubt, gave a satisfying feeling of superiority, but he was paying dearly for it. He decided to "become like other men" and descend from his pedestal onto the lower levels. So he took it on himself to call on his old teacher Exner. Exner behaved very rudely to him, but finally disclosed the fact that the Minister was being personally influenced against him by someone and advised him to seek some counter-influence. Freud suggested the name of a former patient, Elise Gomperz, the wife of the man for whom twenty years ago Freud had translated the John Stuart Mill Essays; Gomperz had been Co-Professor of Philology with von Hartel, now the Minister of Public Instruction. The lady was most helpful, but the Minister pretended to know nothing of the old recommendation, so that a new one was necessary. Freud wrote to Nothnagel and Krafft-Ebing, who promptly renewed it. But again nothing happened.

After this, one of Freud's patients, a Frau Marie Ferstel, wife of a diplomat, got to hear of the situation and at once entered into competition with Frau Gomperz. She did not rest till she had got to know the Minister personally and struck a bargain with him. He was eager to get hold of a certain picture by Böcklin (*Die Burgruine*) for the newly established Modern Gallery, and it was her aunt, Frau Ernestine Thorsch, who owned it. It took three months to get it out of the possession of the old lady, but at the end the Minister graciously announced to Frau Ferstel at a dinner party that she was the first to hear he had sent the necessary document to the Emperor to sign. The next day she burst into Freud's room with the cry: *"Ich hab's gemacht* (I've done it) ."

Freud's sentiments about the whole affair can easily be guessed, but he wrote to Fliess that he was the biggest donkey of all concerned, in that he should have wangled things years before—knowing the way of the world in Vienna. (March 11, 1902.) At all events he got some amusement out of it, and wrote to Fliess—in the last letter of their correspondence: "The population is participating extensively. Congratulations and bouquets are just now raining on me as if His Majesty had officially recognized the role of sexuality, the Council of Ministers had confirmed the importance of dreams, and the necessity of a psychoanalytic treatment of hysteria had been passed in Parliament with a two-thirds majority." (March 11, 1902.)

This absurd story had the expected results. Acquaintances who had looked over their shoulder when passing him now bowed even from a distance, his children's school friends voiced their envy, and—the only thing that mattered—his practice took a permanent turn for the better. He had become, if not respectable, at least respected.[12]

Freud was Viennese as well in the breadth of his cultural interests, though they were not as inclusive as Brücke's or Billroth's. He took comparatively little interest in music and the theater, though he admired Mozart and particularly *Don Giovanni*. (One can guess the reason.) He had a deep love for visual art, as his writings on Leonardo and Michelangelo and his enthusiasm for Botticelli and Signorelli demonstrate. He was equally fascinated by archaeology, the excavation of the past seeming to him to relate to the excavation of the ever-present. As soon as he had money he began collecting antique figures, Egyptian, Roman, Greek; some of them stood on his desk. He spent what time he could visiting museums, and he compared the mind to a museum where every experience is stored and nothing is lost or forgotten. With all that, he was an avid reader, not only of the German classics, but of literature as varied as Tasso, Homer, Milton, and Molière. He was particularly attracted to the English novel, *Tom Jones, Tristram Shandy, Vanity Fair. David Copperfield* was his favorite Dickens, and *Tom Sawyer* his favorite Mark Twain. He was fond of Mark Twain and went to hear him lecture in Vienna. According to Jones, the two books which made the deepest impression on him were Flaubert's *The Temptation of St. Anthony*, and *Don Quixote*. He learned Spanish to read *Don Quixote* in the original.

Perhaps it was his extensive reading, in English literature especially, which helped to form his style, a style which treated complex ideas lucidly and vividly and not without the relief of occasional humor. In that style Freud differed markedly from his followers and their exercises in turgidity. On the threshold of the twentieth century he published *The Interpretation of Dreams,* which established his early fame; the year after came *The Psycho-pathology of Everyday Life,* followed by his instruction in psycho-analysis, his thoughts on the connection between wit and the unconscious, on *Totem and Taboo,* on Leonardo, on Michel-angelo's Moses, and on Moses himself, *The Ego and the Id, Group Psychology and the Analysis of the Ego,* an astonishingly prophetic work, and so on.

He lived to be eighty-three and he worked virtually to his last day, in spite of the constant pain caused by cancer of the palate. He underwent thirty-three operations, most of them with only partial anesthesia. He took only aspirin, according to his physi-cian, Max Schur,[13] because he did not want to benumb his mind. His capacity "to love, to give, to feel, stayed with him to the end." Long before he died many of his ideas had entered everyday speech—"Oedipus complex," "transference," "superego," "subcon-scious," "Freudian slip"—to be used all too loosely. Freud is cited for the most casual mental discomfort, rather like shipping a patient to the hospital to cut a hangnail. He would have been the first to disapprove of dilettante diagnosis.

Some of his theories, particularly his ascription of neurosis to sexual origins exclusively, are being questioned today. Freud is experiencing the familiar fate of the discoverer: the discovery has led to new discoveries and the original discovery is being reshaped. Even if as a cartographer his design should eventually shrink to less than the atlas of psychology, his role in the history of civiliza-tion can never be smaller than that of a Magellan of the mind.

Freud meant nothing to Franz Joseph. In November, 1971, Anna Freud, his daughter, answered my inquiry on this point: "To the best of my knowledge, there was never a link between the Emperor of Austria and his circle and the scientific endeavors of the time. The only role which the Emperor had to play in this respect was to confirm appointments to professorships which were followed by a formal 'audience' of the newly appointed men to thank the Emperor."

7

"Two tendencies prevail today," wrote Hofmannsthal, "the analysis of life and the flight from life. . . . Either one performs anatomical examinations of one's soul—or one dreams. . . . What is modern? The dissection of a passing mood, of a sigh, a scruple."

With whatever success Freud's ministration "to a mind diseas'd" met, however clearly he pointed the way "to raze out the written troubles of the brain," and however exaggeratedly his doctrine may have come to be used, to the interpreters of the human condition, the poets, novelists, playwrights, he offered a new challenge. "Man's soul—how like the water," Goethe had written long ago. Literature, concerned from time immemorial with man's soul, now sent its plummet deeper to sound the subconscious. Folly and fault were subjected to new scrutiny. From such study rose new hope and despair. Freud himself was fond of quoting as the leitmotif of his work Milton's lines from *Paradise Lost:*

> . . . consult . . .
> What reinforcement we may gain from Hope,
> If not what resolution from despair.

Freud acted as godfather to virtually all the literature of the West, beginning with the last quarter of the nineteenth century and continuing to this day.

Proust recaptured a world by tasting a madeleine; Gustav Aschenbach met death in Venice; Nina Leeds lived out her strange interlude; and Molly Bloom fell asleep while her unpunctuated thoughts flowed on as if she were lying on a psychoanalyst's couch.[14] From Virginia Woolf's quiet interior monologues to the retching dialogue of *Who's Afraid of Virginia Woolf?*—where was the spirit of Freud not present?

He inspired a whole group of new Austrian writers who called themselves "Young Vienna." They enacted the comedy of their feelings, felt tender and *triste,* never wept openly, dissected the passing mood, listened to almost inaudible sighs, smiled wan smiles, and put it all on paper in exquisitely shaped words and in sentences so finely spun that the web breaks when one attempts to translate them into another language. Because of this frailty and because they were often occupied with playful love relationships which now seem outdated—half-measures of love, erotic hide-and-seek, impulses which arise when the lights are dim and the air is heavy—their work has been largely forgotten. Their literature has been swallowed by tougher times. Yet it was a scintillating group which used to meet at the Café Griensteidl[15] and flick ideas at one another: Peter Altenberg, a poet who wrote in a *pointilliste* technique of passing pains; Karl Kraus, a satirist who scourged the corruption of society in a famous journal, *Die Fackel (The Torch)*, and who like a biblical oracle predicted "the last days of mankind" while he turned his phrases like a circus master; Hermann Bahr, who resembled Brahms a little and who was the group's father figure, a kindly catalyst. There was hardly a phase of Vienna's intellectual life which Bahr did not stimulate and clarify by his essays. One of these, "Vienna," contained such scorn that the censor banned it. Like Freud, he hated the city as much as he loved it. One of his plays, *The Concert,* a comedy revolving around a philandering and conceited pianist, still holds the stage in Austria.

Two of the writers aided by Bahr emerged as important to posterity. One was Arthur Schnitzler, the other Hugo von Hofmannsthal. Although they differed from each other, they both represent the mellifluousness, the irony, the love for love, the pursuit of psychologic minutiae which are characteristic of the Viennese style. They both suffer from the weakness of that style. The face of the mystery is veiled in an elegant veil, but occasionally the face when revealed turns out to be disappointingly bland.

When poems signed "Loris" first began to appear in Austrian periodicals, men like Altenberg and Bahr were impressed by their autumnal beauty. Who was Loris? He was obviously an older man, a man of experience who had acquired mellow wisdom. When "Loris" was bidden to present himself at the Café Griensteidl, he turned out to be a youth in his teens, diffident and frail: he was writing under a pseudonym because he was still going to school and schoolboys were not permitted to publish under their own names. At sixteen he began to write; at eighteen he was famous.

Hugo von Hofmannsthal's (1874–1929) ancestors were Italians, Swabians, Czechs, and one grandfather who was a Jew. He grew up as a Catholic. The multiple combination made him a true Viennese; yet he was not unaware of his mixed heritage:

> Weariness of long forgotten races
> I cannot brush off my eyelids.

As a poet he longed for the past while expressing the new in verse of bitter sweetness. He was a Hugo Wolf of poetry, composing in the minor mode.

He lived in a rococo castle in Rodaun near Vienna. No modern touch spoiled its authenticity: he never permitted central heating to take the place of the white porcelain stove, and often he suffered from the cold of the Austrian winter. He sat in his study on an uncomfortable antique chair, all white and gold, carefully dressed in a black suit, and he kept on his desk a set of colored glass balls which reflected the light and at which he glanced as he was writing. Since his parents were wealthy, he was not put to the necessity of earning a living and was able to live in reasonable luxury at least until his last years, when the German-Austrian inflation of 1920 swept away his fortune in a tornado of paper money. Then he asked his friend Carl Burckhardt to sell for him a Van Gogh, a Picasso, a sculpture by Rodin; and these, plus the foreign royalties he derived from the operas on which he had collaborated with Richard Strauss, permitted him to live on.

In spite of fame and fortune, in spite of being happily married to a "courageous and humorous" woman, he was given to self-doubt, to moods of deep depression which set in when the weather was gray and which led to a touchiness that made his librettist's relationship with Richard Strauss occasionally approach the breaking point. Strauss—in his personality, not of course in his music—was a matter-of-fact, no-nonsense businessman who wanted to get on with the work, and Strauss's wife was something of a vulgarian. Hofmannsthal, while admiring Strauss's genius, avoided social contact with him as much as possible. Altogether the poet was withdrawn and aloof, a bit of an intellectual snob, who would not attend the official banquet after the Stuttgart premiere of *Ariadne auf Naxos,* since he would be forced to rub elbows with "smeary journalists and Stuttgart nonentities." On the other hand, he was quite willing to use these "smeary journalists" to help him publicize his work, and he penned many an essay to explain what he had in mind. He was intensely disturbed by unfavorable reviews, and often Strauss had to soothe him.

Several of Hofmannsthal's works remain half-completed. Most regrettable of all is *Andreas,* a story set in a menacing Venetian atmosphere. He worked on this novella for more than ten years but remained dissatisfied with it. Similarly, he never managed to produce the final version of his most ambitious play, *Der Turm (The Tower)*. In his works he voices the belief that illusion offers us a firmer ground than reality, that awake or asleep our imagination builds our world, and that this imagination is bound by ritual and legend. We are least original when we think ourselves most independent. Here once more one hears the echo of Freud. Another of Hofmannsthal's themes, derived autobiographically, is repression—in speech and action. The central character of his comedy *Der Schwierige (The Difficult Man)* is an Austrian aristocrat so afraid of "vulgar" sentiments that he finds himself unable to express his feelings for the girl he loves. In the end the girl, being almost equally subtle, manages to win him, though Hofmannsthal avoids anything like a love scene in the entire play.

His occupation with fable and legend occasionally led him to overripe symbolism, as in his Oriental story *The Woman without a Shadow,* which, turned into an opera, proves to be even more of a maze of heavy tropical flowers. On the other hand, his librettos for *Der Rosenkavalier* and *Ariadne auf Naxos* are witty, delightful, and glowing with romantic warmth. "Can a single moment be forgotten in the aeons of time?" asks Zerbinetta in *Ariadne.*

Hofmannsthal is remembered because of these operas and because his adaptation of the old morality play, *Everyman,* is still one of the outstanding features of the Salzburg Festival, in the creation of which he acted as one of the guiding spirits. J. B. Priestley, in *Literature and Western Man,* pays him a just tribute:

> He is ultra-sensitive, deeply serious; the mystical strain in him may not be strong, but it is not false, not a literary device like Maeterlinck's, and his feeling that catastrophe is on its way, that

his world is doomed, has about it something genuinely prophetic. On the other hand, it could be argued that he retreated before this intuitive knowledge that the society and culture, of which he himself was the delicate final flower, were already dying, and that he turned in despair to Baroque masquerade and mystical yearning because he could not bring himself to recognize, in all its raw crudity and destructiveness, what had life in it instead of death. So he clings to the tradition he represents like a man tied to the mast of a ship that is breaking up. His search for "the way into life," perhaps his main theme once his prodigious youth had gone, suggests that he knows he has put himself outside it. But he cannot be dismissed as a figure, elegant and autumnal, of Viennese charm and final melancholy; there is in him more steely strength, more depth too, than that; unlike almost all his contemporaries, he is now gaining and not losing stature; and he is far from being merely the poet whose words we cannot hear, above the brass and percussion of the orchestra, in *Elektra* and *Der Rosenkavalier.*

Arthur Schnitzler (1862–1931), son of a physician and himself a doctor, became the greatest master of the "Viennese language," or better, the Viennese languages, a multiple layer cake of speech which ranged from the raunchy rumbles heard in the workers' suburban districts to the spineless palaver whispered in the Palais of the inner city. His *Reigen* (*Round Dance*) is a tour de force whose successive scenes sketch the sexual habits of representatives of various social classes, an impudent procession from bed to bed, beginning with the prostitute and the soldier, ascending to the soldier and the servant girl, the servant girl and the bourgeois young man, the young man and the married woman, and so on, until the circle is closed by the count and the prostitute.

But Schnitzler was far more than a juggler of language, however dazzling. He searched for the connection between feeling and impulse, combining in his work the awareness of the physician and the psychologist. Like Freud, he perceived the force of the libido; like Freud he was concerned with death, who, in those bright and flirtatious comedies, stands in a corner just off stage. Freud was aware of the kinship and refused to meet Schnitzler, fearing that he would "encounter his own double." "I have often wondered," Freud wrote him in June, 1906, "from where you were able to draw the secret knowledge which I have had to acquire through laborious investigation. I have now come to envy the poet whom I had only admired before."

In "The Death of the Bachelor," a short story, three letters are delivered to the three best friends of the dead man. The letters reveal that each of the friends' wives has been the mistress of the bachelor. The three men react variously, but in the end each resolves to forgive, as a tribute to the finality of death. In "The Wife of the Wise Man" the husband opens the door to his wife's room and sees her with a lover. He closes the door softly. Years later, he meets the lover; he tells him that he knew but kept silent, never disclosing his knowledge. It is the husband who is the victor, having preserved the love. It is the lover who is the loser. In his play *Liebelei*—an untranslatable word meaning frivolous love—he writes of the tragedy of a girl who believes herself truly loved and is destroyed by the realization of how little she means to her lover. Again and again Schnitzler deals with the moment of awareness, the instant which liberates, the flash by which one gains illumination and understanding. Because Schnitzler instinctively turned to the psychoanalytic view he was one of the first writers, if not the first, to invent the interior monologue which was later carried forward by Joyce. Leutnant Gustl is sitting in a concert hall listening to an oratorio for no better reason than that somebody gave him a free ticket. He is bored to death, and while the music plays he is thinking of a thousand things, of a duel he will have to fight the next morning, of the army drill, of how many of those serious girls standing there and singing away could be slept with easily, and so on. Finally the concert is over. In the cloakroom, while the crowd is rushing to get out, a casual acquaintance, a baker, objects to Gustl's shoving and lays his thick hand on Gustl's sword. Gustl ought to have "punished" him at once, but he momentarily loses his presence of mind and before he can think out the "correct behavior" the baker disappears. In his own eyes Gustl is dishonored. If the incident reaches the ear of his colonel, Gustl will have to quit the army, but even if it doesn't, Gustl cannot face himself. He can hardly challenge a baker to a duel. What is left for him to do? There is but one way out: he must kill himself. All night Gustl wanders in the streets of Vienna. He waits for dawn to kill himself. He decides to eat breakfast, his last, in his favorite café. While he is munching a roll, the waiter comes over and tells the Herr Leutnant the latest neighborhood news: during the night the man who baked the roll died of a heart attack. Gustl is saved, his shame buried; the joy of life rushes over him. He is going to hack his adversary to mincemeat in the forthcoming duel, and in the evening, well, in the evening his current girl will have to make herself free to stay with him. Gustl's code of honor, Schnitzler shows, is a sham. All along Gustl has acted not according to inner conviction, but out of the need to keep up appearances, a mannikin in a uniform. When the story first appeared, in 1901, it created a sensation. Schnitzler, who was an officer in the Reserve, was promptly dismissed.

His major novel, *Der Weg ins Freie* (*The Path into the Open*), is a portrait of Viennese society, as well as a study of two very different intellectuals, two friends: one, Georg, an aristocrat, young, handsome, cultured, free of prejudices, aspires to become a composer and struggles to get away from the café-house life, the endless discussions, the do-nothing and know-everything existence which Vienna offers him, a city where it is fatally easy to postpone one's work and stroll in the surrounding woods. Georg's friend, Heinrich, is a playwright who seeks the path away from Judaism, a religious and a racial classification in which he feels demeaned and most of the traditions of which he finds "ridiculous and tasteless." Both men, both high-minded, possess what Schnitzler regards as the tragic fault: the inability to become totally involved. The actress who loves Heinrich kills herself when Heinrich cannot forgive her a passing infidelity. Georg has an affair with a sensitive girl who becomes pregnant. He knows within himself that he does not want the child, but when the baby is stillborn, he is overwhelmed with regret. Both men are guilty—and are not:

> Heinrich shrugged his shoulders. "Yes, I felt without guilt. Somewhere in my soul. Yet in another layer, a deeper one perhaps, I felt the guilt . . . and in one still deeper, guiltless. It depends always how deeply we look into ourselves. And when the lamps are lit on all floors of the house, then we appear to be everything together, guilty and not guilty, cowards and heroes, fools and wise men. . . . In the end, of what use is it that the lights are burning in

all the windows of my house? What help is my knowledge of humanity and my excellent intelligence? None . . . less than nothing.
What I really wish for, Georg, is that all the terrible events of the
last days had turned out to be nothing but a nightmare. I swear to
you, Georg, that I would trade my future and whatever else you can
think of to undo what has been done. Yet had it not happened, I
would probably still be as miserable as I am now."

The range of the novel includes several complex characters and
themes. Schnitzler does not shrink from attacking the Jewish chip-
on-the-shoulder attitude. Georg, who loathes any form of anti-
Semitism, is yet offended by Jews who are self-consciously proud of
being Jewish, or ashamed of it or ashamed of being thought to be
ashamed. He finds it difficult to establish a completely open relationship with his Jewish friends, because they do not wholly trust
him, but also because he himself feels a sense of separation. Understanding them—or anything else—does not help:

> "Understanding" doesn't help at all. Understanding is a sport
> like other sports. It is an elegant sport and quite expensive. One
> can pay for it with one's whole soul—and remain a poor devil.
> Understanding has nothing whatever to do with our feelings, almost
> as little as with our actions. It does not protect us from suffering,
> from disgust, from destruction. It leads nowhere. It is a dead-end
> street.

Heinrich, the intellectual Jew, is accused by Georg of "being a
worse anti-Semite than most Christians." He answers:

> Every race is abhorrent to me as a race. Only the individual is
> able, through his personal virtues, to reconcile us to the race. But
> I will not deny that I am exceptionally sensitive to Jewish faults.
> The reason probably lies in the fact that all of us, I mean we Jews,
> are systematically brought up to feel such sensitivity. . . . If a Jew
> behaves crudely or discourteously in my presence, I am filled with
> such discomfort as to want to sink into the earth.

Veering into politics, Schnitzler tells an anecdote—based on a
true-life incident—in which a Jewish member of Parliament who is
voicing social-democratic ideas "perhaps too energetically" in a
speech is grossly insulted in the Chamber: "Yid, shut your

mouth!" After the session his adversary meets him in the buffet, approaches him in a friendly fashion, and offers him a drink.

"Unbelievable!" exclaimed Georg.

"Unbelievable? No, Austrian. With us indignation is as little genuine as enthusiasm. Only delight at the troubles of others and hatred of talent, those are genuine here."

Such bitter commentary is balanced by Schnitzler in the figure of Court Councillor Wilt, worldly-wise, tolerant, kindly, a true servant of the state he loves:

For him Austria represented an infinitely complicated instrument which only a virtuoso should play and which emits ugly sounds so often only because every bungler thinks he can play it. "They will go on bashing at it," he added sadly, "until all the strings snap, and the case as well."

In the end Georg finds his path to the open, though he carries a part of Vienna with him. To many, many other Viennese the path was to be closed, and the time came when Schnitzler was no longer read. He is not read widely today. He may well experience his day of revival when we turn away from the hammer blows of ferocious fiction.

8

In the year that Rudolf died—the year Hitler was born—Bertha von Suttner published a book which described in passionately vivid prose the sufferings of Russian soldiers during the Russo-Turkish War of 1877. She was a Countess Kinsky—of the same Kinsky family which had aided Beethoven—born in Prague, educated in aristocratic elegance, and accustomed to a life of leisure. When the family met financial reverses, she went to Vienna and got a position in the home of a Baron von Suttner. She fell in love with the son of the house. But the baron strongly objected and Bertha fled to Paris, where she became the secretary of Alfred Nobel. It was she who persuaded Nobel to establish the Nobel prizes; she herself was to become, in 1905, the fifth recipient of the

Peace Prize. After two years of separation, her beloved Arthur Suttner joined her and they eloped to Russia, to Tiflis, where she devoted herself to the care of wounded soldiers and determined to spend the rest of her life writing and lecturing for peace. Her book was entitled *Away with Weapons!* (*Die Waffen Nieder!*). It was translated into almost every European language, and was read as propaganda as avidly as *Uncle Tom's Cabin*.

Two years later, Arthur Suttner took the leading part in founding in Vienna the Union for Defense against Anti-Semitism, an organization which Billroth and Johann Strauss joined. Three years after that, Alfred Dreyfus was condemned. Two more years elapsed; Zola was writing *J'Accuse* when a handsome Hungarian journalist came forth with the proposal that the Jews be granted a home state and form themselves into an autonomous people: this was Theodor Herzl, an adroit and tireless propagandist, who won respect for his cause in much of Europe and organized six world congresses of Jewry before he died. The point is that there were many voices heard in Austria—as there were in other countries but perhaps particularly in Austria—pleading for reason. Not all was introspection, not every writer withdrew from life, not all the talents felt resigned or nihilistic. Ambition for mankind and hope for betterment coexisted with lassitude and resignation.

Rainer Maria Rilke was a poet of resignation, using a strange new poetic instrument, as if German music were played on an Oriental flute in a fog-bound landscape. He was born to a well-to-do family in Prague in 1875. His mother had wished for a girl, and for five years the boy was treated as if he had been a girl, but his father wanted him to become an officer, and he was sent to a military academy, where he suffered until he broke loose and began a life of wandering. He met and fell in love with one of the strongest-willed and freest-acting women of the epoch, the highly intelligent and sensual Lou Andreas Salomé, who numbered Nietzsche among her lovers and to whom polyandry was a way of life, the only way.[16] For a time Rilke lived with her in Berlin. Then he voyaged to Russia, where he met Tolstoy, and to Paris, where he became Rodin's secretary. Still later he worked in the Duino palace near Triest, which the Duchess Marie of Thurn and Taxis had put at his disposal, then in Spain, and in Munich, almost always a bird of passage. He died in 1926 in Montreux, of leukemia.

He carried Hofmannsthal's tradition further, and spoke in lyrical ecstasy of the interconnection between all things, beauty and ugliness, the despicable and the holy. Unpoetic subjects inspired him to the most musical of verses; two of his finest poems are addressed to the Carousel in the Jardin de Luxembourg and to a panther in the Paris zoological garden. Maturing slowly, he finished his most important work in 1922, the *Duino Elegies,* a cycle in free verse.

Often, like Schnitzler and Hofmannsthal, he transferred himself into a self-built world of dreams; the world around him became a chimera. Gone were Schnitzler's worldly irony and Hofmannsthal's cosmopolitan humor. In the end, Rilke's dreams were visions which did not even possess the strength of grief. In his late *Sonnets to Orpheus* he found conciliation and comfort in "quiet disappearance." In *Letters to a Young Poet* he wrote what has become a famous quotation: "Works of art are of an infinite loneliness and to be reached by nothing so little as by criticism. Only love can grasp and hold and fairly judge them."

The Austrian genius unearthed its darkest—and perhaps final—treasure in Franz Kafka. It is easy to trace his lineage, out of Freud to Hofmannsthal to Rilke; yet Kafka seems to stand alone, incomparable, isolated, having no antecedents and no followers, but being present as a man who speaks in a soft voice and the simplest of declarative sentences of phantasmagorical fears and the "nasty sty" of our existence. In a special sense he seems not to have died when he did, in 1924, but to be seated beside us, telling us bedtime stories of horror. W. H. Auden said of him: "Had one to name the artist who comes nearest to bearing the same kind of relation to our age that Dante, Shakespeare and Goethe bore to theirs, Kafka is the first one would think of."

His text, wrote one of our best critics, George Steiner, "comes back from within us like an absolutely familiar, necessary part of our own selves. But it also queries and contradicts. It edges us away from self-consciousness when that has stiffened to cliché, when our mind is banal or inert."[17]

Symbolism has a way of becoming as out of date as yesterday's moral sermon. But Kafka's symbolic tales, such as "The Metamorphosis," the story of an ordinary man turned overnight into a huge insect, or *The Castle,* in which "K" seeks admittance to a stronghold which he can never enter, or "The Burrow," which digs the tunnel in vain, seem to become more relevant as time goes on. As for his major work, *The Trial,* in which Joseph K, "an important functionary in a bank," is summoned before a court to be accused of he knows not what and is never to know, until he feels himself truly guilty of a crime the nature of which he cannot divine—of that book, which has been translated into more than a hundred languages, André Gide wrote, "The anguish that it gives off is at moments almost unbearable, for how can one fail to repeat to oneself constantly: 'That haunted creature is I'?"

Like Freud, he has entered our language: we speak of the "Kafkaesque" complication of modern life. Kafka wrote: "The chains of tormented mankind are made of red tape." In more ways than one he was curiously prophetic. In "The Penal Colony" he envisioned the Nazi concentration camp:[18] the story was written in 1914, and dreadful as it is, it contains more than just cold sweat; it contains, to quote Steiner again: "not only the deepest analysis we have had of the relations between victim and executioner in the world of totalitarian politics but a foreshadowing—whose accuracy we are only beginning to gauge—of the suicidal tensions between technology and human design." That suicidal tension, the urge to open a door which we know may lead toward destruction, is a recurring theme in Kafka:

> Behind the poplars on the far side of the railway track there was the landscape, so massive that it took away one's breath. Was it a dark view through a gap or was it woods, was it a pool, or a house in which the people were already asleep, was it a church steeple or a ravine between the hills? Nobody must dare to go there, but who could restrain himself?[19]

He was born only eight years after Rilke and died two years before Rilke, at the age of forty-one (1883–1924). He was the son of a successful Prague merchant who of course disapproved of the boy's daydreaming. Yet Franz spent his first thirty-two years at home before he summoned enough strength to break away. He studied law and finally took a minor post in an insurance company which left him time enough to write. But he was never sure of his talent, accused himself of being infirm of purpose, and felt guilty toward his father. He wrote because "it was impossible not to write," feeling alternately "fearful strain and joy." But he did little to further a "literary career." He was not a truculent man; quite the contrary, he was gentle, tolerant, good-natured. When he died, he was virtually unknown. A few men, such as Martin Buber, Rilke, Hofmannsthal, and Franz Werfel, could and did value him. At his death, a good part of his work, including the three novels, was still unpublished. Kafka instructed Max Brod, a poet and essayist and his best friend, to destroy all of it. Brod decided to disobey. *The Trial* was published in 1925, a year after its author's death, *The Castle* was published in 1926, and the unfinished novel, *Amerika,* the following year.

Thus, while Kafka lived in Franz Joseph's time and wrote *The Trial* in 1914 (nearly twenty-five years before Stalin's purges) , and though chronologically he belongs to the period of intellectual surge which began in the latter half of the nineteenth century in Vienna, we think of Kafka as being of more recent date than Hofmannsthal or Rilke. His signals sound as if they were going off next to our ears, right now.

Chronology aside, he, Freud, and Mahler are the three Austrians who, ruled by the unsuspecting Emperor, have most potently influenced modern thought and feeling.

9

Less was accomplished in the visual arts. Why Austria, preeminent in music, should never have produced a painter of the first water, while England, preeminent in drama and novel, should never have given birth to a composer of highest genius—that is one of those historic riddles. But there it was—and at the time when the Impressionists, Monet, Sisley, Pissarro, developed in France a new vocabulary for painting, in Vienna a Ferdinand Waldmüller painted sentimental scenes in which shepherdesses dressed in gingham minded immaculately clean sheep. The young men who eventually formed the *Sezession* had less territory from which to secede. Still, once the influence of the oversexed and undertalented Makart had waned, a new school did arise to further Art Nouveau—they called it *Jugendstil* (Style of Youth)—and from it three remarkable artists arose. The leader was Gustav Klimt (1862–1918). Like Wagner's Tristan and Isolde, he meditated on the continuity of love and death—"From where I sprang there must I return"—and, as in *The Kiss* of 1908, placed his lovers in patterns of strange flowers and stranger geometrical shapes, surrounding their embraces by colors as pellucid and vivid as those of a Persian manuscript. As do certain works by Schnitzler and by Hofmannsthal, Klimt's canvases give out the indeterminate shimmer of dreams. Yet he was eclectic enough to learn the joy of innocent color from Renoir, and he demonstrated that joy in *The Sunflower* of 1907 and *Fruitgarden with Roses* of 1903–1905; while his portraits of elegant women are reminiscent of Whistler. Klimt was commissioned to paint murals of *Philosophy, Medicine,* and *Jurisprudence* for the aula of Vienna University. He exhibited the first of these, *Philosophy,* in 1900, a gigantic picture in which floated misty nudes. It created a cloudburst of scandal. Thirty-four thousand visitors came to gape at it and eighty-seven professors signed a petition protesting against it: "At a later time this picture may serve as testimony of the yeasty process pervading the creation of art in Vienna around the turn of the century—but we do not wish to see such a picture on the ceiling of the aula." One professor of theology threatened to resign. Klimt promptly returned his fee and refused to exhibit the other murals. That same year *Philosophy* won the Grand Prix in Paris. All three murals were removed to Immendorf Castle near Vienna, which the Nazis burned in 1945.

Some critics believe that Egon Schiele, born in 1890, might have become one of the important artists of the twentieth century, had he not succumbed at the age of twenty-eight to the influenza epidemic of 1918. His eroticism was more overt and perverse than Klimt's, his women more active. He was a master of line and of the nude. One of his most beautiful paintings is a study in browns, *Autumn Trees,* 1911. Equally fine is *Portrait of a Boy,* 1910, now in the Belvedere. Insufficiently appreciated for a time, he is now considered one of the most original talents of our century; his pictures have sharply risen in value, particularly since the Albertina Museum in Vienna published a monograph reproducing his work.

The strongest of the three, and the best known, is Oskar Kokoschka, born in 1886 and still alive at the time of this writing. He began as an Expressionist of great force, often merciless in his portraits: *The Steward* (around 1900) or *Adolf Loos* (same year), as psychologically perceptive as El Greco. Kokoschka had to win his fame outside of Austria—the old story!—emigrating after Archduke Franz Ferdinand, that great art expert, stated publicly, "The fellow deserves to have every bone in his body broken." His most famous work, now in the Kunstmuseum, Basel, is *The Tempest,* also called *The Wind's Bride,* which he painted just before the start of World War I. Two lovers, presumably himself and Alma Mahler, are enclosed within turbulent forms suggesting storm clouds and jagged mountains. At the heart of the whirlwind the lovers have found peace in each other.

Two architects of talent and daring showed European builders the way toward a new, dryer style, which came to be known as functionalism. Otto Wagner proposed plans for cities which would replace slums with clumps of simple apartment buildings grouped around an "air space" housing shops and places of recreation. His disciple, Adolf Loos (1870–1933) scorned ornament as sickly and outdated, "no longer an organic expression of our culture"—a locomotive was beautiful and had no need of ornament—and wanted to reform not only architecture but dress and all the appurtenances of living. He built on the Michaelerplatz, one of Vienna's oldest squares, a building which the Viennese called "The House Without Eyebrows."

10

The men and women mentioned here by no means represent all the seminal Austrian talents of the Franz Joseph era. One could proceed to Felix Salten, who late in life became famous through his charming animal story *Bambi;* or Rosa Mayreder, one of the

earliest and most effective propagandists in the cause of womanhood; or the important philosopher Franz Brentano, born on the
Rhine, who renounced the priesthood to become a teacher at
Vienna University and to whom most of the leading intellects of
Vienna, including Freud, Breuer, and Masaryk, paid their re-
spects; or Ernst Mach, the physicist who so greatly impressed Wil-
liam James, and is remembered now by the term used to define the
speed of supersonic aircraft; or the social philosopher Josef Popper-
Lynkeus, who proposed that armies of soldiers be replaced by
armies of farmers producing food enough for all; or Christian
Freiherr von Ehrenfels, the progenitor of Gestalt psychology; or
Sandor Ferenczi, one of Freud's most creative partisans.

It was during the Franz Joseph period as well that Vienna
heard the first compositions of Arnold Schönberg (1874–1951) —
Gurrelieder in 1911 and *Pierrot Lunaire* the following year—which
caused such controversy at one performance that a riot broke out
and an ambulance had to be sent for.

Some of the hundreds of ideas, proposals, and plans spawned
by Viennese thinkers were inept to begin with and remained in
the coffeehouse discussion stage. Karl Kraus laughed at the Austrian habit of discussing all sides of a question and never arriving
at an answer: "We dispatch world traffic on narrow-gauge brain
tracks."

All the same, during the reign of Franz Joseph Austrian minds
achieved an astonishing record in the arts and in medicine, spur-
ring later minds to explore in new directions. Freud alone would
have made the era extraordinary, but there were examples enough
to demonstrate that Austrian civilization could be pictured as a
pair of scales, intellectual achievement heavy in one tray, political
achievement light in the other. Whether there was a causal connection in this imbalance one can only conjecture. It has happened often enough to make one suspect that the disproportion,
the odd asymmetry, may not be due to mere happenstance.
Strength and weakness, delight and dole, have frequently coexisted in history.[20]

Karl Lueger, "Handsome Charles," Mayor of Vienna, a despicable man
and a great executive

CHAPTER XII

Din in the House

EXTERNAL PEACE, INTERNAL WAR—such was the condition of Austria in the two last decades of the nineteenth and the first of the twentieth century. External peace, internal war—such was the condition of Franz Joseph's personality in the same period, the king a paradigm of the kingdom.

Franz Joseph sounded as calm as the chairman of the board at a stockholders' meeting in a good year, as he went through the routine of the precisely scheduled meetings with the ministers, the workers' delegates, the foreign ambassadors, and those men and women from the university or the opera house whose achievements merited some sort of acknowledgment, however superficial, and who were now admitted to His Presence, while he smiled and said, "Very nice. I am very pleased." Everything had a shiny gloss, the buttons of the uniforms, the parquet floor, the white kid gloves, and the Emperor's face. The whiskers were perfumed and the face was noncommittal. Yet when he retired at the ungodly early hour at which he invariably did retire, and as he lay alone— often alone now, for Elisabeth soon resumed her absence—in that army cot which he insisted on retaining,[1] he could not have pushed away thoughts of uncertainty over the future, those thoughts which give sharper pain to nighttime meditation. Who was to succeed him? To whose hands was he to pass the scepter? His brother Karl Ludwig? A genuflecting, Bible-quoting follower of the clergy who when he met people did not simply say, "Good day," but made the sign of the cross and who would certainly cause open revolt among the liberals, and who, anyway, was but three years younger than Franz Joseph. Karl Ludwig's eldest son, Franz Ferdinand? An ordinary young man, quite unsympathetic to Franz Joseph, who liked to slaughter game wholesale, whose chief hobby was collecting statues of St. George, the patron saint of hunters, who, though not politically stupid, came complete with a set of prejudices, growing maxims of bias in his fat brain. He had been sent traveling to broaden his viewpoint, and he undertook a voyage to the United States without being much impressed by anything except Niagara Falls. Ludwig Victor, Franz Joseph's youngest brother? He was even then beyond or beneath consideration, having made his existence in Vienna impossible by his escapades. He would serve sumptuous dinners at the "ghastly hour of five o'clock"[2] and then roam the streets in search of handsome boys. Because of an incident in a public bath, he was dubbed "the Archduke of the Bath" by the Viennese. Otto, Franz Ferdinand's brother? Redlich says he was "famed for his male beauty," but he had made himself a laughingstock, providing the populace with comic relief. They called him "the Habsburg fornicator."

One after another, family sorrows sought out Franz Joseph; about the time of Rudolf's death came the revolt of Archduke Johann Salvator (uncle of Valerie's husband), who had been Rudolf's friend and was a highly gifted soldier and statesman. As early as 1875 Johann Salvator had taken it upon himself to criticize the army publicly, pointing to its superannuated regulations and its waste of man power. An enraged Franz Joseph, hurt where he took greatest pride, had immediately chastised and demoted him:

> A brochure entitled, "Reflections on the Austrian Artillery," of which Archduke Johann Salvator has acknowledged himself to be the author, has recently been published. In it he discusses circumstances relating to official and personnel matters in that branch of the service to which he belongs, in a manner incompatible with and severely damaging to order and discipline, the foundations of the army.
>
> I have therefore found myself compelled to transfer this Arch-

duke from the Artillery which he has denigrated to Infantry Regiment Wilhelm No. 12 and personally to punish him with a severe reprimand.

I draw your attention to this incident,

FRANZ JOSEPH
Vienna,
February 17, 1875

Later the Emperor forgave him. Then, in 1886, when Prince Alexander of Bulgaria was kidnaped and, after his return in triumph, refused to serve his lacerated country any longer, a Bulgarian delegation made some secret overtures to Johann Salvator. Nothing came of them; yet Franz Joseph knew about the affair, and the archduke's continued refusal to obtain his Emperor's permission for his moves led to the inevitable break. Not only was he the Emperor, but he controlled the Habsburg fortune (a fund set up by Maria Theresa), could distribute up to two-thirds of its income, and consequently apply financial sanctions against a rebellious archduke. In the very year of Mayerling, Johann Salvator voluntarily renounced his title and his income. No longer a Habsburg, no longer an archduke, he assumed the name of Johann Orth, left Austria forever, became captain of a ship, and perished, perhaps purposely, in a storm off Cape Horn in 1890. (His mistress was supposed to have died with him.) No trace of ship or man was ever found, though rumors persisted that he had been seen in this or that South American republic.

Johann Salvator's brothers behaved strangely as well: Karl was a harmless eccentric who wanted to pick and repair locks and liked to travel incognito on trams; Ludwig, known as "the learned" because he wrote and spoke fourteen languages, dressed like a vagrant, lounged about unwashed and unshaved, and was probably homosexual. Later Johann's niece, Louise, Crown Princess of Saxony, left her home to follow a lover, while his nephew Leopold repudiated his origin and assumed the Wagnerian-sounding name of Leopold Wölfling. Indeed, the House of Habsburg was breaking into pieces.

The question of succession grew more troublesome within the next few years. Brother Karl Ludwig, having in religious ecstasy drunk a cup of water from the river Jordan, died of typhoid.

Nephew Franz Ferdinand suddenly developed tuberculosis. He spent two years in mountain air, stretched out in one sanatorium or another. Nobody expected him to live. Yet, tougher than his medical soothsayers believed him to be, he recovered. He now became the heir presumptive. Was he fit for the task?

2

From the outside looking in, from Paris or St. Petersburg, Austria looked good. Business was better, Vienna was growing. There were war scares, but no wars. Prices on the Vienna stock market rose, and in the foreign press Franz Joseph was beginning to be called "the Peace Emperor."

At home, in the neo-Greek building of the Parliament, things didn't look so pretty. Centrifugal pressures increased within the Iron Ring. At elections held in 1890 the "Young Czech" delegates, zealots all, captured the seats of the conservative Czechs. The German Liberal party was pushed into a corner by the representatives of the Christian Socialists, a rising group which represented the interests of the small shopkeeper and artisans, and the humbler section of the white collar workers. The Christian Socialists were fought by Viktor Adler's Social Democrats, the laborers' party. The Pan-German group made threatening noises against the Jews, the Polish deputies voted against the Hungarian agrarian interests. Parliamentary sessions became cockfights which Taaffe could no longer control.

The makeup of the Parliament did not represent the needs or the wishes of Austria's population. The men who were chosen to serve in the upper and the lower houses were not chosen by a process of universal suffrage but according to a system whereby deputies were elected in four curiae (districts). In the favorite curiae relatively few voters could elect many deputies, while an enormous popular vote in an unpopular curia would result in numerically small representation. Taaffe knew how hopelessly antiquated the system was; he proposed certain reforms which would give the vote to every male citizen twenty-four and older, able to read and write, regularly employed or having served in the army. But he kept the principle of voting by curiae, nor did he change the excessive number of deputies—425 of them.

It was a weak compromise. Nobody was pleased. Just the contrary: the intramural fights became worse, the nationalistic ax-grinding got louder. Franz Joseph knew that Taaffe's Iron Ring had become rusty and was about to break apart. Regretfully he dismissed Taaffe.

He appointed Prince Alfred Windisch-Graetz, the grandson of the general who had helped to save the monarchy in 1848. He was a man of good will, but quite unable to comprehend the temper of a world in which a prince—even a Prince Windisch-Graetz—could no longer be wrapped in cotton wool. Viktor Adler organized the second of the great workers' demonstrations. On a mild October day of 1894 all business stopped in Vienna and crowds paraded in such enormous numbers as to dwarf all previous manifestations. People carried banners demanding "full voting rights." It was a peaceful and orderly demonstration which filled the Ringstrasse, and no one was hurt. In other cities the day went off less peacefully; street fighting broke out, and in Prague the houses of German-Bohemians were broken into and their owners beaten. Windisch-Graetz said he would not be moved by "the arguments of the streets."

It was an insignificant incident that wrote a fast finis to Windisch-Graetz's ministry, even before he had much of a chance to show what he could do. The incident centered around a tiny Styrian town, Cilli, a town which few of the men sitting in the Vienna Parliament had ever visited or worried about. For years the educated Slovenes living in that region had demanded a high school, a Gymnasium, with Slovene teachers. The German liberals had replied that the German Gymnasium there was perfectly adequate; no use spending money to build another school or hire more teachers. But in the budget of 1895 the ministry authorized the expenditure as a gesture of appeasement to the Slovenes. At once the German deputies screamed "betrayal" and Cilli became a symbol of German-Slavic hatred, a speck in the eye which blinded Parliament's sight, or rather made them see red. Without the support of the still-powerful German party, Windisch-Graetz had but one course open to him: he gave up and resigned.

Franz Joseph had let it be known that Parliament was either going to stop behaving like a gang of street urchins or he was going to choose a new cabinet himself, staffing it with men loyal to him—and he would personally override party politics and the rules he himself had set. What he proposed was, of course, illegal. But he was the Emperor. Carrying out his authority, he chose as the new minister-president Count Casimir Badeni, who as Galicia's governor had shown that he knew how to suppress rebellion and govern a province effectively. A "strong man," his well-wishers called him the Polish Bismarck, whom he resembled in stature and aristocratic manners. But he was far from a Bismarck; he was a man who "knew all the answers," when in point of fact he knew little about Austria's internal needs. He found that the sort of family browbeating which worked in a little province didn't work in a large and conglomerate state. In German eyes his greatest fault was being a Pole, and as soon as he had appointed a few of his compatriots to important positions, the German and Czech representatives, temporarily agreeing, shouldered their spades to dig his grave.

Three major problems confronted Franz Joseph and Badeni: (1) reform of the suffrage; (2) appeasement of the Young Czechs; (3) renewal of the *Ausgleich* agreement with Hungary, which was just then due for its periodic decennial negotiation.

As to the first, Badeni did propose the extension of the voting right. But he, too, compromised, combining the principle of popular voting with the old curia scheme, and adding a fifth to the four existing ones.

Badeni's bill was full of intricate absurdities, from a democratic point of view, and full of complicated discriminations. The gross inequities were fully revealed in the way in which the law would operate in the provinces of Bohemia and Moravia; whereas between 40,000 and 50,000 electors there would choose a deputy in the new fifth curia, nineteen landed aristocrats, 3,000 bourgeoisie, and about 9,000 peasants would each elect a representative in their respective spheres. This measure failed utterly to meet the expectations of the advocates of equal and direct suffrage—the Social Democrats and the Christian Socialists—nor did it satisfy the desires of the German Liberals who stood to lose in relative importance, or the rabid Jew-haters, who would deny every Israelite the franchise. Nevertheless, the proposal attracted the support of a majority of the deputies, was passed, and was sanctioned by the Emperor.[3]

The law only created new confusion. In the election held in March, 1897, representatives of no fewer than twenty-five parties were sent to Parliament. It was a disunited-nations assembly, like the French Chamber after World War II.

In that election the Young Czechs made a strong showing. Badeni decided to cater to them. The siege with which Prague had been punished for the recent disturbances was lifted, press censorship lightened, political prisoners pardoned, and a few of the Old Czech officials who had earned the displeasure of the young ones were dismissed. This was but a prologue to two Language Ordinances published in April, 1897, which substantially extended the concessions granted to the Czechs in the eighties.

Within four years every civil servant in Bohemia would be required to speak and write Czech as well as German. "Civil servant" meant high and low, the railroad brakeman and the judge, the letter carrier and the district attorney. Obviously this represented a victory for Czech interests.

It was difficult to foresee that the Language Ordinances, summarily decreed as law by Badeni with Franz Joseph's approval, would cause the severest seismographic disturbances since the revolution of 1848. The quake was felt in city and farm, down to the humblest sun-dried village.

The German Austrians burst with fury. How dared a Polish count, a highhanded and presumptuous aristocrat, who understood nothing of the attempts to achieve solidarity by the people who represented—at least to themselves—the bones and marrow of the body politic, how dared he derogate their importance? It was an insult, a reckless, wayward affront. It was absurd to force Czech, a "mere dialect," on Germans. And surely such a proposition should have been first presented to Parliament.

The wounds gaped anew. The Badeni law reopened underlying jealousies. All over Austria people massed, shouted, hissed insults; the Viennese students waved German flags and carried Bismarck's picture in the streets, while the Czech students unfurled banners bearing the portrait of Huss. In Graz soldiers attacked an anti-Badeni assembly, killing one man who promptly became a national hero. So excellent a historian as Theodor Mommsen let his judgment be swayed sufficiently to publish an open letter in which he urged the Austro-Germans to hold steadfast. A Czech poet answered him by addressing him as "Overweening spokesman of slavery!"

But it was in the Parliament itself that the worst excesses were committed. There was no question any more of doing constructive work. Franz Joseph, by an extraordinary decree which had not been invoked for twenty-eight years, closed Parliament in June, 1897. It didn't help: when Parliament reconvened in the autumn, conditions only became worse. The delegates organized an "Obstruction Concert." They provided themselves with noisemakers, rattles, bells, harmonicas, cymbals, toy trumpets, small and large drums, and just plain pot lids. The Germans filibustered, delivering long speeches to which nobody listened; one delegate, a Dr. Lecher, spoke for twelve hours.

The object of the filibuster was obviously to make it impossible to press the Language Ordinances through the House. Mark Twain was present at the sessions; possibly because he had been trained as a reporter and because his interest in politics was keen, he, a foreigner, understood the situation and wrote a vivid account of the proceedings in "Stirring Times in Austria":

> One half of the great fan of desks was in effect empty, vacant; in the other half several hundred members were bunched and jammed together as solidly as the bristles in a brush; and they also were waiting and expecting. Presently the Chair delivered this utterance: "Dr. Lecher has the floor."
>
> Then burst out such another wild and frantic and deafening clamor as has not been heard on this planet since the last time the Comanches surprised a white settlement at midnight. Yells from the Left, counter-yells from the Right, explosions of yells from all sides at once, and all the air sawed and pawed and clawed and cloven by a writhing confusion of gesturing arms and hands. Out of the midst of this thunder turmoil and tempest rose Dr. Lecher, serene and collected, and the providential length of him enabled his head to show out above it. He began his twelve-hour speech. At any rate, his lips could be seen to move, and that was evidence. On high sat the President imploring order, with his long hands put together as in

The "Obstruction Concert" in the Vienna Parliament (contemporary drawing)

prayer, and his lips visibly but not hearably speaking. At intervals
he grasped his bell and swung it up and down with vigor, adding
its keen clamor to the storm weltering there below.

Dr. Lecher went on with his pantomime speech, contended, untroubled. Here and there and now and then powerful voices burst
above the din, and delivered an ejaculation that was heard. Then
the din ceased for a moment or two, and gave opportunity to hear
what the Chair might answer; then the noise broke out again. Apparently the President was being charged with all sorts of illegal
exercises of power in the interest of the Right (the government
side). *Wolf* (a rabid pan-German delegate): "I require an ad-
journment, because I find myself personally threatened. (Laughter
from the Right.) Not that I fear for myself; I am only anxious
about what will happen to the man who touches me."

The Ordner. "I am not going to fight with you."

Nothing came of the efforts of the angel of peace, and he
presently melted out of the scene and disappeared. Wolf went on
with his noise and with his demands that he be granted the floor,
resting his board at intervals to discharge criticisms and epithets at

the Chair. Once he reminded the Chairman of his violated promise to grant him (Wolf) the floor, and said, "Whence I came, we call promise-breakers rascals!" And he advised the Chairman to take his conscience to bed with him and use it as a pillow. Another time he said that the Chair was making itself ridiculous before all Europe. In fact, some of Wolf's language was almost unparliamentary. By-and-by he struck the idea of beating out a *tune* with his board. Later he decided to stop asking for the floor, and to confer it upon himself. And so he and Dr. Lecher now spoke at the same time, and mingled their speeches with the other noises, and nobody heard either of them. Wolf rested himself now and then from Speech-making by reading, in his clarion voice, from a pamphlet.

I will explain that Dr. Lecher was not making a twelve-hour speech for pastime, but for an important purpose. It was the government's intention to push the *Ausgleich* through its preliminary stages in this one sitting (for which it was the Order of the Day), and then by vote refer it to a select committee. It was the Majority's scheme—as charged by the Opposition—to drown debate upon the bill by pure noise—drown it out and stop it. The debate being thus ended, the vote upon the reference would follow—with victory for the government. But into the government's calculations had not entered the possibility of a single-barreled speech which should occupy the entire time-limit of the sitting, and also get itself delivered in spite of all the noise. Goliath was not expecting David. But David was there; and during twelve hours he tranquilly pulled statistical, historical, and argumentative pebbles out of his scrip and slung them at the giant.

Badeni was sufficiently insulted to fight a duel in which he was wounded, though not seriously. To try to restore order, he resorted to a trick: he had one of his minions introduce a bill proposing that any deputy who continued to disturb a session after being called to order twice could be suspended from the House. Few, if anybody, heard the proposal amid the din, and arbitrarily it was rushed into law. When the delegates realized what had happened, they set up a protest which passed from name-calling and clamor to bodily assault: the young deputies fought with their fists, the older ones hurled inkstands and desk drawers, while one Czech professor of law, who had got hold of a fireman's bugle, blew it into his neighbor's ear. Georg Schönerer cut the upholstery of the chairs with a pair of shears. The chairman summoned sixty policemen, who, with the "cold unsentimentality of their trade" (Mark Twain), grabbed what delegates they could and dragged them away. Schönerer, held fast by a gendarme, kicked and screamed, "Hail, Germania!"

The chaos inside the House had its counterpart in the streets.

Sunday, November 28, 1897, was a gray and rainy day. Low dirty clouds hung over Vienna; they added melancholy to the heavy mood of the people. It was the kind of weather which serves as a setting for revolution. Meetings were scheduled everywhere; the Social Democrats had planned ten separate meetings for that morning, after which they were to march to the Parliament and demand Badeni's dismissal. Parliament itself was blocked off by a cordon of soldiers on horseback. All entrances to the Hofburg were similarly secured. At eleven o'clock the workers appeared marching up the Ringstrasse. The students met them marching from the opposite direction. Thousands of spectators surrounded them; some joined in the singing. They all milled aimlessly around, many not knowing why they were there or what they were supposed to accomplish. Everybody was cold and wet. Suddenly, a few minutes before twelve, a loud command sounded through the rain. The soldiers stationed in front of the Parliament building drew their sabers and at once galloped their horses straight into the crowd, hacking right and left. An immense panic ensued; men fell in the mud cursing, women screamed, young boys were bleeding. The panic lasted all afternoon and spread through the city. Badeni hurried to Franz Joseph and counseled: "Let us not give in to the mob." The mayor and police president declared that they could no longer maintain order without resorting to extreme force. That meant shooting. "I cannot reconcile myself to the use of guns in the streets of Vienna," said Franz Joseph. Badeni had to go. There was no help for it. That night "extras" were hawked in the streets announcing Badeni's resignation. The *Neue Freie Presse* later called the day "a day of shame for every one."

It was, in fact if not in pretense, the end of any attempt at parliamentary government. Parliament continued to exist, the delegates in the lower house continued to shout, the members of the upper house continued to make fulsomely erudite speeches garnished with Latin quotations, but the obstructionists, both on the Czech and on the German sides, had learned only too well that it was possible to scuttle all progressive measures. They talked governing to a standstill.

Now Franz Joseph returned to doing what came naturally to him psychologically, authoritarian reign. He could make himself believe that he had honestly attempted a constitutional monarchy but that it had not worked. What he attempted henceforth was the exercise of absolute authority within a legal structure of constitutionalism. He changed no laws; he laid down the law. It was strong medicine, yet it was a mere palliative, and henceforth to the end of his reign, whenever parliamentary agreement could not be reached, Franz Joseph fell back on Article 14 of the Constitution, which enabled the Emperor to rule by emergency. Article 14 was employed too often in the coming years.

But the dead spirit of Metternich could not get along with the living spirit of a Viktor Adler. The textbook from which Franz Joseph had learned his lesson was no longer valid. Joseph Redlich, one of Austria's most perceptive historians, himself a member of Parliament, wrote of the November Sunday: "From that moment on the realm of the House of Habsburg was destined for perdition." Whether we date the destiny from that "day of shame" or from the January night in Mayerling is unimportant. Certain it is that the denouement was foreordained.

Two years after Badeni proposed the Language Ordinances, they were buried.

3

While the politicians wrangled the city expanded. In twenty years its population grew by more than 50 percent; a census of 1890 showed that it had reached 1,300,000 inhabitants, which made good its claim as a major metropolis. Vienna was now to become one of the world's most glorious and ravishing cities. One man contributed so much to the city's well-being that he came to be known as the "King of Vienna."

Karl Lueger (1844–1910), a famous name in the annals of the

city, was as hateful a man as he was an adroit politician and an admirable administrator. He came from a poor backgroud; his father was a servant employed in a laboratory, who managed to give the boy a good education by sending him to the Theresianum. There he became proficient at debating and mediating. He became a lawyer, turned to politics, briefly entered the Liberal party only to abjure it, and spent his evenings in suburban inns, drinking *Heurigen* wine, eating fried chicken, and talking politics to "my people" until the innkeeper let it be known that it was time to close for the night. He never married and lived with two adoring sisters. He was tall, broad-shouldered, his forehead high and free, his face framed by a small and fine beard, the very picture of a manly man. The Viennese called him "Handsome Charles" (*Der Schöne Karl*). He became the catalyst and driving force of the Christian Socialist party, which he represented in Parliament. There he unloosed his oratory. He spoke a language new to politics: no Burgtheater German for him, no quotations from Latin poets, no rotund phrases: he adopted the Viennese dialect of the fruit vendor and the mason, sentences that in the simplest of syntax pushed forth lies with folksy openness. When he berated his opponents, he did so with the epithets of the fiacre drivers, though he could also command a good-natured joshing. His style was what the Viennese call *fesch* (dashing), and it is easy to understand why he became the darling of the people: he was what Franz Joseph was not, one among them.

His political platform contained two planks, both constructed to please a large section of Vienna's lower middle stand. One was anti-Semitism; the Jews were the international capitalists, and it was they who siphoned off the profits which legitimately belonged to the Vienna shopkeepers. He was going to "get rid of Rothschild," "reform all commerce and create community projects, awarding the work to Christian businessmen." His second resolution was "Get Budapest out of Vienna," and combining both spites, he coined the shibboleth "Judeo-Magyars," which was as meaningless as it was effective, rekindling animosity against the country which was supplying much of Vienna's increasingly expensive food.

The industrialists were incensed at him, the Social Democrats mistrusted him, the nobility disdained him, the intellectuals thought him a peacock. Franz Joseph could not stomach him; he believed that putting him in power would adversely affect the Hungarian negotiations then in progress. What is more, Franz Joseph was jealous of Lueger's popularity; "Handsome Charles" was anything but handsome in *his* eyes. As Lueger was climbing the political ladder to the mayoralty, Franz Joseph said to Count Erich Kielmansegg, the governor of Lower Austria: "You may count on it—as long as I reign I will never confirm Lueger as the mayor of my imperial and residential city." Soon enough he had to take back his word.

There was no stopping Lueger. He rushed from one coffee-house to the next, from one beer hall to the other, from one little social function to the nearby family reunion; there he was, at weddings, at christenings, at confirmations, always the jovial guest. Somebody calculated that by 1904 he had attended fourteen hundred golden wedding anniversaries. An 1895 police report to Franz Joseph stated:

> Medallions with his portrait, photographs and busts of Leuger are being sold en masse. At concerts people call for the "Lueger March" and it is stormily applauded. The women are being caught by dangerous excitement. . . . Anti-Semitism therefore is carried into the bosom of the family; the result is a coarsening of sentiment and a poisoning of social life.

That same year Lueger was elected mayor of Vienna, a post equivalent in importance to that of the mayor of London, and the Christian Socialist party obtained a majority in the city council. Promptly Franz Joseph vetoed the appointment, dissolved the city council, and ruled the city for two years through a commission chosen by himself. During these two years Lueger was elected three times, and each time Franz Joseph, showing the courage of his conviction, vetoed the appointment. After the fourth election, in April, 1896, people massed in front of City Hall to pay hysterical tribute to the "martyr." Franz Joseph held out for another year; after the fifth election he gave in. Lueger became mayor on April 8, 1897. He remained mayor for thirteen years.

If Lueger's rise seems reminiscent of that of a later demagogue, let me add that Hitler acknowledged Lueger as his master.

Here the parallel ends. Once elected, Lueger turned out to be a superb statesman. He did an about-face: he hung up his mantle of hate and put on Solon's cloak. He never lost his earthy suburban manner, remained the simple man, and became not only a wise arbiter but the instigator of innumerable projects for the public weal. He got things done, using everybody's talent, including Jewish talent.[4] He made friends with several Jews; accused of this by a rabid anti-Semite, he was supposed to have replied: "*I decide who is Jewish.*" Incorruptibly honest, he saw to it that contracts were awarded and fulfilled without graft. A British firm, the Continental Gas Company, had been supplying gas to Vienna at high prices. Lueger had municipal gasworks built and lowered rates. He electrified the street cars, established electric street lighting, built a public market, and completed a second aqueduct which brought water to the growing city from 150 miles away. The Viennese always "enjoyed an interment": funerals were elaborate affairs and very expensive, with many a family paying the bill for years after the grave had been closed. Lueger bought two funeral companies and had them run as municipal enterprises, charging reasonable prices. He had new schools built and saw to it that poor children were given free lunches. He opened a retreat for the aged near Schönbrunn, had a new public hospital constructed, and brought under the city's control a life insurance company, a savings bank, and an old-age pension fund. He established an employment agency and a housing agency. He beautified his city by expanding the parks, putting a tub of flowers around each lamppost, and building an easily accessible beach on the shore of the Danube which became one of Vienna's most popular Sunday excursions. He worked with Otto Wagner, who built, among other edifices, a badly needed insane asylum, Steinhof. He did all this without greatly increasing taxes. Less admirable was his stubborn insistence on reintroducing compulsory religious instruction in the schools. Every schoolroom was supplied with a cheap crucifix.

Wearing the mayor's golden chain, he continued his visits to those golden wedding celebrations, and in the evenings would sit down, take off the chain, unbutton his collar, and play tarok. Then he would drink a glass of wine, but it had to be Austrian wine, never Hungarian. Anybody could talk to him, he was considered everybody's friend—and that included the industrialists against whom he had campaigned. Franz Joseph became reconciled to him, at least outwardly. Lueger kept on working and planning, until the diabetes from which he had suffered for years and to which he paid little attention killed him in 1910. He was almost blind in his last years.

In sum, he was instrumental not only in making Vienna more attractive but in putting into operation a social system unexcelled by any other European metropolis. In spite of the demonstrations, the parliamentary quarrels, the ever-present economic problems, the people of Vienna—particularly the simple people he called "his people"—lived in reasonable security during his thirteen years. A despicable man—a great executive! His memory is still green in the minds of the Viennese.

4

Franz Ferdinand recovered. His tenacious love of life, his unslaked ambition, combined with a quantity of luck to accomplish what was then considered a miracle, a victory over the tuberculosis bacillus. He descended from the magic mountain, and in the year that Lueger became mayor, Franz Ferdinand reported himself ready to reassume his military post, one largely nominal, with the rank of lieutenant field marshal. His father dead, he now began to prepare himself for the succession. Franz Ferdinand, like Rudolf, had been kept idle by Franz Joseph. Unlike Rudolf, his response was positive and challenging. At the Belvedere Palace, which had been assigned to him, he gathered a group of advisers to work out future plans: it is of academic interest only to note that had he lived he probably would have provoked further tragedy for his country. He detested the Jews, disliked the Italians, distrusted the Hungarians, and thought Serbia ought to be absorbed into the Habsburg empire.

How curious it is that this man, in whom so much hatred was stored, dared an open clash with Franz Joseph, dared loss of rank, privileges, succession, all that mattered to him—and all for love.

He was now thirty-five years old: it was high time to choose a wife, and it was his duty to select her among the princesses of royal blood. However, he was in love with a girl of lesser lineage, a mere countess, the Countess Sophie Chotek, an intelligent but far from seductive woman. Rumor had it that Franz Ferdinand had become impotent and Sophie Chotek was the only woman who could still arouse him. But so personal a problem, of course, mattered little to a Habsburg ruler: Franz Joseph forbade the union. Franz Ferdinand pleaded with him—without result. Either renounce the woman or renounce the succession as well as the archducal title— such was the ultimatum. It was inconceivable to Franz Joseph that love could outweigh dynastic considerations. It was inconceivable to Franz Ferdinand to abjure the throne he so greatly desired. He turned to what friends he could muster. Among others, Ernest von Koerber, then Prime Minister, who enjoyed the confidence of both uncle and nephew, was beseeched by Franz Ferdinand to act as mediator:

> I beg Your Excellency to plead with His Majesty to have pity on me. I am at the end of my physical and moral force and no longer responsible for what I may do. . . . You are one of the few who sympathize with me. Do everything you can to prevent a catastrophe. . . .[5]

It was only when the Minister of the Exterior, Count Agenor Goluchowsky, had the nerve to declare roundly, "Your Majesty, if you do not give in we shall live through another Mayerling," that Franz Joseph consented to compromise. Franz Ferdinand would remain in the line of succession if he were willing to renounce all royal rights for the children of his morganatic marriage. He was willing.

The "Act of Renunciation" took place on June 28, 1900. Franz Joseph, wishing to give the widest possible publicity to his disapproval, had summoned fifteen archdukes, the chief ministers of Austria and of Hungary, the governors of various provinces, church dignitaries, high officials—all in all more than a hundred men. They assembled in the throne room of the Hofburg. Franz Joseph stood under the baldachin, Franz Ferdinand stripped off his right glove, placed his hand on a Bible which the Archbishop of Vienna held for him, and repeated in hoarse, veiled tones the ritual words: "We bind Ourselves with Our word never to attempt to nullify Our present declaration . . . ," and so on. Then deep silence filled the room, broken only by the scratch of the pen. Franz Joseph inclined his head, turned, and left the room without a word. The archdukes followed.

The following Sunday Franz Ferdinand was married to Sophie Chotek in his castle in Reichstadt in Bohemia. No male member of the Habsburg family was present, not even Franz Ferdinand's two brothers. In future years Sophie was made to feel her inferior status by a hundred humiliations; she was not allowed to sit in the royal loge at the Opera, she could not use any of the court carriages, at table she was seated below the youngest archduchess, when she entered an assembly only *one* of the wings of a double door was opened for her, and when in 1901 Franz Ferdinand gave an official banquet to the German Crown Prince at the Belvedere, she could not act as the hostess in her own home.

Elisabeth in the year of her death, painted by Leopold Horovitz

CHAPTER XIII

Assassination

CAUX IN SWITZERLAND (near Montreux and now the seat of the Moral Rearmament Conference) was a small and fashionable spa. Visitors to Caux in the early days of September, 1898, were speculating as to the identity of a tall woman dressed in black whom they frequently encountered on their early morning walks. She was sometimes accompanied by two or three female companions who treated her with deference, and she carried a large white parasol, holding it low over her head, the obvious purpose of which was to discourage an approach by strangers. When she spoke to anybody, particularly to the children who were everywhere, since school had not yet started, she did so simply and charmingly, in a French which was neither Parisian nor Swiss. With her companions she conversed in Hungarian. Occasionally she carried a book, an English book. She was reading a new novel by Joseph Conrad, *The Nigger of the Narcissus* (retitled in America *The Children of the Sea*). People were aware she was staying at the Grand Hotel, where the concierge let it be known that she had taken fifteen rooms. Her entourage of servants seemed to be a large one. She never appeared in the dining room but took her meals in her apartment, served by her own waiter. The woman in black furnished a topic of lazy conversation on an idle holiday. Who was she? Probably the wife of an immensely wealthy Hungarian nobleman, on leave of absence from her husband.

2

Caux was but an inconsequential point touched in the course of Elisabeth's roving. Like a female Sinbad she voyaged in ever wider circumferences and zigzag peregrinations, carrying on her shoulders the burden of confusion and guilt. She fled from the deaths of others to a wish for her own death which, as soon as it emerged in her consciousness, would be downed by a frantic desire to live, to be young again, to recapture the beauty she once possessed. She was still magnificent, though her long walks and exposure to sun and wind had hardened her skin, and she was now plagued by intermittent rashes that cosmetics could not quite conceal nor her starvation diet—at times madder than ever—wipe away.

It was as if Death, a careful and patient strategist, removed one by one those for whom she cared, to make his way to the capture of the central figure. Rudolf became but a memory, as unreal to her as he had been in life. According to Lady Walpurga Paget, wife of the British ambassador, she wore "a necklace of black wooden beads, with a large medallion containing a lock of Rudolf's hair," and she worshiped her dead son in unrealistic recollection. Andrassy's death left a deeper vacancy. In May, 1890, she lost her eldest sister. Nené had been the only one of the five sisters whose marriage had turned out well, but her husband, Prince Maximilian of Thurn and Taxis, died early, followed by her son, only twenty-one years old. Finally, Nené herself succumbed, ending the pains of cancer, pious and resigned, Elisabeth by her bedside. Two years later mother Ludovika died, and then there was no longer any reason for Elisabeth to visit Possenhofen and reconstruct her youth. In 1897 her youngest sister, Sophie, wife of the Duke of Alençon, was officiating at a charity bazaar in Paris. One of the attractions of the bazaar was a magic lantern, lighted by gas. It exploded, the fire caught a huge curtain which formed a tented ceiling, and spread so rapidly that hundreds lost their lives. In the panic Sophie tried to help with the rescue. She burned to death, her corpse unrecognizable until it was identified by her dentist's chart.

Franz Joseph's eyes still lighted up when Elisabeth came home, though soon enough her melancholy got on his nerves: "She speaks of death so often that I become quite depressed," he confided to the German ambassador. He was now growing slightly deaf, and Elisabeth—perhaps in unconscious revenge—spoke in a voice lower than ever. Valerie urged her mother to speak up, but Elisabeth protested that she could not shout.

She felt herself useless, she said, standing between her husband and Katherina Schratt. Yet from time to time, even though she allowed herself to be painted as the "Mater Dolorosa," she smothered her dolorous mood and made an honest effort to come to terms with life. She did not lose her desire to learn, to read, to write poetry. And to shop. Marie Festetics helped her to bargain. "I would be sitting in a debtors' prison," Elisabeth joked in a letter to Valerie, "were it not for Marie Festetics, who is so good at bargaining that we got things fabulously cheap." The bargains she bought turned out to be second-rate stuff. The Achilleion, which survives as a gambling casino, looks like the showroom of a not quite respectable "art store."

Whatever love still lay in her heart was expended on Valerie. Valerie was much in love with her handsome Franz Salvator, but the wedding had to be postponed twice because of the period of mourning after Rudolf's death. When they did get married, in Ischl on July 31, 1890, Elisabeth summoned strength enough to be there, to cast her nighted color off, to dress in white, to pretend gaiety, and to drive through the throng of cheering villagers, sitting erect in an open flower-decked carriage, bowing to the girls dressed in their Sunday dirndls and to the men waving hats into which they had stuck the precious edelweiss they had plucked on mountain heights. It was only after the ceremony, when mother and daughter were alone and Elisabeth helped Valerie change into traveling clothes, that the Empress broke down and wept. The sad disillusion of her own life overwhelmed her. She doubted the institution of marriage. She said, "At the age of fifteen one swears an oath the meaning of which one does not understand. Forever after one is imprisoned by that oath." In the midst of her happiness, Valerie worried about her mother; she made Karl Theodor, Elisabeth's brother, swear that he would watch over her. She knew that her father could not. But it was no use; Elisabeth would not be watched. Almost immediately after the wedding she announced that she would go away on a long sea voyage. Neither Valerie nor Franz Joseph could hold her.

None of the available Austrian yachts being sturdy enough to brave the open Atlantic, it was arranged for her to charter a British cutter, the *Chazalie*. She boarded it at Dover with a retinue which included a doctor, a Greek teacher,[1] her hairdresser, her chamberlain Baron Nopcsa, Marie Festetics, and the customary staff of servants. At the outset the ship ran into a storm which the crew said was beyond any they had experienced. Marie Festetics wrote her friend Ida Ferenczy: "It was a miracle that we were able to return to shore. . . . What I suffered in the last eighteen hours beggars description. . . . The thought of going on that ship again is terrible. I only pray that my strength will hold out . . . it is really too much for me." Indeed too much for her: she was fifty years old and had grown very stout, and seemed years older than Elisabeth. She felt her life had been wasted in the service of this labile queen. During the storm the ship was damaged and had to be repaired. Then, once more, they set out on a voyage none knew where to or for how long. Again they ran into storms, Elisabeth and the Greek being the only ones not confined by seasickness. When the teacher finally succumbed, Elisabeth complained: she missed her Greek lessons. There was no fixed goal: they went to Portugal, to Gibraltar—where Elisabeth walked for eight hours in the heat, exploring town and fortress, while Marie dragged along— to Tangier, Oran, Algiers, where having barely touched the coast she decided to swerve to Corsica to visit Napoleon's birthplace, to Marseilles, Florence, Pompeii, and Capri. They were all cooped up on the small boat, half-dead from the heat, bickering among themselves. Finally at Naples she declared she had had enough of the *Chazalie*. She ordered her purchases—which included a goat and a Brazilian parrot—loaded in hundreds of crates on board the *Miramar*, to come to rest at Corfu. She had bought marble statues for the Achilleion, a "Peri" (the beneficent fairy of Milton's *Paradise Lost*) , a Sappho, a Homer, a Plato.

Franz Joseph went to Corfu to meet her and beg her to return, if only to stop the ugly rumors which were being whispered, and more than whispered, in all of Austria about the "mad Empress."

She did return, ending the long period of mourning in Vienna. At the first court reception she still wore black, her only jewels a string of black pearls. She then visited Valerie in her new home, but true to her determination not to act the mother-in-law to Valerie's husband, she refused to accede to her daughter's plea to stay: "A seagull has no place in a swallow's nest." Even when Valerie gave birth to her first baby—a girl christened Elisabeth, of course, and called Ella—grandmother soon lost interest. The role of a doting grandmama did not suit her. She could not bear to see Valerie's figure "inflated by pregnancy." No doubt this was a projection of her narcissism. Franz Joseph adored Ella, as he did Rudolf's child, little Erzi (likewise an "Elizabeth") and all the other children born later. He loved to dandle his grandchildren on his knees. He liked to play the role of the magic grandfather, a kind of all-year Santa Claus, without bothering in the least to try to understand the children. Elisabeth had not much use for Erzi, because she disliked Stephanie, Erzi's mother, and she seemed to feel ill at ease with her own grandchildren, natural though she could be with strange children. She bought them expensive gifts, but she would not sit on the floor to play with them. When in 1893 Valerie gave birth to a boy, Elisabeth was again away and Franz Joseph sent off two telegrams with the news: one to her and one to Katherina Schratt. He wrote to Elisabeth: "I don't know why, but I am thinking of Rudolf. It is a weak recompense but a recompense all the same." It was many months before Elisabeth could be persuaded to see her grandson. She, too, was reminded of Rudolf.

In search of sun and warmth—such at least was her excuse to herself—she went to Egypt. There she haunted the bazaars, walking at such a pace that the policemen who were secretly detailed by the Austrian Ministry in Cairo to follow and protect her could not keep up with her and demanded carriages, protesting it was impossible to shadow her on foot. In Alexandria she met Frederic Barker, a handsome young man of a prominent Anglo-Greek family. She was attracted by his looks, his youth, and above all by his knowledge of languages. A year later she asked him to join her on an eight-week voyage, to teach her Greek literature. The eight weeks stretched into thirteen months, and later Barker became her official reader. That was the end of Christomanos. She now found his open-mouthed adoration as enervating as the *Föhn,* the depressing south wind. Everybody in Elisabeth's entourage was delighted to see him depart, most of all the captain of her yacht, who told Elisabeth's new chamberlain, General Adam Berzeviczy—who had replaced old Nopcsa—that Christomanos had behaved so overbearingly that "nothing would give him greater pleasure than to dump the little Greek overboard." The little Greek was awarded a professorship at Vienna University. Royal wishes could make professors. Barker, who could discuss English literature with her as well as Greek, who like Elisabeth wrote verses—which were no better than those of his mistress—and who amused her by playing the guitar, remained with her to her death.

She seemed to live the lines of Heine's poem: "Where I am not, there lies happiness." Her mania for movement lapsed only rarely, and only very rarely did her conscience recall her to the duty of representation. She did consent to take part in the great 1896 celebration of the millennium of Hungary's constitution:

> There she is, seated in the throne room of the royal palace in her black, lace-embroidered Hungarian gown. Everything, everything about her is somber. A black veil cascades from her black hair, held fast by black pins, black pearls, everything black, only her visage white as marble and ineffably sad. . . . It is the same face as long ago, a face we know from charming portraits: the same open, noble features, with the hair cut short in front and framing the forehead like a silken fringe . . . but grief has engraved its traces there. It is the same portrait but wrapped in fog. . . . She sits silent and unmoving as if she saw or heard nothing. . . .
>
> Now the president of the Parliament, Desider Szilágyi [famous as an eloquent orator] begins to speak. Slowly, thoughtfully, respectful before the throne. The King listens. But in Elisabeth's face not a sign can be noticed. It remains pale and motionless. Suddenly the speaker mentions the name of the Queen. Her face does not respond, but at once a shout of *Eljen* roars through the hall, such as had never been heard in the Ofen palace. It was as if a tempest had been let loose, springing from everybody's heart. It was a sound, wonderful and strong, which can neither be described nor explained. A prayer lay in that *Eljen.* Now the silent head moves, and slowly, and hardly noticeably, it inclines in thanks. . . . Stronger

and stronger thunder the shouts; they seem to make the beams tremble. The magnates of the land swing their calpacs. The shouting cannot be stopped, the speaker cannot continue. A flush spreads over the snow-white cheeks of the Queen, the white becomes pink, like milk seen in a rosy light, then red, very, very red, red as life. . . . Her eyes open wide, they shine in former luster. For a moment only. Then those eyes which long ago could smile so seductively that they comforted a sad country, brim with tears. . . .[2]

The same year Queen Victoria had seen her:

. . . I received the Emperor and Empress of Austria. She is much altered and has lost all her beauty, except her figure, which remains the same. The Emperor was very kind . . . and I asked him to accept the Colonelcy in Chief, of the King's 1st Dragoon Guards, which seemed to please him very much. The Empress left sooner, saying she thought I might like to speak to the Emperor. He expressed the hope that our two countries would be on the best of terms—understood that we could not bind ourselves to any particular action beforehand, though I think he regretted it, but I tried to reassure him. He regretted the state of Turkey,—William's imprudence, but trusted England and Germany would always keep well together.[3]

3

At the beginning of the last year of her life, Elisabeth left Paris, having lost confidence in her Parisian physician, and traveled by way of Marseilles to San Remo. She hoped to undergo still another cure there. She felt weak, her shoulders and arms pained her, she walked at an unaccustomed invalid's gait, and she seemed to herself "eighty years old." "Even this," she wrote to Valerie, "will end sooner or later, and I will enjoy eternal peace." Now of a sudden she longed to see Franz Joseph again. It was impossible for him to get away, in the midst of the Badeni troubles, and impossible for her to face coming to Vienna. Instead she submitted docilely to still another cure and additional medical advice,[4] now in Kissingen, then in Bad Brückenau, then in Bad Nauheim, until she gave it all up as useless and hastily went to Switzerland, to Caux, where she had been before. There, in the mountain air and favored by late-summer weather, which the local people said was extraordinarily mild and lucent, her health and mood improved. She took up her usual walking tours, accompanied by Barker and Countess Irma Sztáray, thirty-four years old, who had taken the place of the aging Marie Festetics. She smiled again; Barker read to her; she discussed Bertha Suttner's book, of which the author had sent her an autographed copy.

One day she decided she would visit Julie de Rothschild, who belonged to the Austrian branch of the multitudinous Rothschild clan, her husband Adolph Rothschild belonging to the Neapolitan branch. She was a very good friend of Elisabeth's sister Maria, whom Adolph had aided when she fled from Naples. Julie owned an estate at Pregny on the shores of Lake Geneva which had been described to Elisabeth as a magic castle. Elisabeth announced her visit for the ninth of September, to Julie's great joy, and Julie offered to send her yacht to fetch her. Ordinarily traveling privately would have pleased Elisabeth; nevertheless she thought it tactful to refuse the offer, since she knew that the Rothschild servants were forbidden to accept tips or presents and she felt that she could not put the crew to extra trouble without any recompense. She decided to take the public steamer to Geneva and asked Berzeviczy to arrange rooms at the Hotel Beau-Rivage in Geneva for her, so that she could stop there overnight on her return from Pregny and the next morning do a little shopping in Geneva, before going back to Caux. Berzeviczy begged her not to stop in Geneva. He knew the city was a hiding place for terrorists. At least she ought to have police protection.[5] Did she remember Sadi Carnot, President of France, who four years previously had been assassinated by an Italian anarchist? What about Émile Henry, who had set off a bomb in the Café Terminus in Paris, killing one man and wounding seventeen? The creed of anarchism, a concept which demanded the end of all government and the destruction of high-placed persons, was gaining strength. Assassination was in the air. Elisabeth laughed: "Who would want to harm an old woman like me?"

Early on September 9, a magnificent Indian summer day, Elisabeth's party started out. On the steamer to Geneva she was as placid as the weather; she sat on deck and played with a little boy to whom she gave cakes and fruit. When she arrived at Pregny, Julie was there to greet her enthusiastically. The villa and the gardens were at their best; the leaves were turning, the fat yellow flowers were still in bloom, everything shone in the noon light, while the mountains around had donned their caps of snow, as if they were getting ready for a special parade. The table was laid with old Meissen porcelain, somewhere a hidden orchestra played Italian melodies during lunch, and the lunch itself consisted of two menus, a kosher one for Julie and a French creation for Elisabeth, who forgot her diet for once and even drank champagne. The two women discussed Heine and exchanged court gossip as well. After lunch Elisabeth visited the aviaries, the aquarium, and the greenhouses, to which she returned again and again to admire the orchids. She had had no idea, Elisabeth said to Julie, how many shapes and colors orchids could assume. Entering the villa— one of Switzerland's "museums"—the hostess asked that Elisabeth sign the guest book. She did so on an empty page, writing merely one word, "Elisabeth," and handed the pen to Countess Sztáray. The Countess leafed through the book and seeing on an earlier page the name Rudolf she hastily closed the book and handed it back to Julie. Elisabeth and her lady-in-waiting returned to Geneva around five, stopped at the hotel, but left shortly after to amble through the streets of the city, consume several portions of water ices at Geneva's famous *Konditorei,* Désarnod (that was Elisabeth's supper) , and then went to buy a small inlaid table to be sent to Valerie. Night had fallen, they were still walking through narrow old streets, and they lost their way. But Elisabeth, who had an excellent sense of orientation, soon found the way back to the Beau-Rivage. Nobody noticed them, nobody bothered them.

It was arranged that the servants would take the train back to Caux, while Elisabeth and Countess Sztáray were to return by the steamer scheduled to leave Geneva at 1:40 P.M. In the morning they visited the shop of Monsieur Baecker, who dealt in mechanical contraptions. What Elisabeth wanted to see was the famous "Orchestrion," which reproduced music mechanically (on the principle of a music box or the later pianola) and had been introduced to an admiring British public at the Exhibition of 1851.

Monsieur Baecker appeared and demonstrated the instrument, which played melodies from *Aïda, Carmen, Rigoletto,* and *Tannhäuser.* Elisabeth was enchanted and at once ordered an Orchestrion to be sent to the Archduchess Valerie Salvator, Castle Wallsee. Monsieur Baecker concluded that this customer who made so expensive a purchase lightly must be somebody of importance; he asked her to sign his guest book. Instead, her companion signed "Erzébeth Királyne," which is Hungarian for "Queen Elisabeth." Elisabeth said to her companion in Hungarian: "He won't understand what this means, and by the time somebody translates it we'll be far away." The two women returned to the hotel, and Elisabeth went to her rooms. She had not emerged by 1:25, so the Countess knocked at her door, entered, and found her on the balcony looking at the landscape while she drank milk from a silver cup. "I never saw Mont-Blanc as clearly as today," she said.

"Your Majesty—the steamer is leaving in a few minutes. We must hurry."

"You seem nervous, Irma. You take your duties too seriously."

"It is unthinkable that we two be left alone in Geneva."

Elisabeth put on a black hat in front of the mirror, took her gloves, her fan, and her parasol, and walked with her lady-in-waiting to the landing place.

What happened then is best described in Countess Sztáray's own words, as she gave her testimony to the examining magistrate of the Geneva police, Charles Léchet.[6]

> LÉCHET: I would now like to ask you to describe the details of the crime, beginning with the moment when you and the Empress left the hotel today at midday. When was that?
>
> SZTÁRAY: Exactly 1:35. We crossed the street and walked along the lake front to the dock. The sun was shining and Her Majesty had opened her parasol.
>
> LÉCHET: Were the Empress and you alone?
>
> SZTÁRAY: Yes. Her Majesty was in the best of humors. She called my attention to the chestnut trees which were blooming for the second time. "Just look, Irma!" she said and stopped to admire the blossoms. I said: "Your Majesty, the chestnuts are exceptionally beautiful, but if we want to make that steamer we had better move on!" The Empress laughed. Near the Hotel de la Paix, across the street from a stand for carriages and their

drivers, a man came toward us. Directly in front of us he seemed to stumble. He made a movement with his hand—I thought to prevent himself from falling. In that second I noticed nothing else.

LÉCHET: You saw no weapon in the man's hand?

SZTÁRAY: I would have been ready to swear that he had nothing in his hand. Absolutely nothing.

LÉCHET: Then what happened?

SZTÁRAY: The Empress sank down. Without a sound. Only then the thought came to me that this horror could have struck Her Majesty. Terrible enough. But anything more terrible I could not guess, as I bent over her, thoroughly scared. At once she got up again. A couple of carriage drivers helped her. Straight as a ramrod and smiling she stood again before us. "How does Her Majesty feel?" I asked nervously in Hungarian. "Did anything happen?" "Nothing happened," responded the Empress calmly. In the meantime the concierge of the Hotel Beau-Rivage came running; he had witnessed the frightful scene and begged us to return to the hotel. "Why?" asked Her Majesty, and added, "Let us hurry a little or else we'll really miss our boat." She put on her hat, which she had lost in the fall, accepted with thanks the fan and the parasol which the bystanders handed her, and we proceeded.

LÉCHET: As if nothing had happened?

SZTÁRAY: As if nothing had happened. She marched on with her elastic step and refused my arm. The concierge came after us with the news that the culprit had been apprehended. "What is the concierge saying?" asked the Empress. Since Her Majesty had perfect hearing, I wondered about that and I looked at her. I noticed that her features had suddenly contracted with pain and I implored her to tell me what was the matter. "I think my chest hurts me a little, but I am not quite sure," she replied. We had reached the dock. She walked up the gangway still with a light step. But hardly had she entered the ship when she said to me in a choked voice: "Your arm, now, please, quickly." I could not hold her erect and both of us sank down, her head on my breast. "A doctor, a doctor!" I screamed. The Empress lay in my arms deathly pale. A lackey who had carried our coats to the ship brought water. I moistened her face and temples and she opened her eyes. With horror I saw death in those eyes.

LÉCHET: What did you think had happened?

SZTÁRAY: I was sure that Her Majesty had suffered a heart attack. Somebody said it would be better to transport the unconscious woman to the upper deck. With the help of two men we carried her upstairs and placed her on a bench. In the meantime the ship had sailed. The Empress, in fact, did revive in the fresh air. She opened her eyes and looked around her for a minute or so with an unsteady gaze. Then with my help she slowly sat up. "What has happened to me?" she asked. Immediately after she fell unconscious. I opened her blouse and her silk corset to let her breathe easier. As I tore the ribbons, I saw on her chemise a dark spot, about as large as a silver gulden. I pushed the chemise aside and discovered near her heart a tiny wound, with a drop of dried blood. Now in this moment the incredible truth came over me. . . . I asked that the captain be summoned. "Sir," I said to him, "on your ship lies Empress Elisabeth of Austria, Queen of Hungary, mortally wounded. One cannot allow her to die without medical and priestly assistance. Kindly give orders to return at once." The captain hurried away without saying a word, and immediately the ship changed its course back to Geneva.

The unconscious Elisabeth was carried back to the hotel, to the very room she had left a little while ago. Two physicians and a nurse attending one of the hotel guests volunteered their services. A priest came and performed the last rites without Elisabeth's regaining consciousness. She died at 2:40 P.M., exactly an hour after she had walked onto the boat with the wound in her heart. She died a senseless and useless death, a political victim of a fantastic creed, she who for many years had been as little concerned with politics as a baker's wife in a Tyrolean village.

After the deed the assassin had fled, but several bystanders ran after him and caught up with him. He halted and without any show of opposition followed the policeman who arrested him.

From the first interrogation:

LÉCHET: You are charged with the attempted murder of Her Majesty the Empress of Austria. Do you admit the deed?

LUCHENI: Yes. . . .

LÉCHET: Your name?

LUCHENI: Lucheni.

LÉCHET: First name?

LUCHENI: Luigi.

LÉCHET: Born when?

LUCHENI: April 23, 1873. [He was therefore twenty-five years old.]

LÉCHET: Where?

LUCHENI: In Paris.

LÉCHET: But you are Italian.

LUCHENI: Yes.

LÉCHET: First name of father?

LUCHENI: I don't know.

LÉCHET: Illegitimate?

LUCHENI: Yes. . . .

LÉCHET: Occupation?

LUCHENI: Day laborer. . . .

LÉCHET: Why did you come to Geneva?

LUCHENI: [No answer.]

LÉCHET: Well? You surely know why you came to Geneva.

LUCHENI: That I know exactly. I read in the paper—I mean in the Lausanne paper—that the Prince of Orléans is staying in Geneva.

LÉCHET: And?

LUCHENI: I came here to kill him.

LÉCHET: You mean, the French pretender to the throne?

LUCHENI: Yes. . . . But I did not find him. . . . I swore to myself to kill some high-placed person or another, prince, king, or president of a republic—it's all the same. They're all made of the same stuff.

At this moment, the telephone rang.

LÉCHET: The Empress of Austria has this moment died of her wounds.

LUCHENI: All hail to anarchism!

The interrogation continued.

LÉCHET: Describe your deed now.

LUCHENI: It was just half past one when I saw the Empress come out of the hotel with the woman who had accompanied her in the morning and yesterday.

LÉCHET: You said, "the woman who had accompanied her in the morning and yesterday"?

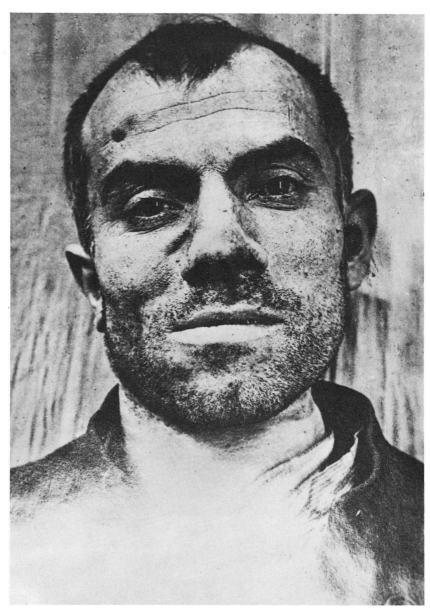

Luigi Lucheni, the assassin

LUCHENI: Yes, that's it.

LÉCHET: How did you know?

LUCHENI: How did I know? Because since yesterday I spied on her. How else?

LÉCHET: Fine—continue. You saw the Empress and her court lady come along.

LUCHENI: Yes, they walked along the lakeside of the Quai du Mont-Blanc. A little while before, a servant, a man with two coats—the kind of coats that belong to women of society—came out of the hotel and went to [the ship] *Genève*. I knew the *Genève* left at 1:40 for Territet below Caux. And in Caux, I knew, the Empress was staying for a cure. . . .

LÉCHET: And?

LUCHENI: Then everything went as I had planned.

LÉCHET: It wasn't *you* who planned it.

LUCHENI: Who else?

LÉCHET: You only executed a command. You acted under orders. We know that exactly. [This was pure bluff on Léchet's part.]

LUCHENI: You can believe what you like. Everything went as *I* had planned. I *alone*. . . . I ran toward her and barred her way. I bent down and looked under the parasol. I didn't want to catch the wrong one. They were both dressed in black. She wasn't very beautiful. Quite old already. Anybody who says different doesn't know what he is talking about. Or he lies.

LÉCHET: And then? What happened then?

LUCHENI: Nothing. I stabbed. That was all.

LÉCHET: With what?

LUCHENI: With a very pointed and sharp weapon. . . .

LÉCHET: Did your flight have a goal? Where did you want to flee? Don't hesitate. Answer!

LUCHENI: I had no intention of fleeing.

LÉCHET: No intention of fleeing? Then you ran as fast as you could just for the exercise?

LUCHENI: I was going to the police. That was my intention from the beginning. I wanted to declare openly why I did it.

LÉCHET: Then why didn't you simply stand still? That would have been more logical.

LUCHENI: I had no wish to be lynched by an infuriated mob, like Caserio [the assassin of President Carnot] before the police could get to me. . . .

LÉCHET: Have you anything to add concerning your deed?

LUCHENI: I confess that it was my deliberate intention to kill the Austrian Empress. I was glad to hear the news of her death. I am an anarchist.

LÉCHET: Did you practice this confession all by yourself?

LUCHENI: Nothing to practice. The great Bakunin[7] showed us how to break our chains.

LÉCHET: What chains?

LUCHENI: The chains with which a degenerate aristocracy and a capitalistic bourgeoisie have bound us.

Later he stated that it had been his original intention to kill the King of Italy, Umberto, but lacking the necessary fifty francs to go to Rome, he chose Elisabeth as second best. The assassination of Umberto was now to be accomplished by another, "another comrade."

Countess Sztáray sent an urgent telegram to Count Paar in Vienna, Franz Joseph's chief adjutant. It was dispatched shortly before 3 P.M. (Elisabeth was already dead): "Her Majesty the Empress dangerously wounded. Please inform His Majesty the Emperor as tactfully as possible." At four o'clock she sent a second telegram: "Her Majesty the Empress has expired."

At five o'clock Paar went to Schönbrunn to tell Franz Joseph, who was on the point of departing for maneuvers in Bohemia. When he heard the news he buried his head in his hands and remained for long moments in total silence. Then he said in a husky voice: "I am spared nothing in this world." Presently he stood up and commanded: "The maneuvers are not to be canceled. Beck [Chief of Staff] is to lead them." (This was later countermanded.) He remained standing, his body stiff and erect. When Paar and the others withdrew and he was left alone, Franz Joseph is supposed to have fallen into a convulsion of weeping, calling Elisabeth's name and sobbing, "Nobody knew how much I loved her." But there were no witnesses to this scene.[8]

About 6 P.M. the news spread through Vienna. The "extras" were hawked to the horrified people standing in the streets; they read the news aloud to those who had not been able to buy a paper. Women and children were weeping. "Murdered!" "Our Empress murdered!" On the Stephansplatz a huge crowd assembled. Traffic came to a standstill. Hidden hatreds again rose to the surface: a mob went to the Rennweg restaurant frequented by the foreign laborers employed by the city to lay new gas pipes; the men shouted, "The Italians steal our bread and kill our Empress." A free-for-all ensued, until the police managed to disperse the people. There were demonstrations all over Vienna and in other parts of the monarchy, particularly in Triest, where, at an open-air concert, Austrians threw chairs and glasses at the Italian musicians. Other rowdies marched to the office of the *Piccolo,* a Jewish-owned newspaper, threw stones, and chanted, "Down with the Jews, down with the Italians, down with the Liberals!"

The whole world shared the sorrow. To the world which knew her not, Elisabeth had been a romantic figure, a fabled queen. Telegrams of condolences flew in. Among the first to arrive were those from Kaiser Wilhelm, Queen Victoria, and President McKinley (who was to become the victim of another anarchist just three years later). The day after, telegrams arrived from Umberto, Leo XIII, Nicholas and Alexandra, the Khedive of Egypt, the King of Siam, the Presidents of the South American states, Abdul-Hamid II, the Emperor of Japan. In Geneva people stood till past midnight gaping at the Hotel Beau-Rivage, though everybody knew that there was nothing to be seen. During the night posters were printed suggesting to the people of Geneva that Monday be observed as a day of mourning and that all offices and stores be closed.

Katherina Schratt was somewhere near Salzburg. She rushed back to Vienna, arriving there on the morning of the eleventh. Franz Joseph sent her a note:

> Dearest friend: How good that you came! With whom could I speak more openly about the transfigured one (*Verklärten*) than with you? I expect you at 11. Please come not through the garden but through my chamber. *Auf Wiedersehen!*
> Your Franz Joseph

It was announced that Elisabeth's body would be brought to Vienna for a state funeral. As the train passed Lausanne, Bern, Zürich, Innsbruck, thousands greeted it silently and in each city the church bells tolled their tribute. The Viennese forgot how little their queen cared about them, how purposefully she had turned her back on the Imperial City. The lambent colors in which the dead are bathed now turned indifference into sentiment, and even those who had whispered salacious slanders about her spoke of "our wonderful Empress." The lights of the city were extinguished; only torches illuminated the procession as Elisabeth returned for the last time to the Hofburg.

Mark Twain wrote to the Reverend Joseph H. Twichell in Hartford:

> Sept. 13, 1898
>
> That good and unoffending lady the Empress is killed by a madman, and I am living in the midst of world-history again. The Queen's jubilee last year, the invasion of the Reichsrath by the police, and now this murder, which will still be talked of and described and painted a thousand years from now. To have a personal friend of the wearer of the crown burst in at the gate in the deep dusk of the evening and say in a voice broken with tears, "My God, the Empress is murdered," and fly toward her home before we can utter a question—why, it brings the giant event home to you, makes you a part of it and personally interested: it is as if your neighbor Antony should come flying and say, "Caesar is butchered—the head of the world is fallen!"

Rebecca West remembered:

> . . . my life had been punctuated by the slaughter of royalties, by the shouting of newsboys who have run down the streets to tell me that someone has used a lethal weapon to turn over a new leaf in the book of history. I remember when I was five years old looking upward at my mother and her cousin, who were standing side by side and looking down at a newspaper laid on a table in a circle of gaslight, the folds in their white pouched blouses and long black skirts kept as still by their consternation as if they were carved in stone. "There was the Empress Elizabeth of Austria," I said to the nurse, thirty-six years later. "She was very beautiful, wasn't she?" she asked. "One of the most beautiful women who ever lived," I said. "But wasn't she mad?" she asked. "Perhaps," I said, "perhaps, but only a little, and at the end. She was certainly brilliantly clever. Before she was thirty she had given proof of greatness." "How?" she asked. To her increasing distress I told her, for I know quite a lot of Hapsburg history, until I saw how bored she was and let her go and leave me in darkness that was now patterned by the lovely triangle of Elizabeth's face.[9]

4

Léchet had a difficult task before him. In the first place he had to prove that Elisabeth had died of her wounds and not of a sudden heart attack. He had to obtain permission to have an autopsy performed, and this permission was, after some hours of reluctance, telegraphed from Vienna at noon of September 11. When the autopsy was performed a consortium of physicians found that the weapon had punctured the left ventricle, but that the wound was so tiny that the blood oozed out only gradually and therefore she had been able to live on for sixty minutes. The cause of death was clearly established, but Elisabeth's body—that body of which she had been so proud—was now mutilated.

Second, the murder weapon had to be produced; Lucheni had thrown it away as he ran. For some reason it could not be found, in spite of the fact that the police had closed the section near the dock and searched every inch of ground. It was eventually brought in by an innocent citizen. Not only that, the roundup of all those whom Lucheni could have known uncovered a notebook, hidden under a mattress, in which a friend of his had sketched the home-made weapon, a file honed to a sharp point and affixed to a sturdy handle.

Third, and most important, Léchet was convinced from the first that Lucheni had acted as a member of an organized conspiracy.[10] The sketch of the weapon confirmed his belief that Lucheni had had the help of others. Who were the others? Who had aided him? They had to be found, if only to prevent further assassinations. Some evidence pointed to the possibility of attempts against Franz Joseph, Umberto, and Wilhelm.

In pursuit of the investigation, the police of Switzerland, Italy, France, and Austria cooperated. In Geneva a wholesale roundup of shady characters took place; the known anarchists were brought in, as were the proprietors and waiters of cheap restaurants and cafés, the inhabitants of the shoddy boardinghouse where Lucheni had passed some days, the prostitutes, an Italian journalist, Pietro Gualducci, who had once been the editor of an anarchist weekly and who had found asylum in Geneva, and many others. Léchet attempted to reconstruct all the details of Lucheni's life.

He had been a decent enough soldier in the Italian army, serving in a regiment under the command of the Prince of Aragona, living in Palermo. The Prince testified that he was "one of the best of the soldiers of his detail," and that he had served as a musician in the regimental band. After he had discharged his military duty, the Prince hired him as a valet. He was unfailingly cheerful, popular not only with the members of the family but with the servants, and not entirely uneducated. He could speak French and a few words of German. Nothing, said the Prince, indicated that he was an anarchist or had any connection with known anarchists. After a short while in the Prince's service, he suddenly quit. The Prince thought it was an ungrateful action because he had shown him much kindness, but made no comment. Later he got a letter from Lucheni begging his pardon and asking whether the Prince would take him back. The Prince replied that he seemed to be more suitable for other tasks than those of a servant but that he remembered him fondly and wished him good fortune. For quite a time after that the correspondence continued, Lucheni writing from Switzerland. It stopped when the Prince discovered that Lucheni had sent several subversive periodicals to some of his former comrades who were still serving in the regiment.

Through a police spy who had penetrated the anarchists' circle, Léchet found out that a meeting had taken place in Lausanne earlier in the year. The purpose of this meeting was to move the office of the anarchist publication *Agitatore* to Zürich. It was estimated that there were about four hundred comrades willing to make financial contributions to the anarchist cause. The Zürich contingent was willing to harbor the office of the newspaper, an undertaking which entailed a certain risk, but they demanded in return that a prominent person be murdered on Swiss territory. This demand was agreed to in a further meeting at the end of August, which was held in Thonon in France, just across the Swiss border. Lucheni, who had previously asked that the cause look on him as "a man of action," was summoned to Thonon. After some discussion, which did envision the possibility of killing Franz Joseph or Umberto or the Prince of Orléans, Elisabeth's death was decided upon. The police spy closed his report by saying that the leaders seemed to consider Lucheni as a not overly bright tool. He was not admitted to their regular meetings and was known by the nickname "Lo Stupido."

In many hours of probing, Léchet unrolled the story of the illegitimate child entrusted to the care of foster parents, who expended on him little love and less food and attempted to put the few lire they received from the government to their own use. He was brought up in a small village, sent to school at six, but after school hours had to work as a gardener's assistant and bring the money home. When he was ten he finished school and was apprenticed to a stonemason. At sixteen he carried on his shoulders the ties and rails of a section of railroad which was being built between Parma and Spezia. He then wandered north, having been told that work was easier to get and better paid in Switzerland, but he found that he often had to starve and was as frequently homeless. He became filled with hate against society, a hate that waxed with every weight his shoulders carried. His stint in the army was his happiest time. What he liked particularly was caring for the horses; he learned to ride. He later made some use of that knowledge by getting a job in a stable, but again he became restless, threw it up, and wandered on. He had no relatives; no woman cared for him; his sexual needs were satisfied by this or that prostitute when he had a little money to spend. It was uncertain when exactly he became an anarchist, but it was certain that he embraced the doctrine passionately.

He was in jail now and had gone there smilingly, proud of the crime he had committed. In the hours between the sessions of interrogation, he busied himself writing letters. Léchet saw to it that he was supplied with paper and pen, believing that one of these letters might be addressed to a co-conspirator. However, Lucheni was too smart for that. On September 11, that is, one day after his arrest, he wrote to a Signor Turco, editor in chief of the leftist newspaper *Don Marzio* in Naples:

DEAR SIR:

Since I want to give a few explanations, I address myself to your newspaper, because it seems to me exceptionally fitting for what I wish to say. And besides, most of my acquaintances are in Naples. I ask you in my name to contradict all the newspapers (or I could say to contradict everybody) who dare to classify me as a born murderer, according to the theory of that professor (if I am not mistaken his name is Lombroso) who has the effrontery to declare that certain human beings are born criminals. Very sorry, but it is my duty to tell this man, who prides himself on having discovered the sixth continent, that he is very much mistaken, certainly as far as I am concerned.

I ask you further to contradict all those who declare that Lucheni acted because of his personal misery. That too is altogether wrong.

To sum up, I declare: If the ruling classes do not cease to be the bloodsuckers of humanity, the just retributions, such as the one performed by the signer of this letter, will repeat themselves more frequently, not only against kings, presidents, or ministers, but against anybody who suppresses a human being for his own benefit. The day is not far off when the true friends of humanity will erase everything which is written today. To build a new world, only one sentence is required. That sentence is: Only he who works may receive.

> Sincerely yours,
> LUIGI LUCHENI, very convinced anarchist

To the wife of his former employer, he wrote three days later:

Signora Dolores de Vera D'Aragona
Principessa della Guardia
via Torre Arza (Palazzo Aliata)
Palermo/Sicilia, Italia

Geneva, September 14, 1898

I confess with these lines to be unworthy to write to you at all. If I do it nevertheless, it is because I must battle against the unspeakable injustices which people of your class have committed against their fellow human beings while they have the nerve to call themselves brothers. As a true Communist, I can no longer support the shame of these injustices. And as a true friend of humanity, I wish to let you know that the hour is not far off when a new sun will shine on all, without difference. As far as I am concerned, I know that I will never see this new sun nor the old one. I have seen enough of it in the twenty-five years which I have spent in this world. Princess, I assure you with my whole heart (my wild heart, or if you like, my reasonable one) that never in my life have I been as much at peace as I am now. And I say openly that if it would be possible to judge me after the law of the canton of Lucerne, which I asked the President of Switzerland to do, I will jump up the steps of the beloved Guillotine and I will need nobody to push me. If my petition is granted, I shall ask the judge to let me have a hole underneath the wonderful Lake of Geneva so that never again will I have to meet the nefarious kings who bathe themselves at their leisure in the light of today's sun. . . .

> LUIGI LUCHENI, conscientious Communist

P.S. If you feel like answering this letter, it is hardly necessary to inform you of my address.

The explanation of the above is this: the canton of Geneva had abolished the death penalty. Lucheni had sent a petition asking to be judged by the laws of Lucerne, where the death penalty did exist. He wanted to die a martyr's death.

He received many more letters than he wrote, many of them anonymous or signed with fake names, and many of them congratulating him on his deed. One or two berated him. Here are two typical examples:

> Murderer, beast, monster, rabid animal! The women and girls of Vienna long to revenge the horrible crime which you committed against our beloved Empress. Rabid animal, do you know what you deserve? Listen, you monster: we want to stretch you out on a table and we, who are so soft-hearted, want to look on while both your arms and your feet are hacked off.

> Dear comrade: The working men, the honest men, all who do not shamefully exploit the labor of others, all who fight for the benefit of humanity, admire your noble deed. It promises the certainty of a victory soon to come! We still have heroes! Others will follow your example! You have killed a woman—and all the slaves and crooks, all those belonging to the class who live by stealing, declare in the newspapers that your deed was senseless. They are out of their minds. They are mad with rage, fear, and panic. That is good. . . . The people will open the portals of your prison! You will not be forgotten! You will live on in our hearts! Remain steadfast! Hope!
>
> One Among Many

All letters were read by Léchet and his assistant. Yet Léchet was not able to find out whether Lucheni had acted on the instruc-

tion of a group or which of Lucheni's acquaintances were implicated in the assassination.

The investigation lasted for some time, and it was not until the
tenth of November that Lucheni faced judge and jury. He had
refused legal counsel, but under the laws of Geneva an accused
person had to have a defense attorney, and one was assigned to
him.

When he entered the court filled with curious spectators at
9:15 on the morning of November 10, he greeted judge and jury
and the spectators smilingly. He was neatly dressed and freshly
shaved. Forty-nine witnesses had been summoned. The prosecut-
ing attorney, Georges Navazza, read the charge. Asked why he
murdered the Empress, Lucheni anwered, "My misery compelled
me to do so." When the question was repeated, he answered, "As
revenge for my life." Asked if he had any accomplices, he said, "I
have none. My accomplice is here," pointing to himself.

Supporting Léchet's theory, the district attorney wanted to
make it clear that Lucheni could not have acted alone. He wanted
to show that he must have been part of a conspiracy, prompted by
the spell which the philosophers of anarchism cast on him.
Lucheni had mentioned Bakunin. Mikhail Bakunin had written
in *The Philosophy of the Dead* that "the passion to destroy is a
creative passion." Similarly his follower, Paul Brousse, had postu-
lated, "We must now begin with the propaganda of action. The
road to revolution leads through the breast of a King."

Yet while Navazza laid stress on Lucheni as the almost snake-
charmed follower, he pictured him as a man perfectly responsible
for his action, adroit in his lying, and not in the least incapable of
understanding that he had committed a crime, which inspired in
him an almost childlike pride and the belief that his name would
go down to posterity. Lucheni did what he did as much from
motives of self-love as from motives of philosophical conviction.
Navazza's address to the jury was a model of close reasoning and
calm presentation. He did not try to skimp an analysis of the
typical behavior of the fanatic, which in cases like Lucheni's
amounted to a psychosis. But he thereby allowed the picture of
Lucheni as an accountable criminal to come to the fore all the
more clearly. Passages from his speech are given here:

My first words are dedicated to the memory of Her Majesty the Empress of Austria, who came to Switzerland to find health. Instead she found the icy rest of death.

Lucheni has confessed. But he has suppressed a part of the truth. . . . He lies when he asserts that he learned from the newspapers about the arrival of the Empress in Geneva on Friday, the ninth of September. The investigation has shown beyond a doubt that her arrival was not mentioned in any paper until Saturday the tenth. Yet on Friday afternoon Lucheni was already waiting for her in front of the Hotel Beau-Rivage. Therefore he must have had another source which informed him of the planned arrival. He was standing there long before the Empress entered the hotel for the first time, around six o'clock.

Lucheni lies when he testifies to having seen the Empress four years ago in March or June in Budapest. We have proved that in the year 1894 she did not visit Budapest before October. At that time Lucheni was performing his military service in Italy. Why this lie? Was the Empress, whom he had never seen before, pointed out to him either on the day or on the eve of the crime, pointed out by somebody who is supposed to remain unknown to us?

Lucheni lies when he testifies that he arrived in Geneva on the fifth of September and that he went to Évian on the seventh of September. In spite of careful research, no trace of him has been found in Évian. . . . On Friday Lucheni was observed [in Geneva] in the company of several persons whom he denies knowing. All this points to the fact that Lucheni assiduously attempts to conceal his meetings and actions during the time of preparation for the crime. Never does Lucheni attempt to spare himself. When in certain instances he withholds truth from us, he does not do so for his own benefit. He does so because the truth might damage other persons.

This brings up the question whether Lucheni, who actually performed the crime, was its moral instigator—and whether he had accomplices. Our researchers were concentrated on this unknown region. Following the example of his predecessors in anarchist crime, he asserts that the deed sprang completely from his own conception. He is sacrificing the liberty of his entire future life to the wild satisfaction which he feels today. He alone wishes to carry the total responsibility, and he is unwilling to cede to anybody else the smallest part of his shabby fame. This is exactly how all anarchist assassins have acted up to now. In spite of his obstinate denials, it is, as I have said, quite possible that we are confronted by a conspiracy. Yet I cannot guarantee this, because we are unable to prove it. If our hypothesis is correct, then there are several indications that we are not dealing with a local affair. We know that the anarchists do a lot of traveling. They wander as ambassadors from one locality to the next. If a conspiracy is to be executed in a certain city, it is planned in another and prepared in still another. You may imagine how difficult it is to uncover such conspiracies. . . .

If it is correct to say that Lucheni had accomplices, would it be fair to state that he was merely a passive and a blind tool? Did he merely carry out orders? Was he a marionette of those anarchist apostles who sit in their dressing gowns at the hearth and stir the embers with their writings so that by and by the fire blazes high? Such men clothe themselves in the mantle of a putative scientific or philosophic belief and then deny their solidarity with those who translate into deeds the doctrine of which they are the prophets and preachers. I have no sympathy with these desk anarchists, who seduce others and ought in truth to be captured themselves. Yet surely one cannot proceed against them effectively by being lenient with those of their disciples who commit murder. . . .

If indeed a planned conspiracy against Her Majesty the Empress of Austria existed, then Lucheni did not play a secondary role in it. Without the shadow of a doubt he was completely in agreement with those who persuaded him to act. He proved this some time ago, when of his own free will he tried to arm himself with whatever weapon he could procure, a dagger, a revolver, or a file. Thus, even if a conspiracy existed, he was no passive or blind fool. His determination and the audacity with which he distinguished himself formed him into an arm of the collective will. And if after all he had been only a tool, then he was a most dangerous one, one that ought to be put away. Gentlemen of the jury, Lucheni is no born criminal. He is—and I quote his own words—a champion of anarchism. The anarchists, who are the cancer of the second half of our century, recognized his proud and determined nature and entrusted him with the execution of a senseless and disgusting crime.

Anarchism is a deceptive, inhuman, and false creed, and like an octopus it entwines many strong and intelligent young men. It pulls them away from their social duties, it destroys in them any feeling for country and family. . . . Anarchism is a doctrine without dogma, without goal, and without *Carta*. It consists of a single slogan: Death to rulers. It is the product of hatred and envy. . . .
Lucheni, have you succeeded in capturing the attention of the

world by thrusting a file into the heart of a sixty-year-old woman? Is your self-love now satisfied? Judge the degree of your cowardice by the ease with which you found your target. Yes, the admiration of those who share your convictions will certainly be yours. It will have to compensate you for the eternal loneliness awaiting you, as well as for the fact that you will be denied the apotheosis of the guillotine. . . . If Lucheni were to stand before a court in one of our neighboring cantons, then he could be certain of marching to those gallows which he cynically pretends to desire. Here his life will be spared. But his liberty he must lose forever. He must disappear from the eyes of mankind. He must receive the punishment which we have substituted for the death penalty. . . . It is no less a severe punishment to be condemned to be forgotten by the world, and to have to live every day and every hour with his crime and with his conscience.[11]

The jury brought in the expected verdict a few minutes before 7 P.M.: lifelong imprisonment. Lucheni once more shouted, "Long live anarchy! Death to aristocracy!" Then he was led away. At 7:05 the court was declared closed.

Yet Léchet could not be satisfied. He continued from time to time to visit Lucheni in prison and to question him. About six months later Lucheni confessed that he had been a member of a conspiracy. Two Italians whom the porter Gilbert had observed at the railroad station at the very hour of the assassination were his direct accomplices. One of them was armed with a revolver, the other with a dagger. Nevertheless Lucheni persisted in his assertion that he knew neither the names of the two Italians nor any of the others of the conspiracy. The investigation therefore ended in failure. Eleven years later, on October 19, 1910, Lucheni committed suicide in his cell. He hanged himself by his belt. (I suggest that the belt was made available to him, to get rid of him.) Virtually nobody paid any attention. He was, as Navazza predicted, forgotten by the world.

A French caricature of Franz Joseph: "New conquests at my age!"
The female figures represent Bosnia and Herzegovina.

CHAPTER XIV

Betrayal

THOUGH YEARS HAD PASSED since any true communion had existed between man and wife, she still had been around, somewhere, somehow, a being Franz Joseph loved to look at. It was more of a mirage than a marriage, yet from time to time she could be comforting and reachable at least by a letter. He used to begin his letters with superscriptions in Hungarian, because he knew that would please her: *"Edes Lelkem"*—"My darling heart." But even when his letters could not get to her, even when she was at sea, she was some place. Now she was no place, and that ineluctable negative was a grief hard to bear. Over his desk hung a large portrait of her, and during the long work hours he looked at it with a gaze in which lay almost a half-century of recollection, idealizing the figure even as the painter had idealized the portrait. He told Katherina Schratt that it consoled him to write to her and speak to her of his dead wife. He tried "to find refuge in sleep." In May of the year following Elisabeth's death he wrote:

> . . . Friday I was hunting in Badat, though without success, and suddenly I heard the first cuckoo of spring. The last time I heard it was with the Empress in the Villa Hermes. She loved the call of that bird. At first the thought came to me I ought to write her about it. Then, as the call of the cuckoo wouldn't stop, it seemed like a greeting from her.[1]

The time was to come when he no longer heard any greeting from her. The time was to come when he looked at the portrait and no longer saw it.

In a way, Elisabeth's death helped him. The people gathered more closely around their bereaved ruler. They were going to help the man who had lost his beautiful wife. He needed "his people"—well, they were not going to disappoint him. The women, once they finished the more important business of exchanging recipes, fell to being sorry for "the kindly old gentleman." He must be so very lonesome in that big Burg. Could a Katherina Schratt substitute for an Elisabeth? Of course not. We, all of us, must show him that we pity him. He became a venerable figure, not by age alone. Sentiment braced his throne. Even those radicals who went the legal limit in attacking Habsburg principles knew that it would be useless to speak of abdication or of turning Austria into a republic.

Schratt felt uncomfortable. After Elisabeth's death she removed herself from Vienna for longer and longer periods, gambling in Monte Carlo or climbing mountains in Switzerland. She felt that her position at court had become too equivocal, because the third corner of the triangle was missing. Elisabeth's approval had given an aura of respectability to the relationship. Valerie was being distinctly unfriendly to her; the old antipathy asserted itself.

Schratt had been promised a high decoration of which she was covetous, the "Elisabeth Order." Now Franz Joseph had to renege on the promise, feeling that such an award would be construed as tactless. The decoration was one which Elisabeth herself was supposed to bestow. Although Franz Joseph now took over the decision as to who was to be cited for the honor, he believed that he could not give it to his "friend" without creating a situation which the malicious would exploit to harm her as well as him. Katherina could not see it his way. She was hurt. The relationship became tense and nervous.

Yet he needed her more than ever. A little more than a month after Elisabeth's death he wrote to her from Hungary:

> Yesterday was a specially sad day for me. I saw again so much which reminded me, partly painfully and partly with melancholy satisfaction, of our dear departed one. In Ofen I wandered through

all her rooms. . . . Everything had been readied to receive her, as usual every object was in place, even the scale on which she weighed herself daily. The new balcony with the beautiful view of Pest and the Danube which had pleased her so much last year was now elegantly furnished. And yet everything empty, lifeless, no hope to see her again in this life! . . .

I feel most at peace when you are present, because with you I can talk about the unforgettable woman whom we both loved so much, and because I love you. I long to see you again.[2]

Less than two years later they quarreled. The direct cause is not certain, but it was probably Franz Joseph's refusal to interfere at the end of her contract with the Burgtheater. According to Thimig, Schratt complained that she was not being given enough leading roles. Well, she was nearing fifty, and she could hardly have been a model member of the organization, insisting on long vacations and special privileges. Thimig noted in his diary for January 7, 1900: "When the Emperor . . . appeared in his loge for the first time since the death of the Empress, Schratt gave no sign from the stage of acknowledging his presence, as she usually did." Thimig thought it would be "a blessing" for the theater if Schratt left. Nine months later she did leave. Thimig noted: "Schratt probably was afflicted by a morbid (or should I say healthy?) thirst for liberty. The slavery of being the favorite, bound by golden chains, seems to have ruined her nerves. Perhaps she'll return after a few months of independence. She even wants to leave Austria. . . ."

After the quarrel Franz Joseph wrote her a letter which in its humble and almost desperate pleading shows how much he needed her:

My dear good friend: I really do not know whether I may still use this form of address or whether I ought to write "Honored Lady." All the same, I cannot relinquish the hope that the black thunder cloud of yesterday will pass and that our old and happy friendship will be restored. You refused stubbornly and passionately all my suggestions and pleas, though they were well meant and offered in both our interests. Finally I lost control of myself with a vehemence which I regret and for which I beg your pardon with all my heart. I wish to forget the peremptory, insulting, and deeply wounding way in which you took leave of me yesterday. Now, let the voice of your good heart speak. Reflect on the situation calmly, and you will find that we simply cannot part, that we must find each other again. Remember the long years of our serene friendship, the happiness and sorrow which we shared—unfortunately more of sorrow, which you helped me bear—remember that dear departed woman whom we both loved and who watches over us as a guardian angel, and then I hope you will be in a forgiving mood. I am unspeakably sad. The thought that the one who comforted me in all my many troubles, the one who was my solace, the one with whom I could talk about everything, would be lost to me is too horrible. Early in the morning whenever I awoke you were always my first thought. The prospect of seeing you during the day gave me equilibrium. When pain and anxiety overwhelmed me, the hope of seeing you and enjoying your company gave me strength. And now, in my old age, am I to live on alone? That you cannot wish, your good heart would not permit it. The way in which you left me yesterday, it is true, raises in me the doubt whether you still love me. Yet if you still feel in you a remnant of our old friendship, think how terrible uncertainty is, how terrible it would be for me not to hold communication with you. Give me a sign which lets me hope that everything will turn out well, that we will be able to see each other again —I hope before long—either here or in your house. God bless you. . . .

Your profoundly loving

FRANZ JOSEPH[3]

The quarrel was patched up, but afterward they were never so close as they had been.

All this, while not officially made known, could not be kept secret, and the shopkeepers passing the Emperor's window on their way to work thought: We ought to stick by him.

Nonetheless there were voices enough to predict the demise of the monarchy. Bismarck died in the year of Elisabeth's death: his memoirs were given to the public. He had predicted that the German Austrians would continue to lose power, and since it was they who held the realm together, the Czechs and the Hungarians would become more effective in widening the division. That would render Austria ripe for the Russians to proceed to war. Let Germany beware of aligning itself too closely with Austria: "It is vain to ally oneself with a corpse." Similarly, the French writer Pierre Paul Leroy-Beaulieu published in the same year an analysis

(*La France, La Russie et L'Europe*) in which he argued that Austria was the key to European peace and that its disintegration would make Germany too powerful while weakening France. But disintegrate it would.

Austrian statesmen resembled a family of sore sons and back-biting cousins, each one of which wanted by hook or by crook to leave the family business and open a business of his own. In every national zone were to be seen and heard perspiring orators who preached separatism; they ranged from sincere professors of sociology to out-and-out demagogues. The Hungarians were the loudest. They, and especially certain wealthy magnates who for centuries had regarded themselves as lords not to be questioned, were damned if they were going to be asked to pay attention to those effete Viennese. They were damned if they would allow themselves to continue to be saddled with a portion of the expenses of running a monarchy, of contributing to building a railroad that would run from Vienna to some place *not* in Hungary, of paying for that big army in which German was spoken.

Still, economics were not, and hardly ever are, the mainspring of the drive toward nationalism. Were one to ask a country: "Would you still like to be independent even if you knew that you would become poorer?" the answer would be yes.

Ludwig Kossuth, long ignored, died in 1894 at the patriarchal age of ninety-two, and was immediately used as a symbol, as France used Napoleon as a symbol of the dauntless hero, once he was safely dead. His son Franz Kossuth became one of the leading spirits of the Hungarian "Independence party." They were against the customs union, wanted a separate army, recommended that teachers require their pupils to hand in their homework only on Hungarian paper, that houses be heated only by Hungarian coal, and similar nonsense. A boycott of Austrian goods began. Men wore porcelain tulips in their buttonholes, women on their dresses: the tulip was to be the flower of independence. Nobody minded that the tulip was not a Hungarian flower but had been brought there by Turkish invaders, nor that the porcelain tulips were manufactured in foreign factories. In the year Elisabeth died Budapest celebrated the fiftieth anniversary of the 1848 Revolution. On the day set aside as a holiday, the Hungarian flag flew from the houses, and on this or that square somebody made a long, impassioned, let's-get-away-from-Vienna speech.

Yet in spite of the orating, the bunting, the placards, the incendiary poems, the hue and cry of jingoism—in Hungary, in Bohemia, Dalmatia, Galicia—the house did not collapse. The quakes were sufficient to keep things tottering but not powerful enough to destroy. The majority accepted the status quo, if only because they feared change might make life worse. Most of the population remained loyal to Franz Joseph, even after the sympathy over Elisabeth's death paled, if only through inertia born of habit. Reasonably good business and several good harvests helped. The boycott was forgotten by and by, as boycotts usually are; the tulips were thrown away.

Franz Joseph now showed political cunning. He put his trust in the people and their respect for tradition. Let the people decide! He threatened the Hungarian magnates with a universal plebiscite, shrewdly guessing that if it did come to a general vote the people would support the status quo. He was quite right: the Hungarian aristocrats knew he was right and shook in their polished boots.

Strangely enough, what Franz Joseph had grasped as a political cudgel he later embraced as a conviction: the people must be given the right to vote. They wanted it, they should have it; and he felt sure that the old, old Habsburg prestige was strong enough to favor him. Giving them the unrestricted vote was a curious idea for an authoritarian monarch to hold. But hold it he did, and once he thought its consequences through he kept insisting on it. We have here the paradox of an emperor acting like a republican. In effect Franz Joseph sided with the Socialists, though he did not like them any better for all that. The method of achieving the suffrage reform proved to be exceedingly complicated, and it took several years and several changes of ministers—from Baron Paul Gautsch, to Ernest Koerber, to Prince Konrad Hohenlohe, to Baron Max Vladimir Beck—before the idea could be translated into law. In 1905 Franz Joseph was deeply disturbed by what he observed in the Russian uprising, a bloody though not a very effective protest, and his consciousness of that revolt spurred his purpose. "I insist on the voting reform," he announced. Finally, in

January, 1907, he was able to sign the franchise bill. It was hailed by some as "enlightened," condemned by others as a "leap in the dark" and a "petrel of disorder." The old aristocrats in the upper house cooled their brows with eau de cologne. The law of 1907 made it possible for virtually all male Austrians to vote for deputies of their own nationality. Five hundred and sixteen deputies could be elected: of these German voters would elect less than a majority, 233; Czechs, 107; Poles, 82; Ruthenians, 33; Slovenes, 24; Italians, 19; Serbo Croats, 13; Rumanians, five.[4] Similarly a new suffrage law was pushed through in Hungary, though there Franz Joseph had first to dissolve the Parliament. The "Independence party" captured half the seats, but Franz Kossuth and his associates thereupon decided that they had better cooperate economically and militarily. This did not please the extremists, and strife ensued within the party; all the same, Hungary did not break away and the Hungarian Parliament limped along.

In Austria the first free election under the new law was held in May, 1907.[5] It produced startling changes: these changes, too, Franz Joseph had foreseen. In the main they were to the good: the radicals, such as the Young Czechs and the Pan-Germans, lost influence. Schönerer, that acrid firebrand, was kicked out. The Christian Socialists, Lueger's party, gained, as did the Social Democrats. In the following years—few enough were left—the Austrian Socialists behaved sensibly and moderately, working for a reasonable improvement of the condition of labor. The bourgeoisie, it would seem, could consume their pastry with *Schlag* (whipped cream), the women wore their coquettish hats, *Hofräte* and nonentities paraded on the Kärntnerstrasse, the cafés were crowded, and in the evening the Viennese could go and listen either to Mozart or to *The Merry Widow*. Now, in the first years of the twentieth century, Vienna was a gay and brilliant city. The gaiety was short-lived.

2

As in old age we often revert to original love, so did Franz Joseph, turned seventy in 1900, revert to the love he felt as a boy when he first donned a major's uniform and swung himself onto a horse. No human being could now fill his need for companionship, but in the army, in those serried rows, the discipline of which he made so punctilious an observance, he felt loneliness annulled. The machine for war gave him a sense of peace. It is significant that the only person outside his immediate family whom Franz Joseph invited to his birthday celebration was Count Friedrich Beck-Rzikowsky, Chief of Staff, a military leader whom he had known since the Prussian war. Franz Joseph's speeches of those years were spiked with such phrases as "our glorious fighting forces" or "the brave defenders of our frontiers," and his pyschological bent made him lean toward men who thought that guns were the answer, who believed that external victory would glue together the internal fragments. Such a man was General Franz Conrad von Hötzendorf, appointed Chief of Staff in 1906, who was as enthusiastic when he read Goethe as he was fanatic when he studied Clausewitz's *On War*. He initiated reforms in army discipline and was heart and soul for the military. "A one-idea man," the British military attaché in Vienna called him; his one idea was that only a preventive war[6] could save Austria. He pointed to the ominous changes in the European equilibrium. France lived for the day of revenge against Germany; England watched in alarm Germany's round-the-clock building of warships; Russia was stabbing against Turkey. Where did all this stress and strain leave Austria? A prey to the lust for expansion of the major nations, Conrad believed. Franz Joseph must move before he was moved against: Austria must take the offensive against false friends. Franz Joseph listened to him.

But Franz Joseph listened as well to Baron Alois Lexa von Aehrenthal, his Foreign Minister. It was Aehrenthal's ambition to lift Austria's stature by diplomatic negotiations, to give new meaning to the Three-Emperors' League, and to have Franz Joseph play a stellar part in the drama of the continental powers for which, he thought, he could contrive a "happy end." Franz Joseph need only be diplomatically artful and he would be able to act as the *deus ex machina*—without the war-*machina* firing a shot.

Aehrenthal was a tall, powerfully built man who walked with the bent gait of the near-sighted, thought a lot, said little. What he said was precise, to the point, unadorned. Behind that professorial look and manner lay a mind which was intensely wily. The stooping posture concealed an erect ambition, a hunger for fame, a patriotic drive which did not stop at dubious methods to reach his goal. He hated to write official memoranda. The written page was inimical to the half-truths and evasions he was capable of employing. He advocated "open diplomacy," as long as he could keep his own secrets. It has been said of him that he represented the characteristics of the old Austrian aristocrat, a combination of smiling ease and reserved arrogance. Yet his aristocracy was of recent origin: his grandfather had been a grain merchant in Prague—the name "Aehrenthal" means "wheat valley"—and it was his grandfather who had been ennobled.

It was this duo of a "one idea" general and a diplomat of many ideas which stood at the Emperor's side at a crucial moment in Austria's history.

3

Bosnia had been administered with reasonable intelligence almost from the day Austrian functionaries had opened offices there. While other European powers sent their fleets to far-off continents to pounce on appetizing territories, while they "colonized" and subjugated, with or without the pretense of Christianity, Austria was content with a relatively unimportant strip of the Balkans. Ethics did not prompt such modesty: Austria did not possess a navy strong enough to frighten the natives of remote lands. Such overseas expeditions as were undertaken were of a peaceful nature; they were explorations and excavations, with the result that the Vienna museums contain superb treasures from Ephesus and from Egypt.

Having once assumed the government of Bosnia-Herzegovina, bureaucratic skill did well. Bosnian carpet weavers and craftsmen of metalware found new markets, the forests which covered the land were sensibly managed to provide wood without being wantonly destroyed, new primary schools and agricultural colleges were built and subsidized, plain but decent hotels were constructed and operated, physicians were sent into the region and hygienic measures were decreed to conquer the cholera prevalent in the Balkans. Where the map of the region had previously shown little but blank spaces, new villages sprang into being, and the standard of living rose above that of the goat sharing the peasant's bedroom. Ilidze, a spa near Sarajevo, became a fashionable vacation spot for Viennese who ventured a little farther than the Semmering. Austrian policemen, backed by the army, did good work in stamping out bloody family vendettas and decreasing the incidence of theft and rape. Some of the Bosnian Robin Hoods came down from the mountains.

But it was of no use. The government could not solve the problem of freeing the tenant peasants from the cupidinous landowners. Nor would most of the tenants listen to proposed new methods for improving the yield of the soil; they insisted on farming as their fathers had farmed, turning each furrow slowly and painfully with a wooden spike. Machinery was godless. The tenants were preponderantly Christians, the landowners Moslems; the difference in religion furnished a good excuse for continued murder and mayhem. The peasants objected to the prohibition against carrying weapons. They objected to increased taxes. They objected to the forestry laws. Most of all, they objected to compulsory military service, which dragged their young men into "wicked foreign lands." And even when they had to serve in the Austrian army, they insisted on retaining a costume which set them apart, wearing garish, homespun trousers and flower-pot hats.

The rebellious spirit of Bosnia was nurtured by Serbia, a country whose youth was inflamed by the idea of a pan-Serb state. A Sarajevo newspaper circulated in Bosnia was confiscated on seventy occasions, or more, for vicious attacks on the Habsburgs. But the propaganda could not be stopped. Starry-eyed young men wandered all over Bosnia, sermonizing for Serbia. A bishop told a visitor from England, "Don't send us Bibles, send us cannons." The danger of revolution was not illusory, and it increased early in 1908, when the Young Turks staged a successful revolt in Constantinople. That upheaval served as inspiration to the Moslem element of Bosnia particularly. But whatever their religious beliefs, men in the Balkans obstinately continued their overt and covert fighting, Serbia against Bulgaria, Serbia against Hungary, Turkey against all its neighbors, trying to recapture parts of Greece it had lost, Italy eyeing Dalmatia. Armed conflicts took place in Macedonia in 1903, the Bulgars, Serbs, and Greeks each wanting to tear a piece from the Turkish-owned region. Had Russia not been fully occupied in its war with Japan in 1905, it, too, would have interfered, the various treaties of "sacred friendship" notwithstanding. As it was, Russia bided its time.

Franz Joseph acted. His answer to the Balkan machinations was to turn occupation into annexation. It was tantamount to wiping out the pretense that Bosnia and Herzegovina were integral countries on the map of Europe. By melting the provinces into the empire, he would be able to govern them as he governed Bohemia or Carinthia. It would be a great coup for the monarchy. It was his answer to Austria's lack of colonies. He did not expect that such freebooting would be accomplished without some show of resistance; here he could give his army something to do, something useful but something short of war. It was a gamble worth risking: the annexation, the increase in territory, would reassert Habsburg strength. It would show the other major European powers that Austria was still a force to be reckoned with. He was also quite aware of the two countries' importance in securing Austria's position on the Adriatic coast. These reasons—rather, these excuses—sufficed to salve his conscience.

Yet an international agreement did exist, the Treaty of Berlin, which stipulated a measure of independence for Bosnia and Herzegovina. Aehrenthal was charged with the task of circumventing the agreement and obtaining approval from the major powers. What were the chances? Turkey and Serbia would protest, but Austria could handle them. France was occupied in quarreling with Germany over Morocco and would not interfere, not effectively at any rate. Britain would probably be content with a parliamentary protest, well worded in clipped English; and Italy would do nothing at all. Of German support Austria could be sure. Russia—there was the rub. Russia could not look with indifference on Austria's gulping down a Balkan dish. Such was Aehrenthal's reasoning, and he proceeded to work out a deal with the Russian Foreign Minister, A. P. Izvolsky. That deal stands as a model of diplomatic cheating, both participants being the cheaters. The long and short of it was that Russia would approve the Austrian move in return for Austria's help in obtaining permission for Russian battleships to pass unhindered through the Straits. The two diplomats met secretly in the castle of Buchlau, the Moravian country estate of Count Leopold von Berchtold, Austrian ambassador to Russia. The two men kept no record of their bargaining, so that each later claimed the other "misunderstood," the diplomats' word for "lied." There is little question that Aehrenthal never intended to take the Straits request seriously, and Izvolsky on his part was pretending "an amicable spirit of reciprocity," waiting to see which way the other powers would jump. Izvolsky claimed that Aehrenthal promised to notify him before he took any action. Instead, Aehrenthal acted swiftly and unilaterally. On October 6, 1908, an Austrian edict, bearing Franz Joseph's signature, announced that Bosnia-Herzegovina would be annexed: to raise the province to a "higher level of political life" it was necessary for Austria to obtain "a clear and unambiguous juridical position." Words, words, words. Clearly, it was betrayal.

Austria's arm stretched and Austria's hand pounced. To give that cutpurse gesture some *post factum* justification, the police "discovered" that a group of Serbs and Croats living within the monarchy had conspired with Serbia to incite a Balkan revolt, with the object of uniting Croatia and Bosnia with Serbia. Bad—if true. Was it true? Fifty-three members of the group were arrested and accused of "high treason." This monster accusation was argued before a tribunal in March, 1909, in Agram. In due course it appeared not only that the accusatory documents were out-and-out fakes, but that some of the witnesses were out-and-out liars. All the same, many of the accused were condemned to prison at hard labor—and this on the shabbiest of evidence, the tribunal being thoroughly prejudiced. The convicted men appealed to a higher court. Masaryk undertook their defense and was able to prove that the documents had been forged, forged not by some guttersnipe counterfeiter but in the precincts of the Austro-Hungarian Embassy in Belgrade itself. There was then no choice but to set the accused free.

Before the Agram trial finished, another unsavory scandal was smeared over Europe's front pages. Heinrich Friedjung, the distinguished historian (who was a good friend of Aehrenthal), wrote an article claiming that certain Croat and Serb politicians were disloyal to Austria in favor of a Greater Serbia. The politicians brought libel suits against Friedjung. They showed that the documents on which he had based his article were patent forgeries. Friedjung at first maintained that his evidence was irreproachable; in the end he had to admit that he had been completely wrong. He acknowledged his mistake, bowing his head. But the harm had been done. As Arthur May wrote in *The Hapsburg Monarchy:*

> Friedjung declined to reveal in court the actual source of the documents he had used, but that the foreign office had furnished them few doubted, and it was this aspect of the affair that gave it European notoriety. . . .
>
> The Austrian foreign office never admitted that it had anything to do with Friedjung's article. It seems not improbable that Foreign Minister Aehrenthal thought the documents that were turned over to Friedjung authentic and that he was as badly deceived by them as the historian. In the light of revelations from Hapsburg diplomatic archives it appears that the authorities in the Ballplatz were ignorant of the fact that the documents were fabrications when Friedjung was given access to them. However that may be, the ill-starred Friedjung trial seriously damaged the reputation of the Ballplatz for reliability and simple honesty in foreign countries; many an informed foreigner believed that Aehrenthal had deliberately winked at the manufacture of documents and had cynically exploited Friedjung as his cat's-paw in an endeavor to fan ill will and hatred of Serbia and to justify his aggressive Balkan diplomacy.

That aggressive Balkan policy smelled bad, the Agram and the Friedjung cases being symptoms of putrefaction. Honest men turned their faces away.

Neither Franz Joseph nor Aehrenthal foresaw the enormity of the ruckus Austria's move would create in Europe. All hell broke loose. In Austria itself strong disapproving voices were heard, the criticism ranging from "imprudence" to "utter immorality." In Prague the Austrian flag was dragged into the gutter by students.

Masaryk made one of his great speeches and called Aehrenthal "Annexander the Great." On the day of the sixtieth anniversary of Franz Joseph's accession, Prague was once again placed under martial law. Yet serious though internal protests sounded, the shouts emitted in self-righteous voices by the other nations rang with a more blatant cacophony. Izvolsky screamed that Aehrenthal's action was "nothing short of treachery." In Rome a mass demonstration was staged before the Austrian Embassy. France, worried over Morocco, merely issued a formal protest, though Clemenceau heaped reproaches on Izvolsky for keeping a secret from France, "your supposed ally." Turkey fumed and the Young Turks swore not to buy Austrian goods. Condemnation was strongest in Great Britain. Sir Edward Goschen, Britain's ambassador in Vienna, refused to have anything further to do with Aehrenthal and called him "a plain liar." Sir Edward Grey, Foreign Minister, said that the annexation made a mockery of all political principles. London's *Daily Telegraph* wrote that if those two men had shuffled cards so trickily in their club they would have been expelled. Even Wilhelm, in a temper, felt insulted that he had been left out: "Aehrenthal's deed resembles the prank of a little subaltern." The Russian press called Izvolsky a "stupid dupe."

Most of this was merely talk, some of it holier-than-thou talk. But real consequences were soon to follow. British policy changed decidedly, taking a long step toward rapprochement with Russia. Britain's suspicion of Germany deepened, the British being convinced that Franz Joseph's move was secretly dictated by Wilhelm, that the Hohenzollern was the lead horse dragging the Habsburg along. The greatest fury flamed in Serbia, naturally; the leading newspaper called Franz Joseph an old ass who was all the more dangerous because he was senile; and in the succeeding weeks the Serbian government spoke ever more openly of war against Slav-suppressing Austria, that war to be fought—hopefully—with the help of Serbia's "fatherly friend," Russia. The Serbian Premier took the next train to St. Petersburg to ask for aid. In the meantime Serbia mobilized. How great was their disappointment when Russia backed down. The Russians would not help and they warned Serbia not to proceed, lest the alarums and excursions give

Austria an excuse to march into Serbia and annex *that* country as well. The Premier left the Russian court weeping bitterly. Serbia then knocked on other doors, sending messengers to Rome, Paris, London, Constantinople. Everywhere they found "sympathy," nowhere a willingness to draw up the cannons. Nobody wanted to risk a European war. Aehrenthal threatened to publish a full report of his conversations with Izvolsky which would prove that he had acted according to agreement. Izvolsky, whose conscience was far from clear, paled and pleaded with the Czar for peace and compromise, saying that Russia was in no shape to undertake another foreign war. That was true enough.

In Austria itself a strong pro-war party existed; for a time their policy prevailed so far as to persuade Franz Joseph to draw up troops along the Serbian border. Then his closer judgment made him see the danger, made him realize the strong likelihood that blood shed in the Balkans would spread like a filthy flood and that the other European powers could not sit calmly in their palaces or parliaments while his troops assaulted an independent kingdom, even one as "unimportant" as Serbia. A series of negotiations followed, Turkey was fobbed off with quite a few million gulden, France and England turned back to their internal affairs, Russia received a few concessions, though never the longed-for access by sea, and Austria emerged as a major power still, Bosnia-Herzegovina in its grasp. Yet it was a Pyrrhic victory. As Izvolsky hated Aehrenthal—and vice versa—so did the major countries hold Austria in suspicion, uneasy about the big boy who was all too ready to hit the small boy. Franz Joseph became so disliked that for the first time precautions for his safety were taken: in his Budapest palace all rooms were kept locked from the inside, the building was surrounded by guards, and during his audiences detectives stood in the corners.

The Serbs swallowed their humiliation. Like a heavy lump revenge lay in their stomachs, and it got heavier as the years went by. Russian propaganda saw to it that Austria's betrayal of a treaty would not be forgotten and promised that some day "joy would come to the Slavic world." What Austria had obtained was to prove no bargain.

"It is very obvious, and no more than natural," Machiavelli

wrote in 1513, "for princes to desire to extend their dominions, and when they attempt nothing but what they are able to achieve they are applauded, at least not upbraided thereby; but when they are unable to compass it, and yet will be doing, then they are condemned, and indeed not unworthily."

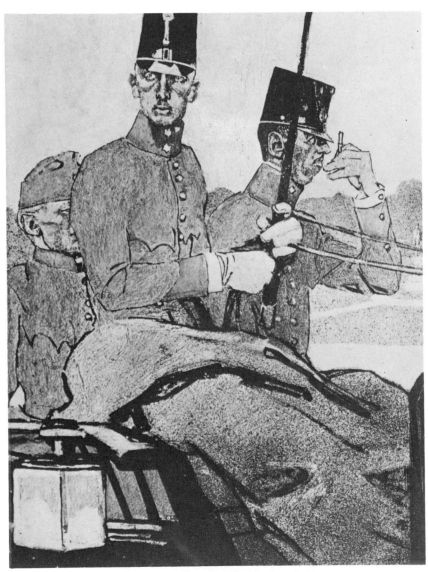

Satirical sketch of Austrian army officers by Wilhelm Thony

CHAPTER XV

Franz Ferdinand and the Redl Affair

AFTER THE ANNEXATION, Franz Joseph lost perspective. He was like a man who tries to imagine the course of a brook by examining a drop of water under a lens. Or, to change the simile, he saw the leaf but not the tree, let alone the forest. He knew what was happening day by day. He was exceptionally well informed about the particles of history. But he failed to understand the broader aspects of those political and social tendencies which were withering and those which were developing in Europe. If a little learning is a dangerous thing, a lot of learning can be just as dangerous, once synthesis and interpretation are missing.

Austria's intelligence system furnished him with reports of the secret deliberations held in Paris, Rome, or St. Petersburg; Wilhelm II and his Chancellor Bernhard Bülow were in almost daily communication with the Ballplatz, sometimes telling the truth, sometimes not; the documents were stuffing the archives; Franz Joseph's ministers were frantically busy being busy—but neither he nor Aehrenthal nor most of the other Austrian experts traced the causes of the European fermentation.

They worried about "the Balkan Powder Keg," all those "uncivilized" people who were making a lot of noise, the Serbs and Montenegrans and Bulgarians and Albanians who spoke incomprehensible languages and made unintelligible demands. Oscar Straus had turned Shaw's play *Arms and the Man* into an operetta, *The Chocolate Soldier*. It spoofed a war of the Bulgarians against the Serbians. Prince Danilo in *The Merry Widow* wore a costume which duplicated the costume of the real Prince Danilo of Montenegro: the Balkan people did not think it was funny. Franz Ferdinand called Serbia a country of "rascals, fools, and prune trees."

While the Austrians' view squinted toward the Balkans, they did not perceive that the deep altercation lay between England and Germany. Wilhelm II was constructing a fleet to challenge England's mastery of the sea. Such rivalry could not be tolerated by the British government, since it endangered not only England's political standing in its world—which meant India, Australia, Canada, and so on—but its ability to compete in the international market and to sell Manchester coal and Birmingham steel. England had to emerge from its "splendid isolation," while Wilhelm—who loved a polished phrase as much as a polished helmet—launched in Vienna in 1910 the frightening words about Germany being a nation "decked in shining armor." And in his mind Austria was now part of Germany. To oppose the German-Austrian complex England concluded a treaty with France, and, later, another with Russia. Russia signed a secret agreement with Italy, ostensibly fabricated to assure the status quo in the Balkans, but actually directed to prevent further Austrian expansion. In turn these treaties thickened the flux of Germany's paranoia: the country was being "encircled," Wilhelm claimed in his loud voice.

Wilhelm put his arm around Austria's shoulder and declared that the two countries would henceforth be inseparable. Franz Joseph did not push the arm away. Nor did the other powers help disentangle Austria. On the contrary. As Professor Paul W. Schroeder wrote:

> The basic point is that everyone saw the central threat to the European system in the decline of Austria, and no one would do anything about it. Russians, Serbs, Rumanians, Greeks, and Italians all exploited it: the French thought only of their security. Even Germany made the problem worse by promoting Austria's survival not as a European independent great power, but as a German state and Germany's satellite, and by insisting against Austrian protests that war, if it came, must be fought as a great duel to the death be-

tween Germans and Slavs. The British, meanwhile, did not want Austria to die, but hoped that if she must, she would at least do it quietly. In 1914 Austria decided not to die quietly, and once this long-postponed decision to recover her position by violence was taken, there was no stopping short of a general holocaust.[1]

Everybody prepared for war and everybody talked peace. Nobody believed that an encompassing war would still be possible. They armed, partly because they were afraid, partly to keep up with the Joneses, partly because the war machine, once begun, somehow grew of its own accord—and grew and grew, as if it had swallowed Alice's expanding cake. War threatened because more and more bayonets were stored in the barracks. The Peace Conference in The Hague in 1907—originally Theodore Roosevelt's idea —failed to stop the arms race. The apothegm by Vegetius, the Roman expert, is false: *"Qui desiderat pacem praeparet bellum"* ("Let him who wants peace, prepare for war"). It is truer to say, "Let him who wants peace, prepare for peace." Austria's generals were fond of quoting Vegetius as they asked for increased budgets; they had had eight years of Latin in school and had not forgotten all of it.

It is possible to ascribe the origins of World War I as much to psychological factors as to economic and political causes. Emotion was the coach driver.

Nephew Wilhelm II and Uncle Edward VII got along only a little less inimically than Hamlet and Claudius. "There never were two men," wrote André Maurois,

who were worse constituted to understand each other. . . . The Prince [Edward] was benevolent, modest, and matter-of-fact, the Kaiser moody, loud, and fantastic. The Prince's conversation lacked brilliance but never tact; the Kaiser shone, but often in an offensive style. The Prince loved Puccini, the Kaiser Wagner. When the Kaiser wore mufti, he looked as if he were wearing a uniform; the Prince was equally at ease in civilian as in military dress. To the Kaiser the Prince represented one of those typical Englishmen whose calm and sureness disconcerted and angered him. Wilhelm hated him . . . even when he was young.

Maurois quotes the Berlin saying, "God knows everything, but the Kaiser knows better." Edward did not know everything.

When Edward died in 1910, he was given so glittering a funeral that all Europe thought it a superb show, and Franz Ferdinand was there to represent Franz Joseph. These trappings and suits of woe were to demonstrate that the rulers loved one another. However, and though muted, the British-German discordance murmured on under George V. Whatever Franz Joseph's opinion of the German Kaiser was, an opinion but half disguised, Franz Ferdinand thought Wilhelm wonderful, the very model of a strong ruler. As the heir to the throne gained influence, the connection with Germany became closer. Count Eduard Paar wrote secretly: "We are no longer capable of independent action. Everything happens according to the men who pull the strings in Potsdam."

Franz Joseph rather liked dull and stuffy Nicholas II, but Nicholas could never trust anybody—except his wife; he even refused the services of a secretary and himself sealed the envelopes which contained official documents—and he was being pulled hither and thither by his own uncertainty and by the conflicts within his realm, conflicts a Romanoff could not possibly understand. Nicholas, too, hated Edward VII; he called him "the greatest mischief-maker and the most dangerous intriguer in the world." (Which did not prevent him from signing the treaty with England.) Franz Ferdinand counseled friendship with Nicholas. "Does it make any sense," he said as late as 1913, "to have the Emperor of Austria and the Czar unsaddle each other and open the portals to revolution?" But Nicholas, just as he could not trust, could not be trusted, one moment agreeing with England, in the next embracing Wilhelm, in the next whispering in Franz Joseph's ear.

It was, then, suspicion, distrust, jealousy, envy, and a frantic desire not to lose power which motivated the behavior of the rulers; they taught these fears—for what were their maladies except forms of fear?—to their subjects. The subjects—all but a few—swallowed the lessons and were subsequently reduced to living in trenches like rats, and like rats were exterminated, some eight million of them. Yet none of the rulers, with the exception of Wilhelm—and even he possessed one or two redeeming traits—none of them was vicious. They were serfs of atavism.

In the early years of the twentieth century Franz Joseph sought to keep the peace by frequent meetings with the other sovereigns. He deluded himself into thinking that these royal visits of three or four days' duration, these mutual compliments, these drawings up of honor guards and booming salutes, these ceremonies of donning the uniform of the country of the visitor—it was always the latest uniform, so that when Franz Joseph greeted the King of Sweden in a new Swedish uniform, the King exclaimed that he himself did not yet possess one—these spectacularly organized hunts, these supersecret talks would lead to understanding. In 1903 Franz Joseph entertained Edward VII in Vienna and the two went to the Opera to hear *I Pagliacci*, with Demuth, Schmedes, Gutheil-Schoder. Schalk was conducting. It must have been boring for both of them: Edward would much rather have been at Maxim's dining with one of his favorite cocottes, *La belle Otero*, whom he had once bidden to a rendezvous simply by sending her his visiting card with a watch sketched on it, the hands pointing to five o'clock. And Franz Joseph would much rather have been in bed.[2] Some two weeks after Edward's visit came Kaiser Wilhelm. They greeted each other fervently, Franz Joseph dressed as a Prussian field marshal, Wilhelm as an Austrian general, while twenty-four cannon shots rang out. All traffic stopped in the inner city as the military paraded. They banqueted together, Wilhelm talked, Franz Joseph listened. Ten days later Nicholas appeared, the police filled the road from the railroad station to Schönbrunn with their men to make sure that no anarchist would try his marksmanship, and the two well-groomed emperors changed to well-fitting hunting clothes and went off to the Imperial Hunting Lodge of Mürzsteg, where they were received by the brass section of the Vienna Philharmonic blowing a Russian fanfare as well as they could in the frosty autumn evening. Nicholas discussed policy with Franz Ferdinand and shot deer with Franz Joseph. The subject again was peace. Four months later Russia was at war with Japan, and the Japanese destroyed the better part of the Russian fleet at Port Arthur. Wilhelm, who had no concern whatever with the Russo-Japanese war, sent the same mark of approval to the attacking Japanese and the defending Russian general, the order *pour le mérite*.

It is customary for historians to speak of the nine or ten years of the twentieth century which preceded World War I as a sunny era, beneficent to burghers, an era of adorable women and growing families—in short, an era of peace. Was it really peace? I, too, have used the word, describing how secure and melodious life seemed in Vienna, with the old gentleman in Schönbrunn watching over one.

Was it really peace?

Today, as we look at the timetable, the "glorious prewar period" does not look so serene, the era not quite so healthy:

1905	Jan. 22:	"Bloody Sunday" in St. Petersburg. Abortive Russian revolt.
	March 30:	Greeks in Crete revolt against Turkish rule.
	May 27:	Japanese annihilate Russian fleet.
	Oct. 26:	Mutiny on the *Potemkin*. First Soviet formed.
1907	March 5:	Revolt in Rumania, suppressed bloodily.
	Aug. 4:	French fleet bombards Casablanca.
	Oct. 18:	Hague Peace Conference fails substantially.
1908	Feb. 1:	King Carlos I of Portugal and the Crown Prince murdered.
	July 6:	Young Turks successfully revolt in Macedonia.
	Oct. 6:	Austria annexes Bosnia and Herzegovina.
	Dec. 2:	Riots in Bohemia (sixtieth anniversary of Franz Joseph's accession).
1910	Oct. 4:	Revolution in Portugal. Manuel II flees.
1911	July 1:	Arrival of German warship *Panther* in Agadir creates international crisis.
	Aug. 21:	Wilhelm orates at Hamburg of Germany's "place in the sun" to be secured by German navy.
	Sept. 29:	Italy declares war on Turkey, bombards Tripoli.
1912	April 18:	Turkey closes the Dardanelles.
	Oct. 8:	Montenegro declares war on Turkey.
	Oct. 17:	Turkey declares war on Bulgaria and Serbia ("First Balkan War").
1913	Feb. 3:	Bulgarians renew Turkish war ("Second Balkan War").
	March 18:	King George I of Greece murdered at Salonika.
	July 10:	Russia declares war on Bulgaria.
	Oct. 17:	Serbs invade Albania.

If this was peace, it was, in Dryden's phrase, "War in Masquerade." How many of these events could have been unmasked by reason?

They were not unmasked. As the second decade began, Europe slithered toward a quagmire of unreason. The Agadir incident, brought on by Wilhelm's truculent ambition; the election of an

irredentist President in France, Raymond Poincaré, which resulted in lengthening compulsory military service to three years;
the Balkan wars; the deterioration of Russo-Austrian relations—all
these contributed toward the final and fatal decision that the
cannons be brought out of the store rooms. World War I had a
long period of gestation.

2

Behind gray eyes which looked as if they had been fished from
some cold northern lake, Franz Ferdinand worried over the preservation of the monarchy for his own future. He had never
forgotten the humiliation of having to renounce his children's
rights to the succession; but the realm was still there, and some
day it would be his to govern, his and his wife's, and he would
govern it not like his "weak" old uncle but like a strong man, a
stern ruler, a man of discipline. Those Viennese—how they needed
discipline! Now things were lax because Franz Joseph was a
compromiser and old, so very old. It could not go on like this.
When would Franz Joseph die? Franz Ferdinand brooded, kept his
temper, and only rarely broke out in rages; when he did, they
were so ungovernable that they frightened even his wife. To her
and to the children he was utterly devoted, but even with the
children he smiled but seldom, and when he smiled his mustaches,
which looked like antlers taken from one of the thousands of stags
he had killed, parted grotesquely. Like his uncle, he almost always
wore uniforms. But unlike his uncle, he looked awkward in them,
unpressed and paunchy. He was never easy with people; he himself admitted that he thought everybody guilty until proved innocent. A mordant and a dour man.

Austria was tumbling downhill, because the Socialists, the
Jews, and the Freemasons were ruining the country, he thought.
The German part of the empire had lost control. With Germany's
help he would wipe out democratization, annul the duality of the
Ausgleich, govern from and by Vienna, and form Austria again
into a Habsburg land. The *Ausgleich* was a disaster, he stated as
early as 1895 and as late as 1913, because it gave the Hungarians a

Franz Ferdinand, his family, and retinue on a hunting expedition

privileged status which they used to lord it over the non-Magyars. Yes, the Hungarians were the chief culprits: force would tame them. He wrote to Franz Joseph:

> The terrible quarreling of the nationalities in Austria, the radical antidynastic current in Bohemia, the South Tyrol, Styria, Triest, and Dalmatia, the extremely poor spirit among the greater part of the bureaucracy, the continuing incitements against the army, the adoption of universal suffrage, and the emergence of revolutionary parties such as the Social Democrats, all of this has its cradle in

Hungary, and only energetic interference there can procure a remedy that will help the whole monarchy.[3]

He proposed that central government could be reaffirmed by granting autonomy in *local* administration to all the nationalities of the monarchy equally, while in policy touching the state Vienna would have the last word. And the first word. There was to be no nonsense about party politics, "such as the Social Democrats."

He made no secret of his feelings. When Franz Joseph gathered court and Parliament together in the ceremonial hall of the Hofburg to announce the plan of universal suffrage—the solemn meeting took place on June 19, 1906—Franz Ferdinand was pointedly absent. Not suffrage—sternness was the solution. The army had to be reformed and modernized, to make "energetic interference" practical. The army could help to govern the Slavs—rendering them loyal to the Habsburgs by uniting them and prying them loose from Hungarian pressure; the army could check the Hungarians; and the army would protect the frontiers of the monarchy. Similarly, the navy needed to be strengthened. (Franz Joseph never had any use for a navy and never wore a naval uniform.) He obtained new budgets for shipbuilding and asked the citizens to contribute; ladies went around selling "navy bonbons." Most important, in order to reform the military Franz Joseph's old guard must be got rid of.

With a tenacity born of bitterness, Franz Ferdinand began to wrest military command from his uncle. Franz Joseph could no longer act as the army's overlord; he could no longer ride into the field to supervise their exercises. True, in 1910 he did, at the age of eighty, insist on appearing in Bosnia and reviewing a parade. It was brave and foolish of him. The police made sure that he was vociferously hurrayed and he got away unscathed, though eleven days after his return a young student attempted to kill the governor of Bosnia—he failed and shot himself—and though it was proved that the student had been present both in Mostar and in Sarajevo during Franz Joseph's visit. In the same year he received a visit from Theodore Roosevelt, who called on the Emperor dressed in striped trousers, a gay cravat, and an old raincoat, scandalizing the

Imperial valet. Franz Joseph told Roosevelt that he considered himself "the last monarch of the old school" and "the protector of my peoples against themselves."

Franz Ferdinand would not have used the word "protector." He saw himself as a surgeon; he was going to eradicate. Beck had served Franz Joseph for over forty years, for twenty-five of them as Chief of Staff. Franz Joseph called him "friend" and publicly shook his hand. Very seldom did Franz Joseph shake hands with a subordinate. In 1906, Beck was seventy-six years old. During a maneuver held that year an embarrassing confusion arose as to quarters for the night. Members of the staff did not know to which post they were assigned. On the following day Beck had an accident: he fell from his horse into the water in full view of the troops. A few days later naval exercises were held on the Adriatic. They were inspected by Franz Ferdinand, Franz Joseph being absent. Franz Ferdinand did not address a single word to Beck; he watched, and what he saw did not please him. At the end of the exercises, when Beck was to give his staff a review of success or failure, Franz Ferdinand ordered the military band to defile and play so loudly that Beck could not be heard. Franz Ferdinand then hurried on to Vienna, called on Franz Joseph, and insisted that the "feeble old fellow" be retired. A day or two later Beck returned to report to Franz Joseph. He asked his chief whether it was true that he had consented to relieve him of his post. Franz Joseph whispered, "Yes." Beck clicked his heels and left. Now the least lieutenant knew where the center of gravity was to lie. Conrad, whose ideas of "energetic interference" chimed with Franz Ferdinand's, was appointed Chief of Staff.

Franz Joseph no longer liked Conrad, and Aehrenthal detested him. Aehrenthal felt that Conrad was interfering with the work of diplomacy. Franz Joseph felt that Conrad's gladiatorial advice was selfishly motivated, and he resented the fact that Conrad's predictions assumed an ever more dire tone: if Austria did not clean up in the south, "if we miss our great chance," in the end "nothing would remain of the monarchy except Vienna and a few suburbs." The Foreign Minister and the Chief of Staff fought outright, and all attempts at reconciliation between them proved futile. Asked to write a letter of apology, Conrad said, "I'd rather cut off my right hand." He was dismissed by Franz Joseph. Moritz von Auffenberg was named his successor.

This represented a setback for Franz Ferdinand. Conrad was his man and Conrad was going to be reinstated. He stormed at Franz Joseph and by sheer persistence—or the Emperor's weakness—made his will prevail. He took delight in personally telling Auffenberg, who in the meantime had inaugurated some progressive measures, that he was through. Conrad was recalled. In February, 1912, Aehrenthal died. Hours before his death Franz Joseph bestowed on him the highest distinction he could confer, the Grand Cross of St. Stephen. Now Conrad's enemy was dead.

The Conrad-Aehrenthal division was mirrored by the growing split between Franz Joseph and Franz Ferdinand. Redlich wrote that Schönbrunn and the Belvedere seemed like the headquarters of rival armies. "And then Franz Joseph decided—the opposite of whatever the successor thought." Here again emotion, not reason, shaped decisions which affected millions.

Franz Ferdinand talked big about the glorious cavalry and the "new fleet"—one dreadnought, the *Viribus Unitis,* was launched in 1911—but he was not so sure as he sounded. He was not so blind as not to see Austria's weakness. His neurosis caused him to blast at those around him, including even Conrad, with whom he quarreled and whom he treated so offensively that Conrad resigned— only to be at once appealed to by Franz Ferdinand, begged to return and to continue "to lend his inestimable force and patriotic dedication" to Austria's cause. Conrad had received a taste of what Franz Ferdinand was capable of when the heir presumptive had rebuked him in front of some officers for not appearing at church: "When *I* go to church, you make it your business to be there too!" All the same, Conrad resumed his post.

Franz Joseph looked on with half-closed eyes. Katherina Schratt had returned to Vienna after a long absence. "I am very tired," he wrote her in May, 1912; "the weakness of my age increases. My mood is sad and bored. I am afraid I will bore you too." The following year he appointed Franz Ferdinand "General Inspector of all the Armed Forces." It was tantamount to resignation. Officially as well as unofficially the power now belonged to the successor. The fat man was now the commander.

Franz Joseph may have been prompted to this step by reasons other than fatigue and age. A scandal had been uncovered which undermined the reputation of his beloved army. It tormented and disgusted him. Let someone else deal with it! Let someone else clean the repulsive spot! He had had enough.

3

The main scandal had been preceded by a lurid murder case. A first lieutenant, Adolf Hofrichter, having failed in his ambition to be appointed a staff officer and forced to remain in provincial Linz, sent ten of his comrades little boxes of cyanide pills. His motive was revenge, revenge against the army, which he thought had treated him unjustly. Obviously it was the action of a madman. A circular went with the pills which urged the recipient to sample them: they were aphrodisiac pills and the results would be "sensational." One man died immediately; the others did not trust the pills. It took the police seven months before they succeeded in tracking down the guilty man and obtaining a confession. The readers of the *Neue Freie Presse* had an enticing time; as the investigation proceeded, it uncovered details of adultery and other scandals in which the officers were involved. The newspaper published more than twenty pages before Hofrichter was condemned to twenty years of imprisonment.

The case occurred in 1909.[4] Worse was to follow.

The Vienna Evidence Bureau—a euphemism for "spy system" —made it a practice to watch letters sent to any post office box and mailed from certain locations which they suspected to be centers of espionage activities. Early in 1913 a letter lay in the General Post Office, addressed to Box——, which had not been claimed. It had been sent from Berlin, and in due time it was returned to the Berlin post office. There it was opened in an effort to find the sender. It contained no clue as to the sender, but it did contain 6,000 kronen and the names and addresses of several men, probably spies. Berlin notified Vienna, the letter was returned to Vienna, and the General Post Office was put under surveillance. Nothing happened, nobody came to claim the letter. Weeks went by. Then on May 24, late on a Saturday afternoon, a man appeared to collect the letter. Two detectives assigned to the case were not at the post office, as they should have been, but they were notified by a code signal. They rushed over only to find that the man had just left. He took a taxi outside the post office and the two hapless detectives just caught a glimpse of his back as he rode away. They did manage to get the number of the taxi.

What followed was a series of totally improbable coincidences. As the detectives tood there deliberating what to do next, the self-same taxi drove up. They hailed it and learned that the driver had taken his previous fare to the Café Kaiserhof. They took the taxi and told the driver to go there as fast as he could. During the brief trip they found in the taxi a small felt sheath, apparently a container for a pocketknife or a comb. When they arrived at the Kaiserhof, the man had left, but they got his description from the waiter. They then went to the nearest taxi stand and questioned the drivers. One of them said that he had taken a gentleman answering to the description to the Hotel Klomser. There the detectives asked the concierge whether such a man was in the hotel. "Yes," replied the concierge, "I think you mean Colonel Redl. He came in about a quarter of an hour ago with two gentlemen. He is in room number one." Redl? Alfred Redl, colonel of the General Staff, a high officer attached to Conrad's retinue, commander of the Eighth Army in Prague and formerly head of the counterespionage service, four times decorated for exceptional merit—it was impossible. One nervous detective now went to the telephone to ask his chief for further instructions; the other handed the concierge the felt case. The concierge was to ask whether it belonged to one of the three men. At this moment Redl came down the stairs. "Colonel, did you lose this?" asked the concierge. "Yes," said Redl, "thank you." Suddenly, out of the corner of his eye, he saw the other detective, studying the hotel register with apparent nonchalance. Redl guessed at once that he was trapped; he lost his nerve. He wheeled around and fled, the detectives after him. They chased him through the city and finally arrested him.

Conrad was sitting at supper in the Grand Hotel; the company was pleasant, the food superb. Of a sudden Colonel Urbanski, head of the Evidence Bureau, appeared, excused himself for the disturbance, and asked Conrad if he mght speak with him alone.

He unrolled the story, to Conrad's horror. Without thinking the problem through and anxious at all costs to avoid a military scandal, Conrad decided that a commission should be formed at once, under Urbanski's leadership, to call on Redl, confront and examine him, and then leave a loaded pistol with him. He would know what to do.

At midnight four men appeared in Room 1 of the Hotel Klomser, where Redl was being kept under guard. He confessed willingly enough. He was a practicing homosexual; his male companion, a "beautiful" young lieutenant whom he had passed off as his nephew, cost him a great deal of money. (Later, when the police searched Redl's flat in Prague, they found a collection of life-sized and obviously expensive female dolls; whether the collection belonged to him or his "nephew" was not certain.) His secret had been discovered by a Russian agent, a Moscow aristocrat, another homosexual, who had first introduced Redl into a shadowy society and then blackmailed him. Redl had been in Russian pay for at least seven years. The head of the Russian secret service, a Colonel Batiouchine, had supplied Redl with a few tips and given him the names of several Russian spies working in Austria, deliberately sacrificing them so that Redl could have them arrested and confirm his own reputation for efficiency and zeal. In turn Redl had betrayed Austrian war secrets to Russia, including the important "Plan Three" dealing with a surprise attack on Serbia, the organization chart of the Austrian espionage system, and the blueprint of the fortress of Przemysl in Galicia. As chief of the Austrian counterespionage service, Redl had been able to obtain such data. He confessed that his bribes, while not extravagant, had been sufficient to enable him to live among a fashionable homosexual group—homosexuality was widespread in the Austrian army, he asserted—and to keep an automobile.

All this, and more, came out during the midnight interview, though Redl to the last said that he had worked alone, without Austrian accomplices. At dawn the men departed and left the revolver. Shortly after they heard a shot.

Nothing having been learned from Mayerling and other experiences, an attempt was made to suppress the news of the Redl affair. It failed. The scandal spread its miasma through the country, and the warmongering clique exploded with indignation at

Russia's spying—as if Austria was not acting similarly. When Franz Joseph heard about it, he exclaimed bitterly: "Our modern age— and these are the creatures it spawns!" It was the "it-could-not-have-happened-in-my-days" sigh of an old man. He was so horrified that he could not sleep; the next day, wrote one of the generals who saw him, he looked "decayed."

Franz Ferdinand reacted differently. First he poured out his indignation on Conrad: he had made both an asinine and an immoral decision. Even a criminal such as Redl was entitled to the services of a priest before execution, and by encouraging Redl to use that revolver they had silenced him, instead of probing further into the Russian intelligence system and uncovering other sore spots in Austria. It just showed that the entire command of the Austrian army was rotten, contaminated, vitiated; he was going to clean house, get rid of everybody, appoint his own generals. So he shouted, his bull neck swollen with rage. He knew he wouldn't succeed; even he could not break through the military clique, as protective of one another as doctors are. He vented his fury on Colonel Urbanski, a man Franz Joseph esteemed. Urbanski was dismissed, but the decision was kept secret from Franz Joseph.[5]

The Redl scandal, though essentially an individual act of corruption, did point to the canker which lay beneath the *Waffenrock*, the military tunic. Exaggerated beyond its actual importance, it left a bitter taste on Austria's lips. But most of the people, as they lapped up the details, simply ordered another portion of Sachertorte.

Perhaps it pushed the military party one step nearer war. The unifying force of war would cut away internal contamination and stop necrosis. Redl would be forgotten. In the meantime Franz Ferdinand made the most of the affair. The split between him and Franz Joseph widened even more, and the messengers of state, wending their way from Schönbrunn to the Belvedere and back again, were confused and fearful.

4

Strange contrast—the dimness of political morality against the light of artistic and philosophic achievement—and between them a void, a no man's land. The life force of the spirit turned its gaze away from the death struggle of the state, as a healthy man hates to look on an invalid lying in an untidy bed.

The poets, writers, musicians, painters, and architects continued to stride ahead, looking only at their companions, without a glance at the other road along which the soldiers were grouping into march formation. The "intellectuals" saw nothing to threaten their existence.

> "I see nobody on the road," said Alice.
> "I only wish I had such eyes," the King remarked in a fretful tone. "To be able to see Nobody! And at that distance too!"

"Nobody" was coming—but many thinking men and women, and particularly the young ones, had no eyes for sorry sights. It is substantially true that the more the distance grew between governmental life and artistic life—the distance so to speak between Franz Ferdinand and Hofmannsthal—the richer became Austria's achievement. Stefan Zweig wrote:

> We young people, completely absorbed in our literary ambitions, took little notice of the dangerous changes in our land. We peered only at books and pictures. We took not the least interest in political and social problems. What did we care about those shrill squabbles? The city became turbulent on election day—and we went to the libraries. The people protested—and we wrote and discussed poetry. We did not notice the fiery handwriting on the wall; like Belshazzar of yore we continued to dine happily on the delicious nourishment of art, without glancing ahead. Only decades later when roof and walls had crashed over us did we realize that the fundament had long been undermined. . . .[6]

Vienna contributed remarkably to the "nourishment of art." The Opera and the Burgtheater stood at an artistic level higher than any other theater in Europe and never equaled since. The Burgtheater had Josef Kainz, unruly, nervous, and intensely poetic, one of the great Hamlets. His monument shows him in the role, contemplating the skull of Yorick. In 1910 Max Reinhardt came to Vienna and showed an enraptured public his staging of *A Midsummer Night's Dream, The Merchant of Venice, Twelfth Night, Lysistrata,* Lessing's *Minna von Barnhelm,* Hebbel's

Judith, and three new plays by Hermann Bahr, Richard Beer-Hofmann, and Hofmannsthal.

It was Hofmannsthal who offered Vienna a declaration of love, at once delicate and robust, which along with that misnamed waltz became the signet of the city. *Der Rosenkavalier,* a joyful journey through the strata of that long-ago society when Maria Theresa was Queen, presents a Vienna imagined and beautified; yet it is truer than accurate description, it is the essence of Vienna. It gave Richard Strauss a temporary visa; inspired by so excellent a libretto, the magician from Munich turned Viennese and made a Wagnerian orchestra perform in three-quarter time. In the figure of the Marschallin one may perceive the personification of Vienna, reflective, world-wise, hiding a drooping spirit under a brocade of gaiety—"half merry, half sad." Paradoxically, this work for which Hofmannsthal himself predicted only parochial appeal, its jokes and allusions being incomprehensible at large, became the most popular international opera of the twentieth century.

It was not only in music and literature—Bartók's *Bluebeard's Castle,* Schönberg's *Pierrot Lunaire,* and Rilke's best poems belong to that period—but in other endeavors of the mind that Austria continued to extend her influence beyond her own frontiers.

Ludwig Wittgenstein, whom many consider the most stimulating philosopher of the twentieth century, offered in his major work, the *Tractatus Logico-philosophicus,* an investigation into the structure of language, which greatly influenced subsequent philosophers, including Bertrand Russell and Alfred North Whitehead. Wittgenstein aimed at clearing philosophic thought of the obtuseness of philosophic expression, insisting that meaningful language must relate to everyday experience. His leitmotif is often quoted: "Whatever can be said can be said clearly, and that of which one cannot speak, one must be silent about."

Ludwig was the youngest of the eight children of a brilliant Jewish father (who had embraced Protestantism) and an almost equally brilliant mother who was a Catholic. His mixed heritage may have prompted him to explore wide fields and dissimilar projects: aeronautic engineer, schoolteacher, gardener, architect, medical orderly during the war, laboratory technician, literary critic—this Ludwig-of-all-trades attempted much. His brother Paul, the pianist, lost an arm during World War I, but Ravel and others composed concertos for the left hand for him and Paul continued his career. Ludwig showed equal determination. Having inherited a fortune from his father, he resolutely gave it away, using most of it to aid young writers. He was one of those Viennese who hated Vienna, only to be attracted back to it time and again. Restlessly he wandered over Europe, to Berlin, Italy, Ireland, the Soviet Union, Norway, finally to find his place as a teacher in Trinity College, Cambridge. There he became a beloved figure, carelessly attired—he was supposed never to have worn a necktie after he reached the age of twenty-three—living in a cluttered room, whistling Schubert melodies, reading cowboy stories, reciting passages from *The Brothers Karamazov* by heart, and discussing philosophy with whoever would come along, including the chambermaid. His disciples gathered around him and urged him to publish his ideas, but he published little during his lifetime and his fame has grown since his death in 1951.

The Jews contributed far more to the intellectual life of Vienna than their number warranted (according to the 1910 census 1,300,000 Jews lived in Austria, representing about 5 percent of the empire's population; about 400,000 lived in Vienna). Here, too, compensation played a role. Only exceptionally did a Jew take part in governmental affairs, only exceptionally did a Jew hold an important post in the military, and never did Franz Ferdinand have a good word to say about them. Yet, in Vienna at least, they were not "oppressed" in the strict sense of the word. They lived a good life and were merely excluded from certain clubs, tangibly or tacitly. None of them foresaw the violence that was to come. Many of them were ardent Austrian patriots—or at least Viennese patriots—and some of them became narrow chauvinists. Perhaps this was a form of wish fulfillment, or an expression of self-derogation. It found a bitter example in a book by Otto Weininger, raging against women as well as Jews. *Geschlecht und Charakter* was published in 1903, created enormous controversy, and went through edition after edition. The author of this malodorous compound of Strindberg and misread Freud committed suicide less than a year after it was published.

The artistic and scientific Jews of the prewar epoch gave "the most intensive meaning to what is Viennese," as Stefan Zweig wrote. "An intellectual energy, unanchored for centuries, here combined with a tradition which had become a bit tired; they nourished that tradition, enlivened and heightened it, refreshed it with new force."

Yet that force, Jewish or Christian, was doomed. It was not strong enough to counterbalance the drive of a Franz Ferdinand or a Conrad. Intellect does not dull the edge of the sword. Mozart is no match for the "Radetzky March." In 1910 the British economist Sir Norman Angell, in *The Great Illusion,* spoke of the futility of war. The book was read eagerly, everywhere, but it was read by the wrong people.

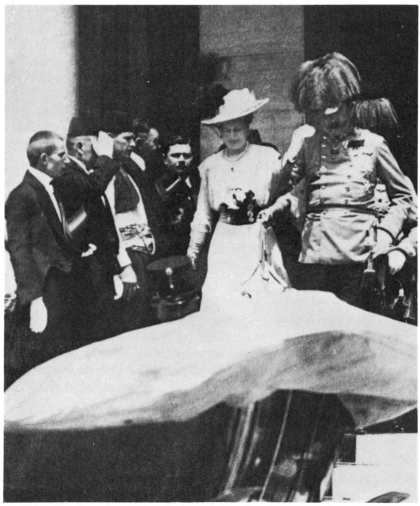

Franz Ferdinand and his wife leaving Sarajevo City Hall after the first
assassination attempt and a few minutes before the fatal incident

CHAPTER XVI

Sarajevo

SO MUCH HAS BEEN WRITTEN about the murder at Sarajevo, so often and everywhere has the phrase "the shot heard round the world"* been repeated, so punctiliously have the details of the crime been investigated, that a mere recapitulation of the drama should now suffice.[1] One question does remain only half-answered, one puzzle not entirely solved. What prompted Franz Ferdinand to undertake a journey against which he had been warned? What was the reason for his obstinacy? What loomed so large to him that he threw caution aside? And why did he take his wife along, surely not the customary action of a military commander going into the field?

Serbia had emerged from the Second Balkan War a strengthened state. It had scored a local victory. By the Treaty of Bucharest of August, 1913, Bulgaria was deprived of parts of Macedonia and these were ceded to Serbia. It had gained about a million new subjects, as well as important new trade routes leading east, though it had failed to achieve what it so badly wanted, an outlet to the Adriatic Sea. There, at Austria's insistence, a new independent state, Albania, acted as a dune. Treaty or no treaty, it was perfectly clear that Serbia would not long be content with its

---

* The phrase was originally written by Emerson in a poem celebrating the completion of the Concord Monument in 1837. Later it was used about the start of World War I.

gains. And if that wasn't clear, if any doubt remained as to the future of Serbian policy, Serbia's premier, Nikola Pašić, made no secret of his intention: "The first round is won. Now we must prepare for the second round—against Austria." Serbian troops marched into Albania. Vienna promptly sent a stiffly worded ultimatum to Belgrade threatening war. Germany endorsed that ultimatum, though hesitantly. At once the other leading nations, including even Russia, urged the Serbs to withdraw their troops. They did so, convinced that Austria was not to be trifled with. But surely they would try again. The truce was but a temporary one.

Serbian youths had formed themselves into secret irredentist groups, the most virulent of which was popularly known as the Black Hand. The organization was founded in 1911, and its intention was to achieve a union of all the Serbs, including those who were still "suffering" under Turkish or Bulgarian rule and especially those living in Bosnia under Austrian rule. They wanted to be known as the "Piedmont of the South Slavs," meaning that they wanted to play the same role in their orbit as Piedmont had played in Italy's liberation. Members of the Black Hand behaved as if life were an opera-libretto. Like the conspirators in *A Masked Ball*, they stalked dark alleys and midnight trysting places. If there was anything a Balkan group dearly loved, it was a conspiracy. Members were known to each other only by number. They swore mystic oaths of secrecy and bound themselves to blind obedience. They indulged in subterranean rites, diabolized but very patriotic —and very melodramatic. To the saner statesmen of Serbia, to Pašić himself, the Black Hand proved to be a nuisance. Pašić knew better than to pin his hopes on the mumbo jumbo of youths who knew nothing about economics or military logistics and whose one solution for all problems was to draw the dagger hidden in the riding boot.

The leader of the Black Hand was a Colonel Dragutin Dimitrijević, at one time chief of the military intelligence of the Serbian army. He was known in conspiratorial circles as Apis. He seems to have been typecast for the role: a man with a frozen, sallow face from which sprang a luxuriant handlebar mustache of intense black, he was not overly endowed with brains, but he was a reckless and romantic hero. He excelled as an organizer, bullying and cajoling men who wanted to be bullied and cajoled. His stern fanaticism was infectious. His private life was that of a devoted family man, but in public life he acted with brutal force. He achieved such success in guerrilla warfare in Macedonia, probably supported by Russian money, that he became the most powerful man in Serbia, too powerful for comfort. Pašić quarreled with him after having supported him.

If a man like Apis resembled the fictional villain—"Thoughts black, hands apt, drugs fit"—if the plots and counterplots carried with them an aspect of ludicrous lubricity, they nevertheless had to be taken seriously. They were the Balkan peoples' riposte to foreign ownership of their lands and institutions, now Turkish, now Venetian, now Austrian. Within Serbia were to be found sensible, honest, and public-spirited men. All the same, conniving and intriguing came naturally to those who lived in an ambiance of suspicion and unrest. Pašić himself, judicious and honest though he appeared, dissimulated and deceived. Whenever something decisive was about to happen, such as in 1903, when the plot against King Alexander I and Queen Draga came to a head—they were murdered and their mutilated bodies thrown from the balcony of their palace—he managed to be absent. He was conveniently absent when the Sarajevo assassinations took place.

Conditions in the Balkans were known to Franz Ferdinand. He knew about the operation of the Black Hand. He knew that Apis had forged a multiple link of terrorists, which reached into the annexed territory. Franz Ferdinand's own military and intelligence staff, housed in the Belvedere, warned him. It is absurd to believe, as several historians have stated, that these warnings did not come to his attention. Such a signal appeared on December 3, 1913, on which day a Chicago newspaper published in Serbian wrote: "The Austrian Heir Apparent has announced his intention of visiting Sarajevo next year. . . . Serbs, seize everything you can lay your hands on—knives, rifles, bombs, and dynamite. Take holy vengeance! Death to the Habsburg dynasty!" Did nobody show Franz Ferdinand this article?

A warning was transmitted by Pašić himself to the Serbian ambassador in Vienna, Jovan Jovanović. Through an informer planted in the Apis organization, Pašić had found out that the

Black Hand planned to kill Franz Ferdinand. Such an act did not at all suit Pašić's schedule, since he was not yet in a position to meet open revenge by Austria. The Serbian forces had not recovered their fighting strength after the Second Balkan War. The warning Pašić sent to Vienna was couched in oblique language; he did not name the Black Hand or specify details (if he knew them), since that would have exposed him to Apis's vengeance and been tantamount to writing his own death sentence; but he said enough for the Serbian ambassador to take action. He should have talked to Count Berchtold, since the matter came within the province of the Foreign Office; but Berchtold could not abide Jovanović and vice versa. So he went to see the Minister of Finance, Leon Bilinski, who was responsible for the administration of Bosnia-Herzegovina. It is inconceivable that Bilinski suppressed the message.

A Dr. Sunarić, president of the Bosnian delegation, telegraphed Bilinski asking him to "use his influence to prevent the journey." Franz Ferdinand's intelligence service recommended that if he did insist on going, he not appear in Sarajevo on the day of the Feast of St. Vitus. To the Balkans, this day was a holiday carrying an especially grave significance. For centuries it had been a day of mourning, commemorating the battle in 1389 when the Turks destroyed medieval Serbia, while recently it had become a symbol of resurgence, the day of the defeat of the Turks in the First Balkan War.

Franz Ferdinand did not walk unawares into a house where mayhem sat in the corner. Why then did he ignore the warnings? "It is my duty"—such was his rationalization for what he longed to do. An important maneuver was scheduled to take place in Bosnia, and he, as the head of the military, needed to be there and form his own impressions of how well or badly the army and the new navy were performing. True enough, yet it was only a factual clothing for a psychological need.

Franz Ferdinand went to Bosnia because he was disliked in Vienna and ignored by the Viennese. The Viennese didn't know how to take this man who didn't compose waltzes, didn't stop to chat with a journalist on the Graben, and whose name was never connected with a ballerina at the opera house. The Viennese said:

"Once he gets to be Emperor we'll have nothing to laugh about" (to which they later added, "He didn't get to be Emperor and we still have nothing to laugh about").

Franz Ferdinand needed approval; he needed a sign of assertion; he needed the pomp and circumstance of a procession in which the men would turn their heads sharp right as they passed him. He needed some tribute or other to bolster his ego. If not in Vienna, under the shadow of Franz Joseph, then in a province, as far away from Schönbrunn as possible. What better stage for displaying himself as the heir presumptive than the newly acquired territory? There, in Bosnia, he could show off Austria's might, of which he saw himself the symbol. You are now and in the future part of the Habsburg land, his presence would indicate to the South Slavs, and you had better make the best of it. An idea was forming in his mind: once Emperor, he would unite the Slavs and form a tripartite monarchy. That move would extinguish or at least weaken Slavic aspirations to independence. It was important that the Slavs get to know him personally. In addition, his going to Bosnia would anger the Hungarians. Perfect—anything which angered the Hungarians pleased Franz Ferdinand.

However intricate his motives, the decisive swing lay in his desire to affirm his eminence, his prestige, his authority. His ear sought the shouts of the populace; he didn't inquire too deeply whether these shouts were induced by an Austrian claque or rose spontaneously. Because of his need he made himself believe that those warnings were nothing: only a coward would heed them.

At the last moment he did have some misgivings. He told Franz Joseph that he did not want to go because it was hot in Bosnia and he suffered in hot weather. Perhaps what he wanted to hear was Franz Joseph saying, "I forbid you to go." But Franz Joseph—who could not have been entirely ignorant of the warnings and surely knew of Serbian propaganda in Bosnia—simply said to him, "Do as you like," and indicated that he wished to wash his hands of the whole affair. Thereupon Franz Joseph moved to Ischl, not to have to receive Franz Ferdinand immediately upon his return. Franz Joseph had got to the point where he avoided as much as possible personal meetings with his successor. It would be too much to say that Franz Joseph desired to expose Franz Ferdinand to danger; such a desire, even in a subconscious form, would have been inconsistent with his personality. He simply wanted to separate himself as often and as much as he could from a man who had become thoroughly uncongenial to him.

Franz Ferdinand took Sophie along. She was not only to witness the fine reception for which he hoped, but the occasion would furnish for the first time a legitimate reason for her to be received in queenly splendor. That prospect swayed him as much as other considerations. A tribute to his wife after many snubs—what could be sweeter? It was arranged that she would go directly from Vienna to Spa Ilidze and wait there for Franz Ferdinand; then the two would drive through Sarajevo in an official procession, a rehearsal for kingship, she at his side, receiving for the first time honors equivalent to the honors extended to him.

2

The maneuvers went well, and Franz Ferdinand, quite satisfied, met Sophie on the twenty-fifth of June, 1914, in Ilidze, where the entire Hotel Bosnia had been put at their disposal, newly furbished, with one room turned into a private chapel. At five o'clock in the afternoon of the next day, the couple and their retinue drove to Sarajevo to visit the bazaar. He was in uniform; the people recognized him and crowded around him; nothing untoward occurred, and everybody seemed friendly and in holiday mood. On June 27 Franz Ferdinand and Sophie gave a dinner to the local functionaries. The official ride through Sarajevo was scheduled for the following morning, a Sunday, the Day of St. Vitus; it included an inspection of military installations and a visit to City Hall and to the new Folk Museum. At dinner Sophie said smilingly to Dr. Sunarić: "You were wrong after all. . . . We have been received with friendliness and sincere warmth by everybody, including the Serbian population." She said it in a tone of relief, making it evident that she had not been unaware of danger.

The arrangements for the procession were the responsibility of a military committee headed by Oskar Potiorek, the Austrian military governor of the province. The chief of police of Sarajevo,

Edmund Gerde, had previously appeared before the committee, recommending that a cordon of police guard the road over which Franz Ferdinand proposed to travel. Potiorek's answer was: "We, the military, have the responsibility for his safety. It is none of your business." Somebody else told Gerde, "You see specters everywhere."

The result of this division between military and civil authority, a division characteristically Austrian, was that the procession began without enough protection, Potiorek disposing only a handful of soldiers to watch and hold back the crowd. The motorcade of six automobiles entered Sarajevo at 10 A.M. Franz Ferdinand and Sophie were in the second car, he in gala uniform, the heavy feathered helmet on his head, she in white with a large white hat, white gloves, a white parasol, a little bunch of flowers stuck in her belt. They must have been thoroughly uncomfortable in the heat. Potiorek sat in front of them, pointing out the sights, and Franz Ferdinand's aide-de-camp Count Franz Harrach sat next to the chauffeur. They were passing along the embankment of the river Miljacka, the time was 10:10 A.M., when a dark young man standing among the crowd on the sidewalk made a peculiar motion with his hands. There was a sound no louder than the popping of a champagne cork; Harrach thought he heard the whistle of a bullet, Sophie felt something in the back of her neck, and Potiorek saw a black ball rolling toward Franz Ferdinand's car. It was a bomb which glanced off and landed underneath one of the following cars: the front tire of that car blew, the car swerved, the officers riding in it were thrown into the street and one of them, Lieutenant Erich Merizzi, put his hand to his face and felt that it was dripping blood. On the embankment some people shouted, "Grab him!" while the young man jumped over the parapet down to the bed of the river, raised a hand to his mouth, and swallowed a capsule. At once the police were after him and dragged him up. The cyanide he had swallowed proved ineffective, he vomited all over his clothes, and he was being beaten by the policemen with the flats of their sabers. His name was Nedjelko Cabrinović, nineteen years old, a member of the Black Hand. The bomb he had thrown was a serviceable weapon, though Cabrinović had handled it so inexpertly that it had caused no major harm. It was of

Serbian manufacture. The piece which had grazed Sophie was the fuse cap; it turned out that she got away with only a superficial scratch. Sophie must have been very brave to go along with the program after such a scare. Merizzi was taken to a hospital, the damaged car was hastily pushed aside, and the other cars proceeded to City Hall, though at greater speed than before.

The mayor greeted Franz Ferdinand, a prepared speech in his hand. Franz Ferdinand was furious and would not let him begin. "What is the meaning of this?" he blustered. "We come here on a peaceful mission and we get bombs thrown at us." Nobody answered. The Bosnians who had gathered at City Hall knew or guessed that the bomb did not represent an isolated incident. It had failed, but another man somewhere, someplace, was ready to throw another bomb, and still another, should the second fail too. Potiorek, however, assured Franz Ferdinand that what had happened was the deed of a lunatic. There would be no repetition. Franz Ferdinand believed him because he wanted to believe him, and presently he let the mayor's speech splash over him and replied with a few words of thanks. While the ceremony was taking place at City Hall, Cabrinović was being given a thorough going-over at the police station. He knew the names of his fellow conspirators (contrary to the usual practice of the Black Hand), but he kept silent and betrayed no one.

Before leaving City Hall, Franz Ferdinand said that the next thing he wanted to do was to stop by the hospital to see how badly Merizzi had been wounded. He again asked Potiorek, "Do you think that there are going to be any more bombs?" Potiorek's answer has been variously reported. According to the most reliable of these reports, he answered, "You may continue without worrying. I accept the entire responsibility." He thought at any rate that the ride to the hospital would be safe because it meant retracing part of the road traversed before, the one along the embankment, and that surely was the last spot where an assassin would look for the Archduke. All the same, it might be advisable to drive to the hospital at the best speed the automobile could manage; it might even be advisable to cancel the rest of the day's program. This, said Potiorek, would be a proper punishment dealt out to the inhabitants of Sarajevo. Franz Ferdinand agreed: he really believed that the Bosnians would consider it a punishment to be deprived of a glimpse of his august person, feathers, medals, and all. Perhaps after the hospital visit he would reconsider: he still longed for that triumphal procession. He was told that Cabrinović had been captured alive. He said, "Hang him as soon as you can, or else Vienna will send him a medal."

Franz Ferdinand and Sophie left City Hall, and some nameless photographer took their picture. No longer did they look spruce and calm. Franz Ferdinand's uniform was rumpled and Sophie's face was drawn. Count Harrach stood on the left-hand running board, on the side from which the bomb had been thrown. The Archduke's car was preceded by the lead car, which carried the chief of police and other officials.

Once again the caravan set off. The time was 11:15 A.M.

What no one among those bumbling Austrian officials knew was that the assassination plot had gone thoroughly awry. The Italian historian Luigi Albertini, after careful research, came to the conclusion that the plot had been engineered by Apis without active participation by the Serbian government. On the other hand, officials in the Serbian regime knew that such a plot existed and did nothing to stop it other than the warning given out by Jovanović. Apis wanted to kill Franz Ferdinand because he knew of Franz Ferdinand's plan to unite Austria's Serbo-Croat citizens and set them up on a basis of equality with the other national groups. Such a plan would have ended the Apis dream of secession and alignment with Serbia, and might indeed have ended the Black Hand altogether. Therefore Franz Ferdinand's death was to Apis a necessity of life. The Black Hand had chosen six young men, none of whom knew Apis personally (but they did know one another), to station themselves along the embankment that Sunday morning. The one who could manage to obtain the clearest view of the Archduke's automobile—in other words, whenever a break in the procession occurred—would do the killing. But when the first bomb fizzled, the five other men were gripped by panic and fled their posts. By the law of probability, Franz Ferdinand was now safe. But probability was replaced by improbability, so coincidental that were one to relate the story as fiction one would be accused of manufacturing the absurd.

Nobody had bothered to inform the chauffeur of the lead car that the route had been changed. As the car reached the Latin Bridge (now called the Princip Bridge), it turned right to go up what was then named Franz Joseph Street. That was the originally scheduled itinerary. Naturally, the Archduke's chauffeur followed the lead car. At this moment Potiorek stood up and yelled at the first chauffeur, "Not that way, you idiot! Go straight!" The chauffeur, flustered, stopped the car so that he could shift into reverse.

On the corner there was a coffeehouse, and before the coffeehouse stood a young man who had just that moment come out after having steadied his nerves with coffee and slivovitz. He was filled with despair over the failure of the first attempt and fear at the probability that soon the police would get to him for questioning. His name was Gavrilo Princip, a poor, frail misfit who, like Lucheni, had imbibed the teachings of Bakunin and was obsessed with a vague and mystic longing to strike a great blow for what he conceived to be freedom. In his pocket he carried a loaded pistol. He did not think that he was ever going to be given the opportunity to use it. And now, there were the Archduke and Sophie sitting straight in the open car, not moving, fewer than ten feet away, and nothing at all between him and his target, since Harrach stood on the other side of the car. It was frighteningly easy. It was preordained. He took careful aim and fired twice. The first shot hit Franz Ferdinand in the chest, the second hit Sophie in the abdomen. For a moment or two both of them continued to sit straight. The assassin was pinned fast by bystanders just as he was raising his pistol to put a bullet through his own head. He was nearly beaten to death by the police, one arm so badly mauled that eventually it had to be amputated.

The chauffeur finally got the car turned around, and as it lurched forward Sophie collapsed against Franz Ferdinand. He remained upright, but a blob of blood stained the front of his white tunic and blood oozed from the corners of his mouth. "Sopherl, Sopherl, don't die! Live for our children!" Franz Ferdinand managed to stammer as he tried to hold her unconscious body. Harrach asked him how bad the wound was. He answered, "It's nothing." Six times he repeated, in a voice growing ever more feeble and incoherent, "It's nothing." Then he was dead. And the "nothing" developed into a something which affected the whole world.[2]

3

The weather was glorious in Vienna that Sunday; the Viennese were out walking or bicycling in the woods. During the afternoon the first "extras" appeared with the gruesome news. It caused no real grief among the Sunday strollers, most of whom had never even caught a glimpse of Franz Ferdinand. They thought the assassination a barbaric act committed by a barbaric people, but not one which would involve them personally. Redlich noted in his diary: "No mood of mourning pervades the city. Music continues to be played in the Prater and out here in Grinzing." Franz Ferdinand's adherents—the Belvedere crowd—knew it was all over for them, and the Hofburg crowd secretly rejoiced, hiding their elation behind a proper melancholy mien.

Franz Joseph put Prince Albert Montenuovo in charge of the funeral arrangements. Montenuovo was grand master of the imperial royal court, a fish-blooded martinet who fulfilled his function with stiff-necked formality, unrelieved by kindness. His favorite bedside reading must have been the Almanach de Gotha. He was the grandson of Marie Louise, Emperor Franz's daughter, whom Napoleon had taken as his second wife, and of a Count Neipperg, whom Marie Louise had married after Napoleon's death, and he let nobody forget his royal grandmother. He had hated Franz Ferdinand for years, despising his infra dig marriage. He now had the opportunity to revenge himself on a dead man.

He arranged it so that the remains of Franz Ferdinand and Sophie did not arrive in Vienna until the second of July, and at ten o'clock at night, dispensing with public ceremony, almost clandestinely. Franz Joseph was not at the railroad station but was represented by the new presumptive heir, Archduke Karl. During the night the coffins were transferred to the Hofburg chapel. There they were placed side by side, but the Archduke's coffin was placed on a higher level than his wife's. On top of Franz Ferdinand's coffin rested the symbols of his rank: the crown of an imperial prince, the cap and saber of an Austrian general, and the hat of an archduke. On Sophie's coffin they placed a fan and a pair of white gloves, a snide reminder that she was once merely a lady-in-waiting.

The next morning the public was admitted, but only between the hours of 8 A.M. and noon. Those four hours did not suffice to satisfy the curious; nevertheless on the stroke of twelve the chapel was closed. At four o'clock a brief service took place. Franz Joseph attended, along with the archdukes and archduchesses who happened to be in Vienna, but most of the foreign heads of state or their representatives did not appear, having been told that Franz Joseph's frail health permitted only a curtailed ceremony. Wilhelm, who had wanted to come, was kept away by hints that a plot to kill him was being hatched by the same assassins who had operated against Franz Ferdinand. There was no truth whatever in that rumor.

Franz Ferdinand would have been entitled to burial in the Capuchin crypt along with the other Habsburgs. But Sophie could not be buried there. Montenuovo, who had previously objected to the viewing of both coffins and had given in only when Karl pleaded that at least this simple honor be paid both of them, knew the way out of the dilemma. Franz Ferdinand had left a will specifying that he wished to be buried in his castle in Artstetten on the shore of the Danube. Why not? Let them both be buried there; let Franz Ferdinand be the exception to the ancient usage. Once more, as night fell, the two coffins were transported, this time to the West Railroad Station. On Montenuovo's orders there was to be no procession, no tolling of the bells, no bearers of candles, no solemn incantations. Military honors to which any plain lieutenant would be entitled were refused. This was too much. The insult was too obvious. Accordingly more than a hundred members of the Austrian aristocracy formed an impromptu procession and, uninvited, followed the corpses on foot to the station. The train arrived at two in the morning at the tiny station of Pöchlarn from where the coffins were to be ferried across the river. A fierce thunderstorm broke, with the rain pelting down on the small group who had been brave enough to remain for the last rites.

They huddled silently and miserably in the dingy waiting room of the station. The ferry arrived just as dawn broke and the hearse was loaded onto the barge. At that moment a delayed thunderclap frightened one of the horses, the horse shied, and only by sheer luck did the funeral carriage not plunge into the Danube. The obsequies had assumed a phantasmal aspect. It was a bad dream, foretelling a worse reality to come.

The ceremony at the church of Artstetten was a brief one. Karl and his wife Zita had arrived there in the morning, and so had Franz Ferdinand's and Sophie's three children. A special train had been sent from Vienna to carry everybody home. Karl and Zita occupied one carriage in the train, while the children, along with a relative of Sophie's, traveled in another carriage. Even at that moment it was made clear that the children were not Habsburgs.

4

When Franz Joseph was first told of the events at Sarajevo, he was supposed to have said (according to Eduard Paar) : "Terrible! The Almighty may not be challenged—a higher power has restored the order which I was unable to maintain." Did he really say that? It doesn't sound like him; Franz Joseph was not given to pronunciamentos uttered extempore. He did not pretend to a grief he did not feel. In purely human terms, he did not sorrow over the death either of his nephew or of his nephew's wife. As Marie Valerie noted in her diary on June 29, 1914: "I found Papa amazingly fresh. He was certainly shocked, and when he spoke of the poor children [Franz Ferdinand's] he had tears in his eyes; but, as I had imagined in advance, he was not personally stricken." He made a special point of publicly commending Montenuovo. In the draft of the letter which had been prepared for him, which spoke of Montenuovo's "at all times carrying out My intentions," there was a passage which read:

> The death of My beloved nephew, a death painful to me . . . made extraordinary demands on you just now and again gave you the opportunity to demonstrate your devotion to Me personally and to My house. . . .

Franz Joseph crossed out the words "a death painful to me."

Why, then, did he proceed against Serbia with an energy, sharpness, and inclusiveness which far exceeded the chastisement of a fanatic who, at that time, had not been shown to have acted with official—that is, government—approval? Why could he not have been content with a full Serbian apology—which Serbia was willing to tender—and the punishment of Princip and the other conspirators? Why did he rattle the Balkan balance, knowing how precariously it sat? Why did he drive toward war?

It has become customary to depict old Franz Joseph as a victim of circumstances, doddering toward a crater into which Wilhelm pushed him. At eighty-four he no longer knew what he wanted. Misled and misguided, he signed the declaration of war with a trembling hand. He was coerced by the war party around him and around Wilhelm, and he was but dimly conscious of his own act. For the spectator of posterity Wilhelm is cast in the role of the villain, Franz Joseph in that of the dupe.

The casting is incorrect, the picture false. True it was that Wilhelm behaved like a saddled steed, snorting for the race to begin. No doubt he saw Germany's future mystically illumined by artillery fire. No doubt he spoke of Germany's mission as "holy." Raids and plunderings are always "holy." But when Wilhelm looked reality square in the face, when he had to give the marching order, when he had to carry out the plan of invading Belgium, a plan for which he knew he was going to be cursed by civilized men, in short when the armored tank took over from the rousing phrase, he was filled with fear and foreboding. In the last moment, when the troop transports were already rolling, he would have dearly loved to withdraw. It was too late. He could not stop, partly because an army on the march could not easily be turned back, partly because his people, whipped to frenzy, would feel deluded, a delusion which would prove dangerous to his regime, and finally because his partner Franz Joseph insisted on action. Franz Joseph cannot be absolved from his share of guilt; he cannot be let off the judgment that he was the co-perpetrator of the war.

He was not at all the somnolent sufferer, enduring the machinations and the scheming of the Conrads and their ilk. Once more Franz Joseph took the reins into his own hands—hands which did not tremble, once more he became the emperor in deed as in name. It was as if Franz Ferdinand's death had rejuvenated him. It was as if he was fired with new ambition to strengthen the monarchy. If that could no longer be done by peaceful means, very well, then war it must be. It was true that Serbia in the last years "had grown bigger, more self-assured, and more exasperating." Yet exasperation could have been met with measures short of armed conflict. It was true that Serbia was now a proud and passionate country, yet pride and passion did not necessarily mean that war was unavoidable. Franz Joseph thought otherwise. The first thing he did was to assure himself anew that Wilhelm would not abandon him. He knew his partner: he could not be trusted implicitly. He wrote to Wilhelm on July 5, 1914:

> In the future the goal of My government must be to isolate and diminish Serbia. . . . You yourself must have arrived at the conviction that a real reconciliation of the opposites which divide Serbia and Ourselves can no longer be considered and that the pursuit of peace by the European monarchs will remain menaced as long as this hotbed of criminal agitation in Belgrade is allowed to exist unpunished.

It was specious reasoning: nobody even remotely thought of *not* punishing the assassins. Wilhelm did hesitate, though only for a moment or two. Then, feeling strong after an excellent lunch, he told the Austrian ambassador that Austria-Hungary could count on full support by Germany, should a serious European complication ensue. He would keep the faith. Even if the conflict in Serbia would lead to a war between Austria-Hungary and Russia, Germany would stand at Vienna's side. He counseled immediate occupation of Serbia. Wilhelm was a specialist in occupation. Just then he was in his challenging phase, his chin stuck out.

At that time Aehrenthal's successor in the foreign office was Count Leopold Berchtold. Vastly wealthy—it was said of him that his estates were so extensive that he had never visited all of them— he was a bit of a dandy, a sportsman, an automobile enthusiast, and a not overly perspicacious thinker. Churchill wrote of him in *The World Crisis:* "Berchtold is the epitome of this age, when the affairs of Brobdingnag are managed by Lilliputians." History has accused him as being to a high degree responsible for the war.

This is unjust; it was not he but Franz Joseph who made the decision. Perhaps Franz Joseph listened to Berchtold more than he did to another of his close advisers, Count Stephen Tisza, son of Coloman, an honest if dictatorial statesman whom Franz Joseph appointed Prime Minister of Hungary three times. (Tisza was murdered in 1918.)

On July 7, Tisza and Berchtold met in solemn council with Conrad and Stürgkh, the Austrian Minister President (murdered in 1916), the Minister of Finance (Bilinski), the Minister of War (Krobatin), and a substitute for the Chief Admiral (Kailer). Significantly, Franz Joseph was not present, though it was the custom for him to preside at decisive sessions at all times. Two hours before the ministers were to meet, he removed himself from Vienna and once again went to Ischl. It looks as if he had made up his mind.

The council session lasted seven hours. All but Tisza voted for "a resolution by force." Tisza held his ground against the other ministers. Bitter words were spoken. Even when Tisza was voted down, he insisted on preparing a memorandum which was to be handed to Franz Joseph. Berchtold, who was to go to Ischl to apprise the Emperor of the results of the conference, promised to hand him the dissenting opinion. Tisza's memorandum read in part:

> Most Gracious Sovereign! The glad news from Berlin, as well as the entirely justifiable wrath over the events in Serbia, ripened at yesterday's ministerial conference the decision to provoke a war with Serbia. It would once and for all settle accounts with this arch-enemy of the monarchy. I found myself unable to agree entirely with such a procedure. As far as a human being can predict the future, an attack on Serbia would bring about intervention by Russia, which in turn would conjure up a world war. . . . Far be it from me to recommend a weak and do-nothing course toward Serbia. By no means do I plead that we ought to swallow the provocation. But I believe that Serbia must be given an opportunity to enable them to rectify their grievous fault by diplomatic means and thus avoid a war. If nevertheless it should come to a war, we must have proof to show the whole world that we acted defensively. I suggest that we send Serbia a memorandum, written in a severe but not in a menacing tone, in which we enumerate concretely our accusations. . . .

A wise memorandum, indeed! Franz Joseph read and reread Tisza's plea. Then he said—and his voice was strong—"No. . . . We must confront Serbia with the sharpest kind of ultimatum. If they do not knuckle under we will go to war."

A complex of motives determined his decision.

Summarizing the political motives first, it was clear to him that the only possibility for Austria's expansion lay in the Balkans. To the west nothing could be done—there Wilhelm was operating. To the north—he probably underestimated Russia's strength, or else he would not have taunted it by the Balkan moves, but he was perspicacious enough to realize that he could not in the long run risk a direct attack against the bear's lair. He remembered Napoleon's fate in 1812. No—if anywhere it was to the south and east, in the torn Balkans, that he could find aggrandizement. He hoped to "bring order to the disorderly peoples," to nullify Turkish influence completely, and to free commercially the shores of the Danube, Austria's aortic artery.

He was prompted by a consideration more immediate: an expedition against a foreign foe would lame his domestic foes, would unite his people, would quiet the Hungarians, who just then were pressing him with new exigence. When things get bad internally, a dictatorship looks for an external excuse to draw attention away from the danger within. Franz Joseph's reasoning was not so very different. He was aware that he was taking a huge chance. "If the monarchy is doomed, let it at least go down honorably," he said to Conrad. Finally—another immediate consideration—he felt that only a thorough defeat of the Balkan enemies, specifically Serbia, would leave Austria's vitally important Adriatic harbors safe.

His was a win-all-or-lose-all decision, and the evidence shows that as he made it his heart ached. There was little of the piratical spirit left in the old man and none of Wilhelm's braggadocio. But make it he did. He did not shrink from this most accursed of gambles, perhaps casting his mind back to that day sixty-six years ago—so long ago—when Schwarzenberg had advised a *va tout* gamble to save the monarchy.

Aside from political thoughts, there were other motives—should they be called emotional?

He had to preserve the stature of the house of Habsburg. A

Habsburg was a being apart, appointed by God to rule. Once destined for the throne a Habsburg was no longer just a man, but a sacrosanct person above persons. In harming one, *all* Habsburgs, past, present, and future, were dealt a blow. That blow needed to be avenged. The fact that he hated Franz Ferdinand was beside the point. Franz Ferdinand had been the successor, the representative of the crown, a steward of that personal rule which the family had maintained for six hundred years. During his long reign Franz Joseph had observed the absolutism of the monarchy being diluted. He had experienced government by shouting, and he had watched the exchange of ideas perverted by the throwing of inkwells. He had tried to accommodate himself to modern times by accepting, and indeed encouraging, suffrage. But one concept had to remain immutable: Habsburg sanctity. The pistol shot which hit Franz Ferdinand attacked that sanctity: war was the only adequate answer.

Finally, the incident at Sarajevo may have unloosed in Franz Joseph's heart a rancor long muffled. It may have been the one drop of blood too many. First his brother, then his son, then his wife, and now his nephew—they all had been snatched away by violence. The cumulative force of these tragedies may have shattered that prudence which was his stock in trade. That is conjecture, but a reasonable one.

So on the ninth of July Franz Joseph told Berchtold to draw up the ultimatum. It was to be done in the greatest secrecy, and to allay the fears of the public the leading personalities were to depart on their summer holidays, pretending that nothing exceptional was brewing. Wilhelm was already on his yacht in the North Sea, Franz Joseph stayed in Ischl, Helmuth von Moltke, the German Chief of Staff, went to Karlsbad for his cure, his counterpart Conrad traveled to Styria to visit the woman with whom he was in love. The subterfuge worked: people everywhere were breathing more easily and saying it would all blow over.

In the meantime, the Austrian command needed to gather more facts about the assassination, facts which would furnish the proposed ultimatum with the spine of righteousness. As soon as Cabrinović was arrested, an investigation was started, a local judge by the name of Pfeffer in charge. Pfeffer was not very peppery: it soon became clear that as an investigator he was no match for the well-drilled Cabrinović or Princip. He worked for twelve days without uncovering much that was significant. The police, who were rounding up all suspects, had taken into custody one Danilo Ilić, a friend of Princip and a member of the Black Hand. It was he who spilled the story—or some of it—in return for the promise to spare his life. On July 9, more than a week after the deed, Vienna decided that the investigation was too important a matter, and too complicated, to be left in the hands of a small-town judge. Yet—and incredibly—no commission of expert investigators or detectives was sent to Sarajevo. They sent one man only, a minor functionary of the Foreign Office named Wiesner, who in two days plowed through the reports, interviewed a slew of people, worked not only all day but much of the night, and then rushed back to Vienna. He found that the plan to kill Franz Ferdinand had been prepared many weeks ahead, that it had begun with three conspirators, that Princip had recruited four others, all young (Ilić, who was twenty-four, was the oldest), that all through May they had practiced bomb throwing and pistol shooting, that on May 27, that is, a month before Franz Ferdinand's visit, they had been given their weapons and their poison and that the weapons had come from the Serbian army arsenal. An Austrian citizen born in Bosnia, one Milan Ciganović, employed by the Serbian State Railways, had aided the conspirators, as had a Major Voja Tankosić of the Serbian army. It was he who had supplied the weapons. The report failed to establish any connection between the conspiracy and the Black Hand or Apis. It failed to specify who it was who had originally conceived the plan. It failed to trace Jovanović's warning to Bilinski. It failed to explain why the three original conspirators, who had been in Belgrade, had been smuggled across the border: they were Austrian citizens holding Austrian passports and could perfectly well have come to Sarajevo openly like any normal travelers.

What about the totally inadequate protection Franz Ferdinand had been given? Potiorek said that the precautions were no worse than the measures taken for Franz Joseph's safety on the occasion of his visit in 1910. Anyway: "Only the complete evacuation of the inhabitants of the city would have given protection against conspirators."

As to Serbia's "official" implication in the plot, Wiesner, an honest man, reported: "There is nothing to indicate, or even to suspect, that the Serbian government knew about the plot, its preparation, or the procurement of arms."

We have no direct evidence that Franz Joseph read the report. Chances are a hundred to one that he did read it. As will be seen below, his ministers took from it what suited their purpose and ignored what did not. Then the report was buried: Austria's use of it was, to say the least, self-serving.

On Sunday July 19 the ministers met again. In order not to arouse journalistic suspicions, they met in Berchtold's house, arriving there not in court equipages but in ordinary taxis. At this meeting the text of the Serbian ultimatum was completed. It was then brought to Franz Joseph, who approved it, but it was decided not to send it to Serbia until the twenty-third, because by that time Poincaré, who was visiting the Czar, would have left St. Petersburg and the French and the Russians would not be able to put their heads together immediately. It is evident that Franz Joseph realized from the beginning that the ultimatum could entail European consequences.[3]

The ultimatum was a long document. Compressed, its points were:

1. Serbia admits that its interests have not been diminished by the Bosnian annexation and guarantees to cease all propaganda encouraging such a view. All publications inimical to or detrimental of the Austrian monarchy are to be confiscated and suppressed at once.

2. The "Black Hand" and similar groups are to be dissolved. The Serbian government is charged with the responsibility of making sure that the disbanded groups do not re-form under another name.

3. School books and other instruments of education are to be cleansed of all anti-Austrian propaganda.

4. All officers and functionaries guilty of inciting hostility against Austria are to be dismissed. The Austrian government reserves the right to inform the Serbian government of specific persons against whom evidence of guilt is found.

5. Serbia is to agree to allow "organs of the imperial and royal government" (policemen and detectives) to act within Serbia's frontiers and to aid in stamping out subversive movements.

6. Serbia is to inaugurate at once an investigaton of all those who took part in the plot of June 28 and who are now within Serbia's confines. In this investigative procedure officials appointed by Austria are to be permitted to take part.

7. Major Voja Tankosić and Milan Ciganović, in Serbia's employ, are to be arrested. They are compromised by the findings of the Austrian investigation.

8. Serbia is to undertake effective means to stop the smuggling of weapons and explosives across the border. Certain custom officials who aided the instigators of the crime at Sarajevo are to be dismissed and severely punished.

9. Serbia is to denounce all government officials, however highly placed, who have expressed themselves in belligerent interviews or speeches against Austria. Their names are to be given to the Austrian government.

10. The Austrian government is to be notified as to how Serbia intends to fulfill all nine of the above demands.

Austria expected the answer to this ultimatum at the latest on Saturday the twenty-fifth at 6 P.M. In other words, within forty-eight hours. It was a foregone conclusion that Serbia could not meet the demands. To allow access to Austrian police investigators within its frontiers amounted to a concession that Serbia was no longer a sovereign state. Furthermore, it was quite impossible to ferret out all officials inimical to Austria or to stamp out clandestine gangs at once.

The ultimatum—and it must be emphasized that Franz Joseph was cognizant of every word of it—was characterized by Lord Edward Grey as "the most formidable document ever addressed by one state to another." (We have become accustomed to more formidable documents since.) The Austrian ambassador in Belgrade, Vladimir von Giesl, handed the document to the Serbian Finance Minister, since Pašić happened to be out of town. The Finance Minister protested that it was election time, that most of the ministers were away on tours, and that it was impossible to call together a cabinet meeting at such a moment. He pleaded for more time. Giesl replied that to the best of his knowledge the telephone and the telegraph were still in working order in Serbia. Not one minute after 6 P.M., July 25, would he concede. Giesl anticipated the answer: he had the secret files of the embassy burned, and he loaded his and his staff's possessions onto several automobiles, ready to depart.

A few minutes before 6 P.M. on Saturday Pašić himself walked to the Austrian Embassy, a thick envelope in his hand. It was of course not the custom for a premier to act as messenger. But at the cabinet meeting which did take place, all ministers having been recalled to Belgrade in great haste, Pašić scanned the countenances of his co-workers, and observing how sad and desperate they looked, he decided to undertake the terrible task himself. The document was a messy piece of paper. It had been changed, erased, reworded up to the last moment; and under the strain of the continuous meetings and the interminable hours a secretary had become so nervous that she put the typewriter out of commission. Several copies had to be written in longhand.

Now Pašić approached Giesl with a slow and halting step, bowed, and handed him the Serbian note. The time was 6:02 P.M. It was an astonishingly placatory reply, indeed an obsequious one. Serbia gave in in almost every respect. They were willing to do all Austria wanted, insofar as it stood in their power, except that they could not accept points five and six: "As far as the collaboration of special delegates appointed by the [Austrian] imperial and royal government is concerned, we cannot grant this, since it would represent a violation of our constitution and our criminal code. However, we would be willing to inform representatives of Austria-Hungary in specific instances of the results of our investigation." The note ended with a plea that "it would be to our mutual benefit not to act rashly in trying to solve the present problem. . . . We are ready to accept a peaceful solution, whether it be arrived at through the international commission at The Hague or by [a meeting of] the major powers."

Read dispassionately, the note removed any substantial justification for going to war. Giesl, who had received Pašić in his traveling clothes, read it differently. It is probable that nothing the Serbians could have written would have been satisfactory, so high had the war fever risen in Austria. In spite of all the secrecy, the news of the challenge flung at Serbia had leaked. How could it not? Somebody, somewhere—in a coffeehouse or the bedroom of a little actress or a porter's lodge—had talked. (One result of the leak was a sinking of the shares on the Vienna Bourse, July 12.)

The temper of a large section of the Viennese public changed in the last days as rapidly as the mood of the Romans after Mark Antony's speech. First fearful, they now were seized by the tipsiness of hatred, a mindless enthusiasm for "doing something." Young men who had no understanding of what war could mean and did not know how it felt to have to lie in freezing mud, thought it a *Hetz*. The army was impatient to draw their sabers.

Giesl, aware of the intentions of Vienna, said to Pašić, "Unsatisfactory." It was the fateful word. Within an hour he was across the border and telephoning the Ballplatz that he had severed diplomatic relations with Serbia. Level-headedness abdicated.

Kaiser Wilhelm had been sent a copy of the Austrian ultimatum. It was forwarded to his yacht; he received it one evening while playing cards and put it aside to read the next morning. He rather enjoyed reading it: he called it "a spirited note." But he saw no reason to interrupt his pleasant cruise in the Norwegian fiords; he still believed that at worst the affair would turn out to be a provincial war. He was not ready for the big war, which he both desired and feared. The Kaiser's Chancellor, Theobold von Bethmann-Hollweg, kept pushing Austria toward war, reasoning that if Austria acted decisively and won a Balkan victory, the major European powers would accept a *fait accompli* and go about their usual business, thus lessening the danger of an international conflagration. It was criminally false reasoning. How tragic it was that neither Germany nor Austria possessed a statesman of vision, Bethmann-Hollweg being only one among many—Berchtold was another—who arrived purblind at decisions they themselves had not desired. Originally Bethmann-Hollweg worked for peace, yet later it was he who said that the treaty guaranteeing Belgian neutrality was nothing but "a scrap of paper." A few days after the outbreak of the war, his predecessor Bülow saw Wilhelm "pallid, frightened, I might almost say desperate," and he asked Bethmann-Hollweg how it all had come about. The Chancellor raised his arms to heaven and replied, "I wish I knew." As Golo Mann wrote: "The men who to the world appeared as the ruthless authors of the war did not know what had happened to them."[4]

Even at the last hour calls to reason were sounded. Sir Edward Grey—one of the few European statesmen unequivocally desirous of peace—called on the German ambassador in London, Prince

Karl Lichnowsky, and pleaded that the German foreign office persuade Franz Joseph to accept the Serbian reply in good faith and
continue negotiations. On the same day, July 27, all leaves in the
British navy were canceled, by order of First Sea Lord Winston
Churchill. That ought to have served as sufficient warning that a
war could not be contained within the confines of the Balkans.

Lichnowsky understood and immediately reported to Berlin.
His dispatch arrived more or less simultaneously with the top-
secret information that Austria intended to declare war the next
day or at the latest on July 29. Wilhelm sensed that a crisis was
developing, cut his cruise short, and returned to Berlin on July 27.
He was nervous and angry. He ordered that Sir Edward Grey's
warning be transmitted to Franz Joseph. Bethmann-Hollweg did
so, but in how shocking a fashion! He expurgated the report,
omitting a passage dealing with the seriousness of Britain's concern, and he failed to say that Wilhelm approved Grey's offer of
British mediation. He even sent one of his colleagues to call on the
Austrian ambassador in Berlin to drop a hint that Austria need
not pay any attention to the British proposal; it had been passed
on merely to preserve the usual diplomatic courtesy. This was
trickery, plain and not simple.

On the afternoon of July 27, Wilhelm received for the first
time a copy of the Serbian reply to the ultimatum. It had purposely been withheld from him. The war party feared the effect of
the conciliatory document on the Kaiser—he did not read it till the
morning of the twenty-eighth—and indeed when he did learn its
contents Wilhelm deemed it a moral victory for Austria and said
that "all reason for war is gone and Giesl ought to have stayed
calmly in Belgrade."

It was too late.

As in Wilhelm's mind, so also in Franz Joseph's the scruples
and doubts which follow decision jolted and lashed about. Did he
at the last moment hope for a cleansing miracle? Had Tisza been
right, Berchtold wrong?

On the Saturday on which the reply from Serbia was due, a
lunch in honor of the Duke of Cumberland was scheduled at the
Ischl villa. In the morning Franz Joseph wrote out instructions as
to the livery to be worn by the servants in attendance at table. He
himself was going to wear a British uniform. He was still inter-

ested in ceremony. Shortly after two, Franz Joseph's retinue assembled, as well as some of the guests. He was not to be seen. Then at a quarter to three he appeared from the garden, but instead of greeting everybody as he always did, he merely nodded perfunctorily and then walked in great agitation, his hands crossed behind his back, up and down the path leading to the villa's entrance.

When the Duke and his family finally drove up, Franz Joseph mastered himself with an effort, and led his guests into the dining room. During the meal he tried to act the host and make conversation. It would not go. Everybody was ill at ease, though the word Serbia was never spoken. At the earliest possible moment, scarcely an hour after he had arrived, the Duke bade Franz Joseph goodby, the other guests following in great relief.

Franz Joseph retired to his workroom, the staff to theirs. Everybody sat and waited. Silence pervaded the villa. About half past five Berchtold stuck his head into the room where Albert Margutti, the aide-de-camp, was sitting, and asked, "Any news?" There was none. Margutti stared at the telephone; it was silent. The clock sounded six o'clock, quarter past, half past. At ten minutes to seven the telephone rang. It was Vienna, the War Ministry. They reported Giesl's break with Serbia. Margutti wrote the telephone message on a piece of paper and hurried to Franz Joseph's room. He needed to see His Majesty at once, he told the guard. He was admitted at once. Franz Joseph stood there, saying nothing, just staring. Margutti reported. In a choked voice, which could hardly make its way through his throat, Franz Joseph said, *"Also doch"*—two historic words which might be translated "Well, then."

He took the paper, and like a man infinitely weary sat down at his desk to read the message. This time, at this moment of crisis, his hands trembled so that only with difficulty could he place his spectacles on his nose. Then he read, bent closely over the page. He remained silent. At last, having seemingly forgotten Margutti's presence, he said to himself: "Well, breaking off diplomatic relations does not necessarily mean war." It was not a convincing soliloquy. Two hours later, 9:23 to be precise, Franz Joseph issued the command for mobilization.

Two days later, Franz Joseph signed the declaration of war

against Serbia. Berchtold had returned to Vienna and had sent a telegram to Franz Joseph reporting that a Serbian detachment had attacked an Austrian regiment stationed at the border. This was untrue. Was Berchtold misinformed—or had he deliberately lied to force his sovereign into action? *Something* untruthful was being cooked up. In the draft of the declaration of war against Serbia the Serbian border attack was mentioned as "one further reason" for Austria's action. Franz Joseph approved the wording of this draft. In the actual declaration that was sent, the words dealing with a Serbian attack were *omitted*. Why? Did they strike the passage because the Serbian government could have proved it a lie? Who changed the text? Did Franz Joseph see the final version as well as the draft? We will never know.

On July 28, the day on which Wilhelm said that "all reason for war is gone," Austria's declaration of war was telegraphed to Belgrade. World War I had begun.

Two days later Franz Joseph left the villa in Ischl where he had spent most of whatever happy hours had been vouchsafed him and went to Schönbrunn. He was to leave Schönbrunn castle only three times in the remaining two years of his life, and all three times for the same purpose: to visit the war-wounded.

Leon Trotsky, who was then living in Vienna, described the mood of the Viennese:

Quite unexpected was the elation of the broad masses of Austria-Hungary. What prompted the shoemaker's apprentice, the half-German half-Czech Pospischil, or our vegetable seller Frau Maresch, or the fiacre coachman Frankl to appear in front of the War Ministry? A national concept? Which? Austria-Hungary represented the negation of the national idea. No, another force motivated them.

So many people in this world live their entire lives, day in, day out, in monotonous hopelessness. The alarm-bell of the mobilization sounded to them like a revelation. It threw over the humdrum, the routine, the boredom. . . . Something new, something extraordinary appeared on the scene. The future promised change. Change for the better? For the worse? But of course for the better. Could the lot of the Pospischils become worse than it had been in "normal times"?

I walked along the main streets of the familiar city and observed the crowds which had gathered in unusual density on the magnificent Ringstrasse. They were fired by hope. A particle of that hope, had it not become reality? At this time the porters, the laundresses, the shoemakers, the apprentices, and the youngsters of the suburbs, all of them believed themselves to be masters of a fate common to all. The war captured all and therefore those who were oppressed, those whom life had cheated, felt themselves on a parity with the rich and the mighty. . . . Mobilization and the declaration of war seemed to wipe out all national and social differences. It was but a historic postponement, a political moratorium, so to speak. The mortgage was written to contain a new due-date, but it was not forgiven.[5]

On the day when Franz Joseph's declaration of war was published, Wilhelm telegraphed the Czar offering to mediate between Austria and an angry Russia. He reminded the Czar of the "sincere and intimate friendship which has united us for years." He signed the telegram, "Your very faithful and dedicated friend and cousin Willy." The telegram crossed a missive by the Czar: "In this extremely grave moment I appeal to you for help. An unworthy war has been declared against a weak country. The fury in Russia, which I share, is enormous. . . . I beg you in the name of our old friendship to do your utmost to persuade your ally to retreat from a step which will lead to the disaster of a European war." He signed "Nicky."

Both Willy and Nicky, as well as Franz Joseph, were captives of their own malfeasance. They could do nothing now. The warmongers had taken over to execute what they did not and *did* want. It was they who incarnadined the minds of the people. The blood wave could no longer be held back. On August 1 Germany declared war on Russia, on August 3 on France and Belgium, on August 4 England declared war on Germany, on the fifth Austria on Russia, on the twelfth England on Austria, and so on and on in a chain of self-destruction.

Statistics: 8.7 million died in World War I; 20.8 million were wounded. Germany lost 1.81 million men; Austria, 1.20; Russia, 2.25; France, 1.25; England, 0.68; Italy 0.6; U.S.A., 0.1. These figures must be augmented by at least 20 percent if deaths due to hunger and disease are included.

The old Emperor, turning to Katherina Schratt

CHAPTER XVII

If—

BECAUSE UNLIKE CATO he did not conclude his every speech by
intoning, "Carthage must be destroyed," because unlike Wilhelm
he did not strut in a spiked helmet, Franz Joseph has been judged
"a peaceable ruler" by his benevolent biographers.[1] That judgment is applicable only to his middle years, which, to be sure,
represented a long period and included the first years of the
twentieth century. But when, toward the end of his life, the problems grew ever more complex, when his advisers included warmongering militarists, when the animosities around him seemed so
severe that he despaired of sane solutions, when he felt that the
prestige of Austria needed to be saved by action, when he himself
was provoked, he *did* provoke a war. He began it: no question
about that; though later the world half-forgot who it was who first
opened the gates of the lock. He had a cause for quarrel with
Serbia. He could say, with justice, that as long as the Balkans, with
Russian help and Russian subsidy, were continuing their clandestine ploys, Austria could not rest easy. But in proceeding against
Serbia he ignored not only the Russian threat, against which he
had been warned, but the danger of an engulfing European flood.
Quickly—indeed, almost before he fully realized what was happening to him—he was drawn into Germany's conflict with France and
England. He couldn't get out of it, though Austria had no quarrel
with France or England. He was committed to the partnership

with Germany. He needed Germany's help; Germany needed his help—so they drowned together.

Corroboration of Franz Joseph's attitude came in 1971 from a new source, the notes of a Viennese journalist and editor, Dr. Heinrich Kanner. He was a writer of reputation, respected by Austria's leading political personalities, as was the periodical he edited, *Die Zeit* (*The Times*). His records, in three typewritten volumes, were bought by the Hoover Institution on War, Revolution and Peace in Stanford, California. They were examined by Robert A. Kann of Princeton, New Jersey, professor at Rutgers University and one of the most knowledgeable historians of Austria-Hungary, who presented his findings to the Austrian Academy of Sciences.[2]

Kanner interviewed Leon Bilinski several times, and Professor Kann believes Bilinski to have been a trustworthy informant. Here, in part, is Kanner's report of an interview with Bilinski on November 3, 1916:

> I asked him: "Do you believe the Emperor foresaw a European war?"
>
> Bilinski replied: "Absolutely."
>
> "Is that so?" I said. "I am astonished. I would not have believed it."
>
> Bilinski: "I can assure you, it is so. I can even recount to you a detail which will interest you. The morning after the ministerial council of July 19th . . . I had an audience with the Emperor. He had with him the memorandum which we had completed the day before. In the conversation I referred to it and said to the Emperor, 'Your Majesty now has to approve a weighty act which may lead to a European war.' The Emperor answered, 'That certainly! It is inconceivable that Russia will stand for this note.' "
>
> I replied that this seemed convincing enough, but nevertheless I remained astonished.
>
> Bilinski: "Yes, the Emperor was always for the war. Don't you know that he already wanted war in the previous year? . . . When we had that quarrel over Scutari[3] everything was ready."
>
> "Well," I interposed, "that time it was only a question of Montenegro."
>
> Bilinski: "Oh no, we were supposed to begin with Montenegro but we had already determined to march from Montenegro into Serbia and settle our accounts with Serbia, once and for all."

I ventured to reply: "In that case the European war would have begun earlier, at that very moment."

Bilinski said, "Indubitably." . . .

Bilinski: "The successor [Franz Ferdinand] was always against the war."

I replied that the public was of the opposite opinion.

Bilinski: "No, I can assure you of that. Even more determined than he was his wife. As a woman the Duchess feared for the safety of her husband. She had a great influence on him. . . ."

As Professor Kann wrote, we must not be misled by our picture, "perhaps too caricatured, of a psychopathic personality [Wilhelm] against our deep respect for the personal dignity and integrity [of Franz Joseph]."

Would that personal dignity and integrity have led to a better decision if he had been surrounded by men more perspicacious than a Berchtold and a Conrad? If Elisabeth had remained by his side and worked, as she did for Hungary, would she have been able to guide him toward peace? Would Franz Joseph have gone to war even if Franz Ferdinand had not been assassinated, snatching at one pretext or another? Was Wilhelm telling the truth when he said that Franz Joseph was rattling the sword, "using the sword of the German Reich"? If he had died and Franz Ferdinand had succeeded him, would World War I not have taken place?

These unanswerable questions are posed to underscore once more the all too obvious fact that over and over again millions of lives have been influenced, diverted, and destroyed by the rulers who made the critical decisions. Some of these decisions were arrived at carefully and with reasoned judgment: history has not always been changed by Napoleon's having a stomachache. Yet the "if," the element of chance, played too large a role in important decisions, and chance was often conditioned by personal motives buried in the psyche of the man who gave the orders. In the prewar years "the terrible if's accumulate," Winston Churchill wrote.

There needs no ghost, my lord, come from the grave to tell us this. Nor is it the whole truth.

Even had Franz Joseph been more "modern" in his thinking— it could be said that he was already out of date when he ascended the throne—even had he been more adaptive in temperament, he could not have escaped two changes which impinged on him and twisted his reign awry. As the years progressed, more and more people came to disbelieve the divine sanction for the crown: "I think the king is but a man, as I am." One could step up to the pedestal, and though the "intertissued robe of gold and pearl" was still impressive, it now appeared evident that it was man-woven. Deification of the ruler was doomed and, with it, absolute rule.

The other influence was the one so often mentioned in these pages, the nationalistic drive. This drive operated not only within Austria, but outside it, and separated the man who said *"das Vaterland"* from the man who said *"la patria"* from the man who said "my country."

The structure of the European system, which had proved sturdy throughout the nineteenth century, was now in danger:

> For a century Europe had managed to avoid a general war. None of the European wars of the century after the Congress of Vienna had involved the survival of the system of relatively independent great powers, between which a number of small states could peacefully live. In all war crises the abstention of some of the great powers was an important element in the eventual restoration of the fundamental structure of the European system. Although shifts of power had occurred, the greatest in connection with the wars of Italian and German unification, they did not destroy the European system. But the division of the great powers of Europe into permanent camps made it likely that every future conflagration would envelop all of Europe. Moreover, the political situation became more inflammable by the growth of a nationalism that left no room for the recognition of a common responsibility for European peace.[4]

This is not to absolve Franz Joseph nor the other rulers nor their advisers from their ugly acts. In spite of the pressures, they might have prevented a world war, had they recognized "a common responsibility." Joseph Redlich, a man who loved Austria, which he served as Minister of Finance in 1918, wrote to his old friend Hofmannsthal that "the crash of the realm was not due to the old concept of Austria itself but to Franz Joseph's hopeless concept of governing." Luciano Magrini, who assisted the historian Albertini and who wrote the introduction to *The Origins of the War of 1914,* gives the refrain of Albertini's inquiry:

An Austrian propaganda picture of 1914. Wilhelm II is pointing toward the map of France.

The Governments of the various countries found themselves suddenly faced with a crisis which nevertheless for years had been foreseen, expected, dreaded. Yet not one of those in authority at the last moment mustered the strength and ability to save the world from disaster. None of the statesmen was capable of learning a lesson from previous experience and, in the action they took, they found themselves victims and slaves of a series of mistakes which had their roots in the past. While fearing a European war, they deluded themselves that they could avert it by not showing fear of it, and thus, in Lloyd George's words, they staggered and stumbled into war. When the diplomatic game had been played to its limits, they found the situation had got beyond their control. They believed, not what hard facts and obvious portents foreshadowed, but the wishes and fears of their own hearts, which in turn fathered their acts.

The "wishes and fears" led them so far astray that Wilhelm and his echo, Bethmann-Hollweg, could talk themselves into believing that England would remain neutral; they believed that even as they began to march into Belgium on August 2.

Digging beneath the social, political, and egocentric causes, does still another cause emerge from the depths?

Continuing along the paths of the nineteenth century, the early twentieth century evinced bright evidence of man's progress, if not philosophically, then medically, technically, psychologically, and in exploring the nature of the universe. How many benefits had been disclosed, how many riddles solved through cooperation which disregarded frontiers! In the Mephistophelean year of 1914, the Nobel Prize winner for physics was a German, Max von Laue, for his work on X-rays; for chemistry Theodore Richards, an American, for determining atomic weights of elements; for medicine Robert Bárány, a Hungarian, for his work on the inner ear. J. H. Jeans, the English physicist, published *Report on Radiation and the Quantum Theory*. The Panama Canal, on which both French and American engineers collaborated, was opened. Einstein was readying his general theory of relativity, which he published in 1915. It seemed as if the poet's apostrophe to man was true:

> He can always help himself.
> He faces no future helpless. There's only death
> that he cannot find an escape from. He has contrived
> refuge from illnesses once beyond all cure.
> Clever beyond all dreams
> the inventive craft that he has
> which may drive him one time or another to well or ill.

The words are Sophocles'—in *Antigone*—441 B.C.

Yet along with man's cleverness, courage, and "inventive craft" grew his pompous righteousness, his need to lord it over others. The current of cruel instincts swelled and, flowing against the current of civilization, created a whirlpool. The primitive self spurted forth. Tribal memories reawakened. People, weary of law and restriction, became drunk on jingoism. They seemed to want upheaval. They seemed to want to hit out, hurt somebody. Even educated men listened to the drums, though they may have listened to the Ninth Symphony as well. Freud wrote of it in *Civilization and Its Discontents*. How the men cheered in 1914, marching into Belgrade and Belgium!

Those *"gemütlich"* Viennese—why were they so recalcitrant? Virginia Cowles wrote in *The Kaiser:*

> After years of being referred to as a weakling Austria was thrilled by her own spirit. When she broke off relations with Serbia Vienna burst into a frenzy of joy, and huge crowds roamed the streets all night singing patriotic songs. Even the old Emperor, so timid at first, was now so buoyed up by the warm response of his people that he was not even deterred by a personal telegram from the Kaiser asking him earnestly to reconsider his decision. Indeed, the tables had been turned so completely that now the Austrians were beginning to jeer at the Germans for having cold feet.

Here, too, "compensation" was to be found, though in its negative phase. In 1915 man's "inventive craft" led to the first use of chlorine gas in warfare, the first bombing by air of London and Paris. The negative phase—the death wish—predominated.

The four-year debacle did not, of course, wipe out all talent or thought. Freud (who published little during the war) took up his work again. So did others. But where was the new growth, where were the young recruits? Where was the refreshment? Sparse, indeed. As to Austria specifically, its end calls for a brief dirge only: intellectual life sickened, never to recover. "What should we Austrian writers do now?" Hofmannsthal asked at the end of the war. And he answered himself: "Die."

In 1915 Rilke wrote to a friend in Paris:

> You will believe me when I tell you that for a year now I have been dragging myself step by step through a desert of incomprehension and pain. I can do nothing but suffer, finding no solace in activity. I could only fight for all, not against anybody. Will any god ever dispose of sufficient balm to heal the horrendous wound which has been dealt to all of Europe?

Whether Western European civilization can fully recover from World War I—a war which in effect has not ended—is quite beyond my ability to predict. As it looks today, the Vienna of the mind is a feeble place, neither its university nor its artistic institutions having brought forth in our times creative talents comparable to those which flourished when its political weakness was outweighed by its intellectual strength.

The history of Austria under Franz Joseph shows a curious, though abridged, parallel to the history of the Byzantine Empire in its final phase.[5] Steven Runciman wrote in *The Last Byzantine Renaissance:*

> If there is any meaning in the concept of decadence, there are few polities in history that better deserve to be called decadent than the East Christian Empire, the once great Roman Empire, during the last two centuries of its existence. It was a period when a crumbling administration, directed by an inept and short-sighted government and centered in a city whose population was rapidly diminishing, vainly attempted to ward off increasing impoverishment and the steady loss of territory. . . .
>
> Yet was it a period of decadence? In strange contrast with the political decline, the intellectual life of Byzantium never shone so brilliantly as in those two sad centuries. . . .

William M. Johnston, associate professor of history at the University of Massachusetts, has written an examination of *The Austrian Mind.* It is a formidable work of research, a copious catalogue, containing more names of creative minds than Leporello's catalogue contains of women. In his concluding chapter Johnston writes: "Although it may be too early to assess everything that thinkers of Austria bequeathed us, clearly their talent for integrative thinking is dying out." His final paragraph reads:

> It remains to be seen whether a global civilization can approximate conditions that once made Austria a beacon of modernity within a drifting world. Now that mutability has become our daily bread, no one has more to teach us than these connoisseurs of metamorphosis. Yet in at least one respect, we ought not to emulate the Habsburg Empire. More than most creative ages, the Gay Apocalypse[6] regarded itself as marking an end rather than a beginning. Indeed Karl Kraus or Stefan Zweig would be astonished to learn that civilization has survived at all, and if we have foiled their expectation, it is no thanks to therapeutic nihilism such as theirs. By heeding more constructive voices, we may yet have time to invalidate their despair. Taken by itself, however, the Gay Apocalypse teaches that time effaces more than it sustains.

Can we find an antidote to the despair of Austrian thinkers? Did the struggle of 1914 to 1918, did Franz Joseph's and Wilhelm's misreckoning, produce any kind of compensation? Was anything gained by the war? In answering "Nothing" let me cite the latest of the seemingly endless number of examinations of the question—a book by the historian Leo Valiani, *The End of Austria-Hungary*.

> A number of arguments can be adduced in favour of the view, now prevalent among Austrian and also American historians (though it is sharply contested by most historians of the countries of eastern Europe) that the harm done by the break up of Austria-Hungary distinctly outweighed the advantages derived from the attainment of national unity and independence by the peoples who ceased to feel free under the Habsburgs. Apart from the material damage done by the fragmentation of a vast unified economic area and the replacement of a conservative monarchy by dictatorships, first of the Right and then of the Left, in some of the successor states, perhaps the weightiest argument is that relating to the 1919 demarcation of frontiers. At the peace conference, the governments of the successor states allied to the Entente, obeying nationalist impulses, aimed at and succeeded in including within their frontiers territories inhabited by large, compact masses of Germans and Hun-

garians, provoking a virulent irredentism among them which played a part as important in the developments that led to the Second World War as Yugoslav irredentism had played in the developments that led to the tragedy of 1914.

Yet it may be claimed that something—a great deal—of Viennese civilization remains, and it is obvious that the contributions of its thinkers—a Freud, a Kafka, a Mahler, a Wittgenstein, a Billroth—have not been lost. Progress can grow in the soil of decay. Civilization can feed on the debris of history. Even the nihilism of Franz Joseph's Vienna can lead to positive new organization and a forward-looking philosophy. It is a truism to say that civilizations die. They do not. Not altogether.

2

In the last two years of his life he sank as a fog sinks over a heath. He sat at his desk, his face almost touching the papers, his weak eyes perusing documents which were submitted to him to give him something to do. The part of the park adjacent to the Schönbrunn palace was closed; the public no longer caught a glimpse of him. From time to time people in the know said he had died and his death was being kept secret.

His eighty-sixth birthday—August 18, 1916—was hardly celebrated at all, in contrast to the large and glittering festivities which used to take place on that day when "there was as much eating and drinking as on that of the Saviour."[7] Franz Joseph worked on his last birthday: he occupied himself with a plan for a revision of the Austrian constitution. It was an exercise in futility.

The war was first conducted by Conrad; later the supreme command passed to the Germans, under Hindenburg and Ludendorff. Franz Joseph took no part in strategic decisions, suffering the humiliation in silence.

He still arose before dawn, one of his three valets giving him a rubdown with cold water. He still dressed carefully and put on his medals. He sorrowed on the day of the declaration of war against Russia when he had to lay aside the medal he particulary treasured: it was the Cross of St. George, given him by Czar Nicholas

I. He had worn the jewel since 1849, the year when together they put down the revolution.

The last note from Franz Joseph to Katherina which is extant is undated but was probably written in April, 1915:

> Most heartfelt thanks, dearest friend, for the beautiful flowers and for the good wishes, which I reciprocate with all my heart. God save you and protect you in these heavy times and preserve your friendship for me! I hope to see you tomorrow at one o'clock. With best greetings,
>
> Your profoundly loving
> FRANZ JOSEPH

Katherina Schratt lived on until 1940: she reached the age of eighty-seven, one year more than Franz Joseph. She was often urged to publish her memoirs; considerable sums were offered her. Yet, tactful as ever, she preserved her silence and left unclear the nature of her relationship with her "profoundly loving" imperial royal friend.

In the beginning Germany scored successes and even the Austrian forces achieved a few victories, as in the battle against the Russians at Limanova in December, 1914, or the occupation of Belgrade in the same month. These were fleeting; soon Franz Joseph had to realize that the war was going badly and that far from Wilhelm's boast that the soldiers would be home by the time the leaves were falling, the end was nowhere in sight, and, when it did come, it would be one of tragic finality. He was deeply pessimistic, not to be fooled by the glib reports of the generals.

To the end he maintained the Habsburg fiction: he gave the title "Supreme Commander" to a member of the family, Archduke Friedrich, who was then told that his sole function was to approve the decisions of the General Staff, and not to ask questions.[8]

When Italy threatened to join the Allies, Austria tried to make substantial concessions; Franz Joseph was forced to agree that the southern Tyrol would be ceded to the Italians. No use—Italy, wanting more and foreseeing that it would be wise to sit at table with the probable victors, declared war on May 23, 1915. The proclamation Franz Joseph issued still sounded the old imperial note. It began: "The King of Italy has declared war on Me." It then went on to say in effect that the hand which held the dagger plunged it into a neighbor's back.

The huge losses of men and material grieved him less, perhaps, than the instances of individual misfortune, since to him, as to most of us, statistics were less comprehensible than the accident which befalls a friend. He was fond of his current Prime Minister, Count Karl Stürgkh, who treated the old Emperor with delicacy and consideration, but who was a reactionary who did not hesitate to dissolve what was left of the Parliament and provincial diets. Franz Joseph's reign, which had begun with the dictatorial guidance of a Schwarzenberg, ended with the autocratic advice of a Stürgkh. On the twenty-first of October, 1916, Stürgkh was shot in a restaurant by Friedrich Adler, the son of Viktor. It was the last of the assassinations which had come within his experience, and Franz Joseph was bowed down by heartache and bewilderment. Exactly a month later he was dead.

"For God's sake, let us sit upon the ground/And tell sad stories of the death of kings." At the beginning of November he was suffering from a bronchial catarrh which made breathing difficult. He got better, then he got worse. Margutti brought him the mail and began to read him the documents. He no longer seemed to understand the matters before him. In a weak voice he said to Margutti: "Leave all the papers, I'll read them myself." Marie Valerie came—it was the twentieth of November—and he complained of feeling feeble. That night he slept fairly well, but he was at his desk at half past three in the morning. Dr. Ernst Seydl, the bishop of the Hofburg, came to hear his confession. Karl and Zita came at half past eleven and he said to them that he *had* to get well, he had no time for being ill. His fever mounted, but he refused to go to bed. His head sank onto the desk, the pen dropped from his hand, he slept. At four in the afternoon he awoke, signed all the documents, and locked his desk. Shortly after six Valerie tiptoed in and found him in his armchair, cheeks inflamed, his hands hot, his uniform carelessly unbuttoned. They put him to bed. He no longer had the strength to kneel, and he said his prayers sitting up. His valet repeated the daily formula: "Your Majesty, what are your wishes?" In a determined voice Franz Joseph answered: "Tomorrow morning, half past three." He then fell unconscious, but awoke to ask for something to drink. They gave him a few drops of tea. Barely audibly he murmured, "Fine." Seydl came at half past eight to bless him and to put the ancient Habsburg crucifix to his lips. Valerie held his hand. At five minutes past nine o'clock in the evening of November 21, 1916, he died.

Katherina Schratt had seen Franz Joseph for the last time on November 19, Elisabeth's name day. She knew how ill he was. Montenuovo now was asked to telephone to her. She hurried to Schönbrunn. According to one report, Valerie and Gisela turned their backs on her, but that seems improbable. Karl received her, took her hand, and led her into the room. She placed on the bed the two white roses she had brought; they were buried with him.

He who had cried that he was spared nothing was spared the knowledge of the final defeat and the breakup of "His" Empire.

3

Several writers (Zessner-Spitzenberg, McGuigan, Saint-Aulaire, and others) have told the story of the ritual used for the burial of a Habsburg. Arrived at the iron gate of the Capuchin crypt the Lord Chamberlain knocked three times with his golden staff, whereupon a voice within demanded:

"Who knocks?"

"His Apostolic Majesty, the Emperor of Austria."

"Him I know not."

Again three raps of the staff, again the voice:

"Who knocks?"

"The King of Hungary."

"Him I know not."

Once more the same gesture, the same demand:

"Who knocks?"

"Franz Joseph, a poor sinner."

"Enter, then!"

It was a touching ceremony; unfortunately further inquiry discloses that the ritual had by Franz Joseph's time long fallen into disuse, if indeed it had ever been used.

On November 25, 1916, the funeral procession, escorted by a

hundred mounted soldiers and by monks bearing torches, made its way down the Ringstrasse, the street which Franz Joseph had built. Only a few of Europe's rulers took part in the procession, and those were of small importance: the King of Bavaria, the Czar of Bulgaria, and others, followed by representatives of some neutral countries such as Sweden and Denmark. Wilhelm could not come: he sent the Crown Prince. The Lord Chamberlain (Montenuovo) accompanied the coffin to the crypt, raised its cover, and demanded of the prefect: "Do you recognize this dead man?" Upon receiving an affirmative answer, the coffin was closed and its two locks locked. One key was given to the prefect "for conscientious custody in all eternity." The other key was preserved in the Hofburg.

The people of Vienna who had followed the procession stood in silence around the church. If they felt grief, the grief was numbed. They were hungry.

A
FRANZ JOSEPH–ELISABETH
CALENDAR

By no means does this calendar give a comprehensive summary of all that was happening in the world between 1848 and 1916. Its purpose is to relate the events of Franz Joseph's and Elisabeth's lives to contemporaneous political and cultural events, or in other words to serve as a frame for the biography. I have given preference to books, compositions, paintings, inventions, etc., which are likely to be familiar to the reader, and to those occurrences which impinged on Austria's fate.

Date	Life	Historical Events	Cultural Events	Scientific Events, Discoveries, etc.
1848	Ascends throne, Dec. 2 (18 years old).	Insurrection in Vienna. Metternich flees. Revolution in Hungary under Kossuth. Vienna Court flees first to Innsbruck, later to Olmütz. Czech revolt suppressed by Windisch-Graetz. Italian revolt suppressed by Radetzky. Third revolt in Vienna (Oct.) crushed by Windisch-Graetz. Revolutions in Berlin, Paris, Rome, the Two Sicilies. France becomes a republic, Switzerland a confederation.	Nicolai: *The Merry Wives of Windsor* (opera). Cavour's newspaper *Il Risorgimento* published. Marx and Engels publish the *Communist Manifesto*. Smetana founds music school in Prague. A. Dumas, fils: *La Dame aux Camelias*. J. Grimm: *History of the German Language*.	
1849	Schwarzenberg his mentor. Appeals to Czar Nicholas I for help against Hungarian insurrection. Signs severe sentences against revolutionaries. Frederick William IV declines German Kaiser crown. Tentatively offered to Franz Joseph. He refuses as well. Negates attempt at formulating a constitution.	Austrian Constitution granted—immediately withdrawn. Hungarian army capitulates. Austrian victory at Novara, Italy. Radetzky conquers Charles Albert of Sardinia, who abdicates in favor of Victor Emanuel. Venice submits after prolonged siege.	C. Dickens: *David Copperfield*. Johann Strauss, Sr., dies. Wagner takes part in Dresden uprising and must flee to Zürich.	Telegraph is more widely used for dissemination of news. P. J. Reuter uses carrier pigeons as well.
1850	After troubles with General Haynau, Franz Joseph takes over supreme command of army. Reigns autocratically. Meets Nicholas I in Warsaw.	Prussia tries to assume leadership in German union. Rising in Hesse-Cassel: Austria supports the Elector, Prussia the insurgents. War threatens, but as a result of Russian mediation, the "Punctation of Olmütz" is signed, by which Prussia subordinates its demands to Austria and recognizes the Frankfurt Diet. Sunday rest-day legalized in Austria.	Liszt performs *Lohengrin* in Weimar. E. B. Browning: *Sonnets from the Portuguese*. W. M. Thackeray: *Pendennis*.	R. W. Bunsen's burner. R. Clausino formulates second law of thermodynamics. First submarine cable.

DATE	LIFE	HISTORICAL EVENTS	CULTURAL EVENTS	SCIENTIFIC EVENTS, DISCOVERIES, ETC.
1851	Throws "constitutional life overboard." Metternich recalled by him. Sentences Andrassy to death (in exile).	Coup d'état by Louis Napoleon.	Verdi: *Rigoletto* J. Ruskin: *The Stones of Venice.* H. Heine: *Romanzero.* H. Melville: *Moby Dick.*	I. Singer patents sewing machine. "The Great Exhibition" opens in London's Crystal Palace.
1852	Death of Schwarzenberg. Goes to Berlin to visit Frederick William IV. Meets Princess Anna, but she refuses him.	Second French Empire is proclaimed with Napoleon III as Emperor. Cavour becomes Prime Minister of Piedmont. Mazzini active in propaganda for Italian unification. Semmering railroad, leading south, is built.	Harriet Beecher Stowe: *Uncle Tom's Cabin.* L. Ranke: *History of France.* Turgenev: *A Sportsman's Sketches.*	D. Livingstone embarks to explore Zambesi. H. Spencer coins the term "evolution."
1853	Attempted assassination by Libényi. Meets Elisabeth of Bavaria (15) and falls in love with her. Czar Nicholas I visits him in Olmütz to win support against Turkey. Further meeting in Warsaw. He decides to remain "neutral."	Russia claims protectorate over Christian citizens of Ottoman Empire. Turkey rejects Russian demands. Czar Nicholas I orders occupation of Danube provinces. Turkey declares war on Russia. British fleet assembles at the Dardanelles.	Haussmann begins reconstruction of Paris. Verdi: *Trovatore* and *Traviata.* Brahms: Opus 1 (Piano Sonata). T. Mommsen: *History of Rome.*	Vienna–Triest railroad completed. W. Ostwald perfects electrolysis.
1854	Marries Elisabeth. Troubles with mother Sophie. Quarrel with Nicholas I. Signs alliance with England and France on Eastern problem. Signs defensive alliance with Prussia. Concludes Austro-Turkish treaty to enable Austria to occupy Danube principalities till war's end.	Crimean War. Austria occupies Danubian principalities. Battle of Balaclava (Charge of the Light Brigade). Siege of Sebastopol begins. U.S.A.: Founding of Republican party, with antislavery and protective tariff policies.	R. Wagner begins composition of *Ring* (finished 1874). F. Liszt: *Mazeppa.* H. D. Thoreau: *Walden.*	A. Gesner manufactures kerosene. R. Burton and J. Speke go to Somaliland.

Date	Life	Historical Events	Cultural Events	Scientific Events, Discoveries, etc.
1855	Daughter Sophie born. Visits Paris World's Fair. Concludes concordat with Pope (probably influenced by his mother) which gives the clergy extraordinary power over Austrian education, censorship, marriage laws, and annuls the reforms of Joseph II. Issues ultimatum to Russia, unless Russia relinquishes claim to protectorate of the Sultan's Christian subjects, and agrees to freedom of the Dardanelles and the mouth of the Danube. Russia is to guarantee integrity of Serbia and Danubian principalities. Is severely criticized by allies for his "neutrality" in Crimean War.	Czar Nicholas I dies, succeeded by Alexander II. Piedmont, under Cavour, joins allies against Russia. Sebastopol falls. Crimean War continues.	H. W. Longfellow: *The Song of Hiawatha.* Walt Whitman: *Leaves of Grass.* Courbet, Daubigny, Daumier, T. Rousseau at height of their creativity. Liszt: Piano Concerto in E Flat Major, *Faust Symphony.*	H. Bessemer perfects fabrication of steel. Livingstone discovers Victoria Falls. Telegraph between London and Balaclava completed.
1856	Gisela, daughter, born. Appoints Ferdinand Maximilian as governor of Lombardy and Venetia. Voyage to Italy with Elisabeth (continued in 1857). Construction of Votivkirche in Vienna begun (finished in 1879). Grants amnesty to many Hungarian revolutionaries of 1848.	Treaty of Paris ends Crimean War. In a further treaty Austria, along with Britain and France, guarantees Turkey's integrity.	J. D. Ingres: *La Source.* G. Flaubert: *Madame Bovary.*	H. Helmholtz: *Physiological Optics.* Neanderthal skull found. Burton and Speke discover Lake Tanganyika.

DATE	LIFE	HISTORICAL EVENTS	CULTURAL EVENTS	SCIENTIFIC EVENTS, DISCOVERIES, ETC.
1857	Elisabeth and he go to Hungary. Elisabeth takes along little Sophie, who dies suddenly. The voyage is terminated. Issues decree to begin widening of inner city of Vienna, new buildings, and beautification.	Frederick William IV suffers stroke and abdicates following year. Succeeded by Wilhelm as King of Prussia in 1861 after regency. Bismarck is at his side. Ferdinand Maximilian marries Carlotta of Belgium. Andrassy returns to Hungary. "Italian National Association" formed by Garibaldi.	C. Baudelaire: *Les Fleurs du Mal.* A. Trollope: *Barchester Towers.* Dickens: *Little Dorrit.*	L. Pasteur proves that lactic fermentation is caused by a living organism. J. Wagner-Jauregg treats paralysis with malaria. Transatlantic cable begun.
1858	Son Rudolf born. Orders strengthening of army against Italian threat. Construction of Ringstrasse begun.	Radetzky (92) dies. Attempt to assassinate Napoleon III by Orsini. Napoleon III and Cavour meet at Plombières to plan consolidation of Italy.	E. Manet: *Le Concert aux Tuileries.*	
1859	Goes to Italian war front. Meets Napoleon III at Villafranca. Terms of Armistice agreed are: Austria cedes Parma and Lombardy, keeps Venetia. His popularity at nadir, after the defeat in Italy.	Death of Metternich. Austrian ultimatum to Sardinia rejected by Cavour. Austria begins war. France declares war on Austria. Various battles at which Austrian forces are defeated, culminating in bloody rout at Solferino. Treaty of Zürich confirms terms of Villafranca.	Dickens: *A Tale of Two Cities.* G. Eliot: *Adam Bede.* E. Fitzgerald: *Rubáiyát of Omar Khayyám.* G. Meredith: *The Ordeal of Richard Feverel.* A. Tennyson: *Idylls of the King.* L. Ranke: *History of England.* C. Gounod: *Faust.* Verdi: *A Masked Ball.* Ingres: *Le Bain Turc.* Manet: *Absinthe Drinkers.* Millet: *L'Angélus.*	Construction of Suez Canal begins. C. Darwin: *On the Origin of Species.*

Date	Life	Historical Events	Cultural Events	Scientific Events, Discoveries, etc.
1860	Appeals to Hungarians when renewed signs of secession appear. Attempts conciliatory compromises, with few results. Meets Czar in Warsaw. No results. Increases number of Imperial Council (*Reichsrat*) through the "March Patent." In October grants constitution, with limited concessions. After Garibaldi invades Naples, Elisabeth's sister has to flee. Franz Joseph is unable to help her. Elisabeth falls ill. First split in the marriage. She goes to Madeira. Discovers corruption in army. Several high officers commit suicide; 82 persons arrested. Removes laws limiting the rights of Jews.	Cavour recalled. Nice and Savoy ceded to France. Various plebiscites vote for Italian unification. Victor Emanuel proclaimed King of Italy. Lincoln elected President of U.S.A.	G. Eliot: *The Mill on the Floss.* J. Turgenev: *On the Eve.* J. Burckhardt: *The Culture of the Renaissance in Italy.*	
1861	Tension with Elisabeth worsens. She goes to Corfu. Orders construction of Vienna Stadtpark.	Frederick William IV dies. King and Queen of Naples surrender to Garibaldi at Gaeta. Hungarian Parliament dissolved after it shows its opposition to Vienna reforms.	Dickens: *Great Expectations.* G. Eliot: *Silas Marner.* Brahms: First Piano Concerto.	H.M.S. *Warrior,* first all-iron steamship, completed. Pasteur develops germ theory of disease.
1862		Bismarck Prime Minister. France sends expedition to Mexico. Lincoln declares freedom of slaves. Civil War (begun 1861) continues.	Brahms arrives in Vienna. Anton Rubinstein founds St. Petersburg Conservatory.	L. Foucault measures speed of light.

DATE	LIFE	HISTORICAL EVENTS	CULTURAL EVENTS	SCIENTIFIC EVENTS, DISCOVERIES, ETC.
1863	Arranges meeting of German potentates in Frankfurt, in an effort to reform and reactivate German Confederation. Elisabeth in Kissingen. Ferdinand Maximilian is offered crown of Mexico. Franz Joseph makes him agree to renounce rights of succession.	U.S. Civil War: Battle of Gettysburg. Lasalle forms "Union of German Workers."	New group of painters exhibit in the Salon des Refusés. Manet: *Le déjeuner sur l'herbe.* Berlioz: *The Trojans,* Part I.	The Red Cross formed. T. Billroth: *General Chirurgic Pathology.* Alfred Nobel manufactures nitroglycerine.
1864	Makes pact with Prussia. Together they send ultimatum to Denmark re incorporation of Schleswig. Ferdinand Maximilian becomes Emperor of Mexico.	War of Austria-Prussia against Denmark. Settled by Peace of Vienna; Denmark cedes Schleswig-Holstein. Ludwig II becomes King of Bavaria. Pope Pius IX issues decree claiming Church's control over science and education.	Bruckner: Mass in D Minor. Tchaikovsky: "Romeo and Juliet Overture."	Geneva Convention re treatment of war prisoners.
1865	Break between Elisabeth and Franz Joseph. She demands authority over her children. Opens first part of Ringstrasse.	U.S. Civil War ends. Lincoln assassinated.	Wagner's *Tristan und Isolde* performed. Manet: *Olympia.* Lewis Carroll: *Alice in Wonderland.*	J. Lister begins antiseptic surgery.

DATE	LIFE	HISTORICAL EVENTS	CULTURAL EVENTS	SCIENTIFIC EVENTS, DISCOVERIES, ETC.
1866	Meets war and defeat by both Prussia and Italy-France. Bismarck appears as his adversary. Fear in Vienna, discontent in Empire. Elisabeth rejoins him. Meets Napoleon III for peace conference. Cedes Venetia. Later, in Peace of Prague, is forced to agree to Austria's exclusion from German affairs. Year of misfortune for him.	Bismarck provokes war, Schleswig-Holstein as overt cause. Prussians defeat Austrians at Sadowa, employing new "needle gun." War against Italy: Italian fleet destroyed at Lissa. Archduke Albert victorious at Custozza. Austrians decisively beaten by Italian-French forces in North Italy. Bismarck dissolves old German Confederation and forms "North German Federation." Austria loses Holstein to Prussia.	Smetana: *The Bartered Bride.* F. Dostoevsky: *Crime and Punishment.*	A. Nobel invents dynamite. G. Mendel formulates laws of heredity.
1867	Elisabeth tries to persuade Franz Joseph to conciliate the Hungarians. Recommends he listen to Deak and Andrassy, for whom she entertains warm feelings. New Prime Minister, Beust, finally persuades him. Elisabeth and he are crowned King and Queen of Hungary. "The Hungarian Compromise." They meet Napoleon III in Salzburg. He visits Paris World's Fair.	Austria is formed into a double monarchy: Austria-Hungary. Andrassy Hungarian Prime Minister. Ferdinand Maximilian is shot in Mexico. U.S. purchases Alaska.	Ibsen: *Peer Gynt.* Premier of J. Strauss, Jr.: "Blue Danube Waltz." Liszt: *Coronation Mass.* Verdi: *Don Carlo.* Karl Marx: *Das Kapital,* Volume I, published. É. Zola: *Thérèse Raquin.* Manet and Courbet show at Paris Fair. Japanese art is introduced to Europe.	Typewriter invented. T. Billroth begins to teach at Vienna University.
1868	Elisabeth in Hungary two-thirds of the year. Marie Valerie born.	Austrian civil marriage law. Concordat loosened. Austrian-Hungarian army increased to 800,000. Disraeli becomes Prime Minister.	Premiere of Wagner's *Die Meistersinger* in Munich. Brahms: *A German Requiem* (first version). Renoir and Manet begin to paint outdoors. F. Dostoevsky: *The Idiot.*	

DATE	LIFE	HISTORICAL EVENTS	CULTURAL EVENTS	SCIENTIFIC EVENTS, DISCOVERIES, ETC.
1869	He journeys to opening of the Suez Canal. Andrassy with him.	Establishment of Social Democratic Labor party at Eisenach.	Tolstoy: *War and Peace.* Vienna Opera House is opened.	E. Skoda establishes ironworks in Bohemia.
1870	Suspends concordat with Vatican because of promulgation of papal infallibility. Causes first aqueduct to be built (completed 1873).	Franco-Prussian War. Napoleon III capitulates at Sedan. Rome incorporated into Kingdom of Italy and made capital.	H. Schliemann begins to excavate Troy. Wagner: *Die Walküre.*	T. Billroth develops esophagus operation.
1871	Appoints Andrassy Minister of the Exterior. Elisabeth with Marie Valerie in Merano. Meets Wilhelm I to discuss treaty.	Wilhelm I proclaimed Emperor of Germany in Versailles. Third Republic in France, Thiers, President (to 1873), after "Bloody Week" in Paris.	J. Whistler: *The Artist's Mother.* A. Bruckner: Second Symphony. G. Verdi: *Aïda* premiere. É. Zola: *Rougon-Macquart* (series of novels). R. Emerson: *Essays.* F. Nietzsche: *The Birth of Tragedy.*	C. Darwin: *The Descent of Man.* Stanley meets Livingstone at Ujiji. J. Maxwell: electromagnetic theory of light.
1872	Sophie, Franz Joseph's mother, dies. Elisabeth lives mostly alone, spending much time in Gödöllö. Meeting of three Emperors in Berlin: Germany, Russia, and Austria. Bismarck as treaty maker.		Building begun of Vienna Museums and City Hall. Turgenev: *A Month in the Country* (play). J. Verne: *Around the World in 80 Days.* S. Butler: *Erewhon.* Eleonora Duse's debut. Bruckner: Mass in F Minor.	
1873	Opens Vienna International Exposition. Visits from Czar, Shah of Persia, Prince of Wales, King of Italy, Emperor of Germany. 25th anniversary of his reign. Gisela marries Leopold of Bavaria. Signs Three-Emperor Alliance.	Cholera breaks out in Vienna. Exposition financial disaster. "Black Friday" on Stock Exchange. Financial crisis spreads to Europe and U.S.A. Bakunin publishes *State and Anarchy.*	Building begun of Vienna University and Parliament. E. Manet: *Le Bon Bock.* Tolstoy: *Anna Karenina.* Bruckner: Third Symphony.	Jean-Matin Charcot: *Leçons sur les maladies du système nerveux.*

DATE	LIFE	HISTORICAL EVENTS	CULTURAL EVENTS	SCIENTIFIC EVENTS, DISCOVERIES, ETC.
1874	Journey to St. Petersburg—first time for an Austrian Emperor. Elisabeth becomes a grandmother (Gisela's child). Flirtation with Fritz Pacher. She visits Queen Victoria and goes hunting in England.	Gladstone resigns. Disraeli forms ministry.	First Impressionist Exhibition in Paris (Cézanne, Degas, Pissarro, Sisley, etc.). J. Strauss, Jr., *Die Fledermaus.* Wagner completes *Götterdämmerung.* Moussorgsky: *Boris Godunov* and *Pictures at an Exhibition.* Verdi: *Requiem.* F. Smetana: *My Fatherland.* T. Hardy: *Far from the Madding Crowd.* New Burgtheater and Stock Exchange building begun in Vienna.	Establishment of a World Postal Union.
1875	Elisabeth in Normandy. Suffers concussion in riding accident. She is away from Franz Joseph for most of the time. Death of Ferdinand, former Emperor, Franz Joseph's uncle.	Tisza forms ministry in Hungary. Rising in Bosnia and Herzegovina against Turkish rule. England buys Suez Canal shares.	Hans Richter, Vienna Philharmonic conductor, leads performances of Wagner's works. Bizet: *Carmen.* Dvořák: Third Symphony. Tchaikovsky: First Piano Concerto. Gilbert and Sullivan begin collaboration with *Trial by Jury.* Hermes of Praxiteles found in Olympia.	
1876	Elisabeth in England meets and is attracted to "Bay" Middleton. Before that she makes excursions to Corfu, Athens, Hungary, etc. Franz Joseph meets Czar Alexander II to discuss attitude toward Serbia and Montenegro in case of war.	Turkish troops massacre Bulgarians. Serbia and Montenegro declare war on Turkey. Murad V, Turkish Sultan, deposed, succeeded by Abdul-Hamid II. Queen Victoria becomes Empress of India. Bakunin organizes Russian secret society.	Brahms: First Symphony. Bruckner: Fifth Symphony. Bayreuth Festspielhaus opens for complete premiere of *The Ring.* Mark Twain: *Tom Sawyer.* Renoir: *Au Théâtre* and *Le Moulin de la Galette.* P. Gauguin: Landscapes.	Lombroso: *The Criminal.* A. G. Bell invents telephone. T. A. Edison invents phonograph.

Date	Life	Historical Events	Cultural Events	Scientific Events, Discoveries, etc.
1877	Elisabeth again in England. Franz Joseph declares himself neutral in Russo-Turkish War.	Austria and Russia agree that no large state be constructed in the Balkans. Russia declares war on Turkey. Serbia and Rumania on Russia's side.	Brahms: Second Symphony. Disastrous first performance of Bruckner's Third Symphony in Vienna. Third Impressionist Exhibition. Cézanne shows 16 pictures. Ibsen: *The Pillars of Society.* G. Keller: *A Village Romeo and Juliet.*	A. Hall discovers two moons of Mars.
1878	Andrassy and he propose European conference. Lord Salisbury suggests concerted action against Russia. Franz Joseph evades commitment. Franz Karl, his father, dies.	Turkey capitulates; asks Russia for armistice, which is granted. Britain sends fleet to Constantinople (the word "jingoism," is coined), later withdraws fleet. Greece declares war on Turkey. Preliminary Peace of San Stefano. Secret Anglo-Turkish agreement to stop Russian advance in Asia Minor. Anglo-Austrian agreement on Bulgaria. Congress of Berlin re Balkans. Austria given mandate to occupy Bosnia and Herzegovina. Austrian troops meet strong resistance in Bosnia-Herzegovina.	Dvořák: *Three Slavonic Rhapsodies.* T. Hardy: *The Return of the Native.* H. James: *Daisy Miller.*	

DATE	LIFE	HISTORICAL EVENTS	CULTURAL EVENTS	SCIENTIFIC EVENTS, DISCOVERIES, ETC.
1879	Elisabeth continues to ride and hunt passionately. Goes to Ireland. Silver wedding anniversary—Makart organizes grand festival. Andrassy resigns and Franz Joseph appoints Taaffe as Prime Minister. Bismarck comes to Vienna to discuss German-Austrian alliance. The Dual Alliance signed for five years—but in effect continues to 1918.	Austrian troops break the insurgents in Bosnia-Herzegovina. Three attempts to assassinate Czar Alexander II prove unsuccessful.	Brahms: Violin Concerto. Tchaikovsky: *Eugen Onegin*. Grieg: Piano Concerto. Renoir: *Mme. Charpentier and Her Children*. Rodin: *John the Baptist*. Dostoevsky: *The Brothers Karamazov*. Ibsen: *A Doll's House*. G. Meredith: *The Egoist*. H. Treitschke begins *History of Germany in the XIX Century* (to 1895).	Edison invents electric lamp. Saccharin produced. Henry George: *Progress and Poverty*.
1880	Franz Joseph fiftieth birthday. Travels to Polish Austria, Bohemia, etc. Declares Czech "official second language."	Schönerer becomes prominent in Austrian Parliament—the "Linz Program."	Bruckner revises Fourth Symphony. Mahler: *Das Klagende Lied*. Zola: *Nana*. Rodin: *The Thinker*.	Pasteur discovers streptococcus. Canned food marketed. Breuer begins treatment of "Anna O."
1881	Rudolf marries Stephanie of Belgium. Three-Emperor League signed (Franz Joseph, Wilhelm I, Alexander III). While in Gödöllö gets news of burning of the Ringtheater. Hurries back to Vienna for investigation. Exonerates Taaffe. Decides to build "House of Atonement." Concludes secret treaty with Serbia.	Czar Alexander II assassinated. Boer War. Severe pogroms in Russia.	Brahms: "Academic Festival" and "Tragic" overtures. Offenbach: *Tales of Hoffmann*. H. James: *Portrait of a Lady*. A. France: *The Crime of Sylvestre Bonnard*. D. G. Rossetti: *Ballads and Sonnets*.	E. Brugsch-Bey discovers "Valley of the Kings" in Egypt. Gotthard tunnel completed. First electric tramway (Berlin). Vienna Museums completed.

DATE	LIFE	HISTORICAL EVENTS	CULTURAL EVENTS	SCIENTIFIC EVENTS, DISCOVERIES, ETC.
1882	Elisabeth and Franz Joseph in Triest. Escape an assassination plot. Celebrates 600th anniversary of the establishment of the House of Habsburg.	Insurgents rise in Bosnia-Herzegovina. Sharpened conflicts between Germanophile and Slavic parties in Austrian Parliament. Italy joins German-Austrian alliance. With Austrian support Prince Milan proclaims himself King of Serbia. British occupy Cairo; establish Franco-British control of Egypt.	Brahms: Second Piano Concerto. Wagner: *Parsifal.* Manet: *Le Bar aux Folies-Bergères.*	G. Daimler builds gasoline engine. F. Lindemann proves impossibility of squaring the circle. Edison builds first electricity generating station in New York. A. Bertillon makes anthropometric measurements. R. Koch discovers tuberculosis bacillus. Vienna City Hall completed.
1883	Sees Katherina Schratt on Burgtheater stage. Rudolf and Stephanie have a daughter, Elizabeth.	Riots in Croatia; object, separation from Hungary. Separatist movement squelched politically. Secret Austro-Rumanian alliance. Nationalist party revolts in Serbia.	Brahms: Third Symphony. Dvořák: *Stabat Mater.* Bruckner completes Seventh Symphony. Stevenson: *Treasure Island.* Nietzsche: *Also Sprach Zarathustra.* New York Metropolitan Opera opened.	First skyscraper (Chicago). Freud becomes assistant to Meynert. Vienna Parliament and University completed.
1884	Elisabeth is enamored of antique Greece. Studies *Iliad* and *Odyssey.*	Renewal of Three-Emperors Alliance. Berlin Conference on Africa organized by Bismarck; 14 nations attend. Agree on abolition of slave trade.	Bruckner completes second version of *Te Deum.* Rodin: *Citizens of Calais.* Ibsen: *The Wild Duck.* Mark Twain: *Huckleberry Finn.* L. Sacher-Masoch: *Die Messalinen von Wien.*	Fabian Society formed. G. B. Shaw member. G. Eastman develops photographic film. O. Mergenthaler develops linotype.

Date	Life	Historical Events	Cultural Events	Scientific Events, Discoveries, etc.
1885	He is much occupied with troubles in the Balkans. Serbia invades Bulgaria. Bulgarians then beat Serbs but are forced to withdraw because of Austrian intervention. Conference in Moravia with Bismarck and Czar Alexander III. Elisabeth makes Greek voyage on yacht *Miramar*. Visits Schliemann excavations of Troy, then to Egypt, returns to Gödöllö, suffers much pain in legs.	Germany's colonization policy active: annexes Tanganyika, Zanzibar, North New Guinea, etc. Death of General Charles Gordon at Khartoum. British relief force arrives at Sudan. Leopold II of Belgium establishes Congo as personal property.	Mahler: *Lieder eines fahrenden Gesellen.* Bruckner: Successful premiere of Seventh Symphony in Munich. Brahms: Fourth Symphony. J. Strauss: *The Gypsy Baron.* Marx: *Das Kapital,* Volume 2. G. de Maupassant: *Bel Ami.* G. Meredith: *Diana of the Crossways.* G. Moore: *A Mummer's Wife.* W. Pater: *Marius the Epicurean.* Tolstoy: *The Power of Darkness.* Zola: *Germinal.*	Freud at Vienna University, then studies in Paris under Charcot. G. Daimler and K. Benz build first automobiles.
1886	Meets Katherina Schratt. Relationship becomes firm. Breaks with Archduke Johann Salvator. Hermes Villa finished for Elisabeth. Ludwig II dies—Elisabeth mourns him.	Differences between Austria and Russia become more acute. Peace of Bucharest between Serbia and Bulgaria, but Serbian conditions remain worrisome. W. E. Gladstone Prime Minister. Introduces Home Rule bill for Ireland.	Seurat: *Le Grande Jatte.* H. James: *The Bostonians* and *The Princess Casamassima.* Nietzsche: *Beyond Good and Evil.* Stevenson: *Dr. Jekyll and Mr. Hyde.* Tolstoy: *Kreutzersonata.* Statue of Liberty erected in New York.	Krafft-Ebing: *Psychopathia Sexualis.* Welsbach invents gas mantle.
1887	Elisabeth in Corfu and Mediterranean voyages. Stays away almost the whole year.	Lueger forms Christian Socialist party. Austrian army budget increased. Bismarck expands German army. Triple Alliance renewed. Queen Victoria's Golden Jubilee. Secret treaty between Russia and Germany.	Brahms: Double Concerto. Verdi: *Otello.* Paderewski gives first recitals in Vienna.	

Date	Life	Historical Events	Cultural Events	Scientific Events, Discoveries, etc.
1888	Elisabeth in England. Later in Bayreuth. Begins construction of Achilleion in Corfu.	Wilhelm II becomes Emperor of Germany. Visits Vienna.	Mahler appointed director of Budapest Opera. R. Strauss: *Don Juan.* Tchaikovsky: Fifth Symphony. Van Gogh: *Sunflowers* and *The Yellow Chair.*	Eastman's Kodak camera. Dunlop's pneumatic tire. F. Nansen crosses Greenland. Pasteur Institute opened in Paris. New Burgtheater completed.
1889	The Mayerling tragedy: Rudolf kills Mary Vetsera and then himself. Elisabeth, in deep depression, observes year of mourning. Franz Joseph to Berlin to visit Wilhelm II to discuss alliance.	Social Democratic party formed in Austria.	Dvořák: Fourth Symphony. G. Hauptmann: *Before Dawn.* B. Suttner: *Die Waffen Nieder!* H. Bergson: *Time and Liberty.*	Eiffel Tower built for Paris World Fair. Mehring and Minkowski prove cause of diabetes.
1890	Andrassy dies, mourned by Elisabeth. Marie Valerie marries Franz Salvator. Elisabeth begins long sea journey on yacht *Chazalie.*	Bismarck dismissed by Wilhelm II. "Young Czechs" win against "Old Czechs" in Parliament. "Reinsurance Treaty" canceled by Caprini, Bismarck's successor. First international May Day celebration in Germany.	Bruckner completes third version of Eighth Symphony. Tchaikovsky: *Pique Dame.* Mascagni: *Cavalleria Rusticana.* Cézanne: *The Card Players.* Ibsen: *Hedda Gabler.*	W. James: *The Principles of Psychology.*
1891	Elisabeth in Corfu. Then in Cairo. Christomanos her Greek teacher and companion. Franz Joseph renews the Three-Emperor Alliance. He sends Franz Ferdinand to St. Petersburg to improve Russian relations.	Famine in many parts of Russia.	Bruckner receives honorary degree, Vienna University. Mahler: Premiere of First Symphony. Strauss: *Death and Transfiguration.* Wedekind: *Spring's Awakening.* Wilde: *The Picture of Dorian Gray.* A. C. Doyle: *Adventures of Sherlock Holmes.* Hardy: *Tess of the D'Urbervilles.* Carnegie Hall, New York, opened. Toulouse-Lautrec: Posters for Montmartre music halls.	J. Stoney introduces "electron" concept. Trans-Siberian railroad begun. Freud begins to collaborate with Breuer.

DATE	LIFE	HISTORICAL EVENTS	CULTURAL EVENTS	SCIENTIFIC EVENTS, DISCOVERIES, ETC.
1892	Elisabeth tires of Christomanos, chooses Frederic Barker. Valerie's first child born (Elisabeth).	Austria financially prosperous. Pan-Slav Conference at Cracow.	Dvořák in New York. Leoncavallo: *I Pagliacci.* Bruckner: First performance of Eighth Symphony in Vienna. Hauptmann: *The Weavers.* Shaw: *Mrs. Warren's Profession.*	R. Diesel patents his engine.
1893	Because of severe inner political conflicts caused by "Language Reforms" he dismisses Taaffe as Prime Minister. Elisabeth wants to sell the just-completed Achilleion.		Dvořák: *Symphony from the New World.* Tchaikovsky: Sixth Symphony. Verdi: *Falstaff.* A. Schnitzler: *Anatol.* A. France: *La Reine Pédauque.* Wilde: *A Woman of No Importance.*	Nansen begins expedition to North Pole. Chicago World's Fair.
1894	He is very much alone, grappling with centrifugal problems. Declares civil marriages in Austro-Hungary legal.	L. Kossuth dies and becomes Hungary's national hero. "Independence party" formed. Czar Alexander III dies, succeeded by Nicholas II. President Sadi-Carnot of France assassinated by Italian anarchist. Alfred Dreyfus arrested on treason charge.	H. Wolf: *Italian Serenade.* Debussy: *L'Après-midi d'un Faune.* R. Kipling: *The Jungle Book.* Shaw: *Arms and the Man.*	S. and B. Webb: *Trade Unionism.*
1895	He appoints C. Badeni Prime Minister. He vetoes K. Lueger's election as Vienna's mayor.	Political rowdyism continues with "Badeni scandals" in Parliament, Anti-Semitism increases. Italy wars against Ethiopia. Massacre of Armenians in Constantinople. Austria recommends international naval action against Turkey.	R. Strauss: *Till Eulenspiegel.* Wolf: *Der Corregidor.* H. G. Wells: *The Time Machine.* Wilde: *The Importance of Being Earnest.*	T. G. Masaryk: *The Czech Question.* W. Röntgen discovers X-rays. G. Marconi invents wireless telegraphy. S. Freud: *Studies of Hysteria.*

DATE	LIFE	HISTORICAL EVENTS	CULTURAL EVENTS	SCIENTIFIC EVENTS, DISCOVERIES, ETC.
1896	He and Elisabeth appear in Budapest to celebrate the millennium of the Kingdom of Hungary. Elisabeth prodigiously honored. He confers with Czar and Czarina, with German Emperor and Empress at Vienna. Death of his brother Karl Ludwig, the heir presumptive. He and Elisabeth visit Queen Victoria. Elisabeth on an ever stricter diet; her melancholy deepens.	Wilhelm II sends "Kruger Telegram," provoking crisis in Anglo-German relations. Cretans revolt against Turkey. Ethiopians defeat Italians. Bismarck publishes a secret Russo-German Reinsurance Treaty, hitherto unknown to Austria. T. Herzl proposes state for Jews.	Brahms: *Four Serious Songs.* Bruckner: Ninth Symphony (incomplete at death). Mahler: Third Symphony. Puccini: *La Bohème.* R. Strauss: *Thus Spake Zarathustra.* Henri Bergson: *Matière et Mémoire.* A. E. Housman: *A Shropshire Lad.* Schnitzler: *Liebelei.* Hauptmann: *Die Versunkene Glocke.* Chekhov: *The Sea Gull.* Rodin: *The Hand of God.*	Completion of city railway of Vienna with stations designed by Otto Wagner. Nobel Prize established. W. Ramsay discovers helium.
1897	Serious disturbances because of Language Ordinances. Franz Joseph dismisses Badeni and, in effect, resumes autocratic government. Parliament closed. Is forced to agree to Lueger's becoming mayor. Goes to Petersburg to visit Nicholas II and discuss Balkan troubles. Agree to status quo.	"Day of Shame"—riot in Vienna—Nov. 28. War between Turkey and Greece. Bernhard von Bülow appointed German Foreign Secretary. First Zionist Congress in Basel. Russian secret police publishes *Protocols of the Wise Men of Zion,* which accuses Jews of seeking world domination. The document is proved utterly spurious.	Mahler becomes director of Vienna Opera. J. Conrad: *The Nigger of the Narcissus.* E. Rostand: *Cyrano de Bergerac.* Rilke: *Poems* Pissarro: *Boulevard des Italiens.* Rodin: *Balzac.* The *Sezession* of artists founded in Vienna.	Great Ferris Wheel constructed in Vienna Prater. R. Ross discovers malaria bacillus. Freud describes "Oedipus complex."
1898	Fiftieth anniversary of his ascendancy. Political agitations continue in Styria and Bohemia. Forms new cabinet under Thun. Anti-Semitic and Nationalistic riots in Galicia. He invokes martial law. Assassination of Elisabeth. Mourned by the world.	Spanish-American War. Zola writes *J'Accuse.* German naval expansion begins. Hawaiian Islands to U.S. Bismarck dead (83 years old). His *Reflections and Memoirs* published posthumously.	Rodin: *The Kiss.* Chekhov: *Uncle Vanya.* James: *The Turn of the Screw.* Wilde: *Ballad of Reading Gaol.* Tolstoy: *Resurrection.* Rilke: *Advent.*	Pierre and Marie Curie discover radium. F. Zeppelin builds airship.

DATE	LIFE	HISTORICAL EVENTS	CULTURAL EVENTS	SCIENTIFIC EVENTS, DISCOVERIES, ETC.
1899	K. Schratt departs from Vienna for a protracted period. "Language Ordinances" annulled. He reigns autocratically. Appoints Ernest Koerber Prime Minister, beginning 1900.	Mass meetings of Social Democrats in Vienna. "Young Czechs" against Germans. Riots in Moravia. Jewish and German houses looted. Troops called out. Peace Conference at Hague; 26 nations participate. Anglo-Boer War begins. New trial ordered in Dreyfus case.	R. Strauss: *A Hero's Life*. Sibelius: First Symphony. Berlioz: *The Trojans*, Part 2. H. Hofmannsthal: *Der Tor und der Tod*. K. Kraus: *Die Fackel* (periodical). J. Kainz at the Burgtheater. Monet: Rouen Cathedral (12 paintings).	Aspirin invented. E. Rutherford discovers alpha and beta rays of radioactive atoms. Freud: *The Interpretation of Dreams* (dated 1900).
1900	In spite of Franz Joseph's protests, Franz Ferdinand marries Sophie Chotek, thereby renouncing claims to succession of any children born from his "morganatic" union. Shah of Persia visits Vienna. Deadlock in nationalistic quarrels continues with noisy scenes. He threatens suspension of constitution if obstruction continues. Estrangement from K. Schratt. She departs from the Burgtheater.	Boxer rising in China. Umberto I of Italy assassinated. Succeeded by Victor Emanuel III.	Mahler: Fourth Symphony. Dvořák: *Rusalka*. Puccini: *Tosca*. Charpentier: *Louise*. J. Conrad: *Lord Jim*. L. Tolstoy: *The Living Corpse*. Rilke: *Geschichten vom lieben Gott*.	E. Mach: *Analysis of Sensations*. A. Evans: Excavation at Crete. M. Planck perfects quantum theory. W. Crookes isolates uranium.

Date	Life	Historical Events	Cultural Events	Scientific Events, Discoveries, etc.
1901	Franz Ferdinand as successor begins to assemble his own group, the "Belvedere Group," in opposition to Franz Joseph. Franz Joseph's Emperor's speech proposes industrial, economic, social reforms and pleads for unity among nationalities. He is very much alone.	Death of Queen Victoria. Accession of Edward VII. Lueger and Anti-Semitic Vienna party weaken at elections. Attempt at Anglo-German-Japanese agreement over Manchuria fails. Britain upholds policy of isolation. W. McKinley assassinated. Theodore Roosevelt becomes U.S. President. Strikes and anarchist movement become more widespread in Europe.	T. Mann: *Buddenbrooks*. Schnitzler: *Leutnant Gustl*. Shaw: *Caesar and Cleopatra*. Strindberg: *Dance of Death*. Chekhov: *Three Sisters* S. Zweig: *Silberne Saiten*.	Freud: *The Psychopathology of Everyday Life*. Marconi sends messages by wireless across Atlantic.
1902	He renews Triple Alliance for six years.	Conflict between Britain and Germany increases. Boer War ends. Increasing troubles in Macedonia—Bulgarians, Serbs, and Greeks.	Year of much intellectual activity in Austria. Mahler: Fifth Symphony. Sibelius: Second Symphony. Debussy: *Pelléas et Mélisande*. A. Gide: *The Immoralist*. G. D'Annunzio: *Francesca da Rimini*. Rilke: *Buch der Lieder*.	B. Croce: *Philosophy of the Spirit*. W. James: *The Varieties of Religious Experience*.
1903	Negotiates renewed troubles with Hungary over demand for separate army. Appoints Stephen Tisza Hungarian premier. Pope Leo XIII dies; Franz Joseph is instrumental in having Pius X elected. Receives Edward VII in Vienna. Discusses with Czar program for quieting Macedonia (Mürzsteg Agreement).	King Alexander I of Serbia and Queen Draga murdered. Peter I succeeds.	Schönberg: *Gurrelieder*. G. Klimt: Paintings for Vienna University. Hofmannsthal: *Elektra*. Schnitzler: *Reigen*. Hauptmann: *Rose Bernd*. H. James: *The Ambassadors*. S. Butler: *The Way of All Flesh*.	Flight of Wright brothers. Henry Ford forms company in Detroit. O. Weininger: *Geschlecht und Character*.

Date	Life	Historical Events	Cultural Events	Scientific Events, Discoveries, etc.
1904	Internal disturbances continue. Parliament meets again. Koerber presents 60 ordinances decreed by Franz Joseph which await approval. This is followed by clashes in Prague and Vienna between German and Slav students. University of Vienna closed by imperial decree. Parliament adjourns without accomplishment. Franz Joseph goes to Budapest, where he personally is enthusiastically greeted, though the Hungarian "Independent party" causes violent scenes in Parliament and nullifies new conciliatory measures. He increases army and navy budgets. Ultimatum presented to Turkey demanding punishment and dismissal of Turkish officials who had interfered with the dispatch of Austrian mails at Scutari.	Russo-Japanese War begins. Japanese cripple Russian fleet at Port Arthur. Entente Cordiale settles several Anglo-French differences (Morocco, Egypt, etc.). Anti-Austrian ministry formed in Serbia (under Pašić).	L. Janáček: *Jenufa.* Puccini: *Madame Butterfly* (premiere). Mahler: *Kindertotenlieder.* L. Hearn: *Japan.* W. H. Hudson: *Green Mansions.* R. Rolland: *Jean-Christophe* (begun). Chekhov: *The Cherry Orchard.* H. Adams: *Mont-St.-Michel and Chartres.* P. Cézanne: *Mont Sainte Victoire.* O. Wagner builds Steinhof in Vienna (to 1907).	E. Rutherford and F. Soddy state theory of radioactivity.
1905	Hungarian fights continue. Franz Joseph threatens to settle them by introducing universal suffrage, believing that the people would side with him. Summons Franz Kossuth and others and lays down demands. Attends army maneuvers, with Chief of Staff Beck.	Russo-Japanese War ends. Japan victorious. Peace of Portsmouth mediated by T. Roosevelt. Wilhelm II visit to Tangier triggers Moroccan crisis. Crete revolts against Turkish rule. Sinn Fein party founded in Dublin. Russian revolt begins with "Bloody Sunday" (Jan. 22). Petersburg workers form first Soviet. Mutiny on battleship *Potemkin.* Nobel Prize for peace to B. Suttner.	Debussy: *La Mer.* R. Strauss: *Salome.* F. Lehár: *The Merry Widow.* *Die Brücke* (The Bridge) group of artists formed in Munich. Matisse and Derain form the Fauve movement. Cézanne: *Les Grandes Baigneuses.*	Einstein states his first theory of relativity. G. Santayana: *Life of Reason.* Freud: *Three Treatise on the Theory of Sex.* Mach: *Recognition and Error.*

DATE	LIFE	HISTORICAL EVENTS	CULTURAL EVENTS	SCIENTIFIC EVENTS, DISCOVERIES, ETC.
1906	He succeeds in forcing Vienna Parliament to accept the principle of universal suffrage (becomes law in 1907). Appoints new ministry. Appoints L. Aehrenthal foreign minister. Franz Ferdinand opposes Beck and insists on appointment of Conrad von Hötzendorf as Chief of Staff.	Parliamentary Reforms in Austria increase number of deputies to 516, with Germans predominating. Liberals' decisive victory in British elections. Dreyfus exonerated in France. Algeciras agreement giving France and Spain control of Morocco. Maximilian Harden attacks Count Eulenburg, friend of Wilhelm II, and uncovers rampant homosexuality at German court.	Bartók: *Hungarian Folk Songs.* Shaw: *The Doctor's Dilemma.* Picasso: *Les Desmoiselles d'Avignon.*	E. Fischer: *Investigations of Amino Acids.*
1907	Suffers bronchial infections. Edward VII visits him to plead that he use his influence to moderate German shipbuilding. He remains noncommittal.	Austrian general elections held, 4,600,000 voting. Peace Conference in Hague; no substantial results. Lenin founds newspaper, *The Proletarian.* Rasputin gains influence on Nicholas and Alexandra.	Crisis in Mahler's life: his daughter dies; he is told he has heart disease; intrigue undermines his position at Vienna Opera. He accepts conductorship at Metropolitan Opera, New York. O. Straus: *A Waltz Dream.* Delius: *A Village Romeo and Juliet.* J. M. Synge: *The Playboy of the Western World.*	C. Pirquet isolates tuberculin. H. Adams: *The Education of Henry Adams.*
1908	After secret conference at Buchlau between Russian Minister, Izvolsky and Aehrenthal, Franz Joseph decides to annex Bosnia-Herzegovina. 60th Anniversary of his ascendancy celebrated.	"Young Turks" stage revolt in Macedonia. Europe is "shocked" by Austrian annexation of Bosnia-Herzegovina. War looms. Bulgaria declares itself independent with Ferdinand I as "Czar of Bulgaria." H. H. Asquith British Prime Minister, with David Lloyd George as Chancellor of the Exchequer.	Bartók: First String Quartet. Mahler: *Das Lied von der Erde.* A. Bennett: *Old Wives' Tale.* E. M. Forster: *A Room with a View.* A. France: *Penguin Island.* Schnitzler: *Der Weg ins Freie.* Monet: *Ducal Palace, Venice.* J. Epstein: Sculptures for the British Medical Association. C. Brancusi: *The Kiss.*	A. Bethe: *General Anatomy and Physiology of the Nervous System.* General Motors Company formed in Detroit.

DATE	LIFE	HISTORICAL EVENTS	CULTURAL EVENTS	SCIENTIFIC EVENTS, DISCOVERIES, ETC.
1909		War with Serbia threatens, but is prevented by intervention of major European powers. Serbia yields to Austria. Clemenceau resigns. Aristide Briand forms ministry. T. Bethmann-Hollweg becomes German Chancellor. Treason trial in Agram, Croatia, 53 partisans of Serbia are convicted. Friedjung libel suit scandal.	Mahler: Ninth Symphony. R. Strauss: *Elektra.* H. Bahr: *Das Konzert.* Rilke: *Requiem.* H. Maeterlinck: *The Bluebird.* O. Kokoschka: *Princess Montesquieu-Rohan.*	P. Ehrlich prepares salvarsan as a cure for syphilis. Freud lectures at Clark University. Lenin: *Materialism and Empiric Criticism.* H. Ford: Model T car. R. E. Peary reaches North Pole. L. Blériot crosses English Channel by monoplane.
1910	80th birthday celebrated throughout Austria. He disagrees more and more with Franz Ferdinand. He voyages to Bosnia-Herzegovina.	Edward VII dies. George V succeeds him. Wilhelm II uses the phrase "decked in shining armor," causing European concern. Japan annexes Korea. Republic proclaimed in Portugal, after flight of Manuel II. Lueger, mayor of Vienna for 13 years, dies, ending an era.	Mahler conducts first performance of Eighth Symphony. Consults Freud, who helps him. Returns to New York to conduct Philharmonic. Stravinsky: *The Firebird.* R. Vaughn Williams: *Sea Symphony.* A. Berg: Third Quartet. Rimsky-Korsakov: *Le Coq d'or.* Kokoschka: *Frau Loos.* F. Molnar: *Liliom.* Rilke: *Aufzeichnungen des Malte Laurids Brigge.*	Freud: *On Psychoanalysis.* A. Evans excavates Knossos. M. Curie: *Treatise on Radiography.*

DATE	LIFE	HISTORICAL EVENTS	CULTURAL EVENTS	SCIENTIFIC EVENTS, DISCOVERIES, ETC.
1911	Plans reorganization and strengthening of military. Conrad tries to persuade him toward a "preventive war." He negates the idea. Is present at wedding of Archduke Karl to Zita of Bourbon. Once again dissolves Lower Parliament because of nationalistic fights. Appoints Karl Stürgkh Premier and reorganizes cabinet.	Economic depression in Austria. Riots in Vienna's laborers' district, suppressed with bloodshed. Christian Socialist party loses against German Nationalists in new general election. British Labor party elects Ramsay MacDonald as chairman. Arrival of German gunboat *Panther* in Agadir creates international worry. Wilhelm II speaks in Hamburg of Germany's "place in the sun." Germany then agrees to let France have free hand in Morocco in return for territory in Congo. Italy declares war on Turkey and bombards Tripoli. Annexes Tripoli and Cyrenaica. A. Tirpitz appointed First Admiral by Wilhelm II. Churchill First Lord of Admiralty in Britain. J. Joffre French Chief of Staff.	Mahler: *Das Lied von der Erde* (premiere). Mahler dies. Bartók: *Bluebeard's Castle.* R. Strauss: *Der Rosenkavalier.* I. Berlin: "Alexander's Ragtime Band." W. Kandinsky and F. Marc found *Blaue Reiter* group of artists in Munich. G. Braque: *Man with a Guitar.* Hofmannsthal: *Jedermann.* K. Mansfield: "In a German Pension." Rilke: *Duino Elegies* (begun). E. Wharton: *Ethan Frome.* M. Beerbohm: *Zuleika Dobson.* T. Dreiser: *Jennie Gerhardt.* R. Brooke: *Poems.*	Amundsen reaches South Pole. Einstein publishes findings on influence of gravity on light. F. Brentano: *The Classification of Psychic Phenomena.*
1912	On death of Aehrenthal appoints L. Berchtold Minister of Foreign Affairs.	First Balkan War; Bulgaria, Serbia, Montenegro against Turkey. Peace Conference at London inaugurated by major powers, arrives at settlement, creating Albania as autonomous state. Count Stephen Tisza becomes President of Hungarian Chamber. Vienna International Socialist Congress.	Schönberg: *Pierrot Lunaire.* R. Strauss: *Ariadne auf Naxos.* Stravinsky: *Petroushka.* M. Duchamp: *Nude Descending a Staircase.* F. Léger: *Woman in Blue.* Sculpture of Nefertiti found. Schnitzler: *Professor Bernhardi.* Shaw: *Pygmalion.*	A. Adler: *The Nervous Character.* *Titanic* sinks on maiden voyage. B. Russell: *The Problems of Philosophy.*

Date	Life	Historical Events	Cultural Events	Scientific Events, Discoveries, etc.
1913	Withdraws more and more from public life. Appoints Franz Ferdinand as "General Inspector" of Austrian military forces. Is much perturbed over Redl scandal—espionage—and Redl's suicide. Suspends autonomy of "Kingdom of Bohemia."	Serbian troops invade Albania; withdraw when Austria and other powers protest. Bulgarians renew war against Turkey. Later Turkey accepts recommendations of major powers for peace. King George I of Greece murdered. Second Balkan War, Bulgaria attacking Serbia and Greece. Russia declares war against Bulgaria. Turkey reenters war. Later (end of 1913, beginning of 1914) Balkan peace treaties agreed to. Relations between Germany and England-France worsen. German army increased. A. Schlieffen develops "Schlieffen Plan" for invasion of France through Belgium. S. Parkhurst leads British suffragettes. S. and B. Webb found the publication *The New Statesman.* Woodrow Wilson U.S. President. Federal income tax introduced in the U.S.	Stravinsky: *The Rite of Spring.* M. de Falla: *La vida breve.* Armory Show in New York of Post-Impressionism. D. H. Lawrence: *Sons and Lovers.* M. Proust: *Swann's Way.* T. Mann: *Death in Venice.* Schnitzler: *Frau Beate und ihr Sohn.*	Niels Bohr examines atomic structure. H. Geiger research on radiation. B. Russell and A. N. Whitehead: *Principia Mathematica.* Freud: *Totem and Taboo.*

DATE	LIFE	HISTORICAL EVENTS	CULTURAL EVENTS	SCIENTIFIC EVENTS, DISCOVERIES, ETC.
1914	After Franz Ferdinand and his wife's assassination in Sarajevo, he takes reins of government once more into his hands. Approves decision of ministers to send stiff ultimatum to Serbia. Though Serbian reply is conciliatory, decides to declare war.	World War I begins (July 28) with Austrian declaration against Serbia. Major European war declarations follow, after frantic and futile last-minute efforts to confer and negotiate. Austria begins bombardment of Belgrade. Hostilities begun at Polish frontier. Germany invades Belgium and France. German advance halted by battle of Marne (Sept. 5–12).	J. Joyce: *Dubliners.* G. Moore: *Hail and Farewell.* T. Dreiser: *The Titan.* T. Mann: *Tonio Kröger.* O. Kokoschka: *The Bride of the Wind.* Renoir: *Tilla Durieux.*	A. Eddington: *Stellar Movement and the Structure of the Universe.* J. H. Jeans: *Report on Radiation and the Quantum Theory.* Panama Canal opened.
1915	Conduct of war largely taken out of his hands. Retires to Schönbrunn.	First German submarine attacks. British blockade Germany. Russians take Przemysl. Germans use poison gas. Germans sink *Lusitania.* After vain conferences, Italy declares war on Austro-Hungary. First Zeppelin attack on London (and later on Paris). Austro-German armies take Lemberg and Belgrade. Germans enter Warsaw and Brest-Litovsk. Four battles are fought at the Isonzo: Italy-Austria (eventually nine battles). Food is rationed in Vienna.		Einstein's general theory of relativity.

DATE	LIFE	HISTORICAL EVENTS	CULTURAL EVENTS	SCIENTIFIC EVENTS, DISCOVERIES, ETC.
1916	Issues plan for future organization of Galicia. He and Wilhelm II announce plan for creating Kingdom of Poland. Dies in Schönbrunn on November 21.	Battle of Verdun rages Feb. 21–Dec. 18. Battle of the Somme. Russians take Czernowitz. Austrians withdraw from South Tyrol. Rumania declares war on Austria-Hungary and begins offensive in Transylvania. Karl Stürgkh, Austrian Premier, assassinated. Sea battle at Skagerrak. Wilhelm II's peace feeler rejected as unsatisfactory by Allies. Bureau of Food Control established in Vienna. Lloyd George British Prime Minister. Rasputin murdered.	E. W. Korngold: *Violanta*. C. Monet: *Water Lilies* murals. F. Hodler: *A Glance at Eternity*. K. Kollwitz: *Mother and Child*. Dadaist art movement. J. Joyce: *Portrait of the Artist as a Young Man*. G. Moore: *The Brook Kerith*. H. Barbusse: *Le feu*.	M. Buber: *The Spirit of Judaism*.

Notes

Foreword

1. *New York Times,* February 6, 1972.

I. *Franz Joseph's Viennese*

1. W. E. Delp, *The Oxford Companion to the Theatre.*
2. Allardyce Nicoll, *World Drama.*
3. *"Was ist der Erde Glück?—Ein Schatten!*
   Was ist der Erde Ruhm?—Ein Traum!"
   (*Medea,* 1820)
4. *"Wer spricht von Siegen?*
   Überstehen ist alles!"
5. Stefan Zweig, *Die Welt von Gestern.*
6. Viennese artists loved to portray beautiful women with their hats: Gustav Klimt, Max Kurzwell, Maximilian Lenz, Egon Schiele.
7. The Palais Liechtenstein was demolished in 1913. On its site stands the ugly Hochhaus, Vienna's skyscraper.
8. About the same time as the New York Philharmonic was established (1842).
9. Joseph II had established it in 1776 as a "National Theater for the Edification of Morals and Taste," in the style of Comédie Française.
10. Friedländer, *Letzter Glanz der Märchenstadt.*

II. *Fever in Europe*

1. Yet as long ago as the fourteenth century a wave of revolts, similar to the wave of 1848, spread across Europe: Siena in 1371, Florence in 1378, the

493

peasant rebellion of Wat Tyler in England in 1381, preceded by a peasant uprising in France, the *Jacquerie* of 1358. Perhaps communication existed to a greater degree than most historians have believed.

2. Guizot, *Études biographique sur la révolution d'Angleterre* (1851).

3. Metternich to Ficquelmont.

4. See Harold Nicolson's brilliant book, *The Congress of Vienna.*

5. After his abdication, Ferdinand lived on in his castle in Prague. He died at the age of eighty-two.

6. Edmond Taylor in *The Fall of the Dynasties* writes that Metternich escaped "hidden in a laundry cart." That seems to be a romantic invention.

7. It was actually not called Budapest till 1872. Before that the city consisted of Buda, Pest, and Ofen.

8. This description is based on a report of a man who was there: Karl Vitzthum von Eckstädt. *(Berlin und Wien in den Jahren 1845–1852: Politische Privatbriefe,* Stuttgart, 1886).

9. Golo Mann, *The History of Germany since 1789.*

10. Lady Jane had a child by him. She cared nothing for the child, and Schwarzenberg, a bachelor, brought her up. After Lady Jane and Schwarzenberg separated, she left Paris, had several adventures in Munich, Athens, Damascus, and at an advanced age fell in love with a wealthy sheik, with whom she lived contentedly.

11. An English translation was published in London in 1849 under the title *A Narrative of Events in Vienna from Latour to Windisch-Graetz.*

12. It was rumored at the time that Sophie forced Ferdinand to abdicate by refusing to allow him to be fed. This seems too melodramatic to be probable.

III. *The Education of an Emperor*

1. Quoted by Joseph Redlich, *Kaiser Franz Joseph von Österreich.*

2. "Your Majesty, do not say to Yourself that to govern is more difficult today than in ordinary times! At all times the task is the same. . . . If the throne knows how to assume the stance which belongs to it by divine and human right, the people will gather around it." Metternich to Franz Joseph. From a letter dated January 17, 1849.

3. Kübeck said that Bach "had the mentality of a pettifogger." He considered Schwarzenberg "arrogantly ignorant."

4. Undated memorandum. Quoted by Corti.

5. Franz Joseph to Nicholas. Confidential letter, written from Olmütz, April 16, 1849.

6. The thousand-year-old "Crown of St. Stephen" represented a mystic symbol to Hungarians. Its hiding place was discovered a year or so after Kossuth had buried it. At the end of World War II it was delivered to the United States Army for safekeeping. At the time of writing, it is preserved in a secret

place "known only to the United States President, the Pope, and a handful of officials" (*New York Times,* February 9, 1972).

7. Figures given by Jászi. They may be understated, but exact figures are now impossible to obtain.

IV. *Years of Mixed Blessings*

1. *War and Peace,* Book IX, Chapter I.
2. Franz Joseph to Sophie, August 26, 1851.
3. Bruck, along with Schwarzenberg, wanted to draw even Switzerland, Belgium, and Denmark into the union of "70 million people" and visualized a "United States of Central Europe."
4. Metternich to Hübner, December 8, 1850.
5. Nicholas to Franz Joseph, July, 1853.
6. Nicholas to Franz Joseph, January 16, 1854.
7. Franz Joseph to Sophie, October 8, 1854.

V. *The Young Elisabeth*

1. The meeting took place on August 15, 1853. Franz Joseph was twenty-three years old, Elisabeth not yet sixteen.
2. Quoted by Saint-Aulaire in *François Joseph.*
3. Both quotations are taken from *Die Weckbeckers* (Wilhelm Weckbecker's memoirs).
4. It is the gift about which Baron Ochs makes such a fuss with the notary in Act I of *Der Rosenkavalier.*
5. Wilhelm Weckbecker.
6. Quoted by Karl Tschuppik, *Elisabeth, Kaiserin von Österreich.*
7. Quoted by Corti.
8. From a memoir of Count Louis Rechberg. The quotation belongs to a slightly later period, when Elisabeth's mood had worsened.
9. Letter to Sophie, August 30, 1856.
10. Luisa di Toscana, *La mia Storia.*

VI. *The Realm Diminishes; Elisabeth Grows Up*

1. Ferdinand Maximilian to Franz Joseph, April 10, 1858.
2. Ferdinand Maximilian to Sophie, 1858.
3. Ferdinand Maximilian to Franz Joseph, January 7, 1859.
4. It was probably Metternich's last advice. He died a little more than a month later.
5. Steiger to Staempfli, June 11, 1859. Quoted by Corti.
6. Franz Joseph to Elisabeth from Verona, June 9, 1859.
7. Franz Joseph to Elisabeth, from Italy, July 5, 1859.

8. Erich Kielmansegg, *Kaiserhaus.*

9. I was astonished to learn upon inquiry at the Austrian State Archive that some time after World War I Marie Valerie, Franz Joseph's and Elisabeth's youngest daughter, had come to the Archive and been permitted to abstract from it certain letters and documents which she judged injurious to her parents' reputation. Marie Valerie died in 1924, and the material is presumably destroyed.

10. Alma Mahler, *Gustav Mahler: Memories and Letters.*

11. Later she opened a subscription for a monument to be erected in Düsseldorf, Heine's birthplace. Kaiser Wilhelm II opposed the monument because Heine was "subversive." The monument was never erected.

12. Elisabeth to Collett, November 27, 1863.

13. Elisabeth to Ludovika, May 26, 1866.

14. Elisabeth to Rudolf, March 31, 1865.

15. Various reports from Blome to Vienna.

16. Ludwig to Rudolf, November 28, 1875.

17. Ernest Newman, *The Life of Richard Wagner,* Vol. III.

18. Sir A. Morier to Lord Bloomfield, February 4, 1866. Quoted by Corti.

19. Franz Joseph to Sophie from Budapest, February 17, 1866.

20. Elisabeth to Franz Joseph, July 15, 1866.

21. Franz Joseph to Elisabeth, July 17, 1866. Written at five in the morning.

22. Franz Joseph to Elisabeth, July 18, 1866, at 5:30 A.M.

23. Franz Joseph to Elisabeth, from Schönbrunn, August 7, 1866.

24. He became Minister of the Exterior of Austro-Hungary in 1871, after Beust, thus finally achieving the position to which he aspired and to which his ability entitled him.

25. The Leitha, a river flowing into the Danube, separated two parts of the realm.

26. Golo Mann, *The History of Germany since 1789.*

27. Bismarck learned something about spy systems from Metternich. Later, during the war, he managed to send a Hungarian spy right into Austria's headquarters: the man masqueraded as a war correspondent.

28. Maximilian's life story is superbly told in Joan Haslip's *The Crown of Mexico.*

29. Ferdinand Maximilian to his brother Karl Ludwig, July 10, 1864.

30. Ferdinand Maximilian to Karl Ludwig, February 24, 1865.

31. Ferdinand Maximilian to Dr. Jilek, February 10, 1865.

32. The rumor spread through Europe that she had been poisoned by an Indian herb (talavatchi) which destroys the mind while leaving the body intact. This was supposed to have been given her by one of her Mexican attendants. No proof of poisoning exists. Carlotta was an enormously wealthy woman. Her father, Leopold I of Belgium, had invested his private fortune of five million francs with the Rothschilds; it grew to twenty million. After her

father's death in 1865, she inherited it, and when she became insane her brother was appointed custodian. Another rumor had it that she regained her sanity and was kept imprisoned by her brother because he wanted the use of the fortune for himself. Several attempts by the Habsburg court, though not by Franz Joseph himself, to get hold of the money failed. Most of the money finally disappeared through speculations in Panama and the Congo.

33. The news traveled slowly because it was brought by couriers across Mexico toward Texas. At Laredo, Texas, a telegraph office was found and the facts were telegraphed to Washington. From there the news reached Europe via the new underseas cable.

VII. *Linden Trees in Vienna*

1. Franz Joseph to Elisabeth, from Schönbrunn, August 8, 1866.

2. I am speaking of the Champs Élysées as it used to be, not as it is today, a cheap, flickering street. The Ringstrasse's beauty has been preserved, though the subterranean passageways have not improved it.

3. She did attend a week later, hearing Auber's *La Muette de Portici*. Franz Joseph and she entertained the Viceroy of Egypt.

4. They are perhaps slumbering in some museum basement. I do not know their whereabouts.

5. It is remarkable that the Opera lost only a little of its interior glamor after it was rebuilt, the roof and the stage having undergone severe bombing in 1945.

6. Quoted from *Hugo Thimig Erzählt*. The meeting took place in Katherina Schratt's house.

7. Elisabeth to Franz Joseph, August 10, 1870.

8. Quoted by Saint-Aulaire in *François Joseph*.

9. Franz Joseph to Sophie, August 25, 1870.

10. Baron Ludwig Gablenz, one of the leading generals of the Austrian army, committed suicide because of his financial losses. It caused a great scandal.

11. However, Austrian socialism was divided for many years by the conflicts between radical Marxists and partisans of Lassalle.

12. Alexander II to Franz Joseph, November 3, 1876.

13. As Hajo Holborn points out, it was significant that Berlin was chosen as the meeting place, "because the Bismarckian policy was now regarded as devoted to peace" (*A History of Modern Germany*, Vol. II).

VIII. *Elisabeth and the Placid Triangle*

1. Elisabeth to Franz Joseph, November 7, 1869.

2. Maurice Barrès, *Amori et dolori Sacrum*.

3. A picture of her in this riding costume appeared in *Vanity Fair*. The

publication wrote that Franz Joseph "married the most beautiful maiden, who is still one of the most beautiful women in Europe."

4. The belief that they *were* lovers was more prevalent in England than in Austria. It would have been consistent with Elisabeth's personality to "love" without physical fulfillment. It would have been consistent with Middleton's personality to accept such a condition. At any rate, I have been unable to find evidence, one way or the other.

5. It was a beauty recipe which originated in the Balkans. Lola Montez believed in it as well.

6. Elisabeth to Franz Joseph, from Gödöllö, November 2, 1868.

7. The first was a fantastic medieval palace; the second, an overloaded imitation of Versailles. Thirty or forty women spent seven years making the cover for Ludwig's bed.

8. Elisabeth to Franz Joseph from Merano, November 14, 1871.

9. Rudolf to Latour, from Prague, December 2, 1881.

10. Today in the Hofburg the dining room table is shown to tourists, set up for a gala dinner. The appurtenances are splendid: six crystal glasses at each place, gold plates, the silver delicate, the linen of finest Bohemian weave. It all seems very cold.

11. Maria Redwitz, *Hofchronik 1888–1921.*

12. He kept this up to his last years. I remember being told as a child, "The Emperor is coming," when I saw the Ringstrasse being cleared and an empty vehicle speeding along it. By then the carriage was an automobile, which Franz Joseph used in his last years, though reluctantly. He thought horses more reliable.

13. Marie Festetics diary. Entry of November 28, 1873.

14. Stephanie Lonyay, *Ich sollte Kaiserin werden.*

15. The details of this episode were researched by Corti, who interviewed the man involved before his death in 1934, and had access to the letters which passed between Elisabeth and him.

16. I got these facts from Frau Virginia Werner in Ischl. Franz Joseph had noticed Virginia as a child when she handed him a bunch of flowers upon his arrival in Ischl. He took a liking to the beautiful little girl and later suggested to Katherina Schratt that she invite Virginia to be her companion. Virginia— who was known in Ischl as *"das Kaiserdirndl"*—remained friends with Katherina for many years. She was eighty-two-years old when I interviewed her, lively and vigorous. Her little apartment was filled with Franz Joseph mementos.

17. These facts are taken from a monograph on Schratt by Hannelore Holub of the Philosophic Faculty of the University of Vienna (9874-c). It is of incidental interest that during Schratt's tours and guest engagements in various theaters in the period before she knew Franz Joseph, she played at the Deutsches Theater in New York (1882).

18. This includes Jean de Bourgoing, editor of Franz Joseph's letters to Schratt.

19. Valerie's diary. Entry of December 9, 1887.

20. Elisabeth also commissioned him to paint two portraits of Katherina Schratt; they were Christmas presents for Franz Joseph.

IX. *"Muddling Through"*

1. I owe this point to Hanns L. Mikoletzky.

2. *Fremdenblatt,* December 9, 1881.

3. Though in later years Jauner, who was a brilliant impresario, tried to work his way back, though for a time he became director of the Theater an der Wien and in 1885 staged the premier of Strauss's *The Gypsy Baron,* he was never able to recapture the affection of the Viennese public. He shot himself on February 23, 1900.

4. Told by Virginia Werner.

5. Edward Crankshaw, *The Fall of the House of Habsburg.*

6. Gustav Strakosch-Grassmann, *Geschichte des Österreichischen Untericht-swesen.*

7. Hilsner was pardoned after eighteen years by Emperor Karl, Franz Joseph's successor.

8. As a child I heard a recording he made of the parable of the "three rings" from *Nathan.* I was thrilled by it. In 1889 Franz Joseph told Katherina Schratt: "At eleven o'clock a Herr Wagemann demonstrated for me the famous Edison phonograph, which is as astonishing as it is interesting. Quite distinctly I heard Bismarck speak, a Hurrah proffered to me in Berlin, then our national anthem played by the Railroad Regiment, and the 'Radetzky March'; a declamation by Sonnenthal in his most affected manner made me laugh. . . ."

9. Hitler, in *Mein Kampf,* wrote that he had studied Schönerer's technique and used some of his ideas. After Hitler occupied Austria, a street in Vienna, the Heinrich Heine Street, was renamed the Schönerer Street.

10. The "Linz Program" has been carefully analyzed by Adam Wandruszka in his article on Austria in the *Handbuch der Europäischen Geschichte.*

11. Four years before his rowdies invaded the offices of the *Neues Wiener Tagblatt,* the editor of that paper, Moritz Szeps, an intimate friend of Rudolf's, was sued for libel by Schönerer and sat four weeks in jail. Rudolf could do nothing about it and Franz Joseph didn't.

X. *Rudolf's Tragedy*

1. A listing of books and pamphlets dealing with Mayerling, given by Judtmann, occupies eleven closely typeset pages.

2. Albert Margutti, adjutant to Franz Joseph, believed this and stated it in his book *Vom alten Kaiser.*

3. A full report which Taaffe is supposed to have written has never been found.

4. Published originally in German under the title *Mayerling ohne Mythos* (Vienna, 1968). A few details were later added by Professor Adam Wandruszka, in an introduction he wrote to a new edition of the biography by Oskar Mitis, *Das Leben des Kronprinzen Rudolf* (Vienna, 1971).

5. He was supposed to have been engaged to her. Then, when it was discovered that she was mortally ill, Rudolf was forced to break the engagement. In the meantime, the two young people had become lovers and Maria Anna had conceived. Rudolf married her secretly (in Vienna, January 1, 1880). The child, a boy, was adopted by a bourgeois family. He grew up as Robert Pachmann. Documents proving the marriage and the birth were supposedly destroyed by court officials. The matter is by no means certain, and it is most probably untrue. (It is related as a fact by Alexander Lernet-Holenia in *Die Geheimnisse des Hauses Österreich*.)

6. Stephanie Lonyay, *Ich sollte Kaiserin werden*.

7. Quoted by Judtmann from notes by Corti.

8. Rudolf to Szeps, February 4, 1884.

9. *Bulletin* of the New York Academy of Medicine, Vol. 41, No. 2.

10. Adam Wandruszka, from the introduction to the Mitis biography of Rudolf.

11. Still another murder theory—one might well call it Theory 6A—has recently been advanced in a book by Victor Wolfson, *The Mayerling Murder*. Wolfson believes that the instigator of the murder was Bismarck, the reason being that Bismarck saw in Rudolf and his liberal ideas a dangerous threat to Germany. It was Bismarck who sent his agents to Mayerling to murder Rudolf and make the deed look like suicide. Even aside from the medical evidence the theory is highly improbable: Bismarck was too astute a statesman to trigger so raw a deed, nor did he stand in fear of Rudolf; he knew perfectly well that once Rudolf would become Emperor he would be open to reason and negotiation. There was no need for Bismarck to sponsor a crime the originator of which might be discovered.

12. Festetics diary. Entry December 3, 1879.

13. Such surveillance was routinely performed, as I mentioned in Chapter IX.

14. Later she married for the third time, to an A. H. Meyers, a farmer in Florida. She lived to the age of eighty-two, dying in 1940.

15. Quoted by Corti.

16. This letter exists only as a fragment. Though Katherina Schratt preserved most of Franz Joseph's letters intact, she must have destroyed a part of this letter, which presumably said something about the Mayerling affair Katherina did not want known.

XI. *Compensation*

1. Heinrich Kralik: *The Vienna Opera*.

2. "The Mahler paradox is that he wrote tunes that can droop or quiver

with self-indulgent sentiment, wrung out in partamento or appoggiatura; but also he was often a composer of hard bony counterpoint," said Neville Cardus.

3. She was so fascinating that men fell in love with her right and left. She responded to "anybody who was a genius," or, better, she went after what she called "productive" men. Klimt loved her, as did Ossip Gabrilowitsch, Alban Berg, and in his old age Gerhart Hauptmann. Kokoschka had a life-size doll made in her image which he carried with him in his travels. When he went to the theater, he bought two seats, placing the doll beside him. After Mahler's death, she married Walter Gropius, then Franz Werfel. She always knew how to make herself the center of attention, and she invented no end of episodes, invariably flattering to herself, so that one needs to take her memoirs with several grains of salt. S. N. Behrman, in *People in a Diary*, describes how she talked about nothing but her amatory experiences; when Behrman told her that his brother-in-law, who had once met her in her youth, had said that "she was the most ravishingly beautiful creature he had ever seen," she replied: "I was!" . . . "She went on and on till she came to Werfel; she included him in her list as if he weren't there. Finally, looking straight at her husband, she made a grand summation: 'But,' she said, 'the most interesting personality I have known—*was Mahler.*' Werfel nodded fervently. He would be the last person in the world to contradict an authority so eminent or to pretend to rival a genius whose memory he held in awed reverence."

4. His other daughter, Anna Justina, became a sculptress, married successively the composer Ernst Křenek, the publisher Szolnay, and the conductor Anatole Fistoulari.

5. Breuer did not tell Freud the full story of "Anna O." Freud reconstructed it. Later Breuer remembered, and told Freud, that "Anna O" at one moment exclaimed: "Now the child I have produced with Doctor B. is being born." Half a century later Freud wrote Stefan Zweig: "In that moment he had the key in his hand . . . but he let it drop."

6. Following the Mayerling tragedy, Franz Joseph did ask Billroth to check secretly on the medical findings of the official physicians. Billroth is supposed to have gone to Mayerling to view the corpses. He never revealed his opinion; he had promised Franz Joseph not to do so.

7. The New York Public Library lists approximately 2,100 entries under "Freud"; these are not specialized medical works but are meant for the general reader.

8. Letter to Fliess, February 1, 1900.

9. In 1875 there were no fewer than 4,549 prostitutes registered with the Vienna police. They were regularly examined for venereal infection. Nevertheless venereal disease was rampant, necessitating the building of a special hospital.

10. *The Autobiography of Wilhelm Stekel.*

11. Vincent Brome, *Freud and His Early Circle.*

12. Ernest Jones, *The Life and Work of Sigmund Freud*, Vol. I.

13. Max Schur, *Freud: Living and Dying.*

14. "Joyce was close to the new psychoanalysis at so many points that he always disavowed any interest in it" (Richard Ellmann, *James Joyce*). Yet any reader of *Ulysses* is aware of the influence Freud exercised on that modern masterpiece. Joyce was intrigued by the interpretation of dreams, making notes of a number of his own.

15. It was an ugly place, thick with cigar smoke, overheated, the mirrors grimy. Yet when the café was finally torn down in 1897, Kraus wrote that Austrian literature was now demolished.

16. She bore some similarity to Alma Mahler. She was first married to a man with whom she did not cohabit, but soon went after men of talent and genius. Much later, in 1912, when she was in her fifties, she became a trusted member of Freud's circle. Even then; according to her biographer, H. F. Peters, she possessed "the radiance and vitality of a twenty-year-old girl." She had an affair with Dr. Viktor Tausk, one of the early psychoanalysts, who was sixteen years her junior, was madly in love with her, and was miserable when she terminated the relationship. Tausk eventually killed himself. Freud himself admired her, though as far as is known they were friends only.

17. *The New Yorker*, July 15, 1972.

18. What Kafka did not envision was reality: that proved to be as horrible as his imagination. His three sisters died in Auschwitz.

19. Franz Kafka, "Wedding Preparation in the Country."

20. Long after I wrote this chapter, George Steiner, reviewing Allan Janik and Stephen Toulmin's study of *Wittgenstein's Vienna*, expressed in *The New Yorker* of July 23, 1973, similar thoughts: "From the eighteen-nineties until its enthusiastic swoon into Hitler's arms in 1938, Vienna was the foremost generator of our current sensibility. A good deal of the artistic, speculative, erotic tonality of present-day London and New York may, to future historians, look like a post-Hapsburg footnote.

"So much is clear. As is the somewhat banal but reasonable conjecture that political-social decay, whether in Byzantium or in Manhattan, can be related to aesthetic and intellectual dynamism. Swamp fires burn high. The loosening of social cohesion inside Austria-Hungary, the absurd contrasts between bureaucratic façade and private reality, opened vital spaces for the imagination and for analytic thought. A sense of nearing international catastrophe, more acute in Vienna and Prague than anywhere else in fin-de-siècle Europe, sharpened the receptivity of educated men and women to extreme points of view and possibilities. The pressure of official hypocrisy on a sexual atmosphere of intense complication and clandestinity almost necessitated the development of a psychology and sociology of neurosis. Emancipated in crucial areas of education and career, invited to assimilate yet already subject to mounting political menace, the strong Jewish element in Vienna-Prague-Budapest society threw up almost pathological modes of perception, radical criticism, and self-hatred. Each of these factors was present in Freud, Schoenberg, Wittgenstein, and Kafka no less than in Theodor Herzl and the foundation of Zionism."

XII. *Din in the House*

1. Much has been made of the spartan quality of his bed, and it is still being shown to tourists. However, the bed was furnished with an excellent box spring and the finest mattress obtainable.

2. Lützow's memoirs relate that Ludwig Victor invited Princess Metternich to one of these dinners, which took place at an impossibly early hour, and noticing that she refused everything, asked why she didn't eat. She replied, "Monseigneur, j'ai l'habitude de ne jamais rien prendre entre les répas."

3. Arthur J. May, *The Habsburg Monarchy*.

4. Schnitzler wrote: "As unscrupulously as he used mass instincts . . . for his own purpose, so little was he a convinced anti-Semite, even at the height of his popularity." Schnitzler felt that Lueger was to be despised all the more for such hypocrisy.

5. Franz Ferdinand to Koerber, April 22, 1900.

XIII. *Assassination*

1. His name was Rhousso Rhoussopolos. He was an unkempt, shy, and intellectual young man. He was replaced by Frederic Barker, who has half English and half Greek and served Elisabeth as instructor in two languages.

2. From an article in the newspaper *Pesti Hirlap*, June 10, 1896. Quoted by Corti.

3. Entry in her journal, March 13, 1896.

4. But she refused to have an X-ray made of her heart. She did not want to "have an autopsy performed while she was still living."

5. At the request of the Bern government, several police agents had been stationed in Caux to watch over Elisabeth. She found out about it and insisted that they be withdrawn. She did not want her incognito disturbed. Nor were the police notified of her excursion to Geneva.

6. Based on the transcripts preserved in the Geneva State Archives. These and other documents were used by Maria Matray and Answald Krüger, the German authors of *Der Tod der Kaiserin Elisabeth von Österreich*.

7. Mikhail Bakunin (1814–1876). Russian anarchist, founder of the Nihilist movement. He believed that society could be saved through "anarchism, collectivism, and atheism," and he advocated violence as necessary. His writings include *God and the State*.

8. Based on a report in the *Neue Freie Presse*, September 11, 1890.

9. Rebecca West, *Black Lamb and Grey Falcon*.

10. See the excellent presentation of anarchist aims and methods in Barbara W. Tuchman's *The Proud Tower*, Chapter 2, "The Idea and the Deed."

11. Quoted from the *Journal de Genève*, November 11, 1898.

xiv. *Betrayal*

1. Franz Joseph to Schratt, Budapest, May 9, 1899.
2. Franz Joseph to Schratt, October 16, 1898.
3. Franz Joseph to Schratt, March 7, 1900.
4. Figures given by Arthur J. May. In allocating the deputies, taxpaying capacity and other factors were taken into account, as well as size of population.
5. 4,600,000 citizens voted—indicating how great the interest was and how right Franz Joseph had been.
6. Bismarck said: "A preventive war is tantamount to committing suicide because one is afraid to die."

xv. *Franz Ferdinand and the Redl Affair*

1. The article, "World War I as Galloping Gertie," was published in the *Journal of Modern History,* September, 1972.
2. In 1908 Edward persuaded Franz Joseph to come with him for an automobile ride. Gisela came along and offered her father some cotton to stuff in his ears. He declined but said to Edward: "You go first—you know this vehicle." It was the first time he tried the horseless carriage. The ride lasted about forty minutes, attaining a speed of eighteen miles an hour. Franz Joseph enjoyed it, or said he did. After that he used an automobile from time to time. On the sixtieth anniversary of his reign, the Austrian Automobile Club presented him with a gift of two Daimlers. But he still preferred horses.
3. From the draft of a memorandum undated but belonging to 1909. The memorandum may never have been sent.
4. It was used for a novel, *The Devil's Lieutenant,* by M. Fagyas.
5. After Franz Ferdinand's death, Urbanski was reinstated and served in World War I.
6. Stefan Zweig, *Die Welt von Gestern.*

xvi. *Sarajevo*

1. The fullest and most vivid account available in English is Joachim Remak's *Sarajevo.* An earlier treatment of the subject, sympathetic to the Slavs, is R. W. Seton-Watson's *Sarajevo.* An excellent short narration is to be found in Edmond Taylor's *The Fall of the Dynasties,* which is a fine book altogether.

The most authoritative analysis of the causes and events which led up to World War I, I believe to be Luigi Albertini's *The Origins of the War of 1914.* Other books are: *The Coming of the War, 1914* by Bernadotte Schmitt and *The Origins of the World War* by Sidney Bradshaw Fay.

2. Because of his youth, Princip was given a prison sentence of twenty years instead of the death sentence. He died in 1918, a little before the end of

the war whose beginning he had triggered. Another of the conspirators, Vaso Cubrilovic, who did not take any active part, is still alive. On May 26, 1973, he was interviewed by the *New York Times:* he said that he had been condemned to prison, released after four years, and had eventually risen to become director of the "Serbian Academy of Sciences." He was now retired, seventy-six years old, and "still studying the tangled history of the Balkan countries."

3. It is worth noting that it took more than three weeks to send the ultimatum: from June 28, the day of the assassination, to July 23.

4. Golo Mann, *The History of Germany since 1789.*

5. Leon Trotsky, *My Life.*

XVII. *If—*

1. Corti: "In the heart of the old ruler there still [after the severance of diplomatic relations with Serbia] resided a little hope to preserve the peace." Redlich: "No doubt that the strongest feature of his political thought in the last decade of his rule was to preserve peace."

2. They were then published in a pamphlet, *Kaiser Franz Joseph und der Ausbruch des Weltkrieges.*

3. A key city in Albania. The quarrel concerned Serbian troops which had penetrated Albania. Austria demanded (in the ultimatum of October 18, 1913) the withdrawal of these troops.

4. Hajo Holborn, *A History of Modern Germany,* Vol. II.

5. I owe this suggestion to George Steiner.

6. Hermann Broch's name for the period from 1848 to 1918 within the Habsburg Empire.

7. Robert Musil in his novel *The Man Without Qualities.*

8. Metternich: "The Austrians make generals of their dukes. The French make dukes of their generals."

Bibliography

Works of literature of the period—such as those by Schnitzler, Hofmannsthal, Kafka, Rilke, etc.—are not listed here. Nor are the scientific works of Freud, Billroth, etc. Such listings would have lengthened the bibliography unduly. Similarly, articles in such publications as the *Austrian Year Book,* or the Vienna newspapers, are referred to only within the context.

Adler, H. G. *The Jews in Germany.* Notre Dame, Ind., 1969.

Albertini, Luigi. *The Origins of the War of 1914.* 2 vols. London, 1952.

Albrecht-Carrié, René. *Italy from Napoleon to Mussolini.* New York, 1950.

Allgemeine Deutsche Biographie (encyclopedia, 56 vols). Leipzig, 1893.

Andrews, Wayne. *Siegfried's Curse—The German Journey from Nietzsche to Hesse.* New York, 1972.

Auerbach, Berthold. *A Narrative of Events in Vienna* (from Latour to Windisch-Graetz). London, 1849.

Bagger, Eugene S. *Francis Joseph.* New York, 1927.

Bahr, Hermann. *Austriaca.* Berlin, 1911.

Barea, Ilsa. *Vienna.* London, 1966.

Barkeley, Richard. *The Road to Mayerling.* New York, 1958.

Beckett, Walter. *Liszt.* London, 1956.

Billroth und Brahms im Briefwechsel. Berlin, 1935.

Blunt, Wilfred. *The Dream King: Ludwig II of Bavaria.* London, 1971.

Böhmer, G. *Die Welt des Biedermeier.* Vienna, 1968.

Bourgoing, Jean de, ed. *Briefe Kaiser Franz Josephs an Frau Katherina Schratt.* Vienna, 1964.

Brandl, Franz. *Kaiser, Politiker und Mensch.* Leipzig, 1936.

Brion, Marcel. *Daily Life in the Vienna of Mozart and Schubert.* New York, 1962.

Broch, Hermann. *Hofmannsthal und seine Zeit.* Munich, 1964.

Brome, Vincent. *Freud and His Early Circle*. London, 1967.

Brook-Shepherd, Gordon. *Anschluss—The Rape of Austria*. London, 1963.

Cassels, Lavender. *Clash of Generations*. London, 1973.

Channon, Henry. *The Ludwigs of Bavaria*. Leipzig, 1934.

Copleston, F. *A History of Philosophy*. 7 vols. Westminster, 1964.

Corti, Count Egon Cesar. *Elisabeth "Die Seltsame Frau."* Salzburg, 1934.

———. *Franz Joseph*. 3 vols. *Vom Kind zum Kaiser*, Graz, 1950. *Mensch und Herrscher*, 1952. *Der Alte Kaiser*, 1955.

———. *The House of Rothschild*. London, 1928.

———, and Hans Sokol, *Kaiser Franz Joseph*. Graz, 1960.

———. *Die Tragödie eines Kaisers* (Maximilian) . Vienna, 1952.

Cowles, Virginia. *The Kaiser*. New York, 1963.

Crankshaw, Edward. *The Fall of the House of Habsburg*. New York, 1963.

———. *The Habsburgs: Portrait of a Dynasty*. New York, 1971.

———. *Maria Theresa*. New York, 1969.

Engel, Eduard. *Geschichte der deutschen Literatur*. 2 vols. Leipzig and Vienna, 1917.

Fantel, Hans. *Johann Strauss, Father and Son and Their Era*. London, 1971.

Fay, Sidney Bradshaw. *The Origins of the World War*. New York, 1928.

Fischer, David Hackett. *Historians' Fallacies*. New York, 1970.

Flesch-Brunningen, Hans, ed. *Die letzten Habsburger in Augenzeugenberichten*. Düsseldorf, 1967.

Fontana, Oskar Maurus. *Arthur Schnitzler*. Zurich, n.d.

Fontenoy, La Marquise de. *Courts of Europe*. 2 vols. Philadelphia, 1900.

Fournier, August. *Erinnerungen*. Munich, 1923.

Frass, Dr. Otto. *Quellenbuch zur Österreichs Geschichte*. Vienna, 1962.

Freud, Ernst L., ed. *The Letters of Sigmund Freud 1873–1939*. London, 1960.

Freud, Sigmund, and Lou Andreas-Salomé. *Letters*. Ed. Ernst Pfeiffer. New York, 1972.

Friedjung, Heinrich, ed. *Benedeks nachgelassene Papiere*. Dresden, 1904.

Friedländer, Otto. *Letzter Glanz der Märchenstadt*. Vienna, 1969.

Fulford, Roger, ed. *"Dearest Child"—Letters between Queen Victoria and the Princess Royal 1858–1861*. New York, 1965.

Gabillon, Helene Bettelheim. *Im Zeichen des alten Burgtheaters*. Vienna, 1921.

Gahl, Hans. *Johannes Brahms*. New York, 1963.

Haas, Willy. *Hugo von Hofmannsthal*. Berlin, 1964.

Hamerow, Theodore S. *Restoration, Revolution, Reaction*. Princeton, 1958.

Haslip, Joan. *The Crown of Mexico*. New York, 1972.

———. *Elisabeth von Österreich*. Munich, 1966.

———. *The Lonely Empress*. Cleveland, Ohio, 1965.

Hederer, Edgar. *Hugo von Hofmannsthal*. Frankfurt, 1960.

Heindl, Gottfried. *Wien, Brevier einer Stadt*. Vienna, 1972.

Henderson, W. D. *The Industrialization of Europe 1780–1914*. New York, 1969.

Hennings, Fred. *Ringstrassen Symphonie.* 3 vols. Vienna, 1965.
──────. *Solange er lebt.* 5 vols. Vienna, 1971.
Hermann, G. *Das Biedermeier.* Vienna, 1968.
Hobman, Franz. *The Habsburg Empire.* London, 1972.
Hofmannsthal, Hugo von, and Josef Redlich. *Briefwechsel.* Frankfurt, 1971.
Holborn, Hajo. *The History of Modern Germany 1648–1840.* New York, 1964.
──────. *The History of Modern Germany: 1840–1945.* New York, 1969.
Holthusen, Hans Egon. *Rilke.* Hamburg, 1959.
Holzer, Hans. *The Habsburg Curse.* New York, 1973.
Jacob, H. E. *Johann Strauss, Father and Son.* New York, 1939.
Janik, Allan, and Stephen Toulmin. *Wittgenstein's Vienna.* New York, 1973.
Jászi, Oscar. *The Dissolution of the Habsburg Monarchy.* Chicago, 1929.
Johnston, William M. *The Austrian Mind.* Berkeley, Calif., 1972.
Jones, Ernest. *The Life and Work of Sigmund Freud.* Vol. I. New York, 1953.
Judtmann, Fritz. *Mayerling: The Facts behind the Legend.* London, 1971.
Kann, R. A. *The Multinational Empire: Nationalism and National Reform in the Habsburg Monarchy 1848–1918.* 2 vols. New York, 1950.
Keller, Helen Rex. *The Dictionary of Dates.* 2 vols. New York, 1934.
Ketterl, Eugen. *Emperor Francis Joseph: An Intimate Study.* London, n.d.
Kielmansegg, Erich Graf. *Kaiserhaus, Staatsmänner und Politiker.* Vienna, 1966.
Kiszling, Rudolf. *Fürst Felix zu Schwarzenberg.* Graz, 1952.
Kohn, Hans. *The Mind of Germany.* New York, 1960.
Kralik, Heinrich. *The Vienna Opera.* Vienna, 1963.
Kühnel, Harry. *Die Hofburg.* Vienna, 1971.
Kuppe, Rudolf. *Karl Lueger und seine Zeit.* Vienna, 1933.
Lernet-Holenia, Alexander. *Die Geheimnisse des Hauses Österreich.* Zürich, 1971.
Longford, Elizabeth. *Queen Victoria.* New York, 1964.
Lonyay, Stephanie. *Ich sollte Kaiserin werden.* Leipzig, 1935.
Luisa di Toscana. *La mia Storia.* Milan, 1911.
Lützow, Heinrich, Graf von. *Im diplomatischen Dienst der K. u. K. Monarchie.* Vienna, 1971.
Macartney, C. A. *The Habsburg Empire.* London, 1968.
McNeill, William H. *A World History.* New York, 1967.
McGuigan, Dorothy Gies. *The Habsburgs.* Garden City, N.Y., 1966.
Mahler, Alma. *Gustav Mahler—Memories and Letters.* New York, 1969.
Mahler-Werfel, Alma. *Mein Leben.* Hamburg, 1960.
Mann, Golo. *Deutsche Geschichte, 1919–1945.* Frankfurt, 1958.
──────. *The History of Germany since 1789.* London, 1968.
Mannoni, Oscar. *Freud.* Hamburg, 1971.
Margetson, Stella. *Leisure and Pleasure in the 19th Century.* New York, 1969.
Margutti, Albert. *Vom alten Kaiser.* Leipzig, 1921.
Matray, Maria, and Answald Krüger. *Der Tod der Kaiserin Elisabeth von Österreich.* Munich, 1970.

May, Arthur J. *The Hapsburg Monarchy 1867–1914*. Cambridge, Mass., 1951.

Mayerling Original, Das (Offizieller Akt des K.K. Polizeipräsidiums). Vienna, 1955.

Mikoletzky, Hanns L. *Österreich—Das Entscheidende 19. Jahrhundert*. Vienna, 1972.

Miller, Jonathan, ed. *Freud: The Man, His World, His Influence*. Boston, 1972.

Mitis, Oskar Freiherr von. *Das Leben des Kronprinzen Rudolf*. New ed. Vienna, 1971.

Mommsen, Wilhelm. *Bismarck*. Hamburg, 1966.

Morton, Frederic. *The Rothschilds*. New York, 1961.

Nelson, W. H. *The Berliners*. New York, 1969.

Newman, Ernest. *The Life of Richard Wagner*. 4 vols. New York, 1933–46.

Nicoll, Allardyce. *World Drama*. London, 1949.

Nicolson, Harold. *The Congress of Vienna*. London, 1946.

Niemann, Walter. *Brahms*. New York, 1930.

Nostiz-Rieneck, Georg, ed. *Briefe Kaiser Franz Josephs an Kaiserin Elisabeth*. 2 vols. Vienna, 1966.

Pauli, Hertha. *The Secret of Sarajevo*. London, 1966.

Perfahl, Jost, ed. *Wien Chronik*. Salzburg, 1961.

Pleasants, Henry III, ed. *Vienna's Golden Years of Music 1850–1900*. (Essays by Eduard Hanslick.) New York, 1950.

Priestley, J. B. *Literature and Western Man*. New York, 1960.

Redlich, H. F. *Bruckner and Mahler*. London, 1955.

Redlich, Joseph. *Kaiser Franz Joseph von Österreich*. Berlin, 1928.

———. *Schicksalsjahre Österreichs, 1908–1919: Das politische Tagebuch von* —2 vols. Graz, 1951.

Redwitz, Maria Freiin von. *Hofchronik 1888–1921*. Munich. 1924.

Reeser, Dr. Eduard. *The History of the Waltz*. Stockholm, n.d.

Remak, Joachim. *Sarajevo*. London, 1959.

Robertson, Alec. *Dvorak*. London, 1945.

Rudolf (Habsburg). *Politische Briefe an einen Freund 1882–1889*. Vienna, 1922.

Runciman, Steven. *The Last Byzantine Renaissance*. Cambridge, Eng., 1970.

Runes, D. D., ed. *Treasury of Philosophy*. New York, 1960.

Saint-Aulaire, Comte de. *François Joseph*. Paris, 1948.

Santayana, George. *The German Mind*. New York, 1968.

Schaeffer, Emil, ed. *Habsburger schreiben Briefe*. Vienna, 1935.

Schenk, M. G. *The Mind of the European Romantics*. New York, 1966.

Schmidt, A. *Dichtung und Dichter Österreichs im 19. und 20. Jahrhundert*. Salzburg, 1964.

Schmitt, Bernadotte. *The Coming of the War, 1914*. 2 vols. New York, 1930.

Schnabel, F. *Deutsche Geschichte im Neunzehnten Jahrhundert*. Freiburg, 1950.

Schneider, Joseph, ed. *Kaiser Franz Joseph I und sein Hof*. Vienna, 1919.

Schonberg, Harold C. *The Lives of the Great Composers.* New York, 1970.
Schreiber, Wolfgang. *Mahler.* Hamburg, 1971.
Schur, Max. *Freud: Living and Dying.* New York, 1971.
Seaman, L. C. B. *From Vienna to Versailles.* London, 1955.
Sedgwick, Henry Dwight. *Vienna.* Indianapolis, 1939.
Seton-Watson, R. W. *Sarajevo.* London, 1926.
Sieghart, Rudolf. *Kaiser Franz Josef I.* Vienna, 1916.
Sigmann, Jean. *1848—The Romantic and Democratic Revolutions in Europe.* New York, 1973.
Smith, D. Mack. *The Making of Italy 1796–1870.* London, 1968.
Srbik, Heinrich. *Aus Österreich's Vergangenheit.* Salzburg, 1949.
Stefan, Paul. *Gustav Mahler.* Munich, 1912.
———. *The Life and Work of Anton Dvorak.* New York, 1941.
———. *Die Wiener Oper.* Vienna, 1932.
Talmon, J. L. *Romanticism and Revolt: Europe 1815–1848.* London, 1967.
Taylor, A. J. P. *Bismarck: The Man and Statesman.* New York, 1955.
———. *From Sarajevo to Potsdam.* London, 1966.
———. *The Hapsburg Monarchy: 1815–1918.* London, 1941.
Taylor, Edmond. *The Fall of the Dynasties.* Garden City, N.Y., 1963.
Thimig, Hugo. *Hugo Thimig Erzählt.* Graz, 1962.
Thomas, H. *Biographical Encyclopedia of Philosophy.* Garden City, N.Y., 1965.
Toynbee, Arnold J. *A Study of History.* 10 vols. New York, 1934–1961.
Tschudi, Clara. *Elizabeth, Empress of Austria and Queen of Hungary.* London, 1906.
Tschuppik, Karl. *Elisabeth, Kaiserin von Österreich.* Vienna, 1929.
———. *The Reign of the Emperor Francis Joseph 1848–1916.* London, 1930.
Tuchman, Barbara W. *The Guns of August.* New York, 1962.
———. *The Proud Tower.* New York, 1966.
Twain, Mark. *Mark Twain's Letters.* Vol. II. New York, 1917.
Unterer, Verena. *Die Oper in Wien.* Vienna, 1970.
Valentin, V. *Illustrierte Weltgeschichte.* 2 vols. Stuttgart, 1968.
Valiani, Leo. *The End of Austria-Hungary.* London, 1972.
Vallotton, Henry. *Metternich.* Heide, Ger., 1966.
Vogl, Alfred. *Six Hundred Years of Medicine in Vienna.* New York, 1967.
Vogt, Hannah. *The Burden of Guilt.* New York, 1964.
Waldegg, Richard. *Sittengeschichte von Wien.* Stuttgart, 1957.
Wallaschek, Richard. *Die Theater Wiens.* 4 vols. Vienna, 1909.
Wallersee, Marie Freiin von. *Meine Vergangenheit.* Vienna, 1913.
Wallersee-Wittelsbach, Countess Larisch. *Her Majesty Elizabeth.* New York, 1934.
Walter, Bruno. *Gustav Mahler.* New York, 1958.
Wandruszka, Adam. *Das Haus Habsburg.* Stuttgart, 1956.
Wassilko, Theophila. *Fürstin Pauline Metternich.* Vienna, n.d.
Wechsberg, Joseph. *Vienna, My Vienna.* New York, 1968.
Weckbecker, Wilhelm, ed. *Die Weckbeckers.* Graz, 1966.

————, ed. *Von Maria Theresia zu Franz Joseph*. Berlin, 1929.

Weigl, Hans. *Das Buch der Wiener Philharmoniker*. Salzburg, 1967.

West, Rebecca. *Black Lamb and Grey Falcon*. 2 vols. New York, 1941.

Widmann, Josef Viktor. *Johannes Brahms in Erinnerungen*. Basel, 1947.

Wien 1800–1850. Wien um 1900. (Catalogues of the Exhibitions at the Historisches Museum—Vienna, 1964 and 1969.)

Williams, Neville. *Chronology of the Modern World*. New York, 1966.

Wolfson, Victor. *The Mayerling Murder*. Englewood Cliffs, N.J., 1969.

Zuckmayer, Carl. *A Part of Myself*. New York, 1970.

Zweig, Stefan. *Die Welt von Gestern*. Berlin, 1962.

Index

THE HABSBURG MONARCHY FROM 1848 TO TODAY

Lemberg

Cracow

Königgrätz

Prague

Linz

Salzburg

Vienna

Komorn

Budapest

Graz

Agram

Fiume

The Habsburg Monarchy – 1848

(when Franz Joseph ascended the throne)